# Refuge in a Moving Wor

# Refuge in a Moving World

*Tracing refugee and migrant journeys across disciplines*

Edited by Elena Fiddian-Qasmiyeh

First published in 2020 by
UCL Press
University College London
Gower Street
London WC1E 6BT

Available to download free: www.uclpress.co.uk

A CIP catalogue record for this book is available from The British Library.

ISBN: 978-1-78735-319-0 (Hbk)
ISBN: 978-1-78735-318-3 (Pbk)
ISBN: 978-1-78735-317-6 (PDF)
ISBN: 978-1-78735-320-6 (epub)
ISBN: 978-1-78735-321-3 (mobi)
DOI: https://doi.org/10.14324/111. 9781787353176

*With love to Bissan-María Fiddian-Qasmiyeh, to whom this book is dedicated:*
bisous *for our Bisou.*

# Contents

# List of figures and tables

# List of abbreviations

AAH:         Action Africa Help International
ACT:         Adults and Children Together
AHRC:        Arts and Humanities Research Council (UK)
BBC:         British Broadcasting Cooperation
BME:         Black and Minority Ethnic
CAS:         Centro Accoglienza Straordinaria (Emergency Accom-
             modation Centres)
CIE:         Centres for Identification and Expulsion
CFS:         Child Friendly Space
CJEU:        Court of Justice of the European Union
EASO:        European Asylum Support Office
EBPU:        Evidence Based Practice Unit
ECD:         Early Childhood Development
ECHO:        European Community Humanitarian Office
ECtHR:       European Court of Human Rights
ESOL:        stands for 'English for speakers of other languages'
ESRC:        Economic and Social Research Council (UK)
EU:          European Union
HBECD:       Home-Based Early Childhood Development (ECD)
HEART:       Healing and Education through the Arts
IASC:        Inter-Agency Standing Committee
IDPs:        Internally displaced persons
INGO:        International Non-Governmental Organization
IRMO:        Indoamerican Refugee and Migrant Organization
IS (or ISIS) Islamic State in Iraq and al-Sham
LAWRS:       Latin American Women's Rights Service
LDA:         Local Democracy Agency in Zavidovići (Ambasciata per la
             Democrazia Locale a Zavidovici)
LGBT:        Lesbian, Gay, Bisexual and Transgender
LGBTI:       Lesbian, Gay, Bisexual, Transgender and Intersex

| | |
|---|---|
| LMICs: | Low- and Middle-Income Countries |
| MEP: | Member of the European Parliament |
| MSF: | Médecins Sans Frontières, (Doctors Without Borders) |
| NEF: | New Economic Foundation |
| NGO: | Non-Governmental Organization |
| NHS: | National Health Service (UK) |
| PTSD: | Post-Traumatic Stress Disorder |
| SPRAR: | System for the Protection of Asylum Seekers and Refugees (Sistema di Protezione Richiedenti Asilo e Rifugiati) |
| UKBA: | United Kingdom Border Agency |
| UKLGIG: | UK Lesbian and Gay Immigration Group |
| UN: | United Nations |
| UNESCO: | United Nations Educational, Scientific and Cultural Organization |
| UNGA: | United Nations General Assembly |
| UNHCR: | United Nations High Commissioner for Refugees |
| UNHRC: | United Nations Human Rights Council |
| UNRWA: | United Nations Relief and Works Agency for Palestine Refugees in the Near East |
| UNU EHS: | United Nations University Institute for Environment and Human Security |
| UWCC: | Unofficial Women and Children's Centre (Calais, France) |
| WASH: | water, sanitation and hygiene |
| WFP: | World Food Programme |
| WHO: | World Health Organization |
| WPC: | Women's Programme Centre (Talbiyeh camp, Jordan) |

# List of contributors

**Elena Fiddian-Qasmiyeh** is Professor of Migration and Refugee Studies and Co-Director of the Migration Research Unit (MRU) at University College London (UCL), where she is also the Director of the 'Refuge in a Moving World' interdisciplinary research network. She is currently leading a number of major research projects, including 'Local Experiences of and Responses to Displacement from Syria' (AHRC-ESRC-funded, www.refugeehosts.org) and 'Analysing South-South Humanitarian Responses to Displacement from Syria: Views from Lebanon, Jordan and Turkey' (funded by the European Research Council, www.southernresponses.org). Elena is the author and co-editor of a number of books, including *The Ideal Refugees: Gender, Islam and the Sahrawi Politics of Survival* (Syracuse University Press, 2014); *The Oxford Handbook of Refugee and Forced Migration Studies* (Oxford University Press, 2014); *South-South Educational Migration, Humanitarianism and Development: Views from the Caribbean, North Africa and the Middle East* (Routledge, 2015); *Intersections of Religion and Migration: Issues at the Global Crossroads* (Palgrave Macmillan, 2016); and *The Handbook of South-South Relations* (Routledge, 2018). She is also co-editor of the *Migration and Society* journal.

**Nerea Amorós Elorduy** is an architect and researcher with extensive experience in sustainable, educational and health projects in East Africa, southern Europe and in post-conflict environments. From 2011 to 2014, she taught architecture and urbanism at the College of Science and Technology at the University of Rwanda. In 2012, she co-founded ASA studio, coordinating the construction of more than 30 educational and health facilities across Rwanda and its refugee camps in over two years. Her PhD research at The Bartlett, UCL, examined the impact of the built environment on young children living in long-term refugee camps in the East African Rift. In 2018, she founded the interdisciplinary practice and think tank Creative Assemblages based in Kampala, Uganda. Her work, individually and as a team member, has been internationally recognized with publications, exhibitions and awards, including the Curry

Stone Foundation Social Design Circle awards and exhibiting at the Museum of Modern Art at Louisiana in Denmark.

**Rula Al-Asir** is a graduate of the UCL Bartlett School in the field of Environmental Design and Engineering, and a member of the Association of Energy Engineers, the National Green Building Council and Jordan Green Building Council. In 2007, she founded Alasir Architects-Sustainable Solutions and she is also a founder member and Vice Director General of GNREADER 'Global Network for Renewable Energy Approaches in Desert Regions'. Rula is also an elected member of the Jordanian Board of Architectural Division Council, Council of Engineering Offices and the Jordanian Architects Society.

**Giovanna Astolfo** is senior teaching fellow and research associate at The Bartlett's Development Planning Unit (DPU), where she combines teaching and research on a variety of global projects in Latin America, West Africa and Southeast Asia, with a focus on informal urbanisms, continuous displacement and refuge, and housing rights. Her PhD research focused on land and housing practices in border cities, which triggered a three-year collective design investigation for the radical reappropriation of abandoned military land with a multi-stakeholder participatory process in different small and medium cities in Italy.

**Tom Bailey** is an English theatre maker, creating work through his award-winning company Mechanimal (www.mechanimal.co.uk). He creates work both nationally and internationally, with recent projects including *Possession* (D-CAF Festival, Egypt); *Ghost Sonata* (Samovar Teateret, Norway); *Zugunruhe*; and *Vigil* (UK and international tours). In 2015–16, Tom worked with the Good Chance Theatre in Calais, and in 2016 was Leverhulme Artist-in-Residence at UCL's Migration Research Unit (MRU) in the Department of Geography. He is currently Artist-in-Residence at Earth Sciences, Bristol University.

**Mette Louise Berg** is an anthropologist and associate professor at the Thomas Coram Research Unit within the Department of Social Science at UCL. Her research interests include migration, diasporas and transnationalism, urban diversity and conviviality, gender and generation, and ethnographic methods. Mette has conducted fieldwork on diversity in London, and has worked on the Cuban diaspora for many years. She is the co-editor of the journal *Migration and Society*, and of *Studying Migration, Diversity and Urban Multiculture*, also published by UCL Press.

**Camillo Boano** is Professor of Urban Design and Critical Theory at The Bartlett Development Planning Unit (DPU). He is Co-director of the UCL

Urban Laboratory and Co-director of the Building and Urban Design in Development MSc at the DPU. Camillo's research has centred on the complex encounters between critical theory, radical philosophy and urban-design processes – specifically engaging with informal urbanizations, urban-collective actions and crisis-generated urbanisms. He is working on a series of interconnected research projects in Latin America, Southeast Asia and the Middle East on urban infrastructures, habitability and citywide upgrade.

**Beverley Butler** is a reader in Cultural Heritage at the UCL Institute of Archaeology. She is the Heritage and Wellbeing Lead at the UCL Centre for Critical Heritage Studies, and also directs the MA in Cultural Heritage Studies. Her key research interests include Critical Heritage perspectives; 'Heritage Wellbeing'; Archive Studies, Cultural Memory; and the transformative 'Efficacies of Heritage' – particularly in contexts of marginalization, displacement, conflict, illness and extremis. Beverley has conducted ongoing long-term fieldwork research in the Middle East – notably, in Egypt, Palestine and Jordan. Outcomes include the monograph *Return to Alexandria – An Ethnography of Cultural Heritage, Revivalism, and Museum Memory* (Left Coast Press, 2007). Her research collaborations include the project *Dislocated Identities and 'Non-places' – Heritage, Place-making and Wellbeing in Refugee Camps* (2011–ongoing).

**Estella Carpi** is a research associate in the Migration Research Unit, Department of Geography (UCL), where she is currently working on a European Research Council-funded project examining Southern-led humanitarian responses to displacement from Syria in Lebanon, Turkey and Jordan (www.southernresponses.org). She received her PhD in Social Anthropology from the University of Sydney (Australia).

**Helen Chatterjee** is Professor of Biology in UCL Biosciences. Her research includes biodiversity conservation and evidencing the impact of natural and cultural participation on health. She co-founded the Culture, Health and Wellbeing Alliance; is an adviser to the All Party Parliamentary Group on Arts and Health; and sits on the Royal Society for Public Health's Special Interest Group in Arts and Health and the International Union for Conservation of Nature Section on Small Apes. Her interdisciplinary research has won a range of awards, including a Special Commendation from Public Health England for Sustainable Development and, most recently, the 2018 AHRC-Wellcome Health Humanities Medal and Leadership Award; she received an MBE in 2015 for Services to Higher Education and Culture. Helen has written three books: *Touch in Museums: Policy and Practice in Object Handling* (Berg

Publications, 2008); *Museums, Health and Well-being* (Routledge, 2013); and *Engaging the Senses: Object-Based Learning in Higher Education* (Routledge, 2015), as well as more than fifty research articles.

**Clelia Clini** is a research associate at Loughborough University, where she works on the project 'Migrant Memory and the Postcolonial Imagination: British Asian Memory, Identity and Community after Partition'. Prior to joining Loughborough University, she was a research associate at UCL, where her research focused on forced displacement and cultural interventions (2017). She has taught Media, Cultural and Postcolonial Studies at John Cabot University (2012–16) and at the American University of Rome (2013–16). Her research focuses on migration and diaspora studies (South Asian in particular); gender, feminism and the media; media and multiculturalism; Indian popular cinema and the Indian diaspora.

**Sarah Crafter** is a senior lecturer in the School of Psychology and Counselling at the Open University. She has a PhD in Cultural Psychology and Human Development, and her theoretical and conceptual interests are grounded in sociocultural theory, transitions, critical or contested ideas of 'normative' development and cultural-identity development. She is currently leading an ESRC-funded research project that seeks to investigate separated child migrants' experiences of care, and caring for others, as they navigate the complexities of the immigration–welfare nexus in England. Her other strand of work focuses on the practice of child language brokering (translating and interpreting for parents who do not speak the local language following migration), which was supported by the AHRC and the Nuffield Foundation. She is lead author of *Developmental transitions: Exploring stability and change through the lifespan* (Routledge, 2019).

**Dominic Davies** is a lecturer in English at City, University of London. He holds a DPhil and British Academy Postdoctoral Fellowship from the University of Oxford, where he also established and convened the TORCH Research Network 'Comics and Graphic Novels: The Politics of Form'. He is the author of *Imperial Infrastructure and Spatial Resistance in Colonial Literature, 1880–1930* (Peter Lang, 2017) and *Urban Comics: Infrastructure & the Global City in Contemporary Graphic Narratives* (Routledge, 2019). He is also the co-editor of *Fighting Words: Fifteen Books that Shaped the Postcolonial World* (Peter Lang, 2017); *Planned Violence: Post/Colonial Urban Infrastructure, Literature and Culture* (Palgrave Macmillan, 2018); and *Documenting Trauma in Comics: Traumatic Pasts, Embodied Histories, and Graphic Reportage* (Palgrave Macmillan, 2019).

**Christophe Declercq,** whose great-grandfather fled in 1914, first to the UK and then to the Netherlands, obtained his PhD from Imperial College London on the subject of Belgian refugees in Britain during the First World War. He has spoken widely about the subject and has been involved in many commemoration and Centenary projects, both in the UK and in Belgium, including several local-community projects (Vredescentrum Antwerpen, Amsab-ISG Ghent, Flanders House London, Wales for Peace, Twickenham, Royal Tunbridge Wells and Tracing the Belgian Refugees). Together with Julian Walker, he edited two volumes on *Languages and the First World War* (Palgrave Macmillan, 2016), and with Federico Federici he has edited *Intercultural Crisis Communication* (Bloomsbury, 2019). Christophe manages several social-media outlets on the subject of Belgian refugees in Britain. He has had multiple involvements with both the BBC and the Flemish public-service broadcaster VRT on Belgians in Britain.

**Alice Elliot** is a lecturer in the Department of Anthropology at Goldsmiths, University of London, where she convenes the MA in Migration and Mobility. She was formerly a Leverhulme Trust Early Career Fellow at UCL Anthropology. She has been conducting ethnographic research since 2006 between North Africa and Europe on the social and intimate dimensions of migration and, more recently, on those of economic crisis and Arab revolutions. She works in Morocco, Tunisia and Italy on themes of gender, kinship and intimacy, Islam and theological/political imagination, hope and indigenous conceptions of movement. She is co-editor of *Methodologies of Mobility: Ethnography and Experiment* (Berghahn, 2017).

**Tyler Fisher** is Associate Professor of Modern Languages and Literatures at the University of Central Florida (UCF). He holds a DPhil in Medieval and Modern Languages from the University of Oxford. Since 2012, he has served as an adviser and visiting scholar at Soran University in Iraqi Kurdistan. By establishing a partnership between Soran and the UCF, he was instrumental in founding the UCF's Kurdish Political Studies Program in 2015. Fisher's long-standing research interests in the intersections of folklore, oral history and the anthropology of religion led to his work on the Yezidis and Kurds of northern Iraq. His most recent publications in this interdisciplinary area of inquiry include 'Haunted Histories and Ambiguous Burial Grounds in Iraqi Kurdistan' in the journal *Oral History* (2016), and 'Yezidi Baptism and Rebaptism' in the *Routledge Handbook on the Kurds* (2019).

**Michela Franceschelli** is a lecturer in Sociology at UCL. Her research focuses on cultural and political sociology, social inequalities, migration, the life course and transitions to adulthood. She is the author of *Identity and Upbringing in South Asian Muslim families* (Palgrave Macmillan, 2016). She recently produced a documentary film (*CCÀ SEMU. Here we are, lives on hold in Lampedusa*) as part of the dissemination of her research on how the local community on the Italian island of Lampedusa has responded to the increasing arrivals of migrants via the Mediterranean Sea.

**Adele Galipò** is honorary research associate at UCL Department of Social Science. She holds a PhD in Anthropology and Sociology of Development from the Graduate Institute in Geneva, and is a former Swiss National Science Foundation Fellow and visiting academic at the Centre on Migration, Policy and Society (COMPAS), University of Oxford. She is the author of *Return Migration and Nation Building in Africa. Reframing the Somali Diaspora* (Routledge, 2019). Her research interests include return migration, transnationalism, diasporas and refugees, gender, humanitarian action and international development.

**Tamar Garb** is Durning Lawrence Professor in the History of Art and Director of the Institute of Advanced Studies at UCL. She has written extensively on questions of the body, sexuality and gender in modern and contemporary art. Key publications include *The Painted Face: Portraits of Women in France, 1814 – 1914* (Yale University Press, 2007) and *Bodies of Modernity: Figure and Flesh in Fin-de-Siècle France* (Thames & Hudson, 1998). More recently she has curated a series of exhibitions on African photography including 'Figures and Fictions: Contemporary South African Photography' (V&A, 2011) and 'Distance and Desire: Encounters with the African Archive' (Walther Collection, 2014).

**Semhar Haile** worked as a research assistant on the ESRC-funded 'Becoming Adult' project, and has a wide interest in refugee and migration studies. She has experience of working in research, ranging from migration to gender studies and climate change. Semhar's reflections on refugeehood and migration are largely shaped by her own migration trajectories and background, as well as her interaction with members of her community.

**Eva Hoffman** grew up in Krakow, Poland before emigrating in her teens to Canada, and then to the United States. After receiving her PhD in Literature from Harvard University, she worked as a senior editor and literary critic at the *New York Times* and has taught at various British and American universities. Her books, which have been translated widely, include *Lost in Translation, Exit Into History, After Such Knowledge* and *Time*, as well as two novels, *The Secret* and *Illuminations*. She has written and presented programmes for BBC Radio and has lectured internationally on the subjects of exile, historical memory, cross-cultural relations and other contemporary issues. Her awards include the Guggenheim Fellowship, Whiting Award for Writing, an award from the American Academy of Arts and Letters and the Prix Italia for radio work. She is a Fellow of the Royal Society of Literature and holds an honorary doctorate from Warwick University. She is currently a visiting professor at UCL and lives in London.

**S. Tahmineh Hooshyar Emami** is an architectural practitioner, design tutor and writer in the field of humanitarian aid and response. She has graduated from Newcastle University and the UCL Bartlett School of Architecture, and is currently working in architectural academia and practice. In her research, she investigates the spatial implications of refuge in the context of enforced mobility using critical creative writing as a tool to explore transitory European refugee camps, focusing on their liminality and transitory geopolitical and demographic position.

**Cornelius Katona** is Medical Director of the Helen Bamber Foundation, a human-rights charity working with asylum seekers and refugees, and honorary professor in the Division of Psychiatry at UCL. He has published about 250 peer-reviewed papers and written/edited 16 books. He led a Royal College of Psychiatrists working group providing guidance on writing psychiatric reports in the immigration and asylum context, and was a member of the committee that recently updated National Institute for Health and Clinical Excellence guidelines on post-traumatic stress disorder (PTSD).

**Ilan Kelman** is Professor of Risk, Resilience and Global Health at UCL and a Professor II at the University of Agder, Kristiansand, Norway. His overall research interest is linking disasters and health, including the integration of climate change into disaster research and health research. This covers three main areas: disaster diplomacy and health diplomacy (www.disasterdiplomacy.org); island sustainability involving safe and healthy communities in isolated locations (www.islandvulnerability.org); and risk education for health and disasters (www.riskred.org).

**Karolin Krause** is a PhD student of Evidence-Based Child and Adolescent Mental Health at UCL and the Anna Freud National Centre for Children and Families, and a research fellow with the International Consortium for Health Outcomes Measurement. Her work focuses on the conceptual definition and measurement of treatment outcomes for childhood depression in routine mental-healthcare settings. Karolin previously spent four years working as an evaluator of UK aid programmes targeting children and adolescents in low- and middle-income countries, and is currently advising Save the Children on the evaluation of a 'sports for resilience' programme in Indonesia and Jordan. She holds an MSc in Political Sociology from the London School of Economics and Political Science.

**Charlotte Loris-Rodionoff** is a social and cultural anthropologist. She works with Syrian revolutionaries and displaced families in the border city of Gaziantep (southern Turkey). Her PhD thesis, titled 'Of Revolutionary Transformations: Lives in Displacement at the Syrian-Turkish Border', examined the (un)intended consequences of the 2011 revolution in all parts of Syrians' lives. She is part of the CARP project (Comparative Anthropology of Revolutionary Politics), an ERC-funded project comparatively examining revolutionary politics and subjectivities in Latin America and the Middle East.

**Samar Maqusi** is an architect and urban specialist with over 11 years of professional experience in international development and refugee camps, including urban design in conflict areas. As part of her PhD research at the UCL Bartlett School of Architecture, Samar built and exhibited spatial installations in refugee camps in Jordan and Lebanon – and also, with support from a UCL Grand Challenges grant, in the P21 Gallery in London. Before her PhD, Samar held the post of architect/physical planner at the headquarters of the UNRWA in Amman. She is currently a postdoctoral researcher at the UCL-RELIEF Centre, where she is working on the Vital City theme.

**Francesca Meloni** is a lecturer in social justice at Kings College London. She has a background in anthropology, and more than ten years of experience conducting ethnographic research with young migrants in contexts of social exclusion. Francesca is particularly interested in the interface between age, illegality, access to services and social belonging. She was a postdoctoral researcher at the University of Oxford and UCL, where she conducted research on former unaccompanied minors and transitions into institutional adulthood in the UK. She received her

PhD at McGill University, Montreal, where she examined the influence of undocumented legal status on youths' social belonging and access to education in Canada.

**Richard C.M. Mole** is Professor of Political Sociology at the School of Slavonic and East European Studies, UCL. His research focuses on the relationship between identity and power, with particular reference to nationalism, sexualities, migration, diaspora and asylum. His current research examines Polish, Russian and Brazilian queer migrants in London and Berlin, exploring their diasporic consciousness and their engagement with and queering of their ethno-national diasporas.

**Muslih Mustafa** holds a PhD in Islamic Theology (Salahaddin University, Erbil, Iraqi Kurdistan, 2008) on the topic of neutralizing and eradicating extremism. A governing member of the Kurdistan Regional Government's Ministry of Higher Education and Scientific Research, he served as the founding president of Soran University from 2009. He also co-founded the Council of Islamic Thinking in Erbil, in 2005.

**Fatima Al-Nammari** is assistant professor in the College of Architecture, Petra University, Jordan. Her research addresses integrated studies of the built environment, including disasters, heritage and development. She has rich and diverse experience spanning several countries with local, international and UN organizations. Her professional work has included projects in refugee camps, urban and refugee heritage management, and disaster preparedness.

**Marta Niccolai** is a senior teaching fellow in European Theatre in Translation and in Translation and Intercultural Communication at UCL. She is the co-author of the book *Nuovo Scenario Italiano. Stranieri e Italiani nel teatro contemporaneo,* on the presence of migrants and refugees in contemporary Italian plays. She is currently writing a book on the performances of Hidden Theatre/Teatro di Nascosto, an Italian theatre company working internationally in war zones, and she is part of the Refuge in a Moving World research network at UCL. Since 2018, she has directed the SELCS theatre group, with a cast and crew of students from UCL's School of European Language, Culture and Society and a performance at the end of the academic year.

**Yousif M. Qasmiyeh** is a Palestinian poet, translator and DPhil researcher at the University of Oxford, where he is examining multiple conceptualizations of time and containment in the burgeoning field of 'Refugee

Writing'. In addition to teaching Arabic at the University of Oxford, Yousif is Writer-in-Residence for the AHRC-ESRC funded Refugee Hosts research project (www.refugeehosts.org), the Arabic-language researcher on the Prismatic Translation strand of the Open World Research Initiative-funded Creative Multilingualism project, and the 'Creative Encounters' editor for the *Migration and Society* journal.

**Thibaut Raboin** is senior teaching fellow in French at UCL. His research focuses on the study of public discourse about social suffering around the configuration of social problems, with a particular focus on migration, sexuality and nationhood. His book, *Discourses on LGBT asylum in the UK* (Manchester University Press, 2017), explores how the social problem of LGBT asylum is conceived of in relation to questions of nationhood, human rights and forms of neoliberal optimism. He is currently working on the cultures of deindustrialization in the Lorraine region in France – evaluating how, since the steelworker marches of 1979, writers, film-makers and artists have found the changing region of Lorraine a fertile ground for conflicting visions of work, migration, poverty, ruination and memory.

**Habib Rezaie** is a Master's student in Data Analytics at De Montfort University, Leicester. He currently works as a project assistant for two projects: the ESRC-funded 'Becoming Adult: Conceptions of Futures and Wellbeing among Migrant Young People in the UK', and 'The Education of Unaccompanied Asylum-Seeker Child'.

**Rachel Rosen** is an associate professor in the Sociology of Childhood at UCL. Her current ESRC-funded research with Sarah Crafter (Open University) explores separated child migrants' experiences of care, and caring for others, as they navigate the complexities of the immigration–welfare nexus in England. Her work is located at the intersections of the sociology of childhood and materialist feminist thought, with a focus on social reproduction, migration and the impact of intersecting inequalities on children's everyday lives. She is co-author of *Negotiating Adult–Child Relationships in Early Childhood Research* (Routledge, 2014) and co-editor of *Reimagining Childhood Studies* (Bloomsbury Academic, 2019) and *Feminism and the Politics of Childhood: Friends or Foes?* (UCL Press, 2018). She has been a leading member of the education committee of Refuge in a Moving World (UCL), involved in participatory projects with migrant women and children designed to open up spaces of knowledge production at UCL.

**Maureen Seguin** completed her PhD in Public Health and Policy at the London School of Hygiene and Tropical Medicine in 2016, working within the Centre for Health and Social Change research group. Prior to commencing her PhD in 2011, she obtained an MA and BA (Hons) in Sociology from the University of Saskatchewan, Canada. She joined UCL in 2015 – first in the Centre for Sexual Health and HIV Research, and then relocating to UCL's Primary Care E-Health Unit within Primary Care and Population Health. Her research has focused in particular on the mental health of Georgian women internally displaced by the 2008 Russo–Georgian war. Although her primary research interests specifically lie in the area of mental health among refugees, she has also contributed to numerous projects examining access to healthcare among marginalized populations.

**Evelyn Sharples** is a senior research and evaluation officer at the Centre of expertise on child sexual abuse (CSA Centre). She is currently leading on the perpetration strand of work to develop a typology of child sexual-abuse offending, alongside leading on the work to build an evidence base on effectiveness of services that respond to child sexual abuse. With a background in children's mental health and well-being, she has been involved in multiple national research and evaluation projects with a primary focus on resilience. Through working for the Anna Freud Centre and as an honorary research assistant at UCL, she secured additional grants to carry out research exploring perceptions of resilience for children in international and development settings. This included working with 'World Awareness for Children in Trauma' to carry out research with looked-after children in Indonesia, building a cross-disciplinary working group of academics and running workshops on building resilience for children in low- and middle-income countries.

**Tom Snow** is a critic and art historian based in London. He completed his PhD in the History of Art Department at UCL in 2017, examining the intersection of critical art practice, activism and the politics of globalization, with a particular focus on tensions between the Istanbul Biennial, artists and activists, leading to the event's partial boycott and the occupation of Gezi Park in 2013. He is consultant editor at *Ibraaz*, a research forum focused on contemporary art and visual culture in the Middle East and North Africa, and his writings have appeared in various books, journals and magazines, including *Afterall*, *Art Monthly* and *Frieze*.

**Jonny Steinberg** is the author of several books about everyday life in the wake of South Africa's transition to democracy. Two of them – *Midlands* (2002), about the murder of a white South African farmer, and *The Number* (2004), a biography of a prison gangster – won South Africa's premier non-fiction award, the *Sunday Times* Alan Paton Award. In 2013, he was among the inaugural winners of the Windham-Campbell Literature Prizes, awarded by Yale University. His latest book, *A Man of Good Hope*, was published in 2015 and records the life history of a Somali man who fled Mogadishu as a child in 1991. He teaches at the Centre for African Studies at Oxford University.

**Huda Tayob** is History and Theory Programme Convener at the Graduate School of Architecture, University of Johannesburg. She received a Master's degree in Architecture (with distinction) from the University of Cape Town, and subsequently worked in architectural practices prior to completing a PhD at the UCL Bartlett School of Architecture in 2018. Her doctoral research looked at the spatial practices of African migrants, immigrants, refugees and asylum seekers in Cape Town, with a particular focus on mixed-use markets established and run by these populations. She was the recipient of a Commendation from the RIBA President's Medal Research Award committee for her PhD in 2018. Her recent publications include 'Architecture-by-migrants: The Porous Infrastructures of Bellville' (Anthropology Southern Africa, 2019).

**Robin Vandevoordt** is Assistant Professor in Migration and Refugee Studies at Ghent University. As a cultural and political sociologist, his research interests are in the lived experiences of forced migration, humanitarianism, solidarity and migration policies. He received his PhD from the University of Antwerp.

**We Are Movers:** The We Are Movers project team includes staff and students from UCL and women from the Helen Bamber Foundation and Lewisham Refugee and Migrant Network in London. The team originally came together in 2017 as part of efforts of the UCL-wide 'Refuge in a Moving World' initiative, bringing together staff and students to make UCL a refugee-friendly university. Its activities include advocacy with senior management at UCL and informal staff–student initiatives, such as *We Are Movers*, designed to open the doors of the university in a spirit of solidarity, knowledge co-construction and widening access. *We Are Movers* was funded by a bursary from UCL Culture and the Department of Social Science at the UCL Institute of Education, and was made possible by support from the Helen Bamber Foundation, Lewisham Refugee and Migrant Network and Britt Permien Design, as well as Rachel Silander and a dedicated group of volunteers who ran an accompanying children's programme.

**Ralph Wilde** is a member of the Faculty of Laws at UCL. He writes and teaches on international law and politics, adopting cross-disciplinary methodologies. His research on migration has included work on UNHCR's administration of camps housing refugees and IDPs, and the extraterritorial application of human rights and refugee law in the migration context, from sea rescues to the extraterritorial posting of border officials. This is part of his broader work on the extraterritorial application of human-rights law, the 'Human Rights Beyond Borders' project.

**Nahro Zagros** is Vice President for Scientific Affairs at Soran University in Iraqi Kurdistan. Born in Kurdistan in 1974, he completed his doctorate in ethnomusicology, on the subject of Yezidi folk music in Armenia, at York University (UK). In addition to his academic and administrative duties at Soran University, he writes for regional newspapers on Kurdistan's sociopolitical affairs within the wider Middle Eastern context. His research interests include politics, higher education, music and conflict, cultural musicology, and music in social rituals. He writes frequently for the Kurdish and international press about the ongoing threats facing the Yezidi ethno-religious community.

# Acknowledgements

This book is the culmination of a series of interdisciplinary research and action-research initiatives convened since 2015 as part of the Refuge in a Moving World network at UCL. These include the 2016 Refuge in a Moving World conference, 'Hospitality and Hostility in a Moving World' (kindly supported and funded by the UCL Institute of Advanced Studies, the UCL Grand Challenges Programme and the UCL Department of Geography); a UCL-wide 10-week seminar series with more than thirty speakers; and a wide range of small-scale interdisciplinary and cross-faculty research projects funded by the UCL Grand Challenges Programme.

Directed by Elena Fiddian-Qasmiyeh as an initiative of the UCL Institute of Advanced Studies – and with a current membership of over a hundred researchers, students and staff from across UCL – the network was born with two main aims. First, it intended to redress and challenge the limitations (and dangers) of the unequal representations of and responses to displacement processes unfolding (or becoming increasingly protracted) around the world. Second, it aimed to recognize that working together, across disciplines and boundaries, can lead to more nuanced understandings of the history, causes, experiences, representations and implications of diverse shifts in people, politics and perceptions – and can, in turn, stimulate more meaningful ways of responding to the human, material and representational effects of the moving world around us.

A collective commitment to opening up informed conversations around different ways of engaging with, and responding to, displacement was thus accompanied by the determination to bring together insights and findings from the numerous studies, projects and initiatives taking place across and through our university by, with, for and about people experiencing and responding to conflict and displacement.

This book is therefore the outcome of a truly collaborative endeavour, and I am grateful to all of the speakers, chairs, participants and members from UCL and further afield who have contributed to the Refuge in a Moving World (RiMW) network, including all of the authors and artists who share their important research and reflections in the following pages (the majority of whom contributed to the above-mentioned 2016 RiMW conference and/or seminar series).

Prof. Tamar Garb (Director of the UCL Institute of Advanced Studies) unconditionally and wholeheartedly supported the birth and development of our interdisciplinary network and its activities, fostering and engaging in intellectual debate and exchange, awarding small grants and hosting our seminars, workshops, exhibitions and conferences. I am both personally and professionally deeply thankful for her mentorship since I joined UCL. Alongside the Institute of Advanced Studies, Dr Ian Scott (Director of the UCL Grand Challenges Programme) and Prof. Andrew Barry (Head of the UCL Department of Geography) have enthusiastically and generously supported our network and our events; UCL Grand Challenges also kindly provided funding to help support the development of this volume.

Special thanks are due to my dear friend and colleague, Prof. Claire Dwyer. From the moment I joined UCL, Claire was unwaveringly generous with her energy and time, offering unmatched encouragement and commitment to the activities and events that we convened together through the UCL Migration Research Unit, which we co-directed until Claire's death in the summer of 2019. I am deeply grateful for her friendship, and I will remember her always.

I would like to thank Chris Penfold at UCL Press for believing in and backing this project from its inception (and for his patience throughout); the anonymous reviewers of the volume for their endorsement and constructive feedback at different stages of this project; and Tom Brocket and Suriyah Bi for their editorial and organizational support.

The framing of this volume draws on insights and processes emerging throughout the AHRC-ESRC-funded interdisciplinary research project 'Local Community Experiences of and Responses to Displacement from Syria: Views from Lebanon, Jordan and Syria', known by its short title 'Refugee Hosts' (www.refugeehosts.org), on which the editor is Principal Investigator (Grant Agreement Number: AH/P005438/1). The book could not have been possible without support from the AHRC-ESRC and the Leverhulme Trust (PLP-2015–250).

The energy and commitment that colleagues from across UCL have dedicated to advance understanding and more meaningful responses to displacement around the world has extended to numerous activities designed to encourage and support UCL as a leading *global* and *local* university, in developing a sustainable approach to supporting prospective and current students and staff with personal and family histories of displacement. Through dynamic staff–student initiatives, working groups, and extensive meetings and consultations with UCL management, since 2015 we have lobbied UCL to commit to widening access to our courses, departments and faculties, including by removing a series of implicit and explicit barriers to access. UCL's research environment has been extremely supportive in advancing interdisciplinary knowledge regarding displacement, and has been a keen advocate for building bridges so that this knowledge can inform policy and practice – and we have encountered many 'Refugee Champions' across UCL. However, after nearly five years of advocating for change within our own university, at the time of writing, UCL has still not committed to developing a central, institutional response to support people with migrant, refugee and asylum-seeking backgrounds in accessing our university. It is my hope that by the time this book is published, the slow process of institutional change will have gained the necessary momentum to make this paragraph redundant. For now: #UCLCommit.

# Introduction
# Refuge in a moving world: Refugee and migrant journeys across disciplines

Elena Fiddian-Qasmiyeh

## Setting the scene[1]

People have been displaced throughout history and across all geographies, and yet attention to displacement ebbs and flows across time and space. Since the mid-2010s across Europe and North America, for instance, various political, humanitarian, media and civil-society spotlights have shone on particular displacement situations, including people from the Middle East and from South and Central America seeking sanctuary at and within the borders of, respectively, European and North American states. At the same time, other people and conflicts have been left in the shadows, their very existence often ignored or overtly denied. In effect, the everyday lives of most of the world's displaced people – who have sought sanctuary in cities, towns and camps in their countries and regions of origin for protracted periods of time, and who are often 'stuck' in contexts of forced *im*mobility – continue to be invisible from the vantage point of European and North American states precisely because they are of no consequence to powerful states and regional bodies. This invisibility is only punctured, and punctuated, when moments interpellated as 'crises' – including cases perceived to be 'exceptional' and particularly 'newsworthy' – arise, demanding immediate, if only short-term, attention (see Snow, and Davies, both in this volume).

The increased visibility of particular people affected by conflict and displacement in diverse public spheres has not necessarily led to people or peoples being granted the rights (or the right to *access* the rights) to which they are entitled. Nor has it led to the development and implementation of political solutions to the violence, occupation, exploitation and discrimination that underpin conflict and displacement situations. Instead, across the globe – whether in Australia or Bangladesh, Chile or Denmark – increased public and political attention to people seeking asylum has been characterized by framing people on the move as 'waves' and 'masses' threatening individual, communal, national and international security, leading to policies and practices of control, surveillance, rejection and expulsion (Pallister-Wilkins, 2019; see Wilde in this volume).

Indeed, the hyper-visibility of refugees and migrants has often been accentuated due to the ways that people on the move have been *securitized*, a framework through which refugees' and migrants' agency has been represented, and constituted, as threatening in nature. In the context of migration and displacement, hyper-visibility and agency are not benign terms: as Jacques Derrida noted, 'The blessing of visibility and daylight is *also* what the police and politics demand' (Derrida, 2000: 57).

While many people who are refugees enact 'strategic invisibility' for multiple reasons (Haile, this volume), humanitarian actors have widely projected and circulated a range of counter-narratives as an apparent corrective to widespread xenophobic and violent responses to the real, anticipated or imagined arrival and presence of migrants and refugees around the world. 'Pro-refugee' narratives and images typically represent, and therefore *constitute*, refugees as suffering victims, grateful recipients of aid and/or as unique 'ideal refugees' who are *truly* worthy of international sympathy, assistance and protection (Fiddian-Qasmiyeh 2014a, 2017).

These 'worthy' refugees fit humanitarian narratives of victimhood, suffering and – more recently – of what I elsewhere (Fiddian-Qasmiyeh, 2017) call 'the super-refugee': the Olympian swimmer who has overcome herculean feats (Jones, 2017), the hyper-successful multilingual entrepreneur (Kuper, 2017), the genius who changed the world (UNHCR, 2009). However, the projection of such figures – vulnerable and suffering, or *appropriately* resourceful and *positively* contributing to the local and global neoliberal economy – is, of course, itself not an apolitical depiction of reality. While such narratives may lead to compassion – even acts of solidarity – they nonetheless actively *constitute* problematic and at times deadly *realities*: both for the 'worthy' refugees and migrants who are forced to fit into this narrative of exceptionalism (and who must accept being instrumentalized in different ways), and for the 'unworthy' refugees and migrants against whom they are explicitly and implicitly compared and contrasted (Fiddian-Qasmiyeh, 2014a, 2016, 2017; see Snow's, Davies', and Mole's chapters, all in this volume).

On the one hand, these representations and responses are permeated by hierarchical processes of inclusion and exclusion, including on the basis of gender, age, sexuality, ethnicity, religion and location: only certain faces, bodies, identities, voices, stories or words are seen, heard, read and empathized with, while others continue to be constituted as threats or remain – or are purposefully rendered – invisible and ignored (Fiddian-Qasmiyeh, 2017; see Part II of this book). On the other hand, these representations and responses tend to position refugees as particular 'types' of people who require external intervention to variously 'save', 'assist', 'protect' or 'control' them. Whether humanitarian agencies, states, NGOs or civil-society organisations use these narratives and images to elicit citizens' donations, compassion or solidarity, or to justify the cessation of sea-rescue missions or the closure of borders, these representations position *non*-refugee actors as actual and potential agents, while refugees are, and have to be, acted upon.

These representations and discourses position humanitarian agencies, states, NGOs and citizens as being necessary and paradigmatic responders. Such an approach constitutes certain people and places as requiring external intervention precisely because they are assumed to be either violent or oppressed, and resolutely incapable (Rajaram, 2002; Fiddian-Qasmiyeh, 2014a, 2014b, 2018). Such discourses and justifications for certain modes and directionalities of response put and keep displaced people 'in their place' (see Malkki, 1992, 1995) and are simultaneously underpinned by and reproduce diverse forms of epistemic violence. Concurrently, state and non-state actors not only fail to acknowledge, but in fact erase from view, the ways that people who have been displaced do not merely 'experience' displacement, but also actively respond (where structural conditions do not prevent them from doing so) to displacement – whether their own or that of other people. As demonstrated by many authors in this volume, such responses are enacted by people with personal or family experiences of displacement in their capacity as researchers, writers and artists, teachers, solidarians, first responders, NGO practitioners, neighbours and/or friends.

This acknowledgement powerfully disrupts rather than reproduces the frequent framing of who 'we' and 'they' are in relation to understanding and responding to displacement (see Qasmiyeh, 2016). It challenges, rather than taking for granted, the implicit and at times explicit assumption that 'we' are active (non-refugee) responders while 'they' are passive (refugee) problems to be fixed through 'our' interventions. This acknowledgement encourages us to critically reflect on 'who we are' and 'who we are to one another' across a range of fields of thought, practice and (in)action (Fiddian-Qasmiyeh, 2018). In the powerful words of Yousif M. Qasmiyeh, the Palestinian poet and scholar who has been writing into literature the situation of different groups of displaced people in North Lebanon:

Refugees ask other refugees, who are we to come to you and who are you to come to us? Nobody answers. Palestinians, Syrians, Iraqis, Kurds share the camp, the same-different camp, the camp of a camp. They have all come to re-originate the beginning with their own hands and feet. (Qasmiyeh, 2016, and in this volume)

In effect, the process of 're-originat[ing] the beginning' in 'the same-different camp, the camp of a camp', through an encounter between refugees, as explored through a process of 'writing the camp, writing the camp archive' (the title of Qasmiyeh's chapter in this book), powerfully invokes four intersecting themes emerging throughout this volume: time, space, relationality and interdisciplinarity.

The first two themes relate to the necessity of being attentive to history, time and temporalities, on the one hand, and to space and spatialities, on the other. This is essential in order to challenge the current tendency to (re)produce ahistorical and presentist accounts of displacement, a tendency that has framed the current situation through a 'lens of historical and geographical exceptionalism and a narrative of "crisis"' (Fiddian-Qasmiyeh and Berg, 2018: v). Instead, it is urgent that we continue tracing 'historical and geographical resonances, relationalities, continuities, and discontinuities' in processes of displacement (ibid.). The importance of spatial modes of analysis – underpinning, *inter alia*, the contributions in Part IV of the book – includes acknowledging the multiple geographies and directionalities of displacement, including but transcending the recognition that the vast majority of displaced people seek safety either within their country of origin (and are known as internally displaced people, IDPs) or in neighbouring countries. It involves developing nuanced understandings of the ways that spaces such as cities, towns, camps, reception centres, markets and schools are (re)constructed, shared and controlled by different actors throughout processes of displacement – and of the significance of scale, which requires that equal attention be given to actors and processes across micro-, meso- and macro-levels.

The third, related theme is that of the need for analyses to be relational in nature (see Fiddian-Qasmiyeh, 2016, and in this volume). On the one hand, this involves carefully tracing the nature and implications of the many encounters, connections, mutualities and both modes of solidarity and of rejection that exist and emerge between different groups of people, organizations, states and systems throughout displacement. On the other hand, it enables us to directly challenge the rhetoric of exceptionalism and crisis by demonstrating the above-mentioned continuities and discontinuities that exist across diverse 'situations' of displacement: those of the past and the present; across different geopolitical regions; and spaces of arrival, (co)habitation, immobility and rejection.

A pivotal form of 'relationality' arising throughout the volume is that of intersectionality (*inter alia*, see Mole, Tayob, Berg and Vandevoordt, all in this volume). Intersectionality was first developed as a means of exploring, explaining and resisting the overlapping experiences of oppression and marginalization faced by African-American women by virtue of their race and gender in a society characterized by everyday, institutionalized racism and patriarchy (see Crenshaw, 1989, 1991). A commitment to intersectionalist analysis simultaneously entails sensitivity to the importance of race and processes of racialization, gender, sexuality and age as being mutually constitutive rather than independent markers of identity, and careful attention to diverse and overlapping power structures and systems of inequality, marginalization, exploitation and violence. In the context of displacement studies, intersectional modes of analysis demonstrate the ways that experiences of displacement and seeking refuge are framed by a range of intersecting and overlapping identity markers (including race and ethnicity, religion, gender, sexual orientation and age) and also by a range of power structures (such as racism and xenophobia, Islamophobia, patriarchy, homophobia and capitalism). Importantly, the relative significance of these identity markers and related power structures shift across time and space, including in processes of displacement, demonstrating the extent to which vulnerability is contextual rather than related to particular 'categories' of identity.

In effect, as suggested above, an intersectionalist mode of analysis pushes us away from homogenizing and reductive depictions of refugees as passive victims waiting to be 'saved', 'assisted' or 'protected' by non-refugee others. Instead, it highlights the extent to which power structures – including those of international and national institutions and humanitarian agencies – *create* situations of violence and marginalization, and prevent displaced people from finding and enacting solutions to their own problems (with the kinds of externally provided support that they themselves prioritize).

In turn, the preceding lenses – historical, spatial and relational/intersectional – point to the necessity of the final approach flagged here: that of interdisciplinarity. As demonstrated below and throughout this volume, it is by building, and opening up critical space and conversations across multiple disciplines and fields of research and practice – including the social sciences, the humanities and the arts, and with and through art, advocacy and activism – that we can develop more nuanced understandings of the history, causes, experiences, representations and implications of diverse shifts in people, politics and perceptions, and in turn stimulate more meaningful ways of responding to the human, material and representational effects of the moving world around us.

Invoking the concept of *refuge*, rather than centralizing the figure of 'the refugee' per se, and thinking through the notion of a 'moving world' centralizes both an interest in critically tracing the nature of and connections between processes of mobility and migration (in addition to their frequent corollary: immobility) and to engaging with processes and experiences that can and do 'move us' – inviting, demanding and requiring different forms of emotional and political engagement with questions of displacement.[2] In so doing, we go beyond a focus on 'the refugee' as a figure or a particular kind of subject – whether as the 'ideal' victim to be assisted or potential threat to be controlled – and beyond the fetishization of either this discursive figure or the numerical figures that are so central to the responses prioritized by politicians; policymakers; and, indeed, many humanitarian practitioners (also see Elliot, Declercq and Maqusi, all in this volume). Instead, this multidisciplinary and interdisciplinary endeavour draws together multiple perspectives, including those of people who conduct research about, or on the margins of, refugee, displacement and hosting situations; and those who respond in different ways, through academia, activism, art and a combination of these.

## Part I: Researching and Conceptualizing Displacement in a Moving World

The eight chapters that form Part I of this volume critically reflect on the complexities of conducting research into, and conceptualizing, diverse processes and experiences of (forced) migration. Part I opens with Semhar Haile, Francesca Meloni and Habib Rezaie exploring the paradoxical nature of participatory research approaches. They delineate and explore ethical challenges arising from the perspective of researchers who share many of the characteristics and life experiences of their interviewees, many of whom were simultaneously friends and peers. Noting the epistemic violence that often underpins and arises through research, they 'highlight the need to problematize the ways knowledge is produced', advocating for the usage of creative methodologies – including photography and art – to ensure that interlocutors '[are] in control of the narrative' they share with researchers. In turn, in her sole-authored chapter, Semhar Haile starts from the acknowledgement that during her participation in a theatre-based research exercise, 'few of us expressed the desire to be seen, under the light of refugeehood or migration stories'. Through challenging the notion of the 'refugee voice', Haile argues that 'in the realms of refugee experiences and social interactions that reiterate the violence of storytelling in establishing the legitimate refugee, strategic invisibility is often a necessary coping mechanism'.

The following two chapters, covering a range of historical periods and geographical settings – from Eastern Europe to North America, East Africa to southern Africa and the Middle East – explore the ways in which refugee and migrant journeys and histories can be written into literature, thereby tracing the roles that the humanities can play in creating nuanced understandings of processes of recognition, inclusion and exclusion. A conversation between the authors Eva Hoffman and Jonny Steinberg and art historian Tamar Garb provides a dynamic opportunity to explore the roles that autobiography and non-fictional reportage can play in providing insights into what it is to be displaced. Reflecting on the process of writing *Lost in Translation*, Hoffman describes 'the contours of a personal experience of movement and migration that can be traced to 1959' while Steinberg discusses the process of chronicling, in *A Man of Good Hope*, the travels of Asad from Somalia across and beyond Africa. Through their exchanges around writing about and through migration, Garb in turn suggests that writing, including through the use of the present tense, 'is used to chronicle something of the past' in a way that 'brings that into a vivid relationship with the present'. Subsequently, Yousif M. Qasmiyeh 'assesses the ways in which refugees *write* the camp into their own multiple narratives vis-à-vis markers (and beings) of temporality, permanence and liminality'. Qasmiyeh's project vis-à-vis the camp of his birth, Baddawi camp in North Lebanon, aims to 'document the lives of its residents in both life and death through processes that would privilege the ordinary and the everyday at the expense of the extraordinary and the unique, which rarely belong to the community itself but to those who claim its representation'. In so doing, Qasmiyeh asks, 'Could there be, after all, an archival writing or a writing of an archive by and for the refugee in a time when neither the camp nor its inhabitants, as always suggested, are born to remain in their writing?' His chapter concludes with a series of Qasmiyeh's poems and creative fragments, including the eponymous fragment, *Writing the camp*, cited above.

Further challenging the ahistorical and decontextualized crisis narrative that pervades many popular accounts of displacement, Christophe Declercq explores local and national-level responses to the arrival and presence of Belgian refugees in the United Kingdom during the First World War, asking whether the history of Belgians in the UK has 'been excluded from public memory not only because it was a temporary one but also because it was successful'. In so doing, Declercq traces a series of continuities and discontinuities between this historic case – in which 250–265,000 Belgians were largely welcomed in the UK – and current-day representations of and responses to displacement – which have been much less hospitable in nature. In parallel with other chapters that explore diverse spaces and places of encounter between different groups of people affected by displacement (including in Parts III and IV), both Declercq and, in the subsequent chapter, Michela Franceschelli and Adele Galipò, draw on interdisciplinary approaches to study local community members' perceptions of and responses to the arrival and presence of refugees in their villages, towns and cities. Recognizing that research is itself a particular form of sociopolitical encounter, Franceschelli and Galipò explore the role that film can play – in the broader context of an ethnographic research project – in documenting and sharing the stories and 'experiences of Lampedusans as they position themselves in the polarized representations of the island as a community of hospitality or hostility'. By offering 'reflections on the intersections between academic modes of knowledge production and artistic expressions', their chapter documents the ways in which visually recording 'Lampedusans' responses to the arrival of migrants relates to their diverse performances in front and behind the video camera, and so between the unequal fields of visibility and audibility'.

The final two chapters in Part I critically engage with a key question: What processes are, and are not, conceptualized as being linked to 'forced migration', and with what effect? Alice Elliot – an ethnographer of migration and mobility in, across and from North Africa – draws on her research with people who are neither defined (by others) nor define themselves as 'refugees' in order to explore the '"distinction work" actualized by the idea – and category – of "forced migration"'. By critically engaging with 'forms of movement that are legally and socially defined as distinct', she examines the dangerous implications of 'paradoxical hierarchies and artificial distinctions ... between moving subjects'. Where Elliot explores the significance of 'the force of hope', conceptualizations of 'force' in relation to (im)mobility are also explored by Ilan Kelman, whose chapter challenges the conceptual and methodological framework of direct causation that underpins many media and popular accounts of so-called 'climate refugees' and 'climigration'. Far from denying the multifaceted significance of climate change in relation to migration-related decisions, including in relation to the cases of low-lying islands and coastal communities in the Pacific, Kelman draws on insights from the physical and social sciences to challenge the causal framework that journalists and politicians often use in their responses to specific forms of migration, carefully 'exploring the nuances, subtleties, complexities and provisos that have always pervaded human choices and lack of choices for migration and non-migration'.

## Part II: Responding to Displacement: Advocacy, Aesthetics and Politics in a Moving World

Part II includes artistic interventions and chapters based on the social sciences and humanities in order to explore how different people, organizations, states and international systems have responded, and encouraged particular forms of response, to displacement.

The opening contribution, by the We Are Movers collective, is the creative outcome of an arts-based collaboration between migrants from the Helen Bamber Foundation and Lewisham Refugee and Migrant Network in London, and a group of researcher-activists at UCL. Established as a way of bridging 'academic research and the lived experiences of migration', the project and accompanying museum exhibition present the collective's response to mainstream depictions of migrants and to concepts such as integration; collective members have also lobbied for universities such as UCL to develop proactive and meaningful institutional responses in support of migrants, asylum seekers and refugees. In the following chapter, Thibaut Raboin explores the discourses and strategies used by NGOs and refugee advocates to 'engage a wide public in caring for the plight of LGBTI asylum seekers'. Focusing in particular on how NGOs mobilize discourses of distance and proximity, Raboin then traces the ways in which LGBTI asylum seekers are constituted as 'deserving subjects', and with what effect. The chapter concludes by arguing that '[e]ngaging and constituting responsible publics in relation to LGBTI asylum might also involve orienting their attention (their ears, their gaze) towards the cracks of social invisibility through which queer asylum claimants may fall because of their systemic exclusion from participation … by the asylum apparatus'.

Shifting from a national focus on the UK, Ralph Wilde in the next chapter explores the ways in which states and regional bodies have been responding to the actual and prospective arrival of people seeking international protection, ranging from push-backs to border closures and restrictions on the resettlement of refugees to third countries. Noting the extent to which such responses have coincided with changes in international law – in theory, becoming more progressive – Wilde examines the ways in which refugee-law protection seems to be simultaneously expanding *in theory* and contracting *in practice*. The chapter thus argues that holistic and multiscalar analyses are essential when examining the changing nature of international protection systems.

The next two chapters in this section explore the ways in which journalists, photographers and graphic artists have responded to particular scenarios of displacement, and how representations of people who have been displaced are developed and mobilized in the political and cultural spheres. Tom Snow analyses the visual politics surrounding the death of Alan Kurdi, tracing the nature and limitations of state, journalistic and artistic responses to the widely circulated photograph of Kurdi's lifeless body. Ultimately, Snow argues that we must 'treat images themselves as traceable agents that urgently require responding to, acting in some sense as antagonists that intercede with popular consciousness and imagination and which might move against the grain of the more ambiguous discursive forces that come to frame them'. Concurrently, Dominic Davies explores the ways in which journalists and photographers have sought to 'accurately' depict the perils of sea crossings in order to consciously build 'empathetic solidarity' among readers/viewers, before turning to 'testimonial comics' as a particular, slow and contextualizing mode of documentation. Davies argues that this medium, 'which differ[s] from written journalistic non-fiction or single photographs by combining both visual and narrative components ... might be especially effective at reconstructing the human rights' of refugees.

The roles of theatre in responding to displacement are then explored by Marta Niccolai and Tom Bailey in their respective chapters. Niccolai examines the processes through which the founder and director of the Teatro di Nascosto theatre company, Annet Henneman, has developed her approach to 'Theatre Reportage', a form of theatre that combines 'facts and performance' and which explicitly 'aims to influence people's opinions on fundamental social issues'. Niccolai describes the processes of preparing and performing two plays – *Lontano dal Kurdistan* (Faraway from Kurdistan) (1998) and *Rifugia-ti* (Refugees/find refuge) (2005) – both of which involved actors who arrived in Italy as refugees, and which have been informed by the director's visits to Afghanistan, Iraq and Turkey. Another model of theatre making, which also involves the mobility of theatre makers and directors, is explored by Tom Bailey in his account of his involvement with the Good Chance Theatre in the so-called

'Jungle' camp in Calais. Where Teatro di Nascosto has performed in the European Parliament among other venues, the Good Chance Theatre operated in a very different space – a space documented, in the second part of his reflection, by Bailey and photographer Tom Hatton through a creative intervention in the form of a natural historical 'Field Diary' guide to the Calais *Zone Industrielle des Dunes*. The theatre (based in a geodesic dome) was one of the only covered public spaces available in the precarious space of the Calais camp, and Bailey aimed not 'to direct a show but to provide a space where people could express themselves spontaneously in a safe environment'. In this sense, Bailey's approach to theatre in the Calais camp 'was not about "performing one's journey" or returning to a site of trauma to process it; it was about opening awareness to the here, the now, the emotion in your body, the partner's hands touching your hands with acceptance'.

In the second of four reflections included in this book on the Calais camp, Sarah Crafter and Rachel Rosen explore the complex 'ecolog[ies] of emotion' and caring landscapes that have developed in the camp, including caring practices delivered by women for women. To explore the question 'What does it mean to care in the context of extreme adversity', Crafter and Rosen use Sophie Bowlby's framework of carescapes and caringscapes to examine the case of Liz Clegg – a volunteer who started the Unofficial Women and Children's Centre in the Calais camp in 2015 – and to trace the nature and power dynamics underpinning and resulting from 'her care relationships with some women refugees and their children, as well as unaccompanied children living in the camp'. While tracing the potential for a feminist ethics of care, the chapter carefully 'speaks to the inequalities of "caring for" in these situations'. Highlighting the precarious nature of such situations, Part II concludes with a poem written by Yousif M. Qasmiyeh in response to the demolition of the 'Jungle' camp in 2015; while the camp was subsequently rebuilt, the poem was originally published in June 2016 – shortly after the camp had been demolished once again, in March 2016.

## Part III: Ongoing Journeys: Safety, Rights and Well-being in a Moving World

Part III examines the ways in which different people – including across axes of religion, sexuality, gender and age – experience and respond to their own situations, and how these responses intersect with initiatives developed by others on their behalf.

The first chapter – by Tyler Fisher, Nahro Zagros and Muslih Mustafa – offers a nuanced reading of the ways in which members of the Yezidi people, who have been persecuted and displaced in and from northern Iraq, make sense of the violence that they and their communities have historically experienced. Through a focus on Yezidi interlocutors' perceptions of the roles played by shamans in the past and present, Fisher, Zagros and Mustafa argue that 'the religion that has rendered them a target for extremists has also proved resilient and adaptive in significant ways'. The chapter thus 'foregrounds the personal and communal aspirations, nuanced apprehensions, and complex human experiences' of members of this ethno-religious minority. The following chapter, by Richard Mole, focuses on the ways in which 'international refugee law and national asylum regimes create "worthy" and "unworthy" queer refugees'. Through a close analysis of the 'personal narratives of two queers from Russia who are going through the asylum process in Germany', and attentive to the ways in which sexual orientation intersects with (real or imputed) political activism and religious identity, Mole highlights 'how the different forms of harm that they have suffered prompted them to apply for asylum and the impact that their different experiences may have on the likelihood of their applications being successful'.

The next three chapters apply a psychosocial lens in order to examine the ways in which people navigate their everyday lives in situations of displacement, and how people's resilience and ability to cope in situations of precarity is viewed, evaluated and – it is hoped – supported through different means.

Maureen Seguin starts by exploring the ways in which internally displaced women in Georgia deal with the trauma and loss resulting from the 2008 conflict in South Ossetia. In addition to highlighting women's gender-specific challenges *and* problem-solving strategies, Seguin delineates the importance of holistic responses being attentive to power structures when aiming to support the well-being of people affected by displacement. Indeed, a psychosocial approach 'examines the economic, social and cultural influences on mental health' and 'favours non-medical interventions for mental-health problems, based on the assumption that the mental-health impact of armed conflict is largely or completely mediated by the stressful social and material conditions that it creates'.

The limitations and possibilities of psychosocial interventions to support displaced *children* is then explored by Karolin Krause and Evelyn Sharples. Their chapter traces the ways in which different responses are developed and implemented to support the well-being of children and their families, and broader communities. Indeed, advocating a multiscalar, multidimensional and systemic approach that is attentive to 'the interplay of risk and protective factors at the individual, family, community and sociocultural levels', the authors stress that people's experiences and approaches to coping with trauma and violence are 'both historically and culturally embedded'. In turn, they agree that the 'development of interventions should be based on a detailed understanding of the cultural, political and social context', and must 'address chronic stressors, and … structural risk and protective factors'.

Helen Chatterjee, Clelia Clini, Beverley Butler, Fatima Al-Nammar, Rula Al-Asir and Cornelius Katona then examine the 'social and psychological impact of cultural and creative activities on displaced people', by bringing together the authors' findings from two collaborative and participatory case studies: the cultural activities led by the Helen Bamber Foundation in London and the Heritage Project established by the Women's Programme Centre in Talbiyeh refugee camp in Jordan. The chapter – which draws on approaches from the social sciences, psychology, critical heritage and the health sciences – concludes:

> whether you are an individual who is a second- or third generation long-term refugee, such as residents from Talbiyeh, or a first-generation 'new' refugee, as with Helen Bamber Foundation clients, the value of creative-arts activities to improve psychosocial well-being, provide a sense of belonging, develop skills and make meaning of your life is potentially profound.

In all, Part III reminds us of the different ways in which people affected by displacement understand and respond to their own situations, and the extent to which external interventions must be historically and contextually grounded, attentive to intersecting power inequalities and based on interdisciplinary modes of analysis.

## Part IV: Spaces of Encounter and Refuge: Cities and Camps in a Moving World

The final part of this book draws together in-depth empirical research with refugees and migrants in cities, towns, camps and informal settlements in southern and eastern Africa, the Middle East and Europe, to offer critical insights into the ways in which people inhabit and negotiate living, working and learning in diverse spaces of refuge.

Huda Tayob's socio-spatial analysis focuses on the roles played by two particular buildings in Cape Town as 'part of an emerging landscape of hospitality and support in the city' for Black African migrants, asylum seekers and refugees who have been subjected to deadly xenophobic violence since 2008. Drawing on the work of AbdouMaliq Simone and bell hooks, and attentive both to processes of racialization and the reproduction of gendered hierarchies across time and space, Tayob develops the concept of Black Markets to explore the intersections between spaces of Blackness and refuge. In so doing, she argues that 'these markets are marginal spaces that act to disrupt entrenched apartheid racial divisions in space – and they therefore … act as radical spaces'.

Nerea Amorós Elorduy then examines the significance of formal and informal learning spaces for young children's learning and development in refugee camps in Uganda, Kenya and Rwanda. Grounded in an interdisciplinary, participatory and collaborative research project that involved 'architects, urban planners, encamped parents, caregivers, children and humanitarian-education experts in a collective effort to create new knowledge on the cases', the chapter documents the barriers faced by children in these camps, how camp residents develop informal learning spaces across the camps, and how UN agencies and NGOs do – and do not – work to promote children's safe access to appropriate spaces for play and learning.

The subsequent two chapters examine different spatial and political dimensions of the Palestinian refugee camps in Lebanon and Jordan. Through a nuanced analysis, Samar Maqusi traces the 'spatial, architectural evolution of the Palestinian camp', examining 'what happens on the ground when displaced people inhabit spaces of refuge that are "designed and operated" by both host governments and UN relief agencies'. She explores cases of camps being destroyed and reconstructed, surrounded by cement walls and controlled via metal gateways, and subjected to the 'softer spatial mode of rescaling the camp' by the Lebanese and Jordanian governments – and of Palestinian refugees' construction of elevated walkways between buildings 'to safeguard their spaces and their lives' during the War of the Camps (1985–8). In so doing, Maqusi explores 'refugee acts and responses to conflict inside the camp space, and both host state's and refugees' own use of the architectural scale of the camp'. Subsequently, Elena Fiddian-Qasmiyeh explores the ways in which Palestinian refugees in Baddawi refugee camp in North Lebanon have responded to the arrival and presence of refugees from Syria since 2011. Fiddian-Qasmiyeh argues that acknowledging the complexities of 'refugee-refugee relationality' 'shift[s] our gaze away from relationships that have become archetypal in the field of refugee studies and refugee response: … between refugees on the one hand and INGOs, UN agencies, states and citizens on the other'. Such an approach neither denies the roles played by non-refugees nor idealizes the responses developed by people who have been displaced; indeed, the chapter sets out numerous ways in which 'bifurcated [aid] structures and external interventions … [create] tensions in this refugee camp' and (re)create inequalities between the camp's residents.

Also in the context of northern Lebanon, Estella Carpi's chapter examines the encounter between NGOs that are 'supporting' Syrian refugees in the villages of the Akkar region. As one of the key 'international' humanitarian principles, 'neutrality' pertains to the imperative not to take sides in conflict – and yet precisely how aid providers, and people who have been displaced by conflict, conceptualize and engage with this principle has received scant attention. Through her ethnographic research with representatives of secular local and international organizations and of Arab Gulf-funded NGOs, Carpi explores the hybrid and nuanced ways in which 'Humanitarian and political actors in northern Lebanon adopt diverse strategies to bring humanity into politics and politics into humanitarianism'. The ways in which Syrians in the city of Gaziantep negotiate the fluctuating politics and policies of refugee response in the context of Turkey is then explored by Charlotte Loris-Rodionoff. In particular, Loris-Rodionoff examines 'the multilayered effects of state policies and legal status on Syrians' everyday lives, their future-oriented decisions, their intimate and family lives, and the construction of a community in exile'. As such, the chapter highlights the importance of time and temporalities in displacement, tracing the ways in which people experience daily challenges, how these challenges have changed since their arrival in Turkey, and how they imagine and seek out 'migratory horizons and paths', including to Europe, in order to navigate the acute insecurity of both the present and the future.

The final four chapters in the book then shift to Europe in order to examine the 'spatial politics of refuge'[3] and the everyday encounters that characterize life in camps, towns and cities in France, Italy, the UK and Belgium.

S. Tahmineh Hooshyar Emami complements Part II's chapters by exploring the Calais camp through a creative spatial intervention that takes Lewis Carroll's *Alice's Adventures in Wonderland* and *Through the Looking-Glass* as a starting point for exploring 'various scales of spatial inhabitation' in the camp. Through a focus on the bed, the door, the house and the corridor/passage, Hooshyar Emami examines these 'four motifs as metaphors to analyse architectural spaces and their significance in the context of the journey or that of the encampment'. In so doing, she investigates the ways in which these objects 'stand in for larger-scale notions of checkpoints, borders and countries' (as is also explored in Maqusi's chapter). Processes and practices of dwelling in the Italian city of Brescia are then explored by Giovanna Astolfo and Camillo Boano, who draw on their teaching-based research in partnership with the Local Democracy Agency in Zavidovići, to explore urban systems of reception, assistance and hospitality towards migrants and refugees. Noting that 'One of the mechanisms through which conditional hospitality works is that of spatial and social separation', the chapter examines the spaces that are inhabited by asylum seekers and refugees in Italy, and how these spaces are conceptualized by their residents, asking the question: 'Where do refugees find home?' The authors conclude by arguing that it is essential 'to unpack and problematize not the simple, given space of hospitality in the form of assistance (camp, centre or house) but the micro, banal, humble and everyday practices of the spatial politics of refuge'.

The final two chapters then turn to the barriers and opportunities that frame migrants' and refugees' experiences of living, working and building (or attempting to build) relationships in European cities and towns. Mette Berg explores the case of Latin American migrants and refugees in the 'super-diverse' London borough of Southwark, against the backdrop of the UK's hostile environment towards racialized non-citizens and the politics of austerity. The chapter documents the ways in which a range of barriers (including access to employment, housing, schooling, health services and English-language classes) 'interact with each other' and with gender and immigration status, to 'creat[e] different degrees and conditions of precarity for men and women, children and adults, EU and non-EU citizens, and between individuals subject to different legal statuses and with different migration trajectories'. This serves as a poignant reminder of the importance of contextually grounded analyses that are attentive to the intersectionality of identity makers and systems of inequality alike.

The book's last chapter, by Robin Vandevoordt returns us to the case of Belgium – explored in Part I by Declercq in relation to the experiences of Belgian refugees who sought safety in the UK during the First World War – by focusing on the ways in which Syrian refugees have sought to build social relations with Belgians since 2011. While physically sharing spaces with Belgian citizens, Vandevoordt's informants explain that Syrians 'are trying to find the key to open the door to Belgian society. They want to break [down] that wall. But [for] now, they're still outside. They can't get in.' The barriers that Vandevoordt's interlocutors navigate, with greater or lesser success, include linguistic ones but also racial and religious discrimination, thereby reminding us that sustainable encounters in spaces of refuge require 'a hospitable social environment that is void of racial and religious discrimination', and that 'forging … social bonds … can only be done by a party of two'.

Indeed, the challenge that endures beyond the chapters in this book is how to promote equitable forms of mutuality and the constitution of social, political and spatial systems that challenge rather than reproduce such systems of discrimination, exclusion and violence.

## Conclusion

As stressed throughout this volume, a commitment to centralizing the interests and rights of people who have been displaced – rather than serving the interests of those in power – must precisely be grounded in a recognition of the inequalities and structural barriers that characterize and frame encounters in displacement situations. Responses to displacement – whether by academics, artists or advocates, politicians, practitioners or people with or without personal or family displacement histories – must be acutely critical of, rather than risk reproducing, paternalistic and neo-colonial discourses and practices, including the drive to 'help' and 'save' 'them'. As part of the process of questioning the locus of our gaze – and of considering the implications of our positionalities, privileges and potential investment in and complicity with diverse power structures – looking critically through different lenses emerges as a priority. Such lenses must, *inter alia*, be attentive to time (the histories and temporalities of displacement) and space (including camp and non-camp settings, and across scales, from the international level to the individual home). They must simultaneously be cognizant of the importance of relationalities and intersections between differently positioned people, power structures and displacement scenarios – recognizing the ways in which people with displacement backgrounds interact with and respond to their own needs and those of other displaced people; barriers interact to create new forms of precarity; and situations from the past and present, and from different parts of the world, connect to and constitute one another. Finally, working collaboratively through inter-disciplinary approaches and methodologies – from poetic to spatial interventions, ethnographic research, theatre, discourse analysis and visual methods – has the potential to more carefully, and creatively, document the complexities of refugees' and migrants' journeys, and to develop more sustained and sustainable modes of responding to our moving world.

# Notes

1. The first part of the introduction to this book – the foundations of which emerged through a series of events and projects hosted by the Refuge in a Moving World network at UCL, as discussed in the Acknowledgments – builds upon Fiddian-Qasmiyeh (2016, 2017). This introduction and the framing of the volume are indebted to insights and processes emerging throughout the AHRC-ESRC-funded interdisciplinary research project 'Local Community Experiences of and Responses to Displacement from Syria: Views from Lebanon, Jordan and Syria', known by its short title 'Refugee Hosts' (www.refugeehosts.org), on which the author is Principal Investigator (Grant Agreement Number: AH/P005438/1). With sincere gratitude to Yousif M. Qasmiyeh for his feedback on earlier drafts of this chapter.
2. This is also the rationale for the title of the 'Moving Objects: Stories of Displacement' project and exhibition led by Helen Chatterjee, Beverley Butler and Elena Fiddian-Qasmiyeh with support from the UCL Centre for Critical Heritage Studies, the UCL Grand Challenges Programme and the UCL Department of Geography. See https://refugeehosts.org/2018/06/08/moving-objects-heritage-in-and-exile.
3. This term is used both by Hooshyar Emami, and Astolfo and Boano in their respective chapters.

# References

Crenshaw, Kimberlé. 1989. 'Demarginalizing the Intersection of Race and Sex: A Black Feminist Critique of Antidiscrimination Doctrine, Feminist Theory and Antiracist Politics', *University of Chicago Legal Forum*, 138–67.

Crenshaw, Kimberlé. 1991. 'Mapping the Margins: Intersectionality, Identity Politics, and Violence against Women of Color', *Stanford Law Review* 43 (6): 1241–99.

Derrida, Jacques. 2000. *Of Hospitality: Anne Dufourmantelle Invites Jacques Derrida to Respond*, translated by Rachel Bowlby. Stanford: Stanford University Press.

Fiddian-Qasmiyeh, Elena. 2014a. *The Ideal Refugees: Gender, Islam, and the Sahrawi Politics of Survival*. Syracuse, NY: Syracuse University Press.

Fiddian-Qasmiyeh, Elena. 2014b. '"Transnational Abductions and Transnational Responsibilities? The Politics of "Protecting" Female Muslim Refugees Abducted from Spain', *Gender, Place and Culture* 21 (2): 174–94.

Fiddian-Qasmiyeh, Elena. 2016. 'Refugee–Refugee Relations in Contexts of Overlapping Displacement', *International Journal of Urban and Regional Research*. Accessed 10 January 2020. www.ijurr.org/spotlight-on/the-urban-refugee-crisis-reflections-on-cities-citizenship-and-the-displaced/refugee-refugee-relations-in-contexts-of-overlapping-displacement/.

Fiddian-Qasmiyeh, Elena. 2017. 'Representations of Displacement Series, 1 September–30 November 2017: Disrupting Humanitarian Narratives?', *Refugee Hosts*, 1 September. Accessed 10 July 2019. https://refugeehosts.org/representations-of-displacement-series/.

Fiddian-Qasmiyeh, Elena. 2018. 'Reflections from the Field: Introduction to the Series', *Refugee Hosts*, 16 November. Accessed 10 January 2020. https://refugeehosts.org/blog/reflections-from-the-field-introduction-to-the-series/.

Fiddian-Qasmiyeh, Elena, Z. Grewal, U. Karunakara, A. Greatrick, A. Ager, C. Panter-Brick, L. Stonebridge and A. Rowlands. 2020. *Religion and Social Justice for Refugees: Insights from Cameroon, Greece, Malaysia, Mexico, Jordan and Lebanon: Bridging Voices Report to the British Council*.

Fiddian-Qasmiyeh, Elena and Mette Louise Berg. 2018. 'Inaugural Editorial', *Migration and Society* 1 (1): v–vii.

Jones, Sam. 2017. 'Film to Follow Teenager Who Crossed the Mediterranean and Competed at Rio', *The Guardian*, 17 March. Accessed 28 June 2019. www.theguardian.com/world/2017/mar/17/yusra-mardini-syrian-refugee-and-olympic-swimmer-inspires-film.

Kuper, Simon. 2017. 'The Power of a Syrian Success Story', *Financial Times Magazine*, 12 April. Accessed 28 June 2019. www.ft.com/content/ea7c9414-1f01-11e7-a454-ab04428977f9.

Malkki, Liisa. 1992. 'National Geographic: The Rooting of Peoples and the Territorialization of National Identity among Scholars and Refugees', *Cultural Anthropology* 7 (1): 24–44.

Malkki, Liisa H. 1995. 'Refugees and Exile: From "Refugee Studies" to the National Order of Things', *Annual Review of Anthropology* 24: 495–523.

Pallister-Wilkins, Polly. 2019. 'Walking, Not Flowing: The Migrant Caravan and the Geoinfrastructuring of Unequal Mobility', *Society and Space*, 21 February. Accessed 3 July 2019. https://societyandspace.org/2019/02/21/walking-not-flowing-the-migrant-caravan-and-the-geoinfrastructuring-of-unequal-mobility/.

Qasmiyeh, Yousif M. 2016. 'Writing the Camp: Vis-à-vis or a Camp', *Refugee Hosts*, 30 September. Accessed 8 July 2019. https://refugeehosts.org/2016/09/30/writing-the-camp/.

Rajaram, Prem Kumar. 2002. 'Humanitarianism and Representations of the Refugee', *Journal of Refugee Studies* 15 (3): 247–64.

UNHCR (United Nations High Commissioner for Refugees). 2009. 'Einstein Poster – UNHCR Collaboration with Nicosia Bus Company'. Accessed 28 June 2019. http://unhcr-cyprus.blogspot.com/2009/03/einstein-poster-unhcr-collaboration_2788.html.

# Part I
# Researching and Conceptualizing Displacement in a Moving World

# 1

# Negotiating research and life spaces: Participatory research approaches with young migrants in the UK

Semhar Haile, Francesca Meloni and Habib Rezaie

## Introduction

In the past few decades, participatory approaches have been widely used in research with young people and migrants, pointing to the importance of doing research *with*, rather than *about*, research subjects (Thomas and O'Kane, 1998; Kindon *et al.*, 2007). Departing from traditional research approaches, they are predicated on the principles of action, participation and social justice, by engaging research participants in different stages of the process (for example, design, fieldwork, analysis, dissemination). In this line, many scholars have argued that participation could help to overcome (or at least to minimize) ethical dilemmas in terms of power differentials and, in so doing, would make research more ethically responsible and socially relevant (Porter, 2016).

However, a critical literature has emerged in recent years, problematizing the process of participatory research and its ethical purposes. This literature has mainly centred around two key issues: power relationships and the complexity of representation (Horgan, 2017; Strohm, 2012). Cooke and Kothari (2001), for instance, see participation as a 'new tyranny', in the name of which vulnerable subjects are 'coerced into activities and decisions for which they are unprepared, which almost always overburden them in the name of (limited and largely spurious) empowerment'. Individuals are then constrained into spaces of participation – spaces that have often not been designed in their own terms. Paradoxically, people might then experience participatory research as disempowering, as this may systematically facilitate certain dominant voices while silencing others (Kapoor, 2002).

Our aim here is to examine these ethical dilemmas associated with participatory research from the perspectives of research participants or 'co-researchers', highlighting the need to problematize the ways knowledge is produced (Ansell *et al.*, 2012). This chapter is written from our three different voices, which dialogue in the space of this text as well in the space of research and our lives. While ethical dilemmas are presented in the first voices of Habib Rezaie and Semhar Haile, our reflections have emerged from a dialogue between our respective experiences and questions. In what follows, we will begin by briefly presenting the research project, and then we will delve into Habib's and Semhar's insights.

## The research context

We worked together on a three-year project aiming to analyse the life-worlds of unaccompanied asylum-seeking minors in the UK, and their transitions into institutional adulthood.[1] Beside more traditional qualitative and ethnographic methods, the project also included a participatory methodology: ten former unaccompanied minors were recruited as co-researchers and became an integral part of the research team. With ongoing support, training and supervision, their role was to participate in each stage of the research through to the analysis of findings. More specifically, they acted as intermediaries with potential interviewees, facilitated contact for longitudinal work interviews and ethnographic work, discussed emerging research findings and participated in the research-dissemination stage. During interviews with research participants, a senior researcher (Elaine Chase or Francesca Meloni) and a co-researcher conducted the interview together. Often, as we will see from Habib's experience in what follows, co-researchers acted as cultural translators and interpreters, but had to navigate a difficult double role as both insiders and outsiders.

## Habib's experience: Negotiating roles

Let me start from the beginning: how I became a member of this research project. I was introduced to this research by a community organization in Leicester. I was told that there was a project that aimed to examine what happens to young people who migrate to the UK on their own, when they turn 18. I found this question very interesting, and I thus applied for the position. However, at the moment of the job interview, it was all very confusing. I was not sure about the nature of the research and what my potential role and responsibilities were in this project. Although Elaine Chase, the project leader, explained everything to me during the interview, it was still confusing for me. However, as the project started, we had our first training and we got to know other team members. Slowly, it became clearer to me what the work was about and what our roles were.

During the research process, we participated in regular trainings, where we were given the opportunity to ask questions and share experiences. Over many group discussions, I could raise my concerns, and we could collectively reflect on our work, learning and gaining new knowledge from each other. We also attended workshops with academics, NGOs and policymakers who are experts in various fields of migration. As co-researchers, we were given a chance to share our thoughts with them, and to see how they viewed the issue of young migrants from their point of view – compared with how we looked at that issue as researchers who also had insider knowledge as former unaccompanied minors.

Yet, many things were also challenging. First of all, it was sometimes difficult to convince potential participants to take part in this project. Some people I contacted were sometimes unfamiliar with the nature of the research and felt uncomfortable in talking about their life experiences. They were sometimes very anxious and cautious about taking part. Many preferred to not reveal any information about themselves because of the precariousness of their current immigration status and the fear that we could give their details to the Home Office. Many participants who took part in the research were people whom I knew from my community – we went to the same college, played in the same football team and some of them were good friends of mine. As I was a trusted member of their community or I was their friend, many people were often willing to take part in the research. Some of them openly told me that they decided to participate because they trusted me and because they knew that I would be there during the interview – otherwise, they would not have chosen to participate.

Organizing the research interviews was often a difficult task. Getting hold of participants and finding a convenient time that suited everyone was tricky. I often had to change date and location several times, as people had other commitments and were unable to attend, or they were unsure about taking part in this project. When someone did not show up at a meeting, I was quite frustrated that the situation did not go as I had originally planned. I felt I had wasted my colleagues' time and resources. But then, as I discussed this more with Elaine and Francesca, I learnt to adapt to the complex nature of the process, and I accepted the fact that things did not always go according to plan.

## Research and life spaces

One of the most challenging situations that I have struggled with was when, during interviews, my friends shared their childhood experiences of migration and the troubles they faced in their lives. What was particularly challenging for me was my complex role, as a researcher who had also experienced circumstances that were similar to the ones shared by research participants themselves. This meant that I was very sensitive and self-aware about the issues that my friends spoke about, and this sensitivity was created by the close relationship that I had with them. I felt emotionally close to what they were saying; I knew and I understood their feelings and their worries.

Being in the middle – as academic researcher, friend and research participant – was a demanding role to play. I had to make sure that my friends felt safe and were willing to speak without any fear. During the interviews, a vital task for me was to create a friendly and safe space for engaging my friends in research. I wanted to give them a space for their voices to be heard, and I also wanted to help to build trust with my colleagues, in order to overcome the potential barriers of sensitive questions, culture differences and language.

Managing my multiple positions was sometimes very difficult. Once, a friend of mine whom I had just interviewed with Elaine for the research told me something that I did not expect. He told me that he wanted to commit suicide. This broke my heart. I felt the need to engage him in a deeper discussion. I took him to one of his favourite restaurants, where we spent long hours discussing the general issues of our lives, our childhood and our migration journeys. This was the first step to let him open up to a deep-hearted discussion about his suicidal thoughts. Sharing with him my own journey made him feel more relaxed. I told him how I dealt with it, how I tried to be strong and to not self-harm. After that evening, I am still in regular contact with him. I often invite him to my house and I offer him my support and help, which I hope is making a positive impact on his life.

Although we had research training on how to deal with ethical issues, I did not expect to face such a personal and powerful event. It made me reflect on my own life and appreciate it more than ever. I felt that the way I dealt with this ethical dilemma came naturally: I used my heart to talk to my friend. It took me several weeks to decide whether I had a right to share what I have learnt about my friend with my colleagues. I felt that the story was so personal that I was haunted by this dilemma for quite a long time. In the end, I considered what was the greater good for my friend and I informed Elaine. In this way, I made the right decision, as I was able to receive Elaine's and the team's advice on how to further support my friend. Overall, being part of this research was very demanding and yet a very enjoyable experience that allowed me to gain new knowledge and to work together with amazing people.

## Semhar's experience: What stories to tell?

This is the first participatory research programme that I have been part of, and before joining it I had little understanding of what participatory research might entail. Through this process, I have come to learn the various complexities that such research presents, especially with regard to issues of cross-cultural translation and the dynamics of migration processes. At first, I was enthusiastic about the idea of having an active role as someone who could serve as a bridge between the research programme and potential participants. However, as the project progressed, I came to realize some of the difficulties that participation may involve. For instance, the very notion of 'recruiting' potential interviewees caused some discomfort for me. The idea of selecting potential interviewees based on the fact that they satisfied a few criteria made me feel as if I was already defining who the interviewee was meant to be, or to represent. Most importantly, I had an extensive debate within myself: When does the label of 'refugee' or 'migrant' cease to be relevant? And to what extent do these labels essentialize identity, almost becoming synonyms for one's story?

As these questions occupied my mind, my role in the research became even more difficult to fulfil. The potential participants were my own friends whom I know deeply through their various facets, beyond their experience of refugeehood. As a friend, I had the responsibility to protect their identities and stories. I had to understand that the label 'refugee' was for many of them part of their past, or that they now identified themselves through other, different identities. I felt that I could not ask them to participate in research where they had to retell their stories and journeys, and to revive memories of such personal events. Participating ran the risk of replaying the same violence that they have already lived through, and that they were perhaps trying to move on from. In many of my relationships with friends, we have never had a long discussion about our migration or journeys. Instead, everything I knew about their migration history happened in the context of brief casual conversations or discussions, which enabled me to better understand my friends (and what they did not want to say). Asking them to narrate their migration stories in the research space – stories that we often left aside from our conversations – would have completely changed the dynamics in our friendships.

These were not only my concerns. Some of the friends that I approached also shared with me their doubts about participating in the research. There were two main reasons for this. On the one hand, people who had settled and had finally established a 'normal life' were reluctant to reclaim the label of 'refugee' or 'unaccompanied minor'. On the other hand, people whose asylum claims had been rejected did not see any purpose in their participation if this did not lead to a tangible outcome that could help them in their asylum claim. In this case, they were willing to use the categories of 'refugee' or 'asylum seeker' in order to get help in sorting out their legal status.

As I also argue elsewhere in this book (Haile, this volume), the 'refugee' label comes with its own bureaucratic and political weight, and its non-participatory nature needs to be problematized. That is, given that labels play an important role in constructing an identity (especially a political one), refugees ought to be allowed to participate in the labelling process, thus 'enabling [them] greater access to and control over decisions about their own lives' (Zetter, 1991: 60). Issues of labelling and categorization, while they might be useful in their own right, fundamentally 'freeze groups in time' (Polzer, 2008: 493) and obscure the nuances and complexities of people moving between categories. Individuals should therefore be able to decide when and how they want to be recognized under the refugee label, or decide not to be recognized under this label at all (also see Fiddian-Qasmiyeh, 2016). In this sense, many of my friends' reluctance can be understood in relation to their desire to remain invisible from the hyper-visibility that the refugee category creates. By remaining 'invisible', my friends claimed a form of normalcy or a voice outside the refugee or migrant paradigm. This is particularly the case among individuals who have been settled in the UK for a long time, and whose experience of refugeehood belongs to their past, having now redefined their identity away from that of 'refugee'.

## Taking charge of research methodologies

If *what* story people are asked to narrate is important, equally significant is *how* they are asked to narrate such a story. Indeed, research methods profoundly shape how participants convey their message or the ways in which they present themselves (Smith, 2012). During the research process and in the context of many discussions that I had with Francesca, I suggested the use of alternative research techniques such as photography and art. This idea emerged from our mutual discomforts in the use of interviews. While interviews can give us considerable insights about individual experiences, they can also reproduce the violence or distress of the interviews that these people had to face during their asylum process.

Moreover, the interview spaces can fail 'to capture the everyday nuances and complexities of migration and [the] health of refugees' (Guruge *et al.*, 2015: n.p.). Cultural or linguistic barriers can make interview spaces even more constrained. In the context of our research, which focuses on highly subjective concepts such as well-being or the future, it becomes easy to miss the cultural and linguistic nuances in the ways in which different people conceptualize well-being (for other approaches to the study of refugees, health and well-being, see the chapters in this volume by Krause and Sharples, Chatterjee *et al.*, and Seguin).

Using creative research methods such as photography enabled us to capture various forms of knowledge and expressions, including emotional experiences and tacit knowledge (Veale, 2005). In our experiment, it allowed our participants to engage with the research programme in a less restrictive and intimidating manner than in interviews. Encouraging people to take pictures of their everyday lives meant that they could allow us to enter into dimensions of their lives that they were happy for us to see, or aspects of their migration processes that could have easily been overlooked in the context of an interview. Using such creative and participatory methods also meant that people were in control of the narrative that they wanted to share with us. Of equal importance is the accessibility of the final outcome of our research, especially for individuals facing language barriers or who are unfamiliar with academic spaces in which scholarly work is usually disseminated. Indeed, the creation of a final tangible product – a photographic book that people could touch, share and be proud of – was very important for them (see Meloni *et al.*, 2017; on the role of documentary making as research, see Franceschelli and Galipò, this volume).

## Concluding reflections

The experiences presented above show some of the complexities and ethical dilemmas of participation. In Habib's experience, he had to navigate the difficult role of mediator between his life spaces and research spaces. He intimately knew the people who participated in the project, and sometimes he knew them 'too much' and from 'too close'. When a friend shared with him his suicidal thoughts, Habib was suddenly confronted with an unexpected ethical quandary. How to deal with his friend's suffering? Did his friend's pain have to remain in the intimate space of a confession between friends? Or was this also a kind of research material? Should Habib tell the other members of the research team, thus breaking his friend's trust? In the end, Habib resolved these ethical tensions using his double role – 'naturally' and using his 'heart', as he put it. As a friend, he comforted him and shared his own personal story and coping strategies. As a researcher, he also revealed his situation to other colleagues, in order to protect him and to receive further support from the team.

Semhar's experience also sheds light on her complex positioning, going beyond the dichotomy of researcher and researched. Differently from Habib, she did not accept the ethically difficult role of mediating between the research and her intimate relationships. She felt that this role would have replicated the violence of labelling her friends as 'refugees', and that it would change too drastically the rule of silence that she shared with her friends about their respective migratory experiences. In a sense, recruiting her friends as participants would have caused an additional violence to the ways in which she knew them, and the ways in which they wanted to be represented. However, during the research process, she carved out a new research position for herself. She became an active and core part of the team, by taking a self-reflexive role and by critically proposing creative methodologies in order to better understand people's lives.

In our experience, the most haunting (and illuminating) ethical dilemmas are often the ones that we do not expect to happen – the ones that unsettle our positions, our common wisdoms and our understandings. Over the past two years, we slowly discovered what our multiple positions involved, and how we had to navigate the potential tensions arising from them (without necessarily resolving them). Rather than assuming an inequality or a polarized difference between researchers and research subjects, and what the role of people should be, in our case knowledge was co-produced in a third space of encounter (Qasmiyeh and Fiddian-Qasmiyeh, 2013; Strohm, 2012; Meloni et al., 2015). Homi Bhabha refers to the Third Space as a 'contradictory and ambivalent space of enunciation', arguing that 'it is in this space that we will find those words with which we can speak of Ourselves and Others. And by exploring this interstitial space we may elude the politics of polarity and emerge as the others of our selves' (Bhabha 2006, cited in Qasmiyeh and Fiddian-Qasmiyeh, 2013: 133–4).

In this context, we adopted a form of 'collaborative research uncertainty' wherein we were often exposed to the limits of our respective practices and assumptions, and we were forced to open ourselves to new ways of seeing or new ways of doing. The making of a third space does not thus grant a voice or a visibility to the other. Instead, through exposing and discussing dilemmas in resonance, a new space is formed – something that is not entirely ours, but neither is it completely different from ourselves.

# Note

1. Project Research Title: 'Becoming Adult: Conceptions of Futures and Wellbeing among Migrant Young People in the UK', funded by ESRC, grant number ES/L009226/1. Further information available at www.becomingadult.net.

# References

Ansell, Nicola, Elsbeth Robson, Flora Hajdu and Lorraine van Blerk. 2012. 'Learning from Young People about Their Lives: Using Participatory Methods to Research the Impacts of AIDS in Southern Africa', *Children's Geographies* 10 (2): 169–86.

Bhabha, Homi K. 2006. 'Cultural Diversity and Cultural Differences'. In *The Post-Colonial Studies Reader*, edited by Bill Ashcroft, Gareth Griffiths and Helen Tiffin, 155–57. 2nd ed. London: Routledge.

Cooke, Bill and Kothari, Uma. 2001. 'The case for participation as tyranny'. In *Participation: the New Tyranny?*, edited by B. Cooke and U. Kothari, 1–15. London: Zed Books.

Fiddian-Qasmiyeh, Elena. 2016. 'On the Threshold of Statelessness: Palestinian Narratives of Loss and Erasure', *Ethnic and Racial Studies* 39 (2): 301–21.

Guruge, Sepali, Michaela Hynie, Yogendra Shakya, Arzo Akbari, Sheila Htoo and Stella Abiyo. 2015. 'Refugee Youth and Migration: Using Arts-Informed Research to Understand Changes in Their Roles and Responsibilities', *Forum: Qualitative Social Research* 16 (3), Article 15, 1–36. Accessed 10 January 2020. http://dx.doi.org/10.17169/fqs-16.3.2278.

Horgan, Deirdre. 2017. 'Child Participatory Research Methods: Attempts to Go "Deeper"', *Childhood* 24 (2): 245–59.

Kapoor, Ilan. 2002. 'The Devil's in the Theory: A Critical Assessment of Robert Chambers' Work on Participatory Development', *Third World Quarterly* 23 (1): 101–17.

Kindon, Sara, Rachel Pain and Mike Kesby, eds. 2007. *Participatory Action Research Approaches and Methods: Connecting People, Participation and Place*. London: Routledge.

Meloni, Francesca, Elaine Chase and Semhar Haile. 2017. *Walking a Tightrope: Unaccompanied Migrant Young People, Transitions and Futures*. London: University College London. Accessed 10 January 2020. https://becomingadultproject.files.wordpress.com/2015/06/walking-a-tightrope_2017.pdf.

Meloni, Francesca, Karine Vanthuyne and Cécile Rousseau. 2015. 'Towards a Relational Ethics: Rethinking Ethics, Agency and Dependency in Research with Children and Youth', *Anthropological Theory* 15 (1): 106–23.

Polzer, Tara. 2008. 'Invisible Integration: How Bureaucratic, Academic and Social Categories Obscure Integrated Refugees', *Journal of Refugee Studies* 21 (4): 476–97.

Porter, Gina. 2016. 'Reflections on Co-Investigation through Peer Research with Young People and Older People in Sub-Saharan Africa', *Qualitative Research* 16 (3): 293–304.

Qasmiyeh, Yousif M. and Elena Fiddian-Qasmiyeh. 2013. 'Refugee Camps and Cities in Conversation'. In *Rescripting Religion in the City: Migration and Religious Identity in the Modern Metropolis*, edited by Jane Garnett and Alana Harris, 131–43. Farnham: Ashgate Publishing.

Smith, Linda Tuhiwai. 2012. *Decolonizing Methodologies: Research and Indigenous Peoples*. 2nd ed. London: Zed Books.

Strohm, Kiven. 2012. 'When Anthropology Meets Contemporary Art: Notes for a Politics of Collaboration', *Collaborative Anthropologies* 5: 98–124.

Thomas, Nigel and Claire O'Kane. 1998. 'The Ethics of Participatory Research with Children', *Children and Society* 12 (5): 336–48.

Veale, Angela. 2005. 'Creative Methodologies in Participatory Research with Children'. In *Researching Children's Experience: Approaches and Methods*, edited by Sheila Greene and Diane Hogan, 253–72. London: SAGE Publications.

Zetter, Roger. 1991. 'Labelling Refugees: Forming and Transforming a Bureaucratic Identity', *Journal of Refugee Studies* 4 (1): 39–62.

## 2
# Voices to be heard? Reflections on refugees, strategic invisibility and the politics of voice

Semhar Haile

## Introduction

As part of the ESRC-funded 'Becoming Adult' research project – a longitudinal study focused on unaccompanied minors and their perception of well-being[1] – the team[2] engaged in a brief theatrical exercise in which we were to act out our feelings in relation to our migratory experiences. Many of us engaged with our own interpretation of some of the themes, such as 'loneliness', 'being invisible' and 'having no one to speak to'. While some of us reflected on the common experiences of being lonely, or being misunderstood by wider society, others expressed a preference for invisibility. In this scenario, there were two interpretations of 'invisibility': one that was enforced by society and institutions, whereas the second one was a strategic choice to be invisible in the realms of refugee discourses and representations. During the exercise, I was struck by the differences in our interpretations. In my previous experience of discussions around refugeehood in my community, there was often the desire to almost hide the refugee identity in public spaces. On the other hand, during the exercise, few of us expressed the desire to be seen, under the light of refugeehood or migration stories.

These contrasting interpretations defy the homogenization of refugee identities, in which the nuances of culture, religion and gender within the refugee experiences are often overlooked. The theatrical example and the differences in approaches to refugee experiences represent the various ways in which refugees may choose to engage with their 'refugee' label, and exercise agency in more nuanced ways. For some, strategic invisibility meant making an active choice – to avoid the stigma that comes with the label of refugee, but mostly also to avoid being seen through the monolithic lens of the refugee label. Strategic invisibility is a concept that particularly attracted my attention, due to my intersecting identities of being Black, female and migrant, which draw hyper-visibility, and my sensitivities with regard to migration narratives in the media and academia. I am interested in exploring how multiple intersecting identities such as mine can sometimes render individuals (involuntarily) hyper-visible within narratives that are not always representing true selves or identities. Most importantly, I am interested in how individuals can resist such narratives and create a safe space for themselves.

In wider debates in the media, the public arena or academia, notions of refugee agency and voice are often addressed through the binaries of speechlessness and political participation. On the one hand, there is an extensive debate on the need for refugees to 'claim their voices' and much criticism of the ways in which refugees (especially in the context of refugee camps) are misrepresented by various organizations, in 'speechless' or 'powerlessness' forms (Malkki, 1996). On the other hand, there is also extensive evidence of the political participation or activism of refugees, demonstrating their abilities to represent their voices and demand that institutions become accountable for their own actions. For instance, the case of Sudanese refugees' appraisals in Cairo, where they demanded better operation from the UNHCR, is often discussed as a case study to demonstrate the consequences of refugee demands for accountability for the ways in which they are handled and treated by states or international organizations (Sigona, 2014).

In this chapter, I aim to explore other, more nuanced, ways in which refugees can exercise their agency. I argue that refugee voices do not always take place in the binary of victimhood (understood as not having a voice) versus resistance (as claiming voice). In an attempt to challenge the speechlessness-and-agency paradigm, I explore the use of strategic invisibility as an alternative way of claiming agency in a less explicit and performative manner. I focus specifically on how individuals who are categorized under the refugee label can exercise agency through invisibility in the context of the sort of hyper-visibility that is inherently embedded in refugeehood. I want to explore how refugees may chose invisibility to renegotiate their label of refugeehood and to exercise agency. Invisibility can act as a form of resistance, as it is a strategic decision to remain silent or invisible in circumstances that forcibly render individuals (and their voices) visible. Furthermore, individuals may choose to be invisible in some circumstances and be visible in others, based on how the refugee category may help to access resources in some spaces and create barriers to resources in others.

I argue that the representation of refugee identities, both in the media and in bureaucratic practices, has important implications for refugees' choices to remain invisible. For instance, refugees might not desire the spaces of hyper-visibility in which refugeehood and practices of claiming voice are often located. In terms of bureaucratic and policy processes in the humanitarian context, I look at how the process of 'refugee labelling' per se is monolithic and essentialist. As explored by Roger Zetter (1991), the labelling process essentializes, and it also creates and perpetuates stereotypes – thus rendering the refugee identity one-dimensional and rigid.

## Labelling, and rigid refugee identity

In most of our everyday life, as individuals, we are often required to belong to or identify with institutionalized categories – for example, identifying as female or male, as citizen or non-citizen, and so on – and we interact with our surroundings under these categories (Butler, 1993). With each category comes certain forms of subjection or expectation that we are expected to fulfil. In the realms of citizenship and belonging, the refugee identity is a powerful category in its implications for the subjects defined within it.

I am interested in the ways in which the process of labelling impacts on the identity formation of individuals who may not recognize themselves in the pre-established notions of refugeehood, and the ways in which they decide to negotiate the identity placed upon them through various circumstances. In fact, as explored by Zetter (1991) in the context of the humanitarian sector, the process of labelling renders refugees objects of policy discourses and agendas, thus consequently defining or depicting them in 'convenient images' (Wood, 1985: 1, quoted in Zetter, 1991: 44). Most importantly, the process of labelling also entails a 'process of stereotyping which involves disaggregation, standardization, and the formulation of clear cut categories' (Zetter, 1991: 6). Through this process of labelling and categorizing, two identities are formed: first, that of the benevolent institution (the humanitarian organization in the context of the humanitarian sector) and second, that of the refugee, who is presented in terms of his/her needs from the perspective of institutional services. In the process, the refugee is represented through a single lens, in the form of a number or as data, and is seen in isolation from a large part of her/his being (Zetter, 1991: 44, quoting Schaffer, 1977). And yet, such identity formation is a two-way process in which both the institutions and the subjects interact and form. In the case of the refugee, formal institutions such as the state, international organizations and some parts of academia overall formulate the identity of the refugee through the repetition of procedures that appear 'normal, routine, apolitical, conventional' in their programme, but these procedures require the conformity of the refugee subjects to the label in order to access specific services or resources (Zetter, 1991: 46, quoting Batley, 1983).

However, individual refugees also have some space in which to negotiate their various identities, in various circumstances. Unpacking the refugee-labelling process helps us to understand its impact on an individual's process of identity formation in the context of the refugee experience, and how he/she chooses to engage with the institutionalized category. As discussed by Sewite Kebede (2010: 6), identity formation is a 'social process rather than [an] individual process', since the way in which an individual perceives her/himself is 'embedded in society'. As such, how a society relates to refugees, often by perpetuating negative images of either criminality or victimhood, is often internalized – in turn, influencing the ways in which young refugees may perceive themselves.

Furthermore, the issue with institutional labelling, especially refugee labelling, is that it does not keep up with the diverse changes that take place in the process of identity formation. Like many socially constructed identities such as gender, self-formation of identity is a fluid and dynamic process. As individuals, we recreate and reinvent ourselves based on our interaction with society, and our past and new experiences. However, the label of refugee does not allow for fluidity, nor does it allow for the heterogeneity of individuals' identities. As part of new identity formation and new settings, refugees will develop new habits but also may recreate old habits or spaces. For example, the case of Palestinian refugees in Sweden, as narrated by Yousif M. Qasmiyeh (in Qasmiyeh and Fiddian-Qasmiyeh, 2013: 137), is particularly striking. Despite their resettlement in new settings in Sweden, in a social-housing neighbourhood, Palestinian refugees from Baddawi camp in Lebanon have recreated 'estate-camps' with former neighbours and school friends from their 'home-camp'. These recreated spaces have enabled them to maintain a sense of belonging to their common identity, their homeland, and to their religious and cultural traditions. In effect, some continue to migrate to their former home-camps to visit family and friends, including to celebrate religious festivities during Ramadan and Eid (Qasmiyeh and Fiddian-Qasmiyeh, 2013: 138). As explained by the author, the recreation of old rituals in new spaces by these Palestinian refugees defies the 'pure monolithic understanding of specific places, as if these were static and lacked the energy or the ability to change and evolve' (Qasmiyeh in ibid.: 138).

The main difference with the recreation of camp spaces across time and space, apart from better facilities and services, is that in the case of resettled Palestinian refugees in Sweden, they were in charge of consciously recreating spaces that are similar to their home-camps (Qasmiyeh and Fiddian-Qasmiyeh, 2013). This representation of camps as changing and travelling spaces (ibid.) can also be transferred to refugee identities, ones that change and evolve over time while also re-creating spaces for old habits and traditions. However, the refugee label does not take into consideration the ways in which individuals in that category change; rather, the refugee label 'freeze[s] groups in time' (Polzer, 2008: 493). Categories like the refugee label treat groups as static and unchanging through their documented criteria (Polzer, 2008).

Given the above discussion on the presentation of refugees and the lack of nuanced analysis on refugee voices, how do refugees negotiate the stigma and hyper-visibility that the label creates? In the following section, I turn to strategic invisibility, which is deployed by various refugees as a bargaining tool to negotiate the refugee label among the multiple identities of individuals. I contend that strategic invisibility enables refugees to claim 'normalcy' in the context of the hyper-visible labelling and the stigmatization that comes with the refugee identity. Strategic invisibility defies the powerlessness/resistance dichotomy, and demonstrates one of the nuanced ways in which refugees negotiate spaces and new identities in response to institutionalized categories.

## Strategic invisibility and labelling

In migration and refugee studies, the concept of invisibility is often discussed in the contexts in which refugees are rendered invisible by powerful institutions, states or international organizations. That is, refugees that are rendered intentionally invisible for political purposes due to the failure of states to provide recognition and resources to them (for example, Puggioni, 2005; Harrell Bond and Voutira, 2007). Alternatively, academia focuses on ways in which undocumented migrants adopt invisibility to 'stay invisible to the "powers that be" by hiding and obscuring identities and activities that the state or other powerful institutions prohibit' (Polzer and Hammond, 2008: 418). Tara Polzer and Laura Hammond, for instance, discuss invisibility as the relationship between those with power to see (that is, states or international organizations) and those without power and who cannot be seen, or those avoiding visibility to escape the negative impact of 'imposed visibility'. In this context, states impose categorization and labels on individuals to render them visible and controlled, and in the process the individuals in question are disempowered – even in cases where they choose invisibility in a context in which they lack legal, political and social protection. In this analysis, it is assumed that refugee groups are most likely to make themselves visible to powerful institutions in order to access resources. However, the analysis overlooks ways in which labelled or categorized refugees can exercise agency by using visibility and invisibility strategically.

Strategic invisibility, as a conscious decision by settled refugees has hardly been explored. In this context, invisibility is a strategic decision that established individuals with refugee experience may undertake to escape labelling by institutions or other individuals. Along the continuum of powerlessness and political voice, settled refugees may choose strategic invisibility to navigate their newly acquired homes and identities. It is an option that enables 'an act of agency ... the first step towards a stronger act of resistance' (Lollar, 2015: 299). Karen Lollar (2015) proposes two forms of invisibility. The first is in relation to the lack of a comprehensive and inclusive view by those in dominant or powerful positions that includes the absence of viewing the group in question beyond their category or label. The second form of invisibility is one that is strategic: a deliberate response or resistance to the dominant group or to the imposed label. While Lollar (2015) contends that the two forms are not mutually exclusive in the context of refugee identities and labelling, I argue that the second form of invisibility takes place in response to the first form. In many of my encounters with friends and acquaintances, during discussions on the experience of refugeehood, the choice to remain invisible was often made in response to the misrepresentation of their identities through the monolithic lens of refugeehood. Thus, the choice to remain invisible is to 'avoid the stigma, the danger, and the rejection of the [refugee] system' (Lollar, 2015: 306). Claiming invisibility as a form of resistance counteracts the often-assumed notion of visibility as the precondition for resistance. As interpreted by Hannah Arendt, resistance or human agency takes place through (wo)men's 'propensity to act', thus visibility as well as sociality and community is the underlying basis for resistance (Gordon, 2002: 135). However, while visibility as a precondition for agency and resistance may apply in some circumstances, in other situations invisibility as a choice in itself can reflect a form of resistance.

Choosing invisibility does not always mean the rejection of the refugee identity. Rather, for some of those who chose invisibility, they may continue to revisit their memories of childhood; their journey to their new homes; and, ultimately, their desire to visit their old neighbourhoods and cities. However, their choices on whether or not to identify with refugeehood are context-specific. Choosing visibility or invisibility is a response to who the 'spectator' is. In spaces of intimate friendships, or among their own communities, the discomfort of visibility is not as present as it is in other social spheres. Rather, in my own community, the way in which we engage in conversations with regard to journeys and migratory experiences are often framed in an almost 'casual' way. In fact, the narratives of refugeehood are seldom discussed on their own; rather, they are often told as part of wider conversations of migration, diaspora and memories of childhood or home in the country of origin. It is in the intimate spaces of privacy or among friends that refugees dwell on their journeys of refugeehood, while constructing and reforming their new identities. Therefore, within the private sphere the experience of refugeehood will always exist, albeit away from the institutionalized labelling of refugeehood that often leads to hyper-visibility. This is the space in which refugees can make sense of their newly adopted lifestyles, a space in which individuals can go beyond the rigidity of refugeehood, and navigate the fluidity that the refugee experience presents. It is also a space in which individuals can present themselves in the way in which they choose to be seen as whole individuals, whose identities go beyond the rigid walls of refugee labelling but are as fluid as their own imaginations.

In contrast, in other public spaces – or in encounters with non-community members, state and non-state institutions or media and academia – refugees often choose to remain invisible. While on the one hand, in some public spaces visible refugee identity is necessary to access resources or services, in other public spaces visibility can create further marginalization. In spaces in which there are regular social interactions, strategic invisibility is a tool that can help refugees blend in and, most importantly, can enable choice in what and how to present oneself. Strategic invisibility in social spaces may function as a shell, protecting the individual from the judgements and presumptions of spectators. It is a way in which refugees can chose to appear in an identity with which they feel most comfortable: it is not a 'made up' identity; rather, it relates to aspects of their being that the refugee label omits.

The notion of strategic invisibility destabilizes the traditional assumption of what refugee resistance should look like. Rather, it pushes us to think of the nuanced and numerous ways in which agency is exercised by refugees and ways in which refugees navigate established processes of categorization and labelling, as well as demonstrating their resilience in creating their own safe space where they can relive their old experiences and familiarize themselves with their new circumstances.

## Final reflections and conclusion

Throughout my engagement in the Becoming Adult project, one of the most persistent questions that I kept facing in my mind was the question of when one ceases to be a refugee (also see Haile *et al.*, this volume). As argued by Kebede (2010), the bureaucratic procedures of refugeehood, from the process of obtaining refugee status to becoming a naturalized citizen, may have a beginning and end. But when does the feeling of longing and loss of belonging end? This has made me question whether having physical stability – that is, being settled in one place – could erase the in-betweens that the refugee experience creates. Despite newly acquired citizenships or naturalization, rarely does the refugee belong to the newly adopted nation. Rather, the refugee often seeks belonging in the memories of the lost home, while building a new home in the adopted state. So, I wonder whether refugeehood is a defined status that has a start and an end, or whether it will always be part of an individual's identity – one that encompasses old memories, lost homes and newly adopted identities. I am of the belief that the experiences of displacement and loss continue to exist in refugees' lives. The refugee is the one who seeks new places and memories to belong to, while coming to terms with the loss of the old home.

And yet, when it comes to institutional spaces, when is an individual no longer considered a refugee? Throughout the Becoming Adult theatrical exercise referred to in the introduction, as well as through the various interactions that I had both with my fellow research-assistant colleagues and my external friends, I noticed how the representation of refugeehood also has a performative element. That is, in spaces where there is a conversation about refugeehood, there is the assumption that refugees want to be seen or want sympathy from spectators. There is an expectation of telling and retelling the stories of their journeys or their difficulty in integrating in host states. Sometimes, it almost appears as if the storytelling process is a necessary element in order to be seen as a legitimate refugee. This replicates the institutional storytelling that is required for the bureaucratic process, to establish the legitimacy of the refugee's story. For instance, on one occasion when my colleagues and

I were speaking about our experiences in the research project to a class of postgraduate students, some individuals felt the need to demand the logistics of or reasons for our journeys in a very intrusive manner.

Thus, in the realms of refugee experiences and social interactions that reiterate the violence of storytelling in establishing the legitimate refugee, strategic invisibility is often a necessary coping mechanism. It is a powerful tool with which to come to terms with the traumatic experiences of refugehood and migration, in one's own time and spaces. It is an opportunity to humanize oneself, while building a new life and reminiscing on the memories of home.

## Notes

1. 'Becoming Adult' is a longitudinal research project focused on an understanding of the perception of well-being and the future by unaccompanied minors in the UK. https://becomingadult. net/about-becoming-adult *and* https://wordpress.com/posts/my/thewellwishers.wordpress. com
2. The team was composed of senior researchers, as well as research assistants with diverse experiences of migration, from a variety of countries.

## References

Butler, Judith. 1993. *Bodies That Matter: On the Discursive Limits of 'Sex'*. New York: Routledge.
Gordon, Neve. 2002. 'On Visibility and Power: An Arendtian Corrective of Foucault', *Human Studies* 25 (2): 125–45.
Harrell-Bond, Barbara and Eftihia Voutira. 2007. 'In Search of "Invisible" Actors: Barriers to Access in Refugee Research', *Journal of Refugee Studies* 20 (2): 281–98.
Kebede, Sewite Solomon. 2010. *The Struggle for Belonging: Forming and Reforming Identities among 1.5-Generation Asylum Seekers and Refugees* (RSC Working Paper 70). Oxford: Refugee Studies Centre.
Lollar, Karen. 2015. 'Strategic Invisibility: Resisting the Inhospitable Dwelling Place', *Review of Communication* 15 (4): 298–315.
Malkki, Liisa H. 1996. 'Speechless Emissaries: Refugees, Humanitarianism, and Dehistoricization', *Cultural Anthropology* 11 (3): 377–404.
Polzer, Tara. 2008. 'Invisible Integration: How Bureaucratic, Academic and Social Categories Obscure Integrated Refugees', *Journal of Refugee Studies* 21 (4): 476–97.
Polzer, Tara and Laura Hammond. 2008. 'Invisible Displacement', *Journal of Refugee Studies* 21 (4): 417–31.
Puggioni, Raffaela. 2005. 'Refugees, Institutional Invisibility and Self-Help Strategies: Evaluating Kurdish Experience in Rome', *Journal of Refugee Studies* 18 (3): 319–39.
Qasmiyeh, Yousif M. and Elena Fiddian-Qasmiyeh. 2013. 'Refugee Camps and Cities in Conversation'. In *Rescripting Religion in the City: Migration and Religious Identity in the Modern Metropolis*, edited by Jane Garnett and Alana Harris, 131–43. Farnham: Ashgate Publishing.
Schaffer, B. B. 1977. *Official Providers: Access, Equity and Participation*, Paris, UNESCO.
Sigona, Nando. 2014. 'The Politics of Refugee Voices: Representations, Narratives, and Memories'. In *The Oxford Handbook of Refugee and Forced Migration Studies*, edited by Elena Fiddian-Qasmiyeh, Gil Loescher, Katy Long and Nando Sigona, 369–82. Oxford: Oxford University Press.
Wood, G. (ed.) 1985. *Labelling in Development Policy*. London, Sage.
Zetter, Roger. 1991. 'Labelling Refugees: Forming and Transforming a Bureaucratic Identity', *Journal of Refugee Studies* 4 (1): 39–62.

# 3
# Stories of migration and belonging

Eva Hoffman and Jonny Steinberg in conversation with Tamar Garb

*This chapter is based on a conversation between two well-known authors, Eva Hoffman and Jonny Steinberg, and the art historian and Director of the UCL Institute of Advanced Studies, Tamar Garb. Throughout their encounter, they explore the ways in which different forms of writing, including autobiography and non-fictional reportage, can challenge the monolith of the figure of 'the refugee' as it has been constituted in the context of contemporary Europe. They do so in particular through reference to* Lost in Translation, *written by Hoffman and published in 1989 as an autobiographical account of what it is to be displaced, describing the contours of a personal experience of movement and migration that can be traced to 1959, and Steinberg's 2015* A Man of Good Hope, *which chronicles the travels of Asad, primarily across but also beyond Africa. Through critical reflections on the process of writing about and through migration, the chapter provides important insights into migratory processes, movement and belonging across time and space.*

**Tamar Garb**: Eva, I wonder if I could start by asking you to offer some opening reflections on *Lost in Translation*. What kind of story does it chronicle and how can issues of migration be thought about in relation to your book?

**Eva Hoffman:** I wrote *Lost in Translation* when I was living in the United States, and America is, of course, a country of immigrants and one that has produced a very large corpus of 'immigrant literature'. However, this literature almost exclusively wrote of exterior journeys of hardships and triumphs, of making it or not making it. What I wanted to trace was the interior journey, and – having first considered whether to write a novel, essays on language or essays on exile in the work of Eastern European writers – I ultimately decided to write a memoir.[1]

The memoir is particularly suited to combining representations of subjectivity and the external world. It was my intention to reflect on the intersection of the two, partly as a result of my immigrant experience. I was interested in exploring how language and culture – two forces that seem to be external to us – shape us and construct us, and how much loss of self we risk if we are without our language and cultural framework. The circumstances of this immigration – the political and the historical context in which they happen – are critical here. Although different kinds of migration and national movement are often compressed into unitary categories, these are highly heterogeneous, and these differences can have very powerful repercussions, including whether one is categorized as an emigrant, an émigré, an expatriate, a refugee or the contemporary nomad who travels around the globe back and forth.

Our particular emigration took place from Poland to Canada in 1959, at the height of the Cold War era. In the late 1950s, a more liberal government came to power in Poland and – at a time when most people were completely prohibited from travelling outside of the Soviet bloc – it allowed the Jewish population in Poland to emigrate. A lot of people decided to take advantage of this, for various reasons, leading to a significant process of emigration framed by the Cold War, in a very divided and bipolar world. However, it was somewhere between emigration and exile because the Jews were encouraged to leave at that point; it was not an *expulsion*, but there was an *encouragement* to leave. We travelled to Vancouver, which was the antipode of Krakow, from where we had left. Poland was a country that had recently been ravaged by two wars: the war of conquest against the Poles and the Holocaust, which took place largely on Polish territory although it was not a Polish project. It was a country stifled by a very oppressive regime and it was a country in a state of complete economic stasis and relative impoverishment. Vancouver was a new city, almost a frontier town, a boom town in a booming economy: it was all future and very little past. The contrast was extreme, as was the sense of rapture.

As we left on one-time visas, there was no going back; we assumed that we would never return, and my parents, in fact, never did. That kind of bipolar world, that kind of rupture, creates a split internal world. The past is suddenly on one side, the present on the other. One kind of identity, of self, is left behind, and a new self has not yet been created. For me, the project became to try to make myself at home in this new world, just as I had felt at home originally in Poland. For me this was crucially connected to writing and to language. I realized that if I wanted to feel at home, I needed a language that would inhabit me as deeply as Polish inhabited me. This project of acculturation involved a process of self-translation, a translation into a new language and into a new cultural vein.

**Jonny Steinberg:** As you were speaking Eva, I was thinking about the connections between your experience and Asad's, the central character in *A Man of Good Hope*.

Let me start with the question of who a refugee is. There are two rival answers to this question out there and I dislike both of them. The first is that refugees are people who have lost control over their circumstances. They are like flotsam in the ocean. Recently, after he performed *Hamlet* in London, Benedict Cumberbatch spoke to the audience about the refugee crisis. The reason people are getting on boats and drowning, he said, is because it is more dangerous on land. People are fleeing – they don't have a choice. This is one image of people seeking refuge.

The other image out there – the opposite image, really – is to say that refugees are cunning people out to take what is not theirs. They feign crisis because they want something better. They are deceitful.

I struggle with both of these ideas. The first says that refugees are owed hospitality because they have been robbed of some of the fundamental conditions that allow them to live human lives. They have experienced social deaths and we must take them in so that they might live again. That so often is just not true. In fact, migrants are able to move precisely because they have not experienced a social death, precisely because they still have the wherewithal of life, precisely because they can imagine and take action and betray and compromise and be bad to loved ones.

One of the things that I was trying to do in *A Man of Good Hope* is say that you should take this man in because he is so very human, because he is as complex as any figure you might encounter in bourgeois European literature. He is as dark, as capable of hurting others, as torn by existential questions.

Working month in and month out with Asad, I kept noticing the ways in which he and I were very different. One was in our respective relations to our own 'pasts'. If you ask me about my lineage I can tell you who my parents and my grandparents were, but when it comes to my great-grandparents I am getting a little shaky and before that I know nothing. When I ask Asad about his lineage he reels off the names of the last twenty-eight generations of his father's family, which is something that was hammered into his head when he was seven years old. It was a very striking difference between us. Another difference, which kept occurring to me, was the risks that he takes.

A little bit about his background on this: he was born in about 1984 in Mogadishu. Conflict broke out in 1991 when he was seven, and his mother was killed. His father disappeared. He then lived this incredibly itinerant childhood across the Horn of Africa. Without being attached to any particular adult he entered very wily relationships with adults. At the age of seventeen he ended up on the streets of Addis Ababa and started making good as a street hustler, earning enough money to maintain a house. He has stability. He gives it up. He puts $1,200 in his back pocket and heads to Johannesburg. He has no idea what he will find there. He hopes there are riches to be made but he really doesn't know. Nor does he really know how to get there. He doesn't have a passport. He has to move illegally.

So that is one decision that from the beginning interested me. From stability, he moves into danger. In Johannesburg he accumulates money, and one of the things that he does is he gives half of his savings to a human smuggler and he gets air tickets to Brazil on a false South African passport. His idea is to travel from Brazil to Mexico, cross the US border and get arrested. He has this idea that the Americans will not deport him because Somalia is at war. Instead, he imagines, they will keep him in jail for a while and then give him a Green Card. He had no idea whether this was actually true; he had heard a rumour. In the end he doesn't go. The night before his planned departure, the smugglers are caught and the trip is abandoned.

So, I was drawn to these differences between him and me: this deep lineage and his appetite for risk. They are intimately connected, I think. For a consequence of thinking about the deep past – imagining yourself at the end of twenty generations – is that you also imagine a deep future at the same time. Who will my descendant be in twenty generations? What will I have done in my brief time on this earth to shape their destiny? It would have to be something dramatic, would it not? Asad was seeking to trigger a revolution in the history of his lineage, to have his descendants live lives that his forbears could never have imagined. And to do that, he would have to jump into a new life, to take enormous risks.

So here is an image of a refugee, a wildly ambitious man who believes that his life will only have been worth living if he can change the future for generations of the unborn.

**Tamar Garb:** That is really interesting in the sense that this is what literature can do and what skillfully crafted narrative contributes. Potentially it extends the terms of the discussion. It enables us to individualize a story and perhaps produce an empathic relationship to a life told. I think both of you very graphically bring that out because, whether it is a form of self-narration or whether it is a form of description or an account of someone who has lived a life very different to yours, we get the opportunity to witness a life that is animated in prose and a journey that is followed with care. And we as readers are invited to follow these lives with you. And yet both of you made very particular decisions in these two books to tell a story of self or a story of an other. I'm interested, Eva, to know how you figure as the subject of your narrative and why, for you Jonny, you appear to shield yourself behind the story of another.

**Eva Hoffman:** As I indicated earlier, I was somewhat reluctant to write a memoir as I am not a writer of a confessional temperament. *Lost in Translation* is not a confessional memoir. It is a book about the experience of transculturation and self-translation, of coming into a second language and a second culture. That is what it explores, and it only includes the aspects of my trajectory which inform that. So it is highly selective. Nonetheless, the reason that I felt that I needed a memoir is because I needed to talk about this from *within*: I was tracing psychic processes rather than external dramas, and for that I needed a case study. And the case study I had was myself.

The reason for writing in the present tense – and I was actually freed to write it when I came upon the present tense – is firstly because, in my case, the narrative, the continuity of the narrative was disrupted by emigration. The narrative of Asad's journey in *A Man of Good Hope* is a narrative of travelling from one place to another, it really is a literal journey and the drama of it adheres in this turbulent trajectory that he chooses to follow. In *Lost in Translation*, I wanted to write about this internal journey and the psychic processes which, in a sense, were always coterminous, were always present. At the same time, the sense of the past was extremely present. The memories weren't the memories of the first stage of my life, growing up in Poland. They were very much preserved, very much part of the present, as I went on to reconstruct myself in a very different cultural and linguistic way.

With regard to hospitality, on one level my family and I were treated very hospitably: we were taken into safety both in Canada and subsequently in the United States. On the level of institutions, of official life, on what could be called political life, we were treated well. And yet what made this process of transculturation difficult was a lack of *recognition*: a lack of personal recognition. This was when I re-emigrated, and I went to the United States in 1963 and studied there.

During this time, America still had a very unified sense of itself – strong counter-cultures and culture wars had not yet emerged – and it considered itself to be the norm, with the ideology of immigration being the melting-pot ideology. Of course, it was the immigrants who were supposed to do the 'melting' and who were presumably grateful and happy to become American, as instantly as possible.

In a sense, I was, and continue to be, grateful. American institutions, especially American education, delivered on its promises. They partly delivered upward mobility, and, for me, a sense of being allowed to become a part of society and to play a professional role within it. However, I also felt that if I underwent this transformation too quickly, or too automatically, or too externally, that my original identity would be colonized, in a way, taken over. I felt that there was a lack of understanding, at that time, not only about particular cultural differences but about the very fact of cultural difference. This was very difficult to explain to people, that there really are different relations of personality, different experiential maps, different forms of relationship, different qualities, different character traits and values. That culture gives you a first template for what it means to be a person, what it means to have a self.

This was really not understood until later, when there was an enormous swing of the pendulum that we can frame as a kind of privileging of otherness and of cultural difference. In this sense, I believe that what Jonny offers Asad is a kind of full recognition, through entering into a really inter-subjective relationship with him. It is Emanuel Levinas who argues that the recognition of another happens with an encounter with their face, through entering into the subjectivity of another person's face. Jonny truly entered into Asad's face, understands his expressions and gestures, and doesn't idealize him in any way. In other words, Asad becomes a three-dimensional person in Jonny's account, which is quite remarkable – a gift, and also very courageous.

**Jonny Steinberg:** That is very generous, Eva, but let me respond by being a bit more self-critical and then to say something admiring about your work. This question of recognition is very interesting. I am quite certain that when people migrate, when they move, they know that they are going to suffer a deficit of recognition where they are going. In a sense, they know that a part of them is going to die, they are going to be living in a world that doesn't acknowledge them much. This is a very tough thing to be doing. And the question arises: Why do that? And I would argue that they are doing it for future generations, really. They are thus thinking over a long span of time. We will suffer a deficit of recognition so that the next generation, or perhaps the one after that, enjoys a surfeit of recognition.

That is complicated by the fact that they surely must know that their descendants, in the very course of being recognized, will lose their history; they will be Americans, not Somalis. At some point they will lose the language, the memories, the connections. And so people like Asad are preparing the ground for people who will in all likelihood forget him.

It is interesting that you say that I recognize Asad, because when the book was almost finished I gave it to him to read and he found it unreadable. He found it too painful to read. And he did not want to recognize what I saw. He did not like, at all, the idea of his struggles and his life laid down on a page. He could talk to me about them because the very process of speaking has agency. He could anaesthetize the experience as it was coming out of his mouth. Whereas to see it by somebody else's hand, not in his control, the whole catastrophe of it was not just painful, but also not useful. Here is somebody thinking about the present and the future. He only thought about the past insofar as it could be used as a pragmatic resource. He wanted bits and pieces of it, not a clear sighting of the whole thing. And so here was I, thinking that I had, as Eva said, given him this enormous attention, this enormous care, this enormous recognition, having created a record, and yet he didn't like the record at all.

**Tamar Garb:** Did he feel betrayed?

**Jonny Steinberg:** No, not at all. He didn't find the record untrue. It just wasn't useful for him. One reason for writing what I write is that I live in a country that I don't understand. It is a country with deep wells of very different experience. We pass each other on the streets and know almost nothing about what animates each other. As such, part of my aim was to enter into lives that are very foreign to mine and yet are caught up in my fate, and to try and understand them from within as much as I can. The way to understand a strange life from within, I think, is to ask: Why do people decide what they decide? Why would somebody chose to leave his wife, to leave a place where he is doing okay? I think that my self is an enquiring self rather than an included self. I don't write anything like memoir because I don't really trust myself to write honestly about myself. I think that writing about oneself with honesty is a very difficult discipline that most people do not have. And I think it's a discipline that Eva very, very uniquely achieved in *Lost in Translation*. It is a rare ability to write about oneself with that depth of truth.

**Tamar Garb:** It is interesting that you have used the historical present when you write. It is about the reconstruction of that past that we come to inhabit in the present and we seem to witness this as if you are experiencing it now. I think that is very interesting in terms of the way that both of you write and how the present tense is used to chronicle something of the past, how it brings that into a vivid relationship with the present.

But I wanted to ask you both, having been fascinated by your accounts of coming from countries in which people don't understand each other or which we ourselves fail to comprehend: How unique is that? Is there any place where one understands the people that are around one? There might be shared cultural forms and rituals that we recognize, and yet, increasingly, that is not the case: we live in very fractured spaces, very divided societies. In light of this, is this construction of the self and the stranger something that the world we are now inhabiting prompts us to confront more and more graphically? Is this as particular to our times as we may experience it as being?

**Eva Hoffman:** Indeed, it may not be as unique as we experience it as being, and yet it is new to us and perhaps it is evidencing itself in more extreme forms than it did before. For example, Poland had a very long commonality of cultural history in which the word multiculturalism didn't exist. They didn't think of themselves as multicultural, although my parents came from a town that was inhabited equally by Poles, Ukrainians and Jews. My parents both knew four languages just by the virtue of growing up there, so this was quite a normal condition, as has historically been the case across many parts of the world. This was the case in a pre-national context, which prompts us to acknowledge the significance of living with diversity within a national society.

Conceptualizing and enacting hospitality and recognition become complicated when we leap from the individual to the collective. There is no dispelling that difference: the kind of recognition that you give Asad cannot be given collectively, it cannot be accomplished collectively. What can be hoped for is being treated as an equal citizen with the same rights and responsibilities as everybody else, being included in this sphere of citizenship. It is unknown if these very particular differences can be recognized in practice, but we can demand that they should be recognized.

As we live with these very different societies, we may benefit from thinking about the French Enlightenment idea that a person could have their privatized religious ethnic identity at home but be a citizen in public. We need to learn how to allow ourselves and each other our particular identities, our specific pasts, our individual cultural experience, while simultaneously maintaining a sense that we share a society in common, we need to learn how to have mutual regard for each other but also for the society that we want to nurture and share. This remains unresolved in the unhappy leap from individual recognition and individual affection that Asad experiences from quite a few people, to the collective misery of non-recognition that comes when violence thrives in a South African township in which the Somalis are systematically attacked, persecuted, victimized, killed.

**Tamar Garb:** In this regard Jonny, how do you understand that hostility, that xenophobic rejection of the outsider or stranger? Is it hostility based on economic competition as many commentators have been saying, or is it an ethnic hostility? Or is it just part of a general hostility against immigrants in a vulnerable and fragile environment?

**Jonny Steinberg:** Asad goes to South Africa because he has been told that there is money to be made, and there is. The problem is that money is to be made in the peripheral settlements of South African cities among the very poor.[2] A foreigner with a cash business among poor people is very vulnerable, and Asad experiences a great deal of violence. Why? It is very comforting to assert that people like Asad are scapegoats, that the violence committed against them has nothing to do with them. And yet I am not sure if that is enough.

Here is a stranger in our midst. He doesn't belong. He has no desire to belong. He is here for nakedly instrumental reasons. He wants to make some money and then move on. That is what he is performing in front of you, day in and day out. You watch him have nothing to do with you but take your money. He does not share in your collective myths, in your anguish, in your suffering. He shows you, all the time, how little you and he have in common.

There are few culturally homogeneous places in the world, that is true. But that does not mean that every place in the world is as heterogeneous as the next. There are parts of the world where difference is felt in much more extreme ways: places where people have lived side by side for many generations and they understand one another as little as they did five or six generations ago. They are making zero-sum claims on the same history. This is not unique to South Africa, as it is true of many places.

**Tamar Garb:** A kind of hopelessness seems to emerge throughout this conversation. On the one hand, you have suggested that only the politics of citizenship can provide the frameworks in which human beings can be safeguarded. So the rule of law is there to protect people from violence and exploitation, and we believe that the rule of law must be in place for this reason. However, both of your reflections on very different historical and geopolitical circumstances note that, even if one is welcomed with open arms and hospitality resides, there is always the possibility of a failure of recognition, which leads to a deep form of alienation, or an internal kind of crisis of self and self-recognition.

**Eva Hoffman:** In my case, I believe that much has changed since the period of our immigration to North America: there is greater understanding and acknowledgement of diversity in the United States and in certain other countries as well. There was almost a swing of the pendulum for a while, in which having a minoritarian identity was positioned as privileged, romantic, glamorous. There was a body of postmodern theory that privileged the qualities of being displaced: fragmentation, displacement, outsiderness, and so on. As such, it was represented as a glamorous condition, and people identified themselves readily with their ethnic identities and ethnic pasts. It appears that an understanding and a greater tolerance for strangers has taken place in the last fifty or so years; it appears that dealing with diversity takes practice, and these countries have now had several decades of practice and something has been learnt through the process. South Africa has had a very different history in this respect, of course. I would suggest that what still needs to be learnt is to be less timid and less cautious about talking to each other, to give each other the kind of recognition that we would give to ourselves. In other words, what we need is to be engaged in a candid conversation with each other, in which we recognize each other not as oppresser and victim, but as humans – members of different groups who need to live in the same society. We need a much more robust dialogue, because otherwise there is a danger that, while prejudices against various groups may have less-ened, many people live in very fragmented circumstances and this is not good for building a society.

**Jonny Steinberg:** In my case, I am going to be more pessimistic. Tamar, you ask whether all we have is the rule of law, and I think that *if only* we had the rule of law, it would go quite a long way. I think that in societies that hit a certain threshold of inequality, in societies that are particularly unequal, you *don't* have the rule of law. Because the rule of law requires equality of recognition. In a country like South Africa, and not just South Africa, equally in a country like Brazil or Colombia, you have the rule of law at very most for the top 50 per cent of society. I don't think that the bottom 50 per cent get much access to the law.

**Tamar Garb:** Law provides the framework, then, for the possibility of recognition. Without the law to protect and frame the fragility of life, the possibility of empathy and engagement with strangers as like sub-jects becomes that much more difficult. But if the story of Asad tells us anything, it is that this is possible, even in the most challenging of cir-cumstances. I must take some hope from that.

## Acknowledgements

The conversation, which took place at the UCL Institute of Advanced Studies as a 'Refuge in a Mov-ing World' research event in December 2015, was initially transcribed verbatim by (in alphabetical order): Ranjita Dilraj, Aydan Greatrick, Yvonne Green, Paige Isaacson, Iyad Tupcharoen and Ana Visan, who were all MSc Global Migration students at the UCL Department of Geography at the time of the event. The transcript has subsequently been edited, and in parts rephrased, by Eva Hoff-man, Jonny Steinberg, Tamar Garb and Elena Fiddian-Qasmiyeh for this volume.

## Notes

1. For other approaches to 'writing' in/through/from displacement explored in this volume, see Haile (on 'voice' and 'silence'), Qasmiyeh (on 'Writing the camp: writing the archive'), Davies (on representations of displacement in graphic novels and testimonial comics) and Niccolai (on writing and producing theatre as a response to displacement).
2. On markets run by and for migrants, asylum-seekers and refugees in South Africa, also see Tayob, in this volume.

## References

Hoffman, Eva. 1989. *Lost in Translation: A Life in a New Language*. New York: Penguin.

Levinas, Emmanuel. 1987. *Time and the Other*, translated by Richard A. Cohen. Pittsburgh: Duquesne University Press.

Steinberg, Jonny. 2015. *A Man of Good Hope*. London: Jonathan Cape.

4

# Writing the camp, writing the camp archive: The case of Baddawi camp in Lebanon

Yousif M. Qasmiyeh

## Introduction

This chapter consists of a brief introduction to what I refer to as 'writing the camp' and 'writing the camp archive', followed by a series of poems or fragments that I have written in my capacity as the writer-in-residence of a research project examining experiences of and responses to displacement from Syria.[1] Through particular reference to Baddawi refugee camp (my place of birth) in North Lebanon,[2] this chapter assesses the ways in which refugees *write* the camp into their own multiple narratives vis-à-vis markers (and beings) of temporality, permanence and liminality.[3] Importantly, I note from the outset that writing (in) the camp is not assigned a specific outcome as such, so much as it is a response to the very presence of the camp itself.

## Writing the camp archive[4]

Who writes the camp? Who traces the camp's evolution into (a) space? Who demarcates its limbs as they retreat internally in order to accommodate more refugees? The camp has never been entirely a place, but a multiplicity of entwined histories and times (also see Fiddian-Qasmiyeh, 2019). These times bear witness to the construction as well as the dissolution of refugee communities. Baddawi camp in North Lebanon is my home camp and has, since its birth in the 1950s, become home to refugees from across the Middle East at different times – including, most recently, refugees from Syria since 2011. It has become urgent to document the lives of its residents in both life and death through processes that privilege the ordinary and the everyday at the expense of the extraordinary and the unique, which rarely belong to the community itself but to those who claim its representation.

This entails maintaining a healthy distance between 'writing' as a determination to exist despite all the renewed adversities in such places, and as an act of continuous archiving whereby refugees themselves (consciously) narrate the camp in their daily presences in ways that not only instate their solitude but are also essential to remember who they are. Such a practice poignantly resonates with Jacques Derrida's conceptualization of the archive as a creation towards the future and as a domain in which people are its mere agents (Derrida, 1996). We might say that such processes are the only processes that remind the camp's inhabitants that it is their right to write what is deemed theirs in the spatial and territorial sense, even though such markers are never conspicuous, nor are they markers of permanence as such.

In 'Writing the Camp', a series of responses and engagements with and around the camp, its battles with itself, its people and its surroundings, which have appeared periodically on the 'Refugee Hosts' platform (www.refugeehosts.org), I have attempted to turn my sight on the camp in two manners (see Qasmiyeh, 2016a, 2016b, 2017a, 2017b, 2017c, 2017d). First, as a site where the holy and the profane amalgamate, for it is their marriage, forced or otherwise, that keeps inviting as well as shunning people. Second, it is through documenting the camp's innards that we witness what will never be witnessed again, through transforming the relationship between the writer of the camp and the camp itself into a form of unbreakable bond, not in the tribal sense but as a memory that is there simply to keep both the camp and its inhabitants alive. To return to Derrida's notion of the archive (1996: 20–1), it is the body – the body of the refugee, her skin – that becomes the parchment, the very piece of paper or skin, that holds the specificities of being a refugee, of being an outcast in a space that will never go away or stay. As such, the refugee's existence becomes solely contingent on an archive that is 'an impression associated with a word' (ibid.: 29), which is in the process of being written by the refugee herself.

Derrida's engagement with bodily markers as essential components of the archive, those that incise as well as circumcise,[5] appears to presuppose difference on behalf of those who intend to write the archive or those whose 'writing' ought to play a role in reclaiming the age(ing) of the camp by tracing the event therein. Writing in this context becomes an act of bearing witness, simultaneously a testimony to/for the individual and the camp. While it is essential for me to write what is worthy of writing, without delving deeply into the personal but hovering above it, writing emerges as a memory hunting down more memories. So, who is the witness in a refugee camp? Who is the owner of the testimony? Is it the refugee herself or those who (are able to) come and go? As it is the camp itself that validates and corroborates what is going to be narrated, the writer becomes a witness-agent, a gatherer of details, details that continuously refer the refugee to the camp through cumulative memories and sounds.

In the camp, we bear witness to ourselves first and foremost, to our multiple lives and deaths in this space of containment. We do so as if it were our 'duty' to leave something behind, a palpable thing upon which our names are inscribed – the names that tie us to those who have borne us while also giving the latter the opportunity to bear witness to the creation of more refugees as time passes. The trace that we normally leave, intentionally or otherwise, in spaces and through journeys that we, at times, attempt by force to normalize, is what keeps us attached to this state of tentativeness: we are neither fully en route or in an actual place, nor are we promised an arrival.[6] As I have argued elsewhere (Qasmiyeh, 2016c), in documenting the trace – in bearing witness to its presence in the shape of the static, animate or otherwise – we forge a linkage between all the tenses at work (also see Hoffman *et al.*, in this volume). In other words, remembering the camp becomes the prerequisite for remembering ourselves in/outside the camp.

It is after all how '[The archive] opens out of the future' (Derrida, 1996: 68) and the way in which its engagement with the past and the present defines and reconfigures its nature – be it that of the individual or that of the collective. In the same vein, it is the unity between witnessing and archiving in the refugee camp that maintains the momentum of writing, as an overarching means through which details are captured as soon as they leave their source. Such an immediacy is that of the future, the future that is yet to be defined as an upcoming event and yet it is its promise that keeps the camp afloat. Indeed, according to Derrida:

> The question of the archive is not … a question of the past. It is not the question of a concept dealing with the past that might *already* be at our disposal or not at our disposal, *an archivable concept of the archive*. It is a question of the future, the question of the future itself, the question of a response, of a promise and of a responsibility

of tomorrow. The archive: if we want to know in times to come. Perhaps. Not tomorrow but in times to come, later on or perhaps never. (Derrida, 1996: 36, emphasis in the original)

Since it is the archive of the refugee that will (might) be gathered, it is worth briefly stopping at the question of performativity. The refugee has never assigned herself the role of the initiator of the archive. It is a role that has been bestowed upon her by a series of instants: these are the instants of the camp. We might argue that sensing that there should be an archive of/for the camp is what keeps the camp alive for the time being, as it transfers both the person and the place towards the future. Thus, the 'camp archive' ties the refugee, the camp and time together in an insoluble chain, in which in order for the archive to survive its own destiny it should survive its writing:

> The camp is a passing human, a book, a manuscript, an archive ...
> Bury it; smother it with its own dust, so it might return as a holy text devoid of intentions. (Qasmiyeh, 2017b – *Writing the Camp Archive*)

The same question, however elliptical it is, keeps returning: Who writes the archive:

> Only refugees can forever write the archive.
> The camp owns the archive, not God.
> For the archive not to fall apart, it weds the camp unceremoniously.
> The question of a camp archive is also the question of the camp's survival beyond speech.
> Circumcising the body can indicate the survival of the place.
> Blessed are the pending places that are called camps. (Qasmiyeh, 2017b – *Writing the Camp Archive*)

Although it is the writing that reminds us of the value of what we write, it seems that a clear distinction between the divine and the human in writing is urgently needed. Such a distinction would not only equate the status of the camp with that of the 'owner' of the archive, but it would also delineate a total synergy between the 'pending' in the camp and the 'pending' in the archive.

The lack of clarity vis-à-vis what the archive *really* is, and realizing that 'nothing is less reliable, nothing is less clear today than the word "archive"' (Derrida, 1996: 90) should undoubtedly not diminish the archive's capacity to privilege the written at the expense of what is already there. In the end, 'the structure of the archive is *spectral*. It is spectral *a priori*: neither present nor absent "in the flesh", neither visible nor invisible, a trace always referring to another ... ' (ibid.: 84). For it is what can be archived that is worthy of the name 'archive'; it is thus essential to consider the language that is employed in such records. More importantly, as we are seeking to write 'the then', transcending the rhetoric of empathy towards refugees becomes some sort of a 'minor' language – a language that is 'the instrument *par excellence* of that destratification' (Deleuze and Guattari, 2012: xvi). In 'writing the camp', this 'destratification' manifests itself in two different (and yet entwined) ways: in writing the camp and in order to write with the intention of continuity, the means, the language in this context, recoils into itself – not to disappear or shrink, but to reinstate its conditions from within. Finally, inviting an act of writing from within does not necessarily imply a *uni*-writing, which is based upon one 'narrative' or on a language that claims absolute entitlement to the future by virtue of having been born in/to the camp. On the contrary, it is the direct opposite of such an archival monopoly. To put it simply, the writing that we are putting forward is the one that 'deals with the acknowledged doubt of an explicit division ... of the impossibility of one's own place' (De Certeau, 1975: 327, cited in Bensmaïa, 2012: ix). This 'division', or fragmentariness, inherent within these narratives, is exactly what enables us to 're-gather' from different sites (whether it is the camp or its (de) placement) and 'write' at the same time as we write the camp.

## Writing Baddawi refugee camp into literature

Against this backdrop, writing Baddawi refugee camp into literature inevitably means writing both those who have continued life and living in this place – and, I would argue, in this camp-time – since the 1950s and also the newcomers who have perceived the camp, in its ontological and existential sense, as their only place, into narratives that are yet to be complete(d). This writing reasserts these people's belonging to and clashes with a continuum of refugeedom and displacement that has escaped its boundaries into a life (or lives) whose writing presupposes the intimate in the national. In writing the camp, we write the intimate, or what is deemed as such, in its absolute rawness and translucence: the place shredding its innards to assume a new place; the wall that defines the prior to and the post of an event; the gravedigger and his hands handling life and death in equal measures; old, new and green cemeteries; the call to prayer disrupting the void but also echoing it at once; the father, the mother, the brothers and the sisters being discerned diurnally and written (probably despite themselves) into fragments and epithets of time; old and new refugees fighting with time, each other and no one; traces as artefacts; tilted memories as the sun in May; dialects *contra* dialects; pictures as recurrent pasts, framed or imposed on frames; UNRWA;[7] God and the neighbour, Palestinian or otherwise; daily jobs practised, like their prayers, mainly indoors; migratory birds flying or being lost above the camp; young people drowning en route to an abstract Europe; weddings and funerals passing the scene hand-in-hand; other camps but also other people; names and proper nouns baiting a never-happening future; the same illnesses occurring and reoccurring; the camp as a future; the camp as an archive.

We shall write the concrete in the camp. We shall write the camp as a time beneath time but, above all, as its own time suspended from the edges of history and intention. We shall write in anticipation of what is to come – that is, to come, to witness, to write the archive.

But what is the archive in a camp named to bear a name – its name, the name that is at once the history and geography of a name beyond a name? The archive only begins in the camp. It begins in the hope that the camp will return to its cycle safely, with a well-recited text, that of the immediate and the intimate. From my mother drying the life out of vegetables to make them edible in the future, to my father hammering a handcrafted wooden table with uneven legs, with innumerable nails to fix a crack, an invisible crack, a crack, nonetheless – therein lies the archive.

My mother's food jars, her dried vegetables – prepared with the intention of using them at a later date, whenever this date happens – compounded with my father's curses as he remembers a life marked by constant precarity since his flight from Palestine in 1948 as a young boy through multiple places until the creation of Baddawi camp, are not mere transient proclivities but a necessary engagement with the 'then' in a setting that is the closest to a text and a canon.

Could there be, after all, an archival writing or a writing of an archive by and for the refugee in a time when neither the camp nor its inhabitants, as always suggested, are born to remain in their writing?

The camp, the archive, shall remain above memory overseeing the daily and the wild odd plants in the cracks …

## Writing as an eye beyond eyes

The following fragments were composed as part of my project, 'Writing the Camp: Writing the Camp Archive', with the intention of co-seeing in writing what would otherwise reach its end without being remembered as the lived.

## Writing the camp: Vis-à-vis or a camp[8]

To experience is to advance by navigating, to walk by traversing. (Derrida, 1996: 373)

I

What makes a camp a camp? And what is the beginning of a camp if there is any? And do camps exist in order to die or exist forever?

II

Baddawi is my home camp, a small camp compared to other Palestinian camps in Lebanon. For many residents, it comprises two subcamps: the lower and the upper camps that converge at the old cemetery. As I was growing up, it was common for children to know their midwife. Ours, perhaps one of only two in the entire camp, was an elderly woman, who died tragically when a wall collapsed on top of her fragile body during a stormy day in the camp. The midwife was the woman who cut our umbilical cords and washed us for the first time. She lived by the main mosque – *Masjid al-Quds* – that overlooked the cemetery. She would always wait by the cemetery to stop those who she delivered en route to school, to give them a kiss and remind them that she was the one who made them.

III

The camp is never the same albeit with roughly the same area. New faces, new dialects, narrower alleys, newly-constructed and ever-expanding thresholds and doorsteps, intertwined clothing lines and electrical cables, well-shielded balconies, little oxygen and impenetrable silences are all amassed in this space. The shibboleth has never been clearer and more poignant than it is now.

IV

Refugees ask other refugees, who are we to come to you and who are you to come to us? Nobody answers. Palestinians, Syrians, Iraqis, Kurds share the camp, the same-different camp, the camp of a camp. They have all come to re-originate the beginning with their own hands and feet.

V

Now, in the camp, there are more mosques, more houses of God, while people continue to come and go, like the calls to prayer emanating at slightly varied times from all these mosques, supplementing, interrupting, transmuting, and augmenting the voice and the noise simultaneously.

VI

Baddawi is a camp that lives and dies in our sight. It is destined to remain (not necessarily as itself) so long as time continues to be killed in its corners.

## Writing the camp archive⁹

*The camp is a passing human, a book, a manuscript, an archive ... Bury it; smother it with its own dust, so it might return as a holy text devoid of intentions.*

I

Only refugees can forever write the archive.
The camp owns the archive, not God.
For the archive not to fall apart, it weds the camp unceremoniously.
The question of a camp archive is also the question of the camp's survival beyond speech.
Circumcising the body can indicate the survival of the place.
Blessed are the pending places that are called camps.

II

My father, who passed his stick on to me, lied to us all: I slaughtered your brother so you would grow sane and sound.
My mother, always with the same knife, cuts herself and the vegetables.
The eyes which live long are the ones whose sight is contingent upon the unseen.

III

God's past is the road to the camp's archive.
We strangle it, from its loose ends, so we can breathe its air.
Privileging death in the camp is the sacral of the refugee body.
Without its death, the archive will never exist.
In whose name is the camp a place?
It is the truth and nothing else that for the camp to survive it must kill itself.

IV

The transience of the face in a place where faces are bare signs of flesh can gather the intransience of the trace therein in its multiple and untraced forms.
The unseen – that is the field that is there despite the eye – can only be seen by the hand. After all, the hand and not the eye, is the intimate part.
The tense in our bones – the one that emerged in no time, but with the desire to be time – will always be ahead of us.

V

Green in the camp only belongs to the cemetery.
The veiled women crying at the grave are my mother and my sisters.
Once, my mother wanted to bring the grave home with her.
In the solemnity of the place, faces fall like depleted birds.
In belonging to the camp, senses premeditate their senses.

## In mourning the refugee, we mourn God's intention in the absolute[10]

We repeat the repeated so we can see our features more clearly, the face as it is, the cracks in their transcendental rawness and for once we might consent to what we will never see.
They rarely return – those pigeons. The piece of wood that was meant to scare off the pigeons and entice them to return to their home landed by my feet. Not knowing what to do with it, I shut my eyes and threw it back in the direction of God ...
The name is the loneliest of things.

What is recited is the voice and not the text.

In my camp, women slap themselves in funerals to never let go of pain.

Who can see it to say: it is? Who has the eyes to say: it definitely is?

The eternal in the camp is the crack. 'The crack also invites.'

What is a camp? Is it not a happening beyond time?

A camp, to survive its happening, must become almost a camp.

The sublime in the camp, what it is? Can it not be the camp gestating with its impossible meaning?

His feet were in water and the hands were by his side as flat as nothing.

While the tea was brewing, he prodded his father's shoulder to ask about the number of graves he dug today.

Nothing can outlive Nothing when Nothing escapes not the idea of living, living like twigs left alone to decay under the sight of the mother tree.

Does the camp not have a gender?

What speaks in the camp is nothing but the foreskin.

These are not headscarves but heads forever wrapped in themselves.

In mourning the refugee, we mourn God's intention in the absolute.


## The Camp is Time[11]


I

Who writes the camp and what is it that ought to be written in a time where the plurality of lives has traversed the place itself to become its own time.


II

How will the camp stare at itself in the coming time, look itself in the eye; the eye of time, the coming that is continually pending, but with a face – human or otherwise – that is defaced? The camp is a time more than it is a place. Upon and above its curves, time remembers its lapses to the extent that it is its time – the one whose time is one – that preys on a body that is yet to be born.


III

In crucifying time neither it nor we can recognise the crucified.

IV

God, incinerate the camp save the dialect. God, incinerate the camp, save the dialect.

V

The incinerator of time is the camp.

VI

What is it that makes a sight worth a sighting when the seer – the quasi-seer – can only use his only eyes for an enormity that no eyes can actually see? Is it the camp or is it its time that should be (re)turned to its body to (re)claim its body as a dead thing with multiple previous lives and none.

VII

I write for it knowing that this is the last time that I write for it, herein the time is last and the last, it may belong to a no-beginning-no-end, but what it definitely has is its camp. The camp is time and time is the camp.

VIII

The possessive is what possesses the guilt that transcends all guilt and yet co-exists with itself until it becomes an event in its own guilt. But is it, is it my camp?

IX

What am I saying right now, in this specific instant and under the false impression that the camp is mine? I say that it is the autobiography of the camp that is autobiographising the camp, suspended in time it is, while we deliberate the impossibility of narration in that context. In order to think of narration (not necessarily its narration), we follow it discreetly in the shape of ash.

X

In time, the mask takes off its mask.

## XI

The foot that treads is also time.

## XII

In time we impregnate time with its time.

## XIII

Time gives birth to nothing. The nothing that is raging nearby is our only time.

## XIV

Time, tell us where your private parts are?

## XV

Time is the acrogenous of the face. Whenever a face ages, it ages beyond time.

## XVI

In the camp, time is hung like threads of dried okra.

## *A Sudden Utterance is the Stranger*[12]

### I

The moon is the birthmark of the refugee.
His birth equates to the mauling of his entire body.
Nothing is anomalous about the wound.
While waiting, we bite our nails and flesh.
Once I dreamt in God's language. In my extreme ecstasy, I swallowed my tongue.

II

A dialect is a circumcised lip.
A sudden utterance is the stranger.
Only when tongues age, do dialects become old enough to leave.
An utterance en route is the utterance that can never promise.

III

In the camp, measuring air by hand by no means connotes the intimate.

IV

As for time, it is an endeavour to the impossible in the impossibility of an existence devoid of it.

V

In the camp, directions are needles in time's back.

VI

The camp, to sustain its body, shrinks its limbs.
The camp has its own God.
The spectator is whoever cannot see his face.

VII

Death, to carry a meaning, carries its offspring.

VIII

The camp is the tomb that has yet to find its dead.
Could it not be that the tomb is the name?
Only the dead lead us to the cemetery.

## *Flesh when mutilated called God*[13]

Time is God's journey to his shadow.
An incomplete sentence is the place.

In the non-occurrence of birth, aborting the camp becomes the only possibility.

Might the dialects be the place that will be?

The hole is its hole, wailing and waiting for the green to sprout.

In a brass bowl with dangling rings as raw as young earlobes, my mother would pour us water whenever a plane broke the sound barrier, thinking that this would calm our fears and interrupt the deafening cries.

There, they interpret life as a sign of life, no more, no less.

When their old wall collapsed, they erected another using their house plants.

In betraying the static, we narrate water with water.

What we pour on ourselves is also called narration.

The neighbour's tattoo inflicted by another neighbour still bears the faint name of another neighbour's daughter.

Sometimes I wonder how a god would look like if he were to have my mother's broken veins.

A god with broken veins is a god who has ultimately given birth.

The Lebanese shopkeeper on the edge of the camp who used to buy our UNRWA tomato paste tins, once said: I was sorry to hear about your father's death. That was what my mother decided to tell the man to make him pay her on time.

The meaning of time is the meaning of what can and cannot move in time and at the same time.

The elderly woman by the mosque once claimed to have seen time in the flesh.

My camp's gravedigger neither prays nor fasts, he is only capable of digging.

Skinning is separating the skin from the flesh, never the flesh from the skin.

My mother tells me that the butcher who sells her meat still swears on his daughter's life that he slaughters his cows with his own hands.

The same butcher who still sells meat to my mother is, according to our distant relative who knew him from another camp, neither married nor does he have a daughter.

Eye, the orifice of oblivion, the camp is certainly before you.

Ageing in the camp is a rehearsal for ageing in heaven. Neither acts require proof to sustain their time.

Whose consciousness is more reliable: the animal that rarely kills or the man who rarely dies?

When the war ended, my father washed the blood off our threshold and gave us a bath.

And what shall we call a camp that is completely there?

The camp's genesis lies in its consciousness of itself.

My mother used to bake us bread and deliver it to school so we could eat, so we could stop looking with envy at our friends holding their bread filled with things. On that day, the school gate was closed but a hole was there. Desperate to reach us, my mother's hand got trapped clutching the bread. To this day, we do not know why my mother, to free her hand and alleviate the pain, did not let go of the bread.

The camp never ceases to exist. A place it is not, but time inhabited by time's selfishness.

Is it not the visceral which binds us to the camp? The feeling in its rawness which drags us to it – to a breast or a lap so dry, as fossilised as our time?

In our home, in the piles of books and notebooks left to their time, I spot my school book: half-faded letters, lines smudged by dampness and traces of rust, my name thinly written on its own on a line.

In total darkness, with no eyes to see me or faces to lament the non-presence of light, I held her hand tightly, thinking that, sooner or later, that light would be back and our eyes, open and shut, would once again return to guard our hands from our hands.

Nothing arrives in the camp. The neighbour with the prosthetic leg once said: I swear by God (pointing at the artificial limb), it feels like mine.

The camp is grasped in its absence.

To kill time, the camp sheds its innards.

The inhabited and the inhabitant share the same limbs.

Once their sweat was the same. He would throw his jacket over the school wall so his brother would wear it after him. As siblings, their main arguments revolved around whose smell the jacket had kept.

My mother's hands, distant as they are, would intertwine, the right above the left, to press the devil back into her tummy and pronounce the end.

In writing the archive we submit to the perishable in writing.

Yet there is something to hold … The women in the long lines, above their invisible legs, outside the UNRWA distribution centres, with hair hurriedly tied up underneath the headscarves, cannot write. In anticipation of their names being called and their thumbs inked, they would tread slowly holding their hands as if cradling premature babies.

The teacher, who asked me to swear by God three times that my father did pray when he handed me a sealed envelope with a bit of money collected by the school for the poor, did not know that my father never accepted that money but instead returned it to the mosque, claiming that he had just found it.

She would always insist on giving me some. In her hands, she would gently rub the dry mint to softness. From lightness, to falling shades, to lightness again. A sighting of sublime dissipation: the leaf, a fragile wing, becoming its own fragility.

The tree in your name, we will recite. The name chosen hurriedly by your father. You were barely a few hours old when he recited it to himself in front of curious strangers as a beginning for something which would never age to die or die to age. Then, neither of your parents knew how to read or write, it sufficed for them to utter the name for the name to be carried across the arid fields of May into the absolute. The letters are now long dead and the wailing, which has never ceased reverberating in those distant furrows, has come home.

What is it that is not a camp?

When the war ended and before leaving the bomb shelter, my mother asked us to check we had everything.

I am writing the fragment within me, the incompletion I behold as a sense.

In the camp the barest attachment to earth becomes the ultimate survival on earth.

A pending mourning in the name. A pending mourning is the name.

For the concrete in it, for what is there for it from times past, the monumental speaks. It speaks to itself, in its own voice, to what once was. In the hope of an ageless silence, it speaks – a silence which is as imperceptible as time.

There, whenever time comes, we cross from age to intention.

We seize speech from behind our ears like overripe fruit, with care, and once caught we start again.

Flesh when mutilated called God.

In dying, flesh prefigures flesh.

As precise as the body is the wound.

On my uncle's floor, the one who sells second-hand clothes to his Lebanese neighbours, I shook my tooth until it fell out, to make a window like my mother's.

Crossing the threshold is to confess without speech.

In the camp, confessing occurs before knowing.

An avowal to an avowal is silence.

Tense as a tense, persuasive as a mask is the camp.

I once saw her imploring God to rid her of her husband while exposing her old breast to heaven.

In the camp, the foot which outlives the other is called a witness.

## The Camp is the Reject of the Reject Par Excellence[14]

I

It bears multiple meanings, depending on how it is said. For my mother, however, the meaning was clear enough to be taken from my father's mouth to God's and vice versa; without allowing it to pass through a limbo of any sort. They would normally fight over the mundane, the most mundane of the mundane, and those most mundane of things would remind us all that our voices really did exist and if they were to be given the opportunity to exercise noise again, they would do so to their hearts' content. My mother would become silent and to reiterate her silence she would only request to be left alone and be allowed to see God's face. Now, they are both old and frail; my father is still in the company of his voice while the woman, that woman, is still looking for her face and God's.

II

Once, I asked my mother: Mother, in the absence of a place, who invites who? She looked at me and said with a concerned tone of voice: My son has gone mad! Hurry! Hurry up! Summon the imam to recite over him!

III

Madness is what accompanies us to the unpredictable, to the camp. The camp's unpredictability lies only in the eyes of the dwellers.

IV

It is the tremor in the hand that invites. My grandmother, in Nahr Al-Bared camp, used to squeeze our little hands whenever we appeared at her doorstep and say: How did you leave the camp? We never answered.

V

By intending to capture the face, the whole body becomes hostage to intention.

VI

In intention, the prevalent tense is the past.

VII

We never listened to my mother and always insisted on swallowing the chewing gum thinking that it might, one day, become a balloon that would transfer us to God.

VIII

Is the memory of the camp not the camp?

IX

Suddenly, our senile neighbour stuffed her memories in a plastic bag and left.

X

The abstract in the camp is the body.

XI

In the bomb shelter in Baddawi camp, in complete darkness, my mother, to ensure we were by her side, would count us, not knowing that, most of the time, the children she was tapping and uttering the number of belonged to other families.

XII

The man whose sister is also my sister once asked me: who is older, God or the camp?

XIII

The camp has its own sky. When people shoot in the air in happiness and in despair it is to kill the bird that is never there.

XIV

My father who has persisted in writing since a young age has not published a single thing. In his beige room, with eyes trying to see, he showed me one of the magazines with a poem of his that bore somebody else's name.

XV

We look at it to see what it is that is not ill.

XVI

The camp is the reject of the reject par excellence.

## Necessarily, the Camp is the Border[15]

There, the noise is also the religious …
On a day as chilly as the pulses of those who took away our things and left the door ajar, you gave birth to me in darkness: you, the midwife, two whitish towels patterned with dry blood, and a bowl of hot water. I, to my utter surprise, bore you from within, at once, with no pain. Now I know why you used to call me 'my mother' whenever I slipped away from my dialect and pretended I ate that which you served me and my siblings, of the cracked wheat you cooked. You said: Eat it. It's good for you. It's good for your memory. You never said that was what was left of our rations, of your undying walks to the distribution centres. Mother, allow me in your absence, while shrouded in the last sound of your sound, to call you: My mother. Mother, listen carefully, mother: I am your mother.
When we entered, the path was nothingness and nothingness was a path.
O Enterers, depart from yourselves to see in your naked eyes the offspring of the border …
The worst of fates is not to arrive in your place.
The place, to protect itself, surrounds its limbs with spears.
Instead of wheat they grind their memories.
Nobody knows for sure a refugee's age.
The border is not bordered except by the coming death.
Only in the camp is the right age read through the hands.
In the archive everything begins and ends with the archive.
The archive whose writing is yet to happen is also called God.

Necessarily, the camp is the border.

We wait before the place never to claim the seen but to count the eyes of which we dream.

Come to the camp to remember what will never come.

The definite is the shadow and not the owner.

Those feet are the creator of time.

The camp will always remember its birth as the question of the question which never ceases to return to its body.

The singularity of the camp equates to the singularity of God whose existence is predicated on complete solitude.

The body of the camp is the bearer of time. When the camp outlives time it outlives itself for itself.

In other words, the camp is whatever is far from clarity but near itself.

Smells in the camp are the body proper. They arrive in advance of everything including the body.

Refugees to awaken themselves stomp their feet upon arrival.

The obscurity of what a camp is is the obscurity of language whenever confronted by its nothingness.

Even when it is approached, the word 'camp' will always be held at the frontier.

We store our dialects in broken hearts in advance of death. Might we die without our dialects one day?

You err. You recite verses upon which additions float. You say: the host is an addition. Your throat swells up as you squeeze words out of sounds and sounds out of words. You pray while water sweeps the intact point on your forehead. I enter with tentative feet. Past your mat tiptoeing: verses, like running water, fall from above rapidly as though something were to happen. As though I were brothering the devil in my silent whispers and my father's spluttering in his room. You were hardly there, only a handful of words hanging from your long white dress.

The promise contains the promise.

When a promise is uttered language dies.

A bird ploughing the air is the dialect.

In the camp, we can only see the camp's shadow.

Dialects, too, get pregnant.

What is still in the dialect is the name and nothing but the name.

# Notes

1. 'Local Community Experiences of and Responses to Displacement from Syria: Views from Lebanon, Jordan and Turkey' (a.k.a. 'Refugee Hosts'), funded by the AHRC-ESRC (Grant Agreement Number: AH/P005438/1); see www.refugeehosts.org
2. On dynamics within Baddawi camp, also see Fiddian-Qasmiyeh in this volume.
3. Hoffman, Steinberg and Garb also explore the role of literature and writing in relation to displacement (in this volume).
4. The following section has been adapted from Qasmiyeh (2019).
5. The term 'circumcision' is used here to shed light on how marking the body, the refugee body, can be segregational in nature as well as a sign of attesting to the legal and existential limbo that refugees commonly experience. It is precisely in the 'archival strata' (Derrida, 1996: 22) that the skin is centralized; this is the case both memorially and as a layer that exposes as well as conceals the writing that is taking place in the camp.
6. For a rhizoanalysis of refugee camps, and the extent to which refugees are 'always-already-in-the-middle', see Fiddian-Qasmiyeh (2019).
7. UNRWA: the United Nations Relief and Works Agency for Palestine Refugees in the Middle East.
8. First published on 'Refugee Hosts', 30 September 2016: https://refugeehosts.org/2016/09/30/writing-the-camp
9. First published on 'Refugee Hosts', 1 September 2017: https://refugeehosts.org/2017/09/01/refugees-are-dialectical-beings-part-one
10. First published on 'Refugee Hosts', 22 June 2018: https://refugeehosts.org/2018/06/22/in-mourning-the-refugee-we-mourn-gods-intention-in-the-absolute
11. First published on 'Refugee Hosts', 15 January 2017: https://refugeehosts.org/2017/01/15/the-camp-is-time
12. First published on 'Refugee Hosts', 25 April 2017: https://refugeehosts.org/2017/04/25/a-sudden-utterance-is-the-stranger
13. First published on 'Refugee Hosts', 1 October 2018: https://refugeehosts.org/2018/10/01/flesh-when-mutilated-called-god/comment-page-1
14. First published on 'Refugee Hosts', 4 January 2018: https://refugeehosts.org/2018/01/04/the-camp-is-the-reject-of-the-reject-par-excellence
15. First published on 'Refugee Hosts', 5 November 2018: https://refugeehosts.org/2018/11/05/necessarily-the-camp-is-the-border

# References

Bensmaïa, Réda. 2012. 'Foreword: The Kafka Effect'. In *Kafka: Toward a Minor Literature*, by Gilles Deleuze and Félix Guattari; translated by Dana Polan, ix–xxi. Minneapolis: University of Minnesota Press.

Deleuze, Gilles and Félix Guattari. 2012. *Kafka: Toward a Minor Literature*, translated by Dana Polan. Minneapolis: University of Minnesota Press.

Derrida, Jacques. 1996. *Archive Fever: A Freudian Impression*, translated by Eric Prenowitz. Chicago: University of Chicago Press.

Fiddian-Qasmiyeh, Elena. 2019. 'Memories and Meanings of Refugee Camps (and More-Than-Camps)'. In *Refugee Imaginaries: Research across the Humanities*, edited by Emma Cox, Sam Durrant, David Farrier, Lyndsey Stonebridge and Agnes Woolley. Edinburgh: Edinburgh University Press.

Qasmiyeh, Yousif M. 2016a. 'Writing the Camp: Vis-à-vis or a Camp', *Refugee Hosts*, 30 September. Accessed 9 January 2020. https://refugeehosts.org/2016/09/30/writing-the-camp/.

Qasmiyeh, Yousif. 2016b. 'My Mother's Heels'. In *Being Palestinian: Personal Reflections on Palestinian Identity in the Diaspora*, edited by Yasir Suleiman, 303–5. Edinburgh: Edinburgh University Press.

Qasmiyeh, Yousif. 2016c. 'If This is My Face, So Be It', *Modern Poetry in Translation 1: 119–23*.

Qasmiyeh, Yousif M. 2017a. 'Refugees Are Dialectical Beings: Part Two – Refugees Are Dialecti-cal Beings', *Refugee Hosts*, 5 September. Accessed 9 January 2020. https://refugeehosts. org/2017/09/05/refugees-are-dialectical-beings-part-two/.

Qasmiyeh, Yousif M. 2017b. 'Refugees Are Dialectical Beings: Part One – Writing the Camp Archive', *Refugee Hosts*, 1 September. Accessed 9 January 2020. https://refugeehosts.org/2017/09/01/ refugees-are-dialectical-beings-part-one/.

Qasmiyeh, Yousif M. 2017c. 'A Sudden Utterance is the Stranger', *Refugee Hosts*, 25 April. Accessed 9 January 2020. https://refugeehosts.org/2017/04/25/a-sudden-utterance-is-the-stranger/.

Qasmiyeh, Yousif M. 2017d. 'The Camp is Time', *Refugee Hosts*, 15 January. Accessed 9 January 2020. https://refugeehosts.org/2017/01/15/the-camp-is-time/.

Qasmiyeh, Yousif M. 2019. 'Writing the Camp: Death, Dying and Dialects'. In Refugee Imaginaries: Research across the Humanities, edited by Emma Cox, Sam Durrant, David Farrier, Lyndsey Stonebridge and Agnes Woolley. Edinburgh: Edinburgh University Press.

5

# Making home in limbo: Belgian refugees in Britain during the First World War

Christophe Declercq

## Introduction

Ahead of Refugee Week in June 2019, the *Guardian* published *You, Me and Those Who Came Before*, portraits by Jillian Edelstein of people with diverse backgrounds. The main argument behind the portrait exhibition – on display at Tate Exchange in London first, then at the V&A – was to celebrate unity in diversity: how refugees, represented by prominent figures, contribute to life in the UK. The geographical spread and the variety of reasons why people left their homes and found a future in the UK was as wide as the representations of refugee movements over time: among the many portraits were a virtuoso zither player from Damascus, an actor who at a very young age had escaped Rwanda with his family in 1994, a former Young Poet Laureate whose parents left Somalia in 1984, a British-Palestinian chef whose grandparents fled Palestine in 1948, a member of the House of Lords who was one of the 10,000 children rescued by the Kindertransport and a children's author who fled Nazi Germany with her family in 1935 (Edelstein, 2019).

Their successful settlement elsewhere – in this case, in the UK – and the unique combination of diverse background and reception culture transpired in the timeline presented. Arguably, among many others, a member of the Windrush generation should have been included too. Experiences of the Windrush generation easily stand for earlier immigrant arrivals in Britain because of their position 'both as British citizens and visible minorities' (Quille, 2018: 2): under Home Secretary Theresa

May, a hostile environment was created at the Home Office from 2013 onwards (York, 2018) and new rules demanded enhanced evidence of people's immigration status. However, those who had come to Britain – typically to address labour shortages – did not always have the right documentation to prove their British citizenship, and after decades of contributing to British society some found themselves with restricted access to employment and limited or even no health services. The Windrush case could also be extended to the settled status that EU citizens had to apply for when it remained uncertain whether Britain would leave the EU or not, or under what conditions (Sigona, 2018; O'Brien, 2019). *You, Me and Those Who Came Before* demonstrates that, by looking into the history of diversity – here, the condition of being a refugee – both differences and commonalities exist between various groups of people who have arrived seeking refuge in the UK.

However appealing it might be as a newspaper article fitting the narrative of 2019 Refugee Week, comparative refugee history – focusing on the experience of refugees over time – is only emerging as an academic field (Kushner, 2017; Stone, 2018). This chapter therefore aims to develop a comparative historical framework in which elements of the current-day refugee situation in Europe are considered against an existing history of refugees, more specifically that of Belgian refugees in Britain during the First World War.[1] First, aspects of both historic and current media attention are contextualized. This is tied into narratives of commemorations. Next, an appreciation of figures – feeding the desire to quantify refugee streams and translating humanitarian aspects of the issue into dehumanized digits – is needed before a succinct overview of specific elements of the Belgian sojourn in Britain are highlighted, each of which contributed to the very history of their presence disappearing during the war and being omitted from public memory after the war.

The purpose of uncovering the history of Belgians in Britain during the First World War is not only to combat forgetfulness of the past and the ensuing lack of understanding about the present but also to reinstate past achievements in terms of refugee reception, accommodation and lasting inclusion into the receiving society – just as the portraits in the *Guardian* did.[2] As such, a much-needed legacy in which the reception culture acted as a haven for refugees across time is reaffirmed (Townsend, 2014). A perfect validation of this contextualization through parallels and contrasts can be seen in the figures concerned: the number of Belgians in Britain for the period 1914–19 is estimated to be between 250,000 and 265,000. A similar number of asylum applications were made in the UK between 1991 to 2017: a total of 261,056.[3] While these are very similar numbers, this number of refugee arrivals happened over the course of 5 years in the 1910s, and over the course of 27 years more recently.

However, if – other than being omitted from public memory – one social legacy of the history of Belgian refugees in Britain is to be singled out, then it is the mere, but fundamental, fact that refugeedom is a complicated and constantly changing sphere that is, to a large extent, only facilitated when refugees themselves are allowed the space to develop their refugeedom. 'Refugeedom' here refers to Peter Gatrell's matrix of administrative practices; legal norms; but, above all, to social relations and refugees' experiences (Gatrell, 2017: 170) from the point of view that refugees themselves validate those contexts.

Given that the history of Belgian refugees in Britain during the First World War has been long overlooked, this chapter also answers the question of whether or not this historic refugeedom has indeed been excluded from public memory not only because it was a temporary one but also because it was successful.

## A little-known history

In June 2014 – at the time of the emerging humanitarian crisis in the wider Mediterranean region and the advent of the First World War centenary – a poll was conducted by YouGov. When provided with seven options and asked which of the historic refugee groups settling in Britain had been the largest, forgetfulness about the right answer – Belgian refugees' presence in Britain during the First World War – became clear: one in five people believed that the correct answer concerned Ugandan Asians fleeing persecution from Idi Amin. Seventeen per cent believed it to be Jewish refugees fleeing Nazi Germany and Austria in the late 1930s. Only one person in over 2,000 people surveyed indicated rightly that the answer was Belgian refugees during the First World War (YouGov, 2014; Declercq, 2015: 33; Declercq, 2016: 94). Indeed – except for a few academics, archivists and local historians – the history of Belgian refugees during the First World War – characterized by voluntary action and government support through local bodies as well as by humanitarian organizations – is not a very well-known one.[4] Yet, more than 1.5 million Belgians fled their country and the violence of the early weeks of the war there – the same number of people as all the sea and land arrivals in the EU for the years 2015, 2016 and 2017.[5] By November 1918, about 600,000 Belgians still lived in France, the United Kingdom and the Netherlands. Regardless of the duration of this exile, today that sudden story of massive displacement would undoubtedly be labelled with the term 'refugee crisis' and press coverage would probably resonate with sentiments of 'being overwhelmed', along with metaphors invoking 'invasion' (Holmes and Castañeda, 2016: 18).

However, in order to fully gauge the difference in scope between then and now, the ultimate framing can be found in the respective press coverage (on media representations of displacement, see chapters by Snow and Davies in this volume). Online available digitized archives, such as the British Newspaper Archive and the archives of the *Manchester Guardian* and *The Times*, together hold well over 45,000 references for 'Belgian refugees' for the war years alone (1914–18),[6] or more than 1,000 references per month of the war period. In turn, a phrase-based search in Google Advanced showed that the *Guardian*, the *Independent*, *The Times* and the *Daily Telegraph* combined printed nearly 13,000 references to 'Syrian refugees' between March 2011 and April 2019.[7] This translates to roughly 135 references per month during this period. Clearly, the Belgians in Britain during the First World War received more press coverage than Syrian refugees a century later.

It is particularly notable that the vast coverage of Belgian refugees in the British press during the First World War did not leave a trace in public memory afterwards. In fact, one of the main characteristics of the history of the Belgians in Britain is that they had already been omitted from public narratives during the war itself: newspaper coverage dwindled so rapidly that the period August 1914 to December 1915 accounted for over 80 per cent of all mentions in British newspapers, whereas fewer than 20 per cent of all mentions arose in the remaining four years (Declercq, 2015; Hughes, 2016; Declercq and Baker, 2016). A clear disappearance from the British press took place during the course of the war, which anticipated a later forgetfulness: the central message of 'soon gone, long forgotten' (Jenkinson, 2016: 101) echoes Peter Cahalan's conclusion that the Belgian refugees 'disappeared as quickly as they had come' (1982: 3).

However, during the commemorations for the First World War centenary (2014–18) the story of Belgians in exile received increasing attention from local-history groups and academics alike, as well as from Belgian and/or British commemoration initiatives such as those launched by or at Amsab-ISG, BBC's World War One at Home, Birtley, Flanders House London, Folkestone, In Flanders Fields Museum, Laugharne, Leeds, Northwich, Rhyl, Richmond/Twickenham, Royal Tunbridge Wells, the Scottish Refugee Council, Tracing the Belgian Refugees, Vredescentrum Antwerpen and Wales for Peace. The commemoration of the centenary coincided largely with the ongoing humanitarian situation in the wider

Mediterranean region (as an area of departure as well as transit), but also with the increasingly antagonistic political atmosphere in several EU member states.[8] Although many of the aforementioned commemorative initiatives promoted strong awareness, hardly any included today's refugees, except for a project by the Scottish Refugee Council.[9] This local and regional impact is unsurprising: the active inclusion of current-day refugees in the commemoration of a historical subject has proved to be mainly of local relevance.

In turn, national narratives in relation to Britain have been driven by a subtext in which a hostile environment is created for any migrant, old or new. This is consistent with the hostile attitude of the British state to individual rights generally, and the right to asylum specifically, that persisted for the remainder of the twentieth century (De Vuyst et al., 2019: 2) and continued to persist in the 2010s. The contrast of today's situation with Britain's generosity towards refugees during the First World War, most of whom were Belgian, could not be greater. In this respect, there is a palpable distance between our ability to learn from the past in order to understand the present better, and the disheartening hostility of the current attitude towards refugees.

## More than just numbers and figures

By providing clear estimates of the numbers of people involved in forced displacement, one reduces a humanitarian situation to sheer numbers (also see Maqusi, this volume). Attempting to grasp the scale of a refugee movement in this way anonymizes the trauma of displacement and the significance of individual refugee stories. More importantly, it focuses on the host state through reference to the scope of and requirements for reception, accommodation and charity (see Astolfo and Boano, this volume). Or it might indicate the lack thereof, as was the case with British charity in the Balkans prior to the First World War and with those current-day refugees who are turned away from the borderlands of Europe and 'returned' to deplorable circumstances in detention centres in Libya. All narratives deemed authoritative aim for numbers but do not emphasize the experiences and priorities of refugees themselves, let alone create a space in which refugees themselves can develop their daily lives.

For the humanitarian disaster(s) of the 2010s, seemingly declining figures appear to provide a collective soothing sensation, as if the issue will gradually go away on its own when numbers eventually go down again (as is the implied anticipation). A headline from *Euronews* was very clear on this point: 'Illegal EU border crossings at six year low' (Musaddique, 2019). This reduction, however, made sense, as several routes into the EU had become increasingly difficult; NGO support at sea was hampered (and, indeed, criminalized); and attempts were increasingly made to stop refugees well before they could even try and make it into the EU.

In 1914–15, the spirit was quite the opposite. Not only did the British Government support the massive accommodation operation initiated by the War Refugees Committee by aligning it with the Local Government Board, but it also committed to providing any resources that charity and philanthropy were unable to cover. These created a refined symbiosis between the official and voluntary levels: 'It was considered expedient for the state to leave problems needing personal action to voluntary and philanthropic bodies' (De Vuyst *et al.*, 2019: 8). Moreover, when the largest influx of Belgians had dwindled and the winter of 1914–15 had passed, not only did the UK authorities resolve increasing friction about the presence of able-bodied Belgian men by incorporating all 60,000 into the war industry, they even fetched large parties of Belgians who were stranded in the Netherlands, where living conditions were not of the same standard as those in the UK.[10] So, in the case of Belgians in Britain, figures provide much-needed grounds for making analogies with today, ideally adding awareness and scope to the current refugee situation or, in simple terms, highlighting what was possible then but no longer is today.

Public awareness of the start of the current humanitarian situation permeated the European public sphere in the first half of 2015 (Fiddian-Qasmiyeh, 2017), whereas the sheer drama of hundreds of thousands of refugees fleeing diverse conflicts in the Middle East, East Asia and Africa and many thousands losing their lives while attempting to cross the Mediterranean had been a major issue well before that. Between June and mid-September 2014, the UNHCR estimated the number of fatalities in the Mediterranean as being well over 2,200, with 130,000 people having arrived in Europe by mid-September 2014, mainly in Italy (UNHCR, 2017). The number of arrivals there in 2014 was more than twice the figure for the whole of 2013, but still only half the number of Belgians arriving in Britain a century earlier. And, most of the latter arrived over the course of only a few weeks (the second half of September to the third week of October 1914).

Although one can trace substantial numbers of people attempting to cross the Mediterranean all the way to the start of the twenty-first century, ranging from about 20,000 in 2000 to over 70,000 in 2011 (BBC News, 2014), there is indeed a break in the figures when it comes to comparing any pre-2015 arrivals with 2015 or later ones. According to the

International Organization for Migration (IOM), about 200,000 refugees arrived in Greece or Italy in 2014, whereas this was well over one million one year later (IOM, 2016). However, by repositioning the humanitarian crisis within a narrative of annual figures, histories of earlier tragedies and earlier modes of response are also eroded. The focus no longer lies with people, nor with the manifold issues that lie behind the situation. However, figures are useful for scoping humanitarian crises and allocating resources. Number estimations of just how many Belgians stayed in Britain during the First World War vary widely, adding to unclear delineations of this historical narrative.

When Germany invaded Belgium on 4 August 1914, stories about atrocities committed by German troops in the first weeks of the conflict quickly spread; many Belgians fled their homes and eventually one out of five Belgians – some 1.5 million – sought refuge abroad (Declercq, 2014: 56). Just how many people were internally displaced but overtaken by the advancing troops is not clear: estimates range between half a million and 1.5 million. It can therefore be safely assumed that, at the start of the war, at least two million Belgians were dispossessed. Initially, more than a million sought refuge in the Netherlands, Belgium's neighbouring country to the north, but by the end of the war, barely 100,000 Belgian refugees were still in exile there. About 325,000 refugees went to France, the neighbouring country in the south. Most Belgians residing in France stayed there throughout the war. Roughly a quarter of a million Belgians – the most frequently used estimations posit a final figure in the 250,000–265,000 range – crossed the Channel during the war years.

The most striking example of varying figures can be found in the seminal government publication *Report on the Work Undertaken ...*, which provided several consecutive sets of figures, ranging from 'upwards of 200,000' through 225,572 to 'a rough total of 260,000' (Ministry of Health, 1920). *The Times History of the War* gave a figure of 265,000, allowing for erroneous records and convalescent soldiers (*The Times*, 1915).[11] Still, a utopian mirroring of the number of Belgians in Britain with current-day Syrian refugees would mean that Britain could have accommodated nearly twenty times more Syrians: between 2015 and early 2019, Britain accommodated only 13,818 Syrian refugees. Admittedly, Belgians made up about 95 per cent of all refugees in Britain during the First World War, whereas the proportion of Syrians in the overall numbers of refugees in Britain in 2019 does not remotely equal that share.

Two eras can never be compared but juxtaposition appears significant, especially in relation to the current public perception of 'being overwhelmed' (Staples, 2015: n.p.) and the way in which this unfounded fear is currently being used by extreme right-wing groups and parties. Of equal importance is how the three main host nations for Belgian refugees during the First World War currently relate to their historic capacity in terms of receiving refugees. In the table below (5.1), the respective population is measured by means of census details close to 1914 and this is then related to the population as near the time of writing (spring 2019) as possible. Next, the estimated number of Belgians in each of the countries – in the period August 1914 to April 1919 – is used to calculate how many Belgian refugees were hosted per one million inhabitants. That figure is then used to extrapolate today's population, resulting in a specific share of today's capacity for the period 2013 to 2017[12] – which is of a similar duration to the First World War period – in comparison with the historical reception.

Table 5.1 Historic refugee reception calculated towards today's possibilities

| Country | Census 1910s | Belgian refugees | Per million | Current population (2019) | Potential capacity | Actual reception | Share of historic reception |
|---------|------|--------|-------|--------|--------|--------|-------|
| UK | 43m | 265,000 | 6,163 | 66m[13] | 406,758 | 174,735 | 43% |
| NL | 6.5m | 105,000[14] | 16,154 | 17m[15] | 274,615 | 121,680 | 44.3% |
| FR | 39.6m | 325,000 | 8,207 | 67m[16] | 549,873 | 451,000 | 82% |

*Source*: Elaborated by the author.

In terms of welcoming refugees, modern-day Britain is only hosting 43 per cent of the refugees and asylum seekers that it cared for during the First World War years. When looking at the other two main host nations for Belgian refugees, the Netherlands (NL) is very similar to the UK in that it is hosting only 44.3 per cent of its historic numbers. Although the situation for Belgians in Britain is in no way comparable with the rather sterile and at times minimal situation in the Netherlands, both countries currently resemble one another in terms of the proportion of what we might term 'historic hospitality'.[17] The hypothetical calculation results in a different situation for France, however. At the time of writing, as a host nation, France maintains a proportional relation of 82 per cent compared with its historical capacity. Any conclusion in terms of different eras – no World War at the doorstep and the like – for the findings for the UK and the Netherlands is therefore thwarted by the result for France. Clearly, the former two countries have undergone a substantial shift in terms of hospitality towards refugees, whereas France has largely maintained it.

Any figure advocated by the distinctive British – Conservative – governments of the 2010s about the intended number of refugees welcomed in Britain is very different from what has been achieved in the past and what France is still achieving.

## The possibilities of empathy

If one of today's biggest concerns is the marginalization of millions of refugees, who face danger and humiliation on a daily basis (Gatrell, 2017), then the story of the Belgian refugees stands out as its counterpart. In 1914, the number of displaced people was on an unprecedented scale, and these included six million Russians, nearly two million French – most of them internally displaced – and half a million Serbs, but also Jewish, Italian, Croat and Slovene refugees, as well as Armenians (Gatrell, 2014) and over 1.5 million Belgians. Yet, despite the strain on resources, and by extension on society as a whole, no 'crisis' was perceived, most certainly not in Britain. In the war months of 1914 to mid-1915, the Belgians were met by a vast wave of British empathy: thousands of refugee committees were formed, overseen by the War Refugees Committee and the Local Government Board,[18] and were ready to help and support the destitute Belgians. Numerous activities were organized nationally and locally, the proceeds of which were in aid of the Belgians.[19] Official reports, media coverage and political actions were all aligned with the war effort, in which 'Remember Belgium' featured heavily – that iconic and omnipresent poster that used the imagery of atrocities committed by German troops on Belgian civilians to galvanize public support for the war effort and to bolster recruitment in Britain. The refugees from Poor Little Belgium epitomized the reason why Britain had gone to war in the first place (Kushner and Knox, 1999).

Popular perception about the necessity of hosting Belgians was such that a myth emerged: more offers of accommodation were in place than needed and everybody wanted a Belgian. Clearly, despite the scale of the Belgian exodus and subsequent exile, there was no feeling of 'being overwhelmed', a sentiment often voiced today (see above). In October and November 1914 especially, quite sizeable crowds regularly turned up at a local station when a first group of refugees was due to arrive – similar to what happened in Munich train station in Germany in 2015.

At the start of the First World War, Britain had grown accustomed to 'immigration restrictions and the identification of foreigners as bearers of disease, criminal proclivities or dangerous ideas' (Cesarani, 1992: 34) and yet sentiments towards this massive influx of 'friendly Aliens' – in contrast to 'enemy Aliens' such as Germans – was very early on replaced by a strong feeling of compassion, further bolstering anti-German feelings across all levels of society. In stark contrast to today's refugees, the Belgians in Britain were not marginalized. Moreover, by the time animosity had slowly begun to increase towards Belgian able-bodied men who had not initially carried out employment duties, let alone enlisted, the War Propaganda Bureau of Charles Masterman – also known as Wellington House – was in full swing, leaving virtually no space for friction. This was also helped by renowned D-notices, issued by the War Office Press Bureau as a means of censorship, which prevented press stories from being printed or at least controlled them. This form of control of the press also applied to stories about rogue Belgians or unsavoury stories involving Belgian civilians and soldiers alike, but also about refugees 'flooding the countryside' (Lovelace, 1982: 112).

If any organized manipulation of information dissemination, similar to what was in place a hundred years earlier, is being used today, then the common enemy has been translated into a common public enemy in the shape of any entity with a sufficient terrorist connotation, ranging from Al-Qaeda and the Taliban to ISIS, Saddam Hussain and Bashar al-Assad. This added layer of diffuse public enemies convolutes a single cause for which public opinion can be galvanized. The fragmentation of ongoing regional turbulence and internal conflict, continuously shifting power vacuums that regional and global powers seek to fill (Cammack and Dunne 2018), is too complicated to sell to the public. Therefore, empathizing with the realities from which people flee is thwarted to such an extent that a common sense of understanding is lacking. Although the Masterman propaganda machine aimed to have the wider British society accept Belgian refugees locally as the ultimate representation of the reason why Britain went to war, the current situation is quite the opposite. A manifest narrative focuses on keeping multiple conflict-driven issues in the Middle East at bay: 'According to the UN's Arab Human Development Report 2016, the Middle East is home to only 5% of the world's population but, in 2014, accounted for 45% of the world's terrorist attacks, 68.5% of its battle-related deaths and 57.5% of its refugees' (Select Committee on International Relations, 2017). This defensive narrative contrasts starkly with the widespread public support for Belgian refugees, in which there was no concern in relation to ethnicity or religion – let alone concerns about the unknown Other arriving on British shores in droves. Put differently, Belgian refugees were simply of the right religion and ethnicity.[20]

The wilful absence of organized empathy towards today's refugees was also evidenced by a BBC online news article from 2018: only the graphs include the UK in relation to migration and the EU; the text itself does not. The analysis of the humanitarian situation in Europe and the way in which the migration issue is charted therefore wilfully aligns the linked chain of concepts in its readers' minds: refugees and migration are EU, not UK. This *EU=migration* premise permeated public debate in the years of the EU referendum and Brexit division: those in favour of leaving the EU used it as a defensive position in terms of migration ('control of our own borders'), so that there is no longer a sense of being overwhelmed and there is confidence that migration can be halted: narratives in which refugeedom proper disappeared. Those in favour of remaining in the EU focused on the contributions of refugees and migrants to a diverse society, narratives in which refugeedom can thrive. At the time, Belgians who fled their country were given many labels: legally Aliens, they became 'friendly Aliens', and were called 'refugees' by media, political and institutional authorities alike. First World War refugees were never dubbed 'migrants', a term that in the 1910s was almost entirely reserved for people leaving Britain (for Australia for instance), returning to Britain, summer workers and migratory birds.[21]

However, several issues further complicate a clear appreciation of just how many Belgians stayed in Britain during the war. These include registration, transmigration and the flawed line between civilian refugees and soldiers (deserters and convalescents alike). Registration was not compulsory or well organized until early December 1914. Refugees who had somehow 'remained under the radar' prior to that point in time could have moved back to Belgium; or to France; the Netherlands; or, indeed, elsewhere. In their relatively secure transnational mobility, Belgians were transmigrants *avant la lettre*, but of a benign kind, clearly, given that the British Government actually actively sought to attract Belgians who had temporarily settled in the Netherlands in order to fill much-needed war industry employment. Belgians in Britain were not exactly hampered by the 1905 Aliens Act, which restricted immigration into Britain for the first time but which allowed it for refugees.[22] Still, the Aliens Registration Act 1914 required any immigrant to register with the police, including Belgians – despite them being 'friendly Aliens'. Although Belgians had to report their whereabouts to the local police, there was still a substantial degree of freedom of movement, which allowed for a high level of mobility for those Belgians who were seeking employment. It was common for people to relocate up to seven times in a four-year period, and relocating up to twelve times was far from exceptional (Declercq, 2015: 127).

Members of this Belgian transnational community in exile also enrolled in the Belgian Army. This complicated the very nature of the concept 'Belgian refugee': not only did thousands of refugees join the Belgian forces from their displaced location, but thousands of lower-ranking officers and soldiers – those who were not interned in prisoner-of-war camps in the Netherlands after they had sought refuge there in 1914 – moved to Britain and effectively were deserters but became members of the refugee community in exile, and valued resources for the British war industry. The line between a refugee and a soldier in exile simply did not exist, nor was this much of an issue for British public opinion – or at least, this does not emerge as an issue in the many newspaper articles published on the Belgians in Britain. Another dimension also stands in the way of the correct figures for Britain-based Belgians and, as such, the concept of a 'Belgian refugee': long-term convalescent Belgian soldiers were often overseen by local Belgian refugee committees.

Admittedly, the current conflict in the Middle East and North Africa, which is among the main causes for the ongoing humanitarian situation in and around the borderlands of Europe, stems from much more complicated fault lines than an easy First World War alignment of *Central Powers – Allies – Neutral Countries*. However, both the mobility and the military aspects of the Belgian refugees in exile in Britain support the understanding that Belgians in Britain were absorbed into the social fabric in a manner that hardly posed any problems then but would, in all likelihood, pose many today.

## Disappearing from view, and forgetfulness

One year into the war, the powerful and much-used image of the Belgian refugee increasingly diminished in the British press. However, significantly decreased attention by the British press and controlled media output – by D-notices – only partially accounts for the Belgians disappearing from view. This had many reasons. First, support for the Belgians in Britain waned as the war dragged on. Second, the focus on charity and Belgium shifted towards supporting occupied Belgium. This was also driven by the large-scale organization of provisions for Belgians by the American Commission for the Relief of Belgium, managed by J. Edgar Hoover. Third, Belgians established their own intricate web of exile newspapers, journals and magazines, so there was no longer any reason for British newspapers to play the mindful carer and include sections for Belgians. Fourth, and perhaps most importantly, by mid-1915 nearly all

Belgian men were employed, mostly in the British war industry, as were quite a large number of Belgian women. Lastly, with the integration of most Belgian children into the British education system – only one in six enjoyed Belgian education in exile[23] – the presence of Belgian refugees on the streets became much less palpable.

Just how liberal this incorporation of Belgians into the British social fabric was can indeed be seen in the opportunity given to them to establish those own social spaces – not least of which was the establishment of over 100 Belgian schools as well as the foundation of Belgian factories, some of which constituted the most characteristic chapters in the history of the Belgians in Britain. Not only were privileges granted enabling able-bodied Belgian men to work in the war industry but Belgians also started businesses in Britain themselves. In Gateshead, for instance, an entire Belgian community grew out of the workforce of the British-run National Projectile Factory. Elsewhere, communities of Belgian exiles formed around factories such as the Kryn and Lahy factory in Letchworth and Pelabon in Richmond/Twickenham. The presence of over five hundred Belgian enterprises on British soil during the war clearly proves that the reception and care of Belgian refugees was not only a matter for the British but that the Belgians also took care of themselves, if not entirely then at least to a large extent. With Belgian unions also playing a role while in exile and Belgian curriculums at play, the Belgians themselves developed a new identity in exile – that of the British Belgians who actively inhabited the host nation's space carved out for refugeedom.

This set of refugee experiences was intensified through the advent of numerous Belgian shops, the most renowned of which were horsemeat butchers. These Belgian shops stocked exclusively Belgian produce and adhered to Belgian etiquette, and thus appealed mainly to Belgian shoppers. British customers struggled and wondered whether to find foreign customs just different or outright difficult.

However, the very fact that many Belgian shipping companies, mainly from Antwerp and often with existing routes into central Africa, relocated to the UK clearly shows that there was a substantial benefit to British trade and labour to be had from the Belgian community in exile. This is in sharp contrast with today's situation in terms of Britain's relation to the regions where most refugees come from. Using the top five countries of origin of UK asylum applicants in 2017 (Iran, Afghanistan, Iraq, Bangladesh and Sudan)[24] as an example, we can see that virtually no such benefit emerges other than supporting conflict locally through weapons' exports, using cheap labour or harvesting natural resources at the very location from which the people are fleeing.

## Forgetfulness

If Belgians quickly became more self-sufficient and less dependent on support because they were granted the necessary space, then logically a sense of segregation played out, as many Belgians were incorporated into Belgian structures of employment and education. Although relationships between the Belgians and British developed and there were cross-cultural transfers, when the Belgian refugees left, 'there were relatively few inter-personal connections to keep memories alive' (Declercq and Baker, 2016: 162). The Belgians not only became literally erased from living memory but also – often through discarded archive material – from the records (Storr, 2009): 'of the estimated 2500 local Belgian relief organizations, the archive material of a little over 200 is kept in the Imperial War Museum archives' (Declercq and Baker, 2016: 163).

There is, however, another factor to be taken into consideration – one that has not been supported by much research because it is no longer feasible, but one that can be seen mentioned time and again in letters, diaries and testimonies up to decades after the war: a common denominator in family-history research relating to the First World War is that those who returned from the front remained silent on any aspect of the war for the remainder of their lives. Likewise, if Belgians were the embodiment of why Britain had gone to war in the first place, it can be argued that family stories about accommodating and entertaining Belgian refugees disappeared into the same silence (Declercq and Baker, 2016: 163). This can be mirrored in today's situation: the distance between the members of the host society and the very reasons why refugees seek a safe haven in Britain has been substantially widened by the focus on de-humanized figures, by the non-mediating nature of press coverage, through the distancing narrative in relation to yet another public enemy and through the perceived lack of benefits for the receiving society. Or, in short, the overarching framing narratives that surround current-day refugees have created the opposite of a wave of empathy.

The final reason behind this forgetfulness of a historic refugee chapter relates to post-war reconstruction. The organized repatriation of Belgian refugees took place in the period between the Armistice (11 November 1918) and the Treaty of Versailles (28 June 1919). Belgian refugees returned to a post-war society in which both their reintegration and the need for the reconstruction of the infrastructure of a broken nation were paramount (Declercq, 2015: 309). However, they also found themselves lost in a nation that was incredibly fragmented and that, through new divisions, no longer coincided with the imagined community from the period in exile. Belgian refugees returned from different host nations and many prisoners returned from Germany, as did people who had been forced into labour there. Belgium had been mostly occupied and when refugees returned not all were readily accepted back into the renewed social construct.

That re-emerging fabric to some extent even harked back to pre-war social conditions, which collided with the more relaxed time enjoyed by many Belgian refugees, with the social mobility that quite a few Belgians enjoyed while in Britain and with the relative gender equality of exile, in that working women were much more common in Britain than in Belgium prior to the war, and immediately after. Moreover, for the entire duration of the German occupation, any house that had remained empty during the war because its inhabitants had fled, was 'a vivid reminder to the local community that Belgians who were not enduring the hardship of occupation and the deprivations that came with it, had once lived on those premises' (Declercq, 2015: 310). The empty houses, a focal point of increasing irritation during the occupation, led to friction when the occupants eventually returned. To date, little has been written about the return of Belgian refugees into their former native environment. This is particularly relevant, as those who returned often found themselves in situations in which trauma was revisited: destroyed and ransacked homes, fewer employment opportunities and internal displacement (which could be temporary but equally definitive). Despite partially destroyed infrastructure – entire areas were badly affected whereas most hardly suffered at all – there is no comparison, for instance, with the barren world that Syrian refugees might return to, if they do so at all. Understanding the feelings of returning Belgians would add to an awareness not only of their first experiences of displacement at the start of the war but also of the circumstances that current-day refugees find themselves in during resettlement and repatriation.

One more factor relating to repatriation and return convoluted the position of the Belgian refugees in both British and Belgian history: at Versailles, Paul Hymans – the key Belgian negotiator there, who from 1915 to 1917 had served as the Belgian minister to Great Britain – erroneously felt that he could play the card of the German atrocities again, hoping to revive international indignation about these and to resuscitate widespread support for Belgium. However, witness reports about these atrocities were already contested during the war (see Wilson, 1979; Horne and Kramer, 2001) and Belgian refugees, at least those in the UK, had served their (propaganda) purpose. The approach backfired and many Belgian demands were not met. This buried the Belgian refugees under yet another layer of historical dust.

## Conclusion

In the past few years, increasing academic output on the experiences of Belgian refugees in Britain and a growing number of local research projects on the subject have shown that public perception and common knowledge of Belgian refugees in Britain, as well as the sheer size of the community in exile, is still not great. Yet, as evidenced by Ian Hislop in *Who Should We Let In?*, a much-praised BBC broadcast (June 2017), analysing the sojourn of a quarter of a million refugees in Britain is important and – often through contrast – provides a context both for our understanding of the contemporary refugee situation, on the one hand, and Britain's changed relationship to immigrants and refugees, on the other. The overall feeling remains in place that over a century ago, receiving nations were able to do more in terms of welcoming refugees than they are doing now.

Just before he passed away in the summer of 1996, the Ukrainian-British rabbi and Auschwitz survivor, Hugo Gryn, called the twentieth century 'not only the century of two world wars, but also the century of the refugee. Almost nobody at the end of the century is where they were at the beginning of it' (cited in Kushner and Knox, 1999: 1). With that refugee label applied to the past century, one wonders how to designate the current era in which even larger numbers of people are displaced and dispossessed around the world, both internationally and internally. The issue of labelling far transcends the terminological level and poses a quintessential question: To what extent, and how, can providing comparisons between historical displacement and contemporary refugee movement increase awareness? This phenomenon sits at the core of history: it is in overcoming a forgetfulness about a particular past – caused by renewed application – that historical parallels prove their existential value for understanding the present. Understanding historical cases of displacement helps to provide proof of the space that refugees themselves should be able to have in order to provide for their own sense of belonging, for their own refugeedom.

By uncovering a history of displacement and contrasting it with today's situation, this chapter has aimed to bridge a gap between those two voids: a long-forgotten history, which at the time galvanized an entire nation, on the one hand, and the current humanitarian situation on the other. That forgetfulness is no longer reiterated, and instead the proud legacy of welcoming refugees and of allowing refugees the space to reinvent themselves is reinforced, so that they themselves are able to translate the trauma of displacement into an experience of social relations within a new construct.

## Notes

1. In relation to today's humanitarian situation, this chapter deliberately avoids the term 'refugee crisis' wherever possible. On terminology such as 'migration crisis' and 'migrant crisis', and how its use by politicians and the media sets popular perception in support of far-right politics and the fear of 'the other', see Malik (2018) and Federici (2019).
2. For a useful companion piece to this chapter, see Vandervoordt (in this volume) on the experiences of Syrian refugees who have sought refuge in Belgium since 2011.
3. Figures from Migration Observatory (Oxford), 25 May 2019.
4. This point of view is shared in secondary literature published before the centenary of the First World War, including Cahalan (1982); Declercq (2007, 2014); Amara (2008); Gatrell (2008); and Storr (2009).
5. Figures UNHCR 2019, 22 May 2019.
6. Figures ibid., 5 May 2019.
7. Taking the Syrian Army clampdown on protests in March 2011 as a start of the period in which Syrians started to flee their country, the Syrian refugee crisis would – at the time of writing in March 2019 – last for eight years, or 96 months.
8. Such as the United Kingdom (UKIP, the anti-immigration stance of the Leave campaign and resulting Brexit approaches), the Netherlands (far-right parties run by Geert Wilders and Thierry Baudet), Hungary (Viktor Orbán's wall to keep refugees out) and Italy (Lega Nord's election campaign was branded 'racist' and 'xenophobic' in the European Parliament; Gottardi, 2009).
9. In the project 'Lest We Forget', a group of refugees and Scots shared what they had learnt about the forgotten history of Belgian refugees in Scotland. The modern-day refugees related their experiences of rebuilding their lives in Scotland to a historical subject (Scottish Refugee Council, 2016).
10. The Netherlands was a neutral country, and the state's perceived generosity towards Belgians could be interpreted by Germans as a violation of that neutrality.
11. Typically, wounded Belgian soldiers convalescing in locations across Britain were overseen and supported by local Belgian refugee committees.
12. Figures from Europarl: http://www.europarl.europa.eu/external/html/welcomingeurope/default_en.htm, 22 May 2019.
13. Figure Office for National Statistics (ONS) UK: https://www.ons.gov.uk/peoplepopulationandcommunity/populationandmigration/populationestimates, 22 May 2019.
14. This is not taking into consideration the one million Belgians who had fled to the Netherlands by the end of September, early October 1914. Nearly 90% of those had already returned in a matter of weeks.
15. Figures World-o-meters, www.worldometers.info/world-population/netherlands-population, 22 May 2019.
16. Sources include INSEE (French National Institute of Statistics and Economic Studies); ONS UK; and Statistisches Bundesamt, Germany, 22 May 2019.
17. For a fine example of hospitality across historical contexts, see Isayev (2018).
18. In Wales, the War Refugees Committee acted in conjunction with the Local Government Board too, but in Scotland all refugee matters were overseen by the Glasgow Corporation. In London, the War Refugees Committee operated alongside the Metropolitan Asylum Board.
19. With the Memorandum of Understanding with Libya, signed in February 2017, the EU – by means of its key Mediterranean member Italy – effectively externalized its borders with Libya, which clashed with the principle of *non-refoulement*, as refugees and/or asylum seekers

should not be sent (back) to countries where they would be in danger (Plan C London, 2019; Caterino, 2019). This was never the case with the First World War refugees. Nor did any solidarity or charity at the time come to be criminalized.

20. Tim, Marshall *Personal communication*, 2016. For an appreciation of the role of religion in the reception of Belgians in Britain, see Taylor (2018).
21. Findings based on single-term searches in the British Newspaper Archive, 22 May 2019.
22. Belgian refugees did not always obtain the contributions they were entitled (De Vuyst *et al.*, 2019: 9). In this respect, there are indeed parallels with the Windrush generation.
23. On refugee children's access to different forms of education in refugee camps in East Africa, see Amorós Elorduy in this volume.
24. Figures, the Migration Observatory, 22 May 2019.

# References

Amara, Michaël. 2008. *Des Belges à l'épreuve de l'exil: Les réfugiés de la Première Guerre mondiale en France, en Angleterre et aux Pays-Bas*. Brussels: Editions de l'Université de Bruxelles.

BBC. 2017. *Who Should We Let In?* BBC television programme, broadcast June 23.

BBC News. 2014. 'Mapping Mediterranean Migration', *BBC News*, 15 September. Accessed 16 January 2020. www.bbc.com/news/world-europe-24521614

BBC News. 2018. 'Migration to Europe in Charts', *BBC News*, 11 September. Accessed 16 January 2020. www.bbc.com/news/world-europe-44660699

BBC News. 2019. 'Fifth of UK's Syrian Refugees Settled in Scotland', *BBC News*, 16 March. Accessed 16 January 2020. www.bbc.com/news/uk-scotland-47597458

Cahalan, Peter. 1982. *Belgian Refugee Relief in England during the Great War*. New York: Garland.

Cammack, Perry and Michele Dunne. 2018. 'Fueling Middle East Conflicts – or Dousing the Flames'. Accessed 30 January 2020. https://carnegieendowment.org/2018/10/23/fueling-middle-east-conflicts-or-dousing-flames-pub-77548

Caterino, Ginevra. 2019. 'Blood on the EU's Hands: What Happens When "Security" Overshadows Human Rights', SOAS Politics and International Studies blog, 28 March. Accessed 30 January 2020. www.soas.ac.uk/blogs/study/blood-on-eus-hands-what-happens-when-security-overshadows-human-rights/

Cesarani, David. 1992. 'An Alien Concept? The Continuity of Anti-Alienism in British Society before 1940', *Immigrants and Minorities* 11 (3): 25–52.

Comité officiel belge pour l'Angleterre. 1918. *Rapport adressé à Monsieur le ministre de l'intérieur, le 31 août 1917*. Brussels: Adhémar Dumoulin.

Declercq, Christophe. 2007. 'Lost and a Translation: Belgians in Britain during the First World War and the Role of Translation'. In *Through Other Eyes: The Translation of Anglophone Literature in Europe*, edited by Richard Trimm and Sophie Alatorre, 149–58. Newcastle upon Tyne: Cambridge Scholars Publishing.

Declercq, Christophe. 2014. 'Belgian Refugees in Britain, 1914–1919'. In *The Low Countries: Arts and Society in Flanders and the Netherlands*, edited by Luc Devoldere, 56–66. Rekkem: Stichting Ons Erfdeel.

Declercq, Christophe. 2015. 'Belgian Refugees in Britain 1914–1919: A Cross-Cultural Study of Belgian Identity in Exile'. PhD thesis, Imperial College London.

Declercq, Christophe. 2016. 'From Antwerp to Britain and Back Again: The Language of the Belgian Refugee in Britain during the First World War'. In *Languages and the First World War: Representation and Memory*, edited by Christophe Declercq and Julian Walker, 94–107. Basingstoke: Palgrave Macmillan.

Declercq, Christophe. 2019. 'Commemorations for the First World War Centenary (2014–18) That Included the Story of Belgians in Exile in Britain', Online Centre for Research on Belgian Refugees blog, 2 June. Accessed 30 January 2020. https://belgianrefugees.blogspot.com/2019/06/refugees-in-moving-world.html

Declercq, Christophe and Helen Baker. 2016. 'The Pelabon Munitions Works and the Belgian Village on the Thames: Community and Forgetfulness in Outer-Metropolitan Suburbs', *Immigrants and Minorities* 34 (2): 151–70.

De Vuyst, Jolien, Kevin Myers and Angelo Van Gorp. 2019. 'The Paradox of the Alien Citizen? Access, Control and Entitlements of Belgian Refugees in Birmingham during the First World War', *Journal of Refugee Studies*, 1–18. Accessed 16 January 2020. https://doi.org/10.1093/jrs/fey071

Edelstein, Jillian. 2019. 'Prominent Refugees and Their Contribution to the UK – in Pictures', *The Guardian*, 21 May. Accessed 16 January 2020. www.theguardian.com/culture/gallery/2019/may/21/prominent-refugees-and-their-contribution-to-the-uk-in-pictures

Federici, Federico M. 2019. '*Emergenza Migranti*: From Metaphor to Policy'. In *Intercultural Crisis Communication: Translation, Interpreting and Languages in Local Crises*, edited by Federico M. Federici and Christophe Declercq, 233–59. London: Bloomsbury Academic.

Fiddian-Qasmiyeh, Elena. 2017. 'The Faith–Gender–Asylum Nexus: An Intersectionalist Analysis of Representations of the "Refugee Crisis"'. In *The Refugee Crisis and Religion: Secularism, Security and Hospitality in Question*, edited by Luca Mavelli and Erin K. Wilson, 207–22. London: Rowman and Littlefield International.

Gatrell, Peter. 2008. 'Refugees and Forced Migrants during the First World War', *Immigrants and Minorities* 26 (1/2): 82–110.

Gatrell, Peter. 2014. 'Refugees'. In *1914–1918-online: International Encyclopedia of the First World War*, edited by Ute Daniel, Peter Gatrell, Oliver Janz, Heather Jones, Jennifer Keene, Alan Kramer and Bill Nasson. Berlin: Freie Universität Berlin. Accessed 30 January 2020. https://encyclopedia.1914-1918-online.net/article/refugees

Gatrell, Peter. 2017. 'The Question of Refugees: Past and Present', *Origins: Current Events in Historical Perspective* 10 (7). Accessed 16 January 2020. http://origins.osu.edu/article/question-refugees-past-and-present

Gottardi, Donata. 2009. 'Written Question – Subject: Racist, Xenophobic Election Campaign: The Lega Nord Posters', *European Parliament Parliamentary Questions*, 12 May. Accessed 30 January 2020. https://tinyurl.com/yd58jfu6.

Holmes, Seth M. and Heide Castañeda. 2016. 'Representing the "European Refugee Crisis" in Germany and Beyond: Deservingness and Difference, Life and Death', *American Ethnologist* 43 (1): 12–24.

Horne, John and Alan Kramer. 2001. *German Atrocities, 1914: A History of Denial*. New Haven: Yale University Press.

Hughes, Lorna M. 2016. 'Finding Belgian Refugees in Cymru1914.org: Using Digital Resources for Uncovering the Hidden Histories of the First World War in Wales', *Immigrants and Minorities* 34 (2): 210–31.

IOM (International Organization for Migration). 2016. 'Mediterranean Migrant Arrivals in 2016: 169,846; Deaths: 620'. Press release, 1 April. Accessed 30 January 2020. www.iom.int/news/mediterranean-migrant-arrivals-2016-169846-deaths-620

Isayev, Elena. 2018. 'Hospitality: A Timeless Measure of Who We Are?', *Migration and Society* 1 (1): 7–21.

Jenkinson, Jacqueline. 2016. 'Soon Gone, Long Forgotten: Uncovering British Responses to Belgian Refugees during the First World War', *Immigrants and Minorities* 34 (2): 101–12.

Kushner, Tony. 2017. *Journeys from the Abyss: The Holocaust and Forced Migration from the 1880s to the Present*. Liverpool: Liverpool University Press.

Kushner, Tony and Katharine Knox. 1999. *Refugees in an Age of Genocide: Global, National and Local Perspectives during the Twentieth Century*. London: Frank Cass.

Lovelace, Colin John. 1982. 'Control and Censorship of the Press during the First World War'. PhD thesis, King's College London.

Malik, Kenan. 2018. 'How We All Colluded in Fortress Europe', *The Guardian*, 10 June. Accessed 16 January 2020. www.theguardian.com/commentisfree/2018/jun/10/sunday-essay-how-we-colluded-in-fortress-europe-immigration

Ministry of Health. 1920. *Report on the Work Undertaken by the British Government in the Reception and Care of the Belgian Refugees*. London: HMSO.

Musaddique, Shafi. 2019. 'Illegal EU Border Crossings at Six Year Low, Says New Report', *Euronews*, 21 February. Accessed 16 January 2020. www.euronews.com/2019/02/21/illegal-eu-border-crossings-at-six-year-low-says-new-report

O'Brien, Charlotte. 2019. 'Settled Status Scheme for EU Citizens Risks Being Next Windrush', *The Times*, 4 April. Accessed 16 January 2020. www.thetimes.co.uk/edition/news/eu-citizens-settled-status-scheme-risks-being-the-next-windrush-scandal-l333p567v

Plan C London. 2019. 'Blood on the EU's Hands', Plan C blog, 13 March. Accessed 30 January 2020. www.weareplanc.org/blog/blood-on-the-eus-hands/

Quille, Niamh. 2018. 'The Windrush Generation in Britain's "Hostile Environment": Racializing the Crimmigration Narrative'. Master's thesis, University of Oxford.

Scottish Refugee Council. 2016. 'Lest We Forget: First World War – Refugees Then and Now'. Accessed 30 January 2020. https://www.scottishrefugeecouncil.org.uk/lest-we-forget-documentary-now-available-online/

Select Committee on International Relations. 2017. 'The Middle East: Time for New Realism: 2nd Report of Session 2016–17'. Accessed 30 January 2020. https://publications.parliament.uk/pa/ld201617/ldselect/ldintrel/159/15902.htm

Sigona, Nando. 2018. 'Windrush Generation is Not Alone – Children of EU-Born Citizens Could Be Next', *The Conversation*, 18 April. Accessed 16 January 2020. https://theconversation.com/windrush-generation-is-not-alone-children-of-eu-born-citizens-could-be-next-95232

Staples, Kelly. 2015. 'Current Migration Levels: More Than We Can Manage?', *Think: Leicester*, 28 August. Accessed 30 January 2020. https://www2.le.ac.uk/offices/press/think-leicester/politics-and-international-relations/2015/it-is-unclear-why-migration-threatens-to-be-unmanageable

Stone, Dan. 2018. 'Refugees Then and Now: Memory, History and Politics in the Long Twentieth Century: An Introduction', *Patterns of Prejudice* 52 (2/3): 101–6.

Storr, Katherine. 2009. *Excluded from the Record: Women, Refugees and Relief, 1914–1929*. Oxford: Peter Lang.

Taylor, Kieran. 2018. 'Belgian Refugees in Glasgow: Local Faith Communities, Hosting and the Great War', *Refugee Hosts*, 31 January. Accessed 30 January 2020. https://refugeehosts.org/2018/01/31/belgian-refugees-in-glasgow-local-faith-communities-hosting-and-the-great-war/

The Times. 1915. *The Times History of the War, Volume IV*. London: The Times.

Townsend, Mark. 2014. 'First-Time Voters Want Britain to Remain a Haven for Refugees', *The Guardian*, 14 June. Accessed 16 January 2020. www.theguardian.com/uk-news/2014/jun/14/yougov-first-time-voters-refugees

UNHCR Operational Portal – Refugee Situations. n.d. 'Mediterranean Situation'. Accessed 27 January 2020. http://data2.unhcr.org/en/situations/mediterranean

UNHCR Operational Portal – Refugee Situations. 2017. 'Update on Durable Solutions for Syrian Refugees'. Accessed 30 January 2020. https://data2.unhcr.org/en/documents/details/59482

Walsh, Peter William. 2019. 'Migration to the UK: Asylum and Resettled Refugees'. Accessed 30 January 2020. https://migrationobservatory.ox.ac.uk/resources/briefings/migration-to-the-uk-asylum/

Wilson, Trevor. 1979. 'Lord Bryce's Investigation into Alleged German Atrocities in Belgium, 1914–15', *Journal of Contemporary History* 14 (3): 369–83.

York, Sheona. 2018. 'The "Hostile Environment": How Home Office Immigration Policies and Practices Create and Perpetuate Illegality'. Unpublished dissertation, University of Kent, on file with the author.

YouGov. *Survey Results / Refugee Week*. No longer available. Accessed 30 January 2020. http://www.yougov.co.uk/publicopinion/archive/10382

6

# Exploring practices of hospitality and hostility towards migrants through the making of a documentary film: Insights from research in Lampedusa

Michela Franceschelli and Adele Galipò

## Introduction

As the importance of visual culture is increasing, visual evidence has also become more central to social-science research and is the subject of discussion among contemporary social theorists who have started exploring 'vision, sight, display and picture' (Bartmanski, 2014: 166) and the social 'power' of appearance (Seel, 2007 in ibid.). This is particularly true in migration research, where visual approaches are increasingly being used alongside interviews and other ethnographic methods to explore different aspects of migrants' lives and journeys. For instance, Divya Tolia-Kelly (2004a and b) used images and artefacts to understand 'memories' and oral histories in South Asian people in Britain (Tolia-Kelly, 2004a, 2004b, 2006) while Lorraine Van Blerk and Nicola Ansell (2006) analysed Malawian and Lesothan children's representation of migration through their drawings. Yet, images and films dealing with migration also significantly influence public opinion, with the risk of fuelling new fears and also promoting otherness (De Genova, 2013; also see Snow, and Davies, both in this volume). This has arguably been the case since the outset of the Arab Spring in 2011, when video reportages have contributed to exacerbating moral panic about migration in the Mediterranean Sea while increasing a sense of emergency, fear of an 'invasion' and giving rise to a new 'border spectacle' (Mazzara, 2015). The Italian island of Lampedusa has been at the core of such representations.

Lampedusa, Italy's most southerly territory at 205 km off the coast of Sicily, is the first port of arrival for those crossing the Mediterranean Sea to reach Europe.[1] As the number of incoming migrants has increased throughout the years, the island has turned from a mere tourist destination to a site of increasing public and media attention, with images that reify and broadcast contradictory representations of the local community of islanders. Hence, Lampedusa has been presented through these contradictions, depicted either as the island of hospitality (Derrida, 2000, 2005) – exemplified by the provision of essential support to migrants and campaigns for their rights – or as a site of hostility (Orsini, 2015), which, we shall see, has acquired specific meaning and has been addressed to specific actors.

In this chapter, we reflect on the role and contribution of visual evidence in the form of a documentary film – *CCÀ SEMU. Here we are, lives on hold in Lampedusa*[2] – to social-science research. In so doing, we also seek to explore the capacity of visual methods to document how the local community of Lampedusa has responded to, engaged with and also resisted the arrival of migrants and refugees. The film was directed by a professional film-maker and was part of a dissemination strategy of a research project that, based on ethnography and interviews, aimed to explore the views and experiences of Lampedusans living on the island today. By focusing on the community of local residents, the project complements other research that more explicitly concerns migrants' journeys, experiences and views (for example, McMahon and Sigona, 2018). Here, we evaluate in particular the potential of the documentary to disseminate research findings and represent the community's responses to the arriving migrants. We then examine the challenges of making a documentary film and the strategies that we adopted to overcome them. In particular, as we decided to collaborate with an experienced film director, we reflect on the possibilities and challenges opened up by these forms of collaborative and multidisciplinary social-science research, drawing on sociology and social anthropology in addition to the arts.

## Lampedusa and Lampedusans: Context and background

Because of its position, the history of Lampedusa has always been linked to that of the Mediterranean Sea and the people who travel, trade and live around it (Taranto, 2017). An ancient free zone for Christians and

Muslims in their battles on the Mediterranean, the island became a colony for dissidents and political prisoners in the late 1870s, up to 1940. At the end of 2016, Lampedusa's population was approximately 6,572 people.[3] Tourism is the main economic activity today, which employs almost the entire population during the summer season. However, the community relied on fishing for generations, before converting to tourism (Orsini, 2015). Being located 205 km off the coast of Sicily, Lampedusa remains isolated from the rest of Italy, to which it is linked via a ferry service that brings essential goods to the island. Usually, the ferry runs twice a week, but when the sea is rough the island might experience a shortage of fresh fruit, vegetables and meat for weeks. This only adds to a situation of permanent marginality, exemplified by pregnant women who have to fly to the Italian mainland or Sicily to give birth as there is no adequate hospital with maternity care on the island.

Despite being located at the geographical margins of Italy and the EU, Lampedusa has been at the core of Europe's immigration and border discussions (Orsini, 2015; Cuttitta, 2014), turning from a mere tourist site to 'the centre of a growing web of controls' (Dines *et al.*, 2015: 433). Since September 2015, the island has been converted into a 'hotspot' where personnel from the Italian police, together with representatives of the United Nations High Commission for Refugees (UNHCR) and the European Asylum Support Office (EASO) carry out the identification of asylum seekers and process asylum claims. Migrants and asylum seekers only remain on the island for a short time, sometimes only a few days and often less than a week, and they are then quickly transferred to other migration centres in Italy. In 2016, overall 11,399 migrants arrived in Lampedusa (Interni 2016). Unlike Greece, which constitutes the route to Europe for many Syrians fleeing war, the majority of migrants and refugees heading to Italy are mostly from Africa, particularly Nigeria (21 per cent) and Eritrea (12 per cent) (ibid.).

## Representing Lampedusa: The 'Island of Hostility' or 'Hospitality'?

How to be 'hospitable' in a world of rising anti-migrant feelings and xenophobia is an urgent question to address (Germann Molz and Gibson, 2016). Jacques Derrida argues that hospitality namely means to 'accept', 'invite', 'receive' and to 'welcome to one's home' (Derrida, 2000: 6). The term has a long history and tradition: from an ethical and religious duty, hospitality became – during the time of the formation of the nation state – part of the legal apparatus and of the procedures that set out the rights and duties of citizens towards other non-citizens (Benhabib, 2004; for a longer history, see Isayev, 2018). The German philosopher Immanuel Kant highlighted – as part of his writing about cosmopolitan rights – how hospitality eventually becomes institutionalized. Kant defines hospitality as 'the right of a stranger not to be treated as an enemy when he arrives on someone else's territory' (Kant, 1795, in Derrida, 2000: 5). Under this definition, hospitality is a natural and universal right of humanity, which, when it becomes institutionalized, turns into a lawful part of national legislation, acquiring some levels of ambivalence (Derrida, 2000: 6). On one hand, hospitality becomes the legal requirement of welcoming newcomers but, on the other, it introduces a new 'conditionality' (Derrida, 2000, 2005) serving as the demarcation of the 'otherness' of the non-citizens.

In this sense, the idea of hospitality is relevant in the context of international migration in order to address the contradictions emerging in relation to our increasingly mobile world (Germann Molz and Gibson, 2016). John Rawls (1999, in Friese, 2010) argues that in modern democratic societies, hospitality must be negotiated with the need 'of safeguarding borders and protect people's political culture and their constitutional principles' (Rawls 1999, in Friese, 2010: 198). These claims reflect a wider antagonism between national sovereignty and the universal human right to assistance. The ambivalence that characterizes the idea of hospitality as a source of antagonism, but also solidarity (Friese 2010), is reflected in the link that Derrida (2000) draws between 'hospitality and hostility': 'the troubling analogy in their [two words: hospitality and hostility] common origin between *hostis* as host and *hostis* as enemy, between hospitality and hostility' (Derrida, 2000: 13). Derrida argues that hospitality is contradictory in its essence and 'does the opposite of what it initially aimed to do' (ibid.) by producing different levels and degrees of hostility, and so it separates the hosts – those who host and welcome others – and the strangers, who are hosted and welcomed. This ambiguity characterizes attitudes towards outsiders, such as migrants, by defining membership and so patterns of inclusion/exclusion. As Heidrun Friese (2010) clearly notes, in the current migration context these theoretical reflections become relevant to think about legislative acts and rights to mobility and, more specifically, to look at how the 'laws of hospitality versus the laws that limit hospitality' become the equivalent of freedom of movement versus restriction to this freedom. In other words, defining the boundaries of hospitality means accounting for where national borders end and where they begin, and the extent to which, for instance, European treaties (for instance, Schengen) rule. In this context, and because of its geographical location, Lampedusa has become a powerful symbol of the ambivalence of 'migration policies and border regimes that mark the limits of hospitality' (Friese, 2010: 330).

The dualism between hospitality and hostility is relevant for reading the numerous media and visual representations of Lampedusa.[4] On one hand, Lampedusa is portrayed as the place where migrants are rescued and saved. Examples of hospitable Lampedusa draw on stories of compassion for migrants, but also on the commitment of islanders to save human lives and drag people out of the water (for example, Kirby, 2016), as some videos suggest (*Guardian*, 2013). On the other hand, the island is depicted as a community in disarray, incapable of dealing with incoming migrants, fomenting sentiments of hostility among the islanders.[5] In this regard, many online video reportages showcase migrant rescues and shipwrecks, with some locals being interviewed and asked to comment. Migrants are rarely seen as active participants, but mostly presented as silent victims to be rescued.[6] Lampedusans, on the other hand, are only recorded in relation to the rescues at sea – providing accounts of the tragic events.

Although media and video coverage on Lampedusa is abundant, and literature exists about migrant experiences of displacement,[7] there is a lack of research about the perspectives of local residents on the island.[8] Our ethnographic work seeks to fill this gap by collecting the views of Lampedusans as they deal with this complex situation, and explores the ways in which they position themselves in the polarized divide between hospitality and hostility. The documentary film has been crucial for reporting the contradictions in which Lampedusans find themselves while also representing the themes that have emerged from our research.[9]

## The rationale for the film: Capturing interactions or disseminating voices?

Visual methodologies, including the production of films and videos, are often used in social research to gather ethnographic data, particularly everyday interactions. In contrast, less attention is devoted to the role of films and videos as vehicles of dissemination of research findings (Brannen, 2002). Research suggests that visual material has a strong impact both in terms of the content transmitted and the retention of this content.[10] Our documentary film was developed with the specific purpose of presenting our findings to audiences less likely to engage with academic work. By producing a film, we also aimed to promote a collaboration between the social sciences and the arts, and to develop an aesthetic illustration of the research results that is different from the more commonly used strategies to report qualitative findings, such as articles and presentations drawing on extracts from interview transcripts (Brannen, 2002).

The use of films and video in social research for data gathering – particularly in the form of audio-visual recordings – has a relatively long history (Erickson, 2011), dating back to the late nineteenth century. Frederick Erickson (2011) identified the antecedents of video-based research in early studies conducted in the late 1800s to document cultural practices amongst First Nations peoples in North America. With the development of the 16 mm camera in the early 1900s, cameras became more portable and easier to use in fieldwork settings. Hence, anthropologists started using video resources to film different activities (for instance, Balinese dancers in Bateson and Mead, 1942: 44–7) as part of the process of data collection and generation.

More recently, technological developments of audio-visual media have increased the use of video tools to generate data in social-science research. Videos and films continue to be mostly used in ethnographic studies to record social actions while they are taking place and to capture the spontaneity of human interactions – hence the 'taken for granted' (Heath *et al.*, 2010). There is an important distinction to make in the use of visual evidence in research. Films were initially introduced as part of ethnographic work as a data-generation/-gathering method about a social situation and an interaction as it happened. By contrast, social documentaries are a different genre, more explicitly recognized as an artistic representation and elaboration of a social reality, a 'movie about real life' (Aufderheide, 2007). According to Patricia Aufderheide (2007), 'documentaries are about real life; they are not real life'. Although the boundaries are sometimes blurred, ethnographic film-makers tend to distinguish their work from social documentaries:

> We tried to use the still and moving pictures cameras to get a record of Balinese behaviour, and this is a very different matter from a preparation of a 'documentary' film or photographs. We tried to shoot what happened normally and spontaneously, rather than to decide upon the norms and then get the Balinese to go through these behaviours in suitable lighting. (Bateson and Mead, 1942: 42, in Aufderheide, 2007)

Our documentary film is based on thematically assembling video interviews with participants who agreed to be recorded on camera. Hence, the spontaneity central to ethnographic films is less relevant in our case because of the way in which the interaction between researchers, film director, cameraman and participants took place. The director and the cameraman positioned participants in front of the camera according to the light and the aesthetic framing of the shot, and this inevitably led to 'artificial' interview settings. Yet, this approach remains in line with our research aims and motivation to make the film, which was not to record spontaneous human interactions on the island but to support public engagement through 'visual narratives'. Visual narratives are ways of 'organising people's experiences' (Bach, 2007: 282) – either collective or individual – and so forms of representations that account for visual elements via different types of images. This is to say that research participants produce and attribute meanings to their life experiences not only verbally but also in forms and ways that can be visually captured and reproduced by, for instance, drawings, photographs or films. In accounts of migration, visual narratives have been used to reify the idea of a 'crisis' via images of suffering but also the arrival of migrants portrayed as an invasion (Mazzara, 2015). In our research with Lampedusans, we experienced first-hand both the potentials and pitfalls of visual narratives by making a documentary film. We often found ourselves in uncomfortable situations, particularly when dealing with video-recorded interviews and assessing the diverse effects of the camera on both ourselves and on research participants. We discuss these issues in the following sections.

## Developing the content of the documentary film

As the documentary film was conceived to disseminate the research findings, the visual narratives in the film document the content of our interview data. A sub-sample of research participants who engaged in in-depth face-to-face interviews with the researchers agreed to be video-recorded during a second interview. Most of the video interviews were conducted by the film director and were shorter than the un-filmed interviews. Thematic analysis of interview transcripts and fieldwork notes happened simultaneously in the film editing, and the themes explored in the film were identified in collaboration by the researchers and the film director.

Our overarching research aim was to capture how islanders spoke about life on the island as well as their main priorities and concerns, hence the issue of whether and how migration is affecting their lives was an important theme emerging from the discussion with locals. The interview findings suggest how this theme was elaborated through a number of contradictions exemplified by the divide between hospitality and hostility. Lampedusans identify themselves with the word 'hospitality'. This is expressed by Gianni, one of our informants who appeared in the film saying that '[hospitality] is part of the DNA of all islanders, not only Lampedusans'. Other participants, like Francesca, echo this point: 'We have always welcomed people'. Hospitality was described as rooted in the tradition and history of the island and is therefore part of the cultural heritage of the islanders. Our participants explained that the sense of hospitality relates to the 'insularity' – intended here as the condition of living on an island – which on one hand involves isolation from the mainland, but also leads to welcoming people arriving from the sea. Another aspect of the link between insularity and hospitality is related to the 'fishermen ethos', which creates internal (among locals) and external (towards those coming from far away) solidarities and relies on a 'community spirit' (Orsini, 2015).

These ideas were supported by Lampedusans' stories about how they mobilized following the Arab Spring emergency in 2011. After the Tunisian president Zine El Abidine Ben Ali fled his country to escape the forthcoming riots, many Tunisians started fleeing their country to reach Europe (Orsini, 2015) and arrived in Lampedusa early in 2011. By March 2011, they started outnumbering Lampedusans and the population of the island grew from just over 6,000 to 15,000 (ibid.). Our participants recounted the difficulties of that time, the lack of government intervention and how they felt the duty to mobilize their own resources and support these people as best they could by relying only on their own personal means. At this point, hospitality was not 'institutionalized', so people did what they could: some opened their second homes to migrants who were sleeping outdoors; they brought blankets, food and allowed them to use bathrooms and showers. At that time, resentment towards the authorities grew strong and islanders denounced the inhuman conditions in which these people were left while also complaining about the negative consequences on the economy of the island, which heavily relies on tourism.

In spite of this resentment and the complaints, forms of hospitality have continued and spontaneous groups of people have formed with the sole purpose of helping migrants and welcoming those who arrive at the Molo Favarolo (Favorolo Harbour) with a smile, a cup of hot tea and some clean clothes.[11] Simultaneously, the feeling of being abandoned by institutions – national, regional but also European – started to produce a sense of resentment, exacerbated by contradictory media representations portraying Lampedusa as either a victim-island or an hostile place. The situation worsened when, in the autumn of 2011, a group of Tunisians fearing deportation threated to set a gas cylinder on fire. The protest ultimately developed into riots with the police and some local islanders. Media representations of these events emphasized the state of emergency of that time.[12]

In our encounters with Lampedusans, the sense of hostility linked to that event was only mentioned as part of the complexity and emergency of that past time, and the term had rather acquired a different meaning and was used in a new context. 'Hostility' was not addressed directly towards migrants but rather towards those responsible for fomenting the arrivals of people and putting their lives at risk – which included not only the Italian Government but also the local authorities and the ineffective action of the European Union (Franceschelli, 2019). Such a sense of frustration and of being abandoned clearly emerged in our documentary film, highlighting how hostility towards institutions and political impasse could coexist with hospitality towards migrants. Many Lampedusans feel abandoned by the state and complain about the ineffective reception system in place for migrants. Moreover, they seem to be particularly concerned by the economic repercussions that the ongoing arrival of migrants might have on local tourism, as there was a significant reduction of hotel bookings following the events of 2011 until about 2015.

## The making of the film: Practicalities, challenges and ways forward

### Doing collaborative research: Working with a film director

From its inception, this research aimed to produce a documentary film on how the local residents of Lampedusa experience and make sense of living on the island today. In particular, the film helped us to shed light on the contradictions and complexities of the island and its inhabitants. As this was an important component of our research, we decided to collaborate with an experienced independent director and documentary-film producer. The decision fitted a double purpose: first, to reflect upon processes of knowledge production, based on a collaboration between academic researchers and artists in analysing social action; and second, to go beyond traditional academic forms of dissemination and reach out to a broader public. Yet, while the possibilities opened up by these forms of collaborative research are diverse, many challenges remain.

As this was the authors' first collaborative experience with a film-maker, we encountered some difficulties in terms of how to conduct video research. From the outset, we – the researchers – informed the design of the short documentary film and identified its main focus. We discussed this with the director and worked together to develop new ideas to best implement and complete the project. Overall, this process was very productive, as exchanges provided us with valuable insights and new viewpoints. For instance, we focused on sociological debates such as the interplay between local issues and global migration or the analysis of Lampedusans' dissatisfaction with the national state. Conversely, the director was able to capture and broadcast more effectively the mood and the feelings of the community caught between a sense of hope, fatalism and resignation and expressed by the title of the film: 'CCÀ SEMU', a fishermen's saying that can be translated as 'here we are'. Yet, in the course of our collaborative journey, some difficulties became quite evident, most precisely when conducting video interviews with research participants.

In the initial phase of our fieldwork, we decided to conduct qualitative video interviews together with the film director and the cameraman. We usually proceeded by arranging to meet the participant in a convenient location for her/him, preparing for video recording by setting the light and microphone, and asking some initial questions – sometimes in the form of a group interview, other times with only one researcher leading the discussion. Obviously, this format required more time for preparation than an un-filmed qualitative interview and had to follow precise rules in order to get the best out of the video recording, involving decisions such as where and how the participant should sit (or stand), how they should look at the camera and who should lead the discussion.

On several occasions, however, we felt uncomfortable in conducting an interview while being filmed. There were clearly some differences about the way in which we – as researchers – are used to interacting with our participants and the director's own way. On many occasions, we felt trapped by the structured format of the video interview and were afraid of losing much of the spontaneity that might have emerged had our interview taken place without the camera. As social researchers, we felt that we were missing the interactive and unexpected side of the research. Similarly, the director was going through the same process. He felt that it was important to manage the space and get a good framing so as to maintain the quality of the recording to a certain standard. We clearly understood that what was important to us to capture ethnographically the noise, the way someone sits and looks at the interviewer, what was behind the stage – was somehow hindering the work of our film director.

As we talked about our respective difficulties, we acknowledged the fact that we had to review our way of filming interviews and how we worked together, so a compromise had to be found. Thinking about potential strategies to overcome such problems, we decided to conduct separate interviews. The idea was for the director to conduct short video interviews with those who agreed to be filmed – based on selected questions decided in advance – and then to follow up with face-to-face interviews without the camera. Overall, this strategy proved to satisfy both academic and non-academic requirements. Moreover, it was interesting to see how people behaved in front of a camera and later on in 'backstage' settings, mirroring Erving Goffman's (1978) metaphor about social life as a theatrical performance. We return to this in the next section.

While these kinds of technical problems were addressed quite easily, other overarching issues remained, such as the question of representation and authority in documentary films. Our case suggests that the collection of visual data is affected by the requirements of the video recording, particularly how participants will be framed by the camera to account for the light and for the background space. These requirements determine where and how the participant is represented in the film and affect the researcher–participant interaction, which becomes less spontaneous and rather staged. In our case, these decisions were taken together with the film director who, like social researchers, has the authority to control what happens on stage and to edit the material collected. Ultimately, the narration was organized during the editing of the film, which also involved cuts of the video interviews with an impact on the final output.

## Performing identities: The video camera and the interviewees

As detailed above, the contribution of films to research are multiple but it often comes together with challenges. First and foremost, the video camera has a specific effect in altering the interaction with the interviewees, clearly influencing their identity and performance (Pink, 2004). In line with Goffman's idea of 'dramaturgy' (1978), social actors act differently according to where they are placed, whether front-stage or backstage.

The importance of performance and representation in the context of migration debates has been documented (Witteborn, 2015) from different perspectives: images and videos may incentivize the creation and also the 'visual production' of, for instance, the 'migration crisis' (Olesen, 2018); they can trigger public anxiety and political apprehension (Snow, this volume); or support specific representations of migration, such as a survival experience (Perl, 2019). Moreover, refugees may engage in different 'identity performances' and representations of their own selves according to specific needs, such as satisfying the expectations of donors and refugee-camp managers (Fiddian-Qasmiyeh, 2011). This section specifically explores how the identity of our research participants and their self-representations were affected by the video camera and the multiple people involved in the interviews.

The lack of personal narrative – including details about participants' more private and intimate lives, such as stories about relationship breakdowns, family issues and ill health, but also strong views and controversial attitudes – was the main pitfall of video interviews. Some participants opened up during the face-to-face un-filmed interviews, but they withheld these personal stories and views while on camera. Visibility and camera were also objects of discussion with our interviewees. During our fieldwork, it emerged that some Lampedusans were perceived by others as taking advantage of the migrants to increase their own visibility through the 'cameras' of film-makers and journalists. This was the case for those people who became involved with the 2016 film, *Fire at Sea*, by Italian director Gianfranco Rosi[13] – a film acclaimed by the critics, which even ran for the Oscars. A young woman in our research told us that migration has also become 'a brand' on which people try to make personal gains. During our fieldwork, we were even offered a 'migration tour' of the island by a local resident driving a small van and waiting to take us around the key symbolic sites such as the Gate of Europe.[14] Overall, participants' narratives about the roles of cameras and visibility were contradictory. Some felt that this attention was a good way to promote the island, others instead felt the opposite and that the focus of media on migration led to them neglecting local issues and complaints about failing public services – particularly healthcare, education and transport.

We found Lampedusans were used to talking to journalists, had been interviewed and had been on camera more than we had initially anticipated. They were very easy to approach and comfortable when talking to us, even in public spaces like cafés and bars. Many people started talking with us out of curiosity, asking who we were and whom we worked for. This was the case of Toni, a man who runs his own car-rental business. When we first met him, we were parking our car near a café and, as he was passing by, we asked him whether it was possible to park in that area. He ironically replied with a strong Sicilian dialect that it was not up to him to say where to park because he was not a policeman. We met him again soon after at the café and he started talking to us spontaneously. Keeping his strong dialect, he spoke about his daughter who had featured in several movies, but also about his family, the lives of his children who had left the island and his local business. When we asked if we could video record his story for our documentary film, he did not hesitate to agree. We then moved closer to the sea to set out the camera and avoid the noise. However, as soon as he found himself in front of the camera, his performance changed and he switched from the Sicilian dialect to Italian also showing concern about how he looked on camera. While talking, he appeared rehearsed and sounded very different from the man we had just heard at the café. Correcting their language while being recorded was also important for how some participants adapted their identity to the 'filming'. For instance, Toni used the derogatory term 'clandestine' while off-camera in the café, and then switched to 'migrant' while we were filming him.

There were many examples – both more and less evident – of how the video camera affected participants' presentation of their self-identities. Maria, a restaurant owner, did not want to be interviewed in her work clothes. For the doctor of Lampedusa, the video interview was a way in which to embrace a specific identity and promote a humanitarian message to support and defend the rights of migrants arriving on the island. Switching the camera on and off also had an effect even on Lampedusans with more experience of being recorded on camera, like local politicians who appeared confident in the recording but also rehearsed. Yet, when the camera was off, the different emotions that were somehow controlled during the interview – a sense of anger towards the current political situation or aversion towards other candidates, as well as some gossip and 'hot topics' – surfaced.

During the fieldwork, it became evident that some Lampedusans held strong negative feelings towards being video-recorded. We also soon became aware that islanders were used to media attention and that some of them had very little sympathy for journalists and their cameras accused of spreading a far too negative image of the island, and so compromising tourism and the businesses. Audio recording was more widely tolerated, and a few Lampedusans who refused to be recorded on camera agreed to be interviewed just by the researchers. One of our them, an activist for a local cultural organization, said that with the video 'he could not control the final output' – but was more lenient and flexible about our audio-recording device, as he understood that it was useful for the reporting. In his case, being in control of the discussion was a major issue. When we met him, we soon discovered that we were not the only researchers and even a French radio station was going to join the interview. This format influenced both the structure of the interview and the interviewee's 'performance', which left little space for interaction. On this occasion, the power balance between interviewer and interviewee shifted towards the participant, who took the opportunity to voice his specific political message. The interview completely lacked the respondent's personal experiences and subjective accounts about life on the island and resembled more a lecture or a previously prepared speech.

In sum, video recording has specific effects on the self-presentation and identity of participants: from changing the language to shaping the presentation of self and of the content disclosed during interviews. It also generated mixed feelings, perceived as an opportunity but also as a possible threat. Moreover, the video camera involved new pressures for us as researchers by not being used to being filmed, by compressing the time we had for the interviews and by affecting the range and depth of the questions that we asked. As detailed above, to moderate these negative effects, we carried out separate filmed and un-filmed interviews. Of course, social interactions and dynamics between participants during all qualitative interviews, irrespective of the presence or absence of different recording devices, are different from 'real world' everyday conversations (Pink, 2004). The video recording adds a level of complexity to this already 'unnatural' interaction, and yet ultimately it is easier to forget about a voice recorder than it is to forget about being in front of a video camera.

## Conclusion

In this chapter, we have examined some of the challenges of making a documentary film and doing collaborative research with a professional film-maker, including how to conduct video interviews and interact with participants who are being filmed. In so doing, the chapter invites reflections on the intersections between academic modes of knowledge production and artistic expressions. In our case, conducting face-to-face interviews with the researchers and separate filmed interviews led by the director was helpful to overcome some of the difficulties of video interviewing. This strategy proved useful and interesting, as it also allowed us to analyse the different ways in which the camera affected participants.

In this chapter, we have also reflected on the potential and complexity of using a documentary film to recount the stories and disseminate the experiences of Lampedusans as they position themselves in the polarized representations of the island as a community of hospitality or hostility. While a complementary analysis is needed to further explore how to develop research-led conversations pertaining to migrants, refugees, displacement and forced migration, the film has brought to light the frustration of Lampedusans as well as the internal tensions within and across the community. In so doing, it complements our interview data by visually recording the themes emerging from the analysis. More specifically, our experience highlights how documenting Lampedusans' responses to the arrival of migrants relates to their diverse performances in front and behind the video camera, and so between the unequal fields of visibility and audibility.

Finally, the process of film-making reproduces the tensions between front-stage and backstage aspects of the participants' selves, and so it illustrates the potential but also the drawbacks of reconstructing and recounting others' experiences through visual tools such as a film. In so doing, this case invites reflections on the role of film-making in nurturing and strengthening the 'spectacle' of migration in its contradictory representations.

## Acknowledgements

We are deeply grateful to the film director Mr Luca Vullo and the project team: Daniele Banzato (Director of Photography), Liana Vullo (Personal Manager at Ondemotive Productions), Voilà Silvia (Animation) and Giuseppe Vasapolli (Original Music). We would also like to thank UCL for funding the project (Seed funding, UCL Grand Challenges: Justice & Equality).

## Notes

1. On processes of reception and 'hospitality' in Italy, also see Astolfo and Boano in this volume.
2. *CCÀ SEMU. Here we are, lives on hold in Lampedusa*: https://youtu.be/yWwklC6yorc
3. Data based on calculations from the Instituto Nazionale di Statistica (ISTAT) concerning residents at 31 December 2016. See https://www.tuttitalia.it/sicilia/82-lampedusa-linosa/statistiche/popolazione-andamento-demografico
4. See, for example, 'Italian police beat migrants in Lampedusa clashes': https://www.youtube.com/watch?v=M5wc6KC6FPI
5. See, for example, 'Lampedusa: Way to Paradise or Hell for African migrants?' RT Documentary: https://youtu.be/NgpldGzumnk
6. An exception is provided by video footage by Al Jazeera, in which migrants are asked to recount their stories about the sea crossing once they have safely arrived in Lampedusa, Al Jazeera English Published on 9 June 2015: https://www.youtube.com/watch?v=tUtlpwsRZYE
7. For example, see Mazzara (2015); Gianfranco Rosi's *Fire at Sea*; and Jakob Brossmann's film *Lampedusa in Winter* or the BBC documentary *Exodus* (2016) shot by refugees themselves.
8. On refugees as members of local communities 'hosting' other refugees (rather than citizens hosting refugees), see Fiddian-Qasmiyeh in this volume.
9. In accordance with the video director, the video focuses exclusively on Lampedusans. This is mainly due to ethical considerations about the use of images portraying migrants at sea and their subsequent 'management'.

10. Retrieved from Forrester Research, https://idearocketanimation.com/4293-video-worth-1-million-words
11. See the work to support migrants of the local community network Forum Solidale Lampedusa.
12. For example, Sky TG News 'Lampedusa, scontri violenti tra polizia, tunisini e lampedusani', 21 September 2011: https://www.youtube.com/watch?v=V5L5MWuyixo
13. Retrieved from https://www.theguardian.com/film/2016/jun/09/fire-at-sea-review-masterly-and-moving-look-at-the-migrant-crisis
14. The Gate of Europe is a memorial monument in Lampedusa designed by the Italian artist Mimmo Paladino and built in memory of thousands of migrants who died while trying to reach Europe.

# References

Aufderheide, Patricia. 2007. *Documentary Film: A Very Short Introduction*. New York: Oxford University Press.

Bach, Hedy. 2007. 'Composing a Visual Narrative Inquiry'. In *Handbook of Narrative Inquiry: Mapping a Methodology*, edited by D. Jean Clandinin, 280–307. Thousand Oaks, CA: SAGE Publications.

Bartmanski, D. 2014. 'The word/image dualism revisited: Towards an iconic conception of visual culture', *Journal of Sociology* 50 (2): 164–81.

Bateson, G. and M. Mead. 1942. *Balinese character: A photographic analysis*. New York: New York Academy of Science.

Benhabib, Seyla. 2004. *The Rights of Others: Aliens, Residents, and Citizens*. Cambridge: Cambridge University Press.

Brannen, Julia. 2002. 'The Use of Video in Research Dissemination: Children as Experts on Their Own Family Lives', *International Journal of Social Research Methodology* 5 (2): 173–80.

Cuttitta, Paolo. 2014. '"Borderizing" the Island Setting and Narratives of the Lampedusa "Border Play"', *ACME: An International e-Journal for Critical Geographies* 13 (2): 196–219.

De Genova, Nicholas. 2013. 'Spectacles of Migrant "Illegality": The Scene of Exclusion, the Obscene of Inclusion', *Ethnic and Racial Studies* 36 (7): 1180–98.

Derrida, Jacques. 2000. 'Hostipitality', translated by Barry Stocker and Forbes Morlock, *Angelaki: Journal of the Theoretical Humanities* 5 (3): 3–18.

Derrida, Jacques. 2005. 'The Principle of Hospitality', translated by Ashley Thompson, *Parallax* 11 (1): 6–9.

Dines, Nick, Nicola Montagna and Vincenzo Ruggiero. 2015. 'Thinking Lampedusa: Border Construction, the Spectacle of Bare Life and the Productivity of Migrants', *Ethnic and Racial Studies* 38 (3): 430–45.

Erickson, Frederick. 2011. 'Uses of Video in Social Research: A Brief History', *International Journal of Social Research Methodology* 14 (3): 179–89.

Fiddian-Qasmiyeh, Elena. 2011. 'The Pragmatics of Performance: Putting "Faith" in Aid in the Sahrawi Refugee Camps', *Journal of Refugee Studies* 24 (3): 533–47.

Franceschelli, M. 2019. 'Global Migration, Local Communities and the Absent State: Resentment and Resignation on the Italian Island of Lampedusa', *Sociology*. Accessed 21 February 2020. https://doi.org/10.1177/0038038519890824.

Friese, Heidrun. 2010. 'The Limits of Hospitality: Political Philosophy, Undocumented Migration and the Local Arena', *European Journal of Social Theory* 13 (3): 323–41.

Germann Molz, Jennie and Sarah Gibson, eds. 2016. *Mobilizing Hospitality: The Ethics of Social Relations in a Mobile World*. London: Routledge.

Goffman, Erving. 1978. *The Presentation of Self in Everyday Life*. Harmondsworth: Penguin.

Heath, Christian, Jon Hindmarsh and Paul Luff. 2010. *Video in Qualitative Research: Analysing Social Interaction in Everyday Life*. London: SAGE Publications.

Interni (2016) Cruscotto Statistico, Ministero Degli Interini. Accessed 3 March 2020. https://immigrazione.it/docs/2016/cruscotto-statistico-giornaliero-12-dic.pdf.

Isayev, Elena. 2018. 'Hospitality: A Timeless Measure of Who We Are?', *Migration and Society* 1 (1): 7–21.

Kirby, Emma-Jane. 2016. *The Optician of Lampedusa*. London: Allen Lane.

Mazzara, Federica. 2015. 'Spaces of Visibility for the Migrants of Lampedusa: The Counter Narrative of the Aesthetic Discourse', *Italian Studies* 70 (4): 449–64.

McMahon, Simon and Nando Sigona. 2018. 'Navigating the Central Mediterranean in a Time of "Crisis": Disentangling Migration Governance and Migrant Journeys', *Sociology* 52 (3): 497–514.

Olesen, Thomas. 2018. 'Memetic Protest and the Dramatic Diffusion of Alan Kurdi', *Media, Culture and Society* 40 (5): 656–72.

Orsini, Giacomo. 2015. 'Lampedusa: From a Fishing Island in the Middle of the Mediterranean to a Tourist Destination in the Middle of Europe's External Border', *Italian Studies* 70 (4): 521–36.

Perl, Gerhild. 2019. 'Migration as Survival: Withheld Stories and the Limits of Ethnographic Knowability', *Migration and Society* 2 (1): 12–25.

Pink, Sarah. 2004. 'Performance, Self-Representation and Narrative: Interviewing with Video'. In *Seeing is Believing? Approaches to Visual Research*, edited by Christopher J. Pole, 61–77. Bingley: Emerald Group Publishing.

Seel, M. 2007. *Die Macht des Erscheinens*. Frankfurt: Suhrkamp.

Taranto, Antonio. 2017. *A Short Story of Lampedusa*. Naples: Grafica Elettronica. Document available in the Archivio Storico di Lampedusa.

The Guardian. 2013. 'Lampedusa Boat Sinking: Fishermen "Prevented" from Rescuing Migrants', *YouTube*, 7 October. Video. Accessed 23 January 2020. www.youtube.com/watch?v=z-ZaqSYegDlc.

Tolia-Kelly, Divya P. 2004a. 'Materializing Post-Colonial Geographies: Examining the Textural Landscapes of Migration in the South Asian Home', *Geoforum* 35 (6): 675–88.

Tolia-Kelly, Divya P. 2004b. 'Locating Processes of Identification: Studying the Precipitates of Re-Memory through Artefacts in the British Asian Home', *Transactions of the Institute of British Geographers* 29 (3): 314–29.

Tolia-Kelly, Divya P. 2006. 'Mobility/Stability: British Asian Cultures of "Landscape and Englishness"', *Environment and Planning A: Economy and Space* 38 (2): 341–58.

Van Blerk, Lorraine and Nicola Ansell. 2006. 'Imagining Migration: Placing Children's Understanding of "Moving House" in Malawi and Lesotho', *Geoforum* 37 (2): 256–72.

Witteborn, Saskia. 2015. 'Becoming (Im)perceptible: Forced Migrants and Virtual Practice', *Journal of Refugee Studies* 28 (3): 350–67.

# 7
# Mediterranean distinctions: Forced migration, forceful hope and the analytics of desperation

Alice Elliot

This chapter offers a reflection about a peculiar resonance, even familiarity, between forms of movement that are legally and socially defined as distinct. I take as my starting point the striking familiarity between the so-called European 'refugee crisis', with its complex historical, racial and mediatic configurations (New Keywords Collective, 2016), and a form of movement that is generally categorized, and indeed explicitly carved out, as distinct: North African migrations across the Mediterranean. This particular transnational movement, which I have been researching since 2009 (Elliot, forthcoming), is not classified as 'forced', nor are Moroccan or Tunisian migrants legally defined, except in very exceptional cases, as 'asylum seekers' or 'refugees'. However, many elements of the 'refugee-crisis' phenomenon are strikingly familiar to me, as well as to my North African interlocutors: the deaths at sea and the makeshift rescue operations; the rhetoric of invasion and the stories of hope; the defiance of fear; and the race, class and gender politics of exclusion and inclusion. While numbers and historical contingencies may be different, for those who have experience of Mediterranean migrations, the 'refugee crisis' is eerily familiar.[1]

In this chapter I reflect on this complex familiarity by focusing on the 'distinction work' actualized by the idea – and category – of 'forced migration', an idea and category that sustains many of the conceptualizations and practices surrounding the 'refugee crisis'. My reflection is in two, brief, parts. In the first part, I trace how the concept of forced migration brings into 'biopolitical being' (Puar, 2017: xix) different kinds of moving subjects by distinguishing certain forces (the force of war, for example, or the force of environmental disaster) from others (for example, the force of relative poverty; the force of colonial history; or, what interests me here, the force of hope). I argue that while this work of classification and distinction of the multiple forces that compel people to move is perhaps necessary at times (though necessary for what, and to whom, remain vital questions), it also generates paradoxical hierarchies and artificial distinctions with tangible, indeed deadly, consequences. In the second part of the chapter, I reflect on the critical labour of interrogating and displacing these legal and social distinctions between moving subjects. In doing so, I trace the possible limitations of analytics that, in an effort to reclaim the 'abstract – rather than historical – humanity' (Danewid, 2017, 1675) of migrants, foreground desperation and vulnerability as determining forces of (some) human movement, actualizing once again specific sets of biopolitical distinctions across the Mediterranean.

## On being forced to move

With over 10 per cent of its total population living abroad, and a global diaspora estimated at between three and four million, Morocco is today one of the major emigration countries in the world (Berriane *et al.*, 2015). Since 2009, I have been tracing how this phenomenon of huge proportions has come to inhabit people's lives in a rural central area of the country where migration to Europe – particularly to southern Europe – is ubiquitous, and in a sense inescapable. Migration towards Europe gained momentum in the area in the early 1980s and initially had a circular character, with Moroccan nationals being able to travel freely back and forth across the Mediterranean. The introduction of visa requirements by Italy and Spain in 1990–1 had fundamental conse- quences on the routes, patterns and composition of migration from the area, and the Mediterranean passage has become increasingly deadly, and part of what Ruben Andersson (2014) describes as a multi-million 'illegality industry'. Indeed, the area where I work is sometimes referred to locally as 'the triangle of death', a chilling reminder of the ceaseless deaths in the Mediterranean Sea of young *harraga* from the region (*har- raga* meaning clandestine crossers – from the verb *haraqa*, 'to burn').

The deadly risks associated with the Mediterranean crossing have not dampened people's desire, or intention, to move. Migration is part and parcel of the very way in which existence, future, and possibility are spoken about and understood, often by younger and older generations alike. *L-berra* – meaning 'the outside' in Moroccan Arabic, and the concept used in the area to refer to Europe and other desired migrant destinations (Elliot, forthcoming) – has become for many synonymous with a life worth living, and many of the actions, thoughts and routines of daily life are infused with a sense of expectation for migratory futures to come.

The hope for migration is particularly forceful in the lives of young men. This is how Aziz, a young unemployed graduate whom I have known for many years, summarized it for me once:

> My life here is nothing [*walu*]. I wake up and I fall asleep but there is nothing that makes it a life. Ask anyone, they'll tell you the same: I need to go to 'the outside' [*l-berra*] so I can live. Here you work like a dog, you study study and study, you bribe like a rich man even if you have nothing ... but still you are stuck, still you are not living, you are not moving anywhere, just going round in circles. I'm not stupid. I don't think there is gold on the street over there, or that people are particularly nice. I know the police beat you up, that even if you have five degrees you'll be in construction, and that some get so lonely they implode. But in 'the outside' there is always something, there is always the hope that, even if today was really bad, tomorrow will be better ...

While young people like Aziz often describe migration, and the hope that it embodies and fosters, as a gripping, and irresistible, force, constitutive of the imagination of life itself, Moroccan migration rarely falls in the official, and normative, category of 'forced migration'. The International Association for the Study of Forced Migration (IASFM) defines forced migration as 'a general term that refers to the movements of refugees and internally displaced people (those displaced by conflicts) as well as people displaced by natural or environmental disasters, chemical or nuclear disasters, famine, or development projects'.[2] None of these dramatic forces necessarily apply to my interlocutors in rural Morocco where I conduct research. There is no war currently raging in Aziz's home town, nor has there been any recent environmental, chemical or nuclear disaster in the region that has displaced vast numbers of people. Indeed, Morocco as a whole is often discussed, if not explicitly treated, as a 'safe country of origin' in a number of European states as they tighten refugee policies, and categories, and streamline deportation regimes.[3] For as long as only disastrous forces such as famine or torture are accorded legal (and social) weight in the administration of migration rights to those moving from non-affluent, non-Western contexts, the forces that animate the movement of people like Aziz remain excluded, and invisible – and so do the moving subjects themselves. And while it may sound logical that someone escaping, say, a civil war should have precedence over someone who feels stuck in an unliveable life, as is always the case with classifications and distinctions (see Douglas, 1966), other problems immediately emerge by thinking this way. Here, I am not solely referring to the racial, historical and social logics that ground the very act of making the right to move and movement of (some) people contingent on classification and distinction in the first place – a point to which I return below. I am also referring, in more immediate terms, to the fact that human movement unavoidably exceeds its formal classification.

While IASFM's definition of forced migration does not seem to apply, at least not obviously so, to the central Moroccan migration with which I am familiar, people from this area aspire to move and sometimes build their lives around moving – and many, denied legal entry by European states, risk and often lose their lives in order to reach the opposite shore. People like Aziz describe their actual or desired migration as something necessary, crucial for their very survival as subjects. The expression 'khassni nemshi' (I have to go), is often uttered in the area, and life without migration can be described as hollowed out, meaningless. This may not be 'forced migration' according to the IASFM's official definition, but the sense of being *compelled*, indeed forced to move, is palpable. Anthropologists of Morocco have analysed this 'force' in different ways. Francesco Vacchiano (2014) has written of the ways in which Moroccan children and adolescents who travel unaccompanied to Europe speak of 'the burning desire' for migration, so burning that it makes them leave family, friends and home in order to undertake an often deadly journey. They also speak, as many of my own interlocutors do, of the compelling sense of responsibility toward one's parents, a responsibility that fuels (forces?) their migratory plans. Similarly, Stefania Pandolfo (2007) has shown how disenfranchised Moroccan youths discuss migration in terms of a religious duty, something that one is required to do when life becomes so unliveable that it parallels a kind of suicide.

How do we distinguish between the different, powerful forces that compel people to move? And what are the consequences of imposing a legal distinction between, say, the force of hope and the force of war? My suggestion is not that these forces are the same (although they do often intimately overlap) but rather that both forces powerfully compel people to move, incessantly defying the classificatory regimes imposed on them. This will always be the case, my sense is, for as long as the right to move of (some) subjects is conceived as *contingent* on specific qualities and properties of the forces compelling this movement.

Discursive framings of *what causes* movement have always shaped how states and other actors have responded, and classified, moving people. Think, for example, of the historically and politically contingent conceptual boundaries between voluntary versus forced migration, migrant versus refugee, economic versus political migrant. On the conceptual distinction between 'refugee' and 'migrant' in particular, anthropologists Seth Holmes and Heide Castañeda have argued how:

> immigrants or migrants, as opposed to refugees, tend to be portrayed in popular, political, and academic discourse as economic opportunists, *voluntarily* leaving their home communities in search for a better life. Because they are viewed as having made a free and autonomous *choice* to cross borders, they are often positioned as unworthy of social, economic, and political rights. (Holmes and Castañeda, 2016: 17)

Importantly, these conceptual distinctions and classificatory regimes quickly become reified into categories of being, erasing the artificiality of the categories themselves. Think, for example, of the category 'illegal immigrant' – the classification that many of my Moroccan interlocutors are given if they survive the perilous Mediterranean crossing into Europe. 'Illegal immigrant' quickly shifts from a formal description of an individual who does not possess the correct documentation in a specific legal regime, and in a specific time and place, to a description of the very quality – even moral fibre – of a person (see, for example, Quassoli, 2013 and Maneri, 2011 on the concept of *clandestino* in Italy). Many have argued that a similar process of moral classification has been taking place with the so-called European 'refugee crisis'.

Nadine El-Enany (2107), for example, has analysed the distinctions between 'the migrant' and 'the refugee' emerging in the media portrayal and popular perception of people seeking entry into Europe. She points to how easily we forget that the legal categories of migrant, asylum seeker and refugee are 'artificial and historically contingent. They do not represent natural or predefined groups of people, but instead construct them' (2017: 30). She argues that much is to be gained from conflating the categories of refugee and migrant:

> if we are trying to understand not only what these categories signify in actuality, but also their effects. All people moving are migrants: people moving out of a desire to better their existence, whether in flight from extreme poverty or from persecution. It is merely that

the law grants some people rights, at least in theory, and others not ... The distinction drawn between migrants and refugees is both false and dangerous in reinforcing the idea that some migrants are worthy of humanisation, while others are not. (El-Enany, 2017: 30)

Holmes and Castañeda make a similar point in their analysis of the idea of 'deservingness' in the contemporary 'refugee crisis'. They argue that because international conventions establish refugees as *involuntarily* displaced by political circumstances (war, famine, violence and so on), they are framed as deserving migrants. This deservingness enables a moral, as much as a legal or social, demarcation between 'people who are understood as worthy of the international community's physical, economic, social and health aid and those who are not' (Holmes and Castañeda, 2016: 17).

## Desperate analytics

In a historical, social and political moment in which distinction and categorization can administer life and death, the work of scholars like El-Enany, Holmes and Castañeda – who interrogate and displace the categories superimposed on, and producing of, moving people – is vital (see also, for instance, New Keywords Collective, 2016; Crawley and Skleparis 2018; Saunders *et al.*, 2016; Sigona 2018; Fiddian-Qasmiyeh, this volume). We have seen how even an apparently straightforward category such as 'forced migration' is not easily discernible on the ground once we take into account the multiple, complex and irresistible forces involved in human movement.

However, my sense is that we also need to pay close attention to the mode in which we (re)categorize and (re)bound moving people (also see Kelman, this volume). When we advocate a critical re-evaluation of the boundary between, for example, the categories of 'refugee' and 'migrant', we often do so on the grounds that both refugees and migrants are moving in a context of desperation, dispossession and poverty. In her critique of the distinction between migrant and refugee, El-Enany states, for example, that 'all people moving are migrants: people moving out of a desire to better their existence, whether in flight from extreme poverty or from persecution' (El-Enany, 2017: 30). We also find this language of desperation and poverty in other critical work. To keep with another previous example, Holmes and Castañeda, in their critique of the distinction between political and economic migration, argue that:

individuals, families, and communities have been driven out of their homes by economic desperation that is politically produced … Indeed, the idea of the 'voluntary' economic migrant elides the realities of structural violence and post-colonial economic inequalities that push people to migrate in order to survive. (Holmes and Castañeda, 2016:17)

Survival and desperation, poverty and structural violence. The case for critical re-evaluation of classificatory boundaries seems to build on pretty depressing grounds. In many cases, this is indeed the context in which people move. And, even when it is not, in specific sociopolitical climates it does make sense to insist on the humanitarian discourse in order to alleviate the strict, and deadly, migration restrictions in place.

However, focusing solely on the desperation of people on the move – whether categorized as 'refugees', 'political migrants' or 'economic migrants' – has its own analytic and political limitations. As I see it, the risk is that we may end up reiterating the idea that the movement of some takes place only in situations of (desperate) *need*. Why is the Mediterranean crossing of young North Africans so rarely framed as a desire to travel? Why are words such as curiosity, adventure, experience so rarely heard when we speak of North Africans, and so often used when describing the transnational movement of, say, young Europeans?

In making my point about the problematic definition of forced migration, I have evoked stories of deep existential and social frustration in Morocco, and the underlying sense of hope that fuels the migratory projects of my interlocutors. But this is just part of the story, as always. Many list, next to the burning need to begin a life worth living, also a wish to see Paris, a curiosity to hear people speak English, a desire to visit an old aunt in Italy, an interest in experiencing different cultures, and the adventure of travel itself (cf. Bachelet, 2019; Nyamnjoh, 2011; Olwig, 2018). Emphasizing frustration, desperation or the need for help, while sometimes effective and sometimes truthful, also reiterates a specific image that Europe has of 'the Other' and of itself, as well as reiterating specific relations of power, hierarchy and charity. It also reiterates the idea that while in the 'Global North' travel may be about curiosity, indecision about the future or love, others may travel – and indeed only *desire* to travel – out of desperation, poverty, fear.

Ida Danewid (2017) has made a similar observation in her analysis of the analytical and political language of hospitality in the Mediterranean. She traces how, in an attempt to resist the dehumanization of migrants embroiled in the 'refugee-crisis' phenomenon, both political activism and academic debate have turned to 'an ethics of hospitality that seeks to disrupt nationalist protocols of kinship and that points towards new forms of solidarity beyond borders' (Danewid, 2017: 1675). She argues that the problem with such 'critical humanist intervention' (ibid.) is that it risks reiterating rather than disrupting specific conceptions of Europe and its (racialized) Others – wherein Europe ultimately emerges as ethical and historically innocent, and migrants ultimately emerge as uninvited guests and charitable subjects. Erasing the 'umbilical cord' (Hall, 1992: 12) that links Europe with the places from which migration originates, 'these discourses contribute to an ideological formation that disconnected connected histories and turns questions of responsibility, guilt, restitution, repentance, and structural reform into matters of empathy, generosity, and hospitality' (Danewid, 2017: 1657). The labour of connecting colonial, imperial and slavery pasts with migratory presents in the Mediterranean (for example, Bhambra, 2017; Broeck and Saucier, 2016; Saucier and Woods, 2014) points in powerful ways to the making of migrants into (racialized and de-historicized) 'charitable subjects' whose desperation, poverty and fear might move Europe to hospitality, pity and protection.

It must not be forgotten, in this respect, that borders and their enforcement often directly foster the kind of desperation, poverty and fear commonly associated with the 'refugee crisis' and the moving subjects that it (re)produces. Nicholas De Genova (2018: 1766) has shown, for example, how 'the EU-ropean legal frameworks governing travel visas, migration, and asylum, together with the externalisation of border policing and transportation carrier sanctions, preclude literally the vast majority of humanity from "legitimate" access to the European Union'. De Genova traces the troubling 'global colour line' of European border regimes, which require (and then systematically deny) visas from travellers from all of Africa and most of Asia, as well as many Latin American and Caribbean countries. The 'inordinate majority' (ibid.) of prospective applicants who do not qualify for visas is required to enter Europe by illegalized means, and only if it survives the perilous journey may it petition for (routinely denied) migrant rights:

> a European border regime that systematically generates and multiplies the conditions of possibility for migrant deaths compels us to reckon with the brute fact that the lives of migrants and refuges, required to arrive to European soil by 'irregular' (illegalised) means, have been systematically exposed to lethal risks. (De Genova, 2018: 1767)

This 'brute fact' is exceptionally clear in the case of North African migrations. The near impossibility for a young Moroccan like Aziz to obtain a visa to enter Europe, which would in turn allow him to board a budget flight at Marrakech Menara Airport rather than pay thousands of euros to travel on a rickety boat that may take his life, is intimately, constitutively linked to the images of desperation, poverty and fear associated with Europe's contemporary borderlands. Here, the European border regime is desperation's very condition of possibility.

## Crisis?

By means of moving towards the conclusion of this chapter, I should reiterate that my reflection on the analytical and political work of 'desperation' should not be read as an erasure or belittlement of the violent forces that are often involved in human movement. Rather, what I am trying to do here is call attention to the ways in which these forces are evoked, and the work that they do by bringing into 'biopolitical being' (Puar, 2017: xix) specific kinds of moving subjects, and, in turn, specific kinds of European imaginations (and actualizations) of itself. While evoking desperation and vulnerability may be necessary at times – although, as I mention above, necessary for what, and to whom, remain vital questions – I am unsure whether the analytics of desperation is ever the most effective way in which to capture the complexity of contemporary human mobility. It definitely was not during an early intimation of the Mediterranean 'refugee crisis'. When young Tunisians started arriving in southern Italy during the Tunisian Revolution of 2010–11, the Italian and international press swiftly adopted a language of crisis – anticipating the systematic mobilization of the concept of 'crisis' that, from 2015 onwards, would bring into being the discursive formations of 'refugee (or migrant) crisis'.[4] These young men arriving on the Italian island of Lampedusa, we were told, were desperate, vulnerable people escaping from the revolution – and, incidentally, they were going to swamp Europe (on Lampedusa, see Franceschelli and Galipò, this volume).

However, many of the Tunisians with whom I have spoken, who crossed the Mediterranean at the height of the revolution, tell a very different story. Since 2014, I have been collecting narratives of the Jasmine Revolution with young Tunisians living on both sides of the Mediterranean, as part of a wider project on the permanence of political ruptures (Elliot, 2017). My young Tunisian interlocutors, who travelled to Europe during or shortly after the national upheaval, never mention escaping from a revolution that many of them contributed in precipitating. They never describe their dangerous crossing to Europe as a desperate act. If anything, they speak of a crossing that was made possible by their experience of the revolution, by the courage and defiance that they learnt from it (see also the testimonies collected by the Italian visual project, CrossingTV – CrossingTV, 2011). Indeed, migration writer and journalist Gabriele Del Grande (2011) has put forward the argument that these young Tunisians were instantiating a second rebellion, this time not against the Ben Ali regime but against a border that they considered unjust and against a legal ban on travel to Europe that they experienced as claustrophobic (see also Garelli *et al.*, 2013).

People move for different reasons, compelled by different personal and historical forces, and animated by different desires and expectations. The language of crisis and desperation maybe works, at times – though it is worth remembering that, in the UK for example, this kind of language (alongside that of 'vulnerability' and 'compassion') produced, at the height of the 'refugee crisis', the acceptance of a dismal 20,000 refugees from Syria over a period of five years, hardly a humanitarian revolution.[5] But the analytics of desperation also risks obfuscating what human movement may be about. It also risks reiterating specific categories of existence and relations (for instance, the curious European traveller versus the desperate migrant Other) while at the same time erasing others (for instance, the 'umbilical' ones between migration and empire – cf. Hall 1992) – a work of reiteration and erasure that fosters rather than alleviates what is periodically defined as 'crisis'.

## Acknowledgements

An earlier version of this chapter was published as 'Forceful hope' on the online platform https://allegralaboratory.net/forceful-hope/. Research for this chapter was partly supported by the ERC Grant ERC-2013-CoG_617970.

## Notes

1. On representations of and responses to sea crossings in the Mediterranean, see the chapters by Franceschelli and Galipò, Snow, and Davies, in this volume.
2. http://iasfm.org
3. See the Asylum Information Database (AIDA) for the definition and application of the 'safe country of origin' concept across EU member states: https://www.asylumineurope.org
4. For critical work on the concept, and politics, of 'crisis' in the context of human movement across the Mediterranean, see, for example, Broeck and Saucier, 2016; Fiddian-Qasmiyeh 2019; New Keywords Collective, 2016; Saucier and Woods, 2014.

5.  BBC News, 'UK to accept 20,000 refugees from Syria by 2020', 7 September 2015: http://www.bbc.co.uk/news/uk-34171148

# References

Andersson, Ruben. 2014. *Illegality, Inc.: Clandestine Migration and the Business of Bordering Europe*. Oakland: University of California Press.

Bachelet, Sébastien. 2019. '"Looking for One's Life": Trapped Mobilities and Adventure in Morocco', *Migration and Society* 2 (1): 40–54.

Berriane, Mohammed, Hein de Haas and Katharina Natter. 2015. 'Introduction: Revisiting Moroccan Migrations', *Journal of North African Studies* 20 (4): 503–21.

Bhambra, Gurminder K. 2017. 'The Current Crisis of Europe: Refugees, Colonialism, and the Limits of Cosmopolitanism', *European Law Journal* 23 (5): 395–405.

Broeck, Sabine and P. Khalil Saucier. 2016. 'A Dialogue: On European Borders, Black Movement, and the History of Social Death', *Black Studies Papers* 2 (1): 23–45.

Crawley, Heaven and Dimitris Skleparis. 2018. 'Refugee, Migrants, Neither, Both: Categorical Fetishism and the Politics of Bounding in Europe's "Migration Crisis"', *Journal of Ethnic and Migration Studies* 44 (1): 48–64.

CrossingTV. 2011. 'La storia di Jihad', *Vimeo*, 1 June. Video. Accessed 11 January 2020. https://vimeo.com/24516251.

Danewid, Ida. 2017. 'White Innocence in the Black Mediterranean: Hospitality and the Erasure of History', *Third World Quarterly* 38 (7): 1674–89.

De Genova, Nicholas. 2018. 'The "Migrant Crisis" as Racial Crisis: Do Black Lives Matter in Europe?', *Ethnic and Racial Studies* 41 (10): 1765–82.

Del Grande, Gabriele. 2011. 'Generazione revolution: La storia di Jihad', *Fortress Europe*, 3 November. Accessed 21 January 2020. http://fortresseurope.blogspot.co.uk/2011/06/generazione-revolution-la-storia-di.html.

Douglas, Mary. 1966. *Purity and Danger: An Analysis of Concepts of Pollution and Taboo*. London: Routledge and Kegan Paul.

El-Enany, Nadine. 2017. 'Asylum in the Context of Immigration Control: Exclusion by Default or Design'. In *States, the Law and Access to Refugee Protection: Fortresses and Fairness*, edited by Maria O'Sullivan and Dallal Stevens, 29–44. Oxford: Hart Publishing.

Elliot, Alice. 2017. *Permanence: Anthropologies of What Stays – An Open Workshop*. University of Bristol. Accessed 21 January 2020. www.bristol.ac.uk/media-library/sites/arts/birtha/documents/Permanence_programme.pdf.

Elliot, Alice. Forthcoming. *The Outside: Migration as Life in Morocco*. Bloomington, IN: Indiana University Press.

Fiddian-Qasmiyeh, Elena. 2019. 'Looking Forward: *Disasters* at 40', *Disasters* 43 (S1): S36–60.

Garelli, Glenda, Federica Sossi and Martina Tazzioli, eds. 2013. *Spaces in Migration: Postcards of a Revolution*. London: Pavement Books.

Hall, Stuart. 1992. 'Race, Culture, and Communications: Looking Backward and Forward at Cultural Studies', *Rethinking Marxism* 5 (1): 10–18.

Holmes, Seth M. and Heide Castañeda. 2016. 'Representing the "European Refugee Crisis" in Germany and Beyond: Deservingness and Difference, Life and Death', *American Ethnologist* 43 (1): 12–24.

Maneri, Marcello. 2011. 'Media Discourse on Immigration: Control Practices and the Language We Live'. In *Racial Criminalization of Migrants in the 21st Century*, edited by Salvatore Palidda, 77–93. Farnham: Ashgate.

New Keywords Collective. 2016. 'Europe/Crisis: New Keywords of "the Crisis" in and of "Europe"'. Near Futures Online 1 "Europe at a Crossroads" (March 2016). Accessed 21 January 2020. http://nearfuturesonline.org/europecrisis-new-keywords-of-crisis-in-and-of-europe/.

Nyamnjoh, Francis B. 2011. 'Cameroonian Bushfalling: Negotiation of Identity and Belonging in Fiction and Ethnography', *American Ethnologist* 38 (4): 701–13.

Olwig, Karen Fog. 2018. 'Migration as Adventure: Narrative Self-Representation among Caribbean Migrants in Denmark', *Ethnos* 83 (1): 156–71.

Pandolfo, Stefania. 2007. '"The Burning": Finitude and the Politico-Theological Imagination of Illegal Migration', *Anthropological Theory* 7 (3): 329–63.

Puar, Jasbir K. 2017. *The Right to Maim: Debility, Capacity, Disability*. Durham, NC: Duke University Press.

Quassoli, Fabio. 2013. '"Clandestino": Institutional Discourses and Practices for the Control and Exclusion of Migrants in Contemporary Italy', *Journal of Language and Politics* 12 (2): 203–25.

Saucier, P. Khalil and Tryon P. Woods. 2014. 'Ex Aqua: The Mediterranean Basin, Africans on the Move, and the Politics of Policing', *Theoria* 61 (141): 55–75.

Saunders, Jennifer B., Elena Fiddian-Qasmiyeh and Susanna Snyder, eds. 2016. *Intersections of Religion and Migration: Issues at the Global Crossroads*. New York: Palgrave Macmillan.

Sigona, Nando. 2018. 'The Contested Politics of Naming in Europe's "Refugee Crisis"', *Ethnic and Racial Studies* 41 (3): 456–60.

Vacchiano, Francesco. 2014. 'Para além das fronteiras e dos limites: Adolescentes migrantes marroquinos entre desejo, vulnerabilidade e risco', *Saúde e Sociedade* 23 (1): 17–29.

# 8
# Does climate change cause migration?

Ilan Kelman

## Introduction: Climimigration?

Media reports and scientific publications are replete with stories of people and communities being forced to flee from their homes as climate change occurs. The notion that climate change must force masses of people to move permeates publications, from Andrew Guzman (2013: 181) writing about 'refugee camps and cities overwhelmed with migrants fleeing climate change and its impacts' to the UK newspaper the *Independent*'s headline 'Climate change could force more than a billion people to flee their homes' (Griffin, 2017). The latter was based on a paper that stated (Watts *et al.*, 2018: 13) 'climate change is the sole contributing factor for at least 4,400 people who are already being forced to migrate, worldwide. The total number of people vulnerable to migration might increase to one billion by the end of the century without significant further action on climate change.' This one-billion figure was further caveated by 'plus or minus' 50 per cent. With presumptions about climate-change migration, Robin Bronen (2008: 31) coined the term 'climigration', which she argues 'occurs when a community is no longer sustainable exclusively because of climate-related events and permanent relocation is required to protect people'.

There is no doubt that human-caused climate change brings major impacts to humanity and Earth, that society is not dealing adequately with these changes and that pathways to improved action are not being implemented at the level needed (IPCC, 2013–14). The 4,400 people who were identified in 2017 as being subject to forced migration caused by climate change (Watts *et al.*, 2018) range from Alaska (Shearer, 2012) to Papua New Guinea (Strauss, 2012), although the latter case study is disputed (Connell, 2016).

These cases demonstrate the wide reach of the challenges, geographically and intellectually, in terms of determining who are climate-change-related migrants and why they might deserve this label; this is especially the case when factoring in Watts *et al.*'s (2018: 14) warning that the 4,400 figure 'is an underestimate because it excludes cases in which more than one factor could be contributing to a migration decision'. Furthermore, if climate-change impacts turn out to be worse than average projections (IPCC, 2013–14), or if melting ice sheets near the poles lead to a sea-level rise of dozens of metres over millennia (Clark *et al.*, 2016), then climate-change migration could become a dominant factor in population dynamics. Denying that climate change and migration have links would be ignoring the reality that many communities involuntarily face, while downplaying realistic scenarios for the future.

It is also, however, to deny reality when authors and commentators focus on climate change only without considering wider contexts. Too many discussions of climate change and migration fail to place the topic within wider and deeper understandings of human mobilities – and, as per Hannam *et al.* (2006) and Lubkemann (2008), immobilities – especially from scientific literature based in realms other than climate change and work that recognizes climate change as a subset of broader disaster, development and sustainability realms. Phrases such as 'climigration', 'climate change refugees' and 'climate migrants' invoke environmental determinism, underlining (even if unintentionally) a linear, causal, direct connection from climate change to forced migration. Yet human population dynamics are, and always have been, complex and multi-factorial. As science quite rightly examines climate-change projections and impacts for 10,000 years and more into the future (Clark *et al.*, 2016), science must also examine human and environmental changes, and their connections, for 10,000 years and more into the past.

This chapter examines the question 'Does climate change cause migration?' by exploring the nuances, subtleties, complexities and provisos that have always pervaded human choices and lack of choices for migration and non-migration.[1] The next section explores human migration, focusing on low-lying and coastal communities and leading to a section demonstrating how migration is often the default human condition. The question then arises: What is the potential impact of climate change on migration? A further section explains how 'climate change migration' is often created or constructed through assumptions of a linear sequence in which climate change *causes* migration. The penultimate section places these assumptions in wider contexts, illustrating the complexities and importance of migration. The conclusions explain how to ensure that the issue of climate change *potentially* causing migration is neither over-blown nor ignored.

## Why migrate from 'paradise'?

Low-lying island and coastal communities are frequently mentioned as being among the locations most needing to prepare for migration linked to climate change. Although they are certainly not the only places discussed as such, the emphasis on them is straightforward in that communities by the sea will be the ones first affected by changes to sea level. All the examples that Watts *et al.* (2018) provide of climate change being the sole contributing factor to people moving are of island or coastal communities. These places are frequently stereotyped as 'paradise' – with many communities called Paradise Island, from Singapore to the archipelago state of the Bahamas. The island names and sanitized images of placid beaches, crystalline swimming pools and lazy palm trees mask difficulties and inequalities such as high unemployment rates for women and youth in the Bahamas (Parra-Torrado, 2014) and racism in Singapore (Velayutham, 2009).

When people experience these social ills, migration is one option that they may consider. Much migration requires some level of resources, with migration studies showing that for forced migration, even in the midst of war and other disasters, the poorest and most marginalized populations tend not to be the first ones to migrate because they lack the resources to do so, although many exceptions exist. Eventually, the poorest and most marginalized people might be faced with the options of dying in place or being likely to die while on the move, leading to the dramatic images that frequently make the headlines, of emaciated children in camps or en route to them (on such images, see Snow, and Davies, both in this volume).

However, not all migration occurs under such dire circumstances. As has long been accepted by migration and mobility studies, the human condition is about movement and migration, as emphasized in the title of Jan Pieterse's (2000) 'We are all migrants'. Migration and non-migration are sometimes forced, sometimes voluntary, and most frequently result from a combination of both, emerging from a multifaceted array of reasons (also see Fiddian-Qasmiyeh *et al.*, 2016a and b).

At times, the degree of migration that is voluntary or forced is subjective. Where someone has resources and chooses to move for fun and adventure, it would be hard to dispute that this migration is voluntary.

Where soldiers provide the choice of marching or being killed, or where land is expropriated for dams (as eloquently described in the fiction of Na D'Souza) or shopping-mall development, the migration is certainly forced.

In other instances, many people migrate for economic reasons or for a specific job. Ultimately, this choice is theirs, but they might feel forced if staying means enduring poor or diminished livelihood prospects. When institutions relocate, they can provide employees with the option of moving or being made redundant, which many would feel is not much of a selection. People often find themselves tied to a location for personal reasons, such as their partner's preference; caring for elderly parents; wishing to remain with their community and culture; or being close to their ancestral home or, after a divorce, to their children. The question of voluntariness is moot in the face of feeling constrained in choices by prioritizing family or identity.

The same balance of being voluntary or forced applies to other reasons for moving. If education and health facilities are desired or felt to be required, then migration is an option to access those facilities, commonly from more isolated areas (such as the outer islands of the Bahamas) to larger settlements (such as Nassau, or in the US or the UK). To open up future opportunities, tertiary education might be deemed necessary, making it difficult to determine whether migration to a location with a college or university is forced by the need for qualifications or voluntary as a choice to acquire qualifications. Distance learning and travelling medical professionals provide different forms of options for these services, further complicating the categorization of the voluntariness or involuntariness of service-related migration.

Islanders exemplify this discussion, whether or not their island is dubbed a paradise. Many island countries do not support extensive tertiary education. If someone from St Vincent and the Grenadines or Dominica is aiming to complete a non-medical university education, then their countries do not have options, so they must use distance education or leave. The same is true for secondary-school education for many Scottish islanders (Gillies, 2014). Even where efforts are ongoing to expand opportunities, such as the University of the South Pacific developing a campus in every member country, a campus cannot be provided for every island: moving hundreds of kilometres (even though within the same island country) may therefore be necessary in order to attend university.

Islands and small communities are not just characterized by out-migration. Singapore is an attractive location for some to move to, with large groups in-migrating to work as international financiers, shipping-industry personnel and care workers (Huang *et al.*, 2012) among other jobs. With both in-migration and out-migration being witnessed in island communities, a fundamental tenet from migration research and island studies emerges that reasons always exist for moving – which is part of the human condition (for example, Keck and Schieder, 2015 for the Pacific, and Brown, 2014 for the Caribbean), even for those who still consider their island the best home in the world.

## Migration as the default

Migrating once does not preclude migrating again, for similar or different reasons. Circular migration occurs when people leave a place for a time and then return, repeating this cycle perhaps seasonally or with each iteration taking several years. Circular migration is a mainstay of many island economies and cultures (Guan and McElroy, 2012), with migrants often sending remittances and sometimes departing from home whenever a job is available and returning once the job has finished.

This 'migration culture' or 'culture of migration' (for instance, Connell, 2008) effectively entails a community viewing the migration process as normal or typical, and generally positive, for life and livelihoods. The acceptance of migration and the challenges to sedentary viewpoints have long been supported by research (for example, Malkki, 1992; Kibreab, 1999 along with the responses and rejoinder in the same issue; and Glick Schiller and Salazar, 2013). Around the Pacific, long ocean voyages enabled people to seek new lands to settle, with an additional purpose of easing resource pressure in their home communities. Leaving does not preclude returning and many islanders were nomads of the sea, sailing among different island communities, spending some time in one place and then moving on. Many subsistence peoples from Arctic and Sahelian communities developed their civilizations as nomads, so that migration became the standard of life and livelihoods, not the exception with a clear decision being necessary in order to move.

Thus, for many peoples, migration can be a continual process rather than a one-off decision and action. Viewing non-migration as the default frequently presents a flawed perspective. As such, examining reasons for not migrating is as important as examining reasons for migrating.

Even many peoples with a large degree of sedentary lifestyles today have rich migration histories and continuing contemporary migration patterns. The Faroe Islanders and Icelanders might have had permanent settlements for little over a millennium, after settling there as migrants, but their peoples never entirely stopped their movement. Today, both nationalities sport extensive diasporas. William Dickinson (1999, 2009) explains how it has been only a few thousand years since some Pacific atolls inhabited today rose sufficiently above sea level and have been sufficiently stable to allow settlement. Settlement typically included actions to try to prevent the islands from changing substantively, even though atolls would naturally shift in shape, volume and area.

Islanders thus have many good reasons for leaving 'paradise', principally that it might not be paradise and, even when it is idyllic, reasons exist to draw people away – such as a roaming life actually *being* paradise (see Cresswell, 1997 for a discussion on perceptions of nomadism as ideal). Nevertheless, removing the exceptionality of migration never justifies forced migration. It merely places forced migration in wider mobility contexts. It is not about judging migration or non-migration but recognizing that people desire and deserve choices to pursue their own mobility or non-mobility pathways, rather than having control and choice removed from their lives – whether by soldiers, expropriation or climate change.

## Constructing climate-change migration

Demonstrating 'climate change migration' has always presented challenges. These challenges include attributing migration to climate change and calculating how many people move due to the phenomenon. Many quantitative estimates fail to stand up to scrutiny by not fully demonstrating (1) how to separate climate change from other influences, especially environmental ones; and (2) how to attribute migration directly to climate change. Finding unambiguous empirical evidence and calculating numbers to track projections have proved to be especially tricky, particularly when aiming to decouple climate change from other environmental factors.

UNU EHS (2005: 1) received wide publicity when writing that 'by 2010 the world will need to cope with as many as 50 million people escaping the effects of creeping environmental deterioration'. However, no empirical methodology existed to monitor or calculate such numbers. The year 2010 arrived with no clear approach to verify or refute the 50 million claim, and as such, much of the public material was removed and then ridiculed at having been published in the first place. A bigger problem arose when M.C. Tirado *et al.* (2010: 1756) claimed that 'The UN projects that there will be up to 50 million people escaping the effects of environmental deterioration by 2020' despite providing no citations to back up this number. Then, Tirado (2011) generated widespread media attention by repeating the figure, again without citations. It might simply have been a misreading of the year cited in UNU EHS (2005).

For climate change more specifically, W. Neil Adger and Jon Barnett (2005: 328) described 'New Zealand's creation of the Pacific Access Category, in response to concerns about climate change'. Even with the website for the Pacific Access Category evolving over the past decade, no official information or documentation was found that mentioned climate change or environmental reasons for instituting this visa category. Instead, it was always framed as a way of annually permitting several dozen healthy and skilled citizens from specific Pacific island countries to emigrate to New Zealand, if they had a suitable job offer. The impetus for the programme might originally have been climate change or it might be a hidden or assumed motivation, but if this is the case then verifiable evidence for the role of climate change in the Pacific Access Category should be presented.

Instead, authors seem to prefer to construct climate-change migration. That is, rather than examining the evidence and concluding from it, the authors appear to have assumed climate-change migration to be an issue for their case study and then they have constructed a 'problem' around this assumption. This assumptive construction of climate-change migration as a current topic (different from future possibilities) has influenced policy and practice.

Some Pacific islanders have tried claiming climate-change-refugee status in New Zealand, but so far all claims on the basis of climate change have been denied (for instance, Burson, 2013) even where other criteria rendered a favourable decision to stay in New Zealand (for instance, Burson, 2014). In December 2017, New Zealand's government announced that it would look at introducing a new visa category for climate-change refugees from Pacific islands. Thus far, there has been no link with the Pacific Access Category. Political and legal regimes are changing in order to construct climate-change migration without taking full account of what science, including migration research, concludes at the moment.

Physical scientists have observed dozens of islands, mainly in the Pacific, to empirically identify changes that might relate to measurable sea-level rise (for example, Rankey, 2011; Kench *et al.*, 2015). This research demonstrates that islands display a combination of accretion (in area and/or volume), changing shape and diminishing in size (in area and/or volume), indicating an absence of evidence for wholescale drowning, sinking or disappearing islands. Some islands are changing rapidly, but not necessarily due to climate change, even where sea level is rising. For instance, Naomi Biribo and Colin Woodroffe (2013) found significant erosion and accretion around Tarawa Atoll, Kiribati, but attributed the observations mainly to local human action rather than to sea-level rise. However, these nuances and combinations of factors are frequently bypassed by the media.

Indeed, when Simon Albert et al. (2016) published their research on changing islands in the Solomon Islands in the context of measurable sea-level rise, numerous media headlines announced that climate change was bringing doom to the atolls. The paper's lead author responded that the media had misrepresented their science because only one-third of the 33 monitored islands had disappeared or severely contracted between 1947 and 2014 despite measurable sea-level rise, not all of which were connected to climate change.

Beforehand, in 2009, a few villages in Vanuatu hit the international headlines as climate-change refugees when they moved inland due to the encroaching sea. Valérie Ballu et al. (2011) researched the cause, discovering that most of the relative sea-level rise in the villages was due to the land sinking naturally rather than to absolute sea-level rise. Climate change has also been attributed as the cause of relocating two villages in Fiji, Narikoso and Vunidogoloa, but the authors making these links (for instance, McNamara and Combes, 2015) do not provide evidence for the actual connection to climate change. Instead, Michael Green (2016) explains how the erosion of these villages' coastlines might have been exacerbated by attempts to stop it, such as through building a sea wall.

Irrespective of these examples, measurable sea-level rise until now does not factor in the majority of sea-level rise projected for the twenty-first century, from thermal expansion of ocean water as it absorbs atmospheric heat, which is expected to become more evident around mid-century. Islands might yet disappear due to climate change – although there is no certitude – and it is sensible to plan for a variety of scenarios, including mass migration while accepting that little evidence exists for it happening so far, despite numerous claims. Rather than either constructing climate-change migration as an overwhelming problem or pretending that it cannot happen at a large scale, a balance is needed that admits the actuality and potentiality of migration linked to climate-change impacts, but that never assumes inevitability. Instead, climate-change-migration analyses should adopt the deep understandings of migration from other fields.

# Contextualizing climate-change migration

The diversity of migrants, and of reasons for migrating and for not migrating, have long been published (Kunz, 1973; Petersen, 1958). While recognizing how migration and mobilities theories have progressed, with discussions becoming less prejudiced and more introspective over the decades (for example, Fiddian-Qasmiyeh *et al.*, 2016a and b), this rich literature yields important lessons for investigating climate change's impacts, or lack thereof, on migration.

The first lesson is in defining migration. How far must someone move in order to be considered a migrant? Moving 10 metres to the next house or next street could be moving out of the projected floodplain over the next century under climate change. Moving 10 metres could also move across an international border while remaining within the same residential block, such as along parts of the France–Monaco and Belgium–Netherlands borders. The Federated States of Micronesia's atoll Pingelap has all its land within 300 metres of the sea, but some of the topography rises higher than 15 metres above sea level. Under a few metres of sea-level rise, the atoll's population would need to reconfigure their island and infrastructure, but would still be living in the same place. Would this count as climate-induced migration? If coastal dwellings were raised, so people effectively move upwards and live in the new tidal zone, would it be vertical migration and would the population be vertical climate-change migrants?

The second lesson is attributing migration. In countries such as St Lucia and Vanuatu, many near-coastal areas are sufficiently above sea level that a short move from coastal homes would, in theory, suffice to avoid inundation from projected sea-level rise until at least 2100. In practice, heritage sites, traditional land uses, ownership and other environmental hazards such as volcanoes and landslides might preclude large numbers of people from resettling anywhere on the same island. If cemeteries, golf courses, wildlife habitat, cropping areas and/or risk assessments force coastal dwellers to leave their country rather than moving 100 metres upslope, is the root cause of the migration actually the impact of climate change, or is it mainly human decisions – no matter how long-standing and legitimate – regarding land use and resource allocation?

Third, are lessons available from other examples of migration in the face of environmental changes? Volcanic eruptions have been involved in dozens of sudden, forced migrations over past decades, incorporating numerous instances when return was not expected to be a definite option. Examples are Tungurahua in Ecuador in 1999 (Lane *et al.*, 2003) and Montserrat after 1995 (Pattullo, 2000). Communities from Greenland (Dugmore *et al.*, 2007) to the Pacific (Nunn and Carson, 2015) display long histories of abandoning communities, possibly through a combination of mass migration and dying out, with one factor among many probably having been climatic shifts. These analogies should assist in contemporary forecasting and planning of movement due to climate-change impacts (Glantz, 1988).

Overall, migration, especially across international borders, has too often been labelled as problematic (for instance, Jansen, 1970), especially if the number of migrants increases because an issue was not addressed, such as an eroding coastline or an economic downturn. With respect to climate change, migration is discussed as both a way to deal with climate-change impacts such as community inundation and failure to deal with climate-change impacts because few other options exist (Stojanov, 2014; Tacoli, 2009). Sometimes, though, the evidence demonstrates that migration is neither an adjustment to climate change nor a failure to adjust, as in a Nicaragua case study (Radel *et al.*, 2018). Consequently, either migration or non-migration itself is not necessarily either a problem or an opportunity. Instead, how migration or non-migration is managed dictates much of how migrants and non-migrants fare along with many of the effects on the communities where migrants pass through, stop over or settle.

This contextual nuance, of how and who migration helps and hinders, renders it difficult to make generic statements or draw overall conclusions – especially for climate change. Migration as a problem, as a solution, as both or as neither depends more on dealing with people than focusing on the migration or non-migration process itself. Even when climate change leaves no other option but to move, the same community will include people who would be delighted to move and people who would be devastated at having to move – and some who would probably refuse to move even at the risk of dying, as often occurs during environmental hazards (Estes and Shaw, 1985; Perry, 1979). Communities in which migrants settle would also inevitably be split between those who welcome newcomers, those who loathe them and those who have little interest. The different degrees to which people wish (or not) to migrate and are able to adjust (or not) to migration or non-migration depends much more on the characteristics of people than on those of climate change.

## Conclusion: Return to paradise?

Does climate change cause migration? As a single, causative, direct factor today, the answer has to be mostly no. As a past and possibly future factor – over decades, centuries and millennia – the answer is that many examples exist and many more are likely to emerge. As a truism often forgotten in the populism of climate change, people make migration-related decisions and do not have opportunities to make migration-related decisions for numerous, complicated, interlinked reasons. These reasons include, but are not limited to, environmental conditions and expectations of environmental conditions, such as climate change.

It is more common to find people moving or unable to move for a host of reasons than a single reason. It is rare to find a community in which everyone has the same migration-related motivations and expresses those motivations in the same way. Scientists, the media and policy- and decision makers have a duty to scale back the rhetoric about climate-change refugees and climate migrants in order to indicate what science does and does not provide according to the current state of knowledge, while articulating how this knowledge might evolve and what is being done to monitor it. An example of doing so is the Lancet Countdown project www.lancetcountdown.org; Watts *et al.*, 2018), which monitors and reports annually on indicators of climate-change effects on health.

None of this denigrates the people and communities who are now moving involuntarily due almost exclusively to climate-change impacts – even when multiple viewpoints are detailed. They need resources, which have generally not been forthcoming, to support their decision-making processes and actions. Climate change, migration, non-migration and the links between migration/non-migration and social/environmental changes are not new. This fact does not justify forced migration of any form, including that from climate change, whether the movement is from or to a paradise – or an assumed-to-be-paradise.

## Note

1. On the complexities of conceptualizing 'forced' migration, also see Elliot in this volume.

## References

Adger, W. Neil and Jon Barnett. 2005. 'Compensation for Climate Change Must Meet Needs', *Nature* 436: 328.

Albert, Simon, Javier X. Leon, Alistair R. Grinham, John A. Church, Badin R. Gibbes and Colin D. Woodroffe. 2016. 'Interactions between Sea-Level Rise and Wave Exposure on Reef Island Dynamics in the Solomon Islands', *Environmental Research Letters* 11: Article 054011, 1–9. Accessed 16 January 2020. https://iopscience.iop.org/article/10.1088/1748–9326/11/5/054011/pdf.

Ballu, Valérie, Marie-Noëlle Bouin, Patricia Siméoni, Wayne C. Crawford, Stephane Calmant, Jean-Michel Boré, Tony Kanas and Bernard Pelletier. 2011. 'Comparing the Role of Absolute Sea-Level Rise and Vertical Tectonic Motions in Coastal Flooding, Torres Islands (Vanuatu)',

PNAS: Proceedings of the National Academy of Sciences of the United States of America 108 (32): 13019–22.

Biribo, Naomi and Colin D. Woodroffe. 2013. 'Historical Area and Shoreline Change of Reef Islands around Tarawa Atoll, Kiribati', *Sustainability Science* 8 (3): 345–62.

Bronen, Robin. 2008. 'Alaskan Communities' Rights and Resilience', *Forced Migration Review* 31: 30–2.

Brown, Laurence. 2014. 'Contexts of Migration and Diasporic Identities'. In *Introduction to the Pan-Caribbean*, edited by Tracey Skelton, 118–35. London: Routledge.

Burson, Bruce L. 2013. *NZIPT 800413*. Auckland: Immigration and Protection Tribunal. Accessed 21 February 2020. https://www.refworld.org/cases,NZ_IPT,5dad6b754.html.

Burson, Bruce L. 2014. *NZIPT 501370–371*. Auckland: Immigration and Protection Tribunal. Accessed 21 February 2020. https://www.refworld.org/pdfid/585152d14.pdf.

Clark, Peter U., Jeremy D. Shakun, Shaun A. Marcott, Alan C. Mix, Michael Eby, Scott Kulp, Anders Levermann, Glenn A. Milne, Patrik L. Pfister, Benjamin D. Santer, Daniel P. Schrag, Susan Solomon, Thomas F. Stocker, Benjamin H. Strauss, Andrew J. Weaver, Ricarda Winkelmann, David Archer, Edouard Bard, Aaron Goldner, Kurt Lambeck, Raymond T. Pierrehumbert and Gian-Kasper Plattner. 2016. 'Consequences of Twenty-First-Century Policy for Multi-Millennial Climate and Sea-Level Change', *Nature Climate Change* 6: 360–9.

Connell, John. 2008. 'Niue: Embracing a Culture of Migration', *Journal of Ethnic and Migration Studies* 34 (6): 1021–40.

Connell, John. 2016. 'Last Days in the Carteret Islands? Climate Change, Livelihoods and Migration on Coral Atolls', *Asia Pacific Viewpoint* 57 (1): 3–15.

Cresswell, Tim. 1997. 'Imagining the Nomad: Mobility and the Postmodern Primitive'. In *Space and Social Theory: Interpreting Modernity and Postmodernity*, edited by Georges Benko and Ulf Strohmayer, 360–82. Oxford: Blackwell.

Dickinson, William R. 1999. 'Holocene Sea-Level Record on Funafuti and Potential Impact of Global Warming on Central Pacific Atolls', *Quaternary Research* 51 (2): 124–32.

Dickinson, William R. 2009. 'Pacific Atoll Living: How Long Already and until When?', *GSA Today* 19 (3): 4–10.

Dugmore, Andrew J., Christian Keller and Thomas H. McGovern. 2007. 'Norse Greenland Settlement: Reflections on Climate Change, Trade, and the Contrasting Fates of Human Settlements in the North Atlantic Islands', *Arctic Anthropology* 44 (1): 12–36.

Estes, Jack and Dennis Shaw. 1985. 'Popular Culture and Mt. St. Helens: A Study of a Response', *Journal of Popular Culture* 18 (4): 135–43.

Fiddian-Qasmiyeh, Elena, Gil Loescher, Katy Long and Nando Sigona. 2016a. 'Introduction: Refugee and Forced Migration Studies in Transition'. In *The Oxford Handbook of Refugee and Forced Migration Studies*, edited by Elena Fiddian-Qasmiyeh, Gil Loescher, Katy Long and Nando Sigona, 1–19. Oxford: Oxford University Press.

Fiddian-Qasmiyeh, Elena, Gil Loescher, Katy Long and Nando Sigona, eds. 2016b. *The Oxford Handbook of Refugee and Forced Migration Studies*. Oxford: Oxford University Press.

Gillies, Donald. 2014. 'Learning and Leaving: Education and Depopulation in an Island Community', *Cambridge Journal of Education* 44 (1): 19–34.

Glantz, Michael H., ed. 1988. *Societal Responses to Regional Climatic Change: Forecasting by Analogy*. Boulder, CO: Westview Press.

Glick Schiller, Nina and Noel B. Salazar. 2013. 'Regimes of Mobility across the Globe', *Journal of Ethnic and Migration Studies* 39 (2): 183–200.

Green, Michael. 2016. 'Contested Territory', *Nature Climate Change* 6: 817–20.

Griffin, Andrew. 2017. 'Climate Change Could Force More Than a Billion People to Flee Their Homes, Says Major Health Report', *The Independent*, 31 October. Accessed 16 January 2020. www.independent.co.uk/news/science/climate-change-global-warming-refugees-migrants-displacement-lancet-study-a8028341.html.

Guan, Jingqiu and Jerome L. McElroy. 2012. 'The Determinants of Migration in Small Islands', *Shima: The International Journal of Research into Island Cultures* 7 (1): 80–95.

Guzman, Andrew T. 2013. *Overheated: The Human Cost of Climate Change*. Oxford: Oxford University Press.

Hannam, Kevin, Mimi Sheller and John Urry. 2006. 'Editorial: Mobilities, Immobilities and Moorings', *Mobilities* 1 (1): 1–22.

Huang, Shirlena, Brenda S.A. Yeoh and Mika Toyota. 2012. 'Caring for the Elderly: The Embodied Labour of Migrant Care Workers in Singapore', *Global Networks* 12 (2): 195–215.

IPCC (Intergovernmental Panel on Climate Change). 2013–14. *Fifth Assessment Report*. Geneva: Intergovernmental Panel on Climate Change.

Jansen, C.J. 1970. 'Migration: A Sociological Problem'. In *Readings in the Sociology of Migration*, edited by Clifford J. Jansen, 3–35. Oxford: Pergamon Press.

Keck, Verena and Dominik Schieder. 2015. 'Contradictions and Complexities: Current Perspectives on Pacific Islander Mobilities', *Anthropological Forum* 25 (2): 115–30.

Kench, P.S., D. Thompson, M.R. Ford, H. Ogawa and R.F. McLean. 2015. 'Coral Islands Defy Sea-Level Rise over the Past Century: Records from a Central Pacific Atoll', *Geology* 43 (6): 515–18.

Kibreab, Gaim. 1999. 'Revisiting the Debate on People, Place, Identity and Displacement', *Journal of Refugee Studies* 12 (4): 384–410.

Kunz, E.F. 1973. 'The Refugee in Flight: Kinetic Models and Forms of Displacement', *International Migration Review* 7 (2): 125–46.

Lane, Lucille R., Graham A. Tobin and Linda M. Whiteford. 2003. 'Volcanic Hazard or Economic Destitution: Hard Choices in Baños, Ecuador', *Environmental Hazards* 5 (1/2): 23–34.

Lubkemann, Stephen C. 2008. 'Involuntary Immobility: On a Theoretical Invisibility in Forced Migration Studies', *Journal of Refugee Studies* 21 (4): 454–75.

Malkki, Liisa. 1992. 'National Geographic: The Rooting of Peoples and the Territorialization of National Identity among Scholars and Refugees', *Cultural Anthropology* 7 (1): 24–44.

McNamara, Karen E. and Helene Jacot Des Combes. 2015. 'Planning for Community Relocations Due to Climate Change in Fiji', *International Journal of Disaster Risk Science* 6 (3): 315–19.

Nunn, Patrick and Mike Carson. 2015. 'Collapses of Island Societies from Environmental Forcing: Does History Hold Lessons for the Future?', *Global Environment* 8 (1): 110–33.

Parra-Torrado, Monica. 2014. *Youth Unemployment in the Caribbean*. Washington, DC: World Bank.

Pattullo, Polly. 2000. *Fire from the Mountain*. London: Constable.

Perry, Ronald W. 1979. 'Evacuation Decision-Making in Natural Disasters', *Mass Emergencies* 4: 25–38.

Petersen, William. 1958. 'A General Typology of Migration', *American Sociological Review* 2 (3): 256–66.

Pieterse, Jan Nederveen. 2000. 'Globalization and Human Integration: We Are All Migrants', *Futures* 32 (5): 385–98.

Radel, Claudia, Birgit Schmook, Lindsey Carte and Sofia Mardero. 2018. 'Toward a Political Ecology of Migration: Land, Labor Migration, and Climate Change in Northwestern Nicaragua', *World Development* 108: 263–73.

Rankey, Eugene C. 2011. 'Nature and Stability of Atoll Island Shorelines: Gilbert Island Chain, Kiribati, Equatorial Pacific', *Sedimentology* 58 (7): 1831–59.

Shearer, Christine. 2012. 'The Political Ecology of Climate Adaptation Assistance: Alaska Natives, Displacement, and Relocation', *Journal of Political Ecology* 19 (1): 174–83.

Stojanov, Robert, ed. 2014. *Migration as Adaptation? Population Dynamics in the Age of Climate Variability*. Brno: Global Change Research Centre.

Strauss, Sarah. 2012. 'Are Cultures Endangered by Climate Change? Yes, but …', *WIREs Climate Change* 3 (4): 371–7.

Tacoli, Cecilia. 2009. 'Crisis or Adaptation? Migration and Climate Change in Context of High Mobility', *Environment and Urbanization* 21 (2): 513–25.

Tirado, Cristina. 2011. 'Global Climate and Environmental Change: Implications for Food Production and Safety Systems'. Paper presented at the American Association for the Advancement of Science (AAAS) Annual Meeting, Washington, DC, 17–21 February 2011.

Tirado, M.C., R. Clarke, L.A. Jaykus, A. McQuatters-Gollop and J.M. Frank. 2010. 'Climate Change and Food Safety: A Review', *Food Research International* 43 (7): 1745–65.

UNU EHS (United Nations University Institute for Environment and Human Security). 2005. *Ranks of "Environmental Refugees" Swell Worldwide, Calls Grow for Better Definition, Recognition, Support*. Bonn: United Nations University Institute for Environment and Human Security. Accessed 3 March 2020. https://www.eurekalert.org/pub_releases/2005-11/unu-ro100405.php.

Velayutham, Selvaraj. 2009. 'Everyday Racism in Singapore'. In *Everyday Multiculturalism*, edited by Amanda Wise and Selvaraj Velayutham, 255–73. Basingstoke: Palgrave Macmillan.

Watts, Nick and 61 others. 2018. 'The *Lancet* Countdown on Health and Climate Change: From 25 years of Inaction to a Global Transformation for Public Health', *The Lancet* 391 (10120): 581–630.

Part II
## Responding to Displacement: Advocacy, Aesthetics and Politics in a Moving World

# 9

# We Are Movers: We are towers of strength

We Are Movers project team: Amalia Pascal, Aminat, Amy North, Ann Oladimeji, Bahati Dan, Becky Ayeni, Claudia Lapping, Debby Kareem, Drucilla Namirembe, Esther O. Odere, Hanna Retallack, Harriet Ibeneme, Ijeoma, Iman Azzi, Neelam, Nneka, Omoh Juliet, Olushola Owolabi, Promise Enabosi, Patricia Akpapuna, Rachel Benchekroun, Rachel Rosen, Raphaela Armbruster, Sara Joiko Mujica, Tabitha Millet, Theresa Ajagu and Zoline Makosso

## Introduction

*We Are Movers* seeks to challenge hostility and discrimination against migrants by offering new ways to see, feel and understand conditions of mobility and settlement.

This image essay, and a linked museum exhibition, was developed through a series of arts-based conversations intended to bridge academic research and the lived experiences of migration. We considered the following issues:

- How can we challenge negative images of migrants?
- How do experiences of poverty, hostility and coercion affect the possibility of 'integration'?
- What does it mean to belong?
- How can our answers inform responses to displacement in universities and beyond?

Project participants included staff and students from UCL and migrant women and children from the Helen Bamber Foundation and Lewisham Refugee and Migrant Network in London.

**Figure 9.1** Members of the We Are Movers project team discuss connections and dislocations between representations of migrants and lived experiences of people on the move. © Tabitha Millet.

*We Are Movers* is the result of these discussions and creative encounters. Photographs, drawings and text from the sessions were developed into a series of three abstracted images that create space for imagination and difference. The accompanying text explains key ideas developed during the collective process.

> Lives on the move are lived in conditions of economic and political precarity
> They are endless periods of waiting, hoping, waiting, and hoping …
> Lives on the move are lived in the public eye
> Subject to control, suspicion and threat
> Lives on the move are filled with hopes, fears, dreams and longings
> …
> They are lived with others, wherever those others might be
> Lives on the move are here, there and in many places at once
> Broken and remade
> Living and loving
> Overcoming barriers
> Contributing and participating
> Lives on the move are lives that move.

## Categories, stereotypes and misrepresentations

Every day, people on the move see themselves represented in the media and government policies. Through examining media coverage of migration, sharing personal experiences and engaging with approaches to researching media, we reflected on how these stories often flatten and simplify complex lives or overextend one negative story as though it applies to all migrants. We scrutinized how these representations are used to justify control, suspicion and punitive measures. They can make deportation, detention, denial of hospitality, exploitation and impoverishment seem acceptable. In contrast, we wanted to make an image that challenges racist and discriminatory messages, and reimagine ways of thinking about people on the move.

> Immigrant, migrant. Where is the line drawn? Why?
> We are not illegals
> We are movers
> We are contributors
> We are here to stay

*We Are Movers* shows that whether people are called migrants, asylum seekers, refugees, immigrants or citizens, they are far more than any of these categories or media representations convey. It speaks to the

**Figure 9.2**  This image, entitled 'Categories, Stereotypes and Misrepresentations', deconstructs and reconstructs representations of people on the move. © We Are Movers.

contributions, commitments and dreams of people on the move. *We Are Movers* highlights the importance of solidarity and collective strength in a hostile environment.

## Questioning 'integration'

'Integration' has become a buzzword for governments globally. However, it is difficult to define and is a highly contested approach to migration and settlement. Who is expected to 'integrate', and what are they 'integrating' into? Who benefits from 'integration'? Through interviewing people, discussing debates about 'integration' in academic research and engaging in interactive forum theatre, we developed an image that depicts the contradictions of 'integration' policy.

Integration is often portrayed as a one-way process, with migrants expected to integrate into 'British society'. Yet there is no singular 'Britain'. The UK is already a diverse and changing society, formed through empire, postcolonial linkages and waves of migration. It is made up of different practices, languages and traditions.

> The migrant needs to learn about the system in order to contribute positively.
> The system needs to learn about the suffering and the sorrow the people go through.
> It's a two-way process and it never stops.

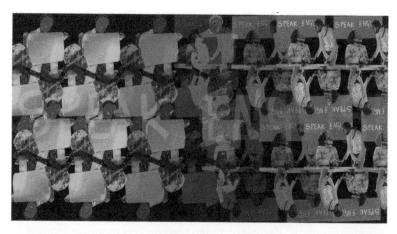

**Figure 9.3** This image, entitled 'Questioning Integration', interrogates policy approaches to 'integration' and highlights the pressures that they place on people on the move. © We Are Movers.

Migrants are expected, and often want, to 'integrate'. However, migrants may be barred from working and studying, trapped in conditions of destitution, marginalization and isolation, because of insecure immigration status in a hostile environment. Waiting to get status that can enable 'integration' takes time. Meanwhile, life is stuck – and the waiting time can become soul breaking. In highlighting control and surveillance, we pose questions about 'integration' in conditions of precarity and suspicion.

## Belonging

This image explores what it means to belong. We developed these ideas through the act of listening, sharing experiences and considering how 'belonging' has been understood in research. 'The dictionary tells us that to belong, we need to "fit in a specific place or environment"', writes Nandita Sharma (2014). 'It is not enough to just be in a particular place: one must fit in and, in order to fit in, one must be seen to belong by others.'

> What is it to fit in?
> You can't do it alone. You need acceptance from the locals.
> You have to make yourself fit in. It is scary.
> Fitting in is status and housing, so you're not looking over your shoulder.
> Fitting in is the ability to contribute and the ability to use your voice.

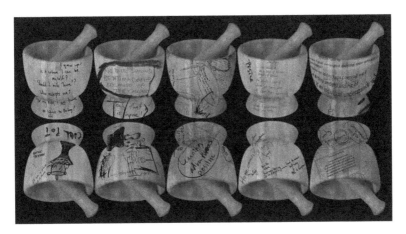

**Figure 9.4**  This image is entitled 'Belonging'. It highlights the ways in which shared experiences, complexity or difference, and transformation can be understood as aspects of belonging. © We Are Movers.

We aim to show that belonging is both deeply subjective and insistently relational. Belonging is grounded in individual memories and family stories, remembered and made real through smells, tastes, sounds, images and relationships. Yet, to belong, people need to be recognized as belonging; feel secure enough to belong; and overcome institutional, social and legal barriers to belonging.

Belonging is a family photograph, a piece of jewellery and a kitchen item reminiscent of long-standing family recipes. Belonging is stories, languages and practices shared and adapted across generations. Belonging is a box or suitcase filled on the run. Belonging is water, food and shelter. Belonging is status, documents and citizenship rights. Belonging is a sense of being at home in the world, and a struggle to achieve.

## Acknowledgements

The We Are Movers project team includes staff and students from UCL and women from the Helen Bamber Foundation and Lewisham Refugee and Migrant Network in London. This staff-student initiative was designed to open the doors of the university in a spirit of solidarity, knowledge co-construction and widening access. In 2019, a version of *We Are Movers* was exhibited at the Migration Museum in London, the Beyond Borders festival at Battersea Arts Centre and at UCL (Teaching and Learning Conference; Refugee Week 2019 in the North Cloisters). We Are Movers was funded by a bursary from UCL Culture and the Department of Social Science at UCL Institute of Education. The project was made possible by support from the Helen Bamber Foundation, Lewisham Refugee and Migrant Network and Britt Permien Design, as well as Rachel Silander and a dedicated group of volunteers who ran an accompanying children's programme.

## Reference

Sharma, Nandita. 2014. 'Belonging'. In *Migration: The COMPAS Anthology*, edited by Bridget Anderson and Michael Keith. Oxford: COMPAS.

# 10
# Advocacy for LGBTI asylum in the UK: Discourses of distance and proximity

Thibaut Raboin

## Introduction

In the UK, asylum rights were granted in 1999 for lesbian, gay, bisexual, transgender and intersex (LGBTI) people.[1] In the 18 years that have followed, advocates, activists and academics have worked continuously to improve the way in which refugee status determined on the grounds of sexual orientation and gender identity is managed by the state – especially in relation to the specific challenges and disadvantages faced by LGBTI claimants. The most pressing issues have included fighting against the requirement – previously made by the authorities determining claims for international protection – that LGBTI claimants return to their countries of origin and be 'discreet' about their sexuality (resolved, albeit with limitations, in 2010); a continuous struggle with both the Home Office, which takes care of refugee-status determination, and the courts in cases of appeal over the plausibility, credibility and overall recognition of claimants as LGBTI people in danger of persecution (Berg and Millbank, 2009; Middelkoop, 2013; Millbank, 2009); and the specific issues and dangers faced by LGBTI people when in detention, and the failure of the state to recognize these (Bachmann, 2016; Lewis, 2013; UKLGIG, 2010, 2013).

The general discursive environment within which these struggles happen is marked by two important trends. First, the reliance on the discourses of LGBTI human rights – understood as the formulation of sexual politics, especially for those who are not deemed sexual citizens (that is, whose rights, insofar as they are not heterosexual and/or cisgender, are not recognized) – on the basis of the universalistic framework of human rights. Present in slogans such as Amnesty International's 'Love is a Human Right', such approaches are central to the legitimation of advocates' discourses on LGBTI asylum. Their efficiency, ability to circulate in public arenas and philosophical tenets have been assessed and discussed in previous literature (Brown, 2004; Kollman and Waites, 2009). The second discursive trend is that of homonationalism, understood broadly as a formulation of nationhood that is open to non-heteronormative sexualities, and sometimes relies on discourses of sexual tolerance to promote the nation's modernity and desirability. Many homonationalist formulations of asylum and queer migration have been examined in scholarship, with critical discourses highlighting the way in which these formulations have become central to regressive discourses concerning immigration, race, international relations or the purported failures of multiculturalism in the UK (Lentin and Titley, 2011; Puar, 2007). Other critiques have also shown the dangers of using homonationalist tropes in progressive discourses and producing racialized distinctions between more or less 'advanced' cultures and civilizations (Brown, 2006; Haritaworn, 2008; Rouhani, 2007). Finally, other works have concentrated on examining in detail the way that homonationalist discourses are in fact used strategically and negotiated for varied reasons and in different contexts by queer[2] migrants, advocates, and so on (Murray, 2016; Raboin, 2017a; White, 2013).

In this wider context, I analyse here discourses on LGBTI asylum from non-governmental organizations (NGOs) and advocates, and examine how they deploy strategies in order to engage a wide public in caring for the plight of LGBTI asylum seekers. In particular, I concentrate on the way in which these discourses negotiate the question of distance. The question of how to bridge the distance in distant suffering has been abundantly discussed in relation to humanitarianism, and here I focus on the specificity of LGBTI advocacy. In doing so, I investigate the roles of sexual citizenship, queer optimism and homonationalism in the configuration of distant suffering. I look at the communication originating from LGBTI asylum advocacy partly as a form of humanitarian discourse – understood as 'the rhetorical practices of transnational actors that engage with universal ethical claims, such as common humanity or global civil society, to mobilize action on human suffering' (Chouliaraki, 2010: 108) – and partly as a strategic field, wherein national and local social actors deploy rhetorical strategies to appeal to the state, in order to open up the question of who has rights and what these rights are.[3]

The corpus examined here is made of sources from heterogeneous material (videos, reports, press releases, blog posts, emails, webpages) produced by six NGOs and civil-society organizations.[4] These discourses are roughly divided into three modes: argumentative, narrative and cartographic. They are also characterized by their strong dependence on events (court decisions, Home Office white-paper publications, particular asylum cases requiring attention, and so on). Their discursive production also includes regular reports that work like snapshots of the current situation. The topics that are most abundantly discussed in the corpus have to do with urgent issues identified by the social actors – and include detention, credibility issues, persecution and HIV.

Rather than analysing the arguments in these discourses and the issues they raise, I examine the rhetorical strategies put into place in order to constitute and engage the public. To do so, I concentrate on the more narrative discourses in the corpus, and on the discourses explicitly addressing and making sense of the idea of 'a public' – this analysis is based on the idea that engaging and constituting audiences are intertwined activities. The notion of 'public' oscillates between passivity (a public exists simply by virtue of being addressed), and activity (merely paying attention to this address is already an intention and an effort to engage) (Lacey, 2013: 14–15; Warner, 2002). In the case of humanitarian discourses, the rhetoric of distant suffering is premised on the need to constitute, through address, a public that is affectively and rationally disposed to act to alleviate that suffering. These two modes (affective and rational) are deployed together: for example, sympathy or compassion for those suffering before our eyes can lead to action only within existing legal frameworks and conceptions of justice (Boltanski, 2007). Finally, such articulations of affect and rationality circulate in the public sphere partly from the publicization of the sexual and affective intimacy of asylum seekers: in questions of sex and gender, privacy is often publicly constructed, and is central to the constitution of a receptive public. This analysis will argue that the rhetoric of LGBTI asylum advocacy shows the frailty of the distinctions between private and public, affective and rational, intimate and political. I will firstly address the way in which NGOs deal with the problem of distance in their discourse, and will then direct my attention to the rhetoric of proximity that accompanies it.

## A rhetoric of distance

As with most humanitarian discourses, the mobilization of a public for LGBTI asylum advocacy is first and foremost based on distance.[5] The aim of these discourses is therefore to bridge the distance, to mobilize publics despite the distance that separates them from suffering bodies. A first way of conceiving of distance is visually: maps, for example, are a useful tool to organize, homogenize and configure the space between publics and those in need of help. In the corpus, the International Gay and Lesbian Alliance (ILGA),[6] Amnesty International and AllOut.org[7] all use maps in their visual materials.[8] With these maps, the nation becomes the central concept for understanding homophobia and queer migration. Alongside colour coding (for example, Amnesty International uses pink and black for its map of Africa), maps visually organize the distance between publics and asylum seekers – notably by distributing homophobia and LGBTI legislation around the world, thereby asserting visually the distinction between countries that are 'there' in terms of rights and those that are not. The main function of these maps is to provide a *semiosis*, to make sense of the world; the map of the world showing the nations that persecute and those that protect their LGBTI populations makes sense of asylum. This simplification constitutes the basis for a homonationalist representation of asylum: the nation becomes the place where the problem of asylum both originates and finds its solution, from countries that persecute to those that will protect LGBTI people.

In the case of AllOut.org, these maps become more interesting rhetorical devices because they are interactive. A phased series of texts appears on the screen ('In 71 countries around the world, it's a crime to be gay. In 10, it can cost you your life. Billions are told their families are not equal. In fact, no country offers full equal rights') and concurrently the map gets progressively covered in red. There are two ways of reading this map: one for optimistic and one for pessimistic readers. An optimistic reading inscribes its gradual covering in red within the teleology of LGBTI human rights: the countries that stay white the longest represent the queer futures that the campaign for LGBTI human rights promises. This reading is optimistic because it proposes a one-size-fits-all approach (afforded by humanitarian universalism) whereby the Global North leads the way towards better futures for the rest of the world. Optimistic NGO discourses rely on a promise of happiness that can be found both in LGBTI human rights and in queer liberalism.[9] Queer liberalism can be understood first as a discourse of rights and citizenship focusing on gay and lesbian liberty. However, I also use it here critically as a specific path towards this liberty, in which freedom tends to be expressed within markets (labour, consumption, and so on), and the category of 'citizen' can exclude racialized queers[10] who do not have easy access to these markets (Duggan, 2002; Eng, 2010). These optimistic discourses, in which the Global North leads the way for queer liberal futures, have been criticized both in relation to the question of homonationalism (the collusion of gay rights in nationalist discourses) and to the blind spots of the promises of happiness (the fact that the promise might not be achievable by those who listen to it) (Ahmed, 2010; Murray, 2016). Homonationalism can be reframed as a discourse of longing for a specific type of happiness that is afforded by queer liberalism: in other words, asylum becomes the possibility of opening up futures as citizens, workers and consumers for persecuted queers, even though this promise is in fact foreclosed by the multifactorial forms of domination that LGBTI asylum seekers endure (economic, racial, sexual, and so on) (Raboin 2017b). This optimism, with its out-of-reach promise, can be described as a form of what Lauren Berlant calls 'cruel optimism' (Berlant, 2011).

In contrast, a pessimistic reading of the same interactive map focuses on the way in which it is gradually filled with red: although not all countries persecute LGBTI people, none of them 'offers equal rights'. This reading rejects the notion of an evolving, better future on the horizon. The public navigating the website is prompted to see persecution worldwide, and the issue of asylum as one struggle in a general and continual deliberation and disagreement over LGBTI people as subjects bearing rights, and over the nature of these rights. For a UK public, maps can therefore, in some ways, eschew a homonationalist reading and engage them not to see themselves as saviours but instead to invite them to think of solidarity and commonality.

However they are read, these maps tend to visually homogenize the possibility of queer politics: sexual politics are not representable on a map as plural, dependent on local geographies, sexual ontologies, histories, and other factors. Rather, even when they are not read as a direct homonationalist teleology, they are still based on the universalist framework of human rights. In order to unpack the ways in which advocates strategically use this universalism in order to engage publics, I will examine calls to action from AllOut.org. AllOut.org has taken up numerous LGBTI asylum cases and asked for public support, usually through signing petitions and donating. Email is a primary mode of engagement with the site's public, such as in the UK campaign for asylum seeker Brenda during 2010–11. The organization asked readers to sign petitions and share Brenda's story, and provided a real-time narrative of the fight over a few days between 28 January and 11 February 2011. The messages themselves are short, and each time repeat the whole story of the asylum case, adding the latest updates. They are typical of the type of engagement practised by such online platforms: they tend to present calls as a matter of urgency, and they presume a fleeting engagement on the part of their public – and as such offer simple, short narratives and argumentations (Chouliaraki 2013; Nyong'o, 2012).

Examining the emails' narratives shows a number of common tropes of LGBTI asylum advocacy and humanitarian discourses in general – chiefly, the way in which the distance between suffering bodies and spectators is bridged: through a rescue narrative. An actantial analysis of the narrative of Brenda's claim is illuminating here. Actantial analysis concentrates on the structure of narratives, especially its acting subjects, asking the question 'who does what in the story?' (Greimas, 2002). In these emails, we can note that the main acting subject is either Brenda (trying to get asylum) or 'we' (trying to get Brenda asylum). There are adjuvants or helpers, which are often 'us' or 'all of us', which seem to variously include AllOut.org and the readers of the email, and sometimes a wider notion of the LGBTI community. The pronoun 'we' is mostly used with active verbs (we need, we talked, and so on) and emphasizes AllOut. org as a legitimate actor deserving support. The pronouns 'she, her' are often associated with passive verbs, as if the acting subject of the story was more likely to be acted upon; there are also a number of possessive forms (her plight, her asylum case, her story, and so on) highlighting this passivity. Finally, the pronoun 'you' is used to interpellate the reader and invite them to act, with one instance of action ('you marched in London'). To sum up, in these emails, Brenda is not the acting subject of the narrative but rather a part of the object of the quest; the acting subjects are in fact AllOut.org and its audience, who try to make it possible for Brenda to stay in the UK. In some emails, the narratives feature helpers (other organizations, advocates and Brenda's local MP) and opponents (mainly the Home Office in the UK, and undefined social actors in Uganda whose threat is made more real with mentions of the murder in 2011 of LGBTI Ugandan activist David Kato). In other words, Brenda has little agency in these narratives despite the fact that it requires huge amounts of agency to claim asylum.

The main criticism directed at such narratives is the way in which they perpetuate colonial imaginaries, and critics of homonationalism have noted a new configuration of sexual rights in the past 15 years within neo-colonial structures. The clearest consequence of this rhetoric is to confer a mediatory position on LGBTI refugees in AllOut.org's discourse on rights. It mediates the representation of both the organization and its projected public on two levels: at a nationalist level, asylum seekers are the necessary migrating victims that reinforce homonationalist narratives about 'our' queer democracy. In other words, queer asylum seekers represent desire for the nation (White, 2013). At the advocacy level, asylum seekers are evidence that LGBTI advocacy remains a legitimate concern, reactivating the wound of being queer in public arenas where strong vested interests fight to disprove this (Puar, 2007; Raboin, 2017a; Rao, 2010). The presence of nationalist tropes should be noted considering that AllOut.org does not present itself as a platform bound to a specific country, making clear that the rescue narrative is a circulating trope: a form of engagement that is premised on (1) making the public feel good about action, and (2) an existing teleology that is not specific to the UK and has been shown to be a potent force in many European and North American contexts.

Not all advocacy discourses are content, however, to perpetuate rescue narratives uncritically and entertain a strategic or ironic relationship with them. In particular, critiques of the detention of LGBTI claimants often revolve around the surprise and turmoil caused to asylum seekers who did not expect it. The UK Lesbian and Gay Immigration Group (UKLGIG) and Stonewall published a report in 2016 about detention that emphasizes that feeling of betrayal, quoting asylum seekers in detention, including the following:

> It felt like I was betrayed because if somebody seeks asylum, they're just trying to get some protection, but then you're detaining them. It's like you're putting them in prison for having come to you for help. It didn't make sense to me. (Bachmann, 2016: 14)

Using such testimonies, advocates infuse the promise of homonationalism with affect: the feeling of betrayal experienced by asylum seekers on the one hand, and a feeling of shame for the public being addressed on the other. Both are affected by their different relationship to the promise of homonationalist rescue, making such a resort to the expression of betrayal a potentially efficient strategic use of homonationalist tropes by activists.

The limits of rescue narratives in their ability to bridge the distance between publics and LGBTI asylum seekers lie in the way that, in order to elicit action, they presuppose a relationship of dependency between a public made up of sexual citizens, and asylum seekers who do not have access by themselves to the language of rights. This is perhaps why, alongside the tropes of rescue, AllOut.org also makes a rhetorical effort to produce the idea of a worldwide community of sexual subjects. On the same homepage as the aforementioned map, scrolling down reveals a short text:

2,213,744 have joined the movement. Are you next? Join Us. We're building a movement ... Gay. Straight. Lesbian. Bi. Trans. Everyone for equality ... No one should be left behind in the fight for equality. That's where All Out comes in. When we come together ... we change conversations ... we influence decisions ... we support the bravest activists in the world ... And with 2,213,744 from every country on earth ... it really works.

At first sight, joining (and helping) AllOut.org is equated with being part of an imagined community of queers around the world: the activist discourse erases the distance between its publics and the people it purports to help by encompassing everyone in the same movement. However, a closer reading indicates the difficulties inherent in a claim for such community: there is for example a tension between 'everyone' and the use of specific, historically and geographically situated identities (however globalized they may be) such as 'gay, straight, lesbian, bi and trans'. There is also a certain vagueness concerning the 'we' of the community: it refers variously to, among others, AllOut.org, all queer people and activists in certain areas of the world. In other words, erasing distance requires publics to join an 'us' that is not a stable entity.

## A rhetoric of proximity

Alongside discourses trying to deal with the distance of humanitarianism, LGBTI asylum advocacy also offers many examples of discourses of proximity. Discourses of proximity and community can be traced back to the French Revolution, when nationhood and community had to be redefined: the Abbé Sieyès then famously offered a definition of citizenship not based on race or culture, but on the adoption of foreigners by a local community (Wahnich, 2013: 260). Although this notion has not concretized in the way in which the law of citizenship works, it is interesting to note that the possibility for foreigners to be adopted by local communities as a sign of their deserving citizenship is in fact an important rhetorical mode of LGBTI asylum advocacy.[11] I call this mode a rhetoric of proximity for it focuses (1) on the pragmatic idea that LGBTI asylum is a domestic problem with a domestic solution, and (2) on the fact that 'we' live together in the same cities and towns (and therefore attention shifts from a worldwide imagined queer community to cohabitation). This means that the notion of shared place becomes crucial, and so I will now look at the way in which spaces and places are described, happy futures envisioned and domesticity depicted.

None on Record[12] offers a series of videos interviewing asylum seek-ers in the UK: an important characteristic is the way in which they show asylum seekers *in situ*, in British landscapes. In the case of John, location is part of the narrative: as he tells his story of migration, we see him near a detention centre, near Heathrow airport and on an underground train, among other locations. Beyond their illustrative function, showing these places reminds the public that LGBTI asylum is a domestic problem, that it is about helping a neighbour; this neighbourliness is also signified in the video with many shots of London suburbs and suburban trains. At the beginning of the video, John explains how when he was young, he had been told that if you stayed under the sun long enough you would become a woman, and he would stay like this for hours; on screen we see the shadow of a woman dancing against a brick wall resembling that of a British house. The video signifies symbolically that the futures dreamed in his country of origin can happen in the UK, thus engaging its public to make sure that this promise is made good: proximity comes to embody the promise of happiness.[13]

Another None on Record video features a lesbian asylum seeker called Skye. She too is shown walking around places, in this case a town on the Isle of Wight, on her own and with her partner, or modelling styl-ish clothes in the pages of lesbian magazine *Diva*. This video plays on the Sieyèsian idea of adoption: in the video, Skye has been adopted by communities (one local, one mediated). Her happy future is represented in scenes of domesticity – for example, having her hair shaved by her partner – and in the pair of them discussing their love of walking in the countryside. The banality and domesticity of her queer happiness is rein-forced by a strong suggestion of Englishness, through the representation of landscape. This video engages the public by showing a very recogniz-able shape of queer happiness; furthermore, Skye becomes more British through her intimacy and private life. Accepted as part of the 'we' of dif-ferent local communities, her account of detention becomes all the more shocking in the way in which it breaks this domesticity and invokes the idea of betrayal. In other words, the rhetoric of proximity, in the way it articulates intimacy and adoption, enhances the feeling of injustice that the public is prompted to recognize.

## Conclusion

Both the rhetoric of distance and of proximity rely on an appeal to a metaphysics of justice – as Luc Boltanski notes, such metaphysics enable public indignation to be converted into action. However, proximity has a very different (if complementary) way of creating a sense of injustice. Bridging distance, as we have seen earlier, relies on universalism: it is based on an abstract queer subject that would encompass, in its imagined community, both the addressed queer liberal public of the advocate's discourse and the asylum seekers that it tries to help. Instead, proximity and the logic of adoption sees the intimacy of asylum seekers being constitutive of their publicness. LGBTI asylum seekers thus become deserving subjects – what Miriam Ticktin calls 'morally legitimate suffering bodies' (Ticktin, 2011) – through the publicization of their domestic, private experiences.

It is nonetheless crucial to remain attentive to the limitations of such modes of engagement: What happens when the happiness of queer liberalism is not affordable to certain asylum seekers? Indeed, the type of private experiences that are recognizable by others as evidence of local adoption may be premised on certain forms of social, cultural and economic capital, including practices of consumption and socialization that are not available to many asylum seekers. In other words, we must not forget that the adoption of queer subjects in communities is neither automatic nor evident. Engaging and constituting responsible publics in relation to LGBTI asylum might also involve orienting their attention (their ears, their gaze) towards the cracks of social invisibility through which queer asylum claimants may fall because of their systemic exclusion from participation (in democracy, markets, and so on) by the asylum apparatus.

## Notes

1. See *Islam* v. *SSHD* (1999) 2 AC 629 (House of Lords). On queer asylum seekers' experiences of seeking refugee status in Germany, see Mole in this volume.
2. The term 'queer' will be used here to denote sexual and gender minorities – including, for example, non-heteronormative sexualities.
3. Following the concept of *dissensus* as developed by Jacques Rancière 2004b.
4. AllOut.org, Amnesty International, International Lesbian and Gay Alliance, None on Record, Stonewall, UK Lesbian and Gay Immigration Group.
5. The question of distance has been central to many theoretical formulations of humanitarianism, especially in the wake of Luc Boltanski's attempts at formulating a sociology of humanitarianism as a relationship to distant suffering.
6. According to its website, the ILGA is 'the world federation of national and local organisations dedicated to achieving equal rights for lesbian, gay, bisexual, trans and intersex (LGBTI) people. ILGA is an umbrella organisation of more than 1,200 member organisations presented in six different regions … ILGA's aim is to work for the equality of lesbian, gay, bisexual, trans and intersex people and their liberation from all forms of discrimination. We seek to achieve this aim through the world-wide cooperation and mutual support of our members … We focus public and government attention on cases of discrimination against LGBTI people by support-

ing programs and protest actions, asserting diplomatic pressure, providing information and working with international organisations and the international media' (ILGA, 2017).

7. AllOut.org often presents itself as a 'global movement' and a 'global team': it mobilizes audiences mostly online (petitions, emails, webpages) for a series of LGBTI-advocacy issues around the world. Its current team and its location can be found on its website (AllOut.org, 2020).

8. In the case of the ILGA, maps, alongside reports, are one of its main yearly outputs.

9. Stonewall's advocacy is a good example, encompassing different forms of optimism with a recurrent theme of advocacy as to what liberates the individual to fulfil their potential (Raboin, 2017a: 130–1).

10. In the context of the UK, by 'racialised queer', I mean queer individuals who are marked as racially or ethnically different from a White British identity.

11. Lise Jacquez has shown how *Réseau Education sans Frontière* in France, in its actions to prevent the deportation of children at school, has relied on such adoption (Jacquez, 2017).

12. On its website, None on Record describes its mission: 'None on Record is an African LGBT digital media organisation that produces documentaries about African LGBT experiences, trains African LGBT community members on digital media and documentation and provides space for African LGBT arts and culture through our Tamasha Festival' (None On Record, 2020).

13. For other examples of how happiness is represented as rooted in a specific place in the country of arrival, see also Amnesty International's success story of a gay Syrian couple who find ways to develop their lives in Germany (Amnesty International, 2018).

# References

Ahmed, Sara. 2004. *The Cultural Politics of Emotion*. Edinburgh: Edinburgh University Press.

Ahmed, Sara. 2006. *Queer Phenomenology: Orientations, Objects, Others*. Durham, NC: Duke University Press.

Ahmed, Sara. 2010. *The Promise of Happiness*. Durham, NC: Duke University Press.

All Out. 2020. 'Our Team'. Accessed 17 January 2020. https://allout.org/en/team.

Amnesty International UK. 2018. 'Gay Syrian Refugee Couple Build a New Future in Germany'. Accessed 17 January 2020. www.amnesty.org.uk/gay-syrian-refugee-couple-build-new-future-germany.

Bachmann, Chaka L. 2016. *No Safe Refuge: Experiences of LGBT Asylum Seekers in Detention*. London: Stonewall.

Berg, Laurie and Jenni Millbank. 2009. 'Constructing the Personal Narratives of Lesbian, Gay and Bisexual Asylum Claimants', *Journal of Refugee Studies* 22 (2): 195–223.

Berlant, Lauren, ed. 2004. *Compassion: The Culture and Politics of an Emotion*. New York: Routledge.

Berlant, Lauren. 2011. *Cruel Optimism*. Durham, NC: Duke University Press.

Boltanski, Luc. 2007. *La souffrance à distance*. Paris: Gallimard.

Brown, Wendy. 2004. '"The Most We Can Hope For … "': Human Rights and the Politics of Fatalism', *South Atlantic Quarterly* 103 (2/3): 451–63.

Brown, Wendy. 2006. *Regulating Aversion: Tolerance in the Age of Identity and Empire*. Princeton: Princeton University Press.

Chouliaraki, Lilie. 2010. 'Post-Humanitarianism: Humanitarian Communication beyond a Politics of Pity', *International Journal of Cultural Studies* 13 (2): 107–26.

Chouliaraki, Lilie. 2013. *The Ironic Spectator: Solidarity in the Age of Post-Humanitarianism*. Cambridge: Polity Press.

Duggan, Lisa. 2002. 'The New Homonormativity: The Sexual Politics of Neoliberalism'. In *Materializing Democracy: Toward a Revitalized Cultural Politics*, edited by Russ Castronovo and Dana D. Nelson, 175–94. Durham, NC: Duke University Press.

Eng, David L. 2010. *The Feeling of Kinship: Queer Liberalism and the Racialization of Intimacy*. Durham, NC: Duke University Press.

Fortier, Anne-Marie. 2003. 'Making Home: Queer Migrations and Motions of Attachment'. In *Uprootings/Regroundings: Questions of Home and Migration*, edited by Sara Ahmed, Claudia Castañeda, Anne-Marie Fortier and Mimi Sheller, 115–35. Oxford: Berg.

Greimas, Algirdas Julien. 2002. *Sémantique structurale: Recherche de méthode*. 3rd ed. Paris: Presses universitaires de France.

Haritaworn, Jin. 2008. 'Loyal Repetitions of the Nation: Gay Assimilation and the "War on Terror"', *Darkmatter*, 2 May. Accessed 17 January 2020. www.darkmatter101.org/site/2008/05/02/loyal-repetitions-of-the-nation-gay-assimilation-and-the-war-on-terror/.

ILGA (International Lesbian, Gay, Bisexual, Trans and Intersex Association). 2017. 'About Us'. Accessed 17 January 2020. https://ilga.org/about-us/.

Jacquez, Lise. 2017. 'De RESF en 2006 à "l'affaire Leonarda" en 2013: Les familles sans-papiers dans l'espace médiatique français', *Études de communication* 48: 21–36.

Kollman, Kelly and Matthew Waites. 2009. 'The Global Politics of Lesbian, Gay, Bisexual and Transgender Human Rights: An Introduction', *Contemporary Politics* 15 (1): 1–17.

Lacey, Kate. 2013. *Listening Publics: The Politics and Experience of Listening in the Media Age*. Cambridge: Polity Press.

Lentin, Alana and Gavan Titley. 2011. *The Crises of Multiculturalism: Racism in a Neoliberal Age*. London: Zed Books.

Lewis, Rachel. 2013. 'Deportable Subjects: Lesbians and Political Asylum', *Feminist Formations* 25 (2): 174–94.

Middelkoop, Louis. 2013. 'Normativity and Credibility of Sexual Orientation in Asylum Decision Making'. In *Fleeing Homophobia: Sexual Orientation, Gender Identity and Asylum*, edited by Thomas Spijkerboer, 154–75. London: Routledge.

Millbank, Jenni. 2009. 'From Discretion to Disbelief: Recent Trends in Refugee Determinations on the Basis of Sexual Orientation in Australia and the United Kingdom', *International Journal of Human Rights* 13 (2/3): 391–414.

Murray, David A.B. 2016. *Real Queer? Sexual Orientation and Gender Identity Refugees in the Canadian Refugee Apparatus*. London: Rowman and Littlefield International.

None on Record. 2020. 'FAQ'. Accessed 17 January 2020. www.noneonrecord.com/faq/.

Nyong'o, Tavia. 2012. 'Queer Africa and the Fantasy of Virtual Participation', *WSQ: Women's Studies Quarterly* 40 (1/2): 40–63.

Puar, Jasbir K. 2007. *Terrorist Assemblages: Homonationalism in Queer Times*. Durham, NC: Duke University Press.

Raboin, Thibaut. 2017a. *Discourses on LGBT Asylum in the UK: Constructing a Queer Haven*. Manchester: Manchester University Press.

Raboin, Thibaut. 2017b. 'Exhortations of Happiness: Liberalism and Nationalism in the Discourses on LGBTI Asylum Rights in the UK', *Sexualities* 20 (5/6): 663–81.

Rancière, Jacques. 2004a. *Aux bords du politique*. Paris: Gallimard.

Rancière, Jacques. 2004b. 'Who is the Subject of the Rights of Man?', *South Atlantic Quarterly* 103 (2/3): 297–310.

Rao, Rahul. 2010. *Third World Protest: Between Home and the World*. Oxford: Oxford University Press.

Rouhani, Farhang. 2007. 'Religion, Identity and Activism: Queer Muslim Diasporic Identities'. In *Geographies of Sexualities: Theory, Practices and Politics*, edited by Kath Browne, Jason Lim and Gavin Brown, 169–80. Aldershot: Ashgate.

Ticktin, Miriam. 2011. *Casualties of Care: Immigration and the Politics of Humanitarianism in France*. Berkeley: University of California Press.

UKLGIG (UK Lesbian and Gay Immigration Group). 2010. *Failing the Grade: Home Office Intitial Decisions on Lesbian and Gay Claims for Asylum*. London: UK Lesbian and Gay Immigration Group.

UKLGIG (UK Lesbian and Gay Immigration Group). 2013. *Missing the Mark: Decision Making on Lesbian, Gay (Bisexual, Trans and Intersex) Asylum Claims*. London: UK Lesbian and Gay Immigration Group.

Wahnich, Sophie. 2013. *La révolution française*. Paris: Hachette Éducation.

Warner, Michael. 2002. *Publics and Counterpublics*. New York: Zone Books.

White, Melissa Autumn. 2013. 'Ambivalent Homonationalisms: Transnational Queer Intimacies and Territorialized Belongings', *Interventions* 15 (1): 37–54.

# 11

# The unintended consequences of expanding migrant-rights protections

Ralph Wilde

## Introduction

One story that can be told about the development of legal protections for certain forced migrants in international law is, in terms of the scope of protection, a progressive one. From expanded definitions of who is entitled to refugee-law protection to the development of complementary protection in human-rights law, the ambit of that which the law purports to cover has moved wider. This might be seen as part of the broader trend in the expanding coverage of international human-rights law generally. Yet a counter-narrative can also be told: a diminished commitment on the part of many states, particularly economically advantaged ones, to inward migration, including of forced migrants, as evidenced in the expanded scope of *non-entrée*, 'closed-borders' measures – from visa restrictions to carrier sanctions, push-back operations and an unwillingness to engage in numerically significant refugee resettlements to their countries.[1] This backlash trend can also be identified in human-rights policy generally.[2] Just as the scope of human-rights legal protection in general, and the legal protection accorded to certain migrants in particular, has expanded, so too have states become less willing to provide such protection.

These two chronologically overlapping, normatively divergent developments are an important feature of global migration law. Given this, how can and should the causal relationship, if any, between them be understood? In particular, have progressive legal developments played a causal role in the broader trend of resistance to inward migration? And, moreover, given the actuality of such resistance, what is at stake when legal developments continue to push in a progressive direction?

## Non-refoulement and extraterritoriality

The present chapter explores these questions through the case study of progressive legal developments in the application of human-rights-law protections, including the *non-refoulement* obligation – the obligation not to send people back to face certain forms of human-rights abuse – and extraterritorially, in relation to states' migration-policy-related actions outside their borders: the extraterritorial operation of border checks, interception and push-back at sea, detention, transfers to third countries, and so on.

The legal developments at issue are at the intersection of two of the main trends in the field of human-rights obligations generally, concerning *non-refoulement* and extraterritorial applicability. They come on the heels of obligations in the former category being accepted, and the scope of their coverage expanding, in the territorial context, and obligations in the latter category also developing in a similar fashion somewhat more recently.[3] Now, in a synthesis of both developments, marking a further development in each, there is an acceptance that human-rights law, including the *non-refoulement* obligation, applies to extraterritorial migration-related policy activities, as affirmed in the *Hirsi* decision of the European Court of Human Rights about Italian maritime push-back operations.[4]

The progressive developments in the extraterritorial application of human-rights law have the effect of grafting onto the migration-policy-related activities similar core protections for migrants as would apply to equivalent activities taking place territorially. This falls short of equivalent protection, given the limited circumstances in which human-rights law applies extraterritorially and important practical impediments in the field of enforcement and third-party scrutiny.[5] Nonetheless, in certain key respects it is a radical shift, introducing substantial constraints on the state. On the issue of *non-refoulement*, this means that, as in *Hirsi*, states can no longer lawfully engage in *refoulement* extraterritorially which would be unlawful territorially, at least as a matter of human-rights law.

## What is at stake

This development potentially constitutes a direct challenge to the very reason for such extraterritorial action in the first place. The way in which such action is, essentially, an extraterritorial manifestation of an activity that would normally take place at or within a state's borders – for example, 'push back' being the extraterritorial equivalent to deporting migrants once they reach the state – requires a consideration of why the extraterritorial locus has been chosen, and what implications such a choice has for the question of protective legal regulation.

The present enquiry forms part of a broader question relating to certain other forms of extraterritorial state activity, wherein states have chosen to engage in an activity extraterritorially that they could have performed, and usually do perform, territorially. Most prominent in the post-9/11 human-rights era is the decision by the US to detain suspected members of Al Qaeda and other militant Islamist groups not in the territorial US but extraterritorially, in its military facility in Guantánamo Bay, Cuba (abbreviated to GTMO, and often pronounced 'Gitmo'), and the initially secret so-called 'black sites'.[6] It was speculated in the case of these arrangements that part of the reason for the choice of the extraterritorial over the territorial locus was that the former offered an arena of relatively less, if any, substantive normative restrictions and associated accountability, including of a legal kind.[7] So, too, a speculation arises as to whether an important reason for moving migration-policy-related activities 'offshore' is to evade normative constraints and scrutiny (Gammeltoft-Hansen, 2011: 3).

The significance of such speculation is heightened when attention is given to the broader context of an increased resistance on the part of many economically advantaged states towards inward migration in general, and the migration of individuals protected from *refoulement* by refugee law and human-rights law in particular – the *non-entrée* policy identified above. Extraterritorial migration-related activities have to be considered, then, not only in a neutral way, aimed at implementing policy that could be, potentially, relatively receptive or restrictive of migration. Rather, the broader context requires a consideration of how these activities might be viewed as a means of furthering *non-entrée* policy.

In consequence, it is necessary to ask whether the objective of circumventing legal restrictions that would operate were these activities to take place territorially might lie behind the move offshore. If this is the case, the question arises: Will the legal move of following state activity to the extraterritorial arena precipitate a counter-response by states? And what might that response look like? And should this matter when considering the merits of the legal move for the field of migration law? What negative blowback consequences for the protection of migrants might be precipitated by the progressive legal developments that have taken place and might take place in the future?

## The potential for worse counter-responses: From 'Gitmo' to drones

The potential risks in the migration context in particular can perhaps be illustrated with an example from the subject of extraterritoriality more generally. It is instructive to consider the shift from the President George W. Bush 'War on Terror' policy of the extraterritorial detention of individuals deemed security threats, to the President Obama policy of the killing of such individuals via strikes by so-called 'drones'. To be sure, this shift has multiple explanations, including advances in drone technology and the lack of a full-spectrum boots-on-the-ground presence in many of the Obama-era theatres of operation like Yemen and the Afghan–Pakistan borderland, compared with Iraq and Afghanistan in the George W. Bush-era. But it is surely important to consider how the general progressivist, human-rights-based critique of Guantánamo and the black sites – shared, of course, by President Obama – might have played a part in the search for and recourse to an alternative and, crucially for the purposes of the present discussion, more extreme means of achieving the same objective of neutralizing security threats.

## Exceptional backlash responses to extraterritoriality

Indeed, there might be something about extraterritoriality that is particularly salient in the backlash debates, precipitating an exceptionally regressive response. It is possible to identify the linked issues of the rights of foreigners, and the rights of people extraterritorially, as a dominant theme in the general backlash debate, with serious consequences for the position of migrants.

In the UK, for example, the long-standing process of periodic assaults on the European Commission (as was) and Court of Human Rights, and the European Convention on Human Rights, has in recent years tipped over into a position, first, in which the Conservative Party committed to replacing the domestic UK Human Rights Act with a 'Bill of

Rights' that would somehow enable a greater diminution in substantive protections from the position of the European Convention, and then, second, whereby the former Prime Minister Theresa May, before taking up this position, expressed a preference not just to alter the domestic-law position but to withdraw from the European Convention on Human Rights.

Significantly, Theresa May's criticism of human rights focused mainly on the impact of the *non-refoulement* obligation territorially, something that operated as a constraint on her decisions as Home Secretary when seeking to deport, expel and/or extradite foreigners from the UK. Moreover, the topic in the UK that has led to the most opposition to the European Convention in recent years, other than the issue of prisoners' voting rights, has been the extraterritorial application of the Convention to the actions of UK soldiers, notably in relation to abuses in Iraq.

Prisoner voting aside, then, extraterritoriality and *non-refoulement* (in the territorial context) are at the heart of an exceptional rejectionist position when it comes to, in the case of the UK, the most significant regime of operative international human-rights law. It is exceptional because it involves not simply objecting to and complaining about positions in certain areas but, rather, proposing withdrawal from the regime in its entirety. It is also notable that one common speculated explanation for the Brexit outcome in the UK referendum on leaving the EU is anti-migrant views, in relation to both inward migration from the EU and (mistakenly, since it is not an EU matter) the reception of refugees.

Returning to human-rights law, there is other evidence that resistance to extraterritorial applicability is of an exceptional nature when compared to resistance on other human-rights topics. In surveying the Turkish Government's responses to decisions by the European Court of Human Rights (ECtHR), which have ranged across many important and controversial topics, Olgun Akbulut places the responses to the cases about the Turkish occupation in Northern Cyprus in an exceptionally negative category, as the 'one group of cases where the government has completely rejected the findings and the judgment of the ECtHR' (Akbulut, 2016: 424).

When considering the special nature of objections to extraterritorial human-rights protections, including for migrants, it is important to bear in mind the identity of the rights holders. Most individuals given the particular right of *non-refoulement* (whether territorial or extraterritorial), and rights generally in the extraterritorial context, are foreigners. Objections to *non-refoulement* and extraterritorial applicability have to be understood, in part, as objections to the legal protection of rights for foreigners – especially given the xenophobic turn that commentators have identified and are identifying for the period corresponding to that under present analysis, when *non-entrée* policies, extraterritorial migration-policy-activities and the backlash against human-rights protection have taken place.[8]

So progressive moves towards the human-rights regulation of extraterritorial state activity in general, and such activity that impacts on migrants, could precipitate a backlash from states of an exceptionally significant character.

## Potential backlash responses

What might happen? In the first place are responses by states that might be understood as still, ultimately, accepting the general idea of needing to provide basic protection, but on the basis of avoiding the implementation of this by allowing migrants to enter and reside in their territories. For example, migrants have been forcibly transferred on their way to, or having arrived at, a state's borders to a third location, allied to the claim that those entitled to protection will not suffer as far as the *non-refoulement* obligation is concerned because the third location is deemed safe. This approach, the spirit of which is captured in the EU-law Dublin 'first country of asylum' regime, can be seen in the Australian policy of intercepting migrants at sea and transporting them to extraterritorial centres such as those on Nauru and Papua New Guinea. It has been discussed in Europe for some time and has resurfaced there during the recent 'crisis', with the possibility of creating such centres somewhere in North Africa. In all these cases, what is being proposed and implemented is the transfer of responsibilities for hosting migrants from relatively economically advantaged countries to relatively economically disadvantaged ones.

Approaches such as these can be seen as responses by states that, on the one hand, gesture to an acceptance of the position that, if migrants fall within their control, whether territorially or extraterritorially, then they do bear an obligation of *non-refoulement*, but, on the other hand, seek to avoid the usual consequence of this, which is that they then discharge the obligation through hosting those individuals entitled to protection within their own territories. The consequent reduction in the numbers hosted is seen as a benefit not only in and of itself, as far as the individuals directly affected by it are concerned, but also as a deterrent to others who might try to travel to the states concerned, not just to obtain protection in general but to obtain protection that would be delivered in those states' territories, and also to all other migrants without a protection entitlement.

For the individuals directly affected, the arrangement is not on its own terms supposed to diminish providing the protection required by the *non-refoulement* obligation if they are entitled to this. But in shifting the provision of protection to an extraterritorial location in a less economically advantaged state, the solution exacerbates the unequal distribution of hosting refugees globally.

That this can be done within the boundaries of the *non-refoulement* obligation indicates the limited nature of international law in this area, which does not provide for a binding regime of equitable refugee hosting among states. In this respect, then, the backlash precipitated by the progressive development in the law may not necessarily lead to a diminution in the additional protection provided by the law, but has come at the cost of the worsening of a separate problem, not covered by the law, in the area of the equitable hosting of refugees between states. More migrants are potentially protected than would be the case without extraterritorial applicability, but responsibility for realizing this through the hosting of such migrants has been added to the already-disproportionately involved developing world.

For those individuals affected in a broader way, whereby the exemplary nature of this arrangement deters them from attempting to travel to the states involved in the first place, the arrangement might have a similar effect if they are able to obtain protection elsewhere. But if they are not so able – if travel to the states implementing these measures is the only route to protection – then the danger is that protection itself will not be realized. Thus, the backlash response reverses the practical significance of the progressive development: the *non-refoulement* obligation might apply extraterritorially, but people have been deterred from travelling into the zone where they would benefit from this. Since the deterrent effect is based on shifting the place where protection will be afforded to a less desirable location, the effect of the backlash response illustrates how the international legal regime only offers core protection, failing to address the broader issues of equitable hosting or, to a large extent, the material conditions in the site of protection. States can respond to the progressive developments by exploiting the lack of effective regimes dealing with these broader issues, to generate disincentives that diminish protection and thereby undermine the practical effect of the progressive developments. It is as if the *non-refoulement* obligation did not apply extraterritorially.

Progressive developments leading to expanded protection may also precipitate backlash measures in other areas that, although not undermining the developments as such, aim to reduce overall inward-migration numbers, including of individuals who would be entitled to protection. Carrier sanctions and visa restrictions could be tightened up. Economically advantaged states could more aggressively seek to contain forced migrants in refugee camps in developing countries, through leverage exercised in relation to UNHCR and host states. In consequence, fewer people would be able to enter zones of protection, or, at least, such zones where the material conditions are better than in initial locations of safety. These measures might have the effect of reducing, and possibly cancelling out, the effect of the progressive developments in expanding the numbers of people protected. Indeed, it might even lead to an even lower number of such people than was the case before the progressive developments occurred.

This possibility – that the backlash responses to the progressive developments are of such an extreme nature that they lead to a position even worse than a situation without such developments – is illustrated by the example of the move from Guantánamo to drones. It would be, obviously, the consequence of a withdrawal from human-rights instruments, as had been discussed in the UK at the time of writing (June 2019), which would drastically diminish legal protections territorially as well as extra-territorially, and in relation to all rights, not just the rights of migrants.

## Conclusion

This chapter neither asserts a clear causal link between progressive developments in migration-law protections and backlash responses by states, nor predicts what will happen in the future. Rather, it speculates about what might be happening and might happen in the future, based on the coincidence between the two phenomena. Ultimately, the clear evidence that many economically advantaged states wish to adopt *non-entrée* measures, in the context of widespread popular xenophobia, indicates that the stakes are particularly high when migration-law developments cut against this. It is not being suggested, necessarily, that the progressive developments are mistaken, nor that efforts to further and deepen them are misguided. Rather, it is important to acknowledge that improvements in particular areas need to be assessed in a broader context. At the very least, the notion of progress itself needs to be approached holistically, and consideration needs to be given to how the combination of improvements in particular areas of migration law with serious regressions elsewhere might leave things, overall, no better or, even, worse.

## Acknowledgements

This chapter is a revised version of an article published originally in the *American Journal of International Law Unbound* 111 (2017), 487.

## Notes

1. On the idea of a general erosion in the commitment to refugees, including the *non-refoulement* obligation, see, for example, Agnès Hurwitz (2009: 178ff.) and sources cited therein.
2. On the trend in human-rights law generally, see, for instance, Popelier *et al.* (2016) and sources cited therein.
3. On the development of the *non-refoulement* obligation in human-rights law territorially, see, for example, Jane McAdam (2007) – *passim*, but in particular, Chapter 4: 'The Scope of Ill-Treatment under the ECHR and ICCPR' – and sources cited therein. On the extraterritorial application of human-rights law in the area of civil and political rights, see, for instance, Ralph Wilde (2013) and sources cited therein.
4. *Hirsi Jamaa and Others v. Italy* (2012), Appl. 27765/09, Judgment of 23 February 2012, 55 EHRR 21 (GC).
5. On the scope of applicability of human-rights treaties in the field of civil and political rights, see Wilde (2013) and sources cited therein.
6. See Wilde (2005: Section II) and sources cited therein.
7. See Wilde (2005: Section IV.C.) and sources cited therein.
8. Indeed, it is notable that the other main issue precipitating an exceptional backlash in the UK, prisoners' voting rights, is also concerned with the rights of individuals who, like foreigners, are placed in a separate, lesser category from citizens, and in which the legal issue challenges this treatment (voting being a right that is quintessentially tied to citizenship, the denial of which being tied up, alongside the deprivation of liberty, with the breaking of the civic bond that forms the basis for a serious criminal conviction).

## References

Akbulut, Olgun. 2016. 'Turkey: The European Convention on Human Rights as a Tool for Modernisation'. In *Criticism of the European Court of Human Rights: Shifting the Convention System: Counter-Dynamics at the National and EU Level*, edited by Patricia Popelier, Sarah Lambrecht and Koen Lemmens, 413–46. Cambridge: Intersentia.

Gammeltoft-Hansen, Thomas. 2011. *Access to Asylum: International Refugee Law and the Globalisation of Migration Control*. Cambridge: Cambridge University Press.

Hurwitz, Agnès. 2009. *The Collective Responsibility of States to Protect Refugees*. Oxford: Oxford University Press.

McAdam, Jane. 2007. *The Evolution of Complementary Protection*. Oxford: Oxford University Press.

Popelier, Patricia, Sarah Lambrecht and Koen Lemmens, eds. 2016. *Criticism of the European Court of Human Rights: Shifting the Convention System: Counter-Dynamics at the National and EU Level*. Cambridge: Intersentia.

Wilde, Ralph. 2005. 'Legal "Black Hole"? Extraterritorial State Action and International Treaty Law on Civil and Political Rights', *Michigan Journal of International Law* 26 (3): 739–806.

Wilde, Ralph. 2013. 'The Extraterritorial Application of International Human Rights Law on Civil and Political Rights'. In *Routledge Handbook of International Human Rights Law*, edited by Scott Sheeran and Nigel Rodley, 635–61. London: Routledge.

# 12

# Visual politics and the 'refugee' crisis: The images of Alan Kurdi

Tom Snow

## Introduction

On 2 September 2015, photographic images began to emerge across multiple social-media platforms and online news networks showing the lifeless body of the 3-year-old Syrian, Alan Kurdi, washed up on the shore close to the southern Turkish resort of Bodrum. Along with his 5-year-old brother, Galip, and mother, Rehen, Alan had drowned at sea just minutes after the family had boarded an underequipped inflatable vessel in the desperate attempt to reach Europe via the Greek island of Kos. Images captured by the Turkish photojournalist Nilüfur Demir working for the Doğan News Agency show the toddler face down in the surf dressed in blue shorts and a red T-shirt. For Demir, 'there was nothing to do except take his photograph' (Fantz and Shoichet, 2015). The sequence also shows gendarme Mehmet Ciplak in an unsettled and perplexed state. In one image, Ciplak carries the child's body away from the scene, cradled as though the devastating situation hadn't fully registered. Ciplak has spoken of his paternal instincts: 'I prayed [to] God to find him alive. I thought of my own son when I saw him.' He apparently had no idea he was under the gaze of Demir's camera lens at the time (Squires, 2015).

Like thousands of other displaced persons – of Syrian nationality, stateless Kurds, Iraqis and Palestinians formerly based in the country, alongside many other communities based in affected regions in the years preceding and following 2015 – the Kurdi family were fleeing a situation of religiously sanctioned, sectarian and political violence. This was related, but not limited, to the Assad regime's brutal suppression of civil-rights demonstrations, which broke out in Daraa in March 2011, and the ensuing rise of umbrella rebel groups, including the Free Syrian Army and other internationally backed paramilitary factions, who subsequently engaged in bloody civil war with presidential forces, their supporters and international allies – and was framed, and to some degree conflated, as a necessary step to attain regional stability in relation to the rise of Islamic State in Iraq and al-Sham (IS) (Sawah and Kawakibi, 2014; Achcar, 2016). The Kurdi family had attempted to reach Europe by contracting the services of people smugglers after their home town of Kobane became besieged by ISIS. The long-term plan included the possibility of reaching the safety and security of Canada, where Fatima Kurdi lives: Alan's aunt and the sister of the family's surviving father, Abdullah. However, after the ordeal of being unable to save his family left him in utter despair, Abdullah returned to Syria, telling CNN, 'I don't want anything from the world'. He added, 'Everything I was dreaming of is gone. I want to bury my children and sit beside them until I die' (Fantz and Shoichet, 2015).

Abdullah Kurdi's experience is a troubling and complex one. This chapter, however, is not concerned with tracing his family's movements or addressing the trauma of Abdullah's current situation, nor the extent to which he became demonized and labelled at one stage as being responsible for his family's deaths (see Fiddian-Qasmiyeh, 2017a). It instead inquires into the politics of the ongoing crisis in relation to photographic reproduction and distribution, foregrounded in the interrelated media and political spheres. The contention here is that the current crisis in the Mediterranean, Europe, and greater Middle East and North Africa region cannot be properly accounted for without analysis of visual (re)production and channels of circulation. Here, I address various responses to the Kurdi images in the political and cultural spheres. The images are then placed in relation to certain anxieties associated with photography and the parallel discourse of visual production. Rather than suggesting that their affective value diminishes over time, however, it is argued that any such interpretation is both framed and delimited by greater political failings, in turn rendering these images emblematic of a broader emergency. What I call 'visual politics', therefore, relates to the way in which visual materials are re-encoded by various rhetorical narratives, which in this context is evocative of larger displacements of contingent political realities.

## The Kurdi images in context

The sequence of images recounted above are determined by a kind of static realism, related to their framing a situation that has been widely debated in the current media sphere. Kurdi's body lies face down on its own, helpless. In that, the images show incapacity in multiple senses. For instance, the absence of family around the child's body deviates from the expected *recognized* constructions of the familial. A representative of the state, in the form of the gendarme, is present. Yet Ciplak is also powerless in his assumed paternal and professional role and thus departs from an expected maintenance of law and order, visually representing a break-down in the civil code.

The emergence of the Kurdi images was nevertheless hailed as a turning point in the crisis of displaced peoples, owing in part to their immediate reproduction and circulation. Estimated to have appeared on 20 million screens in the 12 hours since the discovery of Kurdi's body, researchers at the UK's Sheffield University found that images related to the situation were included in 53,000 tweets, on the social-media plat-form Twitter, every hour (Press Association, 2015). Moreover, follow-ing the publication of the image, language used to describe the larger situation had apparently shifted from the predominant use of the term 'migrant' to 'refugee'. According to Claire Wardle, research director at the Tow Centre for Digital Journalism at Columbia University in the US, '2015 was the year the Syrian refugee crisis hit the European conscious-ness, but it's easy to forget that this was not the case before the Alan Kurdi image' (Press Association, 2015).[1]

Indeed, the United Nations High Commission for Refugees (UNHCR) reported that 13.9 million people were newly displaced by war during the preceding year, 2014, the most since the Second World War. Since 2005, the number of peoples forcibly displaced globally had almost doubled to 59.6 million (UNHCR, 2015). That number increased to 65.3 in 2015, 5.8 million more than the previous year. No fewer than 4.9 million of these people were formally based in Syria (UNHCR, 2016).[2] The total deaths at sea across the Mediterranean region in 2015 were the highest on record, and over half of those recorded worldwide (International Organization for Migration, 2016).

Citing such statistics brings the obscene levels of suffering on a transnational scale into one kind of focus. Yet as Wardle points out, it was apparently via the Kurdi *images* that the 'refugee crisis' entered the con-sciousness of the continent (and the EU) – a continent that many expe-riencing the situation have viewed as the best place to seek refuge and shelter, far from their regions of origin. The humanizing sentiment that characterized multiple mediatized reactions, however, far from matched the long-term reality of policy responses, alongside unfolding and related xenophobia, inclusive of the rise in ethno-nationalisms predominantly across Europe in the aftermath. The perceived iconicity of the images nevertheless describes a world in which political violence continues to be mediated by images on a complex scale capable of effecting a rupture in public sentiment, having only the appearance of effecting a rush to adapt national and international policy.

In the wake of the Kurdi images, European leaders were quick to respond, offering condolences to the surviving Abdullah Kurdi and expressing sympathies to the situation, supplemented by provisional statements concerning the revision of plans to facilitate the safe resettlement of displaced and desperate peoples to predominantly Western European nations. On 3 September, then British Prime Minister David Cameron promised to 'fulfil our moral responsibilities' but gave no explicit details (Dathan, 2015). By 7 September, Cameron announced that he would accept a miserly 20,000 Syrian refugees over a five-year period (Ashdown, 2015). Given this situation, in addition to the toxicity of the EU-membership referendum promised by the prime minister (the cause of his ultimate political demise), it was hardly surprising that by the end of September 2015, the UK's tabloid-mentality sensationalist media machine had returned to its bigoted line of reasoning, suggesting that 'we' have done enough for 'them' (European Journalism Observatory, 2015). The fact that the value of Britain's arms trade to the region has topped £3 billion a year since 2014 was barely publicized in the mainstream press.

German Chancellor Angela Merkel, on the other hand, announced no limits to the number of Syrians entering the country on 5 September, causing rebuttals from Austria out of a feared influx to that country and causing temporary controls along their shared border. The rise in far-right anti-Islamic groups, including Pegida, in the country and across northern Europe would nevertheless force the introduction of restrictions, in addition to following suit with France, the Netherlands, Belgium, Bulgaria and parts of Switzerland in proposing a burqa ban (Oltermann, 2016). The response in Viktor Orbán's Hungary to Merkel's initial compassion was to close its borders with Serbia to stem the potential flow of people on 15 September, alongside the announcement of an official state of emergency claiming to defend Christian Europe from the invasion of Muslims. On 17 September, Croatia and Slovenia followed suit in patrolling their borders with Serbia (BBC News, 2015). There is a difficulty in estimating number of displaced peoples to Gulf states such as Saudi Arabia, given that they have not signed the UN's 1951 Geneva Convention on the status of refugees and that displaced people there are thus not classified or counted as 'refugees' (*Guardian*, 2015). Turkey is thought to now host upwards of three and a half million; Lebanon has taken in excess of one million, the equivalent of a quarter of its population; while Israel has taken only a handful (Al Jazeera, 2017).

The images of Kurdi's body testify to the humanitarian emergency being experienced throughout the southern Mediterranean; yet they are also, depressingly, images that communicate the profound existential disarray related to the furtive and inadequate responses by governmental agencies. The situation, therefore, is not simply a 'refugee' crisis in terms of labelling the precarious situation of millions of displaced people but a crisis of refuge in the sense of apparently developed nations being able to convincingly articulate a political position to satisfy dissenting and divided domestic constituents. Political rhetoric is further foregrounded in the politicization of 'refugees' frequently articulated in a language of movement, yet more aptly described as a 'desultory politics of mobility' (Tazzioli, 2015: xi). That is, a situation underpinned by the immobility of millions of displaced persons, either in camps such as the one on the Turkish border with Syria at Hatay, or the recently dismantled so-called 'Jungle' at Calais at the northern coastal border of France (see also Fiddian-Qasmiyeh, 2017a; on the Calais camp, see the chapters in this volume by Crafter and Rosen; Bailey; Qasmiyeh; and Hooshyar Emani).

## Image and rhetoric

Various reflections on the Kurdi images and the 'power of photography' suggest in multiple ways in which their circulation in various media circles broke with the taboo of publishing pictures of deceased children (Laurent, 2015). Many other writers and commentators concerned with photography have also insisted on the need to consider what is not shown or pointed to in the image of infancy and a symbol of innocence, which might explain projected anxieties onto the images from several quarters. Peter Bouckaert of Human Rights Watch has further proposed a racialized element to public and political responses to the images, suggesting that 'the child looks a lot like a European child' and noting that weeks earlier images had emerged of several African children washed up on a beach in Libya and having nothing like the equivalent response (quoted in Laurent 2015). Such a disconcerting indication demonstrates that photographs are engaged in wider political conversations: in this case, a situation in the mainstream media's projection of the image concerns troubling aesthetico-political standards. On the other hand, the situation exemplifies the growing and formidable traction gained via social media in the circulation of images, in which the way that photographs operate in existing political discourses is difficult to control.

The images are, however, not of a 'European' child, and thus relate back to the facticity that the Kurdi situation represents. The images remain pictures of morbid helplessness in the singular. There is no direct appeal to the viewing public, there is no scream of mortal pain. Only a child's body turned away, lifeless, without speech, beyond vulnerability, utterly destitute. It is, then, also the immobility contained within the images that come to define their role in representing adversity. That is the result of being denied legal rights, of abandonment, statelessness without refuge, being stripped of political identity. The images offer an abeyant sense of grievability, acting as a site to express moral sentiment, which has otherwise done little to properly address the vulnerability of life in the situation (see, for example, Butler, 2010). Although the Kurdi images temporarily punctured a general dehumanizing and intolerant discourse, further indicated here is the fact that a single image or small series of images alone cannot represent the scale of suffering and do not shift discourse or transform the reality of the current crisis.

In broader debates regarding photography, Robert Hariman and John Louis Lucaites have described the way in which certain photographs reinforce media conventions related to image–text circumscriptions – that is, fusing 'individual and collective reference to create a symbol: the iconic representation becomes the event itself', having the capacity to simultaneously 'exceed it to create an additional rhetorical power' (Hariman and Lucaites, 2007: 89). As the authors argue, iconic images have the capacity to effect 'public support for state action on behalf of groups of people' and yet this 'often depends on representations of individuated suffering, just as public celebration of state action culminates in representations of individuated benefit', particularly in the symbol's adapted and re-instrumentalized form (ibid.: 88).[3] A related manifestation of this is the way in which the Kurdi images have been restaged in several instances in the realm of visual and political spectacle, frequently at the specific situation's expense.

In January 2016, the French satirical magazine *Charlie Hebdo*, marking the one-year anniversary of an attack on their Paris offices in which 12 people were killed and 11 injured, published a cartoon asking: 'What would little Aylan [sic] have grown up to be?' and speculating, 'An ass groper?' Under the title 'Migrants', an illustration shows two men with pig-like pug noses and hands extended in front of them chasing two women. Further to this, the publication came both in the wake of the

Bataclan concert-hall attacks of 15 November 2015 in the city, for with ISIS claimed responsibility, as well as accusations of a small number of migrants groping women in Cologne on New Year's Eve. The black-and-white illustration also featured a small circle in the upper right of the spread showing a body lying face down on a beach. Argued by the magazine and other organizations as a gesture supporting 'free speech', the cartoon nonetheless perpetuated rather than addressed or challenged derisory stereotypes, framing sexual assault as an issue of acculturation rather than being embedded in society at large (Meade, 2016; Wilkinson 2016; also on the role of this image in the context of graphic novel/comic illustration, see Davies, this volume).

A separate and less caustic example is the artist Ai Weiwei's black-and-white photograph featuring him lying face down on the beach on the Greek shore in Lesbos. The exhibition of the work at the for-profit Indian Art Fair in Delhi, also in January 2016, was interpreted as a misplaced act of 'solidarity', deemed opportunist and criticized as being reminiscent of contemporary brand ideologies aligning themselves with social causes and discourses for commercial purposes (Archey *et al.*, 2016). Yet equally problematic, in my view, is the way in which both controversy and celebration of Ai's work facilitating 'awareness' distract discussion away from Kurdi and away from the ongoing adversities on the southern Turkish coast and even the larger context throughout Turkey, the Middle East and North Africa.

Other artists have, however, responded to the broader situation in ways that foreground discrepancies between mediagenic representations of the crisis and the ongoing experiences of stateless persons. A recent essay film by artist Oliver Ressler, commissioned by the contemporary-art institution SALT in Istanbul, critically addressed the immobility of peoples in multiple informal situations throughout Turkey (also see Loris-Rodionoff, this volume). *There are no Syrian Refugees in Turkey*, 2016, shows long single shots trained on the monuments and relentlessly expanding metropolis of Istanbul. Disembodied voices inform viewers that there are no refugees in the city, nor 'guests' or 'passers-by', but people that have taken jobs and are renting homes. One interviewee discusses the informal labour practices for Syrians, whose working without permits results in low wages and precarious conditions. 'The game', viewers are informed, is all about the Turkish Government and the EU. Exploitation in this setting facilitates resentment among poorer Turkish communities looking for work, while sustained numbers of Syrians in the country present the opportunity for the Turkish Government to threaten to open its land borders should the EU suspend membership discussions.

The disembodiment of voices is offset against the necessity of both anonymity and non-citizenship statuses. As such, particularly pertinent sequences in the film are those that show the extent of construction work fuelling large parts of the city's economy, in which a large number of Syrians workers toil.[4] The alternative, therefore, is to attempt the treacherous crossing to Kos, like Kurdi's family, to reach the EU.

Photography, then, does little to explain what it shows. Yet it demands that questions are asked of it, as to what kind of work is required in conveying meaning (see, for example, Butler, 2010). At the most cynical level, the outside world is less concerned with the death and rather more concerned with the mediagenic value of the circumstances of death. The cliché that photography lends victims or precarious communities and peoples a voice is not true, either of this picture or others showing the suffering of displaced persons. In spite of this, it does provide a lens through which to view the material reality of the current situation. Photographic devastation is implicit every time we look, providing we continue to look: a politics of visuality that demands not only the right to be seen but also that visual forms be properly addressed (see, for example, Mirzoeff, 1999). This, therefore, is not to think about photography as the great pacifier or as effecting the desensitization of viewers to the image of others' suffering, familiar in expressions of despondency and despair.[5] As Susie Linfield suggests to the contrary, 'photographers have robbed us of the alibi of ignorance' (Linfield, 2010: 46). Rather, it is to treat images themselves as traceable agents that urgently require responding to, acting in some sense as antagonists that intercede with popular consciousness and imagination and which might move against the grain of the more ambiguous discursive forces that come to frame them.

The current political environment is conditioned and constructed in a wider politics of denial and the alienation of humanitarian need in which images are playing a number of roles, with the images of Alan Kurdi at its contemporary apex.[6] In situations like this one, rhetoric centred on the distribution of fear and anxiety towards politically precarious populations can undergo a temporary suspension. Viewed through the lens of a digital world of online circulation, the situation increasingly involves a rhetorical governing of the visual, having the effect of stemming (not quelling) dissent. The result, however, is not the mobilization of political forces. The Kurdi images, therefore, embody a temporality that rehearses a *coming-to-terms* with what is seen or represented and a collective apprehension of it. The visual politics involved in the displacement of millions related to greater proxy warfare in the Middle East are necessarily conditioned by putative notions of movement and immobility, propagated not simply on the conflicted site of image production but also in what is claimed and said about it.

In the growing polarized social and political landscape, then, the larger terrain of image production requires scrutiny on the equivalent level of its textual counterparts. That is, the photograph or image as a constituted form operative in an existing political field rather than being accepted as an anaesthetic tool, or lamenting its failing in the expectancy to represent or prompt action in a much broader crisis. Beyond the political rhetoric in which images are frequently framed, therefore, a greater critical mediation of visual politics is called for – to address what is shown, rather than denying or misappropriating it.

## Notes

1. It is worth emphasizing that there were multiple images of Kurdi's body taken by Demir and in circulation, rather than the single image that many other discussions tend to refer to. Though perhaps a little pedantic, the whittling down of the situation to a single image is broadly representative of the general effort to deal with *the image* rather than the scenario, as I attempt to discuss in the following.
2. What is more, such statistics do not take into account multiple other forms of 'refugee' status including wider and ongoing circumstances of forced economic and environmental migration – see discussions by Elliot, and Kelman, both in this volume.
3. Hariman and Lucaites's work draws attention to photographs that have attained iconic status predominantly in the US over the twentieth century and, importantly, their reproduction and reuse in areas from political cartoons to advertisement culture, demonstrating that the predominant effect is to render the original icon ultimately ambiguous in public or collective memory.
4. For a discussion of the role of documentary films in refugee-related research, see Franceschelli and Galipò in this volume.
5. Earlier theories of despair and desensitization were related to, among other things, the advent of for-profit 24-hour news media in the 1980s and repetition without reflection – see, for example, Sontag (2003) and also, in anticipation, Sontag (1977); Barthes (1981).
6. Take as another example the images emerging roughly a year later, around 18 August 2016, showing 5-year-old Omran Daqneesh sat in the back of an ambulance, dazed, bloodied and covered in dust after his home in a rebel-held district of Aleppo was shelled. As one journalist who filmed the incident, Mustafa al-Sarout, commented, such circumstances were hardly unique. Yet it was the vulnerability of a child in utter shock that most likely brought this image into wide circulation. See Shaheen (2016).

## References

Achcar, Gilbert. 2016. *Morbid Symptoms: Relapse in the Arab Uprising*. London: Saqi Books.
Al Jazeera. 2017. 'PM Hariri: Lebanon at "Breaking Point" Due to Refugees', *Al Jazeera*, 1 April. Accessed 1 December 2017. www.aljazeera.com/news/2017/04/saad-al-hariri-lebanon-big-refugee-camp-170401045951087.html.

Archey, Karen, *et al*. 2016. 'For Photo Op, Ai Weiwei Poses as Dead Refugee Toddler from Iconic Image', *e-flux conversations*, February. Accessed 1 December 2017. http://conversations.e-flux.com/t/for-photo-op-ai-weiwei-poses-as-dead-refugee-toddler-from-iconic-image/3169.

Ashdown, Paddy. 2015. 'Cameron's Offer of 20,000 Syrian Refugees over Five Years is Derisory', *The Guardian*, 7 September. Accessed 1 December 2017. www.theguardian.com/commentisfree/2015/sep/07/cameron-20000-syrian-refugees-offer-derisory.

Barthes, Roland. 1981. *Camera Lucida: Reflections on Photography*, translated by Richard Howard. New York: Hill and Wang.

BBC News. 2015. 'Migrant Crisis: Hungary Declares Emergency at Serbia Border', *BBC News*, 15 September. Accessed 1 December 2017. www.bbc.co.uk/news/world-europe–34252812.

Butler, Judith. 2010. *Frames of War: When is Life Grievable?* London: Verso.

Dathan, Matt. 2015. 'Aylan Kurdi: David Cameron Says He Felt "Deeply Moved" by Images of Dead Syrian Boy but Gives No Details of Plans to Take in More Refugees', *The Independent*, 3 September. Accessed 1 December 2017. www.independent.co.uk/news/uk/politics/aylan-kurdi-david-cameron-says-he-felt-deeply-moved-by-images-of-dead-syrian-boy-but-gives-no-10484641.html.

EJO (European Journalism Observatory). 2015. 'Research: How Europe's Newspapers Reported the Migration Crisis'. Accessed 1 December 2017. http://en.ejo.ch/research/research-how-europes-newspapers-reported-the-migration-crisis.

Fantz, Ashley and Catherine E. Shoichet. 2015. 'Syrian Toddler's Dad: "Everything I Was Dreaming of is Gone"', *CNN*, 4 September. Accessed 1 December 2017. http://edition.cnn.com/2015/09/03/europe/migration-crisis-aylan-kurdi-turkey-canada/.

Fiddian-Qasmiyeh, Elena. 2017a. 'The Faith–Gender–Asylum Nexus: An Intersectionalist Analysis of Representations of the "Refugee Crisis"'. In *The Refugee Crisis and Religion: Secularism, Security and Hospitality in Question*, edited by Luca Mavelli and Erin K. Wilson, 207–22. London: Rowman and Littlefield International.

Fiddian-Qasmiyeh, Elena. 2017b. 'Syrian Refugees in Turkey, Jordan and Lebanon Face an Uncertain 2017', *The Conversation*, 3 January. Accessed 1 December 2017. https://theconversation.com/syrian-refugees-in-turkey-jordan-and-lebanon-face-an-uncertain-2017-70747.

*Guardian* . 2015. 'Saudi Arabia Says Criticism of Syria Refugee Response "False and Misleading"', 12 September. Accessed 1 December 2017. www.theguardian.com/world/2015/sep/12/saudi-arabia-says-reports-of-its-syrian-refugee-response-false-and-misleading.

Hariman, Robert and John Louis Lucaites. 2007. *No Caption Needed: Iconic Photographs, Public Culture, and Liberal Democracy*. Chicago: University of Chicago Press.

IOM (International Organization for Migration). 2016. 'IOM Counts 3,771 Migrant Fatalities in Mediterranean in 2015'. Press release, 1 May. Accessed 1 December 2017. www.iom.int/news/iom-counts-3771-migrant-fatalities-mediterranean-2015.

Laurent, Olivier. 2015. 'What the Image of Aylan Kurdi Says about the Power of Photography', *Time*, 4 September. Accessed 1 December 2017. http://time.com/4022765/aylan-kurdi-photo/.

Linfield, Susie. 2010. *The Cruel Radiance: Photography and Political Violence*. Chicago: University of Chicago Press.

Meade, Amanda. 2016. 'Charlie Hebdo Cartoon Depicting Drowned Child Alan Kurdi Sparks Racism Debate', *The Guardian*, 14 January. Accessed 1 December 2017. www.theguardian.com/media/2016/jan/14/charlie-hebdo-cartoon-depicting-drowned-child-alan-kurdi-sparks-racism-debate.

Mirzoeff, Nicholas. 1999. *An Introduction to Visual Culture*. London: Routledge.

Oltermann, Philip. 2016. 'Angela Merkel Endorses Party's Call for Partial Ban on Burqa and Niqab', *The Guardian*, 6 December. Accessed 1 December 2017. www.theguardian.com/world/2016/dec/06/angela-merkel-cdu-partial-ban-burqa-niqab-german.

Press Association. 2015. 'Alan Kurdi Image Appeared on 20m Screens in Just 12 Hours', *The Guardian*, 15 December. Accessed 1 December 2017. www.theguardian.com/media/2015/dec/15/alan-kurdi-image-appeared-on-20m-screens-in-just-12-hours.

Sawah, Wael and Salam Kawakibi. 2014. 'Activism in Syria: Between Nonviolence and Armed Resistance'. In *Taking to the Streets: The Transformation of Arab Activism*, edited by Lina Khatib and Ellen Lust, 136–71. Baltimore: Johns Hopkins University Press.

Shaheen, Kareem. 2016. '"I Filmed the Syrian Boy Pulled from the Rubble – His Wasn't a Rare Case"', *The Guardian*, 18 August. Accessed 1 December 2017. www.theguardian.com/world/2016/aug/18/i-filmed-the-syrian-boy-pulled-from-the-rubble-his-wasnt-a-rare-case.

Sontag, Susan. 1977. *On Photography*. New York: Farrar, Straus and Giroux.

Sontag, Susan. 2003. *Regarding the Pain of Others*. London: Hamish Hamilton.

Squires, Nick. 2015. 'Police Officer Who Found Syrian Toddler: "I Prayed He Was Still Alive"', *The Telegraph*, 6 September. Accessed 1 December 2017. www.telegraph.co.uk/news/worldnews/europe/turkey/11847321/Police-officer-who-found-Syrian-toddler-I-prayed-he-was-still-alive.html.

Tazzioli, Martina. 2015. *Spaces of Governmentality: Autonomous Migration and the Arab Uprisings*. London: Rowman and Littlefield International.

UNHCR (United Nations High Commissioner for Refugees). 2015. *World at War: UNHCR Global Trends: Forced Displacement in 2014*. Geneva: United Nations High Commissioner for Refugees. Accessed 1 December 2017. www.unhcr.org/556725e69.pdf.

UNHCR (United Nations High Commissioner for Refugees). 2016. *Global Trends: Forced Displacement in 2015*. Geneva: United Nations High Commissioner for Refugees. Accessed 1 December 2017. www.unhcr.org/uk/statistics/unhcrstats/576408cd7/unhcr-global-trends-2015.html.

Weaver, Matthew and Haroon Siddique. 2015. 'Clashes at Border with Serbia as Croatia Says It Cannot Take More Refugees – as It Happened', *The Guardian*, 17 September. Accessed 1 December 2017. www.theguardian.com/world/live/2015/sep/17/refugee-crisis-thousands-enter-croatia-after-hungarys-crackdown-live-updates.

Wilkinson, Abi (2016). 'The White Knight Delusion,' *The Baffler*, 23 February. Online. https://thebaffler.com/latest/cologne-rape-muslim-refugees (accessed 1 December 2017).

# 13
# Crossing borders, bridging boundaries: Reconstructing the rights of the refugee in comics

Dominic Davies

> Europe's birthplace, the Mediterranean, has now become the set-
> ting of its greatest failure ... No other journalists have dared take a
> boat from Egypt, and we are aware of the dangers. We each carry
> a satellite phone to notify the Italian coastguard in an emergency.
> We decided against setting out from Libya or Tunisia. For though
> both are closer to Italy, the boats used there are extremely rickety.
> Egyptian smugglers have to cover a larger distance, so they use bet-
> ter ships. At least that was our hope. We were naive. We thought the
> sea would be the greatest hazard. In fact, it was just one of many.
>
> (Bauer, 2016: 12)

As media coverage of Europe's refugee 'crisis' reached its hysterical apo-
gee in the early months of 2016, German journalist Wolfgang Bauer published these words in the introduction to his journalistic non-fiction book,
*Crossing the Sea with Syrians on the Exodus to Europe* (2016). Accompanied by Czech photographer Stanislav Krupař, Bauer documents his
attempts to 'experience' first-hand, as well as to 'visualize' through photographs, the crossing of the Mediterranean Sea as it has been – and will
continue to be – undertaken by displaced people from Africa and the
Middle East. Though of course migration to Europe is 'by no means new',
in 2014 and 2015 'around 1.2 million people crossed the Mediterranean
in leaking boats' and the European Union estimates that 'between 2016
and 2018 over 3 million more could follow' (Kingsley, 2016: 4–5). Bauer's book reproduces many of the tropes typical of humanitarian-disaster

narratives, particularly those that have arisen in response to this latest crisis. These narratives attempt to mobilize empathy in their readerships and thus to lever tangible political action that translates into a less hostile, more hospitable reception of refugees by host populations – particularly in Western European countries (see, for example, Kingsley, 2015, 2016; Smith *et al.*, 2016; McDonald-Gibson, 2016). They therefore cut against the explicit prejudices that have increasingly shaped representations of migrants and refugees in mainstream-media coverage and public and political discourse in recent years (see Jones, Reece, 2016: 3). It is necessary to understand this representational context in order to see how, as the second half of this chapter will go on to argue, testimonial *comics* – which differ from written journalistic non-fiction or single photographs by combining both visual and narrative components – might be especially effective at reconstructing the human rights of the (particularly Syrian) refugee.[1]

Bauer's intention is to convey with verifiable accuracy – indicated by his prioritization of first-hand experience and inclusion of accompanying photographs – the experience of the migrants as they navigate the crossing of the Mediterranean Sea. Indeed, Bauer emphasizes his efforts to experience *directly*, on behalf of his reader, this most dangerous section of the refugee's journey, writing in the present tense in order to foreground the immediacy both of his and, by proxy, his readers' experience. However, Bauer's attempt to undertake this most perilous section of the journey – the crossing itself – ends in failure, thwarted by the Egyptian coastguard. This means that while *Crossing the Sea* includes photographs taken by Krupař of the (mostly) young Syrian men getting ready for the crossing in Egypt, of the smuggler's buses and boats, the inside of Alexandria prison in Egypt, and the reunited families in Sweden and Germany, notably absent are any photographs of the event of the crossing itself. In the book's conclusion, Bauer shifts from the specific stories of the individuals that he follows to a final polemic plea for a more 'humane' response to migrants and refugees in Western Europe by host governments and populations alike.[2] *Crossing the Sea* is therefore indicative of three tendencies in journalistic documentations of refugee narratives: first, the importance of the photograph in order to verify the refugee experience; second, the obsessive requirement for first-hand accounts, or testimonies, that similarly validate the authenticity of the account of the journey; and, finally, the need for narrative continuity, which plots the migrant's journey along an arc that identifies beginning and end with departure and arrival respectively.

All of these attributes are designed to bring readers closer to the subjective experience of refugees and, through that closeness, to *humanize* the figure of the refugee. That is, they seek to reframe refugees not as displaced *citizens* but as humans who are, subsequently, entitled to human rights. By restricting human movement between nation states, national borders position the rights of the citizen over the rights of the human; subsequently, by allowing different citizenries to be valued differently, national borders necessarily deem some people to be 'more human' or 'less human' than others (Jones, Reece, 2016: 81). 'The migrant has been vilified, considered to be a deviation from the norm', writes Nadine El-Enany, that 'norm being a system of nation states' (El-Enany, 2015: 8). Refugee narratives that are self-consciously geared towards the construction of empathetic solidarity between host populations and arriving displaced peoples attempt to escape this prevalent conception of the refugee as citizen of another nation state, and thus as an interloper in the receiving nation not necessarily entitled to citizen's rights. They do this by emphasizing the humanity of the refugee, reconstructing refugees as humans entitled to their universal – that is, borderless – human rights. If accounts such as Bauer's do not always conclude with the safe arrival of the refugee, this lack of closure cuts against a sense of narrative resolution and in so doing creates a discomfort that can be mobilized into tangible political action.

That Bauer's book was published in the early months of 2016 is significant, and is indicatively the same moment in which the comics with which this chapter is concerned were also researched, written, drawn and published. Efforts such as Bauer's to convey the experience of the migrant seeking refuge in Europe attempted to capitalize on an increased public receptivity that developed when 'the violence of the borders of the EU burst onto the international news through a series of visually shocking stories' in August and September 2015 (Jones, Reece, 2016: 18). Notable among these were the 'shocking images' of Alan Kurdi, a drowned toddler whose body was photographed, washed up on a beach in the Turkish resort of Bodrum on 2 September 2015 (Smith, 2015). This photograph 'went viral and focused the world's attention on the plight of Syria's refugees', and the momentary flood of public outrage in the UK and across Western Europe looked as though it might translate into political action – namely, through larger refugee-acceptance quotas, but also the development of more hospitable policies towards asylum seekers generally. 'At first, the world responded with sympathy', as the 'UK promised to take in 20,000 Syrians; France, 24,000, while Germany temporarily opened its doors without conditions' (Khan, 2015). It seemed that the photograph, by foregrounding the humanity of the refugee *child* – a figure deemed, unlike the adult refugee, innocent and more amenable to cultural assimilation than terrorist threat, benefit scrounger or job stealer – had, despite these discursive qualifiers, finally begun to garner the political response that the refugee crisis so desperately required.

However, in the following weeks the photograph 'was endlessly re-contextualized in memes, morphing and re-morphing on the internet. Some criticized world leaders for failing to act; others condemned [Abdullah Kurdi, Alan's father] himself for putting his child in such a dangerous situation' – an assertion itself indicative of public ignorance around social conditions driving forced migration (Khan, 2015). Further controversies included accusations that the photograph had been faked, that Abdullah Kurdi may himself have been a people smuggler, and even that he 'was profiting from the tragedy' by 'selling his dead son's clothes to a museum in Paris' – absurd stories that, though all swiftly refuted, stuck to the pervasive anti-migrant rhetoric of politicians and pundits alike (Khan, 2015; also see Fiddian-Qasmiyeh 2017).

By June 2016, Kurdi's photograph was all but forgotten, as coverage of migrant populations in Western media outlets was tainted – if not entirely overshadowed – by larger geopolitical shifts, most notably the anti-migrant discourse that flourished in the build-up to Britain's vote to exit the European Union (and, in the following months, Donald Trump's presidential campaign and subsequent election in the United States). This notable shift in media coverage and public consciousness was symbolically encapsulated in another image: a poster released by UK Independence Party leader Nigel Farage that, by depicting hundreds of Syrian refugees arriving in Slovenia in 2015 beneath the words 'Breaking Point, the EU has failed us all', cynically conflated the principle of free movement within the European Union with the refugee crisis in the Mediterranean. As journalist Jonathan Jones pointed out, the poster was 'graphically emotional, as only visual images can be. It portrays an oncoming tide of outsiders at our gate – and they are not European faces. To put it more bluntly they are not white faces' (Jones, Jonathan, 2016). It eradicated the humanity of refugees by emphasizing their 'otherness', epitomizing the more general media, political and public discursive construction of the migrant as 'the vacant point around which ideals clash'; as Hanif Kureishi writes, 'everyone ... has made up their mind that the immigrant is everywhere now, and he is too much of a problem' (Kureishi, 2016: 27–9).

Undoubtedly, the role of photography in twenty-first-century visual culture is changing. For Jean Baudrillard, in the new 'media hyperspace' of 24-hour news channels and the internet, photographic images – especially of conflict and war – have become mundane (Baudrillard, 2000: 50). While news consumers still expect photographic documentation as verifiable evidence for humanitarian disasters, the subsequent bombardment of images of human suffering actually function, Baudrillard continues, to make the events themselves 'more or less ephemeral' (ibid.: 50). This is a sentiment shared by Susan Sontag in her landmark study, *Regarding the Pain of Others* (2003), as wars become 'living room sights and sounds' and the 'catastrophe that is experienced will often seem eerily like its representation' (Sontag, 2003: 18, 21). As Judith Butler explains, Sontag fears 'that photography has lost its capacity to shock, that shock itself has become a kind of cliché, and that photography tends to aestheticize suffering to satisfy a consumer demand' (Butler, 2005: 824). Yet Butler maintains that 'the photograph still interprets the reality that it registers, ... even when it works as evidence for another interpretation that takes place in written or verbal form' (ibid.). That is, the photograph is itself an interpretation, even as it attempts to eradicate its selective framing – both visually and ideologically – through its claim to truthful representation. Theorist of photography Ariella Azoulay is similarly attuned to the fact that 'weak populations remain more exposed to photography, especially of the journalistic kind, which coerces and confines them to a passive, unprotected position' (Azoulay, 2008: 110). However, Azoulay remains more optimistically convinced that photographs are still able to create cross-border solidarity, so that 'what happens "there" is of interest not only to those concerned with it – those who've been struck by disaster – but to onlookers the world over' (ibid.: 99) – an argument to which I will return in this chapter's concluding paragraphs.

It is into this visual culture, both of imagistic ephemerality and of prevalent anti-migrant sentiment, that comics effectively intervene. Indeed, I have outlined these conditions at length because they might begin to explain the recent and sudden surge of the use of comics to document, journalistically, the plight of refugees and migrants in recent years, not to mention other humanitarian disasters. In the age of the internet, viewers in the West are trained on a daily basis to make sense of multiple images spliced with pieces of text, as they log onto Facebook feeds or scan through Twitter. Comics, especially those published online (as is the case for these refugee comics), tap into this constant stream of information, harnessing the experience of information transmission and consumption to which viewers are becoming increasingly accustomed (Gardner, 2006). In addition, however, journalism in comics form is able to do two things: first, it can document suffering that goes un-photographed. It imaginatively visualizes oral and written testimonies in order to document human-rights violations, lending them the 'authenticity' that contemporary news outlets and consumers demand (Smith, 2011). Second, and perhaps even more importantly, comics' sequential and highly mediated form offers an antidote to the 'post-truth' culture of our contemporary world (Mickwitz, 2016), in which photographs are detached from their original context, circulate at lightning speed through multiple framings and re-framings, and are often mobilized towards dubious political ends. The laboured etchings of comics journalism offer an antidote not only to the *lack* of visualization but also the decontextualization of photographic images that, in their proliferation, are reduced to insignificance.

The combination of comics and journalism was pioneered by Joe Sacco in the 1990s and early 2000s, as he collected personal testimonies from victims of conflicts in war zones from Gaza to Sarajevo (Sacco, 2003, 2007). Although comics critic Hillary Chute, in her book *Disaster Drawn*, offers a 'longer genealogy' of the historical relationship between comics and documentary form (Chute, 2016: 5), it is surely no coincidence that Sacco begins documenting human-rights abuses in comics at almost exactly the same time that Baudrillard identifies the transformation of conflict into 'a hyper-real, media-filtered experience' (Knowles *et al.*, 2016: 46–7). As the photographic image circulates with increased speed, its authenticity undermined by the editing capabilities of software such as Photoshop, the laboured depiction of an event in comics form – which, by definition, contextualizes each image alongside others within its sequential-narrative structure – is becoming increasingly popular. Comics slow down a visual culture of proliferating decontextualized images of violence and suffering, the drawn image disrupting the photographic reality to which viewers have become accustomed. Meanwhile, the narratives that comics relate are constructed as much through what is *not* represented, in the gaps between panels, as they are through the drawings that they actually include. They therefore demand a participatory effort on the part of the reader, who has to link up the images that are organized sequentially in order to make sense of the narrative. The comic therefore forces a cognitive engagement with the issues that the journalism explores. Finally, if the internet is a fundamental infrastructure for today's media hyperspace, comics artists too have harnessed the web to reduce their production costs and to reach wider readerships. Comics now document all kinds of human-rights crises in the twenty-first century, from protests in Hong Kong and the aftermath of the earthquake in Nepal to conditions for Bangladeshi factory workers and, of particular concern for this chapter, the plight of Syrian refugees (Mickwitz, forthcoming; Rifkind, 2017, forthcoming).

If only because of the laborious processes of production, then, journalism in comics form offers news in a 'slower time' that contrasts with 'the 24-hour news cycle' and the relentless Twitter and Facebook feed (Orbán, 2015: 124). This slower temporality 'explains why', argues comics critic Katalin Orbán, 'graphic reportage is drawn to wars and conflict particularly in the form of aftermath reportage', taking 'the long view of the consequences of complex and often lasting situations, geopolitical quagmires, long-term ecological processes' and so on (ibid.: 124). Meanwhile, comics' accessibility – attractive image rather than dense prose – allows for 'civic education through information, empathy, and mobilisation' in diverse readerships (Banita, 2013: 51). Constructed from borders and gaps of their own, comics are especially adept at communicating stories across all kinds of linguistic and cultural borders – but especially, I have argued, national ones (Davies, 2019: 259–66). National borders promote citizens' rights over human rights, relativizing the humanity of other citizenries and removing it from those deprived of citizenship through displacement. Conversely, comics, as both a bordered and cross-border form, recover the humanity of displaced people and, in so doing, foreground their rights as human beings. They supply both a visual and a narrative continuity that written or photographic journalism alone often cannot. Meanwhile, their slower time frame conveys a structural understanding of the underlying causes of the humanitarian disasters that they depict, even as they do so through the documentation of individual human experiences.

Comics journalist Josh Neufeld is now one of the world's best established comics journalists, most famous for his long-form comic, *A.D. New Orleans After the Deluge* (Neufeld, 2010), which documents the testimonies of several victims of Hurricane Katrina in New Orleans back in 2005 – a humanitarian crisis of a different kind, the media coverage of which was, however, similarly obsessed with the circulation of striking though often decontextualized visual images of displaced people. For Neufeld, comics are able to 'recreate or bring a scene to life that you wouldn't possibly have been able to witness as the reporter'; but 'what comics can do really effectively in telling journalistic stories is [to make] the reader identify with the protagonists of the stories, and almost put yourself in their place' (Bricker 2016). Neufeld's comic, 'The Road to Germany: $2400', produced in collaboration with journalist and civil-rights lawyer Alia Malek, who collected the testimonies of several Syrian refugees, was published in *Foreign Policy* magazine in the first months of 2016 (Malek and Neufeld, 2016). The idea of conveying

Malek's journalistic research in comics form was inspired by 'a flowchart' that mapped out 'the route from Turkey to Germany' for $2,400, and that was shared via smartphone between Syrian asylum seekers attempting the journey. The fact that sections of this graphic template intervene into Neufeld's comic as panels in their own right repeatedly reminds readers that each individual page conveys only a moment in the broader narrative trajectory of the refugees' journey as a whole. Every image reproduced in the comic is thus emphatically contextualized within a larger narrative arc of the crossing from Turkey to Western Europe.

Importantly, comics can depict scenes from the journey that have not been captured on reliable or good-quality photographs, and Neufeld's first panel throws readers into a scene in which refugees are caught on a defunct boat. The accompanying text locates the scene in 'the Aegean Sea, off the coast of Bodrum, Turkey', implicitly connecting these traumatic images to the photograph of Alan Kurdi. Neufeld stresses that he draws these scenes from first-hand accounts and compilations of witness testimonies – the preface informs readers that even the comic's speech bubbles are direct quotations, or at least paraphrases of direct quotations. As part of this effort to lend the refugee narrative a visual, and thus verifiable, continuity, when reliable photographs are available to the reporters these are interspersed as panels into the drawn graphics. The sudden contrast of drawn and photographic image not only jars the reader into acknowledging the reality of the refugees' experience. It also performs a self-reflexive turn: the sharp distinction between the 'hyper-real' image of the photograph and the obviously 'unreal' image of the drawing highlight the comic's 'mediation-conscious reportage' (Obán 2015, 124), asking the reader to think more carefully about the photograph's context rather than passively consuming it (see Pedri 2017).

This effect is then compounded by the sequential dimension of the comic. As Shane Denson observes, 'visual, material, and narrative frames of various scales and orders irreducibly structure graphic texts, parse their units of significance, and condition the dynamics of their reading', as comics explicitly participate not only in 'naming' but also 'framing' their representations of refugees (2014, 271). Through its formal architecture of borders and panels, readers are asked to actively participate in the threading together of the different segments of the refugees' journey, but also to reflect on what is being presented and, conversely, omitted. Arguably, this self-reflexive, participatory component of the comic might even alert readers to the fact that they are not simply observers of the protagonists' predicament but, as citizens in host countries, are themselves complicit in the structures – namely, militantly regulated national borders – that make the refugees' journey so perilous. Comics journalism, like any other kind of journalism, 'allows distant publics to inform themselves', certainly, but in so doing it also demands from them a 'more contemplative kind of looking' (Orbán, 2015: 127–8).

The second example I want to address here is a trilogy of three testimonial comics compiled by the PositiveNegatives Project, a non-profit-making organization that, like Neufeld, works in collaboration with other NGOs and media organizations to 'combine in-depth ethnographic research with illustration and photography' in order to adapt 'personal testimonies into art, education and advocacy materials' ('PositiveNegatives'). The resulting stories, which 'are adapted directly from first-hand interviews', are designed to educate readers about the reasons driving Syrians out of their country and the difficulties that they face on the journey to Europe. Reproduced in the *Guardian* and *Aftenposten* newspapers, and exhibited at the Nobel Peace Centre in Oslo at the end of 2015 and at the Brunei Gallery at the School of Oriental and African Studies, University of London in 2017, these comics have circulated widely, albeit in already predominantly liberal forums. As for humanitarian refugee narratives such as Bauer's, these comics are self-consciously designed to generate empathy in host populations.

However, several of the stories that the PositiveNegatives depict trouble the simplistic narrative arc of departure and arrival as beginning and end of the refugee story, adding a further layer of complexity to the migrant experience. They begin their narratives with panels depicting their refugee protagonists negotiating the realities of living as a displaced person in a host country. The unique spatial layout of the comics form is then used to intersperse these day-to-day experiences with the traumatic moments of the refugees' 'perilous journeys', many of which have not been documented photographically – most notably, again, these include the actual crossing of the Mediterranean, but also scenes of torture in Syria (see Figure 13.1). This emphasizes not only the difficulty of the journey itself but also the process of integration into the host country after the refugees' arrival. In so doing, they foreground the need for an ongoing hospitable rather than hostile reception for Syrians even after they have received their refugee status. They plot for the reader a careful route across the multiple panels of which the comic is composed, thereby conflating the borders of the panels and the borders of countries, as well as the numerous physical and bureaucratic barriers that the narratives' protagonists are negotiating. As the reader crosses the borders of the comic, then, they are also asked to transcend the national borders that position one citizenry's rights over another's and that thus deny the refugees their rights as human beings.

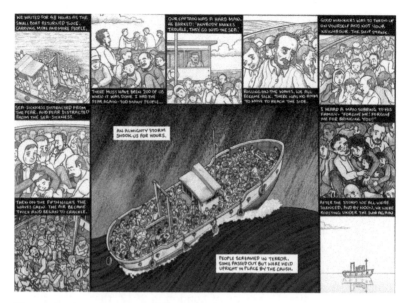

**Figure 13.1**  A large panel from the first story in PositiveNegatives'
'Perilous Journey' trilogy, which depicts migrants aboard a rickety boat
in a storm as they cross the Mediterranean. CC BY-NC-ND.

As with Neufeld's comic, PositiveNegatives assimilate photographic
material into their sequential narratives. However, rather than including these photographic images sporadically throughout the comic, the
stories are told entirely in graphic form before then concluding with
one single photographic image of its refugee protagonist (see Figure
13.2). These photographs sometimes conspicuously avoid showing the
asylum seekers' faces in order to protect their identities – some of them
are still caught in the hostile webs of bureaucratic asylum claims in host
countries and fear for their lives should they be deported back to Syria.
But the result of this sudden and jarring visual conclusion – the spatio-
temporal location of the photograph at the end of the comic – is to even
more forcefully foreground the humanity of the refugee, even as the photographic image also works to verify the various testimonies that have
been related. By conveying the narrative context that leads up to this
final photograph, the comic lends it the sociopolitical weight of much
more shocking photographs such as that of Alan Kurdi. It demands from
readers the empathetic, compassionate response that the refugee crisis
so desperately requires, whilst nevertheless protecting the images from
decontextualization and accusations of falsehood.

Mohammad is still anxiously waiting for a decision to be made under the Dublin agreement if he will be returned to Hungary.

**Figure 13.2**   The concluding panel from the second story in PositiveNegatives's 'Perilous Journey' trilogy, which includes a photograph of its refugee protagonist, Mohammad, yet without revealing his identity. CC BY-NC-ND.

Despite these optimistic claims, it is not my intention to argue that the comics form is *inherently* able to cultivate cross-cultural empathy and understanding, as many have done (see, for example, Polak, 2017). Even as Chute celebrates the fact that comics have 'become a form of almost instantaneous dissemination and accessibility', she also acknowledges that, recently, 'cartoons have been at the centre of major international controversies over images' (Chute, 2016: 256, 265) – consider 'the publication of twelve controversial images of Muhammed in cartoons in 2005 ... through which the Danish newspaper *Jyllands-Posten* inspired world-wide protest', or the similar depiction of the Prophet by the artists at *Charlie Hebdo* and the violent terrorist retaliation in 2015 (Robb and Wanzo, 2010: 212). But there remain dynamics at work in comics that make them particularly adept at reconstructing the human rights of dehumanized populations, and facilitating a borderless solidarity and empathetic community. 'Drawing today still enters the public sphere as a form of witness that takes shape as marks and lines because no other technology could record what it depicts' (Chute, 2016: 265), certainly, but comics also, 'through their distribution of spatial relations, [offer] a potentiality to expose and critique the power inherent in spatial constructions' (Cortsen and La Cour, 2015: 104). Comics' self-reflexive critical capacity, which is concealed by the single, selectively framed photograph, means not simply that comics' 'current power ... is undiminished even in our current age of the camera and digital media' (Chute, 2016: 256–7) but rather that comics' power in fact derives from the alternative modes of looking that the form demands.

As these examples suggest, then, comics journalism has in its repertoire a set of visual-textual strategies that can be deployed to consolidate a much-needed empathetic solidarity between readers in Western Europe and arriving refugees, foregrounding their humanity in order to emphasize their rights as human beings. However, I want to conclude this chapter by suggesting that comics might actually offer a further nuance through their representation of the refugee, one still concerned with the reconstruction of their human rights but that tackles also the potentially damaging hypocrisies of liberal responses both to the refugee crisis and migration more generally. As discussed, while the assimilation of photographic material into these comics might be intended to 'verify' the drawn images, it simultaneously foregrounds the highly mediated form of those drawings. In so doing, even as these comics generate an empathetic solidarity between reader and refugee, they simultaneously emphasize the 'strangeness' of the refugee and the incomprehensibility of their traumatic experience. This has implications for the universalism assumed by Western multicultural liberalism and that is, for a number of commentators, in part responsible for failed attempts at empathy by host communities. If multiculturalism has 'become the container into which Western European nations have poured anxieties whose origins often lie in social and economic changes that are considerably wider than those stemming from the consequences of immigration and multiculturalist policies' (Rattansi, 2011: 5), then the multicultural society – embodied in the figure of the migrant – has come to provide 'a site on which the ontological parameters and political rhetorics derived from the "new" racisms have been laundered' (Lentin and Titley, 2011: 16). Instead, Slavoj Žižek emphasizes the fact that the 'universal dimension is to be sought beyond sympathy and understanding, beyond the "we're all human" level: at another level, which should be designated precisely that of the *inhuman* neighbour' (Žižek, 2016: 77). For Žižek, 'the privileged way to reach a Neighbour is not that of empathy, of trying to understand them, but a disrespectful laughter which makes fun both of them and of us in our mutual lack of (self-)understanding' (ibid.: 79).

By representing refugees in a highly mediated form (a mediation emphasized by the contrast between the drawn image and the apparent verisimilitude of the photograph), these comics actually cut against the grain of self-consciously humanizing narratives such as Bauer's, instead quite literally *de*-humanizing the refugee – after all, visually, refugees are reduced to drawn caricatures, despite the intricacies of the narratives that are related. These comics might be said to quite literally make the figure of the refugee 'inhuman'. Nevertheless, the corresponding effect is not to strip them of their human rights; despite the visual 'strangeness' of the comics characters, the narrative of their 'perilous journey' is still conveyed. Rather, by combining not only two, but *three* contrasting components – visual immediacy (photograph), sustained narrative (plot/testimony) and self-reflexively mediated image (drawing) – these comics are able to emphasize the refugee's difference while simultaneously encouraging host readerships to welcome them as neighbours. They ask their predominantly liberal readerships not simply to contemplate their own location in relation to the arriving asylum seeker but to work through the limitations underpinning the stifling binary political debate – with open borders and racist nationalisms at its two extremes – that dominates mainstream-media coverage of the crisis and discourse around migration more broadly.

I therefore want to conclude by suggesting that the cross-border solidarity and cross-national community that these comics seek to construct might be comparable to, and even an extension of, Ariella Azoulay's concept of the 'citizenship of photography':

> Citizens actualise their duty toward other citizens as photographed persons who've been struck by disaster. The exercise of photography in such situations is actually the exercise of citizenship – not citizenship imprinted with the seal of belonging to a sovereign, but citizenship as a partnership of governed persons taking up their duty as citizens … The camera recognises them as citizens of what I call the citizenry of photograph. (Azoulay, 2008: 99)

While I am more ambivalent about the power of photography to cultivate a cross-national citizenry, by contextualizing the photographic images of refugees with drawn panels the comic is able 'to make them speak', to use

Azoulay's phrase (ibid.: 114), thereby creating a simultaneity of reading experience that encourages cross-border solidarity – or cross-national empathy – through the acceptance of the stranger. That is, in recognizing the humanity of the refugee while also respecting *and accepting* their difference, the reader – as 'citizen' of the host country – is encouraged 'to break away from his or her *status* as citizen and *exercise* citizenship – that is, to turn citizenship into the arena of a constant becoming, together with other (non)citizens' (ibid.: 111). This emphasis on the acceptance of the non-citizen counters what Zygmunt Bauman describes as modernity's liquid 'reality', whereby 'strangers are such people with whom one refuses to talk', and which has led to a 'united front' against '"immigrants", that fullest and most tangible embodiment of "otherness"' (Bauman, 2000: 109; see also Bauman, 2016). Clearly, written accounts and photographic documentation are fundamental in this wider effort to recover and reconstruct the humanity of refugees, and thus to remind readers of the human rights to which refugees are entitled. But comics' multifaceted form – or 'inherently multicultural form, given that the modes of representation that it has available to it implicate both cultures of images and cultures of words' (Ayaka and Hague, 2015: 3) – offers a further insight into the cultivation of a cross-national, borderless citizenship as it is constructed through images (see Davies, 2018). Comics not only reconstruct the rights of the refugee but also reveal that, as Kureishi observes more widely, 'the stranger, with a mixture of naivety and knowing, might be in a position to tell us the truth about ourselves, since he sees more than we know' (Kureishi, 2016: 30).

## Notes

1. This chapter can be usefully read in conjunction with the contributions, also in this volume, by Snow, Hoffman *et al.*, and Qasmiyeh.

2. Given the limited scope of this chapter, I use the terms 'migrants' and 'refugees' more or less interchangeably throughout. The simplistic, binary categorization of moving people into the definitions of either 'asylum seekers' and 'refugees', on the one hand, and 'migrants' on the other obscures the structural violence of poverty that forces many to seek refuge in Europe. This is by no means to downplay the violence of civil wars that have been a major factor in the displacement of Syrians and others to Europe. Rather, it is to emphasize the fact that numerous migrants – though not fleeing the obvious, 'directly visible' violence of conflict – do not travel to Europe out of any simplistic, self-interested 'choice' but because they are subject to the equally 'catastrophic consequences of the smooth functioning of our economic and political systems' (see Žižek, 2008). As Reece Jones observes, 'In the current system, a refugee fleeing political persecution is more legitimate than a migrant fleeing a life in a filthy, crowded, disease-ridden, and dangerous slum where the only option is to work long hours in a sweatshop for very low wages. Focusing only on the limited, state-defined term refugee renders other categories of migrants, who are moving for economic or environmental reasons, as undeserving of help or sympathy' (2016: 22–3). The latter reasons are also explored by Elliot, and Kelman, both in this volume.

# References

Ayaka, Carolene and Ian Hague. 2015. 'Introduction: Representing Multiculturalism in Comics and Graphic Novels'. In *Representing Multiculturalism in Comics and Graphic Novels*, edited by Carolene Ayaka and Ian Hague, 1–16. New York: Routledge.

Azoulay, Ariella. 2008. *The Civil Contract of Photography*. New York: Zone Books.

Banita, Georgiana. 2013. 'Cosmopolitan Suspicion: Comics Journalism and Graphic Silence'. In *Transnational Perspectives on Graphic Narratives: Comics at the Crossroads*, edited by Shane Denson, Christina Meyer and Daniel Stein, 49–65. London: Bloomsbury Academic.

Baudrillard, Jean. 2000. *The Vital Illusion*, edited by Julia Witwer. New York: Columbia University Press.

Bauer, Wolfgang. 2016. *Crossing the Sea with Syrians on the Exodus to Europe*, translated by Sarah Pybus. High Wycombe: And Other Stories.

Bauman, Zygmunt. 2000. *Liquid Modernity*. Cambridge: Polity Press.

Bauman, Zygmunt. 2016. *Strangers at Our Door*. Cambridge: Polity Press.

Bricker, Mindy Kay. 2016. 'The Power of Narrative Comics', *Foreign Policy: The Backstory* podcast, 29 January. Accessed 27 March 2017. http://foreignpolicy.com/2016/01/29/the-power-of-narrative-comics/.

Butler, Judith. 2005. 'Photography, War, Outrage', *PMLA* 120 (3): 822–27.

Chute, Hillary L. 2016. *Disaster Drawn: Visual Witness, Comics, and Documentary Form*. Cambridge, MA: Harvard University Press.

Cortsen, Rikke Platz and Erin La Cour. 2015. 'Opening a "Thirdspace": The Unmasking Effects of Comics'. In *Comics and Power: Representing and Questioning Culture, Subjects and Communities*, edited by Rikke Platz Cortsen, Erin La Cour and Anne Magnussen, 110–30. Newcastle upon Tyne: Cambridge Scholars Publishing.

Davies, Dominic. 2018. '"Welcome to the New World": Visual Culture, Comics and the Crisis of Liberal Multiculturalism', *Albeit* 5 (1). Accessed 26 July 2018. http://albeitjournal.com/welcome-to-the-new-world/.

Davies, Dominic. 2019. *Urban Comics: Infrastructure and the Global City in Contemporary Graphic Narratives*. New York: Routledge.

Denson, Shane. 2013. 'Afterword: Framing, Unframing, Reframing: Retconning the Transnational Work of Comics'. In *Transnational Perspectives on Graphic Narratives: Comics at the Crossroads*, edited by Shane Denson, Christina Meyer and Daniel Stein, 271–84. London: Bloomsbury Academic.

El-Enany, Nadine. 2015. 'On Pragmatism and Legal Idolatry: Fortress Europe and the Desertion of the Refugee', *International Journal on Minority and Group Rights* 22 (1): 7–38.

Fiddian-Qasmiyeh, Elena. 2017. 'The Faith–Gender–Asylum Nexus: An Intersectionalist Analysis of Representations of the "Refugee Crisis"'. In *The Refugee Crisis and Religion: Secularism, Security and Hospitality in Question*, edited by Luca Mavelli and Erin K. Wilson, 207–22. London: Rowman and Littlefield International.

Gardner, Jared. 2006. 'Archives, Collectors, and the New Media Work of Comics', *MFS: Modern Fiction Studies* 52 (4): 787–806.

Jones, Jonathan. 2016. 'Farage's Poster is the Visual Equivalent of Enoch Powell's "Rivers of Blood" Speech', *The Guardian*, 16 June. Accessed 27 March 2017. www.theguardian.com/commentisfree/2016/jun/16/farage-poster-enoch-powell-rivers-of-blood-racism-ukip-european-union.

Jones, Reece. 2016. *Violent Borders: Refugees and the Right to Move*. London: Verso.

Khan, Adnan R. 2015. 'Alan Kurdi's Father on His Family Tragedy: "I Should Have Died with Them"', *The Guardian*, 22 December. Accessed 27 March 2017. www.theguardian.com/world/2015/dec/22/abdullah-kurdi-father-boy-on-beach-alan-refugee-tragedy.

Kingsley, Patrick. 2015. 'The Journey', *The Guardian*, 9 June. Accessed 27 March 2017. www.theguardian.com/world/ng-interactive/2015/jun/09/a-migrants-journey-from-syria-to-sweden-interactive.

Kingsley, Patrick. 2016. *The New Odyssey: The Story of Europe's Refugee Crisis*. London: Faber and Faber.

Knowles, Sam, James Peacock and Harriet Earle. 2016. 'Introduction: Trans/formation and the graphic novel', *Journal of Postcolonial Writing*, 52 (4), 374–84.

Kureishi, Hanif. 2016. 'These Mysterious Strangers: The New Story of the Immigrant'. In *A Country of Refuge: An Anthology of Writing on Asylum Seekers*, edited by Lucy Popescu, 27–30. London: Unbound.

Lentin, Alana and Gavan Titley. 2011. *The Crises of Multiculturalism: Racism in a Neoliberal Age*. London: Zed Books.

Malek, Alia and Josh Neufeld. 2016. 'The Road to Germany: $2400', *Foreign Policy*, 29 January. Accessed 27 March 2017. http://foreignpolicy.com/2016/01/29/the-road-to-germany-2400-refugee-syria-migrant-germany-nonfiction-comic/.

McDonald-Gibson, Charlotte. 2016. *Cast Away: Stories of Survival from Europe's Refugee Crisis*. London: Portobello Books.

Mehta, Binita and Pia Mukherji, eds. 2015. *Postcolonial Comics: Texts, Events, Identities*. New York: Routledge.

Mickwitz, Nina. 2016. *Documentary Comics: Graphic Truth-Telling in a Skeptical Age*. Basingstoke: Palgrave Macmillan.

Mickwitz, Nina. Forthcoming. 'Comics as Refugee Stories'. In *Documenting Trauma in Comics: Traumatic Pasts, Embodied Histories and Graphic Reportage*, edited by Dominic Davies and Candida Rifkind. London and New York: Palgrave Macmillan.

Neufeld, Josh. 2010. *A.D.: New Orleans after the Deluge*. New York: Pantheon Books.

Orbán, Katalin. 2015. 'Mediating Distant Violence: Reports on Non-Photographic Reporting in *The Fixer* and *The Photographer*', *Journal of Graphic Novels and Comics* 6 (2): 122–37.

Pedri, Nancy. 2017. 'Photography and the Layering of Perspective in Graphic Memoir', *ImageText* 9 (2). Accessed 25 February 2019. http://imagetext.english.ufl.edu/archives/v9_2/pedri/.

Polak, Kate. 2017. *Ethics in the Gutter: Empathy and Historical Fiction in Comics*. Columbus: Ohio State University Press.

Rattansi, Ali. 2011. *Multiculturalism: A Very Short Introduction*. Oxford: Oxford University Press.

Rifkind, Candida. 2017. 'Refugee Comics and Migrant Topographies', *a/b: Auto/Biography Studies* 32 (3): 648–54.

Rifkind, Candida. Forthcoming. 'Migrant Detention Comics and the Aesthetic Technologies of Compassion'. In *Documenting Trauma in Comics: Traumatic Pasts, Embodied Histories and Graphic Reportage*, edited by Dominic Davies and Candida Rifkind. London and New York: Palgrave Macmillan.

Robb, Jenny E. and Rebecca Wanzo. 2010. 'Finding Archives/Making Archives: Observations on Conducting Multicultural Comics Research'. In *Multicultural Comics: From Zap to Blue Beetle*, edited by Frederick Luis Aldama, 202–19. Austin: University of Texas Press.

Sacco, Joe. 2003. *Palestine*. London: Jonathan Cape.

Sacco, Joe. 2007. *Safe Area Goražde*. London: Jonathan Cape.

Smith, Ali, Marina Lewycka, David Herd, Chris Cleave, Jade Amoli-Jackson, Patience Agbabi, Inua Ellams , Stephen Collis, Michael Zand, Dragan Todorovic, Avaes Mohammad, Abdulrazak Gurnah and Anna Pincus. 2016. *Refugee Tales*. Manchester: Comma Press.

Smith, Helena. 2015. 'Shocking Images of Drowned Syrian Boy Show Tragic Plight of Refugees', *The Guardian*, 2 September. Accessed 27 March 2017. www.theguardian.com/world/2015/sep/02/shocking-image-of-drowned-syrian-boy-shows-tragic-plight-of-refugees.

Smith, Sidonie. 2011. 'Human Rights and Comics: Autobiographical Avatars, Crisis Witnessing, and Transnational Rescue Networks'. In *Graphic Subjects: Critical Essays on Autobiography and Graphic Novels*, edited by Michael A. Chaney, 61–72. Madison: University of Wisconsin Press.

Sontag, Susan. 2003. *Regarding the Pain of Others*. New York: Picador.

Žižek, Slavoj. 2008. *Violence*. London: Profile Books.

Žižek, Slavoj. 2016. Against the Double Blackmail: Refugees, Terror and Other Troubles with the Neighbours. London: Allen Lane.

14

# Theatre and/as solidarity: Putting yourself in the shoes of a refugee through performance

Marta Niccolai

## Introduction

Since 2015, European citizens have regularly heard the term 'refugee crisis' used to define the arrival of a large number of non-Europeans who have fled persecution, countries at war and the violation of human rights. On the one hand, the media and European governments have tried to make it increasingly difficult for asylum seekers to be seen as people in great danger, regularly portraying them as lying to gain entry to Western countries. On the other hand, theatre practitioners, among others, have created counter-narratives to these official discourses, and have sought to bridge the gap between the audience and refugees or asylum seekers whose life stories are often concealed by the media (with the latter often speaking of them only in political and economic terms).

'Putting yourself in the shoes of the refugee' is an idiomatic expression for developing an empathic point of view, as if one were the other person. As stated by Alison Jeffers (2012: 60):

> [it] is a common way to encourage those who are not refugees to consider the experience of those who have been forced to leave their homes to seek asylum. This approach asks for imagination and empathy and is very commonly used in refugee advocacy literature but it is in theatre that its full potential can be explored with the possibility of a somatic replacement of the refugee body with that of the citizen.

With this in mind, this chapter focuses on Teatro di Nascosto/Hidden Theatre,[1] an international theatre company based in Italy, founded and directed by Annet Henneman. Henneman moved from the Netherlands to Italy over 30 years ago and has since been based in the town of Volterra, Tuscany. Always sensitive to humanitarian issues and crises, Henneman's work exposes events that threaten the well-being and daily life of entire communities. Since 1997, Teatro di Nascosto has placed refugees and their stories at the centre of its work in order to touch the public and influence policymakers. This is done as a double act: on the one hand, Henneman meets asylum seekers and refugees in Italy, and on the other hand, she visits their home countries in order to learn how they live and also to stage theatrical events with the collaboration of local actors. Throughout this process, borders and marked cultural differences make 'hospitality' a complex issue.

More precisely, in this chapter I will first discuss 'hospitality' in relation to Henneman's visits to the Middle East, and to asylum seekers and refugees in host European countries. I will then illustrate the methodology adopted by Henneman to make theatrical events, before analysing two productions: *Lontano dal Kurdistan* (Faraway from Kurdistan) (1998), which deals with the first arrivals of Kurdish refugees in Italy, and *Rifugia-ti*[2] (2005), which included European parliamentarians in its cast.[3]

## Teatro di Nascosto: A methodology informed by hospitality

Boats with asylum seekers[4] started arriving in Italy towards the end of the 1990s.[5] On 19 November 1997, 374 Turkish and Iraqi Kurds reached Monasterace on the coast of Calabria, and on 27 December 1997, 837 would-be refugees disembarked from the cargo boat *Ararat* near Badolato, also on the Calabrian coast.[6] Most of the people on board were Turkish Kurds fleeing ethnic persecution. Henneman travelled to the south of Italy to meet the new arrivals to understand their reasons for undertaking such a dangerous journey. She decided to travel to Turkey, and subsequently to Iraqi Kurdistan in order to gain first-hand experience of what was happening there. In an interview, Henneman recalls that everybody thought she was wealthy, and that those living in unsafe territories believed that she could help them to enter Europe. Even though as an artist she did not fulfil these criteria, she showed her interest in hearing people's experiences of living in a conflict zone. This was Henneman's offer to the refugees' community of origin – simultaneously a community 'hosting' her – whose members responded enthusiastically by sharing their stories and offering her hospitality and assistance as a Western woman travelling alone in often unsafe territories such as Iraqi Kurdistan.

Over the years, Henneman has struck up personal and enduring relationships with some of the families that have offered her hospitality; she lives life at the rhythm of their members and partakes in their rituals, family losses and celebrations such as marriages and births. The relationships with families and, through them, communities in Iraq, Turkey and Afghanistan are based on an exchange: namely, she has developed her experiences and the stories she has heard into theatre events that make geographically distant and culturally different communities visible and known in European countries.

Indeed, hospitality is a complex concept and process, and one that needs to be questioned and redefined with demographic changes in local and national communities. Illuminating Henneman's experience as a guest in a Middle Eastern country is a small act of resistance to the assumption that it is only the West that offers hospitality to 'the other' (also see Fiddian-Qasmiyeh 2016).

The notion of a guest offering something back to the host is implied in the notion of hospitality. However, as noted by Jeffers, 'Unlike tourists, who are seen to contribute financially to the nation, asylum seekers are, to paraphrase Derrida, the wrong kind of guests (Derrida 2000, 61) figured as "takers" but apparently giving nothing in return' (Jeffers, 2012: 50). Indeed, refugees, whose arrival is uninvited, are commonly seen through the lens of a fear of unlimited hospitality, as guests who do not give anything back, parasites who take from the wealth of the host country.

Derrida argues that 'hospitality' inherently contains its opposite in 'hostility' to the extent that he coined the word 'hostipitality' (Jeffers, 2012: 50; Fiddian-Qasmiyeh 2015), a word that points in two directions. It simultaneously contains a meaning and its opposite, and can be applied to refugees as host states will often hold both attitudes towards them. The term 'hospitality' is loaded with complexity – at once 'an ancient classical tradition, a philosophical value, an ethical imperative, a political issue, and also a polymorphous practice' (Rosello, 2001: 6). As well as acknowledging the tension between the difficult coexistence of the ethical and the political, and the impossibility of resolving them, Mireille Rosello adds the fear that both host and guest have to each be changed by the other (ibid.: 176).

For many years now, Henneman has worked with theatre companies and universities in the Middle East, directing theatrical events to explore themes such as memory, loss, and individual and community identity shattered by conflicts.[7] With her approach based on living together and sharing daily life, the hosting community and Henneman have come to know each other intimately, and in this climate the aforementioned tension between the political and the ethical is often overcome – partly thanks to the artistic nature of the projects, which does not seem to alert political institutions to intervene and check on the presence and actions of the guest in the host country, and partly thanks to the help that she receives from the families supporting and hosting her.[8]

Community and collaboration are key components of the methodology of Teatro di Nascosto. The roles of guest and host are reversed when actors from the country that Henneman has visited in the Middle East go to work with her in Volterra, where refugees and asylum seekers living in Italy are also invited to play a role in theatrical events. It can be said, therefore, that these lasting relationships go beyond the professional role of a director, as Henneman comes to know the nuances of the sociopolitical background of the refugee and this leads to the representation of more nuanced emotions and events on stage.

Stories are told as 'Theatre Reportage',[9] a term coined by Henneman to indicate the combination of facts and performance that aims to influence people's opinions on fundamental social issues. The presence of journalistic information within the creative medium of performance has the important function of presenting reality in a form that is different from news channels, the internet and photographic images that, by virtue of their repetition, become ephemeral (see Snow, and Davies, both in this volume). As part of the process of Theatre Reportage, a theatrical event is prepared with refugees, asylum seekers and actors from the Middle East and Europe who live together for at least two weeks and rehearse and live as a community.[10] In this way, the reality represented in the theatrical event is learnt intimately, with experience and emotional involvement.

This is political theatre because it presents the audience with a different perspective on the current affairs that they see on the news every day, and on questions of social justice. It is influenced by the 'epic' theatre developed by the playwright Bertolt Brecht, a term that merely indicates a type of theatre not based on characters' development or catharsis that would involve the spectators emotionally rather than intellectually (Mumford, 2009). A political play should leave the audience feeling motivated to question themselves and the society that they live in. Brechtian techniques of distantiation are used by contemporary practitioners like Henneman, devices that prevent the audience members from losing themselves in the narrative, instead becoming conscious and critical observers.

Even the social aspect of the rehearsals is not divorced from political meaning because the aim is to transform the perception of the spectator from one of distance and indifference to one of empathy and concern for the well-being of the culturally different other. By living together as a community, the boundaries between those who experience pain and discomfort and those who hear about it are more porous. As a result, the actors on stage embody emotions more vividly and for this reason the audience may be touched very deeply, more emphatically, and perhaps for a moment can identify with the pain of a fellow human being who is like them, but from a different culture.[11]

The notion of 'voice'[12] is very important for Henneman who says, 'I want to tell the stories of people who have no voice, so all the stories come from the refugees' (cited in Cooper, 2012).

Indeed, recent research on the media coverage of the refugee crisis has revealed that the opinions of refugees were rarely represented:

> Refugee voices remained in [the] minority ... compared to those who were allowed to speak. In all analysed countries, voices of representatives of national governments, governments of other countries or European politicians were featured in articles significantly more often than voices of asylum seekers ... Women were particularly missing in the journalistic frames. Women were rarely quoted and in descriptions of refugees in the articles men and children dominated the narrative. (Georgiou and Zaborowski, 2017: 10–11)

As outlined by Helen Nicholson, the role of citizens is not necessarily to 'give voice' but to 'create spaces and places which enable voices *to be heard*' (Nicholson, 2005: 163, emphasis added).[13]

The notion of voice presents complexity. Perpetuating refugees' stories of suffering victims can be counterproductive and can create a label imbued with epistemic violence in the community receiving them. Indeed, Semhar Haile discusses how 'settled refugees may choose strategic invisibility to navigate their newly acquired homes and identities' (this volume). Nonetheless, as part of this process of navigation, there are arguably also times when the visibility of the refugee, such as in the 1990s in Italy when their presence was growing, is important to draw the attention of different institutions and diverse groups of citizens. It is in this context that Henneman's work has aimed to build human counter-narratives to the more political, militarized and securitized ones found in the European press, which purposefully silence refugees.

## *Lontano dal Kurdistan* (Faraway from Kurdistan)

The first play performed by Teatro di Nascosto was *Lontano dal Kurdistan*, which premiered in Pontedera (Pisa) in 1998.[14] It tells the journey of three Turkish Kurds who flee to Italy, where they are assigned to the Regina Pacis detention centre in San Foca, Puglia. One of them is a mother, Hedye, acted by Henneman, who refuses to believe that her son Memo is dead. She behaves as if he were still alive, a belief that her two young male fellow travellers, Sipan and Ismail, endorse by pretending that Memo, who died under torture by Turkish police, is wounded and travelling with them.

This is the only theatrical work by Teatro di Nascosto with an entirely Italian cast. During an interview, Henneman said that originally, a Kurdish refugee had planned to act in the play, but shortly before the premiere he was unable to cope with the strong emotions that he experienced when telling of real events in front of an audience, and he ultimately opted out of the play (also see Haile *et al.*, this volume). The true protagonists of *Lontano dal Kurdistan* are the people mentioned by the characters – people who come alive through their names, personalities and daily lives – suddenly gone because of unspeakable circumstances that are sometimes described in detail. The impression is that the stage becomes animated by their presence, while Kurdish music and songs soften the tension and strong emotions that some descriptions may evoke in the audience. Giving people a name and showing their pictures are devices used to bring them closer to the audience, who otherwise only hear of refugees as anonymous groups, and restores the complex identities that are denied by the media, as recent research on media coverage of the 'refugee crisis' have revealed:

> Although much was said for and about the refugees in the European press, their description[s] were highly limited in scope … Refugees thus emerge from these narratives as an anonymous, unskilled group. They are 'the other' to the presumed reader of the press and this limited characterisation shapes the discourse surrounding the refugee crisis for both European audiences and stakeholders (Georgiou and Zaborowski, 2017: 10).

As noted above, the play adopts Brechtian techniques to make spectators less emotional and more intellectually engaged when watching. The staging, for instance, is very minimalist with just a small cart – symbolic of travelling by sea and on land – a few blankets and a bundle of personal belongings.

The characters address the audience, thus eliminating the 'fourth wall' – namely, the illusion of events unfolding on stage as if no one was watching. There are two instances when the mother speaks about the audience.[15] In the first instance, she speaks to one of the fellow travellers:

| | |
|---|---|
| **Hedye:** | *Ismail, io la gente qua la rispetto una per una, ma perché non fanno niente?* |
| **Ismail:** | *Perché non importa a nessuno.* |
| **Hedye:** | *Io voglio sapere perché …* |
| | |
| **Hedye:** | *Ismail, I respect everybody here, but why don't they do anything?* |
| **Ismail:** | *Because they don't care.* |
| **Hedye:** | *I want to know why …* |

In a monologue that comes later, Hedye addresses the audience with a powerful speech using the imperative form to keep the public's attention, exhorting them to become active citizens who react to injustice and suffering [the highlighted imperative form is mine]:

*<u>Guardate</u>! Il mio popolo è senza terra, è stato abbandonato …*
*<u>Svegliatevi</u> amici miei, fin quando volete aspettare con gli occhi chiusi?*
*Non <u>sentite</u> il rumore della Guerra, degli spari, delle bombe?*
*E <u>guardate</u> sono stati uccisi gli amici vittime del desiderio della libertá*
*E vi prego <u>fermate</u> tutto questo! <u>Fermate</u> l'ingiustizia!*

<u>Look</u>! My people have no country, they have been abandoned …
<u>Wake up</u> my friends, how long will you wait with your eyes closed?
Do you not <u>hear</u> the sound of war, shots, and bombs?
<u>Look</u>, friends have been killed, victims of their desire for freedom.
I beg you to <u>stop</u> all this! <u>Stop</u> this injustice!

The voice of the character (the mother) overlaps with the voice of Henneman – the result of having spent a long time living with Kurds in their home regions, experiencing, like them, the fear of dying at any moment and fearing the loss of loved ones. The depth of Henneman's feeling on stage can increase the possibility that the audience will relate emphatically to the story, a feeling that is not encouraged by political discourses and a long tradition of representing the other through cultural representations that are based on Orientalism – an imperial way of constituting Middle Eastern people that distorts differences and places greater distance between the West/ Europeans and the people of, or from, the Middle East (see Said, 1978).

The play has two endings. In the first instance, the audience are unaware that they will experience a metatheatrical moment, whereby the fictionality of the play is revealed in order to draw attention to the reality of an event or statement. The actors interrupt the singing of a Kurdish song to announce the arrival of the police because the use of the Kurdish language is forbidden on stage. They tell the audience to leave before leaving the stage themselves. They soon return on stage, using their character's names but speaking out of character and 'outside' the play as such. The characters/actors are in an in-between space, in the same way as the play can be seen happening in between reality and fiction. Henneman/Hedye announces that the police will no longer be coming, and she explains that the incident really happened to the actors of a Kurdish theatre company in Istanbul, who were arrested and beaten by the police for days. Before knowing the truth, the audience may have felt alarmed, believing that the police were coming. They were briefly put in a space that could have been unsafe, and was certainly different from what they expected. This is a theatrical work with more elements of reality than fiction.

The second ending invites the audience to join the actors on stage for a tea ceremony. This final part of the play is like an epilogue and is also a social moment that can last up to two hours, sharing questions or other stories, with traditional Kurdish music and the actors still dressed as their characters. Before ending the gathering, Henneman would take a picture, with men and women standing separately – a custom that in the 1990s, when the play was written, she encountered among rural families in Turkish Kurdistan. The audience, therefore, is placed in a political as well as a cultural setting that puts them very much 'in the shoes of [the] refugees'.

## *Rifugia-ti* (Refugees/find refuge)

*Rifugia-ti* premiered in October 2005 in Volterra, and then played in Rome, Milan and inside the European Parliament in Brussels. The European Parliament is an unusual place for a performance, and the room where it took place underwent a change, becoming poorly lit and inhospitable. The atmosphere of the place did more to the play than an actual stage ever could. The location in Rome was a former slaughterhouse, with hooks still hanging from its walls; in Volterra, it was a dump and a poorly lit unused underground parking garage; and in Milan, a former psychiatric hospital littered with rubbish. Unusual locations are unfamiliar referents (and a tool of Brechtian distantiation) that can prevent the audience from interpreting what they see and experience through the knowledge they have, thus reproducing what they already know.

The cast of *Refugia-ti* included international actors, asylum seekers, journalists, a lawyer and the exceptional participation of European parliamentarians, who agreed to be part of the play. Two internationally acclaimed actors and directors – Judith Malina and Hanon Reznikov, of the legendary US-based Living Theatre – were also involved.

The play deals with the experiences of asylum applicants who need to prove to the Italian host state that they should be granted refugee status. It is related to a real event, in which nine asylum seekers working and living with Teatro di Nascosto were denied refugee status and asked to leave Italy within 15 days. It also includes stories from a previously staged work, *Dinieghi* (Denials, 2002) that explores a similar topic. Instead of a traditional plot, the play develops the journey of a refugee through several dramatic pieces such as speeches, poetry and songs, together with devices like music, photographs and comical sketches. This variety ensures entertainment and keeps the audience's attention on a very serious topic.

The play opens with a poem written by Henneman, who directed the play and acted in it. This poem anticipates the themes of the play: memory, pain, loss, injustice and danger. The first line begins:

> Voices telling …
> The pain, the silent scream
> Of the ones dying in this moment
> In a war we know about
> Or the one we never heard of

This is followed by a sequence of stanzas starting 'of the ones', a dramatic refrain that line after line increases the amount of suffering and the situations that cause suffering, as well as a list of people suffering because they have been forced to leave home.

The audience walks to the big metal gate of a refugee detention centre, which is shut behind them, with loudspeakers stating the rules of the place simultaneously in Dutch, English, Italian, Turkish, French and Kurmanji Kurdish.

This is another instance in which the audience is placed in the role of refugees. Rosello warns against the fixity of the role of guest and host, because it can mean a deterioration of the relationship whereby hospitality will be replaced by parasitism or charity. She adds that the theatrical event about refugees can provide a fresh perspective that revitalizes the relationship between guest and host (Rosello, 2001: 174 in Jeffers, 2012: 51). Placing the audience in the shoes of the refugees, in an unfamiliar, unsettling and unfriendly space where many languages are spoken at once, as in the scene above, can be a way in which to encourage audience members to develop new attitudes about and feelings towards asylum seekers and refugees.

The rules of the place emanating from the loudspeaker on stage are the rules of the Regina Pacis camp in the southern region of Puglia, where refugees were treated like prisoners with the constant threat of being handed over to the police. The list of rules was provided by Dino Frisullo, an Italian journalist and activist for the Kurdish people, who was arrested and put in a Turkish political prison in 1998 for protesting in favour of Kurdish rights in Diyarbakir. Although the audience does not know this, it demonstrates how much of the play is woven in a political and ethical web that links similar events that have taken place around the fight for human rights.

The plight of those seeking asylum is seen from several angles through real accounts given by different voices. In one scene, an Italian lawyer, Alessandra Ballerini, shares the experience of her visit, together with Henneman as translator, to a detention centre near Rome. The same questions and requests addressed to her then are now addressed to the audience, who are placed in the role of visitors to the centre. The content of the statements is alarming because it raises awareness of the lack of basic human rights (the play was performed in English):

> … my friend has got a hernia, he is in terrible pain but no one has come! … I have no clothes … the clothes sent by my family were stolen … they give us drugs to keep us asleep … Write my name and phone number. I am married and have a daughter. Please contact her.

Ballerini's account of what she witnessed is dramatically given as 'I saw …', a refrain that stresses the reality of her testimony, which cannot be disproved:

> I saw hands burnt with electric truncheons
> I saw legs bandaged with toilet paper
> I saw men's backs burnt by the sun and salt
> I saw rubber dinghies, suitable for children's games, loaded with men
> …
> I saw Red Cross nurses turning jailers and policemen turning torturers
> …
> I saw indolent and bored judges looking impatiently at their watch during hearings.

...
I saw angels. They are doctors, journalists, lawyers, volunteers, artists, men and women whose life is devoted to healing the wounds inflicted by those who despise, torture, reject.

This extract from Ballerini's monologue – mentioning torture in the home country, the journey and life in the detention centre – shares similar dark tones, with pain and lack of care as common denominators. A question arises of whether there is a difference between the perpetrators at home and the people in Europe who have the power to make the life of an asylum seeker more human or a continuation of their hell.

The variety of performances allows the repetition of the same theme without losing the audience's attention or interest in the play. Henneman stresses that the suffering of people in their homeland is not felt and understood in Europe, as noted in an interview: 'I want everyone from all backgrounds to share in the experience that is created. When people are humanised, they will be open to change' (cited in Cooper, 2012).

Two poems then follow: 'Look at My Paradise' – written by Adil Yalcin, a Kurdish refugee tortured in Turkey – is performed by Feleknas Uca, a German MEP originally from Kurdistan; 'Refugee Blues', by W.H. Auden, is then recited by Judith Malina and Hanon Reznikow. Both poems are personal accounts of what it is like to be a refugee.[16] Yalcin laments the loss of his country, subjected to genocide with no justice for his people. His great pain comes from the destruction of his homeland and from realizing that no one comes to help his people who are being killed. The poem is a litany of loss that does not mention a specific place; therefore, it can be applied to any place where injustice is committed. Actors walking slowly towards the audience holding photographs of death, destruction and oppression from the refugees and asylum seekers' home countries dramatically illustrate this. The stark contrast between the poem's title and its content leaves the audience trying to imagine this 'paradise' as it might have been before its total destruction:

> They are burning it
> They are bombarding it
> Why do they burn my paradise?
> Look at me
> I have no land
> They cut off my roads, they isolated me
> How long will the force of evil continue for?
> The colonisation, the torture, the repression
> ...

In turn, 'Refugee Blues' (Auden, 2003) tells the plight of Jews losing their rights and their homes because of their religious and ethnic origins. Malina – who knows the trauma intimately, being herself a Second World War Jewish refugee from Germany who escaped to the United States – recites the poem. As with Frisullo, Malina is part of a web of collaborators whose direct experience of the themes of the play can increase the possibility of it reaching the audience more powerfully.

Each of the 12 stanzas mentions the loss of a human right, as in the following selection:

> Say this city has ten million souls,
> Some are living in mansions, some are living in holes:
> Yet there's no place for us, my dear, yet there's no place for us.

> Once we had a country and we thought it fair,
> Look in the atlas and you'll find it there:
> We cannot go there now, my dear, we cannot go there now.

> In the village churchyard there grows an old yew,
> Every spring it blossoms anew:
> Old passports can't do that, my dear, old passports can't do that.

The poem ends with Malina desperately repeating, 'I cannot travel without a passport!'

This voices the crucial and highly political question of identity. Those who cross borders to flee their homeland become asylum seekers who need to be granted refugee status to be legally accepted – with their rights, and the right to remain, guaranteed. The procedure requires asylum seekers to go through a bureaucratic performance in which, as Jeffers says:

> they must become conventional refugees, those who conform to cultural expectations of refugees, particularly in relation to suffering … The onus is on the individual asylum seeker to prove that they have what the Refugee Convention defines as 'a well-founded fear of persecution'. This is something that the majority of asylum seekers fail to do. (Jeffers, 2012: 17)

Here, the belief is that those claiming refugee status are just economic migrants; therefore, their story must be a 'credible *performance*' (Jeffers, 2012: 30), which persuades the authorities that refugee status should be granted on account of the fact that the persecution would continue were they to return to their home country.

Many asylum seekers fail their bureaucratic 'performance' and are rejected. Jeffers underlines the fact that, paradoxically, 'refugees' bureaucratic performances for the state force them to work hard to create an identity for which they have no desire but which they passionately desire at the same time' (Jeffers, 2012: 37–8). In other words, they have to act 'the refugee' and produce a speech that enacts a believable refugee because their status is decided in that moment by those with the power and authority to do so.

The inadequacy of the system to judge and reach a verdict is dramatized in *Rifugia-ti* with a sequence that includes politicians, parliamentarians, asylum seekers and state representatives. A single actor plays the role of politicians from centre-left and right-wing parties, as well as the mayor of a town in northern Italy. This device signals to the audience that the speeches may be different, but that politics is one body. Each speech documents different attitudes towards refugees, with the centre-left typically viewing immigration as a resource and integration a necessity while the politician from the right is inflexible and speaks of zero tolerance to safeguard democracy.

The sequence alternates a politician's speech with a refugee's account of imprisonment and torture, or with an MEP's memoir of their experience with refugees. One Italian MEP, Vittorio Agnoletto, tells the story of an Iranian doctor who worked for the Red Cross in a detention centre where he witnessed a total lack of medical support and where the police arrived to deport a man in desperate physical condition. The English MEP, Linda McAvan, shares a story that she heard just before *Rifugia-ti* was performed in Brussels. She tells the dramatic account of a woman whose husband died while crossing the Mediterranean. The boat capsized near Malta, leaving many men at sea holding onto crates for two days while politicians from neighbouring countries debated who should send a rescue boat. Many were saved by an Italian boat but neither Italy, Malta nor Libya wanted to take care of the dead. Eventually France took on this responsibility.

In the play, the refugees are heard three times, with questions addressed to them that are supposed to help the state to make a decision about their future. Answers are given collectively unless a specific name is called out:

...
Date and place of departure
All answer at the same time
Date and place of arrival in Europe

All answer at the same time
Have you been in prison in your country for political, ethnic or religious reasons?
All answer yes and no
For how long?
All answer in their own language
Mr Bahram, how much time did you spend in prison?
Mr Bahram: two and half years

...

Mr Ozmen, how many people were torturing you?
Two
Mr Abbas?
Eight
Who has been beaten with a stick?
Some raise their hands
Who has been cut, the wounds covered with salt [who had salt put on their wounds]

The questions are asked summarily, answered with a show of hands, ticking boxes upon which the final decision will be made.

The final speech by the state, calling the refugees one by one, is the climax of the play:

Ridyn Ozmen after a meeting of 40 minutes with the Central Committee of Rome according to the Convention of Geneva of the 28th of July 1951, given the better living conditions in Turkey and the last development towards a democratic republic, your application for political asylum has been rejected. You have to leave Italy within 15 days.

*The stage directions indicate that Ridyn joins again the travellers crossing mountains and borders.*

Miss Aine Shemal after a meeting of 55 minutes with the Central Committee in Rome according to the Convention of Geneva, seen the lack of documentation of your case, taken into account the lack of evidence that the signs on your body come from torture in an Israeli prison, your application for political asylum has been rejected. You have to leave Italy within 15 days.

*Stage directions as before.*

Shakila' Karammudin after a meeting of two and half hours with the Home Office in London according to the Geneva Convention and given the danger to lose your life by death sentence, your request for political asylum has been granted. Granted.
*She leaves the stage and sits behind the audience.*

Since all the stories are tragic, a spectator is bound to find the choice to reject or grant refugee status as being dependent on the perceived goodwill of the speakers. In other words, if the speech act is considered 'hollow' or 'empty' of the thought and feelings that asylum seekers are supposed to have in order to become 'refugees', they are considered liars.

This is not the final speech. The bureaucratic process, which in Italy normally occurs behind closed doors, now has an audience whose members have heard the stories and the verdicts normally pronounced in secret. The refugees' theatrical space happens in the temporal and spatial area of the audience – characterized by proximity between 'us' and 'them' on stage, and proximity, with thin boundaries, with the audience.

The audience hears stories of suffering together with the rejection of refugee status. At that point, the public can be in a different, internal space – perhaps an uncomfortable, in-between space where what they know about refugees from media coverage and what they begin to understand through the play no longer coincide.

## Conclusion

In conclusion, the methodology of 'Theatre Reportage' adopted by Teatro di Nascosto relies on the director's and actors' deep knowledge and empathic understanding of refugees' journeys and barriers to safety, well-being and international protection. In performance, hospitality is no longer the complex and contested space between nation states. The space of the performance becomes a community with a multiplicity of voices – some distinct, like the voices of refugees telling their personal stories – heard together with the voices of the international community of actors who put themselves in refugees' shoes and partake in refugees' enactments of cultural memory as well as the loss of home and homeland. In the theatrical events, the factual and the emotional combine to tell stories that should touch the audience, and move them to act more empathically towards the suffering of culturally distant people, now near to them.

# Notes

1. Henceforth, Teatro di Nascosto.
2. The hyphenated title refers to the two meanings of the word *rifugiati*, a word that means 'refugees' and 'take refuge' depending on the stress.
3. Throughout the chapter, no page references are provided for quotations from the plays as they are drawn from unpublished manuscripts made available by the theatre director.
4. I use the term 'asylum seekers' conventionally, to indicate the people applying for refugee status in a European country, and more broadly, to refer to people making the crossing by sea who may not (yet) have applied for asylum but cannot be called migrants either because they are escaping persecution and conflict in their home countries.
5. In line with most other Western European countries, in the 1990s Italy started experiencing the steady arrival of labour migrants and asylum seekers from countries outside of Europe. The first occasion on which a large number of asylum seekers reached Italy by boat was in 1991, when an estimated 16,000 Albanians fled political turmoil in their country and region of origin.
6. For recent books including Italy and refugees, see Puggioni (2016); Glynn (2016); Castelli Gattinara (2016).
7. One of the most recent events, *The Catwalk*, took place in Basrah's Times Square Shopping Centre in January 2018.
8. During her visits to Iraq and to Iraqi Kurdistan, Henneman has often received phone threats, sometimes she has been isolated by people who put her under a bad light for speaking up about the regime and at other times her plans to stage an event have been disrupted by local authorities.
9. This is different from 'Theatre of Reportage', a non-dramatic technique based on reporting news, real speech and interviews.
10. On the collaborative co-production of knowledge, see Haile *et al.*, Haile, and We Are Movers, all in this volume.
11. Besides Brecht, Henneman's theatrical approach has been influenced by other practitioners engaged with social justice and human rights, such as 'The Invisible Theatre' of Augusto Boal; Judith Malina of the US based 'Living Theatre'; and the methodology adopted by Ariane Mnouchkine of Théâtre du Soleil, who developed a number of performances with refugees.
12. For other approaches to 'voice' in refugee research, see Haile (this volume).
13. Besides refugees, the construction of 'voice' is discussed in the literature on other marginalized groups, such as women (Shaw and Lee, 2015) and the colonized (Fanon, 1952; Spivak, 1993). Gayatri Spivak, in the field of Postcolonial studies, has critiqued the absence of the subaltern voice as a reproduction of power dynamics that perpetuates colonial power (Spivak, 1993).
14. The play has travelled internationally, including to the annual Amnesty International meeting in Boston (US) in 2000/2001.
15. The following extracts include the original text in Italian, followed by my translation into English.
16. For other approaches to 'writing' in response to displacement, see Hoffman *et al.*, Qasmiyeh, and Davies, all in this volume.

# References

**Primary works:** *Lontano dal Kurdistan* (Faraway from Kurdistan) *Rifugia-ti* (Refugees/find refuge) (unpublished manuscripts on file with the author)

Auden, W.H. 2003. 'Refugee Blues', In *Collected Shorter Poems 1927-1957 by WH Auden*. London: Faber.

Carr, Matthew. 2016. *Fortress Europe: Dispatches from a Gated Continent*. New York: New Press.

Castelli Gattinara, Pietro. 2016. *The Politics of Migration in Italy: Perspectives on Local Debates and Party Competition*. London: Routledge.

Cooper, Neil. 2012. '"Hidden" Theatre Offers a Sense of Belonging', *The Herald*, 27 June. Accessed 9 January 2020. www.heraldscotland.com/arts_ents/13063150._Hidden__theatre_offers_a_sense_of_belonging/.

Derrida, Jacques. 2000. *Of Hospitality: Anne Dufourmantelle Invites Jacques Derrida to Respond*, translated by Rachel Bowlby. Stanford: Stanford University Press.

Fanon, Frantz. 1952. *Black Skin, White Masks* (1967 translation by Charles Lam). Markmann: New York: Grove Press).

Fiddian-Qasmiyeh, Elena. 2015. *South–South Educational Migration, Humanitarianism and Development: Views from the Caribbean, North Africa and the Middle East*. London: Routledge.

Fiddian-Qasmiyeh, Elena. 2016. 'Representations of Displacement from the Middle East and North Africa', *Public Culture* 28 (3): 457–73.

Galani-Moutafi, Vasiliki. 2000. 'The Self and the Other: Traveler, Ethnographer, Tourist', *Annals of Tourism Research* 27 (1): 203–24.

Georgiou, Myria and Rafal Zaborowski. 2017. *Media Coverage of the "Refugee Crisis": A Cross-European Perspective* (Council of Europe Report DG1(2017)03). Strasbourg: Council of Europe.

Glynn, Irial. 2016. *Asylum Policy, Boat People and Political Discourse: Boats, Votes and Asylum in Australia and Italy*. London: Palgrave Macmillan.

Jeffers, Alison. 2012. *Refugees,Theatre and Crisis: Performing Global Identities*. Basingstoke: Palgrave Macmillan.

Mumford, Meg. 2009. *Bertolt Brecht*. London: Routledge.

Nicholson, Helen. 2005. *Applied Drama: The Gift of Theatre*. Basingstoke: Palgrave Macmillan.

Puggioni, Raffaela. 2016. *Rethinking International Protection: The Sovereign, the State, the Refugee*. London: Palgrave Macmillan.

Rosello, Mireille. 2001. *Postcolonial Hospitality: The Immigrant as Guest*. Stanford: Stanford University Press.

Said, Edward W. 1978. *Orientalism*. New York: Pantheon Books.

Shaw, S.M. and J. Lee. 2015. *Women's voices, feminist visions: classic and contemporary readings* (Sixth ed.). New York: McGraw-Hill Education.

Spivak, Gayatri C. 1993. 'Can the Subaltern Speak?' In *Colonial Discourse and Post-Colonial Theory*, edited by P. Williams and L. Chrisman. London: Harvester Wheatsheaf, 66–111.

# 15

# The empty space: Performing migration at the Good Chance Theatre in Calais

Tom Bailey

*During 2017, theatre maker Tom Bailey was Leverhulme Artist in Residence at UCL's Migration Research Unit. The following chapter contains two parts. The first is an interview with Tom regarding theatre work in the 'Jungle' in Calais. The second contains extracts from an artistic 'field guide', made with photographer Tom Hatton, presented at the UCL Festival of Culture 2017.*

*What was the Good Chance Theatre?*

The Good Chance Theatre was a community space set up in summer 2015 in the Calais 'Jungle' camp. It was established by two playwrights from the UK, Joe Robertson and Joe Murphy, and received extensive support from established theatres in London like the Royal Court and the Young Vic. Gradually, it grew as an organization with an aim to provide a space for migrants to engage with expressive arts, to provide a safe space where people can work creatively together, and to be a voice in the media advocating for the rights of refugees within and beyond the UK.

*How were you involved with the organization?*

I worked as a visiting artist running workshops and making performance with migrants across 2015–16.

*What kind of work did you do there?*

It varied from time to time. No one day was the same. Most days I would run a theatre workshop that would last from one to three hours. The work would range from theatre games, physical work, massage, song work, ensemble movement and play. My aim was not to direct a show but to provide a space where people could express themselves spontaneously in a safe environment, connect with others in ways they may not have done so before, to build trust among the group, and to provide dramatic avenues for unexpressed tensions and experiences. As I mentioned, no one day was the same. It depended on who was in the theatre space, and what the energy was in the space. In a workshop context like this, one soon found that coming with a plan and trying to execute it was a recipe for failure. It was about trying to capture the mood of the people in the room and see, with guidance, what spontaneous collective action would emerge.

*What was the theatre space?*

The theatre space was called 'the dome' – a geodesic dome donated to Good Chance. It became the focus point for all activities. In the camp, people from different nationalities tended to live near those from the same country, with different areas of the camp named after the main nationality of the people living there. The dome was situated within what was called the Afghan area of the camp. It could hold more than 300 people when full. Previously, before the dome came, activities happened in the Sudanese area of the camp.

*Who used the dome?*

The dome was open almost every day, from sunrise to sundown. There was a policy of always welcoming people; it was a space of no exclusion. Across the day, there was a roster of activities. There were visitors from over 40 different nationalities – many Iraqis, Iranians, Syrians, Kurds, Libyans, Eritreans, Ethiopians, to name a few. One aim of the dome was to be a place where people could meet new people in a safe space, develop friendship through creativity. There was occasionally aggravation between different groups, but this was to be expected when living in a squalid camp with such structural and infrastructural limitations.[1]

*What kind of activities went on?*

Across the day, there were activities ranging from painting, sculpting, martial arts, singing, theatre making, music, film nights, community meetings, volleyball, football and many more things. Several refugees with experience in martial arts ran workshops themselves, while I ran basic capoeira workshops as well.

It should be noted that this all took place in a context where many people were understandably in states of lethargy and ill health. Not only were they exposed to the constant, hacking sea wind across the Calais dunes, but the wind also carried rather nauseating fumes from nearby Calais industrial estates. Nutrition was limited and there was no exercise programme within the camp. People were, needless to say, in a very fragile state, dealing with undiagnosed traumas from their various journeys, and the challenges of living in the camp itself.[2] We had to be acutely aware of this when working within the theatre.

*How did people express themselves within the theatre?*

Theatre has different meanings and importance in different countries around the world. In Britain, theatre has been very close to a collective form of national consciousness since Elizabethan times, and British theatre tends to be literary and text-based because of this. In various European countries this is different – and innovations in France, Poland and Russia across the twentieth century have made strong developments in the use of the body to make theatre.

Within the context of the 'Jungle', we were primarily interacting with people who were either from societies where theatre was not immediately present or where it was not 'accepted' on religious, cultural and/or political grounds; in other cases, they were from societies where, for various reasons, they had little interaction with theatre. Most, however, came with experience of song, music and a cultural dance form. These tended to be the primary forms of performance in the dome.

*Did you link up with theatres in other refugee camps?*

There were other companies that visited, who had in some cases extensive experience of arts work in refugee camps. But many of the artists running work were new to this work environment, and consequently found it very difficult. Everything in the Jungle was ad hoc. This was not an officially organized refugee camp, and had no centrally organizing charity. It was mainly run by volunteers, many of whom were learning on the job and did as best as they could.[3]

Performance in this context worked very differently. As far as I understand, theatre shows in other refugee camps (for instance, those managed by United Nations agencies) are often more organized affairs. Here, our understanding was growing as time went on, as the camp changed continuously, as the theatre constantly had to justify its existence in the camp. Good Chance had to daily argue (to sceptics, media, locals, and so on) that theatre and well-being were as important as the essentials of food, clothing and shelter.

*What is the use of performance in a refugee context?*

I approach the words performance and performativity with caution, because I feel that in academia performance has taken on different connotations and meanings. I understand performance as bodily action. I do theatre for many reasons, but at the core is my belief in witnessing the transformative, expressive power of collective bodily action. My theatre workshops had three functions: to act as a safe environment where play, instinct and spontaneity could emerge; to provide a space for physical exercise and training; and to work together in making theatre performance. In this context, I feel that performance work can lead a participant to be in greater contact with themselves, their instinct, here and now. It is a 'presencing'; an articulation of where you are, as a human, right now. It is an invitation to go deeper into yourself as a human with other humans. I do not wish to theorize about the real value of this performance work to refugees, because it is different to everyone. I do not view it as a magical interventionist tool that can somehow alleviate suffering. People in the Jungle were mostly bored shitless because there was nothing to do, and theatre could do little to alleviate that. But theatre offered a new way, perhaps a kind of 'third space', of relating to each other amid the boredom.

Nor am I qualified to say that my theatre work was intentionally therapeutic (there are many companies whose work is far more in this area). Many refugees did not like the work that we were doing and walked away. But for those who were in need of what we were offering, I feel that performance plays a valuable role in a context of what I have come to call 'suspended identity'. Many of the refugees we were working with were stateless: unrecognized people wandering across continents – some for days, some for weeks, some for years – separated from a homeland, from family, from friends … all with a yet-unarrived-at destination, a place of suspended ending of the journey, a place of possible fulfilment of something. Above all, the Jungle was a space of limbo, temporary suspension of identity and personhood; the work of theatre could assist in the processing of this identity-suspension, in the witnessing and recognition of it by self and others in the act of doing something imaginatively together. It was not about 'performing one's journey' or returning to a site of trauma to process it; it was about opening awareness to the here, the now, the emotion in your body, the partner's hands touching your hands with acceptance. Perhaps the subtext of this work was:

> I know that you have been many places, and you still have somewhere to go. Life is on hold. Here, in the Jungle, is not the place you want to be. Here is not what you want to be, or how you want to live your life. Things are shit. But let's find a way, through moving and playing together, to turn the shitness, for a moment, here and now, on its head.

*What were the most challenging aspects of working in this context?*

1) The wind. The Calais dunes are very exposed to the wind. The wind and rain gets everywhere. Everything sinks into the sand and mud. The best thing about the dome was that it was the only public space that was free and open and out of the wind.
2) Leaving. Working closely with people in a fragile situation, you form strong attachments. It's very difficult to leave, when leaving is so easy for some and so difficult for others.

3) Telling people about the UK. A refugee's primary reason for being in Calais was to get to the UK. Many had travelled thousands of miles with the belief that the UK was better, kinder, freer than other European countries, and that education was free and that jobs would be available. Knowing that this is not the case, it is hard to try and persuade someone, tactfully, that this might not be true – especially when they have travelled so far.

4) Gaining trust. There are so many visitors to the Jungle. Western visitors. Coming and going as easy as birds, looking around, surveying, photographing, recording, documenting. It is hard for refugees to know who is really there to help, or who is a fly-by tourist, or who could be an undercover police officer, or who could be catching your face on their camera for their arts project or academic study. This was an environment where hidden identity is important. As per the EU-law Dublin 'first country of asylum' regime, you are supposed to claim asylum at the first safe country you arrive at. If the UK government were to find evidence that you had been in Calais, or Italy (where many people were fingerprinted against their wishes), you could be denied entry. In trying to work closely, sensitively, artistically with people in this context, gaining their trust is very difficult. And without trust, theatre can't happen.

*What of the Good Chance Theatre now?*

As many will know, the Jungle was demolished by the French authorities in 2015, rebuilt and demolished again in March 2016. The dome had to be taken down and the land cleared in spring 2016. In recognition of its work, in summer 2016 there was an 'Encampment' Festival at the Southbank Centre in London, celebrating refugee performance, and the company has been supported by the Young Vic. The two playwrights who started the theatre, along with director Stephen Daldry, went on to create a Young Vic play called *The Jungle* in 2017, entailing a kind of documentary interpretation of the daily activities of the camp. Although there is no dome in Calais any more, the Good Chance Theatre organization has since developed other refugee-related projects both in the UK and abroad.

*What did you do at the UCL Migration Research Unit (MRU) during your residency?*

During my residency, along with a creative team I developed a new theatre show called *Zugunruhe*. I spent time engaging with a number of researchers from different disciplines to try and understand both human and bird migration. During my research, I became very interested in how the discourses around human migration and animal migration are seemingly so separate. So I ended up asking, through the artwork, how exploring bird migration might offer audiences fresh perspectives on human migration.

The show went on to premiere at the Edinburgh Festival Fringe in 2018, where it received critical acclaim and a Herald Angel Award. It has since toured in both the UK and internationally – most recently in Cologne, Germany.

During my time at UCL, as part of the development of *Zugunruhe*, I also presented an audio-walk experience at the UCL Grant Museum of Zoology. This was created with sound designer Simon Whetham. The experience explored the compositional intertwining of bird songs and human songs (recorded in the Jungle migrant camp). Below, I present some extracts from the 'field guide' that was created to accompany the walk, made in collaboration with artist and photographer Tom Hatton.

## Field Notes: *Zone Industrielle des Dunes*

Text by Tom Bailey

Images from Calais by Tom Hatton. Tom Hatton is an artist based in London. His project NOW HERE traces the lives of asylum seekers within and around the Calais refugee camp. The work was selected for the Bloomberg New Contemporaries, 2017.

**Figure 15.1**   Untitled photograph. © Tom Hatton. Calais.

# Welcome to the *Zone Industrielle des Dunes*. This guide will take you on a short walk through some of the popular viewing spots.

# Situated close to the *Réserve Naturelle Nationale du Platier d'Oye* on the coast of Nord Pas de Calais, it's home to a vast number of migratory birds.

# Geography and irony: These sand dunes were once the killing fields of World War II. They now accommodate a bird wetland, an unofficial refugee camp and chemical factories.

# The architecture of war still sleeps beneath the beaches: pill boxes, rusted machine parts, chains, concrete shells.

**Figure 15.2**   Untitled photograph. © Tom Hatton. Calais.

# A landscape of sand and water twisted and gouged by explosions, like the body of a dead animal in a desert.

# Above this, dead scrub of stinted grass, where nature tries to grow but fails. Water and air bleed into each other.

# A little way back from this: Small, silent villages, shuttered and dead in winter. Open, yet silent, in summer. A holiday land. Long, flat roads snake through fields; little concrete rivers into concrete horizons.

# Few really stay here.

Viewing Hide # 1: An old pill box.

**Figure 15.3**   Untitled photograph. © Tom Hatton. Calais.

Species: Little Ringed Plover (*Charadrius dubius*)

   The Little Ringed Plover is a small plover. The genus name *Charadrius* is a Latin word for a yellow bird. This comes from Ancient Greek *kharadrios*, meaning 'a bird found in river valleys'.

   Conservation status: Least Concern.

   Song: Gives a clear 'peeoo' as common call, a far-carrying sound for a small bird. A short 'peeu' or 'cru' and insistent 'pip' in alarm are usually heard.

   Migration: Between sub-Saharan Africa in winter and Northern Europe in summer. Geolocation methods have shown that the winter flight of the Little Ringed Plover differs from that of many other long-distance migrating shorebirds. The Plover prefers to make multiple stop overs within the Middle East.

*Nature Notes:*

\# While there is symbolic romance in the freedom of the bird flying, migration is a brutal exercise in endurance and survival.

 \# Migration flights, often across thousands of kilometres, require a huge amount of metabolic preparation. During flight one may lose half one's body weight. Many die on the way.

 \# One of the most astonishing aspects of bird migration is the mechanisms they have evolved to be able to navigate vast distances. A quantum biological phenomenon in their eyes permits them to see the Earth's magnetic rays. They navigate by the stars, by land and sea features, and by an internal compass. Genetically, within some species journeys are also able to be encoded. Chicks are known to hatch and then fly thousands of kilometres without prior guidance.

 \# Birds are the only known species on Earth to be able to migrate like this.

Viewing spot \# 2. Beach & reeds.

**Figure 15.4**   Untitled photograph. © Tom Hatton. Calais.

As we emerge from the viewing hide, we'd like to draw your attention to the magnificent reedbed on your left, a popular habitat for the highly endangered Pied Avocet, which can be spotted here below.

Species: Pied Avocet (*Recurvirostra avosetta*).

A large black and white wader, renowned for its elegance, and included in Linnaeus' 1758 *Systema Naturae*. Its large legs are particularly useful in scaling large obstacles, such as fences.

Conservation Status: Endangered in Europe due to loss of habitat. Not globally threatened, and widespread in most parts of Africa.

Song: The Pied Avocet utters a clear 'kluit'. This is loud and often repeated. When alarmed, the same call appears as a somewhat more shrill 'kloo-eet'.

Migration: Some populations live all year round in Africa; others breed in Europe and winter in Africa. Others migrate between central Asia, China and India.

*Nature Notes:*

# Zoologically speaking, migration is understood as a return journey to and from a place.

# Birds, like humans, are one of the few vocal learners in nature. MIT researchers have recently suggested that human language first evolved from the imitation of bird song. The expression of song is a costly metabolic exercise for birds, so it is understandable that they do not sing in flight. Song is used to communicate information about territory, and attract a mate, in specific habitations. The relationship between migration and song is far more prominent in humans, for its mnemonic function – especially in the example of Aboriginal people, where songs themselves are maps of the landscape.

# It is ironic that our rapidly advancing understanding of migration patterns in birds is for a large part due to the growth and popular use of innovative surveillance technology; technology that in other contexts is used to detain humans. Chips, tags, nature cams, body cameras, and GPS devices have assisted in the recent widespread mapping of bird migration routes, and an appreciation of just how astonishing the feat of bird migration is.

# # 3. Art Installation: *Zugunruhe*.

**Figure 15.5**   Untitled photograph. © Tom Hatton. Calais.

# This is a real gem for visitors. Installed by VR artists from Norway, it's our *I'm a Bird Get Me Out of Here* simulator.

# In the 1930s ornithologist Ronald Lockley conducted some of the first migration experiments on birds, with a Manx Shearwater. Taking them from Skokholm Island, Wales, he journeyed to Boston by plane with the bird in a black box, so as to ensure it had no idea where it was. Immediately upon being released it flew East along a 3,200 mile route it had never flown. Twelve days, twelve hours and thirty-one minutes later, Lockley found the bird nestled back on Skokholm.

# This twenty-minute installation offers visitors an outstanding, sensory interpretation of travelling thousands of miles in a box to somewhere unknown.

# Following World War II, German ornithologists coined the term *Zugunruhe* to denote a kind of restlessness in migratory species when contained. ('*Zug*' meaning to 'move', '*unruhe*' meaning 'anxiety or 'restlessness').

# Upon emerging, we invite you to listen closely to your body.

# 4. The Open.

This part of the walk takes visitors from the dunes, further inland, into a section that we call The Open.

**Figure 15.6** Untitled photograph. © Tom Hatton. Calais.

Species: Human (*Homo sapiens*).
Conservation Status:
Song:
Migration:

*Nature notes:*
# Widespread migration movements of today, in the wider context of the sixth great Age of Extinction in the Earth's history, bring the human relationship to place under greater scrutiny.

 # The Anthropocene is witnessing a deepening rupture between humans and evolved nature. This guidebook argues that the present mass movement of refugees and migrants, from the Middle East and Africa, is inseparable from the same destructive political and economic logic that

is driving severe climatic change. The effects of human-induced climate change, currently already in progress, will far outstrip present levels of deprivation and suffering.

# A comparison of animal and human migration, in the present global context, should not be read as degradingly viewing refugees as animals. The aim of this guidebook is to encourage new vantages of the present 'refugee crisis' from a natural historical point of view, as opposed to the dehumanizing economic and political arguments of much refugee discourse in the media.

# Could life on Earth have evolved to its present state without migration? We are dealing with an activity that is central to the evolutionary development of organic life, the movement of organisms and resources across the Earth.

# As the effects of climate change develop, the number of environmental refugees will far outstrip those displaced by war (not that war and 'environmental' reasons are ever separate).

# It appears that, in global governance, there needs to be a monumental rethink of how displaced persons can continue to live in some

**Figure 15.7** Untitled photograph. © Tom Hatton. Calais.

**Figure 15.8**  Untitled photograph. © Tom Hatton. Calais.

form of dignity and prosperity. It is quite possible that, by the end of this century, displaced persons will be the norm.

# For the majority of the existence of *Homo sapiens*, we have not lived in one fixed place, or the notion of home has been fluid. We were nomads long before we were agrarians.

# Why, then, have humans not evolved comparable migratory skills to birds? We cannot see the Earth's magnetic field, and our toddlers cannot migrate to Africa without our guidance. Nonetheless, where biology has not equipped us, technologically we are arguably the most advanced navigators on Earth. Researchers have conjectured that we are not, without technology, poor navigators. Modern humans have simply lost what biological, social migratory skills we had as a species. Remains of navigational skills within indigenous cultures – for instance, the well-documented 'songlines' of the Australian Aboriginal peoples – would seem to confirm this.

# It is not so much about how and why humans move. Humans will always move. It's about how they are hosted when they arrive. This critical interaction requires deep care and attention.

# What we can say is that the journey changes the story.

**Figure 15.9**   Untitled photograph.   © Tom Hatton. Calais.

## # 6: Visitor Centre: *The Empty Space.*

We have been unconventional in the design of our Visitor Centre. Leaning upstream against the current tide of family-orientated gizmos, our Visitor Centre contains an empty space.

> Species: Theatre (*Communitas*).
> Conservation Status: Near Extinct.

**Figure 15.10**  Untitled photograph. © Tom Hatton. Calais.

*Nature notes (in fifteen small thoughts):*

1. The mass global migration movements of today have called into question many things: international governance regarding refugees, cross-border agreements such as Schengen, and the present capacity of international communities to deal with the growing numbers of displaced people.
2. It also calls into question the role of space, and how we share it.
3. Theatre is an art form of *space* and people.
4. An empty space is an empty space. If someone crosses an empty space, it can become theatre.
5. If people spend time in a space, a dynamic between the space and the people will emerge. A new narrative becomes possible.
6. Theatre is an art of *being*. Not doing.
7. There are not many spaces left where you can simply *be*, with others. And let *being* happen. Being is not a static state. It is an opening flower.
8. If the flower opens, revolutions are possible.
9. In simply being, we can listen to ourselves, and listen to others.
10. Theatre in these times becomes a place of refuge.

11. The place of refuge is always open, and always safe, for the cultivation of love and understanding.
12. A condition of the place of refuge is also that it is temporary. It is never one fixed place. It is a place to which one must travel and one must leave. It is the space to speak of that journey. The journey is the story and the story is the journey.
13. The place of refuge is not solely for humans. If it were, the mistakes of the past would continue.
14. We are the first humans to live in a time when natural spaces – the spatial dynamics evolved by nature without human intervention – are no longer a given. All theatre hitherto has been predicated on human action within non-human nature.
15. Human intervention in nature (synthetic biology and climate change) has meant that nature is changing. Quite possibly to a magnitude that we cannot conceive of. The theatre of refuge witnesses this human experience, as we move into an unknown world.

# 7: Gift Shop.

We hope you enjoyed your visit.

**Figure 15.11**   Untitled photograph. © Tom Hatton. Calais.

*After The Jungle. April 2016.*

# Notes

1. On conditions in the camp, also see Crafter and Rosen (this volume).
2. On the diverse impacts of displacement and inhumane reception conditions, see Krause and Sharples (on children and adolescents affected by conflict and displacement) and Chatterjee *et al.*, both in this volume.
3. On the role and experiences of a humanitarian volunteer worker in the camp, see Crafter and Rosen in this volume.

# 16

# Care in a refugee camp: A case study of a humanitarian volunteer in Calais

Sarah Crafter and Rachel Rosen

## Introduction

What does it mean to care in the context of extreme adversity, such as the crisis of hospitality that migrants have encountered in Europe in the past decade? Drawing on a geographies-of-care framework, this chapter follows the case study of a humanitarian volunteer in the unofficial refugee camp in Calais, France.[1] Foregrounding the complexities of care provides a useful entry point to understanding the interactions between formal contexts in which care occurs and informal practices across time and space, including in conditions saturated with precarity and power. However, the assumed figure of the adult as carer in this theoretical approach is challenged by the complexities of lives on the move and the contested nature of childhood.

The wider backdrop to this case study is the movement of more than one million asylum seekers entering Europe in 2015, some of whom made their way to the refugee camp in Calais, France, as a key destination point for entering the UK (Clayton and Willis, 2019). There had been prior settlements in the Calais area since the late 1990s (Reinisch, 2015), but this chapter focuses on the site that was controversially dubbed the 'Jungle' by the media in 2015 and 2016 (Harker, 2016). This was a volatile context, with both the UK Home Office and French authorities prioritizing the securitization of the region, rather than providing assistance or protection for refugees. For example, the camp in Calais was repeatedly demolished and reconstructed in different forms, with mass evictions and demolitions having taken place by October 2016.

The lack of official recognition of the Calais refugee camp by either the British or French authorities meant that larger international charities were not present (Clayton and Willis, 2019). Instead, a smaller collection of charities and volunteer organizations provided essential daily services to fill this void. This chapter is a case analysis of the founder of one such charitable organization, Liz Clegg, who started the Unofficial Women and Children's Centre (UWCC) in the Calais refugee camp in 2015. Notwithstanding the fact that such endeavours are complex and often tenuous, they are inevitably tied to our moral responsibilities towards others (Wilkinson, 2014) and may also be linked with concepts of care. Care, as an interdependent relationship involving both physical and emotional labour (Bowlby, 2012) and ethical questions, may be deeply challenging in the context of an extreme situation such as an unofficial refugee camp and a crisis of hospitality.

This chapter narrates the story of Liz's time in the camp and, more specifically, her care relationships with some women refugees and their children, as well as unaccompanied children living in the camp. In doing so, we draw on geographies of care perspectives and, more specifically, the notions of 'caringscapes' and 'carescapes' (Bowlby, 2012). 'Caringscapes' refers to the social organization of informal care, with particular reference to time, space, shifting possibilities and obligations taking place across time and space (De Graeve, 2017; De Graeve and Bex, 2017). 'Carescapes' is used to refer to 'the resource and service context shaping the "caringscape terrain"' (Bowlby, 2012: 2112), such as the role of institutions or care organizations.

This chapter uses the case study of Liz's experiences to explore care in the context of extreme challenge and adversity in the refugee camp. It begins by introducing her initiation into humanitarian volunteering in the refugee camp. The chapter then considers how the concepts of carescape and caringscape illuminate some of the complexities raised by Liz relating to informal volunteering with women and children living in refugee situations. Finally, as Liz's own work in the camp extended to include children – both with families and alone – we argue that the carescape and caringscape framework would benefit from exploring contested childhoods: extreme situations in which imaginaries of the ideal child as the vulnerable recipient of adult care sit at odds with adults' abilities to enact care relationships. Additionally, we propose that the caringscape framework might be useful for exploring care relationships by children, for other children.

## 'We never realized we'd have to stay' – Liz's introduction to humanitarian aid

In the early summer of 2015, Liz was working as part of the clean-up crew following Glastonbury Festival. The music festival generated thousands of left-behind tents, sleeping bags and cooking equipment. Aware of the growing crisis for refugees and the expanding refugee camp in Calais, Liz had initially planned to simply take this equipment to the camp, drop it off at a charity warehouse and continue on to other work. What she saw led her to stay in the camp for prolonged periods of time until its eventual demolition in the autumn of 2016. The camp had become an epicentre of both a humanitarian and a political crisis. Conditions there were reported to be 'diabolical', with poor water, sanitation, living conditions and emotional distress (Harker, 2016). Census data collected by the non-governmental organization (NGO), Help Refugees, indicates that by autumn 2016, alongside the adult population of 8,241 there were 865 children living in the unofficial refugee camp in Calais, 78 per cent of whom were 'alone'.

When Liz arrived, there were fewer than ten volunteers attempting to sort, manage and distribute goods out of the warehouse. She described how they were overwhelmed by a bottleneck of donated goods which they were struggling to distribute within the camp. She spent hours each day helping to distribute items like clothing, shoes, bedding, hygiene products and food:

> I realized there's nobody handing out food, there's nobody doing this, there's nobody doing that and it was, it just, carried on and I never left … So I started distributing out of the back of a truck and managed to find various random volunteers to help me. And, yeah, line distribution: a bit of a nightmare. Not really ideal, but there was nobody else and it was the only way to get it out there. So that's what we did. Literally hundreds and hundreds, I mean we could have, we did one seven-hour shoe distribution; hundreds and hundreds of people came for shoes because the weather was so bad and it was horrendous. And we just did it.

This was not care at a distance, in which, for example, donors might give money for aid without needing to directly confront the realities of a humanitarian crisis (Silk, 2000). Equally, we get a sense that her time in the camp was not planned but formed from a reluctance to walk away from a desperate situation, so Liz just 'carried on and I never left'. There was a catalyst incident, however, when she first arrived in the camp, which she said 'shocked me, and I guess it's what made me stay out [there]'. Liz was distributing alone from the back of a truck and it was raining hard. A man spotted a roll of bin bags, which he grabbed to use as a rain jacket. Within seconds other people were doing the same and it 'turned into a bit of a scrum'. She said:

> I was shocked that, oh my God, we're in northern France and these people have just had a mini riot over a roll of bin bags. And I was kind of, that kind of brought it home to me how desperate these people were.

Perhaps more noticeable to Liz were the conditions for the women, which she described as 'horrendous'. The small official refugee centre had a space for women, but many were afraid to use it in case they were registered as being in France and therefore forced to claim asylum there, rather than the UK. The border between UK and France is at the edge of the Schengen region of Europe where it is possible to move without a passport, thereby making Calais a key point where mobility regimes change.

Liz had the impression, but was not certain, that the official centre would only allow children up to the age of 12 to enter as long as they were accompanied by an adult. In fact, in 2013 the EU Dublin III regulation stated that refugees should have their asylum claims processed in the EU country where they are first registered, but that unaccompanied minors with close relatives in other European states (known as Dublin III claimants) should be an exception. However, commentators who were in the camp observed that many of the children with strong Dublin III claims were missed (Clayton and Willis, 2019). In the final months prior to the camp's demolition, it was estimated that there were nearly 2,000 unaccompanied young people. Regardless, many women decided to live outside of this official space in other parts of the camp, and Liz realized that they had specific needs that other government and aid agencies were not fulfilling.

Liz described how she wanted to develop a space within the camp where women and children could go '24-7' because some were being raped or injured in the night. She also wanted to ensure that there were appropriate supplies available to women and children, such as sanitary products and small-sized shoes and clothing. Commenting that 'we never realized we'd have to stay', Liz talked about how the reality of life in the camp signified to her a necessary longer-term commitment, which included starting the UWCC.

## The physical and emotional entanglements of care

A central theme in Liz's narrative, although she does not explicitly state it in these terms, is the physical and emotional care labour done by women and children living in the camp and those who volunteered to support them. According to Sophie Bowlby (2012), the labour involved in caring for, and about, others always involves some kind of transactional interdependency. Despite this, there are many situations in which the caring of others brings to the fore the inequalities inherent in any relationship where there may be power differentials or vulnerabilities. Moreover, caring relationships are open to influence from other intersections of diversity such as ethnicity, age, social class and locationality (De Graeve, 2017). Caring practices are also deeply emotional (Atkinson, Lawson, and Wiles, 2011) and linked to both how we feel and how we feel in certain contexts and places (Milligan, 2005). These elements of caringscapes are shaped by, and in turn shape, the carescapes in which such labour occurs. In this case, the carescape was marked by highly precarious lives rendered 'ungrievable' (Butler, 2016) – with the emphasis on securitization, limited resources and infrastructure for basic provisions, and increasingly restrictive immigration regimes in the UK (Rosen, Crafter and Meetoo, 2019).

Liz described herself as a 'humanitarian' who had an informal role providing space and support for people in the camp. We would suggest, however, that many of her activities can also be viewed as a type of informal care, such as using her position as a non-state actor to position herself as a resource to people (Bowlby, 2012), whereas government and state actors' contributions were described as minimal and, by extension, inadequate. Their money went towards fences; perimeters; and, of course, the building of the limited official camp: the Jules Ferry Centre. Liz only ever intended the UWCC to be in operation until state actors stepped in to take up their responsibilities, which arguably never happened. Non-governmental aid agencies such as Médecins du Monde and Médecins Sans Frontières provided necessary care, attempting to help with health-related needs. There was also support from faith-based aid agencies, both Islamic and Christian, with varying approaches to supporting migrants and transformed by migrants in the process of 'living' religion (Saunders et al., 2016). Liz places herself in the role of mediator between the migrants and the aid agencies. Care, in this context, transcends both territorial and familial boundaries (Popke, 2006):

I think because we were based and living in the Jungle we had a better connection with the women, because they saw that we were living in the thick of it. So we kind of built up this kind of trust. So we tried to be the bridge between what was available from the services and the refugees, and educate women that it's OK to go to the doctor … a really nice midwife there, and don't worry about that; that's fine. And [we] started to try to build those bridges between the refugees and the French services.

While the provision of care has sometimes been criticized for being paternalistic (Milligan and Wiles, 2010), Liz's form of care, her own humanitarianism, attempted to work against patronizing and hierarchical relations. Liz perceived the refugee camp as a gendered space where women and children were outnumbered, neglected, invisible and often vulnerable. In contrast, she approached women residents in the camp to ask what the UWCC could do for them. The women asked for a beauty day when they could have a proper shower, do their hair and make choices from the donated clothes. While on the surface this activity may seem flippant, it is worth highlighting the atrocious living conditions of the camp. The camp itself took shape on what was previously a refuse site. The ground was sandy, and the wind would create eddies of dirt-embedded debris. Rats were a major problem, and the temporary toilets were rarely emptied and not well cleaned. Overall, there were significant problems with harmful bacteria and unhygienic conditions (Harker, 2016).

The challenges offered by the physical and material space were matched by the psychological difficulties experienced by migrants (on trauma, resilience and well-being in displacement situations, see Chatterjee et al., and Krause and Sharples – both in this volume). This is discussed by Christine Milligan and Janine Wiles (2010), who talk about care as an emotional landscape full of entanglements – including tensions and feelings of connectedness. Liz described how the women, who came from a diverse set of cultural and religious backgrounds, began to 'bond' with each other through a shared ecology of emotion within the space (Reavey et al., 2017). Liz framed the emotional entanglements as a move from shame to dignity. Dignity is a concept that the care literature around disability has focused on, because being cared for can leave you in undignified positions and often involve an unchosen intimacy with the human body (Watson et al., 2004). For the women involved in the UWCC, ongoing emotional care work took place through stories and experiences of trauma told during caring practices – namely, massage. Tactile massage as a tool for acts of care and compassion has been found to be effective in more formal care relationships – for example, between nurses and patients (Airosa *et al.*, 2016).

These were informal relationships however, and women were both the 'cared for' and the 'caregivers' (Milligan, 2005). The care delivered by women, for women, was a catalyst for emotional entanglements but also a space of physical intimacy:

> And massages: incredible, powerful, a lot of tears. People might think, oh; having a massage, that's nice, but actually the stuff it brings up when a woman is allowed to relax and be pampered and cared for, actually huge amounts of tears, huge amounts of outpourings. Disclosures, lots of disclosures … so when they have this experience it all suddenly comes out that they lost a couple of kids on the way or something like that. And there are a lot of tears. They'll talk about very difficult things. I mean it's all a bit horrendous. Every day, oh look, you know, being raped a lot, a lot have been raped. But it is, it is incredible that you can watch an Eritrean girl with an Afghan woman do each other's hair and you sit and listen and … there was a woman not long ago who was being massaged and she just came out with, she'd been really badly raped and she hadn't, it had caused a lot of damage to her and she … had all sorts of problems. And it all came out when she was having a massage. And there were some other girls who'd had similar experiences and … they were able to go, 'it's all right'. It's just so awful, isn't it, that it just takes … you know, OK, you've got bits hanging out and she was scared about it. And she hadn't told anybody because she was so ashamed of being raped. And some other girl just came over and said, 'no, no, no; that happened to me. OK. I've had this done, that done and it's fine'. And they're able to … we can provide the space and we can provide hair oil and this, that and the other …

It was no coincidence that Liz developed the UWCC to operate outside of the formal socio-structural processes that were evident in other parts of the camp. The development of a caringscape outside the confines of the state and charity-organized spaces was to fulfil, from Liz's perspective, a gap in the care being offered to certain women and children (including those with children over the age of 12 or with children who were considered too 'troublesome' to be accommodated).

Equally, though, Liz was very conscious of the status of her own position in relation to refugees in the camp. She was both an insider and outsider in this relationship – but, notably, one with the ability to leave the situation:

... it's a very interesting dynamic, isn't it, those of us who provide the space with ... people who are receiving the aid and what have you; it's a very interesting dynamic. And on some levels you know, [inaudible] situation; we're very aware of that. And we have access to stuff and, of course, a lot of the refugees think we're government organizations, they think we're all paid and we've got access to an endless amount of everything and of course we don't. And so ... so it's an interesting dynamic to have incredibly close relationships with people and yet it is them and us and we are never going to be equal. And I've found that fascinating to be with that dynamic, that ... yeah, we're never going to be equal. And they know it and we know it and they know that ... we know, oh; these people who are nice to us, they want something. And yet they're wonderful people who are ... and it's a fascinating ... fascinating experience that you can't ... you can't resolve it.

The kind of care work undertaken by the UWCC took place in a public space (Raghuram *et al.*, 2009), but not one within the tight institutional boundaries of structures such as a hospice, nursery or old-people's home. It was also possible that maintaining an explicit strategy to keep care at an informal level gave Liz more room to be creative with the space and for the women to take the lead on how they wanted to use the space. Liz was not there in a formal capacity, and therefore, was not caught within the same tensions that formal care practitioners (such as social workers) may feel when their personal desire to care is at odds with the institution regimes that they are obliged to uphold (De Graeve, 2017).

It is in this regard that the caringscape literature helps us to make sense of Liz's story. She stayed in the camp despite the inequalities that made solidarity very conditional, but she did so because of a moral sense of responsibility to others and to the world (Wilkinson, 2014). Evident in the quotes above is not only a recognition that care relationships are almost never 'equal', even if they are reciprocal, but that reflexivity is a central part of addressing these sorts of issues in caringscapes. While Liz did not describe her motives as being explicitly political, in that she narrated her actions as providing aid for people's everyday survival, she was vocal about wanting the state to take care of its obligations towards the crisis. Her determination to continue working in both an unofficial and informal care space in effect allowed her to take on both of those positions at once. Additionally, we have shown how care is an emotional and existential requirement – and one that is laden with ethical, political and economic implications. By placing intimate actions and relationships in a wider context of 'carescape terrain', we have provided conceptual resources to consider their interactions and tensions, and to keep both personal decisions and structural contexts in the frame of analysis.

## Caring *for* children and care *by* children

Within discussions around migration, children are often talked about as an extension of women and/or families rather than as people in their own right (Orellana *et al.*, 2001). Certainly this has been the approach dominating traditional theorizations of care relationships (Burman, 2008; Rosen and Newberry, 2018). Others have pointed to problems in conflating women and children into one homogeneous group because they have a different set of pressures, particularly around asylum (Bhabha, 2004; Enloe, 1991). Equally, it has been argued that the woman–child relationship shifts across different places, contexts, political situations, class and gendered spaces (Rosen and Twamley, 2018). Therefore, any conflation can mask the experiences of children and young people, making those travelling alone or as a separated minor invisible (Rosen and Crafter, 2018).

It is unsurprising then, that early on in the development of the UWCC, care for and with women was treated as the precursor to care for children. Liz viewed the improved well-being of the mothers as a reflection on children's well-being. Over time, though, she began to build relationships with separated children and those children who were so testing that 'no one wanted to deal with' them. Liz described the care of the unaccompanied younger children (13 and under) as extremely challenging, and when she reflected on her time looking after these children she said, 'I will not lie, don't know how we did that'. Regardless of these challenges, Liz talked about the deep emotional care relationships (Milligan, 2005; Milligan and Wiles, 2010) that she established with some of the separated children, developing a profound sense of responsibility towards them. Liz's growing and ongoing feelings of responsibility towards separated children in the camp resonates with discussions about ethics of care among feminist geographers, in which care is undertaken outside of the family and sometimes at a distance (McEwan and Goodman, 2010). Liz, for example, continued to make herself available to these children by giving them her telephone number so that even when she was away from the camp they could contact her.

When there is a focus on children in the literature, care is usually something that adults do for or to children (Rosen and Newberry, 2018). What has been given less attention through a caringscape lens is care *by* children, particularly in the context of the minority world. The 'carings-capes' literature has largely focused on the care of children by adults, even in the case of separated or unaccompanied children (De Graeve and Bex, 2016). This is perhaps because there has often been an interesting associ-ation between paternalism and care (Milligan and Wiles, 2010) but also because traditional understandings of childhood suggest that children should be cared for, rather than do the caring. The limits of this framework are, however, notable – particularly in the case of unaccompanied migrant children, given the absence of adult kin who might play a caring role.

There are examples in other research areas in which children can be seen as central actors in care labour. Children's work, when widely defined to include both paid and unpaid labour such as domestic work, can involve children caring for others (Crafter *et al.*, 2009). For instance, there is a body of work from the South African context looking at child-headed households born out of the HIV/AIDS epidemic. Fearing abuse, many children choose to live with their siblings without adult support. Research suggests that, on the one hand, some local communities support these children but, on the other hand, these children are also regarded as 'unruly, wild and even dangerous' (Haley and Bradbury, 2015: 399). In relation to migration, the work of Lorraine Young and Nicola Ansell (2003) is instructive. They provide the example of 'fluid households' in the context of the HIV/AIDs epidemic in southern Africa, in which orphaned children migrate alone to be with their 'extended family'. These children are often involved in, and used for, care labour.

Indeed, although she did not immediately speak about children's care for each other, perhaps for the reasons noted above, when pressed, Liz commented:

> … there is a lot of that and there are some incredible examples of children looking after children. There was a boy who's ten, he'd got his nephew with him who's seven and they were separated … and it's gobsmacking; it is gobsmacking when I see … now when I'm with the boys in the UK … they have their own … when … you know, like recently we've had an issue and so I discuss it with some of the boys. And I watch them … they're not related, they've known each other in the camp, bonded in the camp but then they had a big meeting to discuss it all and tell each other. And I watch them and it's … there is an incredible resilience and group … I don't know what it is, a kind of survival-group discussion that goes on amongst them and that is always, you know, is amazing to see. That is an incredible bit of resilience.

Our own observations of children's relationships, both within the Calais camp and in their support networks on arrival to the UK, speak to the importance of children's care relationships with and for each other (Rosen *et al.*, 2019). These observations are supported by Sue Clayton, a film-maker and news producer who worked extensively in the Calais camp and who found the bonds of friendship to be extremely strong (Clayton, 2019). It was not unusual, for example, for the young people to find each other and regularly meet up when they reached the UK. They were willing to cover considerable distances to do so, even when their foster-care accommodation was far apart.

Such relationships are not without their pitfalls, however. While the children were said to provide each other with resources in the form of both knowledge and psychological support (Kendrick and Kakuru, 2012), the information that they shared in their networks sometimes perpetuated misinformation. For instance, some of the NGO/charity workers tried to dissuade the young people from attempting to come to Britain, knowing that there was a high probability of deportation at 18 years of age. However, many of the young refugees in the camp were desperate to get to the UK. There are differences in the national definitions of 'persecution' between the UK and France, which are central to achieving legal recognition as a refugee. France has a far more limited definition, recognizing only government persecution as grounds for refugee status, while the UK's broader definition makes it more likely that people who have experienced persecution by non-state actors will be granted asylum.

Arguably, the challenges brought about by camp life were made more complex in relation to the presence of children, their age-related care and constructions of childhood. For example, Liz described how only children under 12 were allowed in the Jules Ferry Centre, so it was decided that the UWCC would accept a range of ages to make up for this shortcoming. They supplied the younger children with toys but bore witness to a range of 'upsetting' and 'shocking' behaviour, because 'it took quite a lot of managing to enable these children to learn to play with each other, to not have anxiety around toys'.

Commenting on the care provided by the UWCC, Liz explained:

> You know … these children have … were … an absolute nightmare and these wonderful volunteers … And a lot of the women also recognized that we couldn't abandon these children. And they were constantly a nightmare and took a lot of management. But yes, so there are … yes, severe challenges to working with … you know, a lot of children, particular the younger ones that are

unaccompanied. Huge behavioural problems, huge lack of boundaries. They've learnt to do all sorts of stuff to survive, absolute nightmare. Very little respect for adults, obviously, they're all abandoned and you know ... No, if you had the choice you certainly ... certainly wouldn't have done what we did over the winter. But we didn't have any choice; we had no choice.

Liz's quote reflects some of the contradictions and contested ideas about childhood that may be applied to children in camp life – and, in particular, to separated children (De Graeve and Bex, 2017). Set against hegemonic understandings of how children should be, such as particular ways of behaving or having the ability to play in a certain way with toys, these children presented a contradiction in adult imaginaries of childhood. First, they had seen and done 'stuff to survive' that set them outside of assumptions of childhood innocence and, by corollary, notions of children as the objects of (paternalistic) care. It was very probable that they had spent considerable time operating outside of the expectations and boundaries set by adults, and certainly had established relationships with non-kin adults on their own or through relationships with other children. While some adults, such as Liz, attempted to provide care, many had encountered adults on their journey who had done the opposite of care for them. As a result, their encounters with charity workers who attempted to embody an adult–child caring relationship – often based on impossible idealizations of middle-class, minority-world childhoods – became fraught with tension. Such tensions suggest that there is still more to be done within the carescapes/caringscapes framework in the context of contested childhoods.

## Concluding comments

In this chapter, we have drawn on the caringscapes/carescapes literature to help us make sense of a humanitarian aid worker's experiences of life in the camp in Calais. Using the caringscapes/carescapes framework has enabled us to make sense of Liz's decisions to maintain her identity as a humanitarian with a moral responsibility to care in the face of a highly challenging and extreme situation. Previous conceptual work on care had struggled with the blurred lines between informal and formal caring – the former often being problematically associated with familial care in the home, and the latter with the type of care delivered by professionals (Atkinson *et al.*, 2011; Watson *et al.*, 2004). The 'caringscape' framework by Bowlby (2012) offers new ways in which to explore how non-familial care can be socially organized and implicated by its situatedness to time and space. Liz did not begin with the intention of staying for a prolonged time in the Calais camp, but was initially drawn into the struggle felt by other volunteers to distribute charitable donations to all who needed them, and later to the extreme challenges faced by women in the camp and, later still, to the children.

It is notable, though, that Liz deliberately locates herself outside formal care organizations and other services that shape the 'caringscape terrain' in the Calais camp, while simultaneously playing a mediational role between the women and some of the limited formal services that were available. It is no coincidence that she set up an informal care organization with the word 'Unofficial' in the title. This was in deliberate and decided contrast to the official Jules Ferry Centre, which was open to women and children but of which many migrants were suspicious, as discussed above. At the same time, she worked on the margins of carescapes by mediating with medical and religious support groups.

Central to discussions of care, both in the literature and by Liz herself, are discussions about ethical responsibility (Raghuram *et al.*, 2009) and a broader sense of caring about others and the world. Liz also saw herself filling a gap within the carescape terrain where the state, in her view, failed to provide a basic and necessary level of care. It is because of this gap that Liz describes how she felt compelled to care, partly prompted by witnessing a change in people's identities and behaviours born out of the harsh conditions. Liz's own story also speaks to the inequalities of 'caring for' in these situations, of which she is highly conscious herself. It is of note, given how central both power and inequality are to discussions about carescapes, that Liz narrates different positionalities of care throughout her time at the camp. In her initial role as a distributor of charitable goods, she described taking a firm and almost authoritative role in order to avoid conflicts while crowds of people waited for items. On the other hand, in setting up the UWCC she sought out the women's views on what kinds of activities they wish to engage with. The women thus took a lead in both determining the activities that they would undertake and the stories that they told to each other. Even so, Liz is reflexively conscious that there remains an imbalance of equality between her as a provider of care (and someone who can come and go from the camp) and their position in the camp as refugees and, in the context of the UWCC, the receivers of care – not to mention their inability to cross various social and geopolitical borders.

While the caringscapes/carescapes framework was very useful in exploring Liz's relationship with women in the camp, the framework also makes a useful contribution to debates relating to the imaginaries of care when looking at children who are separated or unaccompanied minors. We suggest that contestations surrounding the imaginaries of childhood are inexorably linked to how both the social organization of informal care (caringscapes) and the resource-and-service context (carescape) shaping the 'caringscape terrain' operate. At the level of the carescape *terrain*, the official camp seemed to place boundaries relating to age and lone status. Consequently, over time, Liz saw herself filling a gap in the care of both unaccompanied/separated children and young children whose parents did not want to be part of the official camp spaces and, as she put it, of children that 'no one else wanted to deal with'. On the one hand, Liz saw herself filling a gap in need that others did not respond to, which matches her position relating to women. On the other hand, the UWCC's attempts to manage children in ways that fitted with 'normalized' notions of childhood and care became problematic. Many children struggled to use the UWCC-provided toys in ways that reflected particular ways of behaving, based on the assumption that the natural activity of childhood is playing with toys (Rosen, 2016). In some instances, practices based on constructions of the playful child had the unintended consequence of heightening anxiety and causing rifts between children, and between children and adults.

We also argue here that the caringscapes framework has been developed *by* adults *for* adults, taking adult carers as the assumed norm, and has therefore paid little attention to the care *of* children *by* children. For children living in extreme situations, especially those who are separated or travelling alone, care relationships with other children can be of paramount importance. In a study about unaccompanied asylum-seeking children in Ireland, for example, adults were largely absent from their lives and relationships with other children were a key support from social isolation (Abunimah and Blower, 2010). Liz reported witnessing similar relationships in the refugee camp in Calais. However, less is known about the different forms that this care may take, or what benefits and challenges might be generated by these relationships. One core tenet of the caringscape/carescape framework is the connection of care relationships across time and space. Given that tenuous circumstances of dislocation and forced migration can lead to the physical separation of kin-related adults and children, and a disruption of established patterns of care, we would suggest that care between children represents a significant gap in the research.

# Note

1. This chapter can be productively read alongside the contributions in this volume by Bailey; Qasmiyeh; and Hooyshar Emami (all offering different insights into the Calais camp), and Fiddian-Qasmiyeh (on Palestinian refugees in Lebanon responding in support of people displaced from Syria).

# References

Abunimah, Ali and Sarah Blower. 2010. 'The Circumstances and Needs of Separated Children Seeking Asylum in Ireland', *Child Care in Practice* 16 (2): 129–46.

Airosa, Fanny, Torkel Falkenberg, Gunnar Öhlén and Maria Arman. 2016. 'Tactile Massage as Part of the Caring Act: A Qualitative Study in Short-Term Emergency Wards', *Journal of Holistic Nursing* 34 (1): 13–23.

Atkinson, Sarah, Victoria Lawson and Janine Wiles. 2011. 'Care of the Body: Spaces of Practice', *Social and Cultural Geography* 12 (6): 563–72.

Bhabha, Jacqueline. 2004. 'Demography and Rights: Women, Children and Access to Asylum', *International Journal of Refugee Law* 16 (2): 227–43.

Bowlby, Sophie. 2012. 'Recognising the Time–Space Dimensions of Care: Caringscapes and Carescapes', *Environment and Planning A: Economy and Space* 44 (9): 2101–18.

Burman, Erica. 2008. *Deconstructing Developmental Psychology*. 2nd ed. London: Routledge.

Butler, Judith. 2016. *Frames of War: When is Life Grievable?* London: Verso.

Clayton, Sue. 2019. 'Narrating the Young Migrant Journey: Themes of Self-Representation'. In *Unaccompanied Young Migrants: Identity, Care and Justice*, edited by Sue Clayton, Anna Gupta and Katie Willis, 115–33. Bristol: Policy Press.

Clayton, Sue and Katie Willis. 2019. 'Migration Regimes and Border Controls: The Crisis in Europe'. In *Unaccompanied Young Migrants: Identity, Care and Justice*, edited by Sue Clayton, Anna Gupta and Katie Willis, 15–38. Bristol: Policy Press.

Crafter, Sarah, Lindsay O'Dell, Guida de Abreu and Tony Cline. 2009. 'Young Peoples' Representations of "Atypical" Work in English Society', *Children and Society* 23 (3): 176–88.

De Graeve, Katrien. 2017. 'Classed Landscapes of Care and Belonging: Guardianships of Unaccompanied Minors', *Journal of Refugee Studies* 30 (1): 71–88.

De Graeve, Katrien and Christof Bex. 2016. 'Imageries of Family and Nation: A Comparative Analysis of Transnational Adoption and Care for Unaccompanied Minors in Belgium', *Childhood* 23 (4): 492–505.

De Graeve, Katrien and Christof Bex. 2017. 'Caringscapes and Belonging: An Intersectional Analysis of Care Relationships of Unaccompanied Minors in Belgium', *Children's Geographies* 15 (1): 80–92.

Enloe, Cynthia. 1991. '"Womenandchildren": Propaganda Tools of Patriarchy'. In *Mobilizing Democracy: Changing the US Role in the Middle East*, edited by Greg Bates, 89–95. Monroe, ME: Common Courage Press.

Faulstich Orellana, Marjorie, Barrie Thorne, Anna Chee and Wan Shun Eva Lam. 2001. 'Transnational Childhoods: The Participation of Children in Processes of Family Migration', *Social Problems* 48 (4): 572–91.

Haley, Jeanne F. and Jill Bradbury. 2015. 'Child-Headed Households under Watchful Adult Eyes: Support or Surveillance?', *Childhood* 22 (3): 394–408.

Harker, Joseph. 2016. 'Stop Calling the Calais Refugee Camp the "Jungle"', *The Guardian*, 7 March. Accessed 18 January 2020. www.theguardian.com/commentisfree/2016/mar/07/stop-calling-calais-refugee-camp-jungle-migrants-dehumanising-scare-stories.

Kendrick, Maureen and Doris Kakuru. 2012. 'Funds of Knowledge in Child-Headed Households: A Ugandan Case Study', *Childhood* 19 (3): 397–413.

McEwan, Cheryl and Michael K. Goodman. 2010. 'Place Geography and the Ethics of Care: Introductory Remarks on the Geographies of Ethics, Responsibility and Care', *Ethics, Place and Environment* 13 (2): 103–12.

Milligan, Christine. 2005. 'From Home to "Home": Situating Emotions within the Caregiving Experience', *Environment and Planning A: Economy and Space* 37 (12): 2105–20.

Milligan, Christine and Janine Wiles. 2010. 'Landscapes of Care', *Progress in Human Geography* 34 (6): 736–54.

Popke, Jeff. 2006. 'Geography and Ethics: Everyday Mediations through Care and Consumption', *Progress in Human Geography* 30 (4): 504–12.

Raghuram, Parvati, Clare Madge and Pat Noxolo. 2009. 'Rethinking Responsibility and Care for a Postcolonial World', *Geoforum* 40 (1): 5–13.

Reavey, Paula, Jason Poole, Richard Corrigall, Toby Zundel, Sarah Byford, Mandy Sarhane, Eric Taylor, John Ivens and Dennis Ougrin. 2017. 'The Ward as Emotional Ecology: Adolescent Experiences of Managing Mental Health and Distress in Psychiatric Inpatient Settings', *Health and Place* 46: 210–18.

Reinisch, Jessica. 2015. '"Forever Temporary": Migrants in Calais, Then and Now', *Political Quarterly* 86 (4): 515–22.

Rosen, Rachel. 2016. 'Early Childhood Subjectivities, Inequities, and Imaginative Play'. In *Identities and Subjectivities*, edited by Nancy Worth and Claire Dwyer, 141–62. Singapore: Springer.

Rosen, Rachel and Sarah Crafter. 2018. 'Media Representations of Separated Child Migrants: From Dubs to Doubt', *Migration and Society* 1 (1): 66–81.

Rosen, Rachel, Sarah Crafter and Veena Meetoo. 2019. 'An Absent Presence: Separated Child Migrants' Caring Practices and the Fortified Neoliberal State', *Journal of Ethnic and Migration Studies*, 1–18. Accessed 18 January 2020. https://doi.org/10.1080/1369183X.2019.1608167.

Rosen, Rachel and Jan Newberry. 2018. 'Love, Labour and Temporality: Reconceptualising Social Reproduction with Women and Children in the Frame'. In *Feminism and the Politics of Childhood: Friends or Foes?*, edited by Rachel Rosen and Katherine Twamley, 117–33. London: UCL Press.

Rosen, Rachel and Katherine Twamley. 2018. 'The Woman–Child Question: A Dialogue in the Borderlands'. In *Feminism and the Politics of Childhood: Friends or Foes?*, edited by Rachel Rosen and Katherine Twamley, 1–20. London: UCL Press.

Saunders, Jennifer B., Susanna Snyder and Elena Fiddian-Qasmiyeh. 2016. 'Introduction: Articulating Intersections at the Global Crossroads of Religion and Migration'. In *Intersections of Religion and Migration: Issues at the Global Crossroads*, edited by Jennifer B. Saunders, Elena Fiddian-Qasmiyeh and Susanna Snyder, 1–46. New York: Palgrave Macmillan.

Silk, John. 2000. 'Caring at a Distance: (Im)partiality, Moral Motivation and the Ethics of Representation – Introduction', *Ethics, Place and Environment* 3 (3): 303–9.

Watson, Nick, Linda McKie, Bill Hughes, Debra Hopkins and Sue Gregory. 2004. '(Inter)dependence, Needs and Care: The Potential for Disability and Feminist Theorists to Develop an Emancipatory Model', *Sociology* 38 (2): 331–50.

Wilkinson, Iain. 2014. 'The Problem of Understanding Modern Humanitarianism and Its Sociological Value', *International Social Science Journal* 65 (215/216): 65–78.

Young, Lorraine and Nicola Ansell. 2003. 'Fluid Households, Complex Families: The Impacts of Children's Migration as a Response to HIV/AIDS in Southern Africa', *The Professional Geographer* 55 (4): 464–76.

# 17
# The Jungle

Yousif M. Qasmiyeh

*As we write about the Self, the image of the refugee always floats nearby. It floats palpably and metonymically, as both its own entity and marker. At this moment in time, the refugee has become the conceit of bare survival, the naked survivor whose corpus is no longer a corpus, but its non-elliptical sacrifice. Thus, in writing alone, the refugee can stare at his body (properly) as it disintegrates only to record his own fading and the world's.*

## The Jungle

I

When do shadows sin
by returning to a light that
has suddenly deadened.
Because He lies in stomachs
bearing a void.
Yet you can watch them
chewing sea water,
cooked on stones of wheat.
As if theirs
were a feminine smell
floating in silent alleys.
As if their providence
were a chorus
making coffins
from a remote echo,
hailing a rock that has become theirs.

II

Where will you take me
when the clouds have covered me
with a yellow heart?

III

Places are droppings of the sky.
Bones on the eyelids
and a whiteness like death
lulling the pillars of air.

## Acknowledgements

Qasmiyeh's poem, 'The Jungle', was published in June 2016 on Refugee History: http://refugeehistory.org/blog/2016/12/21/the-jungle, and on Refugee Hosts: https://refugeehosts.org/2017/03/13/the-jungle/

Part III
# Ongoing Journeys: Safety, Rights and Well-being in a Moving World

## 18

# Palliative prophecy: Yezidi perspectives on their suffering under Islamic State and on their future

Tyler Fisher, Nahro Zagros and Muslih Mustafa

## Introduction

On 20 April 2016 (the first Wednesday of Nissan), the Yezidis[1] of northern Iraq celebrated the beginning of their New Year. The holiday is an occasion for the community to reflect on the past as well as on future prospects. The Yezidis' recent past has been fraught with violent persecution, culminating in the attacks by Islamic State (IS) that drove tens of thousands to the mountains of Sinjar, in the northwestern corner of Iraq, in the late summer of 2014. After the fall of Mosul to IS, the aspiring caliphate aimed to expand and consolidate its control over the region by exterminating the thinly protected enclaves of Yezidis and other ethno-religious minorities on the Nineveh Plains. The assault on Sinjar displaced roughly 200,000 civilians and forced almost 50,000 Yezidis to flee to the mountains.

As IS set fire to Yezidi villages, obliterated their shrines with explosives, abducted women and children, and executed men who resisted conversion to Islam, the Yezidis who escaped to the mountains of Sinjar found themselves besieged by IS forces. The week-long siege was broken, if only temporarily, when Kurdish and Iraqi military forces, with support from US airstrikes and humanitarian airdrops, managed to usher most of the displaced Yezidis to the relative safety of camps in Iraqi Kurdistan or Kurdish areas of Syria and Turkey.

In the aftermath, amid mass graves and ongoing efforts to rescue the thousands of Yezidis still in captivity under IS, observers have struggled to take stock of the sheer scale of the atrocities: an estimated 3,100

Yezidis were massacred in the attacks of August 2014, while 6,800 more were taken captive, and as many as 400,000 were forced to abandon their homes – numbers that might ultimately prove to be a conservative estimate (Cetorelli *et al.*, 2017). In short, the Yezidis have been the target of an ongoing genocide that the international community – including the UN, the European Parliament, the Council of Europe, the British Parliament and the United States Congress – finally, formally recognized as such.

The Yezidis survived as a peripheral minority in the upper reaches of Mesopotamia during centuries of the Ottoman Empire, the British Mandate, the Baathist era, the American occupation and withdrawal, and the ascendancy of IS. In northern Iraq, which has long been the centre of Yezidi devotion and the area where their population is most highly concentrated, the shifting political and military tides have been punctuated by recurring hostilities and devastation for their communities. Despite the Yezidis' claims to monotheism, their reverence for angelic beings and the syncretic features of their religion have caused neighbours of other faiths to regard them as apostates or, worse, as devil-worshippers – legitimate prey for persecution.

IS's own propaganda in its slick English-language magazine, *Dabiq*, justifies the mass murder and enslavement of Yezidis on the grounds that they are 'a pagan minority', '*mushrikīn*', whose 'worship of Iblīs [that is, Satan]' makes them fit only for forced conversion, 'the sword' or slavery; 'the Yazidi women and children were then divided according to the Sharī'ah amongst the fighters of the Islamic State who participated in the Sinjar operations, after one fifth of the slaves were transferred to the Islamic State's authority' (Islamic State, 2014: 14–17).

Yet the religion that has rendered them a target for extremists has also proved resilient and adaptive in significant ways.[2] Shamanic prophecy is one feature of the Yezidi religious tradition that has undergone a self-reflexive reinterpretation following genocidal onslaughts by IS. Yezidis maintain that shamanic personages, some in the distant past and some still practising today, had articulated certain prior prophecies concerning a disaster – prophecies that, in effect, had foretold the destruction of Sinjar and, some say, had forecast what would come thereafter. In the light of recent events and the current situation, Yezidis are revisiting their recollection of these prophecies, and some are adjusting their expectations of their future accordingly. Thus, as they hailed their New Year, they conversed about the messages that they had heard in the past and reflected on the implications for the coming year. Taken together, their reflections convey a mingling of credence, doubt and qualified hope – a sense of cautious optimism regarding the prophetic legacy, tempered with disillusion and trepidation born of harrowing experience.

This chapter seeks to document and understand Yezidis' perspectives on their community's recent suffering and on their future. In doing so, it aims to present the perspectives of this ethno-religious minority and to record some of their responses – individual and collective – to their persecution. Providing a space for the voices of Yezidis themselves to be heard (or at least 'read'), on their own terms,[3] is especially important and timely because misrepresentations and misperceptions have, in large part, given rise to the atrocities inflicted on them over the ages, as we have seen most recently in the pages of *Dabiq*.

Recording Yezidi experiences and self-perceptions constitutes, moreover, a critical reminder that they are more than merely numbers in the international newsfeeds' tally of humanitarian crises. By documenting, in particular, their reflections concerning shamanic prophecies in the aftermath of the IS attacks, this chapter foregrounds the personal and communal aspirations, nuanced apprehensions and complex human experiences behind the numbers. The shamanic prophecies about ethnic violence are one aspect of Yezidi culture that has direct bearing on how they perceive and represent themselves, and how they are striving to make some transcendent sense of their situation. This is the rich vein of interpretive insight that the following pages examine.

Although first recorded by an outside observer in the late eighteenth century, the shamanic element in Yezidism has received relatively little scholarly attention. Major ethnographic studies of Yezidism give it little more than a passing mention (Guest, 2010: 34–5; Allison, 2001: 31, 88; Spät, 2005: 48; Spät, 2009: 133). In fact, one of the most thorough, monographic treatments of Yezidi religious culture, *The Religion of the Peacock Angel* (Asatrian and Arakelova, 2014), does not include any discussion of Yezidi shamanism. Philip Kreyenbroek, the scholar who has done the most to document and elucidate Yezidi creeds and customs, characteristically provides a more thorough, albeit brief, treatment of the 'visionaries, diviners and miracle-workers of the community' (Kreyenbroek, 1995: 134–5). He was, however, unable to gather first-hand evidence in relation to these shamanic personages because 'such activities have stopped now', and he reports a taciturn reluctance regarding the subject because the practitioners 'are ashamed' (ibid.: 142, n. 127).

In collaboration with Khalil Jindy Rashow, Kreyenbroek later added an important distinction between the two very different applications of the term *koçek* as 'servants of the sanctuary … at Lalish' and as the 'community's seers' (Kreyenbroek and Rashow, 2005: 8), an aspect that seems to have confounded many previous observers. In short, the lack of a thorough, scholarly treatment of this facet of Yezidi culture is perhaps not surprising. Existing inside and alongside the Yezidis' syncretic religion, the shamanic phenomenon constitutes a quasi-heterodox or unofficial element. It does not, for instance, receive a mention in the Yezidis' own series of school textbooks designed to instruct their children in the principles of Yezidism (Silêman, 2012–13). What follows, then, is an ethnographic approximation, which redresses this relative neglect while also preserving the contemporary perspectives and voices of this vulnerable ethnicity.[4]

## Research methodology

The authors interviewed 39 Yezidis over the course of three days, 19–21 April 2016: the day immediately prior to, the day of and the day after the Yezidi New Year, called *Çarşema Sor* or *Serê Sal* ('Red Wednesday' or 'Head of the Year', respectively).[5] The New Year's celebration afforded optimal circumstances in which to obtain a varied cross-section of the community's perspectives. Not only does the New Year celebration traditionally entail communal gathering – with the largest gathering taking place at Lalish, the Yezidis' principal shrine, in the far north of Iraq – but this occasion also saw the arrival of Yezidis from further afield than would normally be the case, as many have been forced to migrate to the relative security of the regions around Lalish. Some of these displaced people, particularly from the Sinjar District, commented that this New Year's Day marked their first visit to Lalish.

The interviews took place in Lalish itself, and in the nearby towns of Shaykhān and Māmrashān, in the Badinan province of the region called Iraqi Kurdistan at the time of this writing. By deliberately interviewing at least two members (at least one woman and one man) from each of the three Yezidi castes (*mirîd*, *pir* and *sheikh*), we gathered a broad array of perspectives, personal anecdotes and conceptualizations of the Yezidis' shamanic traditions. The interviewees ranged in age from 15 to 70 years old, and varied in the degree of status that they hold within the community, including those who occupy positions of religious and political authority as well as those who have no such rank. Additionally, we conducted an extensive interview with one shamanic practitioner, a 46-year-old *faqra*, who provided key perspectives as a seer who claimed to have foreseen her people's suffering. In spite of the ample variety among our informants, however, this study does not pretend to be in any way comprehensive or definitive, nor does it necessarily reflect the diversity of perspectives in the wider Yezidi diaspora. It does, however, offer an illustrative sampling of dynamic attitudes, memories and beliefs among the Yezidi community at a critical point in its history. Now, before delving

**Figure 18.1**  A shrine on the rooftop of Sheikh Adi's mausoleum in Lalish, the Yezidis' holiest site.  Photograph © Tyler Fisher, 14 December 2018.

into their responses, we must first situate Yezidi shamanism in the context of theory and practice more broadly.

## Shamanism among the Yezidis

The complex of spiritual praxis and religious personae that anthropology conventionally labels *shamanism* takes diverse yet recognizably similar forms across cultures, even among those separated by time and geography. Without digressing into the debates concerning narrow or broad applications of the term, we can usefully apply, with some necessary particularizations, Mircea Eliade's now classic, succinct definition: 'shamanism = technique of ecstasy' (Eliade, 1989: 4). Eliade usefully identifies the ecstatic technique and trance, or altered state of consciousness,[6] as the essence of shamanism, without attempting, as other scholars have done, to tie a definition to the issue of whether the shaman controls spirits or is controlled by spirits:

> the specific element of shamanism is not the embodiment of 'spirits' by the shaman, but the ecstasy [that he or she attains]; incarnating spirits and being 'possessed' by spirits are universally disseminated phenomena, but they do not necessarily belong to shamanism in the strict sense. (Eliade, 1989: 499–500)

In the most general terms, a shaman is a type of 'religious specialist', an extraordinary mediator who acquires and conveys supernatural insight, which may entail clairvoyance (predictions, diagnoses or other kinds of divination) and healing or other supernatural aid; 'the crucial elements of shamanism include direct contact and communication with the supernatural through trance, the use of spirit helpers, the use of a specific culturally recognized and transmitted method and paraphernalia, and a socially recognized special position for the shaman' (Stein and Stein, 2016: 120–1).

With reference to Yezidi shamanism, the particulars of the 'culturally recognized and transmitted method and paraphernalia' are not always entirely consistent. For instance, our informants did not uniformly agree that their shamans' altered state of consciousness is necessarily accompanied by physical, bodily manifestations (for instance, convulsions or fainting) or that their messages are necessarily accompanied by speaking in tongues. Nevertheless, a sufficient number of them acknowledged commonalities among the conspicuous features of Yezidi practice and conceptualization to allow a coherent, composite picture to emerge. We will address, in turn, the persons, the techniques and circumstances, and the messages that constitute Yezidi shamanism today, in relation to the attacks of August 2014.

## Persons

The most common terms for Yezidi shamans is *koçek*, or *faqra* for a female shaman (*faqrya* in the plural).[7] An alternative, generic term, *chavron*, encompasses both sexes and refers to a person who can see the future. They can come from any caste among the Yezidis (ShMS61), and their shamanic status and abilities are not considered hereditary (BaBāFMi46). For some *koçeks* and *faqrya*, fortune-telling is how they make a living (ShMPi64).

The Yezidis frequently mention – sometimes enumerate – particular names of renowned shamans of the past. Their lists are not identical, but there is apparent overlap. 'Koçek Saeed, Koçek Shamo, Koçek Silo, Koçek Hajo, Koçek Hasro, Koçek Karo' is one such list (ShMS68), and of these names, Saeed, Shamo, Hajo, and Karo were most frequently cited as shamans who had attained a significant reputation for efficacy among the Yezidis. The common factor among these is that they all pertain to previous generations and are deceased; some Yezidis named a *koçek* or *faqra* of the present day, even noting one or two that they themselves had consulted, but not in the form of a rote list.

There is a widespread perception among the Yezidis that the shamans of the past were more authentic and credible, and greater in number, power and predictive accuracy. Conversely, Yezidis view those of the present day as fewer in number and more suspect, more likely to be shams than genuine shamans and more likely to be motivated by financial gain – to the extent that some of our informants categorically dismissed anyone who purported to be a *koçek* or *faqra* in the present day. One servitor at the Lalish shrine succinctly expressed this view:

> Don't believe those *koçek* and *faqrya* today. Some of the *koçek* in the past were blind and deaf, yet they could hear voices and see the future. Their predictions were always correct and you could rely on them. People had absolute faith in those *faqrya* and *koçek*, but today there are no genuine ones, and the majority of their predictions are incorrect. People used to believe in them more. (ShMMi60)

'I don't believe in *koçeks* and *faqrya*,' another woman declared, '[but] the ones from the previous generation were very good. Whatever they said was true' (ShFPi68). An elderly *sheikh*, whose father and grandfather had served in Lalish before him, recalled having to chase a charlatan out of the shrine for making fraudulent claims of shamanic abilities within the last two years (ShMS68). 'There are people who have this power, to predict the future, but the majority of them are not genuine. They are doing it for money' (ShMMi50). 'People don't believe in them like they used to. It's like Pepsi-Cola', another *sheikh* quipped, 'It used to taste better before, but now Pepsi-Cola doesn't taste as good. People don't believe in *koçeks* and *faqrya* now because they don't sound genuine' (ShMS61).[8]

Nonetheless, a purported *koçek* or *faqra* in the past was not necessarily above suspicion. One *mirîd* recalled that the shamanic phenomenon 'was very common thirty to forty years ago in Ba'shīqa [his home town]. There were three or four people who would lose consciousness, go into a trance, as if going to another world', and he added the following anecdote:

> My cousin and I once, when we were about fifteen years old, were naughty boys, and a woman went into a trance. She was not a *faqra*, she was cheating people, and she thought she was a spiritual lady or something like that. And we attended that incident. And then I asked my cousin, who's dead now, his name was Asa, 'let's take out her underwear'. And she suddenly came out [of her feigned trance]! (BaBāMMi65)

The practising *faqra* whom we interviewed, a middle-aged *mirîd* mother of five sons, was born in Ba'shīqa Bāzān but has lived in Māmrashān for the past 28 years. No previous shamans, to her knowledge, were in her family line, but her family has been associated with serving at Lalish and as *qawwals*, itinerant singers and musicians who preserve the Yezidis' sacred lore. She identified herself as one of only two *faqrya* practising in the village, and noted as a point of pride that she has been practising for ten years in comparison to her counterpart's three. She claimed, moreover, to have Yezidi, Muslim and Christian clients, some of whom travel from Syria, Iran and Jordan to seek her services. As is typical of shamans across cultures, she associated the onset of her shamanic abilities with a severe illness and recovery:

> It's a gift from God. One day I was ill. I was ill for three years. Very ill, and I was losing my mind. And one day I felt better, but I also felt that I possessed a power. It was like wearing a large, new jacket. You know you are wearing it. It was that obvious I possessed a power. And from then on, whatever I predict, it must happen.

## Techniques and circumstances

The shamanic phenomenon among the Yezidis is often accompanied by unusual behaviour: screaming, trembling, convulsions, sometimes falling down or reclining while receiving spiritual revelation in a trance-like state – these are recurring features in Yezidis' descriptions (ShMPi64, ShMPi65, BaBāMMi65). The tendency of a *koçek* or *faqra* to speak in a foreign or unidentifiable, incomprehensible language was also frequently noted as a feature of their practice (ShMMi30, ShMMi50, ShMPi64). 'Those people speak in a language – it could be English or anything. It is a language we cannot understand' (ShMS61). One widow, who has lived at Lalish as a *faqir* (servitor at the shrine) for three years, described the behaviour as follows:

> It is very strange when you see them fall down, and they speak in French, foreign languages, Turkish, maybe twenty languages. It is baffling. You would be scared to look at them. You listen to them and look at them and are unable to understand what they are saying. (ShFMi55)

Other practices include laying hands on a client's forehead (ShMMi70). A Yezidi shaman may also exhibit uncommon physical strength: 'they go into a trance, and they become physically very powerful. They could lift you and hurl you some distance' (ShMMi50).

In stark contrast to the eccentric behaviour noted above, however, the *faqra* in Māmrashān described more subdued scenes of revelation,[9] yet she does receive her clients in a room specially designated for the purpose and noted that she conceals her face, as Leondardo Garzoni observed in the eighteenth century:

> It's how we are talking to each other now. There is no secrecy about that. I only talk in a normal voice. I will ask questions, and when I receive the message, I will tell it in a normal way. … I am always normal. I sit like I am sitting now. The only thing is, I don't let people see my secrets. I don't let people look me in the eye, when I receive the message. I cover my head. That is the only thing I do.

Although the *faqra* claimed to speak to her clients in an ordinary manner, she asserted her preternatural knowledge of 12 languages, and described herself, in the first-person plural, as part of a prophetic collective:

> We have twelve languages: Hindi, English [here, her voice trailed off as she listed the others], and the most important one is the one no one can understand, the language of the prophets. When we sit together, when the prophets talk – and I can tell you when they gather: when it's a full moon – the prophets from all religions will talk, in a language that only they, and no one else, can understand.

Her special abilities she described as 'possess[ing] God's secret', but made a point of clarifying that God does not communicate with her directly:

I receive voices. God has never spoken to me. [The voices come] from angels, via two birds. When someone comes to me [for sha-manic aid or revelation], one of the birds will bring the message to me in a voice. I see them [that is, the birds] most of the time, and hear the voice.

Birds, of course, have been associated with the spirit realm and as emis-saries between heaven and earth since ancient times. For the Yezidis, whose principal angel is represented as a peacock, the association is even stronger. In addition to the avian messengers, the *faqra* went on to say, 'Sometimes I see Jesus Christ talking to me, and sometimes I see Moham-med advising me. Sometimes when I face a difficult problem, I see all three prophets talking to me.' (The third prophet here is likely Sheikh Adi, the Yezidis' pre-eminent religious figure.)

## Messages

A Yezidi *koçek* or *faqra* can make predictions concerning, among other things, employment prospects and travel (BaBāFMi46), matrimony (ShFMi52, SinFMi60, SiFMi64), conception (BaBāFMi46) and tech-nological developments (ShMS68, ShFP68). They may give prognoses concerning health (BaBāFMi46, ShMMi50, ShMS68), diagnose or cure people who are suffering nightmares (TallQFMi14, ShMMi50), restore personal relationships (BaBāFMi46, ShFMi52), predict the results of aca-demic examinations (even providing supernatural assistance in academic performance [TallQMi19]), predict when people will die (ShMMi50, ShMS61) and forecast cataclysms. This last subject of prophetic fore-knowledge is most relevant here.

## Specifying and spreading the prophetic messages

No single statement concerning the relevant Yezidi prophecy included all of the components that emerged in the course of the interviews. Nev-ertheless, considering the varied responses in the aggregate, we can delineate recurring motifs and configurations, beginning with a notably detailed account as an example. One woman of the *mirîd* caste offered a description of how, 'two months before the incident in Sinjar', a *faqra* from Sinjar came to her in-laws' house in Shaykhān on a Wednesday evening (Wednesday is the holy day of the week for Yezidis) and prophe-sied impending disaster, speaking in the prophetic present tense:

She entered into a trance, fell down, and spoke in a language that nobody can understand. [The *faqrya*] can't control their speech. She was crying and screaming, saying, 'Come, come! Everyone, behold the fire that is burning Sinjar. Dignity is gone, humanity is destroyed, people are fleeing. The fire is so vast it is spreading all the way to Ba'shīqa Bāzān'. She even said, 'Blood is all over the place. They are seizing girls!' (ShFMi47)

This informant was not present when the *faqra* delivered her message but gave a vivid, second-hand recitation. As was typical for those who related prophecies that they themselves did not directly witness, she emphasized her particular, personal connections to the place and to the witnesses present. The site was, specifically, her husband's maternal uncle's home, where her husband's family and her own sister, along with others, were witnesses on the occasion.

Others described having heard such messages in person from a *koçek* or *faqra* in the months just prior to IS's onslaught, and connected those predictions with prophecies that they recalled from decades earlier. The following is a representative dialogue between two Yezidi men from Bahrī, near Sinjar. The older of the two recalled having witnessed a *koçek* deliver his prophecy:

They [that is, the *koçeks*] were correct. They said a *ferman* would come and for three days the Yezidis would see hell. I heard this prophecy around twenty years ago. I was present when this was prophesied. They said after the *ferman*, life would be much, much better. Only God knows, but we hope it will be better. The same *koçek* said there would come a time when the Yezidis would face the most difficult time in their history. And this is a fact, because I was present there. (BahMMi49)

The younger man corroborated his elder's recollection:

Yes, before the *ferman*, a [servitor of the shrine at Lalish] came to [his] house and said that he heard this from them a long time ago, that a *ferman* would come upon the Yezidis. I was there, as well as many other people. (BahMMi30)

This brief exchange also touches on the process by which the messages of individual shamans can be transmitted by non-shamans and become forecasts repeated among the wider community as messages unattributed to particular shamans – although some Yezidis were careful to make a distinction between messages that they had heard directly or via family and those that were simply widespread hearsay. 'I don't know', one pious *pir*, the Yezidis' principal baptismal officiant, admitted, 'I've heard people talking about it, but I have never heard it myself. People are saying that years ago it was widely acknowledged that a *ferman* would come, but I haven't heard it myself directly from anyone. I've never been present in these conversations' (ShFPi68).

*Ferman* (or *firman*), the specific term that these Yezidis used for the wave of attacks of August 2014, denotes a hostile incursion, a campaign of armed aggression. In its strictly literal acceptation, this term – which is found in Persian, Turkish and Kurmanji – refers to an order or edict, historically issued by the Ottoman authorities. *Ferman* is a metonym: the cause (the order to attack) has come to represent the effect (the ensuing massacre, abductions and destruction). It is the word by which the Yezidis designate and conceptualize the recurring outbreaks of persecution that have punctuated their history.

Writing in 2005, Eszter Spät records that 'Yezidis themselves talk about seventy-two *fermans*, or persecutions against them – a term that could aptly be likened to "pogroms".' Spät suggests the following interpretation:

> In fact, this is a symbolic number, for according to Yezidi mythology the nations of the earth are seventy-two, corresponding to the seventy-two sons and seventy-two daughters of Adam and Eve. The Yezidis, created in a unique way, are not included in this number. So repeating the number seventy-two is a way of expressing the Yezidi sense of constant persecution by all outsiders. (Spät, 2005: 26)

The parallel drawn by Spät makes her interpretation persuasive. In the aftermath of IS, however, we found that the Yezidis now number the *fermans* as seventy-three or seventy-four; there is disagreement on the total, although most of our informants seemed to favour the latter number. If we follow Spät's interpretation, the sum now implies not only repeated persecution by all other nations but persecution that has exceeded the limits of any normal expectation or reckoning. In the words of one Sinjari woman now living at an IDP camp in Khanke, on the Mosul Dam Lake, the traditional prediction was 'that the Yezidis would face seventy-four *fermans*. My ancestors had faced seventy-three, and my generation never thought that the seventy-fourth *ferman* would come in our time' (SinFMi60).

## Predictions of flood and fire

As for the particulars of this most recent *ferman*, Yezidis recalled that the prophecies employed imagery of conflagration and deluge, they predicted the geographical directions and parameters of the attacks, and they foretold how the trauma would elicit extreme emotional reactions among the Yezidis. We will now discuss, in turn, each of these various dimensions of the vatic message, which the shamans often couched in figurative language and oblique expression.

In keeping with what we have already seen in one informant's recollection of a Sinjari *faqra*'s message, the imagery of fire on Sinjar was the most commonly repeated. Others recounted the prophecies of conflagration as follows: 'For the last decades and centuries, they have been repeating, "There will be fire upon Sinjar [and] Ba'shīqa Bāzān"' (ShFMi55).

> The first time I saw *koçeks* was in 1957, when I was very young. It was roughly around the same time I was at Pir Jawa's Tomb. I saw a *koçek* shivering and acting in a very strange way. He put his coat on and spoke in a language I did not understand. Then he spoke in Kurdish: 'The fire hit our mountains'. (ShMPi64)

> There was a *koçek* named Sheikh Braimê Awdi. Around twenty years ago he spoke about these *fermans*. He said there would come a time when there would be a *ferman* upon Mount Sinjar and the Sinjar region. Nobody would survive. Even the trees would be burnt. (BorMPi20)

Interestingly, this last young *pir* from Borek, in the Sinjar District, did not see the prediction of utter annihilation as problematic, even though he himself and many others had, in fact, escaped from the area.

A woman from Zorava, also in the Sinjar District, similarly reported a more recent version of this prophecy, and similarly expressed no doubt regarding the absolute assertion: 'Less than a month before the *ferman*, I visited a *koçek* who said that there would be a *ferman* and none of the Yazidis would survive' (ZoFS27). The key matter for these Yezidis was that their shamans had predicted a vast massacre; the prophetic hyperbole, like the imagery of conflagration, gave potent expression to their perception of holocaust.[10]

Imagery of flooding also served a function analogous to that of the fiery representations, in its capacity to underscore the sweeping devastation of the attacks. For the *faqra* whom we interviewed in Māmrashān, deluge was the preferred imagery. Like the Yezidis more generally, she too related her predictions to those of previous generations, and claimed that she could foresee, albeit imprecisely, the atrocities of 2014:

> My father and grandfather always said that [another *ferman* would come], but I could also predict that a disaster would happen, but I did not know it would be Daesh [IS]. A disaster could be a flood or a disease. I never thought that it would be committed by humans.

She then shifted to the first-person plural, as if to diminish any individual responsibility that foreknowledge of the events might entail:

> We could see dark things happening. We knew it was a disaster, but we didn't know whether it was wind, flood, disease, or what it was. We did not know it would be humans devouring [literally, eating, annihilating by consumption] humans. That flood happened.

While imagery of conflagration and deluge allowed for effective indeterminacy in depicting the destructive agent and the sweep of destruction, the prophecies grounded their forecasts in more specific geographical parameters, indicating the direction and frontiers of the attacks. According to one young woman of the *mirîd* caste, 'A *koçek* said the *ferman* of the Yezidis would come from the west of Sinjar [that is, from the general direction of IS's stronghold in Raqqa, Syria]. I was present when the *koçek* made this prediction, and so many other people were repeating the same story' (TallQFMi21). Naweran, a mountain and village of the same name, lay roughly where Kurdish Peshmerga and coalition forces halted the IS advance and, with coalition forces, marked the frontline. 'Our *koçeks* and *faqrya* told us that fire would come to Sinjar and Ba'shīqa Bāzān and would stop in Naweran, and it was proven to be right. This was told us by our ancestors' (ShFMi55). '"The border between Yezidis and others will be Naweran … " That was Koçek Saeed, twenty or thirty years ago. It is deeply rooted in our traditions' (ShMPi65). A Sinjari woman now living in the IDP camp in Baadre recounted the following prophecy, which she had heard from her father-in-law: 'Behind Sinjar there is a long road. If the Yezidis can escape beyond that road, they will be safe. If not, they will be captured by the Muslims. They will be slaughtered just like poultry' (SiFMi64).

In the event, many Yezidis did escape to relative safety behind the front lines during and after the attacks of August 2014, yet their physical safety belies profound feelings of estrangement, displacement and dishonour. Reportedly, *koçeks* and *faqrya* had foretold sentiments that their listeners had found difficult to imagine before the *ferman* and all too apposite in its wake. One young *sheikh*, for instance, was ambivalent about how much credence to grant the shamans, but he explained how their prophecies helped to verbalize the physical and emotional disintegration of families:

> Five to six months before the massacre at Sinjar, people talked about how *koçeks* and *faqrya* repeated this story in the past, about how a *koçek* said that there would come a day when a father would not want to know his son, nor his son want to know his father. It's true: so many people left their family members behind in Sinjar. (SiMS26)

Another woman related an anecdote on this point, concerning a mother:

> who had four daughters and prayed always to have a son. God gave her a son, and when they had to flee, she left her son under a tree and ran away to seek refuge. I can tell you openly that we have seen people leaving their children behind and fleeing. (ShFMi55)

The instinct to preserve one's life, even to the point of forsaking what one most cherishes, had its counterpart in a depleted will to live. The shamans predicted that 'there would come a day when every Yezidi wishes he were buried alive, and it was true. With what we faced, some people wished they were dead rather than alive' (SiMS21). The same woman who reported seeing parents abandoning children in the midst of the terror also concurred with this prediction, and added:

> I wish that our affliction was more like that of Halabja [where Saddam Hussein's regime killed some 5,000 Kurds in a chemical attack in 1988]. It would have been better, less painful, than taking our dignity. We always repeat this: we wish we had been gassed like Halabja. It would have been less painful. (ShFMi55)

Again, the prophecies were apparently vague or silent regarding the factors that would give rise to such sentiments, but their ostensible fulfilment provided these Yezidis some basis for articulating unthinkable reactions to inconceivable suffering.

In summary, the general content, characteristics and contours of the shamans' messages have facilitated retrospective, collective recognition in the aftermath of IS. Their language – which makes use of metonymy, metaphor and other figurative devices – is sufficiently oblique and imprecise to achieve a highly adaptable oracular expression, yet sufficiently specific and explicit to achieve a highly memorable impression of the Yezidis' ordeal, its scale and effects. Alongside the style and substance of the messages themselves, there is a significant element of ellipsis in the shamanic revelation, a sense that the revelations omit or suppress some information.

According to one *mirîd* from Tall Qaṣab, shamans may withhold information: 'Some [*koçeks* and *faqrya*] are correct and some are not. Those who are correct receive messages from God. If they think it is right to tell you, they will do so, otherwise they do not tell you' (TallQMMi42). The *faqra* of Māmrashān likewise maintained that shamans withhold some messages if unable or unwilling to disclose them. As she put it, in addition to not having known how her visions of 'dark things' might apply, there are necessary silences and omissions among her prophecies: 'I can always predict what will happen. Sometimes we know the facts but we cannot say the facts. Sometimes I see people, I know what will happen to them, but I cannot tell them. Some of the facts are bitter.' Such ellipses are naturally capable of granting freer rein to adherents' imaginations.

## Forecasting *fermans*

If the *ferman* of 2014 was indeed the seventy-fourth, as the men from Baḥrī noted, the prophecies tell of a brighter future. Yezidis perceive the seventy-fourth *ferman* as a culminating moment of affliction:

> People were saying this even during the time of my grandfather and great grandfather, that there would come a time when the Yezidis would face a *ferman*. And we saw the *ferman*. We believe that we will face seventy-four *fermans*, and after that peace and stability will come, but it must be God's order. Only God knows when and how. In this instance the *faqrya* and *koçeks* were proven right. (ShFMi52)

In addition to the numerical total of *fermans*, two related events, which we have not yet touched upon, were predicted to mark a turning point in what the Yezidis conceptualize as their serial suffering.

One is the destruction of the tomb of Nabi Yunus (the prophet Jonah) in Mosul, a shrine that ISIS rigged with explosives and demolished in July

2014. In the *koçeks'* and *faqrya's* reckoning, this demolition was to be a sign accompanying the nadir of suffering for the Yezidis, after which their situation would markedly improve (ShMPi39, TallQMMi42, ShMPi64). The second event is the arrival of foreigners of a different complexion. '*Faqrya* and *koçeks* believed that a *ferman* would come to the Yezidis, but when the *sees* [white] and *sorê chawshin* [red-complexioned, blue-eyed] people come, life would become calm. They meant Americans' (ShMS68; the Yezidis apply this description to Westerners generally). This was one prophecy, among others, attributed to Koçek Saeed, who figures so prominently in the Yezidis' recollection of renowned shamans of the late twentieth century:

> Koçek Saeed, said, 'The near future for the Yezidis will be very bad. People with blue-green eyes and blond hair will come. The Americans, the Europeans will come – *chawshin, chawkesk* – and then, after that, a good period of time will come for the Yezidis. But they have to endure these atrocities against them. They will undergo a long, severe process and suffer, but finally will enjoy a good life'. He experienced a kind of hallucination, shivering for a couple minutes, then talking to himself. People around him understood what he said, and then it was over. The people around him talked to others, reciting the message. Nowadays they write down such things. I heard it word of mouth. (ShMPi65)

The sum of seventy-four *fermans* and the accompanying signs, then, point to a more favourable future for the Yezidis – or more positive prospects may be simply a matter of a cyclical or oscillating tendency for good to succeed evil, peace to follow destruction. This was the prediction of the *faqra* of Māmrashān:

> There is no more disaster coming. A brighter future is ahead. Nothing will be worse than what we experienced. After every disaster, there will be better life. From now on there will be a better life. Happiness has no limits. When it rains, our rooftops will be wet (in the sense of an inevitable effect following a cause).

## Actions, inaction and reactions

A prophecy of impending devastation might naturally prompt action in response. The Yezidis' reported responses to the *koçeks'* and *faqrya's* prophecies reflect varying degrees of credence and varying interpretations. Regarding the arrival of ruddy, fair-haired outsiders, the Yezidis did not agree on when or whose arrival fulfilled this prophecy. Was it the US-led coalition's 2003 invasion of Iraq, or the international interventions to relieve the siege of Sinjar and beat back IS's territorial expansion? Those whose interpretation pinned the *sorê chawshin*'s arrival to 2003, long before the *ferman* of 2014, understandably viewed it as a mistaken prophecy in hindsight, but it had once attracted enough adherents to spur a Yezidi delegation to US diplomat Paul Bremer's transitional government in Baghdad.

A participant described the incident and the ensuing disappointment:

> *Koçeks* said many things. There is one thing that they predicted that did not happen. They said *sorê chawshin* would come, and Yezidis and Kurds would be free and face no more sufferings. The Yezidis assembled and said that once the *sorê chawshin* come, we must send a delegation to Baghdad to ask what they will do for the Yezidis. I knew it was pointless because I do not believe in these things. We met Paul Bremer, and Bremer welcomed us. 'Your rights are with Talabani and Barzani [Jalal Talabani, President of Iraq 2006–14; and Masoud Barzani, President of the Kurdistan Region 2005–17]. Ask them', he said. The governor of Shaykhān went with the delegation. 'You are Kurds, you should go there', Bremer said. But our forefathers had told us that things would be better. Freedom and liberation meant that we would live on our own land and no one would question my Yezidism, when my children study in our own language, when there is equal opportunity for everyone, when Yezidis are not discriminated against. (ShMPi64)[11]

On a less eminent but no less momentous scale, Yezidis recounted the choices that individual families faced whether or not to heed advance warnings or bide their time in their homes. Several reported disbelief that led to inaction. 'I visited one [*koçek*] who told me that there would come a time when the Yezidis would face a *ferman*, but nobody believed it. This was not long before the *ferman*. So many *koçeks* before repeated this message, that the Yezidis would face this persecution, but nobody believed them' (SiFMi45). Another Sinjari woman, whose nephew was killed and whose son was wounded in IS's onslaught, said:

> We never believed [the *ferman*] would happen. We said that nothing would happen. But we experienced it. We never thought people

would come to do us harm, but we experienced the worst. Some people said that we should prepare for the worst and that Daesh would attack, but we didn't believe. But one day the electricity went off, and people began to flee. Those who fled survived, but those who did not faced death. (ZoFS46)

Not everyone, of course, was aware of predictions, prophetic or otherwise, concerning imminent attacks. 'We did not hear anything, or people would have evacuated their villages before', claimed a woman from the Sinūnī area (SinFMi44).

If, as the saying goes, hindsight is twenty-twenty, it is only selectively or illusorily so. As such, hindsight can be a potent corroboration of the shamans' foresight, as the faithful tend to recall points of correspondence between predictions and experience while discounting or postponing points of incongruity. One *pir* reflected on this tendency:

> We remembered we were told [about the *ferman*] before. But when it happens, you are more worried about other things. It was said and said again, but did not happen, so people forgot about it, but when it happened the story came back to our minds. When it happens, you don't think back to the prophecy right away. You have to deal with the immediate consequences of the hardships. People are fleeing, crying, facing death. You have to deal with that first when it happens. But afterwards, when you have time to think, these memories will come back – how all these stories were repeated again and again. (ShMPi39)

In this regard, even among those who reported a prior disbelief the prevailing opinion was that the recent suffering had, in fact, reinforced the community's belief in the shamanic traditions that had ostensibly foretold it (TallQFMi21, TallQMMi23, BaBāFMi46, ShFMi55, ShMS61, ShMS68):

> Sometimes when people predict an event, afterwards you wonder if these people possess a spiritual power because what they predicted came true. People who have the ability to predict probably know what will happen, but in the end only God knows what will happen. (ShFMi47)

The distinction between shamans' foreknowledge and God's foreknowledge in the previous quotation points to the manifold complexities of the Yezidis' perceptions concerning prophecy. While a *koçek*'s or *faqra*'s prediction might ultimately have divine origins, it is subordinate to God's will and divine providence. Their statements do not necessarily carry any dogmatic weight. Because of the peripheral nature of Yezidi shamanism in relation to the more central tenets of the faith, Yezidis are free to doubt a shaman without doubting their religion, although some informants cited the shamans' personal religiosity as a reason for placing faith in them (TallQMMi23, TallQFMi19); shamans themselves, however, are not necessarily more religious or pious than their coreligionists (ShMS61).

As we have already seen, belief in the shamans' abilities and messages is by no means uniform among the Yezidis, especially in the present day. The Yezidis do not evince a facile, uncritical acceptance of their shamans' utterances, nor do gradations of scepticism and belief have clear generational correlations. Some drew distinctions between doubts based on personal disappointments in unfulfilled messages concerning their individual circumstances, on the one hand, and belief in the messages that concern the broader community on the other.

Yet certain patterns emerge from this complex composite of individual idiosyncrasies and areas of consensus. From the most credulous to the utterly sceptical, our informants expressed an anticipation of better prospects ahead. Some linked these anticipations to the New Year itself, or to the time that had elapsed since the outbreak of persecution. 'Just yesterday,' reported a Sinjari *mirîd*, 'I met a *faqra* in Zakho who said that after the month of Nissan, onwards into the New Year, signs of peace will appear. She said this year will bring happiness to us. I have always believed in them' (SiFMi45). The same young *pir* who reported the prophecy of *koçek* Sheikh Braimê Awdi noted, 'This was not mere hearsay. My father and uncle and many villagers were around when this *sheikh* predicted it. He said there would be happiness afterwards, three or four years after, and we have now passed two years' (BorMPi20).

As we have already had occasion to mention in relation to the Yezidis' notion of recurring *fermans*, and as Kreyenbroek has demonstrated more widely (2008: 86), the Yezidi concept of history is generally cyclical. 'Koçeks predicted that history would repeat itself. History always repeats itself' (ShMPi64). But a repetitive, cyclical historical paradigm does not require perfectly regular circles. Particular features of this last cycle are notably different. Not only has the tally of *fermans* reached its supposed limit but the destruction of Jonah's tomb and the arrival of *sorê chawshin* herald a meaningful change in the cycle. In the words of one Sinjari *sheikh*:

What can I tell you? We've seen trauma and persecution. We've left our homes, we live in tents, and can't sleep. When I was a child, my father said that there would come a time when the Yezidis would face the most difficulties, but after that life would be normal for the Yezidis. My father and grandfather used to repeat these stories. *Koçeks* also believed and repeated these stories: there would come a time, the next cycle, when we would face a massacre, but after that life would be normal for the Yezidis. (ZoFS46)

As noted by Joy Hendry, '*Explanations of misfortune* form part of the cosmology of a society' (Hendry, 1999: 140, italics in original). In other words, explanatory accounts of suffering can reinforce the broader narratives that a people tell themselves about themselves and about their place in the cosmos. This is especially true of accounts that facilitate retrospective revaluations and anticipatory projections. Such are the recollected messages of the Yezidi shamans in the wake of the 2014 atrocities. If suffering has the capacity to shake one's faith to its core as some of the most faithful Yezidis, including a cousin of Koçek Saeed, admitted, it also has the capacity to provoke vital re-visions of received wisdom. Whereas the Yezidis' shamanic tradition had reportedly come to be regarded as outdated, superseded, even shameful, a reconsideration of past prophecies has reinvigorated their sense of teleology, as they strive to perceive transcendent sense in senseless suffering.

Our close examination of the shamanic phenomenon in Yezidism has revealed an inherent, interpretive flexibility in their methods and messages. This flexibility allows for rich complexity and variations in the interpretation and application of their shamans' forecasts. The patterns of perspectives that emerge, in the midst of variations, point to an enduring coherence in the community's faith system. As we have previously observed (Fisher and Zagros, 2015), the Yezidis' distinctive religion, which has made them a target for so much persecution, is also a source of resilience (Ager *et al.*, 2015). Their traditions of shamanic prophecy, although not central to their religion, are also a component of that adaptive resilience in the Yezidi faith and its cultural manifestations. At the dawn of a new year, a vulnerable community, whose way of life is on the brink of extinction via destruction and displacement, turned to palliative prophecies to articulate a qualified yet hopeful sense of reassurance that the flames and waves of genocidal persecution may subside at last.

## Appendix (Abbreviations used for castes and places of origin)

**Bah** Bahrī
**BaBā** Ba'shīqa Bāzān
**Bor** Borek
**Mi** mirîd
**Pi** pir
**S** sheikh
**Sh** Shaykhān
**Si** Sinjar City
**Sin** Sinūnī
**TallQ** Tall Qaṣab
**Zo** Zorava

## Acknowledgements

This study was made possible by generous financial support from Soran University. The authors' gratitude is also due Luqman Suliman and his family, who, in addition to being consummate hosts in Shaykhān, were invaluable guides to the people and lore of Lalish.

## Notes

1. Among the various transliterations of the name of this ethno-religious group, *Yezidis* is the version that prevails in academic publications, while the United Nations and the mass media – including the BBC, the *New York Times*, the *Guardian*, Reuters and the *National Geographic* – have generally tended to use the alternative *Yazidis*. One unfortunate, inadvertent consequence of spelling *Yazidi* in this way is that it reinforces an erroneous association with the Umayyad caliph Yazid ibn Mu'āwiya, with implications of a primordial Arab apostasy; the association carries peril in a region where extremists seek justification for genocide. See Asatrian and Arakelova (2014: 46–8) for an instance of this error. *Êzidi* perhaps most closely approximates what the Yezidis call themselves. The initial /j/ is probably a reflection of the tendency for native speakers of Arabic to insert this phoneme as a substitute for /ê/. For the transliteration of geographical terms, we follow Cecil John Edmonds's meticulous survey of Yezidi places and populations, produced for the Royal Asiatic Society (1967: 82–7).
2. On different approaches to 'resilience' in studies of and responses to displacement, see Krause and Sharples, and Chatterjee *et al.*, both in this volume; on different forms of significance of faith, religion and spirituality in displacement, see the contributions by Mole, Seguin, and Fiddian-Qasmiyeh, all in this volume.
3. On the importance of 'voice' in refugee studies, see Haile, and Qasmiyeh, both in this volume.
4. Although our informants were willing for us to record their names, we have chosen not to identify them by name here. As the security situation remains precarious at present, the potential for reprisals is real and caution is imperative. Thus, we have adopted and adapted Kreyenbroek's method of encoding Yezidi informants' identities by place of origin, sex, caste and age at the date of the interview (Kreyenbroek, 2009: 13–14); for example, ShFMi47 represents a 47-year-old female Mirîd from Shaykhān. See the Appendix for abbreviations of castes and places of origin.

5. Even the religious authorities among the Yezidis refrain from numbering the incoming year with any certainty. No one knows the number of the current year in Yezidi reckoning, they maintain. This professed ignorance or lacuna reflects, on the one hand, the Yezidis' turbulent history and vulnerability. Relevant records concerning their reckoning of years have been lost, if any ever existed. It also reflects, on the other hand, the Yezidis' traditional resistance to literacy as well as the community's insistence on depicting its origins as stretching back before recorded time.

6. In discussions of shamanic practices, 'ecstasy' is the term favoured in the field of comparative religion and 'trance' is favoured in psychology and anthropology, but 'altered state of consciousness' has gained ground as a usefully elastic designation for the shaman's distinctive experience (Morris, 2006: 19–20). Its elasticity is especially applicable to shamanism among the Yezidis, for they describe altered states of consciousness that range from utter loss of consciousness to visions, into which the shaman more or less wilfully enters.

7. Yezidis apply the term *koçek* to shamans of both sexes, though less often to females. Scholars have previously confused female *faqir* and *faqrya*, probably because of the similarity of the terms, but these are entirely distinct categories that designate distinct roles. A *faqir* is a man or woman – often a virgin or widow – who elects to join the community of servants who maintain the principal Yezidi shrine at Lalish, while the *faqrya*, the female shamans, operate as individuals and do not necessarily have any connection to the holy sites. Examples of this confusion can be found in Allison (2001: 30–1), Spät (2005: 48) and Açikyildiz (2010: 94–6).

8. As for why this degradation in shamanic abilities or reputation has occurred, Yezidis proposed various explanations. For the cynical, it was a result of increasing education levels and diminishing superstition (ShMMi30). Alternatively, diminishing powers correspond to a degenerate age: 'Until the 1980s, the earth was more pure and people could predict the future' (ShMMi60). Others noted a declining reliance on shamans for services that medicine now provides: 'When we were children, we did not have medical doctors and pharmacies here. We would visit *koçeks* when we had a problem' (ShMS68). In this vein, the *faqra* of Māmrashān perceived technological developments as depleting not only reliance on shamans but also their powers: '*Koçeks* and *faqrya* had more power before. People didn't have doctors, couldn't travel far, and didn't have science. But now science, travel, and medical doctors are taking away power from *koçeks* and *faqrya*. Technology is taking power from *faqrya* now.'

9. One *sheikh* explained, 'There are two colours [i.e. two types] of *koçeks*. We have *koçeks* in Shaykhān and Bāzān [an idiomatic way of saying 'everywhere']. Some of them speak normally when you consult them; some [that is, the second type] go into a trance where they see images' (ShMS61). In terms of the *sheikh*'s dichotomy, the shamanic *faqra* in Māmrashān is of the second type, but this was the only informant to make this distinction. Much more common were distinctions between shamans of the past and present, or between genuine and fraudulent shamans.

10. The *faqra* of Māmrashān made a comparable statement: 'We have lost at least one person from every household.' The statement, on the face of it, is inaccurate, but it accurately conveys the Yezidis' all-inclusive sense of loss.

11. Bremer's own account of his time in Iraq makes no mention of this incident. Indeed, he mentions the Yezidis only once, when enumerating the 'sharp ethnic and sectarian differences' that characterize the 'disparate people' of Iraq (Bremer and McConnell, 2006: 38).

# References

Açikyildiz, Birgül. 2010. *The Yezidis: The History of a Community, Culture and Religion*. London: I.B. Tauris.

Ager, Joey, Elena Fiddian-Qasmiyeh and Alastair Ager. 2015. 'Local Faith Communities and the Promotion of Resilience in Contexts of Humanitarian Crisis', *Journal of Refugee Studies* 28 (2): 202–21.

Allison, Christine. 2001. *The Yezidi Oral Tradition in Iraqi Kurdistan*. Richmond: Curzon.

Asatrian, Garnik S. and Victoria Arakelova. 2014. *The Religion of the Peacock Angel: The Yezidis and Their Spirit World*. London: Routledge.

Bremer, L. Paul and Malcolm McConnell. 2006. *My Year in Iraq: The Struggle to Build a Future of Hope*. New York: Simon and Schuster.

Cetorelli, Valeria, Isaac Sasson, Nazar Shabila and Gilbert Burnham. 2017. 'ISIS' Yazidi Genocide: Demographic Evidence of the Killings and Kidnappings', *Foreign Affairs*, 8 June. Accessed 11 January 2020. www.foreignaffairs.com/articles/syria/2017–06-08/isis-yazidi-genocide.

Edmonds, C.J. 1967. *A Pilgrimage to Lalish*. London: Royal Asiatic Society of Great Britain and Ireland.

Eliade, Mircea. 1989. *Shamanism: Archaic Techniques of Ecstasy*, translated by Willard W. Trask. London: Arkana.

Fisher, Tyler and Nahro Zagros. 2015. 'Report from Iraq: Religion Lends Yazidis a Profound Resilience in the Face of Persecution', *The Conversation*, 8 October. Accessed 11 January 2020. https://theconversation.com/report-from-iraq-religion-lends-yazidis-a-profound-resilience-in-the-face-of-persecution-48127.

Fortenberry, Jeff. 2015. 'H.Con.Res.75 – Expressing the Sense of Congress That the Atrocities Perpetuated by ISIL against Religious and Ethnic Minorities in Iraq and Syria Include War Crimes, Crimes against Humanity, and Genocide'. Accessed 12 January 2020. www.congress.gov/bill/114th-congress/house-concurrent-resolution/75.

Guest, John S. (1993) 2010. *Survival among the Kurds: A History of the Yezidis*. London and New York: Routledge.

Hendry, Joy. 1999. *An Introduction to Social Anthropology: Other People's Worlds*. Basingstoke: Macmillan.

Islamic State. 1435 [i.e. 2014]. 'The Revival of Slavery before the Hour', *Dabiq* 4: 14–17. Accessed 11 January 2020. https://clarionproject.org/docs/islamic-state-isis-magazine-Issue-4-the-failed-crusade.pdf.

Kreyenbroek, Philip G. 1995. *Yezidism: Its Background, Observances and Textual Tradition*. Lewiston, NY: Edwin Mellen Press.

Kreyenbroek, Philip G. 2008. 'History in an Oral Culture: The Construction of History in Yezidi Sacred Texts', *Journal of Kurdish Studies* 6: 84–92.

Kreyenbroek, Philip G. 2009. *Yezidism in Europe: Different Generations Speak about Their Religion*. Wiesbaden: Harrassowitz Verlag.

Kreyenbroek, Philip G. and Khalil Jindy Rashow. 2005. *God and Sheikh Adi Are Perfect: Sacred Poems and Religious Narratives from the Yezidi Tradition*. Wiesbaden: Harrassowitz Verlag.

Morris, Brian. 2006. *Religion and Anthropology: A Critical Introduction*. Cambridge: Cambridge University Press.

Silêman, Pîr Xidir. 2012–13. *Perwerda Êzidyatî*. 6 vols. Duhok: Kurdistan Regional Government Ministry of Education. On file with the authors.

Spät, Eszter. 2005. *The Yezidis*. London: Saqi.

Spät, Eszter. 2009. 'Late Antique Motifs in Yezidi Oral Tradition'. PhD thesis, Central European University.

Stein, Rebecca L. and Philip L. Stein. 2016. *The Anthropology of Religion, Magic, and Witchcraft*. 3rd ed. London: Routledge.

United Nations Human Rights Council. 2016. *"They Came to Destroy": ISIS Crimes against the Yazidis* (Thirty-Second Session, Agenda Item 4, 15 June 2016). Accessed 12 January 2020. www.securitycouncilreport.org/atf/cf/%7B65BFCF9B-6D27-4E9C-8CD3-CF6E4FF96FF9%7D/A_HRC_32_CRP.2_en.pdf.

# 19

# Queer Russian asylum seekers in Germany: Worthy refugees and acceptable forms of harm?

Richard C.M. Mole

## Introduction

In June 2011 the United Nations Human Rights Council (UNHRC) approved a resolution expressing 'grave concern at acts of violence and discrimination in all regions of the world, committed against individuals because of their sexual orientation and gender identity' (United Nations, 2011), with Secretary-General Ban Ki-moon emphasizing that such persecution was 'an attack on the universal values that the United Nations and I have sworn to defend and uphold' (United Nations, 2012). Through these actions, the rights of lesbian, gay, bisexual and transgender (LGBT) people were recognized as human rights at the highest level of international society. While respect for LGBT rights is promoted as a universal value, however, this view is far from being universally accepted. More than 2.7 billion people live in states in which being homosexual is a crime: in 13 states, homosexuality is punishable by death; while in a further 73, LGBT individuals can be imprisoned because of their sexual orientation/ gender identity (ILGA, 2017). Even in states in which homosexuality is not a crime, LGBT people often face marginalization, discrimination, hostility and violence. It is therefore unsurprising that sexual minorities from such states seek refuge in countries in which LGBT rights are more widely respected. Yet, while sexual orientation and gender identity are now generally accepted in most European states as grounds for refugee status, only a small fraction of queers fleeing homophobia are considered worthy of asylum.[1] Against this backdrop, the aim of this chapter is to use the experiences of queer[2] Russian asylum seekers in Berlin as a heuristic to think about the ways in which international refugee law and national asylum regimes create 'worthy' and 'unworthy' queer refugees on the basis of the readability of their queerness and the 'acceptable' and 'unacceptable' forms of homophobic harm that they have suffered.

Following a brief explication of my methods, I will set out the key debates on sexual orientation and gender identity in international refugee law. I will then examine how homosexuality has been constructed in post-Soviet Russia in a bid to understand why attitudes in recent years have deteriorated to such an extent that we have seen a rise in the number of LGBT citizens of the Russian Federation seeking asylum overseas (Schreck, 2016). This section closes with an analysis of the personal narratives of two queers from Russia who are going through the asylum process in Germany, with a view to highlighting how the different forms of harm that they have suffered prompted them to apply for asylum and the impact that their different experiences may have on the likelihood of their applications being successful.

## Methodology

The qualitative research on which this chapter is based is drawn from a larger project on queer migration from Eastern Europe to Germany.[3] The research was conducted over a period of four years from 2012 to 2016 and was based on 32 interviews with Russian-speaking lesbian, gay, bisexual, trans* and queer (LGBTQ) migrants – 11 of whom were asylum seekers or refugees – and on the analysis of a range of German, European and international legal documents. For the interviews conducted for this specific chapter, eligible respondents were literate men and women aged 18 or over who self-identified as non-heterosexual asylum seekers or refugees from Russia or one of the post-Soviet states, and whose native language was Russian. The sample was recruited primarily through *Quarteera*, an association of LGBT Russian speakers and their friends, as well as through snowball sampling. A total of 11 interviews were conducted with asylum seekers/refugees, although in this chapter I will focus in particular on the narratives of just two. The interviewees were aged between 20 and 50; six were men and five were women. The interviews were carried out in Russian, took place in cafés or in parks and lasted, on average, 45–50 minutes. Participants were offered €25 as an incentive. Purposive sampling was used for the interviews to ensure a gender balance, but the sample does not otherwise claim to be representative. The interviews were recorded and transcribed verbatim. Data management and analysis were facilitated by the use of the qualitative software NVivo. The verbatim data was coded and ordered within a thematic matrix, which emerged both from reviewing extant literature and the interview data itself. NVivo helped to identify the key themes in the respondents' narratives, around which the chapter has been structured: social attitudes towards homosexuality in Russia, the ability to live one's life openly as LGBT, the reasons for seeking asylum in Germany, going through the asylum procedure and respondents' reflections on the likelihood of their applications being successful. In the text, pseudonyms have been used to protect participants' identities.

## The legal debates: From discretion to disbelief

While Article 1A (2) of the Refugee Convention, which defines a refugee as an individual who has a 'well-founded fear of being persecuted for reasons for race, religion, nationality, membership of a particular social group or political opinion', does not specifically refer to homosexuality as a protected category, sexual minorities are generally understood to constitute 'a particular social group' for the purposes of seeking asylum.[4] This is in view of the fact that they meet the two preconditions:

> First, members of that group share an innate characteristic, or a common background that cannot be changed, or share a characteristic or belief that is so fundamental to identity or conscience that a person should not be forced to renounce it. Second, that group has a distinct identity in the relevant country because it is perceived as being different by the surrounding society. (CJEU, 2013)

That sexual orientation is 'irreversible' [*unabänderlich*], and thus comparable to race or nationality as grounds for seeking asylum, was recognized by the German Federal Administrative Court as early as 1988.[5] Although there is now a general consensus among legal scholars and the courts that sexual minorities should be recognized as legitimate potential refugees, there is less agreement as to whether all persecution of lesbian, gays and bisexuals in their home countries is – as stipulated in the Refugee Convention – *for reasons of* their sexuality, and thus grounds for asylum. Such debates have raised questions as to whether LGBT individuals have a duty to exercise discretion in their home countries in a bid to avoid persecution, whether only specific forms of harm to queer asylum seekers make the latter worthy of protection and, consequently, whether there are 'acceptable' and 'unacceptable' forms of homophobic persecution.

## Discretion

For asylum seekers to be successful in gaining international protection, they need to demonstrate a 'well-founded fear of being persecuted' in their country of origin. Until relatively recently, however, it was common practice in a range of European states to expect queer asylum seekers to exercise discretion about their sexual orientation in their home countries so as to avoid persecution (Jansen, 2013).[6] This would then allow adjudicators to deny the existence of a 'well-founded fear of being persecuted' and turn down applications for asylum, as can be seen in this rejection letter sent by the UK Border Agency to an Iranian asylum seeker in 2010:

> Legislation which renders homosexuality illegal in Iran may cause you to be secretive in the conduct of your homosexual relationships there. However, this does not engage the UK's obligations under Art. 8 [of the European Convention on Human Rights]. This is because it is clear from your own evidence that you have demonstrated neither past nor future intention of publicly engaging in any homosexual conduct which ... would expose you to any real risk on return to Iran ... when an individual's right to pursue his sexuality is placed within the context of a civilised society, the need for discretion in relation to sexual practices is the accepted norm. (UKLGIG, 2010: 4)

The claim that it was reasonable to expect gays and lesbians to return to their home countries and exercise discretion was highly controversial. First, it assumed that discretion on the part of the applicant was a free choice and not the result of 'oppressive social forces' (Millbank, 2009: 392). In addition, sexual orientation was understood as a form of behaviour ('sexual practices'), which one could choose to engage in (or not) rather than part of an innate characteristic of an individual's sense of self. Were sexuality reduced to sexual practice, one could perhaps reasonably expect everyone, both homosexuals and heterosexuals, to be 'discreet' in the sense of not engaging in sex in public. If we understand sexuality as a fundamental aspect of an individual's identity, however, it is clear that homosexuals were being treated inequitably in that heterosexuals are never asked to exercise discretion in expressing their heterosexuality. In this sense, it is not discretion that is asked of homosexuals but rather concealment. As such, it runs counter to the 2012 *UNHCR Guidelines on International Protection with reference to Claims to Refugee Status based on Sexual Orientation and/or Gender Identity*, which specify that 'a person cannot be denied refugee status based on a requirement that they change or conceal their identity, opinions or characteristics in order to avoid persecution'. Moreover, the idea that all LGBT individuals can always conceal their queerness, even if they sought to do so, is erroneous. Among my respondents, for those who did 'not look gay by Russian standards', to cite Boris, the ability to pass as heterosexual did make life easier. But this was not possible for everyone. As Alyosha confirms, 'It wasn't ever possible to tell anyone … But you can tell that I am gay, I can't hide it, it's my nature. What am I supposed to do?'

The discretion argument was abolished in Germany in 2012 on the basis of a ruling by the Court of Justice of the European Union (CJEU, 2013) and following a number of high-profile cases in Australia and the UK. The duty to be discreet was rejected in the UK in 2010 in the *HJ (Iran)* v. *Secretary of State for the Home Department* ruling by the Supreme Court. Recognizing that there was more to being gay than sexual practices, Deputy President of the Supreme Court Lord Hope ruled that 'what is protected is the applicant's right to live freely and openly as a gay man. That involves a wide spectrum of conduct, going well beyond conduct designed to attract sexual partners and maintain relationship[s] with them' (UK Supreme Court, 2010). Acknowledging that his examples of 'gay conduct' were trivial and stereotypical, Lord Hope argued that 'just as male heterosexuals are free to enjoy themselves playing rugby, drinking beer and talking about girls with their mates, so male homosexuals are to be free to enjoy themselves going to Kylie concerts, drinking exotically coloured cocktails and talking about boys with their straight female mates' (ibid.).

While the rejection of the discretion requirement was welcomed by LGBT activists, the ruling itself was criticized for presenting an essentialist and universal understanding of what it means to be gay, defined in specifically Western and consumerist terms. It was also criticized by certain legal scholars. While supporting the repeal of the requirement, James Hathaway and Jason Pobjoy, for example, disagreed with the reasoning given – particularly the idea that not being able to drink colourful cocktails and attend Kylie concerts was grounds for LGBT individuals to claim asylum *for reasons of* their sexual orientation. They argued that 'the "for reason of" clause was included in the Refugee Convention precisely to delimit the scope of the refugee class to those persons at risk of serious harm *for reasons deemed fundamental*' (Hathaway and Pobjoy, 2012:

339, emphasis in original). To suggest that attending a Kylie concert is a fundamental part of a universal gay experience – in addition to prioritizing a very Western understanding of homosexuality – thus cast the net too widely in terms of what the Refugee Convention originally intended. Other scholars, such as Janna Weßels, also criticized the Supreme Court ruling – but for not going far enough. Weßels (2013) argues that the discretion reasoning has not been completely rejected but rather that a distinction has been made between acceptable and unacceptable forms of discretion. As Lord Hope's ruling continued:

> If the tribunal concludes that the applicant would choose to live discreetly simply because that was how he himself would wish to live, or because of social pressures, e.g. not wanting to distress his parents or embarrass his friends, then his application should be rejected. (Weßels, 2013)

Again, this suggests that queers *choose* to adhere to social pressure and, more importantly, implies that the concealment of sexual identity as a result of social pressure does not inflict the sort of serious harm to LGBT individuals that would justify a claim for asylum. As the analysis of my interviews with Russian asylum seekers, below, will demonstrate, neither of these positions is defensible. Nevertheless, despite the fact that other branches of human-rights law recognize that 'acts that cause mental suffering' constitute cruel and inhuman treatment just as much as 'acts that cause physical pain', asylum adjudicators are more likely to be persuaded by evidence of exogenous, physical harm perpetrated by state actors over endogenous, psychological harm resulting from social and family pressures (Hathaway and Pobjoy, 2012: 362; United Nations Human Rights Committee, 1992). As Rachel Lewis confirms, 'it is still the case that the closer one's application conforms to the traditional model of the male political activist fleeing an oppressive regime, the more likely one is able to obtain asylum' (Lewis, 2013: 178).

## Disbelief

Now that most EU member states no longer (in theory) turn down asylum applications for reasons of sexual orientation on the grounds that the applicants could reasonably be expected to return home and be discreet about their sexual identity, the key means of rejecting queer asylum applications has shifted from 'discretion' to 'disbelief' (see Hertoghs and Schinkel, 2018). While few countries have taken the extreme measure adopted by the Czech Republic of using a phallometer to test male applicants' reactions to gay pornography, most EU states have sought to verify the sexual orientation of asylum seekers during the interview process. What research by academics and LGBT-rights organizations has identified, however, is that the sexuality of asylum seekers from non-Western states is being tested against the benchmark of Western consumerist gay and lesbian identities. As Thibaut Raboin (2017: 673) demonstrated with reference to the UK as early as 2010, 'Home Office case owners have sometimes assessed claimants' gayness by testing their knowledge of the commercial gay scene in London, such as describing the layout of Heaven, a large club in central London with multiple rooms':

> You have to ask, what is his behaviour in the UK? If you were a gay man and you had been repressed or ostracised in your home country, then presumably coming to London would give you the chance to go to Soho or Heaven and enjoy the kind of lifestyle and bars and opportunities that that presents. (Nicholas, UKBA senior caseworker, quoted in Miles, 2010: 16)

Similarly, judges in the UK have refused to believe that lesbian asylum seekers were indeed lesbian for not showing interest in lesbian magazines, for having been married or for having children – demonstrating a failure to understand the social pressure on sexual minorities in states outside of the 'West' to conform to heteronormative gender and sexual roles and identities so as to remain invisible and thus safe (see, for example, Miles, 2010: 15; and Lewis, 2013: 175).

To be deemed credible, therefore, LGBT asylum seekers need to be able to translate their identities and 'experiences of persecution into the kinds of asylum narratives that are recognizable to the state' (Lewis, 2013: 176). The process of gaining asylum in the West thus presents a paradox for many queer refugees, who leave their home societies so as to be able to live their sexual lives and fashion their sexual identities in ways of their own choosing, only to then be forced to frame their queerness in ways that are readable by Western asylum adjudicators. While in Germany adjudicators are not supposed to ask individuals to prove their sexual orientation, the credibility of claimants' testimony often hinges on their adherence to specific stereotypes of what gays and lesbians look like and how they behave.

## Fleeing Russia

In Russia, consensual sex between adult men was decriminalized in 1993, while sex between women had never been a crime. Across Russia, LGBT community organizations and publications mushroomed in the mid-1990s but their numbers dwindled to almost nothing by the early years of the new millennium in the face of official harassment and cuts in overseas funding. The fact that the apparently sudden appearance of homosexuality in the public sphere coincided with the political and economic turmoil and the rapid demographic decline of the post-Soviet transition gave the impression that homosexuality was a 'symptom of post-Soviet Russia's decline and ... a threat to Russia's already embattled social order' (Baer, 2013: 40). As a result, social attitudes towards same-sex sexual behaviour remained conservative throughout the 1990s and the first decade of the new millennium, although this was not exclusive to Russia.

However, it was during President Putin's third term that controlling homosexuality was raised to an issue of government policy, with the introduction of the law banning the spreading of 'propaganda of non-traditional sexual relations among minors', passed unanimously by the Duma in June 2013. While homophobia in Russia has a long provenance (see Healey, 2017), it is particularly since the introduction of this law that Russian attitudes towards homosexuality have hardened. In the years 2003–15 – that is, between Putin's first and third presidencies – the percentage of Russians relating to homosexuals with 'apprehension', 'annoyance' or 'disgust' increased from 48 to 65 per cent (Levada-Center, 2015). While 31 per cent of respondents felt that homosexuals should be left in peace, 13 per cent believed that they should be prosecuted (as had been the case during the Soviet period) and 38 per cent thought that homosexuals should be medically treated (ibid.). This increase in homophobia coincided with a re-traditionalization of gender roles (used to legitimize the decriminalization of domestic violence in 2017), as well as the hegemony of the Russian Orthodox Church as the country's ultimate moral arbiter.

In terms of legal protection for LGBT citizens, there are no anti-discrimination laws in employment or in the provision of goods and services, and no anti-LGBT-hate-crime laws. While it is difficult to demonstrate the direct persecution of LGBT individuals by the Russian Government, the latter has without question created an atmosphere – through the introduction of the aforementioned 'homosexual propaganda law' – in which homosexuals are constructed as a threat to Russian society, children, national mores and religious values, fuelling homophobia and legitimizing violence against gays and lesbians (Human Rights Watch, 2014). In addition, certain state institutions – in particular, the police – have themselves been directly implicated in violent attacks on LGBT individuals and groups (ILGA-Europe, 2016: 142; Russian LGBT Network, 2016: 2–4). Even when the police are themselves not responsible for the violence meted out against gays and lesbians, there are numerous reports of their failing to investigate crimes, instructing victims to drop their criminal complaints, failing to arrest the perpetrators or even arresting the LGBT victims of the attacks (ILGA-Europe, 2016: 139).

In the context of living in an increasingly homophobic society, sexual minorities are often faced with the task of deciding how to respond to situations in which they are constructed as not fitting within that society. One could argue that for sexual dissidents, the basic response is one of 'exit', 'voice' or 'loyalty', to use Albert Hirschman's classic paradigm (Hirschman, 1970) – that is, leave the country, engage in public protest to bring about change or attempt to remain invisible. Although eventually, both of the respondents on whose narratives I am focusing chose to exit Russia and claim asylum in Germany, they initially opted for quite different responses – namely, voice and loyalty, respectively. While both suffered physically and psychologically as a result of their choices, their different responses could have a significant impact on their being granted asylum.

Maxim, a 31-year-old gay man from a medium-sized city in the European part of Russia, moved to Moscow after university and soon become involved in political activism. Protests in favour of LGBT rights in Russia inevitably attract counter-protests from the far right and, despite the presence of the police, Maxim was attacked on numerous occasions, resulting in broken ribs and a broken nose. The police repeatedly refused to arrest the attackers, arguing that this was a civil rather than a criminal matter. On other occasions, it was he rather than his attackers who was arrested. At the police station, he was verbally abused and physically attacked by five policemen, who then called his parents and outed him to them in the hope that they would convince him to desist from his political activism.

Such violent treatment from Russian policemen was also reported by Vadim and Konstantin, who, as a result, chose not to report incidents of violence at the hands of homophobic gangs to the police, as they felt no confidence that the attacks would be investigated seriously. Such action could, in fact, even make matters worse. As Vadim commented, when asked if he had reported his attack: 'No, there is no point … I haven't heard of a single case of anyone [in this situation] contacting the police. Firstly, it's pointless, and secondly, it is really dangerous.' As Maxim explained, once the authorities take an interest in you, they are more likely to monitor your activities and out you to others – as had been the case with his parents and then his boss: ' … if you are a public figure, then you face much greater risk because of it'.

In seeking to exercise his constitutional right to free expression and public assembly, Maxim was repeatedly attacked by counter-protesters and the police. His visibility and his refusal to give up his activism made him a target for arrest. After three of the four members of the LGBT collective of which he was a member had been sent to prison or were awaiting trial, Maxim realized that it was only a matter of time before he would be arrested, sent to prison or killed: 'It's not worth waiting to see how this story plays out. I'm not waiting for them to slit my throat.' While visiting Hamburg to give a lecture on protest movements at the university, he discovered that the police had been looking for him at his apartment in Moscow and at his parents' home, and so decided that he could not return to Russia but would seek asylum in Germany.

Asya's story was very different. She is a 23-year-old lesbian from a Muslim-majority republic in the Caucasus region of the Russian Federation. She herself identifies as Muslim. Unlike Maxim, she was not out to anyone but her closest friends. When asked why she was not out, she explained:

> because I come from a religious family. My older brother, in particular, is religious. And, if they knew about my sexual orientation, they would kill me. It's not just that – I don't know – that they would scold me or disown me. They would kill me to cleanse the shame [I had inflicted] on the family.

Unlike Maxim, she was unable to move to Moscow, a large anonymous city with at least some LGBT venues, as living away from the family home would not have been permitted by her parents and brother.

When she was 18, her family attempted to force her to marry a man they had chosen for her. In a bid to get out of the marriage, she entered into a fictitious engagement with a gay man whom she had met through a mutual acquaintance. However, her family did not approve of her choice and insisted that she call off the engagement. Under considerable psychological strain – and fearful that she would be forced to enter another arranged marriage, or that she might be kidnapped by her former fiancé and forced to marry him – she decided that she needed to leave the country. On the pretext that she was eloping with her (fake, gay) fiancé, who had secured a job in Berlin, she fled to Germany. While it is not just past persecution but also the risk of future harm that constitute sufficient grounds for claiming asylum, 'lesbians continue to have difficulties proving persecution in their cases because the harm they suffer does not often take place in the public arena' (Neilson, 2005: 426). Asya's case was even more complicated in that, unlike Maxim, she was not out and no one suspected that she was anything other than heterosexual. She was, therefore, not subject to any persecution for reasons of her sexual orientation in Russia: she did not suffer physical violence or discrimination at the hands of state institutions; nor had she suffered physical violence at the hands of her own family, on which the state institutions had failed to act. Her family still does not know that she is a lesbian.

While German asylum adjudicators are not permitted to ask claimants to prove their sexual orientation, it is clear that the credibility of their testimony often hinges on their adhering to specific stereotypes of what gays and lesbians look like and how they behave. Despite Maxim's public profile as an LGBT activist, it was not until his interviewer had seen a video of a report on him on the German TV channel ARD that she believed him: 'You know, now I understand that you really are gay.' According to Maxim, the interviewer continued, 'I believe that you are gay. But sometimes you get women turning up with six kids and claiming to be a lesbian.' The failure of asylum seekers to adhere to preconceived ideas of what it means to be gay or lesbian can thus result in their being disbelieved and deemed unworthy of asylum. The fact that lesbians in homophobic societies come under tremendous pressure to marry and have children, for example, is not taken into account. In turn, queer Russian asylum seeker, Vadim, was particularly concerned that his sexuality would not be sufficiently readable to German asylum adjudicators: 'Looking at me, you can't tell [that I'm gay] because I'm quite well-built. Because of that I was afraid that they simply wouldn't believe that I am LGBT, they wouldn't believe my story.'

Maxim's and Asya's ability to convince the asylum adjudicators that they had been or would be subject to persecution for reasons of their sexuality would be key to the success of their asylum claims. Again, Maxim's public profile as an LGBT activist who had suffered verbal and physical abuse at the hands of thugs as well as the police and had been arrested on numerous occasions should – according to previous research on queer asylum seekers (see, for example, Lewis, 2013) – make him a worthy candidate for asylum. Nevertheless, while the discretion reasoning for refusing asylum claims had been officially rejected in Germany, it was also evident from Maxim's experience that an adjudicator's assessment of the validity of an asylum seeker's claim can often be coloured by the expectation that the claimant could have done more to stay under the radar in their home country. As his interviewer told him, when Maxim was discussing how hard life was in general for LGBTs in small-town Russia:

> No. Move to Moscow and try to live like a normal person in a city of 10 million inhabitants. What's there to stop you taking an apartment, going to work and keeping quiet about it? If you are the type of person who comes here and says 'I am afraid to live in my country', that is not proof that you are being persecuted.[7]

For Asya, the discretion strategy, as set out by Maxim's interviewer, was the one that she had adopted since she realized that she was a lesbian. Trying to keep her sexual orientation a secret from her religious parents and brother in a homophobic society meant that she was living under considerable psychological strain.[8] However, she had never suffered physical violence or discrimination at the hands of state institutions or her family; she was thus extremely concerned that the discretion that she had exercised in Russia would be used by her adjudicators to dismiss her claim for asylum, despite this reasoning having been rejected by the CJEU and despite the risk of future harm constituting just as sufficient grounds for claiming asylum as past persecution:

> Honestly, I am afraid that they will turn me down. Because, again, I haven't suffered any persecution. Although, of course, when I say that, my friends say: 'Had they [your family] known, they would have killed you.' I reply: 'Yes, but they never bothered me, they didn't hit me, they didn't kill me.' … If you have proof, perhaps a video in which you are being threatened … then the people making the decision, they can look at this proof and see what it is really like here and probably approve your application. But they can simply not believe my story because I haven't presented them with any proof … I'm afraid.

Both these cases demonstrate that the refugee-status-determination processes that frame applicants under the 'particular social group' category – in this case, sexual minorities – may fail to take account of the intersections between the protected categories in Article 1A (2) of the Refugee Convention – that is, the political and sexual persecution experienced, for example, by Maxim as well as the relationship between past persecution and future risk, as in the case of Asya. Moreover, the perceived incompatibility of Asya's sexual and religious identities may also have an impact on the probability of her claim being believed. While, as Elena Fiddian-Qasmiyeh has shown, queers from Muslim-majority states are often seen by adjudicators in the liberal North 'as innocent victims of patriarchal and heteronormative religious frameworks – as "gender outlaws" who are persecuted due to their non-conformity to religious/cultural norms', this is predicated on claimants rejecting their Muslim faith (Fiddian-Qasmiyeh, 2016: 216). Based on Orientalist assumptions about Islamic repression of non-heterosexual sexualities, adjudicators have often dismissed as unbelievable the claims of queer asylum seekers who continue to identify as Muslim – as is the case with Asya (see ibid; Berg and Millbank, 2009; Massad, 2007; Murray, 2016).

At the time of writing, both Maxim and Asya are still waiting for the decision of the German Federal Agency for Migration and Refugees.

## Conclusion

On the basis of in-depth interviews with queers fleeing homophobia in Russia, this chapter has engaged with the relatively recent legal phenomenon of queer asylum, analysing the evolution of legal debates as to whether homosexuality should be a protected category in refugee law, whether all persecution of queers in their home countries is for reasons of their sexuality and thus grounds for asylum, whether LGBT individuals have a duty to exercise discretion in their home countries in a bid to avoid persecution and whether only specific forms of harm constitute persecution. Through an analysis of the narratives of two asylum seekers from the Russian Federation with different backgrounds, experience of different responses to homophobia in Russia and different forms of harm incurred, the chapter has shown how international refugee law and national asylum regimes create worthy and unworthy queer asylum seekers on the basis of the readability of their queerness and perceptions of 'acceptable' and 'unacceptable' forms of homophobic harm. The analysis further highlights the extent to which one's worthiness as an asylum seeker depends on whether one performed one's queerness in the public or the private sphere in the home country and whether one adhered to the cliché of the gay man or lesbian in the eyes of Western asylum adjudicators. Ultimately, the chapter demonstrates that international refugee law and national asylum regimes do not always work in sync – with legal practices agreed at the level of the European Union and national governments not always filtering down to the level of individual adjudicators, thereby rendering the asylum process for already vulnerable individuals even more uncertain.

## Acknowledgements

The research was made possible thanks to funding from the Alexander von Humboldt Foundation.

## Notes

1. On the advocacy strategies used by NGOs to 'engage a wide public in caring for the plight of LGBTI asylum seekers' in the context of the UK, see Raboin in this volume.
2. The term 'queer', when discussed with reference to individual subjects, is used here as an alternative for 'lesbian', 'gay', 'bisexual' and 'transgender' to reflect the fact that the latter Western terms were not adopted by all the individuals whom I interviewed.
3. Ethical approval for the research was provided by the UCL Research Ethics Committee (REC 3596/001).
4. While this is the case, sexual minorities can of course also claim asylum on the basis of one of the other protected categories.
5. German Federal Administrative Court, BVerwG 9 C 278.86, 15 March 1988, last modified 4 June 2017, https://dejure.org/dienste/vernetzung/rechtsprechung?Gericht=BVerwG&Datum=15.03.1988&Aktenzeichen=9%20C%20278.86.
6. According to Jansen (2013: 3, fn. 12), the discretion requirement was used in the adjudication of queer asylum applications in the following states: Austria, Belgium, Bulgaria, Cyprus, Denmark, Finland, France, Germany, Hungary, Malta, the Netherlands, Norway, Poland, Romania, Spain and Switzerland.
7. These are the interviewer's words as remembered by Maxim, rather than taken from an official transcription.
8. On the importance of faith and religion in processes of displacement and return, as discussed with reference to Yezidi displaced people in northern Iraq, see Fisher *et al.* in this volume.

## References

Baer, Brian James. 2013. 'Now You See It: Gay (In)visibility and the Performance of Post-Soviet Identity'. In *Queer Visibility in Post-Socialist Cultures*, edited by Nárcisz Fejes and Andrea P. Balogh, 35–56. Bristol: Intellect.

Berg, Laurie and Jenni Millbank. 2009. 'Constructing the Personal Narratives of Lesbian, Gay and Bisexual Asylum Claimants', *Journal of Refugee Studies* 22 (2): 195–223.

BVerwG (Bundesverwaltungsgericht). 1988. 'BVerwG, 15. 03.1988– 9 C 278.86'. Accessed 28 January 2020. https://dejure.org/dienste/vernetzung/rechtsprechung?Gericht=BVerwG&Datum=15.03.1988&Aktenzeichen=9%20C%20278.86.

CJEU (Court of Justice of the European Union). 2012. 'C-71/11 and C-99/11 *Germany v Y and Z*'. Accessed 28 January 2020. www.asylumlawdatabase.eu/en/content/cjeu-c-7111-and-c-9911-germany-v-y-and-z.

CJEU (Court of Justice of the European Union). 2013. 'C199/12 to C201/12 *Minister voor Immigratie en Asiel v X, Y and Z*'. Accessed 28 January 2020. https://eur-lex.europa.eu/legal-content/EN/TXT/HTML/?uri=CELEX:62012CJ0199&from=EN.

Fiddian-Qasmiyeh, Elena. 2017. 'The Faith–Gender–Asylum Nexus: An Intersectionalist Analysis of Representations of the "Refugee Crisis"'. In *The Refugee Crisis and Religion: Secularism, Security and Hospitality in Question*, edited by Luca Mavelli and Erin K. Wilson, 207–22. London: Rowman and Littlefield International.

Giametta, Calogero. 2017. *The Sexual Politics of Asylum: Sexual Orientation and Gender Identity in the UK Asylum System*. New York: Routledge.

Hathaway, James C. and Jason Pobjoy. 2012. 'Queer Cases Make Bad Law', *New York University Journal of International Law and Politics* 44 (2): 315–89.

Healey, Dan. 2017. *Russian Homophobia from Stalin to Sochi*. New York: Bloomsbury Academic.

Hertoghs, Maja and Willem Schinkel. 2018. 'The State's Sexual Desires: The Performance of Sexuality in the Dutch Asylum Procedure', *Theory and Society* 47 (6): 691–716.

Hirschman, Albert O. 1970. *Exit, Voice, and Loyalty: Responses to Decline in Firms, Organizations, and States*. Cambridge, MA: Harvard University Press.

Human Rights Watch. 2014. 'License to Harm: Violence and Harassment against LGBT People and Activists in Russia'. Accessed 7 June 2017. www.hrw.org/report/2014/12/15/license-harm/violence-and-harassment-against-lgbt-people-and-activists-russia.

ILGA-Europe. 2016. 'Russia'. In *ILGA-Europe Annual Review of the Human Rights Situation of Lesbian, Gay, Bisexual, Trans and Intersex People in Europe 2016*, 138–43. Brussels: ILGA-Europe. Accessed 29 January 2020. www.ilga-europe.org/sites/default/files/Attachments/annual_review_2016-for_web.pdf.

ILGA. 2017. *State Sponsored Homophobia 2016: A World Survey of Sexual Orientation Laws: Criminalisation, Protection and Recognition*, last modified 1 May 2017, http://www.ilga.org/downloads/02_ILGA_State_Sponsored_Homophobia_2016_ENG_WEB_150515.pdf.

Jansen, Sabine. 2013. 'Introduction: Fleeing Homophobia, Asylum Claims Related to Sexual Orientation and Gender Identity in Europe'. In *Fleeing Homophobia: Sexual Orientation, Gender Identity and Asylum*, edited by Thomas Spijkerboer, 1–31. London: Routledge.

Levada-Center. 2015. 'Homophobia'. Press release, 10 June. Accessed 29 January 2020. www.levada.ru/en/2015/06/10/homophobia.

Lewis, Rachel. 2013. 'Deportable Subjects: Lesbians and Political Asylum', *Feminist Formations* 25 (2): 174–94.

Massad, Joseph A. 2007. *Desiring Arabs*. Chicago: University of Chicago Press.

Miles, Nathanael. 2010. *No Going Back: Lesbian and Gay People and the Asylum System*. London: Stonewall.

Millbank, Jenni. 2009. 'From Discretion to Disbelief: Recent Trends in Refugee Determinations on the Basis of Sexual Orientation in Australia and the United Kingdom', *International Journal of Human Rights* 13 (2/3): 391–414.

Murray, David A.B. 2016. *Real Queer? Sexual Orientation and Gender Identity Refugees in the Canadian Refugee Apparatus*. London: Rowman and Littlefield International.

Neilson, Victoria. 2005. 'Homosexual or Female? Applying Gender-Based Asylum Jurisprudence to Lesbian Asylum Claims', *Stanford Law and Policy Review* 16 (2): 417–44.

Raboin, Thibaut. 2017. 'Exhortations of Happiness: Liberalism and Nationalism in the Discourses on LGBTI Asylum Rights in the UK', *Sexualities* 20 (5/6): 663–81.

Russian LGBT Network. 2016. 'Monitoring of Discrimination and Violence Based on SOGI in Russia in 2015'. Accessed 29 January 2020. https://lgbtnet.org/en/content/monitoring-discrimination-and-violence-based-sogi-russia-2015.

Schreck, Carl. 2016. 'Russian Applications for US Asylum Surge Again in 2016', *Radio Free Europe/Radio Liberty*, 6 December. Accessed 29 January 2020. www.rferl.org/a/russia-increase-seeking-us-asylum-in-2016/28159435.html.

Spijkerboer, Thomas, ed. 2013. *Fleeing Homophobia: Sexual Orientation, Gender Identity and Asylum*. London: Routledge.

UKLGIG (UK Lesbian and Gay Immigration Group). 2010. *Failing the Grade: Home Office Initial Decisions on Lesbian and Gay Claims for Asylum*. London: UK Lesbian and Gay Immigration Group. Accessed 1 May 2017. http://uklgig.org.uk/wp-content/uploads/2014/04/Failing-the-Grade.pdf.

UK Supreme Court. 2010. *'HJ (Iran) (FC) (Appellant) v Secretary of State for the Home Department (Respondent) and One Other Action'*. Accessed 29 January 2020. www.supremecourt.uk/cases/uksc-2009-0054.html.

UNHCR (United Nations High Commissioner for Refugees). 2012. 'Guidelines on International Protection No. 9: Claims to Refugee Status Based on Sexual Orientation and/or Gender Identity within the Context of Article 1A(2) of the 1951 Convention and/or Its 1967 Protocol Relating to the Status of Refugees'. Accessed 29 January 2020. www.refworld.org/docid/50348afc2.html.

United Nations. 2011. 'UN Resolution 17/19 on "Human Rights, Sexual Orientation and Gender Identity", A/HRC/17/L.9/Rev.1'.

United Nations. 2012. 'To Those Who Are Lesbian, Gay, Bisexual or Transgender, Secretary-General Says in Message: You Are Not Alone in Your Struggle to End Violence, Discrimination (SG/SM/14145-HRC/13)'. Press release, 7 March. Accessed 29 January 2020. www.un.org/press/en/2012/sgsm14145.doc.htm.

United Nations Human Rights Committee. 1992. 'CCPR General Comment No. 20: Article 7 (Prohibition of Torture, or Other Cruel, Inhuman or Degrading Treatment or Punishment)'. Accessed 29 January 2020. www.refworld.org/docid/453883fb0.html.

Weßels, Janna. 2013. 'Discretion in Sexuality-Based Asylum Cases: An Adaptive Phenomenon'. In *Fleeing Homophobia: Sexual Orientation, Gender Identity and Asylum*, edited by Thomas Spijkerboer, 55–81. London: Routledge.

20
# Aspects of loss and coping among internally displaced populations: Towards a psychosocial approach

Maureen Seguin

## Introduction

This chapter aims to explore resource loss and coping strategies among internally displaced women in the Republic of Georgia (hereafter referred to as Georgia). Internally displaced persons (IDPs) are defined as persons who have been forced to flee their homes as a result of, or in order to avoid, the effects of armed conflict, situations of generalized violence, violations of human rights, or natural or human-made disasters (Kälin, 2008). They differ from refugees as the latter cross state borders, although IDPs often leave their homes for the same reasons as refugees.

The motivation to explore resource loss and coping among internally displaced women is driven by gaps in the existing literature. First, much existing literature focused on mental-health status among populations residing in post-conflict areas employs a narrow definition of mental health, using a trauma-focused orientation (Steel *et al.*, 2009; Miller and Rasmussen, 2010; Ager, 2014 – and see Chatterjee *et al.*, and Krause and Sharples, in this volume). Second, there is a paucity of research devoted to understanding how conflict-affected populations cope in response to exposure to trauma and loss. Moreover, much of the existing research on coping mechanisms among conflict-affected persons focuses on refugees residing in high-income countries, even though most such persons live in low- and middle-income countries (LMICs) (UNHCR, 2017). Third, IDPs remain neglected in research on war-affected populations even though there are substantially higher numbers of IDPs than refugees worldwide (ibid.). Fourth, evidence suggests that conflict-affected men and women in LMICs experience conflict and cope in different ways from each other (Seguin and Roberts, 2017). This may stem from the different sorts of trauma faced by men and women at different stages of a conflict, and the resources available during and after war (Dahl *et al.*, 1998; Kottegoda *et al.*, 2008; Annan and Brier, 2010; Feseha *et al.*, 2012).

To address these gaps, the following research questions direct the chapter: What are the losses experienced by internally displaced women in Georgia (and other IDPs)? How do these women and other war-affected groups cope with these losses? Are there differences according to gender? Such questions lend themselves to a psychosocial approach to mental health, by focusing on agency rather than victimhood, on promoting resilience among conflict-affected children (see Krause and Sharples, this volume) and on the wide social context that shapes both losses suffered and reactions to loss among IDPs.

A psychosocial approach to addressing mental-health needs examines the economic, social and cultural influences on mental health, acknowledging local understandings of distress and the long-term impact of conflict on mental health (Pedersen, 2002). The daily stressors caused by the effect of conflict on income, housing, education, social and cultural networks and practices are examined, rather than focusing on the short-term impact of trauma alone (Summerfield, 1999; Miller and Rasmussen, 2010). Those adhering to the psychosocial paradigm view refugees and IDPs as agents possessing skills and strengths rather than as passive victims (Miller and Rasco, 2004). This orientation favours non-medical interventions for mental-health problems, based on the assumption that the mental-health impact of armed conflict is largely or completely mediated by the stressful social and material conditions that it creates. Measures such as providing jobs, reuniting families, and creating effective justice and education systems are viewed as appropriate treatment responses for populations affected by war (Silove, 2005). In contrast, the trauma-focused paradigm focuses on exposure to violence associated with war and the measurement of mental disorders – most notably, Post-Traumatic Stress Disorder (PTSD) (Ingleby, 2005). This approach is characterized by a universalist understanding of mental disorders based on the Diagnostic and Statistical Manual of Mental Disorders. A movement toward a synthesis of the two approaches has been noted (Miller and Rasmussen, 2010) and promoted in guidelines on mental health and psychosocial support in emergency settings from the Inter-Agency Standing Committee (IASC, 2007). The guidelines recognize that people affected by emergencies have diverse outcomes;

while some may develop mental-health disorders and require specialized treatment, others may retain good mental health or require only limited support.

## The Georgian context

Georgia is a strongly agricultural society, with almost half of the population living in rural areas and depending on subsistence and semi-subsistence farming for its livelihood (Pelkmans, 2006). Displays of generosity and hospitality are important elements of Georgian culture, reflected in the widely held sentiment that 'Guests are a gift from God'. Rituals such as feasts, toasts and gift-giving reinforce national values, and symbolize individual and family social standing within communities (Muehlfried, 2007). The Georgian Orthodox faith is central to the identity of many Georgians – as demonstrated by frequent church attendance, the high status of the Georgian Orthodox patriarch and the strict observance of various religious practices. Strong ties of 'brotherhood' are prevalent among Georgian men, forming spiritual kinship that bestows benefits as well as obligations on members (Frederiksen, 2013: 9).[1]

In conjunction with this strong commitment to the Orthodox faith, Georgia has long been ethnically heterogeneous, composed of a diversity of groups each with distinct traditions, manners and languages (Pelkmans, 2006). The Ossetians are one such group, living in an area that spans Russia and Georgia (North and South Ossetia). South Ossetia comprises 3,900 square kilometres, amounting to 5.6 per cent of the total area of Georgia.

In 1921, Georgia was invaded by Soviet Russia and became absorbed into the Union of Soviet Socialist Republics (USSR). The South Ossetian Autonomous Region was created in 1922, with borders drawn to include several communities composed primarily of ethnic Georgians (Souleimanov, 2013). There were no armed conflicts between ethnic Georgians and South Ossetians in the South Ossetian Autonomous Region during the Soviet era; the two groups lived side by side in a patchwork of villages with high rates of intermarriage. Men's roles in Georgia during this time revolved around supporting loved ones as the family breadwinner. Despite efforts to create a 'New Soviet Woman' who would equal men in the workplace (Crate, 2004), traditional patriarchal gender relations were deeply held in Georgia throughout the Soviet era.

As the Soviet Union started to disintegrate in the late 1980s, there were calls for Georgian independence from the USSR and South Ossetian independence from Georgia. Tensions over South Ossetia's declaration of independence lead to a war in the territory that resulted in several thousand casualties and approximately 10,000 displaced persons, who fled either north to North Ossetia or south into Georgia proper (Asmus, 2010). Ethnic Georgians were largely driven out of the South Ossetian capital of Tskhinvali, with some resettling in undamaged Georgian villages near the capital. A Moscow-brokered ceasefire between South Ossetia and Georgia was signed on 24 June 1992, and demilitarized zones between South Ossetia and Georgia were established. These were to be patrolled by peacekeepers from the newly formed Commonwealth of Independence States and United Nations monitors. Far from being neutral observers, however, the peacekeepers installed in South Ossetia were dominated by Russia, which had itself been part of the conflict that fuelled the need for peacekeepers. In practice, post-conflict South Ossetia was largely run by Russian military and intelligence services while still officially Georgian territory (ibid.).

During the war, the Georgian Parliament declared independence from the USSR on 9 April 1991. A chaotic transition period commenced, characterized by a deep recession that caused a dramatic decline in living standards and the deterioration of the health system to the point that it failed to function into the 1990s (Gotsadze *et al.*, 2005; Scott, 2007). In 1995, a Health Care Reform Package was introduced in Georgia that ushered in health insurance and user fees (Rukhadze, 2013) – part of a 'rationalization' process that radically privatized the health system, which decreased care affordability and quality (Machavariani, 2007).

The next major conflict in South Ossetia occurred from 7 to 12 August 2008. North of Tskhinvali, entire Georgian villages were completely razed as Russian troops entered Georgia through the Roki tunnel (Tsereteli, 2014). It is estimated that 850 people (half of them civilians) were killed in the war and several thousand wounded (de Waal, 2010). At least 158,000 ethnic Georgians and Ossetians fled South Ossetia and the bordering areas, amounting to over half the population of South Ossetia (IDMC, 2009). The vast majority of those displaced were initially accommodated in the Georgian capital, Tbilisi, in public buildings such as schools and universities, and then were settled in the central Shida Kartli region, of which the city of Gori is the capital. A ceasefire was signed on 12 August 2008 and hostilities ended. In the final months of 2008, many of those who were displaced from the 'buffer' zone bordering South Ossetia returned to their homes – as did ethnic Ossetians, who fled alongside ethnic Georgians (IDMC, 2009). However, a substantial group of ethnically Georgian IDPs was unable to return home, with

2009 estimates ranging from 37,000 (IDMC, 2009) to 40,000 (de Waal, 2010), and 17,000 in 2012 (IDMC, 2012). As of the writing of this chapter, Georgia remains locked in a frozen conflict with South Ossetia, with many Georgians displaced by the 2008 conflict still unable to return to their places of origin.

From November 2012 to February 2013, I supervised two female Georgian research assistants as they conducted 42 semi-structured interviews with internally displaced Georgian women. All interviewees resided in one of three IDP settlements near the Georgian city of Gori. The purpose of these interviews was to explore resource loss and coping strategies of the women. Below, I share Latavri's story, a personal account reflecting historical developments in South Ossetia leading to the 2008 war.

## Latavri's story

Latavri was the eldest participant in the study, aged 73 at the time of the interview. She introduced herself at the beginning of her interview:

> I was born in [a village in South Ossetia] in 1940. I was 1 year old when my father went to war, World War II and he never came back. I was the only child in my family and my mother devoted her life to me. By a twist of fate, I married an Ossetian.

When asked by the interviewer to tell her about the events that led to her living at Skra IDP settlement, Latavri stated:

> Well, I'd like to say that these events didn't start in 2008. It all began long before … I don't know. This is my opinion. This is what I think. When the Soviet Union was about to collapse … I'm not a politician or anything, but I'd like to tell you about what was going on in Tskhinvali at the time. Ossetians used to hold demonstrations in Tskhinvali. They didn't want to live with Georgians. They didn't want to be part of Georgia. I could tell it from their banners and everything. From my private conversations with them too, of course. Everything was against Georgia. They wanted their own republic. … It all began during the 90s. In 1989, to be more precise. After this, life there got harder … So, I'm saying that this war didn't start in 2008, but a long time before. The situation had been growing worse

until it escalated into the war in 2008. But even before 2008, things were so tense that we were standing at the verge of war.

Latavri then reflected on the impact of these political developments on her day-to-day life in South Ossetia, including danger to her personal safety and difficulty in conducting animal husbandry:

There were nine Georgian villages. There was no road or anything. Sometimes they would close the road through Tskhinvali. Sometimes they would let us pass through it. They used to stop buses and capture people. I don't know. We've been through a lot. I think anyone can prove it. We've been through hard times. They used to shoot at us. Our gorge was surrounded by mountains and their roadblocks or something, I don't know, they were located uphill … They would shoot at us from there. We were in a really difficult situation. Many houses were destroyed by missiles. Everything was being destroyed. Herdsmen couldn't put livestock to pasture because Ossetians would kidnap both their cattle and herdsmen themselves. This family from Kekhvi here lost a member when he was putting livestock to pasture; four people from Dzartsemi were killed too, they were also kidnapped when they were putting their cattle to pasture. So, things like this used to happen … Younger people used to leave the region with kids, older people would stay there, then they would return but what these Russians and Ossetians did in 2008 was too much. It was just too much.

Reflecting on the loss resulting from the war, Latavria shares:

It's all lost. I was 69 years old at the time. Everything my mother, my grandfather, my ancestors had worked for – and we had earned something too – was lost. We were left without anything … When we wake up … Well, I don't know. I discuss things with other women and I know that we all face the same difficulties. So, we wake up thinking. We look around and think all the time. Personally I and everybody else. So, thinking. Thinking about our village, our corner, our burnt down houses. We go to sleep and dream about being there. Our flesh is here but our soul stayed there … Now, my dear, when I look back at things, it seems that our life was a bed of roses, not a bed of problems. We had jobs. We had gardens full of fruit trees and everything. We had income … We owned livestock, chickens, pigs … We had everything.

The loss described by Latavri resonated in other women's accounts, as outlined in the section below.

## Resource loss among conflict-affected groups

I frame the losses experienced by internally displaced Georgian women drawing on the Conservation of Resources (COR) theory (see also Seguin *et al.*, 2016). The central tenet of the theory is that 'people strive to retain, protect, and build resources and that what is threatening to them is the potential or actual loss of these valued resources' (Hobfoll, 1989: 516). Groups of resources tend to develop or decrease in aggregate in 'resource caravans' (Hobfoll, 2012). Thus, the loss or gain of an important resource has a comprehensive, multilevel impact on other resources. Whether resources increase or decrease depends on external factors largely outside an individual's control that 'support, foster, enrich, and protect the resources of individuals, families, and organizations, or that detract, undermine, obstruct, or impoverish people's resource reservoirs' (ibid.: 229). Sudden losses associated with traumatic events usually have a severe initial impact followed by resource loss and psychological distress, each of which makes the other worse over time (Hobfoll *et al.*, 2009; Heath *et al.*, 2012). Where entire groups have faced trauma, aggregated individual resource losses can manifest as a loss of social capital across an entire community (Ritchie, 2012).

The theoretical tenets above resonated with my data on internally displaced Georgian women. The war-related traumatic events that they experienced while fleeing and in the immediate aftermath of the war (displacement, exposure to combat, separation from family members, and food and shelter challenges) were referenced as causing fear, sleeping problems, neurosis and aggression. However, it was the farther-reaching impacts of the war, beyond the initial trauma, with which women were mostly concerned. Displacement and the loss of property that it entailed had a comprehensive, multilevel impact on other resources: on livelihood, social networks, and physical and mental health. Below, I discuss each of these elements in the 'loss caravan'.

The circumstances produced by the war (notably, prolonged displacement, poverty and its effects) were viewed by the women as detrimental to their mental health. The poverty in particular was a source of constant stress. The loss of their property was deeply felt, not only due to the financial security that the land represented but also due to the sentimental attachment and decades of work invested in their farms.

Moreover, the inability to visit graves and carry out various rites (visiting the deceased on significant dates over the year) was a bitter affront to their Orthodox faith. Georgian IDPs have referred to the loss of their native land as a 'lost paradise', underscoring their deep and passionate attachment to their villages of origin (Makhashvili *et al.*, 2010). The multiple paths to mental distress have been noted in other war-affected groups. The loss of access to land and traditional economic roles among Mozambican refugee women has been linked to decreased self-worth, confidence and status (Sideris, 2003). In a study on social determinants of health among IDPs in northern Uganda, B. Roberts *et al.* (2009) found that displacement from property led to impoverishment, which in turn led to mental health losses – and a similar pattern has been observed among IDP Palestinian women in the West Bank (Al-Khatib *et al.*, 2005).

A deterioration of social networks was interrelated with these losses in livelihood and mental health. Many women viewed their IDP settlements as insecure and unfamiliar, with formerly proximal friends and family now far away. They frequently contrasted their current settlements with their villages of origin, which they characterized as cohesive and familiar (though physically unsafe). A lack of ability to afford gifts socially necessary for visits presented a barrier to maintaining contact with formerly close family and friends, along with the inability to pay for transportation for such visits. Such challenges were often implicated in the deterioration of social networks.

Physical-health losses were also apparent. Such losses were attributed by the women to the conditions in IDP settlements, with dampness, mould and poor water quality blamed for causing respiratory and joint problems. Physical-health ailments were also seen as resulting from mental-health problems (most commonly, from excessive worrying) and from financial difficulties that prevented the purchase of medication. Such linkages have been noted elsewhere: Roberts *et al.* (2009) observed similar pathways to poor physical health among IDPs in northern Uganda, and participants in the research of Mark Eggerman and Catherine Panter-Brick (2010) drew a link between poverty and poor physical health. The losses of livelihood and physical and mental health are interrelated; the former leads to a deterioration in physical health due to the inability to afford medical care and mediation. Poor physical health was also viewed as being caused by poor mental health, with 'worrying too much' commonly perceived as causing health problems.

The widely documented lack of access to health services reported by the participants exacerbated losses in physical and mental health. The largely privatized healthcare system in Georgia primarily relies on out-of-pocket payments from citizens to fund services (Rukhadze, 2013), which deters citizens of low socio-economic status from seeking medical treatment and accessing pharmaceuticals (Karavasilis, 2011). This barrier seems to persist even though insurance is covered for households living below the poverty line (Rukhadze, 2013), which includes most IDPs. The lack of outpatient psychiatric clinics in rural Georgia and poor quality of care in rural compared to urban clinics constitute further barriers to mental-health treatment (Makhashvili and van Voren, 2013).

Although mental-health issues resulting from war-related trauma have been the focus of much research, the findings outlined above underscore the impact of other loss trajectories (loss of employment, social networks and physical health) on mental health. Internally displaced women in Georgia attempted to mitigate these losses in a wide variety of ways, as summarized in the next section.

## Coping strategies among conflict-affected groups

The coping responses reported by IDP women in Georgia are here interpreted according to a typology of coping domains that encompasses problem solving, support seeking, escape avoidance, distraction and positive cognitive restructuring (Skinner *et al.*, 2003; Seguin *et al.*, 2017). Where relevant, I include women's thoughts on the differences in coping strategies between men and women in their IDP settlements. Throughout, I contextualize the findings on internally displaced women in Georgia in relation to findings obtained elsewhere.

Problem-solving coping strategies were the most common types of strategy reported by the respondents, and included seeking employment and working, budgeting, and adopting new roles and responsibilities. Engaging in problem-solving coping strategies generally yielded a sense of hope and relief among respondents, consistent with the findings of a systematic literature review on coping strategies used by conflict-affected persons in LMICs (Seguin and Roberts, 2017). The willingness among internally displaced Georgian women to take on work that is perceived as unappealing resonates within other studies on war-affected women residing in LMICs. For instance, a study on Liberian refugee women in Ghana observed that they were commonly engaged in 'inconsistent subsistence' economic activities, comprising tasks such as hair braiding, selling water and produce, and washing the clothes of others in order to generate income to survive (Hardgrove, 2009). The majority of these women were unable to access work similar to their previous roles in

Liberia – especially those who were trained professionals, such as teachers or nurses.

Women often compared their problem-solving coping strategies with the coping strategies enacted by their male counterparts. The women often stated that they were much more willing to take on petty, temporary and unappealing work than male family members were. Because of this phenomenon, many of the women interviewed felt very strongly that their roles in the displacement era had expanded, with some reporting that they had taken over the breadwinning role in their families from males. Expanded roles among conflict-affected women observed here have been reported in other contexts (Bennet *et al.*, 1995; El-Bushra, 2000; Tummala-Narra, 2004; Saragih Turnip and Hauff, 2007) and in the case of Georgians displaced in conflicts during the 1990s. A study on the latter observed that displaced Georgian women worked determinedly to provide for their families, turning to petty street trade and seasonal agricultural work (Buck *et al.*, 2000). Male counterparts to these women were seemingly unwilling to engage in these income-generating activities, instead reportedly passing time in collective IDP centres with other men, drinking alcohol and socializing (Vivero Pol, 1999). A survey in 1998 concluded that women provided the main sources of income in 72 per cent of IDP families in Georgia (Zurikashvili, 1998). The trends observed in the 1990s have again become apparent with IDPs displaced in/since 2008. Internally displaced Georgian women have observed that men have been doubly traumatized, by the conflicts of the 1990s and in 2008 – first by the war (and the associated loss of territory), and second by the lack of livelihood in the post-conflict era (and loss of the breadwinner role). These losses and trauma are not unique to Georgia. For instance, angry reactions to such losses have been noted among male Burundian refugees in Tanzania (Turner 1999).

Many internally displaced women turned to a variety of sources of social support in response to having lost the social networks described above; this is consistent with the wider literature on coping strategies among war-affected groups (Seguin and Roberts, 2017). In particular, relationships with cherished family members – and, specifically, children – were sometimes held up as the only worthwhile thing left in life. As Nino Makhashvili *et al.* (2010) note, in Georgia children are viewed as the most important part of the community.

Reaching out to peers is also commonly reported in other studies on war-affected groups. In the current study, the support shared by and with 'old' neighbours (that is, neighbours from the IDPs' pre-displacement villages) was of paramount importance, as is reflected elsewhere (Almedom,

2004; Kassam and Nanji, 2006). Drawing support from priests and other religious figures was frequently reported by the respondents in this study, mirroring reports across the coping literature on war-affected persons in LMICs (Almedom, 2004; Hardgrove, 2009; Fiddian-Qasmiyeh and Ager, 2013).

Only a minority of the respondents mentioned reaching out to mental-health counsellors, psychologists or psychiatrists as strategies to address problems. This finding is reflected in other studies, which suggests that appealing for social support from friends, family, neighbours and community members is preferable and a more common way for war-affected persons in LMICs to deal with trauma and loss than resorting to specialized services (Ruwanpura *et al.*, 2006). As Daya Somasundaram (2010) states, social support from family and reliance on social networks more generally is a vital protective factor against poor mental health – especially in non-Western more 'collectivist'-orientated cultures. Similarly to problem-solving coping strategies, the respondents felt that support-seeking coping differed between the men and women in their settlements. In fact, these differences were among the most heavily emphasized when questions were asked about how men's and women's coping strategies differed. Respondents widely felt that women readily engaged in seeking support while men tended to conceal their hardships from others.

Distraction techniques reported by internally displaced Georgian women included reading and watching TV, as well as doing housework. They also distracted themselves through visiting others (overlapping with support-seeking strategies) and seeking employment, working and gardening (overlapping with problem solving). Some Georgian women reported using escapist or avoidant techniques, such as giving up on problems, isolating themselves physically and/or emotionally, crying and engaging in wishful thinking. These tactics represent attempts to avoid unwanted experiences. Makhashvili *et al.* (2010) suggest that avoidance coping resembles 'typically Georgian' ways of dealing with painful memories.

Internally displaced Georgian women saw a large difference between their own avoidance and distraction coping strategies and those used by their male counterparts, which largely centred on the consumption of alcohol. Men socializing and drinking in groups throughout the day was a source of frustration for many of the women, with many reporting that men's alcohol use was very high and had increased after the war. These developments were given as evidence of shifting roles of men in the community, and were viewed as driving women to engage in problem-solving coping strategies by seeking and taking on paid employment. Alcohol use was contrasted with women's distraction techniques, which tended to focus on seeking employment and working, gardening for distraction, engaging in housework, reading and watching TV, and visiting others.

A range of positive cognitive-restructuring techniques, defined as changing one's perspective of a stressful situation in order to see it in a more positive light (focusing on the positive rather than the negative, adopting an optimistic viewpoint, downplaying levels of distress) (see Skinner *et al.*, 2003: 242), were reported by internally displaced Georgian women. Many women recounted their own difficulties and losses, but then often stated, 'but others have it much worse'. Focusing on mental strength was another cognitive-restructuring coping technique reported. The women were proud that they had met the challenges that life had presented so far, contributing to a sense of confidence as they reflected on how far they had come. Concentrating on the future rather than the present was also commonly reported among the respondents, reflected in statements about their hopes for children's prospects.

Coping through faith was nuanced, with women drawing on several aspects of religion in order to cope. Respondents reported that faith enabled them to find meaning in hardships and/or war-related events. For instance, several women viewed the war and displacement as 'God's plan' – thereby assigning an inevitability to the events, which conferred comfort. The meaning-making function of faith-based coping has been reported elsewhere (Ebadi *et al.*, 2009; Hardgrove, 2009; Eggerman and Panter-Brick, 2010; Thomas *et al.*, 2011). Faith also imparted a sense of strength to respondents. Numerous comments such as 'God gives me strength' and 'God makes me stronger' reflect research findings among other female (Badri *et al.*, 2013) and mixed-gender war-affected groups in LMICs (Ruwanpura *et al.*, 2006). Reliance on the Georgian Orthodox faith emerged as a cross-cutting theme throughout the data, functioning as a medium through which to access social support and engage in problem solving through prayer or reaching out to others of the same faith. Faith also acted as a prism through which to view events as 'God's plan'. Activities associated with faith, such as attending church and engaging in religious rites, equally served as avoidance and distraction coping strategies.

## Conclusion

In this chapter, I have argued that a psychosocial approach is particularly relevant for understanding the experiences of internally displaced Georgian women, due to its long-term focus and attention to daily stressors caused by the effects of conflict. Although traumas associated with the war were certainly mentioned by the women who participated in this study (as well as issues that might be symptoms of depression or anxiety disorder), the daily challenges associated with displacement were much more pronounced: these included the loss of income, belongings, ability to grow food, and opportunities for children. As noted by Kenneth Miller *et al.* (2008) and Mark van Ommeren *et al.* (2005), the mental-health impact of armed conflict is mediated by the stressful social and material conditions that it creates. This finding speaks to the need for interventions to be developed from a psychosocial standpoint rather than a trauma standpoint, including through providing jobs, reuniting families, and creating effective justice and education systems.

While refugees are entitled to protection from host national governments and the United Nations High Commission for Refugees, there is no legal obligation for the extension of such rights to IDPs. As a result, IDPs have been marginalized from international humanitarian relief and support (United Nations, 2005: 5). Although efforts have been made to improve the protection of IDPs over the past decade (UNHCR, 2008), they still generally experience less protection and social support than do refugees (Hampton, 2002). This context perpetuates an unequal and arbitrary distribution of resources between IDPs and refugees, though the former often leave their places of origin for the same reasons as the latter.

This chapter focused exclusively on women forcibly displaced by war, rather than both men and women, due to the higher burden of poor mental health in post-conflict settings borne by women (Johnson and Thompson, 2008; Steel *et al.*, 2009), which may stem from the different types of hardships faced during displacement and/or cultural mores framing the treatment of women. These gender-based differences must be acknowledged in order to implement interventions that will be effective in supporting the coping strategies of forcibly displaced women. The evidence base on coping strategies of war-affected groups would benefit from future studies taking a gender-sensitive approach and focusing separately on both female and male participants. Moreover, future work guided by intersectional lines of analysis (see Fiddian-Qasmiyeh, 2014) would equally represent an advancement in the understanding of the day-to-day struggles and coping strategies of conflict-affected women in diverse contexts.

# Note

1. For discussions on the significance of religion, faith and spirituality in diverse contexts of conflict and displacement, see the chapters by Fisher *et al.* (on Yezidi IDPs in Iraq), Mole (in relation to queer Russian asylum seekers' claims for protection in Germany) and Fiddian-Qasmiyeh (on faith-related assistance by and for refugees in Lebanon), in this volume.

# References

Ager, Alastair. 2014. 'Health and Forced Migration'. In *The Oxford Handbook of Refugee and Forced Migration Studies*, edited by Elena Fiddian-Qasmiyeh, Gil Loescher, Katy Long and Nando Sigona, 433–46. Oxford: Oxford University Press.

Al-Khatib, Issam A., Rania N. Arafat and Mohamed Musmar. 2005. 'Housing Environment and Women's Health in a Palestinian Refugee Camp', *International Journal of Environmental Health Research* 15 (3): 181–91.

Almedom, Astier M. 2004. 'Factors That Mitigate War-Induced Anxiety and Mental Distress', *Journal of Biosocial Science* 36 (4): 445–61.

Annan, Jeannie and Moriah Brier. 2010. 'The Risk of Return: Intimate Partner Violence in Northern Uganda's Armed Conflict', *Social Science and Medicine* 70 (1): 152–59.

Asmus, Ronald D. 2010. *A Little War That Shook the World: Georgia, Russia, and the Future of the West*. New York: Palgrave Macmillan.

Badri, Alia, H.W. Van den Borne and Rik Crutzen. 2013. 'Experiences and Psychosocial Adjustment of Darfuri Female Students Affected by War: An Exploratory Study', *International Journal of Psychology* 48 (5): 944–53.

Bennett, Olivia, Jo Bexley and Kitty Warnock, eds. 1995. *Arms to Fight, Arms to Protect: Women Speak Out about Conflict*. London: Panos.

Buck, Thomas, Alice Morton, Susan Allen Nan and Feride Zurikashvili. 2000. *Aftermath: Effects of Conflict on Internally Displaced Women in Georgia* (Working Paper 310). Washington, DC: Center for Development Information and Evaluation.

Crate, Susan A. 2004. 'The Gendered Nature of Viliui Sakha Post-Soviet Adaptation'. In *Post-Soviet Women Encountering Transition: Nation Building, Economic Survival, and Civic Activism*, edited by Kathleen Kuehnast and Carol Nechemias, 127–45. Washington, DC: Woodrow Wilson Center Press.

Dahl, Solveig, Atifa Mutapcic and Berit Schei. 1998. 'Traumatic Events and Predictive Factors for Posttraumatic Symptoms in Displaced Bosnian Women in a War Zone', *Journal of Traumatic Stress* 11 (1): 137–45.

De Waal, Thomas. 2010. *The Caucasus: An Introduction*. New York: Oxford University Press.

Ebadi, Abbas, Fazlollah Ahmadi, Mostafa Ghanei and Anoshirvan Kazemnejad. 2009. 'Spirituality: A Key Factor in Coping among Iranians Chronically Affected by Mustard Gas in the Disaster of War', *Nursing and Health Sciences* 11 (4): 344–50.

Eggerman, Mark and Catherine Panter-Brick. 2010. 'Suffering, Hope, and Entrapment: Resilience and Cultural Values in Afghanistan', *Social Science and Medicine* 71 (1): 71–83.

El-Bushra, Judy. 2000. 'Transforming Conflict: Some Thoughts on a Gendered Understanding of Conflict Processes'. In *States of Conflict: Gender, Violence and Resistance*, edited by Susie Jacobs, Ruth Jacobson and Jen Marchbank, 66–86. London: Zed Books.

Feseha, Girmatsion, Abebe G/mariam and Mulusew Gerbaba. 2012. 'Intimate Partner Physical Violence among Women in Shimelba Refugee Camp, Northern Ethiopia', *BMC Public Health* 12, Article 125: 1–10. Accessed 25 January 2020. https://doi.org/10.1186/1471-2458-12-125.

Fiddian-Qasmiyeh, Elena. 2014. 'Gender and Forced Migration'. In *The Oxford Handbook of Refugee and Forced Migration Studies*, edited by Elena Fiddian-Qasmiyeh, Gil Loescher, Katy Long and Nando Sigona, 395–408. Oxford: Oxford University Press.

Fiddian-Qasmiyeh, Elena and Alastair Ager, eds. 2013. *Local Faith Communities and the Promotion of Resilience in Humanitarian Situations: A Scoping Study* (Working Paper 90). Oxford: Refugee Studies Centre.

Frederiksen, Martin D. 2013. *Young Men, Time, and Boredom in the Republic of Georgia*. Philadelphia: Temple University Press.

Gotsadze, George, Akaki Zoidze and Otar Vasadze. 2005. 'Reform Strategies in Georgia and Their Impact on Health Care Provision in Rural Areas: Evidence from a Household Survey', *Social Science and Medicine* 60 (4): 809–21.

Hampton, Janie, ed. 2002. *Internally Displaced People: A Global Survey*. 2nd ed. London: Earthscan.

Hardgrove, Abby. 2009. 'Liberian Refugee Families in Ghana: The Implications of Family Demands and Capabilities for Return to Liberia', *Journal of Refugee Studies* 22 (4): 483–501.

Heath, Nicole M., Brian J. Hall, Eric U. Russ, Daphna Canetti and Stevan E. Hobfoll. 2012. 'Reciprocal Relationships between Resource Loss and Psychological Distress Following Exposure to Political Violence: An Empirical Investigation of COR Theory's Loss Spirals', *Anxiety, Stress, and Coping* 25 (6): 679–95.

Hobfoll, Stevan E. 1989. 'Conservation of Resources: A New Attempt at Conceptualizing Stress', *American Psychologist* 44 (3): 513–24.

Hobfoll, Stevan E. 2012. 'Conservation of Resources and Disaster in Cultural Context: The Caravans and Passageways for Resources', *Psychiatry: Interpersonal and Biological Processes* 75 (3): 227–32.

Hobfoll, Stevan E., Patrick A. Palmieri, Robert J. Johnson, Daphna Canetti-Nisim, Brian J. Hall and Sandro Galea. 2009. 'Trajectories of Resilience, Resistance, and Distress during Ongoing Terrorism: The Case of Jews and Arabs in Israel', *Journal of Consulting and Clinical Psychology* 77 (1): 138–48.

IASC (Inter-Agency Standing Committee). 2007. *IASC Guidelines on Mental Health and Psychosocial Support in Emergency Settings*. Geneva: Inter-Agency Standing Committee.

IDMC (Internal Displacement Monitoring Centre). 2009. *Georgia: IDPs in Georgia Still Need Attention: A Profile of the Internal Displacement Situation*. Geneva: Internal Displacement Monitoring Centre.

IDMC (Internal Displacement Monitoring Centre). 2012. *Georgia: Partial Progress towards Durable Solutions for IDPs*. Geneva: Internal Displacement Monitoring Centre.

Ingleby, David. 2005. 'Editor's Introduction'. In *Forced Migration and Mental Health: Rethinking the Care of Refugees and Displaced Persons*, edited by David Ingleby, 1–27. New York: Springer.

Johnson, Howard and Andrew Thompson. 2008. 'The Development and Maintenance of Post-Traumatic Stress Disorder (PTSD) in Civilian Adult Survivors of War Trauma and Torture: A Review', *Clinical Psychology Review* 28 (1): 36–47.

Kälin, Walter. 2008. *Guiding Principles on Internal Displacement: Annotations* (Studies in Transnational Legal Policy 38). Washington, DC: American Society of International Law.

Karavasilis, Konstantinos. 2011. 'Georgian Healthcare Reform – Truth or Consequences: What's behind Door Number Three?', *World Medical and Health Policy* 3 (1): 1–5.

Kassam, Azaad and Anar Nanji. 2006. 'Mental Health of Afghan Refugees in Pakistan: A Qualitative Rapid Reconnaissance Field Study', *Intervention* 4 (1): 58–66.

Kottegoda, Sepali, Kumudini Samuel and Sarala Emmanuel. 2008. 'Reproductive Health Concerns in Six Conflict-Affected Areas of Sri Lanka', *Reproductive Health Matters* 16 (31): 75–82.

Machavariani, Shalva. 2007. 'Overcoming Economic Crime in Georgia through Public Service Reform'. In *Organized Crime and Corruption in Georgia*, edited by Louise Shelley, Erik R. Scott and Anthony Latta, 37–49. London: Routledge.

Makhashvili, Nino, Lela Tsiskarishvili and Boris Drožđek. 2010. 'Door to the Unknown: On Large-Scale Public Mental Health Interventions in Postconflict Zones – Experiences from Georgia', *Traumatology* 16 (4): 63–72.

Makhashvili, Nino and Robert van Voren. 2013. 'Balancing Community and Hospital Care: A Case Study of Reforming Mental Health Services in Georgia', *PLoS Medicine* 10 (1), Article e1001366: 1–5. Accessed 25 January 2020. https://doi.org/10.1371/journal.pmed.1001366.

Miller, Kenneth E., Patricia Omidian, Andrew Rasmussen, Aziz Yaqubi and Haqmal Daudzai. 2008. 'Daily Stressors, War Experiences, and Mental Health in Afghanistan', *Transcultural Psychiatry* 45 (4): 611–38.

Miller, Kenneth E. and Lisa M. Rasco. 2004. 'An Ecological Framework for Addressing the Mental Health Needs of Refugee Communities'. In *The Mental Health of Refugees: Ecological Approaches to Healing and Adaptation*, edited by Kenneth E. Miller and Lisa M. Rasco, 1–64. Mahwah, NJ: Lawrence Erlbaum Associates.

Miller, Kenneth E. and Andrew Rasmussen. 2010. 'War Exposure, Daily Stressors, and Mental Health in Conflict and Post-Conflict Settings: Bridging the Divide between Trauma-Focused and Psychosocial Frameworks', *Social Science and Medicine* 70 (1): 7–16.

Muehlfried, Florian. 2007. 'Sharing the Same Blood – Culture and Cuisine in the Republic of Georgia', *Anthropology of Food* S3. Accessed 25 January 2020. http://journals.openedition.org/aof/2342.

Pedersen, Duncan. 2002. 'Political Violence, Ethnic Conflict, and Contemporary Wars: Broad Implications for Health and Social Well-Being', *Social Science and Medicine* 55 (2): 175–90.

Pelkmans, Mathijs. 2006. *Defending the Border: Identity, Religion, and Modernity in the Republic of Georgia*. Ithaca, NY: Cornell University Press.

Ritchie, Liesel Ashley. 2012. 'Individual Stress, Collective Trauma, and Social Capital in the Wake of the Exxon Valdez Oil Spill', *Sociological Inquiry* 82 (2): 187–211.

Roberts, B., K. Felix Ocaka, J. Browne, T. Oyok and E. Sondorp. 2009. 'Factors Associated with the Health Status of Internally Displaced Persons in Northern Uganda', *Journal of Epidemiology and Community Health* 63 (3): 227–32.

Rukhadze, Tamari. 2013. 'An Overview of the Health Care System in Georgia: Expert Recommendations in the Context of Predictive, Preventive and Personalised Medicine', *EPMA Journal* 4, Article 8: 1–13. Accessed 25 January 2020. https://dx.doi.org/10.1186%2F1878-5085-4-8.

Ruwanpura, Eshani, Stewart W. Mercer, Alastair Ager and Gerard Duveen. 2006. 'Cultural and Spiritual Constructions of Mental Distress and Associated Coping Mechanisms of Tibetans in Exile: Implications for Western Interventions', *Journal of Refugee Studies* 19 (2): 187–202.

Saragih Turnip, Sherly and Edvard Hauff. 2007. 'Household Roles, Poverty and Psychological Distress in Internally Displaced Persons Affected by Violent Conflicts in Indonesia', *Social Psychiatry and Psychiatric Epidemiology* 42 (12): 997–1004.

Scott, Erik R. 2007. 'Georgia's Anti-Corruption Revolution'. In *Organized Crime and Corruption in Georgia*, edited by Louise Shelley, Erik R. Scott and Anthony Latta, 17–36. London: Routledge.

Seguin, Maureen, Ruth Lewis, Tinatin Amirejibi, Mariam Razmadze, Nino Makhashvili and Bayard Roberts. 2016. 'Our Flesh is Here but Our Soul Stayed There: A Qualitative Study on Resource Loss Due to War and Displacement among Internally-Displaced Women in the Republic of Georgia', *Social Science and Medicine* 150: 239–47.

Seguin, Maureen, Ruth Lewis, Mariam Razmadze, Tinatin Amirejibi and Bayard Roberts. 2017. 'Coping Strategies of Internally Displaced Women in Georgia: A Qualitative Study', *Social Science and Medicine* 194: 34–41.

Seguin, Maureen and Bayard Roberts. 2017. 'Coping Strategies among Conflict-Affected Adults in Low- and Middle-Income Countries: A Systematic Literature Review', *Global Public Health* 12 (7): 811–29.

Sideris, Tina. 2003. 'War, Gender and Culture: Mozambican Women Refugees', *Social Science and Medicine* 56 (4): 713–24.

Silove, Derrick. 2005. 'The Best Immediate Therapy for Acute Stress is Social', *Bulletin of the World Health Organization* 83 (1): 75–6.

Skinner, Ellen A., Kathleen Edge, Jeffrey Altman and Hayley Sherwood. 2003. 'Searching for the Structure of Coping: A Review and Critique of Category Systems for Classifying Ways of Coping', *Psychological Bulletin* 129 (2): 216–69.

Somasundaram, Daya. 2010. 'Collective Trauma in the Vanni: A Qualitative Inquiry into the Mental Health of the Internally Displaced Due to the Civil War in Sri Lanka', *International Journal of Mental Health Systems* 4, Article 22: 1–31. Accessed 25 January 2020. https://doi.org/10.1186/1752-4458-4-22.

Souleimanov, Emil. 2013. *Understanding Ethnopolitical Conflict: Karabakh, South Ossetia, and Abkhazia Wars Reconsidered*. Basingstoke: Palgrave Macmillan.

Steel, Zachary, Tien Chey, Derrick Silove, Claire Marnane, Richard A. Bryant and Mark van Ommeren. 2009. 'Association of Torture and Other Potentially Traumatic Events with Mental Health Outcomes among Populations Exposed to Mass Conflict and Displacement: A Systematic Review and Meta-Analysis', *JAMA: Journal of the American Medical Association* 302 (5): 537–49.

Summerfield, Derek. 1999. 'A Critique of Seven Assumptions behind Psychological Trauma Programmes in War-Affected Areas', *Social Science and Medicine* 48 (10): 1449–62.

Thomas, Fiona C., Bayard Roberts, Nagendra P. Luitel, Nawaraj Upadhaya and Wietse A. Tol. 2011. 'Resilience of Refugees Displaced in the Developing World: A Qualitative Analysis of Strengths and Struggles of Urban Refugees in Nepal', *Conflict and Health* 5, Article 20: 1–11. Accessed 25 January 2020. https://doi.org/10.1186/1752-1505-5-20.

Tsereteli, Mamuka. 2014. 'Georgia as a Geographical Pivot: Past, Present, and Future'. In *The Making of Modern Georgia, 1918–2012: The First Georgian Republic and Its Successors*, edited by Stephen F. Jones, 74–93. London: Routledge.

Tummala-Narra, Pratyusha. 2004. 'Mothering in a Foreign Land', *American Journal of Psychoanalysis* 64 (2): 167–82.

Turner, Simon. 1999. *Angry Young Men in Camps: Gender, Age and Class Relations among Burundian Refugees in Tanzania* (New Issues in Refugee Research Working Paper 9). Geneva: United Nations High Commissioner for Refugees.

UNHCR (United Nations High Commissioner for Refugees). 2008. *Policy Framework and Implementation Strategy: UNHCR's Role in Support of the Return and Reintegration of Displaced Populations*. Geneva: United Nations High Commissioner for Refugees.

UNHCR (United Nations High Commissioner for Refugees). 2017. *Global Trends: Forced Displacement in 2016*. Geneva: United Nations High Commissioner for Refugees.

United Nations. 2005. *In Larger Freedom: Towards Development, Security and Human Rights for All*. New York: United Nations General Assembly.

Van Ommeren, Mark, Shekhar Saxena and Benedetto Saraceno. 2005. 'Mental and Social Health during and after Acute Emergencies: Emerging Consensus?', *Bulletin of the World Health Organization* 83 (1): 71–6.

Vivero Pol, Jose Luis. 1999. 'Stable Instability of Displaced People in Western Georgia: A Food-Security and Gender Survey after Five Years', *Journal of Refugee Studies* 12 (4): 349–66.

Zurikashvili, Feride. 1998. *The Socio-Economic Status of Women with Children among Internally Displaced Persons in Contemporary Georgia*. Tbilisi: Women's Studies Center of Tbilisi State University.

# 21

# Thriving in the face of severe adversity: Understanding and fostering resilience in children affected by war and displacement

Karolin Krause and Evelyn Sharples

## Introduction

In 2016, close to one in ten children around the world were living in areas affected by armed conflict (UNICEF, 2016). By the end of 2017, nearly 31 million children had been forcibly displaced, including 13 million child refugees and an estimated 17 million children displaced within their countries of origin (UNICEF, 2018). Conflict-related displacement often lasts for years: towards the end of 2014, half of the world's refugees had been in displacement for longer than a decade, and at least half of all internally displaced people had been unable to return to their places of origin for at least three years (UNICEF, 2016).

Children affected by armed conflict and displacement face a host of challenges to their well-being. The World Bank's *World Development Report 2011* (World Bank, 2011) estimates that children living in fragile or conflict-affected countries are twice as likely to be malnourished, to lack access to adequate sources of water and sanitation or to lose their lives before their fifth birthdays than children in other developing countries. Primary-aged children are almost three times more likely to be out of school than their peers in peaceful developing contexts. These extraordinary challenges, in combination with more ordinary stress factors affecting children as they grow up, place young refugees and those still living in active conflict zones at an increased risk of developing mental-health problems (Garmezy, 1988; Bronstein and Montgomery, 2011; Fazel *et al.*, 2012; Reed *et al.* 2012).

Indeed, most available studies show an elevated prevalence of mental-health difficulties in displaced and conflict-affected populations compared with local populations. Exact prevalence rates vary strongly, as many studies are limited by small samples and suboptimal research designs (Bronstein and Montgomery, 2011; Reed *et al.*, 2012). A meta-analysis of 17 studies including 7,920 children from various conflict and post-conflict contexts found that, on average, 47 per cent met diagnostic criteria for Post-Traumatic Stress Disorder (PTSD) with some variation across countries (Attanayake *et al.*, 2009). A systematic review involving 3,003 displaced children from over 40 countries found levels of PTSD between 19 and 54 per cent, and levels of depression between 3 and 30 per cent, as well as varying levels of other emotional and behavioural problems (Bronstein and Montgomery, 2011). Other reviews have found high prevalence rates for psychiatric disorders among displaced children resettled in low- and middle-income countries (Reed *et al.*, 2012), as well as an average prevalence rate of 11 per cent for PTSD in children resettled in high-income countries (Fazel *et al.*, 2005). Despite these differences – with the prevalence of PTSD among conflict- and displacement-affected children ranging from 11 to 54 per cent – these findings clearly showcase the trend for widespread prevalence rates among displaced populations.

Despite the severe challenges facing them, the majority of children affected by war and displacement persevere without developing severe psychological difficulties (Barber, 2013; Masten, 2014; Cicchetti, 2010). The question of why some children develop mental-health problems in the face of severe adversity while others do not has inspired an entire subfield within the discipline of psychology that is devoted to the study of *resilience*. This chapter explores common mechanisms of resilience for children affected by conflict and displacement. We start by providing a brief historical overview of the resilience research field, followed by a discussion of the evidence base about risk and protective factors in the context of conflict and displacement. The second part of the chapter discusses implications and outstanding challenges for psychosocial resilience-building interventions, drawing on insights from an interdisciplinary workshop that was hosted at UCL in January 2017.

## A brief historical overview of the resilience research field

The first resilience studies emerged in the early 1970s within the fields of psychology (for example, Garmezy, 1971; Barclay Murphy and Moriarty, 1976) and ecology (for instance, Holling, 1973). They were strongly influenced by systems theory,[1] and shifted the focus of psychological inquiry from the manifestations and causes of psychopathology to the factors that can strengthen and protect children's mental health (Masten, 2014). The processes that help or hinder resilience were further unpacked over the course of the 1980s and 1990s, as researchers tried to better understand why some children had more positive outcomes than others (for example, Rutter, 1987).

Contemporary concepts of resilience are strongly influenced by the so-called bioecological model developed by Urie Bronfenbrenner (1979, 2005), which conceives of child development as a dynamic process that is shaped by the child's interactions with the different systems surrounding them, such as the family, community and broader society (Miller and Rasco, 2004; Cicchetti, 2010; Masten, 2011; Masten and Narayan, 2012; Tol et al., 2013a; Ungar, 2015). The ways in which these systems interact over time result in a variety of developmental trajectories and resilience outcomes, as described by Dante Cicchetti:

> the pathway to either psychopathology or resilience is influenced by a complex matrix of the individual's level of biological and psychological organization, current experiences, active choices, the social context, timing of the adverse event(s) and experiences, and the developmental history of the individual. (Cicchetti, 2010: 145)

In line with a multi-systemic resilience concept, Ann Masten defines resilience as 'the capacity of a dynamic system (individual, family, school, community, society) to withstand or recover from significant challenges that threaten its stability, viability, or development' (Masten, 2011: 494). Another definition emphasizes agency, by describing resilience as 'both the capacity of individuals to navigate their way to the psychological, social, cultural, and physical resources that sustain their well-being, and their capacity individually and collectively to negotiate for these resources to be provided in culturally meaningful ways' (Ungar, 2011: 10).

Contemporary resilience research is increasingly mindful of the difficulty of identifying universal risk and protective factors that would be relevant across time and space (for instance, Ungar, 2015; Ager et al., 2015). There is a growing recognition that the ways in which children adapt to traumatic events and stressful conditions differ depending on the sociocultural context; the resources available within families and communities at a given point in time; and the children's own skills, experiences and capacities. Nevertheless, there are certain risk and protective factors relevant to children affected by war and displacement that have been evidenced repeatedly in different contexts. We will provide a brief overview of these risk and protective factors and the current evidence base around them, before discussing the implications for developing resilience-building interventions.

## Stressors and risk factors facing children affected by conflict and displacement

Children affected by war and displacement who have experienced a severe traumatic event are at an increased risk of developing mental-health problems (Bronstein and Montgomery, 2011; Fazel *et al.*, 2012; Masten and Narayan, 2012; Reed *et al.*, 2012). They may have lost a close family member; been separated from their family; or experienced injury, torture and abuse. The likelihood of developing trauma or mental-health difficulties increases with the severity of the traumatic experience, and the accumulation of repeated traumatic events.

Direct exposure to trauma, however, does not explain all the variations in mental-health outcomes observed in children with roughly 'similar' experiences of conflict and displacement (Miller and Jordans, 2016). There is a growing body of multi-systemic resilience research that examines the additional, *indirect* pathways through which armed conflict and displacement create stress in children's lives (for example, Masten and Narayan, 2012; Miller and Rasmussen, 2010; Ventevogel *et al.*, 2013). Military conflict and forced displacement often disrupt family units and dynamics as well as schooling, the coherence of peer and community networks, public infrastructure, the rule of law and the wider economy. In doing so, they may exacerbate *daily stressors* that also exist in non-conflict environments, such as overcrowded housing, unsafe sanitation, malnutrition and lack of access to education (Miller and Rasmussen, 2010). Violence may also cascade from the political level down to the family level, and intensify daily stressors such as harsh parenting and domestic violence (Panter-Brick *et al.*, 2014) or parental mental-health problems (Palosaari *et al.*, 2013; Khamis, 2016). Some children may already be experiencing severe adversity in the form of abuse and maltreatment, and have limited resources with which to cope with the additional challenges caused by war and displacement (Fernando *et al.*, 2010). Daily stressors are often pervasive and chronic in conflict and post-conflict settings, and the ongoing exposure to these stressful conditions may gradually erode children's mental health and their ability to process singular traumatic events (Sapolsky, 2004; Miller and Rasmussen, 2010).

On a similar note, research on refugees in high-income countries suggests that daily stressors in the host country are equally relevant or even better predictors of mental-health problems than exposure to traumatic events prior to departure (Miller and Rasmussen, 2010). Such stressors have been found to include living in shelters or mass accommodation for refugees, rather than more private accommodation (Fazel *et al.*, 2012); having an uncertain asylum status for a prolonged period of time, or having to relocate repeatedly (Nielsen *et al.*, 2008); and not feeling supported in the country of resettlement (Bronstein and Montgomery, 2011). Daily stressors further include feelings of being discriminated against; a lack of financial support; having a single parent, or a parent who struggles with mental-health difficulties; or, indeed, arriving in an unfamiliar environment as an unaccompanied minor without any parental support (Fazel *et al.*, 2012).

## Protective factors

While direct and indirect war-related stressors exist at the individual, family, community and wider societal level, so do resources and processes that can help children to cope with adverse conditions and experiences. These factors – which have the potential to offset risk factors, as least for some young people – are generally referred to as *protective factors* (Garmezy, 1985).

### Individual factors

At the individual level, some of the best-evidenced protective factors – both in the general resilience literature and with regard to children affected by war and displacement – are cognitive capacity and flexibility, self-regulation and problem-solving skills (Fayyad *et al.*, 2017; Masten and Obradović, 2008; Qouta *et al.*, 2008; Masten and Narayan, 2012; Tol *et al.*, 2013a), as well as perceived agency (Masten, 2007; Masten and Obradovic, 2008) and competence (Cryder *et al.*, 2006). Children with superior cognitive and coping skills may be better able to process traumatic experiences, but they may also be more effective at negotiating and securing resources within their families and communities that can help them to adapt. Whether individual coping responses effectively build resilience, however, at least partly depends on the type of coping strategy and the psychological symptoms under scrutiny. Raija-Leena Punamäki and colleagues (2004), for example, found that denial and refusal to engage with traumatic memories protected Kurdish children from developing aggressive symptoms, but did not reduce their likelihood of developing PTSD or sleeping difficulties. These were, however, reduced in children who engaged in active help-seeking as a coping strategy. While there is some consistent evidence pointing to the importance of protective processes at the individual level, the exact ways in which these shape resilience trajectories are complex and not yet fully understood.

The role of gender in relation to resilience also tends to be similar for children affected by war and conflict, as for children growing up in less adverse circumstances. A systematic review of resilience in refugee children resettled in middle- and low-income countries suggests that boys are less likely than girls to develop emotional difficulties, such as depression and anxiety, but more prone to developing behavioural problems – especially after experiencing multiple traumatic events (Reed *et al.*, 2012). This is consistent with findings in non-refugee populations. About half the studies of children resettled in high-income countries reviewed by Mina Fazel and colleagues (2012) found similar gender differences.

The extent to which boys and girls are exposed to stressors such as active fighting, gender-based violence or changing family dynamics may differ by gender, as may the ways in which the children, their families and communities interpret and respond to these events (Reed *et al.*, 2012). Risk and protective factors may thus interact differently for boys and girls, and lead to different mental-health outcomes. Theresa Betancourt and colleagues (2010), for example, found that former female child soldiers were more likely to have experienced rape than male peers, and that they reported greater degrees of social stigma as a result of their abuse. Exploring experiences of trauma in the context of the First Palestinian Intifada, Samir Qouta and colleagues (2008) found that in highly traumatized Palestinian families, girls tended to describe their parents as attentive and restrictive, whereas boys perceived them as indifferent and rejecting. Boys who had themselves been politically active in the conflict described their fathers as supportive and affectionate, whereas girls who had been politically active tended to perceive their fathers as being punitive and restrictive. These examples showcase the fact that gender is an important factor to consider when exploring the role of risk and protective factors in shaping children's resilience.

## Family factors

There is a strong evidence base for the importance of the family environment in fostering children's resilience. Having a supportive parent available who can help to process traumatic experiences (see, for instance, Masten and Narayan, 2012), high levels of family cohesion (Laor *et al.*, 1997), positive and non-punitive parenting practices (Punamäki *et al.*, 1997, 2001; Qouta *et al.*, 2008) and a close child–carer relationship have been associated with better mental-health outcomes in children living in conflict-affected contexts (see, for example, Tol *et al.*, 2013a), as well as in children resettled in high-income countries (Fazel *et al.*, 2012).

Based on research with families in Palestine, Punamäki and colleagues (2001) argue that it is not only the case that specific parental attributes shape children's resilience but also that the family environment as a whole conditions the ways in which children utilize their own individual capacities, such as intellect and creativity, to develop coping strategies. Highly creative children, for instance, may fail to translate their skills into coping strategies if their parents are dismissive and unsupportive. The importance of family dynamics is further emphasized by Punamäki and colleagues' (2001) finding that children were most likely to develop symptoms of PTSD and emotional difficulties when there was a discrepancy between positive parenting on the mother's side and negative attitudes and parenting on the father's side – thus emphasizing the complexity of resilience processes within the family system.

## Community factors

At the community level, functioning schools, the availability of childcare, and safe places to play and learn are among the most widely reported protective factors with regard to children affected by armed conflict (Masten and Obradović, 2008; Masten and Narayan, 2012). There is also some consistent evidence that support from friends and positive experiences in school have a protective effect on refugee children resettled in high-income countries (Fazel *et al.*, 2012; see also Miller and Jordans, 2016), even though similarly robust evidence is missing for children resettled in low- and middle- income countries (Reed *et al.*, 2012). A study by Betancourt and colleagues (2013) found that former child soldiers showed higher levels of pro-social behaviour if they lived in accepting communities. The evidence base is, however, not unanimous, and some divergent findings and complexities are discussed by Weiste Tol and colleagues in their systematic review of 53 studies of resilience among children affected by conflict (Tol *et al.* 2013b).

## Sociocultural factors

At the cultural level, spirituality and religious beliefs have been reported as protective factors in a number of studies (Masten and Narayan, 2012; Tol *et al.*, 2013a, 2013b). For example, religiosity was associated with lower levels of antisocial behaviour and depression in Palestinian girls (Barber, 2001), as well as PTSD across both genders in Bosnian and Croatian adolescents, and all psychological symptoms in a Ugandan sample of former child soldiers (Klasen *et al.*, 2010). Religious commitment was also associated with significantly lower levels of anxiety and depression, as well as increased self-esteem among displaced Bosnian adolescents (Sujoldžić *et al.*, 2006). Having interviewed more than a thousand Afghan families, Mark Eggerman and Catherine Panter-Brick (2010) found that many shared the sense of a moral order that was conveyed through cultural values such as faith, family, effort, morals and honour. Feeling grounded within these values was found to act as a 'bedrock' of resilience, as these values fuelled social aspirations, self-respect and dignity (Eggerman and Panter-Brick, 2010: 81). However, these cultural values also represented a source of stress for young people and their families when the realization of social and cultural aspirations was barred by structural inequalities or a lack of resources.

Finally, there is some evidence that political activism and ideological commitment can have a protective function in certain conflict settings. The First Palestinian Intifada (1987 to 1993) was characterized by high rates of youth participation, compared with other political movements (see Barber and Olsen, 2006). Several studies have found that youth who actively participated in the first Intifada had better psychosocial outcomes once active fighting had ceased than young people who had remained passive (Baker, 1990; Barber, 2008; Quota *et al.*, 1995a, 1995b, 2008). Brian Barber (2008), for instance, found that activism during the Intifada was associated with significantly higher subsequent levels of empathy and lower levels of antisocial behaviour among young men, and higher social competence and civic engagement among both men and women. In turn, Punamäki and colleagues (2001) found that those who had actively participated in the conflict had lower rates of PTSD and emotional problems several years after active fighting had ceased.

## Summary

In summary, recent studies suggest that the resilience of children facing extreme adversity is strengthened by similar factors and processes to those that promote adaptation under less extreme circumstances, such as cognitive capacity and intelligence, self-regulation and parental support (Masten, 2001; Barber, 2013; Tol *et al.* 2013a). At the same time, however, the evidence for a particular protective factor often relates to specific psychological symptoms, with variation across contexts, children's developmental stages and the phasing of a conflict. Resilience processes are highly complex and result from the interplay of risk and protective factors at the individual, family, community and sociocultural levels. They are thus both historically and culturally embedded, which makes it nearly impossible to predict trajectories or list protective factors and processes that are universally valid (Ungar, 2011).

Understanding the complex pathways and processes by which children adapt to adverse conditions, and by which they can recover from stress and trauma, is, however, crucial for developing effective psychosocial interventions to support the well-being of young people affected by conflict and displacement. In the remainder of this chapter, we present insights on multidisciplinary working between practitioners and researchers from a recent UCL workshop on the issue of building resilience for children in low- and middle-income countries, and we discuss some of the implications for intervention.

## Insights from an interdisciplinary workshop and the implications for intervention

### Rationale and purpose of the workshop

In January 2017, the Evidence Based Practice Unit (EBPU), a collaboration between UCL's Faculty of Brain Sciences and the Anna Freud National Centre for Children and Families in London held a one-day workshop entitled 'Building Resilience for Children in Low- and Middle-Income Countries'. The workshop was funded through the UCL Grand Challenges Scheme and incorporated the scheme's agenda of developing cross-disciplinary research collaborations to address pressing societal challenges. It was also part of the EBPU's mission to bridge the gap between evidence and practice, and of influencing national and global policy agendas with regard to mental-health provision for children and young people.

Initial conversations with workshop collaborators pointed to an evident disconnect between practitioners who pioneer resilience-building interventions in the context of conflict and displacement in low- and middle-income countries, and psychologists and academics working on trauma and resilience in the UK. The workshop aimed to promote evidence-informed practice and practice-informed evidence, by bringing these parties together for a day of mutual learning. This was based on the conviction that there is ample knowledge, good practice and learning to be gained from low- and middle-income countries that could be brought to light and built on by practitioners in high-income contexts. Over 60 attendees came together to share insights about what works in building resilience for children in low- and middle-income countries, increase understanding of how to demonstrate the impact of resilience-building interventions and build collaborations between stakeholders.

## Examples of resilience-building interventions presented by the speakers

The workshop speakers'[2] focus varied within the parameters of building resilience for children in low- and middle-income countries, but spanned the interconnected themes of conflict, displacement and trauma.

Despite the fact that 250 million children are currently growing up in conflict-affected settings, the evidence on what works in responding to trauma and strengthening resilience is still scarce (a notable exception being Ager and Metzler, 2017). Speakers highlighted the fact that psychosocial models of trauma treatment developed in high-income countries can be ineffective and unsustainable in resource-poor contexts due to the demands that they place on time, financial resources and the standard of mental-health training required. While protracted displacement is widespread around the world and many refugees are rendered forcibly immobile in different camp and non-camp spaces (Fiddian-Qasmiyeh, 2016, 2019), Mark Jordans (2017), for instance, has emphasized the fact that many established psychosocial interventions may require too many subsequent sessions to be successfully implemented with displaced populations – including those who either remain 'on the move' for months, and at times years, after their initial displacement.

While recognizing the importance of providing specific trauma treatment to children suffering from PTSD, speakers also emphasized the need to address more chronic daily stressors. In line with the contemporary debates outlined in the first part of this chapter, they promoted ecological concepts of resilience whereby resilience is not a personal attribute but arises from the interplay between individuals, their families, communities and societies. Jordans (2017) presented a holistic intervention model developed by the charity War Child[3] to strengthen and mobilize resources at all levels of this ecology. War Child's approach involves specialized trauma and mental-health treatments in combination with life- and income-generating-skills training, teacher training, providing temporary education where schools have been closed or destroyed, working with families, and strengthening community cohesion and resources. In doing so, holistic approaches may be able to build a comprehensive system of care and to strengthen resources for resilience at all levels of the child's environment.

Other concrete examples of resilience-building interventions were presented by Tasha Howe (Humboldt State University in California) and Sarah Hommel (Save the Children UK). Howe introduced the ACT (Adults and Children Together) Against Violence Raising Safe Kids programme developed by the American Psychological Association. The programme fosters resilience by reducing sources of toxic stress within the family environment, and by promoting safe, stable and nurturing family relationships through parent-training programmes (Howe, 2017).[4] Hommel discussed the Healing and Education through the Arts (HEART) programme developed by Save the Children UK, which provides psychosocial support for children affected by serious chronic stress in 15 countries around the world. Through arts-based activities, HEART aims to help these children to process and communicate their feelings and experiences (Hommel, 2017).[5] Rather than providing specialized trauma treatment, both the ACT and HEART thus address sources of chronic stress as key risk factors and build up resources within the family and the individual children, respectively.

## Considerations and challenges for effective resilience programming

The concluding panel discussion raised a number of questions around conceptualizing and delivering resilience-building interventions for children affected by war and displacement in ways that are effective, collaborative and ethically sound.

### Resilience building as a 'band aid' solution?

A key issue raised was how to conceptualize resilience and whether it meant to simply survive in the face of adversity, to achieve positive outcomes or to engage in different forms of resistance. In line with predominant definitions of resilience in the literature, the panellists agreed that resilience refers to the ability for an individual to not just survive but to thrive in the presence of risk and adversity (see also Luthar *et al.*, 2000; Barber, 2013; Masten, 2014). However, panellists raised concerns that in actual practice building resilience may serve as a 'band aid' solution where it aims to alleviate distress in the short term, even though this distress is an understandable reaction to structural adversities such as conflict, chronic poverty or human-rights violations that would require longer-term solutions. These concerns resonate with critical voices in the field of global mental health (for instance, Mills and Fernando, 2014) that criticize a 'pathologization' of upset and distress in low- and middle-income countries, stressing that a significant part of suffering is caused by social and political conditions that would need to be restructured in order to promote well-being. This underscores the need for psychologists to work across disciplines – with social scientists, economists, policymakers and practitioners from fields such as poverty reduction and peace keeping – in order to promote resilience in holistic ways that not only strengthen children's individual coping skills but that also build and sustain supportive environments around them.

## Accommodating local resilience concepts and strategies

Panellists also discussed how to avoid imposing universalist understandings developed in high-income countries, and how to accommodate local or group-specific concepts and processes of resilience. Gang membership, for instance, could be considered a sign of maladaptation but might also have a protective function when it promotes self-confidence, a sense of belonging and peer support among young people. Another example is the protective function of participation in armed and non-armed forms of resistance among Palestinian youth discussed above. As emphasized by Michael Ungar (2015), behaviours that might be considered risky or undesirable in some contexts can have an adaptive function in other contexts. At the stage of designing an intervention, such behaviours should thus be considered in terms of their *function* in a context marked by adversity rather than dismissing them as undesirable per se. The risks and benefits of 'atypical' coping strategies will need to be carefully assessed in order to make informed decisions about how to build a resilience intervention around them.

More generally, the development of interventions should be based on a detailed understanding of the cultural, political and social context. This should include an assessment of the dynamics underpinning the conflict, local leadership and power relations (Tol *et al.* 2013a), as well as a detailed mapping of the resources and resilience strategies that already exist in communities (Ager and Metzler, 2017). Interventions must also consider the timing of an intervention with regard to children's developmental stages, and the phasing of the conflict and adverse events – as is evidenced by the examples discussed above. Finally, careful monitoring and evaluation should be embedded along with intervention design and implementation throughout an intervention's lifecycle in order to ensure that it complements existing resources and builds on local knowledge and competencies rather than interfering with local or individual processes of recovery, which would reduce effectiveness and sustainability in the longer term (Tol *et al.* 2013; Jordans, 2017; Ager and Metzler, 2017).

## Concluding remarks

This chapter has attempted to provide a brief overview of the current evidence around mechanisms that endanger or promote the resilience of children affected by war and displacement. It has examined processes of resilience from a multidimensional, systemic perspective exploring frequently evidenced risk and protective factors at the individual, family, community and sociocultural levels, and showcased the complex and context-specific ways in which these factors interact. As discussed in the second part of this chapter, any efforts to strengthen resilience among children affected by war and displacement will need to be highly sensitive to the intervention context, to catalyse rather than undermine the resources and processes already present in communities. In building on contemporary academic debates, holistic interventions will also need to reflect ecological and systemic understandings of resilience – and not only provide direct trauma treatment but also address chronic stressors, and the structural risk and protective factors that shape the child's wider ecological environment.

## Notes

1.  Development systems theory is a theoretical framework that goes beyond looking at nature and nurture influences on patterns or aspects of behaviour separately. Systems-theory proponents argue that behaviour is influenced by multiple factors that are context sensitive, with the influencing developing systems extending beyond the individual (Johnston, 2010).
2.  The speakers included resilience-focused researchers Jessica Deighton and Elena Fiddian-Qasmiyeh from UCL, Tasha Howe from Humboldt State University in California, Mark Jordans from King's College and Panos Vostanis from the University of Leicester, as well as practitioners from non-governmental organizations such as Sarah Hommel from Save the Children UK, Carlotta Raby from Luna Children's Charity and Helen Stawski from Islamic Relief UK.

3. War Child is a non-governmental organization founded in the United Kingdom in 1993 with the aim to protect and educate children affected by war, and to advocate for their rights (www. warchild.org.uk).
4. More information about the ACT is available at http://www.apa.org/act/.
5. More information about the HEART programme is available at https://www.savethechildren. org/content/dam/global/reports/education-and-child-protection/heart.pdf. On the role of the arts in promoting well-being, see Chatterjee et al. in this volume.

# References

Ager, Alastair and Janna Metzler. 2017. 'Where There is No Intervention: Insights into Processes of Resilience Supporting War-Affected Children', *Peace and Conflict: Journal of Peace Psychology* 23 (1): 67–75.

Ager, Joey, Elena Fiddian-Qasmiyeh and Alastair Ager. 2015. 'Local Faith Communities and the Promotion of Resilience in Contexts of Humanitarian Crisis', *Journal of Refugee Studies* 28 (2): 202–21.

Attanayake, Vindya, Rachel McKay, Michel Joffres, Sonal Singh, Frederick Burkle and Edward Mills. 2009. 'Prevalence of Mental Disorders among Children Exposed to War: A Systematic Review of 7,920 Children', *Medicine, Conflict and Survival* 25 (1): 4–19.

Baker, Ahmad M. 1990. 'The Psychological Impact of the Intifada on Palestinian Children in the Occupied West Bank and Gaza: An Exploratory Study', *American Journal of Orthopsychiatry* 60 (4): 496–505.

Barber, Brian K. 2001. 'Political Violence, Social Integration, and Youth Functioning: Palestinian Youth from the Intifada', *Journal of Community Psychology* 29 (3): 259–80.

Barber, Brian K. 2008. 'Contrasting Portraits of War: Youths' Varied Experiences with Political Violence in Bosnia and Palestine', *International Journal of Behavioral Development* 32 (4): 298–309.

Barber, Brian K. 2013. 'Annual Research Review: The Experience of Youth with Political Conflict – Challenging Notions of Resilience and Encouraging Research Refinement', *Journal of Child Psychology and Psychiatry* 54 (4): 461–73.

Barber, Brian K. and Joseph A. Olsen. 2006. 'Adolescents' Willingness to Engage in Political Conflict: Lessons from the Gaza Strip'. In *Tangled Roots: Social and Psychological Factors in the Genesis of Terrorism*, edited by Jeff Victoroff, 203–26. Amsterdam: IOS Press.

Barclay Murphy, Lois and Alice E. Moriarty. 1978. *Vulnerability, Coping, and Growth: From Infancy to Adolescence*. New Haven: Yale University Press.

Betancourt, Theresa Stichick, Ivelina Ivanova Borisova, Timothy Philip Williams, Robert T. Brennan, Theodore H. Whitfield, Marie de la Soudiere, John Williamson and Stephen E. Gilman. 2010. 'Sierra Leone's Former Child Soldiers: A Follow-Up Study of Psychosocial Adjustment and Community Reintegration', *Child Development* 81 (4): 1077–95.

Betancourt, Theresa S., Ryan McBain, Elizabeth A. Newnham and Robert T. Brennan. 2013. 'Trajectories of Internalizing Problems in War-Affected Sierra Leonean Youth: Examining Conflict and Postconflict Factors', *Child Development* 84 (2): 455–70.

Bronfenbrenner, Urie. 1979. *The Ecology of Human Development: Experiments by Nature and Design*. Cambridge, MA: Harvard University Press.

Bronfenbrenner, Urie. 2005. 'Ecological Systems Theory'. In *Making Human Beings Human: Bioecological Perspectives on Human Development*, edited by Urie Bronfenbrenner, 106–73. Thousand Oaks, CA: SAGE Publications.

Bronstein, Israel and Paul Montgomery. 2011. 'Psychological Distress in Refugee Children: A Systematic Review', *Clinical Child and Family Psychology Review* 14 (1): 44–56.

Cicchetti, Dante. 2010. 'Resilience under Conditions of Extreme Stress: A Multilevel Perspective', *World Psychiatry* 9 (3): 145–54.

Cryder, Cheryl H., Ryan P. Kilmer, Richard G. Tedeschi and Lawrence G. Calhoun. 2006. 'An Exploratory Study of Posttraumatic Growth in Children Following a Natural Disaster', *American Journal of Orthopsychiatry* 76 (1): 65–69.

Eggerman, Mark and Catherine Panter-Brick. 2010. 'Suffering, Hope, and Entrapment: Resilience and Cultural Values in Afghanistan', *Social Science and Medicine* 71 (1): 71–83.

Fayyad, John, C. Cordahi-Tabet, J. Yeretzian, M. Salamoun, C. Najm and E.G. Karam. 2017. 'Resilience-Promoting Factors in War-Exposed Adolescents: An Epidemiologic Study', European Child and Adolescent Psychiatry 26 (2): 191–200.

Fazel, Mina, Ruth V. Reed, Catherine Panter-Brick and Alan Stein. 2012. 'Mental Health of Displaced and Refugee Children Resettled in High-Income Countries: Risk and Protective Factors', The Lancet 379 (9812): 266–82.

Fazel, Mina, Jeremy Wheeler and John Danesh. 2005. 'Prevalence of Serious Mental Disorder in 7000 Refugees Resettled in Western Countries: A Systematic Review', The Lancet 365 (9467): 1309–14.

Fernando, Gaithri A., Kenneth E. Miller and Dale E. Berger. 2010. 'Growing Pains: The Impact of Disaster-Related and Daily Stressors on the Psychological and Psychosocial Functioning of Youth in Sri Lanka', Child Development 81 (4): 1192–210.

Fiddian-Qasmiyeh, Elena. 2016. 'Representations of Displacement from the Middle East and North Africa', Public Culture 28 (3): 457–73.

Fiddian-Qasmiyeh, Elena. 2019. 'Looking Forward: Disasters at 40', Disasters 43 (S1): S36–60.

Garmezy, Norman. 1971. 'Vulnerability Research and the Issue of Primary Prevention', American Journal of Orthopsychiatry 41 (1): 101–16.

Garmezy, N. 1985. 'Stress-Resistant Children: The Search for Protective Factors'. Recent Research in Developmental Psychopathology, edited by J.E. Stevenson, 213–33. Oxford: Pergamon Press.

Garmezy, Norman. 1988. 'Stressors of Childhood'. In Stress, Coping, and Development in Children, edited by Norman Garmezy and Michael Rutter, 43–84. Baltimore: Johns Hopkins University Press.

Garmezy, Norman. 1993. 'Children in Poverty: Resilience Despite Risk', Psychiatry 56 (1): 127–36.

Holling, C.S. 1973. 'Resilience and Stability of Ecological Systems', Annual Review of Ecology and Systematics 4: 1–23.

Hommel, Sara. 2017. 'HEART: Save the Children's Global Approach to Arts Based Psychosocial Support'. Paper presented at the Workshop on Building Resilience for Children in Low and Middle Income Countries, EBPU, University College London, 27 January 2017. Accessed 10 March 2020. https://www.annafreud.org/insights/news/2017/01/building-resilience-for-children-in-low-and-middle-income-countries.

Howe, Tasha. 2017. 'ACT Raising Safe Kids Programme'. Paper presented at the Workshop on Building Resilience for Children in Low and Middle Income Countries, EBPU, University College London, 27 January 2017. Accessed 10 March 2020. https://www.annafreud.org/insights/news/2017/01/building-resilience-for-children-in-low-and-middle-income-countries.

Johnston, Timothy D. 2010. 'Developmental Systems Theory'. In Oxford Handbook of Developmental Behavioural Neuroscience, edited by Mark S. Blumberg, John H. Freeman and Scott R. Robinson, 12–29. New York: Oxford University Press.

Jordans, Mark. 2017. 'Resilience in Supporting Children in Areas of Armed Conflict'. Paper presented at the Workshop on Building Resilience for Children in Low and Middle Income Countries, EBPU, University College London, 27 January 2017. Accessed 10 March 2020. https://www.annafreud.org/insights/news/2017/01/building-resilience-for-children-in-low-and-middle-income-countries.

Khamis, Vivian. 2016. 'Does Parent's Psychological Distress Mediate the Relationship between War Trauma and Psychosocial Adjustment in Children?', Journal of Health Psychology 21 (7): 1361–70.

Klasen, Fionna, Gabriele Oettingen, Judith Daniels, Manuela Post, Catrin Hoyer and Hubertus Adam. 2010. 'Posttraumatic Resilience in Former Ugandan Child Soldiers', Child Development 81 (4): 1096–113.

Laor, Nathaniel, Leo Wolmer, Linda C. Mayes, Avner Gershon, Ronit Weizman and Donald J. Cohen. 1997. 'Israeli Preschool Children under Scuds: A 30-Month Follow-Up', Journal of the American Academy of Child and Adolescent Psychiatry 36 (3): 349–56.

Luthar, Suniya S., Dante Cicchetti and Bronwyn Becker. 2000. 'The Construct of Resilience: A Critical Evaluation and Guidelines for Future Work', Child Development 71 (3): 543–62.

Masten, Ann S. 2001. 'Ordinary Magic: Resilience Processes in Development', American Psychologist 56 (3): 227–38.

Masten, Ann S. 2007. 'Resilience in Developing Systems: Progress and Promise as the Fourth Wave Rises', Development and Psychopathology 19 (3): 921–30.

Masten, Ann S. 2011. 'Resilience in Children Threatened by Extreme Adversity: Frameworks for Research, Practice, and Translational Synergy', *Development and Psychopathology* 23 (2): 493–506.

Masten, Ann S. 2014. 'Global Perspectives on Resilience in Children and Youth', *Child Development* 85 (1): 6–20.

Masten, Ann S. and Angela J. Narayan. 2012. 'Child Development in the Context of Disaster, War, and Terrorism: Pathways of Risk and Resilience', *Annual Review of Psychology* 63: 227–57.

Masten, Ann S. and Jelena Obradović. 2008. 'Disaster Preparation and Recovery: Lessons from Research on Resilience in Human Development', *Ecology and Society* 13 (1), Article 9: 1–16. Accessed 29 January 2020. www.ecologyandsociety.org/vol13/iss1/art9/.

Miller, Kenneth E. and Mark J.D. Jordans. 2016. 'Determinants of Children's Mental Health in War-Torn Settings: Translating Research into Action', *Current Psychiatry Reports* 18 (6), Article 58: 1–6. Accessed 26 January 2020. https://doi.org/10.1007/s11920-016-0692-3.

Miller, Kenneth E. and Lisa M. Rasco. 2004. *The Mental Health of Refugees: Ecological Approaches to Healing and Adaptation*. Mahwah, NJ: Lawrence Erlbaum Associates.

Miller, Kenneth E. and Andrew Rasmussen. 2010. 'War Exposure, Daily Stressors, and Mental Health in Conflict and Post-Conflict Settings: Bridging the Divide between Trauma-Focused and Psychosocial Frameworks', *Social Science and Medicine* 70 (1): 7–16.

Mills, China and Suman Fernando. 2014. 'Globalising Mental Health or Pathologising the Global South? Mapping the Ethics, Theory and Practice of Global Mental Health', *Disability and the Global South* 1 (2): 188–202.

Nielsen, Signe S., Marie Norredam, Karen L. Christiansen, Carsten Obel, Jørgen Hilden and Allan Krasnik. 2008. 'Mental Health among Children Seeking Asylum in Denmark: The Effect of Length of Stay and Number of Relocations: A Cross-Sectional Study', *BMC Public Health* 8, Article 293: 1–9. Accessed 26 January 2020. https://doi.org/10.1186/1471-2458-8-293.

Palosaari, Esa, Raija-Leena Punamäki, Samir Qouta and Marwan Diab. 2013. 'Intergenerational Effects of War Trauma among Palestinian Families Mediated via Psychological Maltreatment', *Child Abuse and Neglect* 37 (11): 955–68.

Panter-Brick, Catherine, Marie-Pascale Grimon and Mark Eggerman. 2014. 'Caregiver–Child Mental Health: A Prospective Study in Conflict and Refugee Settings', *Journal of Child Psychology and Psychiatry* 55 (4): 313–27.

Punamäki, Raija-Leena, Abbas Hedayiet Muhammed and Hemen Ahmed Abdulrahman. 2004. 'Impact of Traumatic Events on Coping Strategies and Their Effectiveness among Kurdish Children', *International Journal of Behavioral Development* 28 (1): 59–70.

Punamäki, Raija-Leena, Samir Qouta and Eyad El Sarraj. 1997. 'Models of Traumatic Experiences and Children's Psychological Adjustment: The Roles of Perceived Parenting and the Children's Own Resources and Activity', *Child Development* 68 (4): 718–28.

Punamäki, Raija-Leena, Samir Qouta and Eyad El-Sarraj. 2001. 'Resiliency Factors Predicting Psychological Adjustment after Political Violence among Palestinian Children', *International Journal of Behavioral Development* 25 (3): 256–67.

Qouta, Samir, Raija-Leena Punamäki and Eyad El Sarraj. 1995a. 'The Impact of the Peace Treaty on Psychological Well-Being: A Follow-Up Study of Palestinian Children', *Child Abuse and Neglect* 19 (10): 1197–208.

Qouta, Samir, Raija-Leena Punamäki and Eyad El Sarraj. 1995b. 'The Relations between Traumatic Experiences, Activity, and Cognitive and Emotional Responses among Palestinian Children', *International Journal of Psychology* 30 (3): 289–304.

Qouta, Samir, Raija-Leena Punamäki and Eyad El Sarraj. 2008. 'Child Development and Family Mental Health in War and Military Violence: The Palestinian Experience', *International Journal of Behavioral Development* 32 (4): 310–21.

Reed, Ruth V., Mina Fazel, Lynne Jones, Catherine Panter-Brick and Alan Stein. 2012. 'Mental Health of Displaced and Refugee Children Resettled in Low-Income and Middle-Income Countries: Risk and Protective Factors', *The Lancet* 379 (9812): 250–65.

Rutter, Michael. 1987. 'Psychosocial Resilience and Protective Mechanisms', *American Journal of Orthopsychiatry* 57 (3): 316–31.

Sapolsky, Robert M. 2004. *Why Zebras Don't Get Ulcers*. New York: Owl Books.

Sujoldžić, Anita, Lana Peternel, Tarik Kulenović and Rifet Terzić. 2006. 'Social Determinants of Health: A Comparative Study of Bosnian Adolescents in Different Cultural Contexts', *Collegium Antropologicum* 30 (4): 703–11.

Tol, Weiste A., Mark J.D. Jordans, Brandon A. Kohrt, Theresa S. Bet and Ivan H. Komproe. 2013a. 'Promoting Mental Health and Psychosocial Well-Being in Children Affected by Political Violence: Part I – Current Evidence for an Ecological Resilience Approach'. In *Handbook of Resilience in Children of War*, edited by Chandi Fernando and Michel Ferrari, 11–27. New York: Springer.

Tol, Wietse A., Suzan Song and Mark J.D. Jordans. 2013. 'Annual Research Review: Resilience and Mental Health in Children and Adolescents Living in Areas of Armed Conflict: A Systematic Review of Findings in Low- and Middle-Income Countries', *Journal of Child Psychology and Psychiatry* 54 (4): 445–60.

Ungar, Michael. 2011. 'The Social Ecology of Resilience: Addressing Contextual and Cultural Ambiguity of a Nascent Construct', *American Journal of Orthopsychiatry* 81 (1): 1–17.

Ungar, Michael. 2015. 'Practitioner Review: Diagnosing Childhood Resilience: A Systemic Approach to the Diagnosis of Adaptation in Adverse Social and Physical Ecologies', *Journal of Child Psychology and Psychiatry* 56 (1): 4–17.

UNICEF. 2016. *The State of the World's Children 2016: A Fair Chance for Every Child*. New York: UNICEF. Accessed 29 January 2020. www.unicef.org/publications/files/UNICEF_SOWC_2016.pdf.

UNICEF. 2018. *Child Displacement*. Accessed 10 March 2020. https://data.unicef.org/topic/child-migration-and-displacement/displacement.

Ventevogel, Peter, Mark J.D. Jordans, Mark Eggerman, Bibiane van Mierlo and Catherine Panter-Brick. 2013. 'Child Mental Health, Psychosocial Well-Being and Resilience in Afghanistan: A Review and Future Directions'. In *Handbook of Resilience in Children of War*, edited by Chandi Fernando and Michel Ferrari, 51–79. New York: Springer.

WHO (World Health Organization) and Calouste Gulbenkian Foundation. 2014. *Social Determinants of Mental Health*. Geneva: World Health Organization.

World Bank. 2011. *World Development Report 2011: Conflict, Security, and Development*. Washington, DC: World Bank. Accessed 29 January 2020. https://siteresources.worldbank.org/INTWDRS/Resources/WDR2011_Full_Text.pdf.

22
# Exploring the psychosocial impact of cultural interventions with displaced people

Helen J. Chatterjee, Clelia Clini, Beverley Butler, Fatima Al-Nammari, Rula Al-Asir and Cornelius Katona

## Introduction

This chapter explores the social and psychological impact of cultural and creative activities on displaced people, a process that is of particular importance at a time when understanding how to ease the transition of asylum seekers and refugees to a new place of settlement, and how to improve their lives and their integration in their societies of settlement, is of growing concern.

While the general idea that refugees are entitled to protection is not questioned by European governments, the actual entitlement of individuals to be granted refugee status is – and so migration policies increasingly focus on the protection of borders and the erection of barriers to stop the unplanned and irregular movement of people (Fassin, 2011; Fotopoulos and Kaimaklioti, 2016; Thomas, 2014; Sassen, 2006; Turner, 2015). As is by now widely acknowledged, these borders have a strong impact on the physical and psychological condition of refugees and asylum seekers. Drawing on studies in the field of migration, health, arts and well-being, this chapter discusses the potential of cultural and creative activities to ameliorate the negative impacts of displacement and to improve the psychosocial health of people with refugee and asylum-seeking backgrounds. The chapter is divided into four parts: it begins with an overview of the multiple traumas that many refugees and asylum seekers experience and then discusses the link between forced displacement and mental health. The chapter explores the connection between mental well-being, forced displacement and the arts, by drawing together findings from two site-specific case studies from the UK (the Helen Bamber Foundation) and Jordan (Talbiyeh refugee camp).

## Trauma and violence

The following lines are from the song 'No borders', composed by the music group of the Helen Bamber Foundation, Woven Gold:

> Let's talk about no borders
> Let's sing about no borders
> We are all human
> And this is our world
> Let's say no to borders

These verses point to the centrality of borders, material and metaphorical, in the lives of refugees and asylum seekers. Indeed, borders are not only the territorial boundaries that refugees have crossed to reach their country of destination, they are also, in Avtar Brah's words, those 'arbitrary dividing lines that are simultaneously social, cultural and psychic; territories to be patrolled against those whom they construct as outsiders, alien, the Others' (Brah, 1996: 198). The juxtaposition of borders and humanity made in this song denounces the violence of being systematically excluded from the realm of humanity both at a discursive and at a practical level: several scholars have in fact observed 'the prominence of animal metaphors and imagery in representations of irregular migration at border sites globally' (Vaughan-Williams, 2015: 2; see also Khosravi, 2007) as well as in political discourses over migration,[1] not to mention the dehumanizing conditions in which refugees travel to escape from their countries of origin (Crawley et al., 2016: 43).

Researching the conditions of migration journeys, several scholars have reported a high level of exposure to death and violence, due on the one hand to 'natural obstacles such as seas, deserts or mountain ranges' (Collyer, 2010: 277) and on the other hand to the intervention of traffickers and smugglers (Collyer, 2010; Crawley et al., 2016; Gerard and Pickering, 2013; Turner, 2015). Violence is also met at the hands of employees in detention camps at the borders of Europe or of local-government authorities, with evidence referring in particular to Libya and Turkey (Amnesty International 2017; Crawley et al., 2016; Vaughan-Williams, 2015). Embedded in this violence is a dehumanizing approach that links migrants to animals; Nick Vaughan-Williams's metaphorical reading of the zoo of Tripoli, which in the wake of the Libyan Revolution of 2011 was turned into a detention camp, is a case in point: 'the Tripoli zoo-turned-processing centre is symptomatic of a more pervasive and yet under-examined feature of detention in the field of European border security as experienced by some "irregular" migrants: their animalisation in spaces of dehumanisation' (Vaughan-Williams, 2015: 4). It is often migrants themselves who, in the discussion of their journeys, employ animalizing tropes to highlight the inhuman treatment to which they have been subjected – not only outside of Europe but even in detention camps within European borders, as the 2015 Women for Refugee Women's 'I am Human' report shows (see also Crawley et al., 2016: 43; Khosravi, 2007: 324; Saunders et al., 2016: 35; Vaughan-Williams, 2015).

The connection between borders and violence thus exists both at the metaphorical and the literal level, and this violence has a deep impact on the health and well-being of refugees and asylum seekers for it affects their bodies, their minds and their ability to integrate in the country of settlement.

## Forced displacement and mental health

Considering the traumas that, as previously mentioned, refugees have suffered and/or witnessed, both before being able to flee their countries and during their migration journeys, it is perhaps not surprising that research conducted in the field of displacement and mental health shows that 'asylum seekers and displaced persons worldwide report high rates of pre-migration trauma' (Robjant et al., 2009: 275; see also Silove et al., 1997) and that they display high levels of post-traumatic stress disorder (PTSD), depression and anxiety (Alpak et al., 2015; Katona, 2016; Robjant et al., 2009; Schubert and Punamäki, 2011 – also see Krause and Sharples, and Seguin, in this volume). Research shows that refugees and displaced people are more likely than the general populace to experience a range of mental-health problems, such as major depression and PTSD, even two decades after resettlement (Fazel et al., 2005; Hassan et al., 2016; Marshall et al., 2005). They are also at greater risk of non-affective psychosis (for example, delusional disorder and loss of touch with reality) than other migrants (Hollander et al., 2016). These problems are thought to arise from the trauma associated with exposure to violence (Reed et al., 2012) and difficulties encountered in the migration journey (Collyer, 2010), as well as migration-related difficulties in their countries of asylum and of resettlement – such as difficulties with immigration, employment and income (Carswell *et al.*, 2011). Additionally, refugees and displaced people can be vulnerable to loneliness (Strijk *et al.*, 2011) and loss of identity through the process of acculturation (Colic-Peisker and Walker, 2003; Liebkind, 1996; Phillimore, 2011).

It is important also to note that a considerable number of asylum seekers worldwide (an estimated 20 per cent in 2011) have been victims of torture – a practice that, Carla Schubert and Raija-Leena Punamäki argue, aims at 'deliberately breaking down their personal integrity' and thus heightening the probability of their developing mental-health problems (Schubert and Punamäki, 2011: 175). According to studies conducted in this field, asylum seekers and refugees also display higher rates of psychopathological disorders and they are at greater risk of developing schizophrenia and other non-affective psychoses compared with the non-asylum-seeking population (Katona, 2016; Hollander *et al.*, 2016; Porter and Haslam, 2005).

In addition to pre-migration trauma, asylum seekers and refugees are also exposed to post-migration living difficulties, including socio-economic disadvantage, work difficulties, experience of detention and the situation of uncertainty related to the asylum-application process, which enhance their vulnerability to non-affective psychoses (Alpak *et al.*, 2015: 45; Aragona *et al.*, 2012: 4; Katona and Howard, 2017: 1; Robjant *et al.*, 2009: 276). Indeed, if, as several studies suggest (Allen and Allen, 2016; Fisher, 2012; Griffin, 2010; Marmot *et al.*, 2010; Paul and Moser, 2009), there exists a strong link between social and economic conditions – including income, employability and housing – and health, then asylum seekers and refugees are at considerable risk of developing mental and physical health issues. Refugees' vulnerability to non-affective psychosis is also heightened by racism and hostility, which in turn generate social and emotional isolation (Katona, 2016: 1). As refugees and asylum seekers find themselves isolated from a society that maintains their status as outsiders, they often lack the social networks that could provide support (Allen and Allen, 2016: 31) – hence, the feelings of loneliness that, as reported by a study conducted by the charity The Forum in 2014, are perceived as the major challenge for displaced people living in the UK (Christodoulou, 2014).

## Well-being, creative practices and displacement

In order to understand the link between creative practices, health and well-being, it is useful to focus first on the notion of well-being – a term used extensively, if often in a self-evident manner. A useful definition is offered by the New Economic Foundation (NEF), which defines well-being as 'the dynamic process that gives people a sense of how their lives are going through the interaction between their circumstances, activities and psychological resources or "mental capital"' (NEF, 2008: 3). According to the NEF, there are different components to well-being, including 'personal wellbeing (emotional wellbeing, satisfying life, vitality, resilience, self-esteem and positive functioning) and social wellbeing, including supporting relationships and trust and belonging' (NEF, 2009: n.p.). Well-being is also associated with health; the World Health Organization (WHO) defines health as 'a state of complete physical, mental and social wellbeing and not merely the absence of disease or infirmity' (WHO, 1946: 2). Well-being thus cannot simply be defined either as a matter of happiness or as a lack of illness or disease. As emphasized by Erica Ander *et al.*, 'well-being is associated with a sense of resilience and flourishing, rather than just surviving' (Ander *et al.*, 2011: 243), a point that is crucial to bear in mind when thinking of the well-being of refugees and asylum seekers.

A growing body of research offers evidence of the beneficial effects of arts and creative activities – including dancing, singing, theatre, museum and heritage activities – on health and well-being (APPPGAHW, 2017; Bygren *et al.*, 2009; Camic and Chatterjee, 2013; Chatterjee and Noble, 2013; Clift *et al.*, 2010; Clift and Camic, 2016; Cuypers *et al.*, 2012; Konlaan *et al.*, 2000; Staricoff *et al.*, 2001; Staricoff, 2004, 2006). Studies conducted in the field of museums and health, for example, suggest that 'museum and art gallery encounters can help with a range of health issues, enhance wellbeing, and build social capital and resilience' (Chatterjee, 2016: 286; see also Ander *et al.*, 2013). For instance, Koenraad Cuypers *et al.* (2012) conducted a large population study in Norway involving over 50,000 adult participants in order to assess the role of cultural activities on perceptions of health, anxiety, depression and satisfaction with life. Results showed that participation in both receptive and creative cultural activities was significantly associated with good health, good satisfaction with life, and low anxiety and depression – even when the data was adjusted for confounding or associated factors (such as employment status).

Another example of the benefits of participating in creative practices is offered by Betsan Corkhill and colleagues' study on the effects of knitting on people with depression and sufferers of post-traumatic stress disorder (PTSD): according to their findings, the repetitive movements made by knitters seem to induce a state of meditation and relaxation that can help people manage 'pain spasm, panic and anxiety' (Corkhill *et al.*,

2014: 40). The researchers add, 'automatic movements may also facilitate access to the subconscious and could aid treatments such as cognitive behavioural therapy' (Corkhill *et al.*, 2014: 41). Moreover, even 'symptoms of post-traumatic stress disorder (PTSD) can subside significantly with knitting, even several years after the original trauma' (ibid.). The possibility of choosing whether to knit in groups or not – and, in the former case, to be able to choose whether to join a conversation or to knit in silence – or to make or not make eye contact, together with the fact of being in charge of the rhythm of knitting strengthen the perception of being in control, which adds to the benefits of knitting (ibid.: 40–3).

Given these premises, it is plausible to hypothesize that arts and creative activities can successfully alleviate some of the harmful effects of both pre-migration trauma and post-migration living difficulties. The social dimension of engagement in creative activities can be especially helpful in addressing the question of post-migration difficulties related to racism and hostility, social and emotional isolation and work difficulties. Indeed, this is a hypothesis also advanced by the European Commission, which in a 2005 report argued that engaging in creative activities could reduce poverty and social isolation. The report also highlighted the fact that having access to cultural activities is especially difficult for refugees (Community Action Programme on Social Exclusion, 2005: 3). Several initiatives in Europe seek to address the question of integrating refugees (and migrants more generally) through the arts: recently published research commissioned by the European Union (EU) maps 96 cultural initiatives across the EU that target refugees and migrants with the purpose of easing their integration within the countries of settlement (McGregor and Ragab, 2016: 11). In the UK, a 2008 report commissioned by Arts Council England, the Baring Foundation and the Paul Hamlyn Foundation identified nearly 200 organizations engaged with arts and refugees (Kidd *et al.*, 2008: 5). While stressing the important role that arts can play in integrating refugees and migrants in their societies of settlement, the EU study also maintains that 'artistic expression can be an important tool in therapeutic settings since it promotes self-esteem, facilitates the expression of emotions as well as the processing of traumatic experiences' (McGregor and Ragab, 2016: 8).

Previous research highlights the important role that engagement in cultural activities can play in the integration of refugees and immigrants, and how being involved in cultural activities is a way in which to challenge social exclusion, promote social cohesion and tackle discrimination and the negative representation of refugees and asylum seekers in the dominant discourse – including in the media and policy (Kidd *et al.*, 2008). Notwithstanding these findings, and even if there is general agreement over the beneficial effects of cultural and creative activities on the lives of refugees, previous studies agree that their impact on health and well-being has yet to be evaluated in a systematic way (Kidd *et al.*, 2008: 53; McGregor and Ragab, 2016: 6). Laura Smith *et al.* (2011) also highlight the research gap, noting that there are relatively few studies that have explicitly explored the impact of cultural participation and arts activities on the health and well-being of displaced people. A few studies have been conducted in the field – for example, N. Sunderland *et al.*'s (2015) research on the impact of participatory music on the health and well-being of refugees in Australia – but this is still an emergent field of study. Smith *et al.* (2011) detail three case studies of the impact of arts engagement involving displaced and marginalized people: theatre performances with Sudanese refugees living in Syracuse, New York; Cuban exiles producing art in Miami; and flamenco music with Gitanos, or Roma, in southern Spain. The study reveals that artistic activities help individuals to restore their identity and a sense of community, and to build solidarity. The authors argue that the arts provide 'alternative spaces for the contemplation of the complexities of adaptation', which help communities to navigate the challenges of dislocation, marginalization and integration (Smith *et al.*, 2011: 196), and go on to suggest that the expressive and non-violent outputs of cultural participation demonstrate that the arts and culture should be integrated into all levels of policy pertaining to immigration, conflict resolution and diplomacy.

## Assessing the impact of creative practices on the well-being of refugees and asylum seekers

Assessing the impact of cultural and creative activities on the well-being of refugees and asylum seekers presents challenges – as is the case with assessing the efficacy of any non-clinical intervention in the health arena. The field of arts and health has a vast evidence base, but this evidence has often been limited to evaluation studies that have not been subjected to peer review or small-scale qualitative studies with small sample sizes and no control groups; this has limited its acceptance across mainstream health and social care. In order to address this challenge, UCL and the University of Petra (Jordan) have adopted an interdisciplinary approach to analyse the impact of cultural activities carried out at the Helen Bamber Foundation in London and at the Talbiyeh refugee camp in Jordan, which – drawing on the social sciences, psychology, critical heritage and the health sciences – combines qualitative and quantitative methods.

The collaboration between UCL and the University of Petra was established in order to address the research gap in relation to the impact and efficacy of creative and cultural programming for recently and longer-term displaced people. Funded through the UK's Global Challenges Research Fund (Ref: ES/P003818/1), the work employed a participatory-action research approach. Described 'as a way of opening up space for dialogue and conversation about states of affairs in our worlds' (Kemmis *et al.*, 2014: 28), this method encourages engaged participation in the activities under study and is ideally suited to help break down potential cultural, disciplinary, professional, language or socio-economic barriers among audiences (Chevalier and Buckles, 2013: 9–33; Pope and Mays, 2006: 1–11). Participants are thus treated as co-researchers and co-producers with a view to reducing inequalities, building connections and creating a shared learning experience. Findings from this research are presented in two case studies.

## Helen Bamber Foundation, London: Case study 1

The Helen Bamber Foundation, London provides expert care and support for refugees and asylum seekers who are survivors of torture and/or other forms of extreme human cruelty such as human trafficking. Established in 2005, the foundation has pioneered a model of integrated care that addresses the complex needs and vulnerabilities of survivors. This includes an individually tailored programme of specialist psychological care and physical rehabilitation activities alongside an advisory GP clinic, expert medico-legal documentation, safeguarding, welfare and housing support, and a creative-arts programme. Launched in 2007, the programme offers survivors access to 10 free artistic and skills-development groups within comfortable and safe surroundings at the foundation. Group activities available at the Helen Bamber Foundation include knitting, music, arts and crafts, photography and film-making. Groups are delivered by 25 dedicated, professional volunteers and attended by 100 survivors of torture, human trafficking and other forms of extreme human cruelty from over 30 countries. These groups offer vital opportunities for survivors to explore their independence, reconnect with their pre-trauma identity, and learn new and expand existing skills in order to improve their future employment prospects. Crucially, they also offer the opportunity to socialize and develop supportive peer relationships (also see We Are Movers, this volume).

In pilot research with the Helen Bamber Foundation, the participatory-action research approach was developed with clients, staff and volunteers, who were recruited as co-researchers to help design the research protocol and inform the data-collection approach through a series of informal focus groups. During pilot research, co-researchers were consulted on the wording of draft research questions for use in formal one-to-one interviews and to gather more informal feedback on the best ways in which to demonstrate the impact of creative and cultural activities on psychosocial health and mental well-being. The rationale was to develop the research paradigm through collaboration and reflection; this process of collective inquiry allows ideas and answers to research questions to evolve over time, providing more nuanced and insightful outcomes. The approach also affords an opportunity to compare and contrast the experiences of refugees and asylum seekers from the Helen Bamber Foundation and Talbiyeh refugee camp.

## Co-researching forced displacement and the creative arts

Co-researcher workshops allowed for the emergence of a few key thematic clusters, which were subsequently explored in more detail during the interview phase. Clients, volunteers and members of staff articulated their reflections on the impact of creative activities guided by three topics (skills, social engagement and personal emotions); from this, a number of themes emerged regarding the value of engaging in creative-arts activities (see also Figure 22.1):

- Learning or improving practical skills
- Acquiring technical, language, social and life skills
- Developing new, balanced, social relationships based on respect and mutual recognition
- Having opportunities to meet people, forge friendships, counter loneliness and develop a sense of belonging in a 'safe space'
- Valuing peer-learning and mutual support
- Developing improved mood and self-confidence
- Experiencing freedom of expression and the possibility to develop new identities other than being viewed as refugees or asylum seekers.

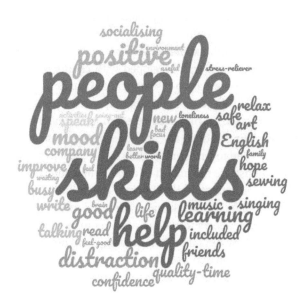

**Figure 22.1**　Emergent themes regarding the value of engaging in creative-arts activities from the Helen Bamber Foundation, London. © Helen Chatterjee *et al.*

Emergent themes were then explored in greater detail during the interview stage. One element that emerged strongly in the interviews conducted with clients is that these groups offer the opportunity to do something useful and productive rather than staying at home and waiting for the government to grant them leave to remain in the UK. All of these clients asserted that attending these groups allows them to have a routine – a 'luxury', one client observed – while learning new (or improving old) skills, and commented on the benefits of such a combination on their mental-health condition. 'Having something to do' and 'something to look forward to' were two recurrent expressions that came up during interviews, usually followed by a strong emphasis on the utility of the skills learnt. As one client remarked:

> There are a lot of skills that you learn and that, you know, you'll keep, that will stay with you for a lifetime … For instance if I go for a job somewhere, where you have to write what skills you have, so I could include all of this. I mean I don't have a certificate or, like, proper qualifications, but I've learned all those skills so I feel like,

it is, in a way, impressive? Because you feel like, you know, rather than just waiting and not doing anything, you have been learning.

This perspective was shared by another client, who commented:

> I've learnt new skills … and you can never waste your time learning new skills. New skills always help you in your life, always. So everything I've learnt will help me. You think like 'film club, learning how to edit, etc.' People pay people on YouTube to edit their films, and I'm, like, I could just do my own, if I wanted to have a YouTube channel I can do my own.

Apart from learning different skills, clients also commented on the impact of attending groups on their mental-health condition. One explained how, by attending creative groups, 'you don't feel like a useless person' and how creative activities help participants to experience:

> A sense of achievement: like every time I come to these classes I make something, I take something home with me, I learn something from my teachers, from other friends, and then I get this … like I have to do more, or, I have to improve myself, that kind of a feeling. So, these classes, I think, are very important: instead of sitting at home, you come here, you feel better.

Another client drew an explicit connection between creative activities and mental health:

> If you are not doing anything with your time, then it's not good for you, you know; depression sets in, anxiety sets in … you become paranoid about everything, you know, but going to an activity helps you release those hormones that bring happiness to you – when you are actually doing something that you are enjoying.

The opportunity to meet people and create friendships emerged as another theme. A client explained how attending the singing group, for example, helped her to learn how to connect with people:

> I didn't know how to communicate … so because of this singing, I know how to communicate now, I know how to sing and I know how to play with people … I [didn't] play with people before, I [didn't] talk to people before, but through this singing I know how

to communicate with people, I know how to sing, I know how to play with people. Now I know how to draw people to myself. Before when I came, because of all [the] things that [were] going on in my life I don't talk to people, I don't go near people. But because of these groups now, when everybody comes together, they would just live together, eat together, then just stay together. So I love it, I love it, being together with people. True, before, when I came to this country I don't move, I don't go near people ... I [didn't] have [a] friend, I [didn't] have anybody in the country, but through this music group now I met many friends.

When asked how she feels when she attends arts activities, one client said, 'I feel so happy and I feel loved, because we are like sisters and brothers ... to see people: you are not alone, you have other people and your situation is not for you only, also others are experiencing such [a] situation'. More generally, it seemed that through arts-activities groups clients were able to create a community characterized by solidarity. The awareness of experiencing similar situations made clients feel free to share their own experiences with one another – but they also felt free not to do so, if they did not feel like opening up:

> There is a sense of community: you know you go there, you know there are people like you in the same situation, you're not going to be judged, so it's that sense of community: we know what's going on, we don't have to talk about it ... But with that opportunity of people meeting up in the groups where there is a therapeutic activity going on, again it's a distraction from immigration and we know we are all going through it, but we don't have to talk about it. There are other things going on in life, and we talked about, for example in the art group, the works we produced and what we could do, what we could achieve and get inspired by each other's work. And learning new things like polishing our existing skills, it's just amazing.

This reflection highlights the importance of expressing emotions through art creation:

> It is more of expressing, more of letting go, it's like getting a spirit out of you, and you don't necessarily have to tell someone 'I've done this because of that and that, and this', you know. Because sometimes you just don't find the voice to talk about it and, I, as a person am really shy and, you know, I feel easily embarrassed, you know ... So ... that's why I'm into arts – yes, I'm doing arts really.

In addition to the opportunity to express themselves without having to articulate their feelings, clients also seemed to agree on the fact that these groups had helped them to 'grow emotionally' and gain 'confidence'.

Building on findings from the above case study, we adopted the same participatory-action framework to explore experiences of residents from Talbiyeh refugee camp in order to assess the psychosocial impact of creative and arts activities.

## Talbiyeh refugee camp, Jordan: Case study 2

Talbiyeh refugee camp in Jordan is one of 13 emergency camps (10 of which are under the mandate of the UN Relief and Works Agency, UNRWA)[2] established to house Palestinian refugees in the aftermath of the 1948 and 1967 Arab–Israeli wars. Jordan houses the largest number of Palestine refugees in the Middle East:[3] the current number of refugees from Palestine in Jordan (more than two million) comprises approximately 20 per cent of the country's current population.[4] Talbiyeh was established in 1968 as an emergency camp, and offers refuge to around 5,000 Palestinian refugees and displaced people, mostly coming from Beer Sheba, Hebron, Jericho, Ramallah and Gaza, in addition to other Palestinian towns. The camp is set up on an area of about 130,000 square metres, 35 kilometres south of the capital, Amman. The official camp boundaries currently include 805 shelters offering refuge to 823 families; however, the camp and its surrounding spillover include 7,262 individuals according to the 2007 estimates of the Jordan Department of Statistics. By 2008, the unemployment rate was approximately 15 per cent and 10 per cent of the shelters housed two to four families, bearing in mind that the average family size is 5.6 and the average shelter size is 71.33 square metres. Furthermore, 12 per cent of families live in abject poverty and 32 per cent are in relative poverty. As is the case in urban Palestinian camps across Jordan, the urban context is severely disadvantaged as there is limited open space, no recreational areas and limited vehicular access to many camp areas (UNRWA 2008 – also see Maqusi, this volume).

Palestinian refugee camps were created in the course of two waves of human displacement. The first wave came in the aftermath of the violent conflict and displacements of 1948 synonymous with the creation of the Israeli state. This event is referred to by Palestinians as *Al-Nakba* ('the Catastrophe') and is a traumatic episode that has had little international recognition and no resolution (Butler and Al-Nammari, 2016).

As a consequence of the displacement of Palestinians into Jordan, the Hussein, Amman New (Wihdat), Irbid and Zarqa camps were created. The second wave of displacement, in 1967, resulted in the creation of Baqa'a, Husn (Azmi al-Mufti), Talbiyeh (Zyzia), Marka, Souf and Jerash camps. Three additional camps are acknowledged by the Department of Palestinian Affairs, but not by UNRWA: Madaba, Prince Hassan and Sukhneh. These camps grew into settlements without any urban planning, resulting in what are effectively temporary cities characterized by low-quality construction and layers of socio-economic issues mixed with high levels of social solidarity (Al-Nammari, 2013, 2014). UNRWA serves the camps by providing basic education, health and relief, and the Jordanian Government offers supportive services in development and infrastructure in addition to camp governance and control, which is carried out in close coordination with UNRWA (Al-Nammari, 2015; see Maqusi, this volume).

Violence in Talbiyeh camp has been identified as a key issue by local camp communities; although not large in scale, issues of vandalism, youth assault, verbal abuse, domestic violence and school delinquency have been cited as significant by local organizations and locals (Al-Nammari, 2013, 2015). During the current research project, participants confirmed that such issues persist, in addition to what they perceived as a spread of drug abuse among the unemployed youth. Reasons, or sources, of violence suggest that the community understands the problem to be rooted in the following issues:

1) Environmental pressures: the cramped conditions and lack of space in the camp creates tensions and puts the inhabitants under great stress. This is compounded by the poor quality of shelters, as the zinc roofing makes the rooms very hot in the summer and very cold in the winter, in addition to leaks and inability to control noise. This is further accentuated by having an average of five to six individuals living in a space of 70 square metres.

2) Economic pressures, including: a lack of job opportunities, limited income for those who do work, a heavy dependency ratio, an inability to meet daily life needs and scarce resources. Studies have shown that youths have a feeling of 'complete despair' as they feel that they have no possibility of a better quality of life as long as they remain in the camp and, furthermore, that some feel that the only solution is to emigrate due to discrimination against Palestinians in Jordan (Al-Nammari, 2015).

3) Social issues, including: pressures of being away from family, low expectations, feelings of insecurity due to the political situation, anxiety, pressure from family or relatives, pressure from the community.
4) Political issues: there is currently no solution on the horizon, creating a lasting 'temporary state' (Al-Nammari, 2015) in which refugees live in a state of 'permanent impermanence' (Butler and Al-Nammari, 2016).

In the light of the above, and in an attempt to offer psychosocial support, the Women's Programme Centre (WPC) in Talbiyeh started the Heritage Project in 2008. The WPC is a local organization functioning via local volunteers and a locally elected leadership; it offers varied training programmes for income generation and support for women's empowerment, but also targets youths and adolescents. The Heritage Project uses video and oral interviews undertaken by youths with the elders on their memories of Palestine, the 1948 and 1967 wars, life prior to the wars, early camp life and memories of the homeland in general. The programme received funding in 2010 and again in 2013 from the German International Development Fund (GIZ), and has successfully developed the heritage initiative including:

1) an objects-based heritage programme, developing themes for exhibits and collections including embroidery and fabrics, domestic and agricultural tools, and old photographs
2) art and photography, which are both used as tools for developing film-making skills through workshops
3) a performing-arts programme including traditional *dabkeh* dancing and a related spin-off in the form of a Palestinian rap group, which is run in collaboration with the Talbiyeh Youth Club
4) a memory project, documenting the memory of elders in the camp, which emerged as a key objective that culminated in the production of short 5–10 minute films
5) a film school developed by young people from the camp to capture, record and investigate their identities as refugees, women, men, camp residents and Palestinian-Jordanians.

Other local organizations also offer sewing, embroidery and macramé classes, but such classes are only offered to women. Males, on the other hand, have limited art exposure and their youth institutions focus mainly on sports (UNRWA 2009); thus, the WPC heritage project has received

**Figure 22.2**  Emergent themes regarding the value of engaging in creative-arts activities from Talbiyeh refugee camp, Jordan.

© Helen Chatterjee *et al.*

significant credit for successfully creating a space that offers diverse arts and culture activities for both genders.

Our work in Palestinian refugee camps in Jordan employed 'heritage ethnographies' in order to address the dynamic and creative relationships between heritage, well-being and place making; the authors argue that these manifest as potent popular and efficacious heritage rites that comprise crucial resources underpinning Palestinian residents' experiences of camp life. Moreover, this study highlights the way in which such heritage rites enable refugees to define themselves beyond 'bare life' and to make moral/ethical claims to well-being in terms of diverse articulations of the 'good life' (Butler and Al-Nammari, 2016).[5,6]

Adopting the participatory-action research approach that was developed with the Helen Bamber Foundation, and building on the above, we worked with residents from Talbiyeh camp and colleagues from the WPC to explore themes of creativity and arts activities through a series of art making, embroidery and film-making workshops. The following themes emerged from these workshops:

- Perseverance and life skills
- Identity and self-exploration
- Joy, combating distress
- Social networks, high moral and peer support
- Self-esteem and pride in achievement
- Economic potential.

A number of themes emerging from research in Talbiyeh overlap with those discovered in London at the Helen Bamber Foundation regarding the value of creative-arts activities. These include the importance of acquiring life skills (which could also be classed as transferable skills), the role of arts activities as a conduit for self-exploration and addressing issues of identity, improving self-confidence and self-esteem, and the value of social networks and peer support.

## Conclusion

If we consider well-being as 'the dynamic process that gives people a sense of how their lives are going through the interaction between their circumstances, activities and psychological resources or "mental capital"' (NEF, 2008: 3), then it appears that creative activities have a positive impact on the well-being of refugees and asylum seekers, and that cultural creative activities can be employed to address pre-migration trauma (as in the case of Talbiyeh camp) and post-migration living difficulties (explored with the Helen Bamber Foundation). In particular, the evidence confirms Jessica Allen and Matilda Allen's suggestion that 'engagement in participative creative arts activities in communities can help to build social capital, address loneliness and social isolation, and build personal confidence and a sense of empowerment' (Allen and Allen, 2016: 32). In addition, our research in the UK and Jordan demonstrates that creative activities afford an opportunity to develop new, and to enhance existing, skills, including those that are transferable and have economic potential. Furthermore, the social and collaborative nature of creative activities provides avenues for individuals to explore personal and psychological challenges, such as anxiety and depression, using non-verbal creative means – and this approach to dealing with psychological trauma may be preferred to standard psychological therapies (including drug and talking therapies) or, indeed, used to augment such approaches.

In a similar vein, studies that pursue co-researched mixed methodologies can make an important contribution by investigating and highlighting novel aspects of the lived realities faced by refugees and asylum seekers while also identifying new creative resources for supporting well-being in its wider sense. As the synergies highlighted by researching across two refugee settings have demonstrated, whether you are an individual who is a second- or third-generation long-term refugee, such as residents from Talbiyeh, or a first-generation 'new' refugee, as with the Helen Bamber Foundation clients, the value of creative-arts activities to improve psychosocial well-being, provide a sense of belonging, develop skills and make meaning of your life is potentially profound.[7]

## Notes

1.  One of the most notable examples of this discursive strategy was offered by the former British prime minister, David Cameron, in the summer of 2015, when he warned of a 'swarm of people' crossing the Mediterranean Sea. https://www.theguardian.com/uk-news/2015/jul/30/david-cameron-migrant-swarm-language-condemned.
2.  Palestine refugees are catered for via UNRWA exclusively, while Syrian and Iraqi refugees (and any other nationality) are addressed by UNHCR – see Fiddian-Qasmiyeh in this volume for a discussion of the implications of this bifurcated system in a camp inhabited by Palestinian in addition to Syrian, Iraqi and other refugees.
3.  Jordan is the country that hosts the largest number of Palestinian refugees (2,175,491 refugees), and, as a result of the arrival of refugees fleeing the Syrian conflict since 2011, in 2016 it was the world's top refugee-hosting country: that year, there were more than 2.7 million refugees in Jordan, compared with 2.5 million refugees in Turkey. By 2017, as the number of Syrian refugees decreased, Jordan became the country hosting the second-largest number of refugees in the world, with 89 refugees per 1,000 inhabitants (Malkawi, 2017; UNHCR, 2017; UNRWA, 2016).
4.  These figures – provided by UNRWA and the Jordan Department of Statistics – do not include displaced persons, as UNRWA does not acknowledge their refugee status.
5.  Beverley Butler and Fatima Al-Nammari (2016) critically explore Giorgio Agamben's concept of 'bare life' (1998), and both his (1995) and Arendt's (1994 [1943]) 'We refugees' theses.
6.  For a discussion of conceptual and ethical relationships between heritage and well-being, see Butler (2012); on the crucial role of Palestinian cultural heritage in contexts of extremis, see Butler (2009, 2009b); and on the efficacies of heritage, see Butler (2016).
7.  Results and creative outputs from this study are available via the project website: https://culturehealthresearch.wordpress.com/forced-displacement-and-cultural-interventions.

## References

Agamben, Giorgio. 1995. 'We Refugees', translated by Michael Rocke, *Symposium: A Quarterly Journal in Modern Literatures* 49 (2): 114–19.
Agamben, Giorgio. 1998. *Homo Sacer: Sovereign Power and Bare Life*, translated by Daniel Heller-Roazen. Stanford: Stanford University Press.
Allen, Jessica and Matilda Allen. 2016. 'The Social Determinants of Health, Empowerment, and Participation'. In *Oxford Textbook of Creative Arts, Health, and Wellbeing: International Perspectives on Practice, Policy, and Research*, edited by Stephen Clift and Paul M. Camic, 27–34. Oxford: Oxford University Press.
Al-Nammari, Fatima. 2013. 'Participatory Urban Upgrading and Power: Lessons Learnt from a Pilot Project in Jordan', *Habitat International* 39: 224–31.

Al-Nammari, Fatima. 2014. 'When the Global Impacts the Local: Revisiting Talbiyeh Camp Improvement Project', *Habitat International* 44: 158–67.

Al-Nammari, Fatima M. 2015. 'Targeting Adolescence Vandalism in a Refugee Camp in Jordan'. In *Community-Based Urban Violence Prevention: Innovative Approaches in Africa, Latin America, Asia and the Arab Region*, edited by Kosta Mathéy and Silvia Matuk, 234–66. Bielefeld: Transcript Verlag.

Alpak, Gokay, Ahmet Unal, Feridun Bulbul, Eser Sagaltici, Yasin Bez, Abdurrahman Altindag, Alican Dalkilic and Haluk A. Savas. 2015. 'Post-Traumatic Stress Disorder among Syrian Refugees in Turkey: A Cross-Sectional Study', *International Journal of Psychiatry in Clinical Practice* 19 (1): 45–50.

Amnesty International. 2017. 'EU: Human rights cost of refugee deal with Turkey too high to be replicated elsewhere'. Accessed 22 February 2020. https://www.amnesty.org/en/latest/news/2017/02/eu-human-rights-cost-of-refugee-deal-with-turkey-too-high-to-be-replicated-elsewhere.

Ander, Erica, Linda Thomson, Guy Noble, Anne Lanceley, Usha Menon and Helen Chatterjee. 2011. 'Generic Well-Being Outcomes: Towards a Conceptual Framework for Well-Being Outcomes in Museums', *Museum Management and Curatorship* 26 (3): 237–59.

Ander, Erica, Linda Thomson, Guy Noble, Anne Lanceley, Usha Menon and Helen Chatterjee. 2013. 'Heritage, Health and Wellbeing: Assessing the Impact of a Heritage Focused Intervention on Health and Wellbeing', *International Journal of Heritage Studies* 19 (3): 229–42.APPGAHW (All-Party Parliamentary Group on Arts, Health and Wellbeing). 2017. 'Creative Health: The Arts for Health and Wellbeing'. Accessed 8 August 2017. www.artshealthandwellbeing.org.uk/appg-inquiry/.Aragona, Massimiliano, Daniela Pucci, Marco Mazzetti and Salvatore Geraci. 2012. 'Post-Migration Living Difficulties as a Significant Risk Factor for PTSD in Immigrants: A Primary Care Study', *Italian Journal of Public Health* 9 (3), Article e7525: 1–8. Accessed 2 February 2020. https://doi.org/10.2427/7525.

Arendt, Hannah. 1994. 'We Refugees'. In *Altogether Elsewhere: Writers on Exile*, edited by Marc Robinson, 110–19. Boston: Faber and Faber.

Bauman, Zygmunt. 2005. 'Who is Seeking Asylum – and from What?', *Mediactive* 4: 90–106.

Ben Jelloun, Tahar. 1976. *La réclusion solitaire*. Paris: Denoël.

Ben Jelloun, Tahar. 1988. *Solitaire*, translated by Gareth Stanton and Nick Hindley. London: Quartet.

Brah, Avtar. 1996. *Cartographies of Diaspora: Contesting Identities*. London: Routledge.

Butler, Beverley. 2009a. '"Othering" the Archive – from Exile to Inclusion and Heritage Dignity: The Case of Palestinian Archival Memory', *Archival Science* 9 (1/2): 57–69.

Butler, Beverley. 2009b. 'Palestinian Heritage "to the Moment": Archival Memory and the Representation of Heritage in Conflict', *Conservation and Management of Archaeological Sites* 11 (3/4): 236–61.

Butler, Beverley. 2012. 'Heritage as Pharmakon and the Muses as Deconstruction: Problematising Curative Museologies and Heritage Healing'. In *The Thing about Museums: Objects and Experience, Representation and Contestation*, edited by Sandra Dudley, Amy Jane Barnes, Jennifer Binnie, Julia Petrov and Jennifer Walklate, 354–71. London: Routledge. Online (2011). https://www.tandfonline.com/doi/abs/10.1080/10632921.2011.598418 (accessed 25 March 2020).

Butler, Beverley. 2016. 'The Efficacies of Heritage: Syndromes, Magics, and Possessional Acts', *Public Archaeology* 15 (2/3): 113–35.

Butler, Beverley and Fatima Al-Nammari. 2016. '"We Palestinian Refugees" – Heritage Rites and/ as the Clothing of Bare Life: Reconfiguring Paradox, Obligation, and Imperative in Palestinian Refugee Camps in Jordan', *Journal of Contemporary Archaeology* 3 (2): 147–59.

Bygren, Lars Olov, Sven-Erik Johansson, Benson Boinkum Konlaan, Andrej M. Grjibovski, Anna V. Wilkinson and Michael Sjöström. 2009. 'Attending Cultural Events and Cancer Mortality: A Swedish Cohort Study', *Arts and Health* 1 (1): 64–73.

Camic, Paul M. and Helen J. Chatterjee. 2013. 'Museums and Art Galleries as Partners for Public Health Interventions', *Perspectives in Public Health* 133 (1): 66–71.

Carswell, Kenneth, Pennie Blackburn and Chris Barker. 2011. 'The Relationship between Trauma, Post-Migration Problems and the Psychological Well-Being of Refugees and Asylum Seekers', *International Journal of Social Psychiatry* 57 (2): 107–19.

Casas-Cortes, Maribel, Sebastian Cobarrubias, Nicholas De Genova, Glenda Garelli, Giorgio Grappi, Charles Heller, Sabine Hess, Bernd Kasparek, Sandro Mezzadra, Brett Neilson, Irene Peano,

Lorenzo Pezzani, John Pickles, Federico Rahola, Lisa Riedner, Stephan Scheel and Martina Tazzioli. 2015. 'New Keywords: Migration and Borders', *Cultural Studies* 29 (1): 55–87.

Chatterjee, Helen J. 2016. 'Museums and Art Galleries as Settings for Public Health Interventions'. In *Oxford Textbook of Creative Arts, Health, and Wellbeing: International Perspectives on Practice, Policy, and Research*, edited by Stephen Clift and Paul M. Camic, 281–9. Oxford: Oxford University Press.

Chatterjee, Helen and Guy Noble. 2013. *Museums, Health and Well-Being*. Farnham: Ashgate.

Chevalier, Jacques M. and Daniel J. Buckles. 2013. *Participatory Action Research: Theory and Methods for Engaged Inquiry*. London: Routledge.

Christodoulou, Panos. 2014. *This is How It Feels to Be Lonely: A Report on Migrants and Refugees' Experiences with Loneliness in London*. London: The Forum. Accessed 24 February 2017. http://migrantsorganise.org/wp-content/uploads/2014/09/Loneliness-report_The-Forum_UP-DATED.pdf.

Clift, Stephen and Paul M. Camic, eds. 2016. *Oxford Textbook of Creative Arts, Health, and Wellbeing: International Perspectives on Practice, Policy, and Research*. Oxford: Oxford University Press.

Clift, S., G. Hancox, I. Morrison, B. Hess, G. Kreutz and D. Stewart. 2010. 'Choral singing and psychological wellbeing: Quantitative and qualitative findings from English choirs in a cross-national survey', *Journal of Applied Arts and Health*, 1 (1): 19–34.

Colic-Peisker, V. and I. Walker. 2003. 'Human capital, acculturation and social identity: Bosnian refugees in Australia', *Journal of Community and Applied Social Psychology* 13 (5): 337–60.

Collyer, Michael. 2010. 'Stranded Migrants and the Fragmented Journey', *Journal of Refugee Studies* 23 (3): 273–93.

Community Action Programme on Social Exclusion. 2005. *The Role of Culture in Preventing and Reducing Poverty and Social Exclusion* (Policy Studies Findings 2). Brussels: European Commission.

Corkhill, Betsan, Jessica Hemmings, Angela Maddock and Jill Riley. 2014. 'Knitting and Well-Being', *Textile* 12 (1): 34–57.

Crawley, H., K. Jones, S. McMahon, F. Duvell and N. Sigona. 2016. *Unpacking a rapidly changing scenario: Migration flows, routes and trajectories across the Mediterranean*. Coventry: Centre for Trust, Peace and Social Relations, Coventry University.

Cuypers, Koenraad, Steinar Krokstad, Turid Lingaas Holmen, Margunn Skjei Knudtsen, Lars Olov Bygren and Jostein Holmen. 2012. 'Patterns of Receptive and Creative Cultural Activities and Their Association with Perceived Health, Anxiety, Depression and Satisfaction with Life among Adults: The HUNT Study, Norway', *Journal of Epidemiology and Community Health* 66 (8): 698–703.

Edwards, Adrian. 2016. 'UNHCR Viewpoint: "Refugee" or "Migrant" – Which is Right?', *UNHCR News*, 11 July. Accessed 10 February 2017. www.unhcr.org/uk/news/latest/2016/7/55df0e556/unhcr-viewpoint-refugee-migrant-right.html.

Fanon, Frantz. 2004. *The Wretched of the Earth*, translated by Richard Philcox. New York: Grove Press.

Fassin, Didier. 2011. 'Policing Borders, Producing Boundaries: The Governmentality of Immigration in Dark Times', *Annual Review of Anthropology* 40: 213–26.

Fazel, M., J. Wheeler and J. Danesh. 2005. 'Prevalence of serious mental disorder in 7000 refugees resettled in western countries: A systematic review', *Lancet* 365 (9467): 1309–14.

Fisher, Mark. 2012. 'Why Mental Health is a Political Issue', *The Guardian*, 16 July. Accessed 24 February 2017. www.theguardian.com/commentisfree/2012/jul/16/mental-health-political-issue.

Fotopoulos, Stergios and Margarita Kaimaklioti. 2016. 'Media Discourse on the Refugee Crisis: On What Have the Greek, German and British Press Focused?', *European View* 15 (2): 265–79.

Gerard, Alison and Sharon Pickering. 2014. 'Gender, Securitization and Transit: Refugee Women and the Journey to the EU', *Journal of Refugee Studies* 27 (3): 338–59.

Girma, Marchu, Isabelle Kershaw, Gemma Lousley, Sophie Radice and Natasha Walter. 2015. *I Am Human: Refugee Women's Experiences of Detention in the UK*. London: Women for Refugee Women. Accessed 10 March 2017. www.thebromleytrust.org.uk/files/wrw_iamhuman.pdf.

Griffin, Jo. 2010. *The Lonely Society?* London: Mental Health Foundation. Accessed 7 March 2017. www.mentalhealth.org.uk/sites/default/files/the_lonely_society_report.pdf.

Hassan, G., P. Ventevogel, H. Jefee-Bahloul, A. Barkil-Oteo and L. Kirmayer. 2016. 'Mental health and psychosocial wellbeing of Syrians affected by armed conflict', *Epidemiology and Psychiatric Sciences* 25 (2): 129–41. Accessed 25 March 2020. 10.1017/S2045796016000044.

Hollander, Anna-Clara, Henrik Dal, Glyn Lewis, Cecilia Magnusson, James B. Kirkbride and Christina Dalman. 2016. 'Refugee Migration and Risk of Schizophrenia and Other Non-Affective Psychoses: Cohort Study of 1.3 Million People in Sweden', *British Medical Journal* 352, Article i1030: 1–8. Accessed 2 February 2020. https://doi.org/10.1136/bmj.i1030.

Katona, Cornelius. 2016. 'Non-Affective Psychosis in Refugees', *British Medical Journal* 352, Article i1279: 1–2. Accessed 2 February 2020. https://doi.org/10.1136/bmj.i1279.

Katona, Cornelius and Louise Howard. *The Mental Health Difficulties Experienced by Victims of Human Trafficking (Modern Slavery) and the Impact This Has on Their Ability to Provide Testimony* (Briefing Paper). London: Helen Bamber Foundation. Accessed 15 February 2017. www.helenbamber.org/wp-content/uploads/2017/02/Briefing-Paper-Difficulties-in-providing-testimony-victims-of-modern-slavery.pdf.

Kemmis, Stephen, Robin McTaggart and Rhonda Nixon. 2014. The *Action Research Planner: Doing Critical Participatory Action Research*. Singapore: Springer.

Khiabany, Gholam. 2016. 'Refugee Crisis, Imperialism and Pitiless Wars on the Poor', *Media, Culture and Society* 38 (5): 755–62.

Khosravi, Shahram. 2007. 'The "Illegal" Traveller: An Auto-Ethnography of Borders', *Social Anthropology* 15 (3): 321–34.

Kidd, Belinda, Samina Zahir and Sabra Khan. 2008. *Arts and Refugees: History, Impact and the Future*. London: Baring Foundation. Accessed 5 February 2017. http://baringfoundation.org.uk/wp-content/uploads/2014/10/ArtsandRefugees.pdf.

Konlaan, B.B., N. Björby, L.O. Bygren, G. Weissglas, L.G. Karlsson and M. Widmark. 2000. 'Attendance at Cultural Events and Physical Exercise and Health: A Randomized Controlled Study', *Public Health* 114 (5): 316–19.

Konlaan, Boinkum B., Lars O. Bygren and Sven-Erik Johansson. 2000. 'Visiting the Cinema, Concerts, Museums or Art Exhibitions as Determinant of Survival: A Swedish Fourteen-Year Cohort Follow-Up', *Scandinavian Journal of Public Health* 28 (3): 174–78.

Leudar, Ivan, Jacqueline Hayes, Jiří Nekvapil and Johanna Turner Baker. 2008. 'Hostility Themes in Media, Community and Refugee Narratives', *Discourse and Society* 19 (2): 187–221.

Liebkind, K. 1996. 'Acculturation and stress: Vietnamese refugees in Finland', *Journal of Cross Cultural Psychology*. 27 (2): 161–80.

Lloyd, Moya. 2015. 'The Ethics and Politics of Vulnerable Bodies'. In *Butler and Ethics*, edited by Moya Lloyd, 167–92. Edinburgh: Edinburgh University Press.

Malkawi, Khetam. 2017. 'Jordan Tops List of Refugee-Host Countries – Amnesty', *Jordan Times*, 8 March. Accessed 20 January 2018. http://jordantimes.com/news/local/jordan-tops-list-refugee-host-countries-%E2%80%94-amnesty.

Marmot, Michael, Jessica Allen, Peter Goldblatt, Tammy Boyce, Di McNeish, Mike Grady and Ilaria Geddes. 2010. *Fair Society, Healthy Lives: The Marmot Review*. London: Marmot Review. Accessed 2 February 2020. www.instituteofhealthequity.org/resources-reports/fair-society-healthy-lives-the-marmot-review/fair-society-healthy-lives-full-report-pdf.pdf.

Marshall, Grant N., Terry L. Schell, Marc N. Elliott, S. Megan Berthold, and Chi-Ah Chun. 2005. 'Mental health of Cambodian refugees 2 decades after resettlement in the United States', *Journal of the American Medical Association* 294 (5): 571–9.

McGregor, Elaine and Nora Ragab. 2016. *The Role of Culture and the Arts in the Integration of Refugees and Migrants*. European Expert Network on Culture and Audiovisual. Accessed 15 February 2016. https://migration.unu.edu/publications/reports/the-role-of-culture-and-the-arts-in-the-integration-of-refugees-and-migrants.html.

Michaelson, Juliet, Saamah Abdallah, Nicola Steuer, Sam Thompson and Nic Marks. 2009. *National Accounts of Well-Being: Bringing Real Wealth onto the Balance Sheet*. London: New Economics Foundation. Accessed 2 February 2020. https://neweconomics.org/uploads/files/2027fb-05fed1554aea_uim6vd4c5.pdf.

Mitchell, Harry. 2017. *The Distinction between Asylum Seekers and Refugees*. London: Migration Watch UK. Accessed 7 August 2017. www.migrationwatchuk.org/pdfs/MW70-the-distinction-between-asylum-seekers-and-refugees.pdf.

Moore, Kerry. 2013. '"Asylum Shopping" in the Neoliberal Social Imaginary', *Media, Culture and Society* 35 (3): 348–65.

NAWB (National Accounts of Well-Being). n.d. 'What is Well-Being?'. Accessed 20 March 2017. www.nationalaccountsofwellbeing.org/learn/what-is-well-being.html.

NEF (New Economic Foundation) 2008. 'Five Ways to Wellbeing: A report presented to the Foresight Project on communicating the evidence base for improving people's well-being', New Economic Foundation, London. Accessed 25 March 2020. https://neweconomics.org/2008/10/five-ways-to-wellbeing.

NEF (New Economic Foundation). 2009. 'National Accounts of Well-being: bringing real wealth onto the balance sheet,' New Economic Foundation, London. Accessed 25 March 2020. https://neweconomics.org/2009/01/national-accounts-wellbeing.

Pace, Paola and Kristi Severance. 2016. 'Migration Terminology Matters', *Forced Migration Review* 51: 69–70.

Paul, Karsten I. and Klaus Moser. 2009. 'Unemployment Impairs Mental Health: Meta-Analyses', *Journal of Vocational Behavior* 74 (3): 264–82.

Phillimore, J. 2011. 'Refugees, acculturation strategies, stress and integration', *Journal of Social Policy* 40 (3): 575–93.

Philo, Greg and Liza Beattie. 1999. 'Race, Migration and Media'. In *Message Received: Glasgow Media Group Research, 1993–1998*, edited by Greg Philo, 171–96. Harlow: Longman.

Pope, Catherine and Nicholas Mays, eds. 2006. *Qualitative Research in Health Care*. 3rd ed. Oxford: Blackwell.

Porter, Matthew and Nick Haslam. 2005. 'Predisplacement and Postdisplacement Factors Associated with Mental Health of Refugees and Internally Displaced Persons: A Meta-Analysis', *JAMA: The Journal of the American Medical Association* 294 (5): 602–12.

Prior, Ross W. 2010. 'Editorial', *Journal of Applied Arts and Health* 1 (1): 3–6.

Reed, R.V., M. Fazel, L. Jones, C. Panter-Brick and A. Stein. 2012. 'Mental health of displaced and refugee children resettled in low-income and middle-income countries: risk and protective factors', *Lancet* 379 (9812): 250–65.

Robjant, Katy, Rita Hassan and Cornelius Katona. 2009. 'Mental Health Implications of Detaining Asylum Seekers: Systematic Review', *British Journal of Psychiatry* 194 (4): 306–12.

Robjant, Katy, Ian Robbins and Victoria Senior. 2009. 'Psychological Distress amongst Immigration Detainees: A Cross-Sectional Questionnaire Study', *British Journal of Clinical Psychology* 48 (3): 275–86.

Sassen, Saskia. 2006. 'Migration Policy: From Control to Governance', *OpenDemocracy*, 12 July. Accessed 2 February 2020. www.opendemocracy.net/en/militarising_borders_3735jsp/.

Saunders, Jennifer B., Susanna Snyder and Elena Fiddian-Qasmiyeh. 2016. 'Introduction: Articulating Intersections at the Global Crossroads of Religion and Migration'. In *Intersections of Religion and Migration: Issues at the Global Crossroads*, edited by Jennifer B. Saunders, Elena Fiddian-Qasmiyeh and Susanna Snyder, 1–46. New York: Palgrave Macmillan.

Schubert, Carla C. and Raija-Leena Punamäki. 2011. 'Mental health among torture survivors: cultural background, refugee status and gender', *Nordic Journal of Psychiatry*, 65 (3), 175–82. Accessed 10 March 2020, https://doi.org/10.3109/08039488.2010.514943.

Silove, Derrick, Ingrid Sinnerbrink, Annette Field, Vijaya Manicavasagar and Zachary Steel. 1997. 'Anxiety, Depression and PTSD in Asylum-Seekers: Associations with Pre-Migration Trauma and Post-Migration Stressors', *British Journal of Psychiatry* 170 (4): 351–7.

Skingley, Ann, Stephen M. Clift, Simon P. Coulton and John Rodriguez. 2011. 'The Effectiveness and Cost-Effectiveness of a Participative Community Singing Programme as a Health Promotion Initiative for Older People: Protocol for a Randomised Controlled Trial', *BMC Public Health* 11, Article 142: 1–6. Accessed 2 February 2020. https://doi.org/10.1186/1471-2458-11-142.

Smith, L., B. DeMeo and S. Widmann. 2011. 'Identity, Migration, and the Arts: Three Case Studies of Translocal Communities', *Journal of Arts Management, Law, and Society* 41 (3): 186–97.

Staricoff, Rosalia Lelchuk. 2004. *Arts in Health: A Review of the Medical Literature* (Research Report 36). London: Arts Council England.

Staricoff, Rosalia Lelchuk. 2006. 'Arts in Health: The Value of Evaluation', *Journal of the Royal Society for the Promotion of Health* 126 (3): 116–20.

Staricoff, Rosalia L., Jane P. Duncan and Melissa Wright. 2001. 'A Study of the Effects of Visual and Performing Arts in Healthcare', *Hospital Development* 32: 25–8.

Strijk, P.M., B. van Meijel and C.J. Gamel. 2011. "Health and Social Needs of Traumatized Refugees and Asylum Seekers: An Exploratory Study', *Perspectives in Psychiatric Care*, 47 (1): 48–55.

Sunderland, N., L. Istvandity, A. Lakhani, C. Lenette, B. Procopis and P. Caballero. 2015. 'They [Do More Than] Interrupt Us from Sadness: Exploring the Impact of Participatory Music Making on Social Determinants of Health and Wellbeing for Refugees in Australia', *Health, Culture and Society* 8 (1): 1–19. Accessed 2 February 2020. https://doi.org/10.5195/hcs.2015.195.

Thomas, Dominic. 2014. 'Fortress Europe: Identity, Race and Surveillance', *International Journal of Francophone Studies* 17 (3/4): 445–68.

Turner, Stuart. 2015. 'Refugee Blues: A UK and European Perspective', *European Journal of Psychotraumatology* 6 (1), Article 29328: 1–9. Accessed 2 February 2020. https://doi.org/10.3402/ejpt.v6.29328.

UNHCR (United Nations High Commissioner for Refugees). 'Protocol relating to the Status of Refugees' [1967 Protocol]. Accessed 27 March 2020. https://www.ohchr.org/EN/ProfessionalInterest/Pages/ProtocolStatusOfRefugees.aspx.

UNHCR (United Nations High Commissioner for Refugees). 'Cartagena declaration on refugees' [1984]. Accessed 27 March 2020. https://www.unhcr.org/uk/about-us/background/45dc19084/.

UNHCR (United Nations High Commissioner for Refugees). 2005. *Refugee Status Determination – Identifying Who is a Refugee: Self-Study Module 2*. Geneva: United Nations High Commissioner for Refugees. Accessed 10 February 2017. www.unhcr.org/uk/publications/legal/43144dc52/self-study-module-2-refugee-status-determination-identifying-refugee.html.

UNHCR (United Nations High Commissioner for Refugees). 2016. *Global Trends: Forced Displacement in 2015*. Geneva: United Nations High Commissioner for Refugees. Accessed 17 February 2017. www.unhcr.org/576408cd7.pdf.

UNHCR (United Nations High Commissioner for Refugees). 2017. *Jordan Factsheet*. Geneva: United Nations High Commissioner for Refugees. Accessed 20 January 2018. https://reliefweb.int/sites/reliefweb.int/files/resources/Jordan%20Fact%20Sheet%20June%202017-%20FINAL.pdf.

UNRWA. 2008. In F. Al-Nammari, ed., Draft Results of the Socio Economic Survey in Talbiyeh Camp. Amman: UNRWA Camp Improvement and BMZ.

UNRWA. 2009. 'Assessment of Assets, Needs, and Constraints by the Community of Talbiyeh: Sustainable Development Guidelines'. In Fatima Al-Nammari, ed., Report on the interviews and focus groups conducted between July 2008 to June 2009.

UNRWA. 2011. *UNRWA Statistics – 2010: Selected Indicators*. Amman: UNRWA. Accessed 15 August 2017. www.unrwa.org/userfiles/2011120434013.pdf.

UNRWA. 2016. 'Where We Work: Jordan'. Accessed 20 January 2018. www.unrwa.org/where-we-work/jordan.

Vaughan-Williams, Nick. 2015. '"We Are Not Animals!": Humanitarian Border Security and zoopolitical spaces in EUrope'. *Political Geography* 45: 1–10. Accessed 12 June 2020. https://doi.org/10.1016/j.polgeo.2014.09.009.

WHO (World Health Organization). 1946. Constitution of the World Health Organization. Accessed 25 March 2020. https://www.who.int/about/who-we-are/constitution.

Part IV

# Spaces of Encounter and Refuge: Cities and Camps in a Moving World

# 23
# Black Markets: Opaque sites of refuge in Cape Town

Huda Tayob

## Introduction

*Imagining the City*, a 2007 anthology of oral histories about Cape Town, begins with a description of this South African metropolis as both the 'Gateway to Africa' and a xenophobic city. This is expanded to explain that while Cape Town is marketed to 'First World' tourists as the welcoming 'Mother City', for many African migrants, immigrants, refugees and asylum seekers, the city is a space of immense hostility and uncertainty (Field *et al.*, 2007: 3). This is a result of the tenuous legal status of many, in addition to local xenophobic attitudes. This anthology was published in 2007. In May 2008, xenophobic violence in South Africa reached a crucial peak, with nationwide attacks that particularly targeted Black Africans from other parts of the continent. The violence began at the end of May in Johannesburg, and within two weeks had spread throughout the country. The resulting 62 deaths included 21 South Africans and left around 100,000 people displaced, many permanently. This has been noted as the worst violence the country has seen since the end of apartheid in 1994 (Steinberg, 2008; Steinberg 2015; also see Hoffman *et al.*, in this volume).

The dismantling of apartheid and the introduction of a non-racial democracy in the early 1990s led to an increasing number of immigrants, migrants, asylum seekers and refugees coming into South Africa from other African countries.[1] Yet, paradoxically, as Sally Peberdy (2001) and others argue, this has been contradicted by the simultaneous institutionalization of draconian immigration policies that particularly target Black African new entrants. On the ground, this has resulted in frequent police raids, in the course of which non-citizens are identified through racial profiling,[2] and often arrested; detained; and, at times, deported or 'repatriated' to their counties of origin. This has corresponded with growing xenophobia from the wider South African public, and has taken the form of physical attacks that target the informal small shops and businesses of Black Africans, many of whom are refugees and asylum seekers. For these populations, due to limited options in formal employment, informal trade is the only way to access a livelihood. The country-wide violence of May 2008 was arguably one of the most severe consequences of this growing sentiment (Peberdy, 2001; Reitzes, 2002). Despite this general condition, certain pockets of hospitality do exist within the city (Abdi, 2011; Abdi, 2015). These are largely centred on the markets and informal shopping arcades run by African arrivals to the city since the 1990s. Many of the new entrants who run these markets arrived in South Africa as asylum seekers, and their trading areas continue to act as spaces of support for new arrivals despite increasing and ongoing xenophobic violence.

**Figure 23.1**   Cartography of xenophobic violence in the Cape Peninsula, 2008–14. Drawing © Huda Tayob. Sources: Crush, 2014; Chimurenga, 2011; Somali, 2012.

## An emerging spatial typology

This chapter focuses on two particular buildings in Cape Town – namely, *Sekko's Place* in the historic city centre of Cape Town and *Som City* in the northern suburb of Bellville.[3] These buildings both form part of an emerging landscape of hospitality and support in the city. My research posits that they also form part of a wider series of markets that offer vital spaces of refuge for those fleeing violent conflicts and economic collapse across the continent, as well as for those who have been displaced by violence within South Africa's borders. As such, these markets could be understood as an emerging spatial typology of **Black Markets**, pointing to the complex nature of spaces of refuge within urban areas in South Africa.

Adrian Forty suggests that there are two common ways of identifying a typology within architecture – namely, by morphology and by function. For Forty, the debate around typology has largely been concerned with the relationship between these two (Forty, 2004). Drawing on his succinct analysis of the use of the term within architecture, I suggest that the markets described in this chapter are a form of an emerging yet contingent spatial typology, as they share a similar kind of morphology and function. The morphology is defined by the multiplicity of small spaces, while a key overarching function lies in the fact that these markets are spaces of refuge. This function of refuge is embedded within various other functions, and is the key characteristic that distinguishes these markets from regular informal markets. As a spatial typology, these markets are rendered invisible as they lie outside of the canon of architecture. These are not spaces designed by architects, but are rather 'everyday' architectures.[4]

A third consistent similarity across these markets is that they are racially Black spaces – referring both to the racialized landscape of post-apartheid Cape Town, and to the tenuous position of the spaces and their inhabitants in the city. This Blackness cuts across the ideas of function and morphology described above, as it locates the markets in the racial and socio-spatial field of post-apartheid Cape Town. The concept of Black Markets draws on AbdouMaliq Simone's reference to 'Black urbanism', along with bell hooks's suggestion that the margin is a site of radical potential (Simone, 2010a; hooks, 1990b). Following Simone, the use of the term Blackness not only refers to the racial characteristic of a space but is, more importantly, an analytical and conceptual tool to 'bring into consideration certain dimensions of urban life that are too often not given their due' (Simone, 2010b: 279). This chapter argues that these markets are part of a broader network of support and possibility as much as they are sites of displacement, noting the importance of recognizing these characteristics together.

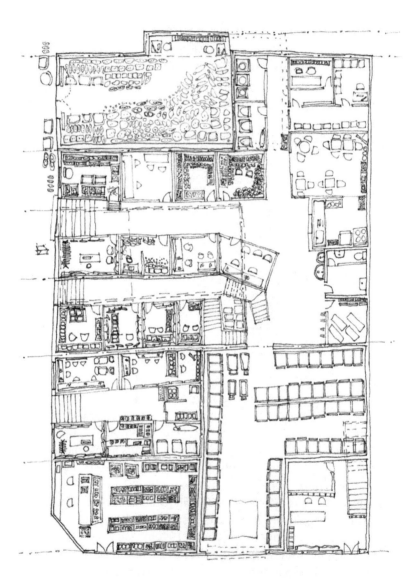

**Figure 23.2** Plan of Sekko's Place. Drawing © Huda Tayob, 2016.

## Sekko's Place

Sekko's Place, as it is called, is a market on the corner of Longmarket and Loop streets in the historic core of Cape Town (see Figure 23.2, opposite). It is housed in a three-storey building and is a labyrinthine space consisting of around 20 small trading rooms, subdivided rooms, wall surfaces and passageways – most of them for individual enterprises. This market also houses storage for nearby street traders, a restaurant and a residential lodge. Most of these spaces are between 2 and 4 square metres in size. This unassuming space is run by the Sekko brothers, along with a third partner. The elder brother, known as Sekko, is deeply rooted in many of the changes that have occurred in the city centre since the end of apartheid. He arrived in South Africa in 1995 as a refugee from Mali, and was initially a street hawker. In 1996, he rented a small space in the recently opened *Pan-African Market* on Long Street, and in 2000 started his own market space incrementally.

The Pan-African Market is a large tourist market, and the first of its kind in the city. It was started in 1996 and, like Sekko's Place, consists of multiple small stalls and shops. Every surface is appropriated, adapted and used. The trade in these markets is in a combination of African art and curios, along with various services. Yet the market is much more than a trading space. The current owner is Vuyo Koyana, and in our interview, when describing Cape Town in the late 1990s, she said:

> The street was lily-white, the city was lily-white. So this became a beacon of Blackness in the city. And this became a space where Black people could come and you know, no matter how big their dreams, could find a space here to make them come true. (Interview with Koyana, 2014)

In 2000, Sekko moved out of the Pan-African Market, and started his own place with his brother. He described the incremental process of acquiring space in the city by initially renting an open garage area, which they sublet to traders. Over the years, as space became available, they slowly managed to lease most of the building. He said of this process, 'we were getting the space from the owner – it was full of White people, and they move out, we came in, they move out, we came in' (interview with Sekko, 2015). Apart from the curios and African arts for sale, the market is host to weekly meetings for Malians in Cape Town every Saturday afternoon. In addition, various informal gatherings take place on the lower floors of this market space throughout the week. For instance, Fatima's restaurant was widely known throughout the Francophone African community in Cape Town (interview with Charles, 2015), and the small prayer room and ablutions area next to the restaurant provided a further important, sacred meeting space within this building.

Both Koyana and Sekko point to the hostile nature of post-apartheid Cape Town. Koyana described the Long Street market as a kind of home, and her own experience in the city as a 'kind of immigrant' from the Transkei (one of the former homelands of the apartheid state).[5] She explained:

> you know if I really think about it, for me personally, and for a lot of the traders in the space, our homes may have changed over the years, you know our actual residential homes. But this place hasn't changed, this has become a constant. So for me coming from the Transkei, and if you like that's also a foreign country, I came into this space as an immigrant as it were. I imagine that it's the same experience for a lot of the traders here, that you have this as a constant, and this, in a way, is your home. (Interview with Koyana, 2014)

Koyana pointed to the importance of the market as a space of Blackness and refuge, in what is often still described as a 'White city'.[6] She articulated the cultural and social importance of a place like the Pan-African Market in a city hostile not only because of more recent xenophobia but also due to a history of racial segregation. This was a view reiterated by various other traders in the market, who asserted the ongoing difficulty of acquiring space in the city as both Black people and non-citizens.[7]

Since 2000, several similar markets have been started in this part of the city – all following a similar trading and spatial typology. These markets are mostly run by African refugees, predominantly from West and southern Africa, and are largely host to small traders and entrepreneurs from these same regions. The main goods sold in these markets are curios and African arts; this aspect of the markets is the most visible. Yet to label these spaces as primarily for trade is a misnomer, as it renders invisible the important social, cultural and service role that these markets play for new entrants. Beyond providing vital access to space, they also host hairdressers, internet cafes, laundries, travel agents, storage spaces, restaurants, grocery stores selling 'African foods' and informal banking services. The status of the population in these markets ranges from those who are more established and have permanent residence permits to refugees, asylum seekers, undocumented migrants and others who are cross-border traders and itinerant. In numerous interviews, a consistent narrative emerged of the safety of this network in the city: safe from xenophobic violence and safe to earn a living (interview with Sekko, 2015). These markets form a network of spaces of 'self-reliance', negotiating hospitality and hostility on a daily basis (Fiddian-Qasmiyeh, 2019).

## Som City

Som City is a market in the northern suburb of Bellville. Bellville was classified as a White area in 1958, under the apartheid Group Areas Act. From the late 1950s, *Cape Argus* and *Cape Times* newspaper articles began to describe the area as the cultural heartland of White Afrikaans speakers in the region.[8] Since 2000, the central area of Bellville has seen a drastic change – this time becoming a hub for pan-African businesses and inhabitants, the majority of whom are Somali refugees. The area also hosts sizeable Ethiopian and Congolese populations. Specifically, it is the few city blocks between the Bellville train station and Voortrekker Road, a key urban artery, that have become the centre of this new pan-African space. The spatial form of these changes is largely visible through the growth of what are known in the area as **Somali Malls**. Som City is one of these markets.

In many ways, Som City is similar to Sekko's Place. As with the markets in the city centre, Som City is a multistorey building that consists of multiple small trading spaces. It contains similar services to Sekko's

**Figure 23.3**  Section drawing of Som City. Drawing © Huda Tayob, 2016.

Place, such as restaurants, internet cafés, laundries and trading stores. However, in the case of Som City, the market largely caters to the resident refugee population in Bellville, the majority of whom are Somali refugees. The markets are therefore more homogeneous than their city-centre counterparts and largely ethnically defined. Other Somali Malls in the area house numerous mosques, madrasas, refugee-run NGOs, an English-language school and nursery schools.

Ahmed, a Somali refugee, started Som City in 2005 with two friends. In an interview, he described passing through Eastleigh in Nairobi when travelling overland to South Africa from Somalia. He described staying in an informal shopping arcade in Eastleigh, a space where he found temporary lodgings and from where he was able to arrange the next phase of his journey. By noting this, Ahmed pointed to the existence of these lodges throughout East Africa.[9] He arrived in Cape Town in 2000, and initially worked as a street trader in various parts of the city. He described arriving in the city, only knowing the address of two friends who had travelled before him. These friends lent him 1,000 rand,[10] with which he bought socks and scarves and began selling these on the street at the taxi rank in Bellville. Three years later, in 2003, he joined three friends in an informal *spaza* shop[11] in a peripheral Cape Town area. In this period, he saved as much as possible – sleeping initially in shared rental accommodation, and later in the *spaza* shop itself. When 20 Kruskal Road in Bellville became available, together with two friends he decided to make an offer to rent the building to start a Somali Mall with a lodge. They converted the ground and first floor into trading spaces and service areas, and the upper two floors into a lodge – subdividing larger office spaces for more affordable rentals.

As with the markets in the city centre, the first floor of Som City is characterized by multiple small spaces, and the dense accumulation of goods. Yet here, the goods were described as 'Somali goods' and 'women's things', which varied from particular clothing items to cosmetics and general food products. The shops on this floor are all run by women, and are an important source of products for special occasions such as weddings and religious celebrations in addition to goods for daily life. The familiar foods and products enabled women to establish a sense of home in the city (Tayob, 2018). These small shops are also important social spaces for women, as a result of long hours spent in these stores and the gendered nature of the market space. The shops in the Somali Malls were open seven days a week, from at least nine in the morning until nine at night. During the course of fieldwork, I was told that these shops were the places where women visited each other to share news of daily life in the area; updates on marriages, births and deaths; or news on the violence surrounding Cape Town (interviews with Fatima, 2014 and Sara, 2015).

On the second and third floor of Som City was the lodge. Like the shops, the lodge consists of multiple small rooms, created from subdivided offices. Most rooms have between two and six beds, which are all rented out independently and cater mostly to Somali men. Some of the inhabitants stay in these lodges on a long-term basis, while many come into the area for one to three days a week. Ahmed himself lived in this lodge in a shared room for the first two years of running it, in Room 208. He repeated this several times during our interview: that he had lived in the space himself, in shared accommodation. Therefore, while the lodge is now a profitable business for him, it is also intimately linked to his own personal trajectory in the country – of arriving as a refugee with nothing. The current occupation of the lodge speaks of the business practices of migrants in Cape Town, high levels of urban violence and the regulations of being an asylum seeker or refugee in the city. Inhabitation patterns reflect days on which one can apply for papers or permits, or visit NGOs. The population of the lodge is thus largely in flux, yet simultaneously regular.

The number of lodges, and their popularity, has particularly expanded along with the increasing xenophobic violence. Demand reached a peak during May 2008, when, as mentioned, there were widespread xenophobic attacks particularly targeting African new entrants. Many from around the province, city and suburbs of Cape Town fled to Bellville. These lodges provided important sites of emergency housing and refuge. Som City, along with neighbouring lodges, opened its doors to those who had been left homeless as a result of the violence, at no cost. Ahmed said that most people stayed for two or three weeks, but many stayed up to four months as they had lost everything in the attacks (interview with Ahmed, 2015). Bellville was described as a 'safe haven' at this time (Nicholson, 2011). For several months, the area became a relief space centred on the Somali Malls, which provided food and accommodation to those in need. The Somali-owned businesses based in Bellville contributed with food in support. The area of Bellville as a whole, and the multiple small spaces within these markets in particular, became important sites of emergency housing and refuge during and after the attacks (interview with John, 2014).

## Conclusion

In conclusion, I want to return to the idea of these markets as an emerging spatial typology. I suggest that the African markets discussed above could be understood as a contingent typology, which I term Black Markets. Here, the key morphological and functional characteristics relate in the first case to the multiple small spaces found in all of these markets, and in the second to the spaces of refuge that the markets individually and collectively form. Both Sekko's Place and Som City are buildings that were initially created for alternative uses. This points to the lack of importance of the physical envelope. Yet in both cases, the adaptation of these generic buildings into multiple small spaces is essential to their transformation into a particular type of market that can support its new population. The small scale of the spaces makes them affordable, while the accumulation of these small spaces results in the creation of an alternative public and a space for inhabitants to 'speak in their own voice' (Fraser, 1990).

This second and related aspect revolves around the function of the markets. As described above, both Sekko's Place and Som City are spaces of trade. Yet equally important, and embedded within these markets, are relationships of care and refuge established by refugees themselves. Although this aspect is not typically designated as a programmatic function, the interviews and fieldwork discussed above reveal the importance of these markets to host and support new entrants, many of whom are refugees and asylum seekers. Under the broader umbrella of relationships of care are included emergency housing in times of need; alternative banking, transport and communication services; and space in which to meet socially.

Simone's concept of 'Black urbanism' is a useful framework within which to think about these spaces as Black Markets. For him, the framework is a way of recognizing the space of African entrepreneurs and migrants, which is often overlooked in urban research. Many of the spaces described by Simone share similar characteristics to the markets discussed above – as the spaces of displaced African populations and entrepreneurs, in which some activities are illicit and others not. Importantly, as with the Black Markets discussed above, these are, similarly, spaces for these marginal populations to 'imagine in' (Simone, 2010b: 263). As a conceptual device, understanding these distinct markets in different areas as a contingent spatial typology enables comparison of their socio-spatial occupation patterns despite the distinct populations that they house. It further enables a reading of these market spaces beyond their topographical understanding as sites of informal trade, and instead leads to an understanding of the spaces as part of a network of refuge and support in the city. It also points to the existence of similar markets elsewhere on the continent and beyond. Some of these sites are urban, such as Eastleigh, while others are refugee camps, such as Dadaab in Kenya (interview with Ifrax, 2015). As a whole, a spatial and typological understanding of these markets leads to a more complex understanding of spaces of refuge within urban areas, as spaces that may be embedded within various other functions, and a blurring of boundaries between private, public, market and spaces of refuge.

We are, however, reminded by bell hooks that Blackness does not inherently signify oppositionality or radicality (hooks 1990a). This is particularly salient to note when considering the gendered field of the market. As noted above, individual shops become key social spaces for women. This is in contrast to restaurants, coffee shops and mosques, which in turn are rendered as public and male spaces. These are all small and makeshift spaces within buildings, yet through spatial practices a normative, gendered understanding of space is reintroduced whereby individual shops run by women are domesticized. However, hooks points out that in certain circumstances the experience of being 'Black' does afford a privileged critical location. Elsewhere, hooks suggests that the margin is 'space of radical openness … a profound edge' (hooks, 1990b: 149). I argue that in the context of post-apartheid Cape Town, these markets are marginal spaces that act to disrupt entrenched apartheid racial divisions in space – and they therefore, I suggest, act as radical spaces.

Despite their tenuous position, both legally and physically, and their location within an often hostile city, these markets offer a safe space for new arrivals. They are small and limited spaces, sometimes profitable and at other times not. Yet while they appropriate existing buildings, they are not wholly disciplined by the state, the city or their architecture. These market spaces disrupt established fixed divisions of understanding the public, the private and the domestic in Cape Town, along with the racialized landscape of the post-apartheid xenophobic city. Yet, they remain isolated examples in the city and are largely contained within the envelopes of individual buildings. They are pockets of hospitality, which play a crucial role in negotiating marginality, Blackness and hostility in the city of Cape Town.

## Notes

1. Exact numbers of refugees and asylum seekers in South Africa are unknown. South African Police Force estimates from 1994 suggested that there were two million undocumented migrants, and in 1995 suggested eight million. Other estimates range between three and eight million non-citizens in the country. The Southern African Migration Programme suggests that these figures are inflated, and that the number of documented and undocumented migrants was closer to three million in 2008 (Segatti and Landau, 2011: 148).

2.   Immigrants are identified through superficial physical features such as having darker skin than Black South Africans, by vaccination marks, language skills and dress (Peberdy, 2001).
3.   The research was approved by the ethics committee of University College London (5505/001) and the data was collected in accordance with the 1998 UK Data Protection Act. All interviews were conducted by the author.
4.   This expanded understanding of architecture to include a recognition of 'everyday' spatial practices has notably been taken up within the field in *Architecture of the Everyday* (edited by Steven Harris and Deborah Berke, 1997) and *The Unknown City* (edited by Iain Borden, Joe Kerr, Alicia Pivaro and Jane Rendell 2000), among others.
5.   The region is currently the Eastern Cape Province.
6.   This view is frequently noted in both popular and academic media.
7.   During research, I was frequently told of the difficulty of acquiring a space to trade and earn a livelihood in the city. Charles, a trader in the Pan African Market, particularly drew my attention to this (interview with Charles, 2015).
8.   Newspaper articles of the time describe Bellville as a place where 'Great plans mature' (*Cape Argus*, 31 October 1957), claimed that 'It was in Bellville … that the Afrikaner had found his feet and become a co-builder of South Africa's future' (*Cape Argus*, 7 April 1982) and noted that it was from Bellville that the 'Afrikaner could play [a] decisive role' (*Cape Times*, 7 April 1982).
9.   In a study of Eastleigh in Nairobi, Neil Carrier and Emma Lochery describe the emergence of Garissa Lodge, the first multistorey shopping-and-residential arcade in Eastleigh. They note that the lodge is said to have started in an old two-storey courtyard building called Garissa Court, which was let cheaply to newly arriving refugees from Somalia. From the late 1980s, following an increasing number of refugees, these residential spaces began to be used for trade during the day and residential accommodation at night. In 1992, the building was converted into the Garissa Lodge Mall. See Carrier and Lochery, 2013; Campbell, 2006; Steinberg, 2015.
10.  Around US$70 in 2017.
11.  *Spaza* shops is the term used to describe informal grocery shops that are located in informal settlements or previously non-White areas throughout South Africa. These are areas that under apartheid were only residential, and in many cases continue to lack formal service provisions. These *spaza* shops are often the only places where residents can access food and groceries in these areas.
12.  All of the names are pseudonyms at the request of the interviewees, with the exception of those marked with *.

# References

Abdi, Cawo Mohamed. 2011. 'Moving beyond Xenophobia: Structural Violence, Conflict and Encounters with the "Other" Africans', *Development Southern Africa* 28 (5): 691–704.

Abdi, Cawo M. 2015. *Elusive Jannah: The Somali Diaspora and a Borderless Muslim Identity*. Minneapolis: University of Minnesota Press.

Borden, Iain, Joe Kerr, Jane Rendell and Alicia Pivaro, eds. 2000. *The Unknown City: Contesting Architecture and Social Space*. Cambridge, MA: MIT Press.

Campbell, Elizabeth H. 2006. 'Economic Globalization from Below: Transnational Refugee Trade Networks in Nairobi'. In *Cities in Contemporary Africa*, edited by Martin J. Murray and Garth A. Myers, 125–47. New York: Palgrave Macmillan.

Carrier, Neil and Emma Lochery. 2013. 'Missing States? Somali Trade Networks and the Eastleigh Transformation', *Journal of Eastern African Studies* 7 (2): 334–52.

Chimurenga. 2011. 'The Chimurenga Chronic, 18–24 May 2008', *Chimurenga* 16. On file with the author. Accessed 10 March 2020. See http://www.mahala.co.za/art/the-chimurenga-chronic.

Crush, Jonathan and Sujata Ramachandran. 2014. *Migrant Entrepreneurship, Collective Violence and Xenophobia in South Africa* (Migration Policy Series 67). Waterloo, ON: Southern African Migration Programme.

Fiddian-Qasmiyeh, Elena. 2019. 'From Roots to Rhizomes: Mapping Rhizomatic Strategies in the Sahrawi and Palestinian Refugee Situations'. In *Refugees' Roles in Resolving Displacement and*

*Building Peace: Beyond Beneficiaries*, edited by M. Bradley, J. Milner and B. Peruniak. Georgetown University Press, 247–66.

Field, Sean, Renate Meyer and Felicity Swanson, eds. 2007. *Imagining the City: Memories and Cultures in Cape Town*. Cape Town: HSRC Press.

Forty, Adrian. 2004. 'Type'. In *Words and Buildings: A Vocabulary of Modern Architecture*, by Adrian Forty, 304–11. London: Thames and Hudson.

Fraser, Nancy. 1990. 'Rethinking the Public Sphere: A Contribution to the Critique of Actually Existing Democracy', *Social Text* 25/26: 56–80.

Harris, Steven and Deborah Berke, eds. 1997. *Architecture of the Everyday*. New York: Princeton Architectural Press.

hooks, bell. 1990a. *Yearning: Race, Gender, and Cultural Politics*. Boston: South End Press.

hooks, bell. 1990b. 'Choosing the Margin as a Space of Radical Openness'. In *Yearning: Race, Gender, and Cultural Politics*, by bell hooks, 145–53. Boston: South End Press.

Nicholson, Zara. 2011. 'Somalis Find a Safe Haven in Bellville', *IOL*, 11 May. Accessed 11 January 2020. www.iol.co.za/news/somalis-find-a-safe-haven-in-bellville-1067228.

Peberdy, Sally. 2001. 'Imagining Immigration: Inclusive Identities and Exclusive Policies in Post-1994 South Africa', *Africa Today* 48 (3): 15–32.

Reitzes, Maxine. 2002. '"There's Space for Africa in the New South Africa (?)": African Migrants and Urban Governance in Johannesburg'. In *Under Siege: Four African Cities – Freetown, Johannesburg, Kinshasa, Lagos: Documenta11_Platform4*, edited by Okwui Enwezor, Carlos Basualdo, Ute Meta Bauer, Susanne Ghez, Sarat Maharaj, Mark Nash and Octavio Zaya, 215–38. Ostfildern-Ruit: Hatje Cantz.

Segatti, Aurelia and Loren B. Landau, eds. 2011. *Contemporary Migration to South Africa: A Regional Development Issue*. Washington, DC: World Bank.

Simone, AbdouMaliq. 2010a. 'Reclaiming Black Urbanism: Inventive Methods for Engaging Urban Fields from Dakar to Jakarta'. In *City Life from Jakarta to Dakar: Movement at the Crossroads*, by Simone AbdouMaliq, 263–333. New York: Routledge.

Simone, AbdouMaliq. 2010b. *City Life from Jakarta to Dakar: Movements at the Crossroads*. New York: Routledge.

Simone, AbdouMaliq. 2012. 'Reclaiming Black Urbanism: Inventive Methods for Engaging Urban Fields in Africa and Beyond'. In *African Perspectives – [South] Africa: City, Society, Space, Literature and Architecture*, edited by Gerhard Bruyns and Arie Graafland, 30–47. Rotterdam: 010 Publishers.

Save Somali Community. 2012. 'Lists of Somalis Killed in Cape Town in 2012'. On file with the author.

Staff Reporter. 1982a. 'PM: Afrikaner Has Decisive Role', *Cape Times*, 7 April.

Staff Reporter. 1982b. 'Bellville', *Cape Argus*, 7 April. On file with the author.

Steinberg, Jonny. 2008. *South Africa's Xenophobic Eruption* (ISS Paper 169). Tshwane: Institute for Security Studies.

Steinberg, Jonny. 2015. *A Man of Good Hope*. London: Jonathan Cape.

Tayob, Huda. 2018. 'Fatima's Shop: A Kind of Homeplace'. In *Architecture and Feminisms: Ecologies, Economies, Technologies*, edited by Hélène Frichot, Catharina Gabrielsson and Helen Runting, 265–9. London: Routledge.

Weiss, R. 1957. 'Great Plans Mature at Bellville', *Cape Argus*, 31 October.

# Interviews[12]

John (2014), 'Interview', August, Bellville.

Charles (2015), 'Interview', January, Cape Town.

Fatima (2014), 'Interview', September, Bellville.

Ahmed (2015), 'Interview', February, Bellville.

Ifrax (2014), 'Interview', November, Bellville.

*Koyana (2014), 'Interview', January, Cape Town.

Sekko (2015), 'Interview', February, Cape Town.

Sara (2015), 'Interview', February, Bellville.

## 24

# Learning in and through the long-term refugee camps in the East African Rift

Nerea Amorós Elorduy

## The long-term camps in the East African Rift

At the beginning of 2019, at least 66 refugee camps existed in eastern Africa that had been running for more than five years and that hosted over 5,000 inhabitants each. Their establishment dates range from three years to six decades (Crawford *et al.*, 2015: 9–10). I call these settlements long-term refugee camps. Some of them are sparsely populated like a rural community, while others are densely built up like a crowded urban area. Some are small like a village, while others occupy areas larger than a city such as Barcelona. Some long-term camps' spatial organizations are grid-like and planned, while others have grown organically over the years. Some grow rhizomatically, located on top of hills and along the valleys of hilly areas thickly covered by jungles and forests, while others grow like an oil stain in the middle of desert plains. Some camps host a few thousand refugees from one or two ethnicities, whereas others host hundreds of thousands of refugees from tens of different ethnicities and tribes, fleeing up to 12 different nation states. The inhabitants of these camps can be civilians, political exiles or even soldiers. In some cases, victims and the perpetrators of the crimes that they have fled live side by side.

Many of these camps fluctuate in population and area covered over the years, their boundaries and their spatial organizations are porous and extremely plastic – with homes, streets and paths continuously changing

**Figure 24.1**   Map with the location of various long-term refugee camps in East Africa. © Nerea Amorós Elorduy.

according to the refugees' needs, resources and wishes, and influenced by humanitarian funds, international visibility, proximity to a border and relationships with their direct local hosts.[1]

Humanitarian organizations perform well in solving well-defined problems through a linear chain of action. However, they sink when problems are complex, intertwined, evolve and cannot be solved through standardized solutions – as is the case of the long-term refugee camps. Hence, in an effort to define concrete problems to solve through standardized solutions, the underfunded humanitarian system – particularly underfunded in protracted situations and refugee education – generalizes geographically and culturally biased, and incomplete, information on refugee displacement and applies it worldwide. One of these solutions is the housing of refugees in isolated, planned camps; another is the provision of formal education.

Since the 1990s, the UNHCR-led humanitarian system and host-nation governments have largely approached refugee assistance through the planning, construction and maintenance of isolated 'camps' or 'settlements' to contain and assist refugees. These planned camps are more the result of geopolitics and transnational power dynamics than a straightforward or logical step after displacement.[2] They linger, becoming a decades-long non-solution for refugees and members of their host communities. This is especially the case as donors are increasingly reticent to fund responses to protracted crises and non-'life-saving' topics – such as the built environment and education (Anderson and Hodgkin, 2010: 3; Crawford et al., 2015: 34; Crisp, 2001, 2003; Nicolai and Hine, 2015; Slaughter and Crisp, 2009; Stoddard et al., 2007) – given the growing number of long-term camps worldwide (UNHCR, 2017) and the increasing number of 'new' humanitarian crises. In the light of this situation, since 2014 the humanitarian system has promoted a policy turn to devise *Alternatives to Camps* (UNHCR, 2014). This policy and other recent international instruments[3] have been devised to address the wishes, needs and rights of refugees who continuously choose to settle outside of these planned settlements,[4] and to gather the attention of the donor community, tapping into new funding sources – such as the private sector or promoting refugees' self-reliance[5] – in order to make humanitarian operations more effective, sustainable and economic.

However, many refugees in East Africa continue to be encamped,[6] receiving standardized assistance that usually disregards their needs and wishes and those of their local hosts. This misalignment between policies and reality is partly due to an extreme lack of information. Moreover, the situation of existing long-term camps will not change in the short or medium-term. In such a context, what can be learned from long-term refugee camps and their spaces in order to actually address the needs of refugees and their hosts? What would policies and interventions look like if long-term refugee camps were understood as what they are de facto: multifaceted human settlements where changes happen catalytically, layers of history overlap, power dynamics change, and relationships are multiple and variable (also see Qasmiyeh and Fiddian-Qasmiyeh, 2013; Fiddian-Qasmiyeh 2019)?

The aim of this chapter is threefold. First – in line with the works of anthropologist Liisa Malkki (1995b: 495–523; 2002), geographer Elena Fiddian-Qasmiyeh (2013: 875–95; 2019), sociologist Elizabeth Holzer (2015) and development expert Roger Zetter (1995) – I argue that detailed, specific information adds complexity and nuance to refugee-encampment studies, depicting a more realistic image of the varied situations of encamped refugees and underscoring the powerful agency of refugees and their direct local hosts. Second, I explain how the built environments of seven long-term refugee camps in eastern Africa that I studied between January 2015 and January 2018 – Nakivale (est. 1958), Kyangwali (est. 1964) and Kyaka II (est. 1983) in southwest Uganda; Kakuma (est. 1992) in northwest Kenya; and Kiziba (est. 1997),

Kigeme (est. 2005) and Mugombwa (est. 2013) in Rwanda – are affecting young children's learning. My analysis presents selected spaces in these seven case studies as learning resources, highlighting the fact that studying these camps' built environments through the lens of early-childhood development is a worthwhile task. Finally, I present these seven refugee camps, which were established between 1958 and 2013, as dynamic places, fully-grown and mature human settlements that many argue display city-like and urban traits.[7] Their spaces, in line with Henri Lefebvre's 'right to the city'(Lefebvre 1968, 1973), modify refugee lives and, in turn, refugees modify those spaces. Among other changes, refugees transform their homes, and create religious facilities and community schools. These changes become prevalent as long-term refugee camps become less visible and controlled, and their humanitarian resources dwindle.

## Studying the built environment and young encamped refugee children's learning

As an architect, my attention lies on the long-term camps' built environment, and its societal roles (Lefebvre, 1973: 73–7). I am especially interested in how the built environment affects young children born and raised in these camps.

For decades, the development–humanitarian divide considered education to be part of the development realm rather than the humanitarian one because it was not considered a 'life-saving' action. This meant that education was not initially incorporated into the humanitarian cluster[8] system (Anderson and Hodgkin, 2010: 1–7). Additionally, for years many host governments were weary of the permanence of refugees and saw the provision of formal education as a 'pull factor' (Dryden-Peterson, 2011: 67). However, with the acknowledgement of the protracted character of refugee crises by the mid-2000s (UNHCR, 2004), the development–humanitarian divide relaxed, allowing education to be recognized as a long-term investment for society, including refugees, and as necessary to achieve many of the other humanitarian actions such as child protection and health (Anderson and Hodgkin, 2010; Consultative Group on Early Childhood Care and Development and INEE, 2010; Newby, 2012). The education cluster was created in 2007 and Early Childhood Development (ECD) became part of it, and of humanitarian practice, in 2009 – and the first ECD programmes began to be implemented in the cases studied here in 2011. Hence, humanitarian-led ECD initiatives are still scarce and in the testing phase. This relative newness creates an opportunity to develop a thorough study of the current ECD situation, assessing and evaluating these initial efforts before ideas and policies are crystallized, scaled up and multiplied worldwide.

Since the early 1950s, it has been known that young children are susceptible to the effects of the sociocultural and the built environments, which are critical for lifelong learning and development at an early age. Specifically, in the early 1950s, Maria Montessori and the Reggio Emilia Approach raised the idea of the 'environment as an added educator' in the school setting (Edwards *et al.*, 1998; Montessori, 1984). Throughout the 1950s and up to the late 1990s, developmental psychologists such as Urie Bronfenbrenner, Lev Vygotsky, Jean Piaget and, later, Gary Evans looked at the effects of spaces outside of formal educational facilities on young children's brains and their socio-emotional development. These research- ers studied the effects of factors such as noise, temperature or crowding – especially in the home – on young children's learning (Bronfenbrenner, 1979; Evans, 1999; Ferguson *et al.*, 2013; Piaget, 1951; Vygotsky, 1978). Later on, built-environment specialists such as Colin Ward studied the streets as learning environments (Ward, 1978, 1986), and in the last decade geographers, urbanists and architects such as Colin McFarlane and Kim Dovey are using post-structural theories to break up the sca- lar understanding of space and conceiving the city as a learning setting (Dovey and Fisher, 2014; McFarlane, 2011). Unfortunately, the effects of the built environment on young children are largely understudied in long-term refugee camps, including in those located in eastern Africa, and therefore remain unknown.

## Research approach

Currently, refugee ECD policies and programmes focus almost solely on the programmatic matters of formal educational facilities.[9] They largely disregard the learning and development that happens outside of them, the role of the built environment and the knowledge of encamped pop- ulations. To investigate forms of learning that stem from the built envi- ronment and that happen outside formal schooling facilities, I involved architects, urban planners, encamped parents, caregivers, children and humanitarian-education experts in a collective effort to create new knowl- edge on the cases that I studied. In this chapter, I present the first compar- ative study related to the ways in which the built-environment elements of long-term refugee camps in Rwanda, southwest Uganda and north- west Kenya are linked to young children's learning and development; in so doing, I map the existing spatial elements that children, their caregivers and the camps' education managers perceive as being relevant for the direct and indirect learning of children aged from three to six.

My research methodologies were inspired by the work of architect Kevin Lynch to gather and map the perceptions of all the actors mentioned above (Lynch, 1960, 1977), architectural and speculative approaches to knowledge creation[10] and the concept of 'lifelong learning' (Coombs, 1989: 57–60; Coombs and Ahmed, 1974). During the research process, I first mapped and analysed the refugee camps' spatial characteristics – observing and sketching the existing spaces as well as collecting, producing and analysing satellite imagery and maps of the camps. Second, I collected and analysed residents' perceptions of these spaces through semi-structured face-to-face interviews, randomized-sample questionnaires at the household level, focus-group discussions with key groups and stakeholders, and transect walks with young children.[11] I contrasted the findings from those methods with existing literature and data sets. I classified the spaces that affect young children's learning into formal schooling settings, non-formal community-organized groups and informal learning settings such as homes and streets. Finally, I collected and tested the residents' design proposals on how to improve the camps' spaces for the betterment of young children's learning. I did so through a combination of action research, design propositions and community workshops.[12]

Due to the lack of data available, budget and time, I focused only on three- to six-year-olds rather than developing a more in-depth research through the lens of age, and I was unable to include water, sanitation and hygiene (WASH) facilities even though they are key for young children's development. Moreover, while I support the critiques of the concept of a 'universal child' (Pence, 2011; Pence and Hix-Small, 2007), in this chapter I use the overarching four pillars of 'children's development' as established by UNESCO since they have guided, and will continue to guide, refugee educational programmes and policies in long-term refugee camps worldwide for at least the next ten years (Global Education Cluster, 2015).

## Formal, non-formal and informal learning settings

### Formal learning settings

In the last decade, international tools devised to guide refugee education have grown in number.[13] A key tool produced in 2011 was the UN's *Education Strategy 2012–2016*, which emphasized the 'integration of refugee learners within national systems' (UNHCR, 2012) and aimed at providing 'more specific country-level education strategies and programmes' (Dryden-Peterson, 2016; UNHCR, 2004, 2008). This alignment with host countries' programmes coincided with the inclusion of ECD in the Education Cluster activities. It also coincided with the development of host countries' own ECD national standards and policies,[14] guided by international institutions, their tools, and conceptions of childhood (Pence, 2011; Pence and Hix-Small, 2007). As a consequence, the NGO-managed formal ECD centres in the camps under study are usually based on host countries' national standards, yet they obviate indigenous understandings of the child and camp inhabitants' child-rearing practices.

One of the main characteristics of the built environment of these formal ECD centres, is the general lack of involvement by designers and planners, by refugee parents, caregivers and children themselves. NGOs and UN agencies lead the design and construction of these formal ECD centres. Off-site predefined designs are the norm, usually developed by foreign consultants or local contractors with little to no involvement by learning-environment-design experts. The location of these centres is usually chosen by camp managers based on numerical data – which is often outdated and partial, as managers lack detailed and up-to-date maps of the camps and do not consult refugee inhabitants about their knowledge of the camp. Only in rare cases are refugees employed in basic construction jobs, and their involvement in these centres is relegated mainly to the eventual organization of PTAs; in some cases, they are employed as teachers or head teachers.

As a consequence of this top-down approach, and due to the prioritization of speed of construction, elements that both the literature and the refugee children and their support networks identify as key for children's attendance and stimulation are overlooked or contemplated as secondary. Little consideration is given to distances and pathways of access, the aesthetics and the materiality of the building, the safeness and security of the compound, access to drinking water, child-friendly toilets or the provision of nutritious food and play materials.

For example, in Kiziba refugee camp in Rwanda, four-year-olds have to walk more than one kilometre with a 300-metre change in altitude to reach their nearest formal ECD centre. Once there, the facility has no play equipment or toilets, and 100 children are educated in a 36-square-metre room with only one caregiver. The situation is even worse in larger camps such as Nakivale in Uganda and Kakuma in Keyna, where, in addition to long distances, young children face speeding vehicles, drunken adults and uneven terrain on their journey to the ECD centre. These centres

**Figure 24.2**  Photograph of the formal ECD centre in Kiziba in Rwanda (September 2015). © Nerea Amorós Elorduy.

might house up to 200 children in a 48-square-metre room with only one caregiver, two at best. They lack proper toilets, furniture and didactic materials, and some of the supposedly semi-permanent structures are crumbling only a few years after their construction.

Additionally, most formal ECD centres are run by international NGOs, with two negative effects: they tend to change every few years, and they provide a 'universal child' approach to education.

On the one hand, the NGOs' strategies and their modus operandi vary – affecting ECD programmes and their consistency, preventing straightforward monitoring and evaluation, and hampering institutional memory and the improvement of programmes over time. For example, in Kyangwali (Uganda) two NGOs are in charge of ECD – Action Africa Help International (AAH) and Save the Children. They use different strategies, and compete for funds and lines of action. In 2010, Save the Children built 10 Child-Friendly Spaces (CFSs)[15] detached from primary schools, and later on added WASH facilities and ECD structures. In contrast, AAH works mostly in primary schools and gives support to already-existing community-organized centres. In 2013, AAH took over the management of five of Save the Children's built CFSs. During my visit in September 2016, the CFSs coordinated by Save the Children were in a perfect state and widely used, whereas those under AAH coordination were crumbling and dangerous as they did not fall under AAH's priorities and lines of action.

On the other hand, the NGOs' top-down, universal and standardized means of education clash with the varied child-rearing practices, languages and needs of the pupils attending the formal ECD centres and their families. This clash is demonstrated, for example, in the general assumption by many NGO members that parents' 'mind-sets' are the reason behind low attendance at formal ECD centres. In several interviews, NGO members related low attendance with parents' laziness, abandonment of their children, and overall culture. Assertions included the following: 'They are not sensitized, they didn't go to school themselves, so they don't see the purpose of it' (interview at AAH offices in Kyangwali refugee camp, 19 August 2016), or 'Congolese do not bring children to get an education'. These assertions are only partially true, if at all. These assumptions, influenced by stereotypes and racialization processes, are partly the consequence of a lack of NGO practitioners' information and knowledge, largely based on preconceptions and generalizations, enhanced by the continuous mobility of humanitarian personnel and a lack of actual data. Taking these assumptions as the truth, humanitarian programmes and strategies overlook other factors that might be affecting attendance, such as the built environment.

In fact, the built environment has a great impact on whether parents bring their children to school. Adults point to dangerous roads and long distances; the lack of proper toilet facilities at the ECD centres, which currently cause children to suffer accidents or abuse; overcrowded classrooms; and the lack of stable and secure constructions. Additionally, children state that they loved attending school but many mentioned the lack of proper pavement, play equipment, colourful charts and sugar in their porridge as their main concerns.

Nevertheless, formal ECD centres and their programmes have a very positive effect on the refugee communities. Adults talk about how they help to raise awareness about the relevance of the early years for a healthy development and for lifelong learning. ECD centres free parents up for a few hours to find jobs and income-generation activities, and they help children to gain socialization skills. Children like going to the centres – especially when these have colourful charts; modelling clay; building blocks; shade in outdoor areas; and clean, child-friendly toilets.

**Figure 24.3**   Photograph of the formal ECD centre in Mugombwa, Rwanda (September 2015). © Nerea Amorós Elorduy.

## Non-formal learning settings

Encamped refugees in eastern Africa are not a homogeneous group. Hence, formal, top-down institutionalized ECD initiatives alone do not meet their needs. In fact, groups of refugees, sometimes in association with their direct local hosts, have always organized their own ECD initiatives and still do so, despite having had formal ECD centres since the early 2010s. This is partly due to the ECD centres' scarcity, standardization and universalized means of teaching. I use the term 'non-formal learning settings' to classify the diverse initiatives whereby community groups, mother leaders, churches and madrasas – sometimes in liaison with smaller and local NGOs – create spaces and mobilize human resources towards young children's learning.

A good example of such non-formal ECD initiatives can be found in Kigeme and Mugombwa camps in Rwanda, where mother leaders organize Home-Based ECD (HBECD) groups, 94 and 61 respectively. These HBECDs began with a collaboration between refugee mother leaders and CARE International, launched by a Rwandese employee from CARE International, who had more than 15 years of experience in ECD programmes in the country – several of them focused on refugee ECD. Individually, she held more experience on the topic than the whole of UNHCR's Rwanda education section, which only started in 2011 and the managers of which rarely remain in post for more than one year.

The HBECDs are initiatives in which groups of 10 mothers take care of around 15 children in a rotation system. Each group chooses the most adequate space available near their homes – these are usually interstitial spaces between two homes, or a home and a path – and conditions them with a floor mat and some toys to develop stimulating activities, such as playing, dancing, singing and providing children with porridge. The spaces available in Kigeme are far from ideal, so when Mugombwa was being built at the end of 2013 the same CARE employee lobbied the UNHCR planners for the enlargement of the available spaces between homes in order to host better HBECD initiatives.

HBECD initiatives are closer to the small children's homes and provide mothers with more control than the formal ECD centres do. However, their proximity to roads, lack of protection from the sun and the rain, and an absence of defined boundaries are not conducive to children's concentration, play and rest.

**Figure 24.4**  Photograph of the home-based ECD initiative at the hangar housing in Mugombwa (September 2015). © Nerea Amorós Elorduy.

Of the camps that I studied, Kakuma in Kenya is the best funded and most controlled. It is also the most insecure due to internal clashes and confrontations with local hosts. In this camp, even the non-formal education initiatives are managed by international NGOs, which have initiated the Furaha centres and the Waldorf initiatives. The two Furaha centres, situated in Kakuma phases III and IV (Kenya), are a joint effort by UNHCR, UNICEF and NGOs in charge of education and child protection, and offer an after-school playground and a referral centre for all ages. They include counselling rooms, a well-equipped playground and toilets, and are fenced spaces. The three Waldorf Kakuma initiatives take place at the camp's protection and reception centres, and in Kakuma phases III and IV. These initiatives are based on Western-initiated pedagogy that uses art as a means of learning and expression. Children come to the Waldorf spaces for a few hours, plant and paint, make clay models and undertake other manual activities.

In Uganda, due to the country's relatively welcoming refugee policies, refugees and local hosts have more freedom to create and choose for themselves the type of education that they want, and the majority of ECD initiatives are non-formal and community initiated. Some non-formal ECD initiatives are developed in churches; some are attached to primary schools; and others are in specifically designed compounds led by either youth groups such as Coburwas, community organizations such as P14 or private initiatives established and run by Ugandan neighbours. In a few cases, these ECD initiatives are developed in very well-built and creatively designed spaces – excellent examples of stimulating ECD spaces. In these cases, a teacher or a head teacher had been trained in, or had had access to, alternative pedagogies such as Montessori, Steiner, Waldorf or Reggio-Emilia – all of which include space as an important factor in promoting ECD.

These non-formal ECD activities greatly depend on local construction materials, geographic and climatic conditions, urban arrangements and the resources of the different refugee groups. In fact, adult respondents complain about insufficient access to material resources in comparison to UNHCR-funded ECD centres. They especially regret the lack of child-friendly toilets, play equipment, access to water, furniture, fencing and food. Children miss play materials, food and protection from the sun and the rain.

However, all of my research interlocutors agreed that these non-formal ECD initiatives improve the overall learning scenario due to being composed of smaller groups that are located closer to the children's homes, and where caregivers speak the same languages as the children

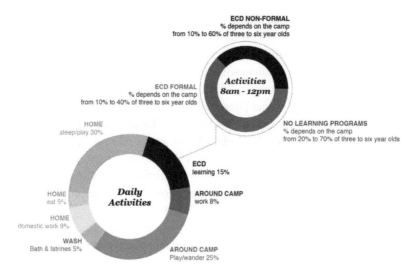

**Figure 24.5** Graphic showing the spaces where children spend most of their time according to refugee research participants. © Nerea Amorós Elorduy.

and understand their cultural upbringings. The likelihood of getting lost or suffering an accident on the way to the ECD initiative is greatly reduced, individual attention to the children increases, more vulnerable children have access to them, and the initiatives strengthen both community ties and refugees' agency.

## Informal learning settings

Finally, the most overlooked but most influential spaces for young children's learning are informal learning settings: homes, streets and common spaces. These environments and the activities developed in them constitute the principal influence on young children's brain development, as well as their emotional, social and physical development. Children spend most of their time in them – sleeping, eating, learning cultural and family habits, playing and fetching water or firewood – and they navigate them in order to reach the ECD centres and bigger playgrounds. In many cases, these spaces are what prevent children from attending formal or non-formal ECD initiatives.

## Homes

Home compounds perform poorly both as homes and as stimulating learning environments, mainly because they were intended and designed to be temporary emergency shelters from the weather and external threats, as defined by international humanitarian standards, rather than long-term homes.

Time and refugee interventions have modified these once-standardized shelters. However, despite these modifications, the lack of space and material resources mean they are lacking on many fronts. One element of concern, especially for adult respondents, is the sleeping arrangements. These are the cause of illnesses among young children due to sleeping on dusty, damp floors without mattresses or mosquito nets in unventilated and overcrowded rooms. In addition, the congested sleeping area is often shared with adults, a situation that can lead to sexual and physical abuse. Other concerns regarding the home environment include the structure and materials, the lack of space, unprotected open-fire kitchens and poor toilet facilities.

Nevertheless, both child and adult respondents agreed that the home environment can also be conducive to children's learning by protecting them from external threats and by enhancing family unity. Parents and caregivers value having control over an enclosed space that provides protection from the weather and external threats. Children state the importance of spending time with siblings, and especially their mother. All respondents agree that being safe and feeling secure at home reinforces children's self-esteem and confidence, which affects direct and indirect learning and prevents risky behaviour later in life.

## Streets

The second most used area in my case studies is the streets. Although children love to play in them with their friends, these are the locations that are most feared by parents and caregivers due to excessive accidents; abuse; and even kidnapping – which has been historically predominant in camps close to borders, such as Kakuma, Kiziba and Kyangwali. The majority of young children are also scared of going to the bush on the outskirts of the camps and to forested areas due to animals.

The roads in the highly dense and steep Rwandan camps become muddy and slippery streams during the rainy season, unmaintained pit latrines overflow, and trash pits are open and fenceless – all of which are serious threats to three- to six-year-olds. At the other end of the spectrum are Nakivale's and Kakuma's big, open, dusty roads exposed to the weather and speeding vehicles. In Kakuma, children also have to deal with the *lagga* – dry riverbeds that flash flood during the rainy season – where troublemakers are often found in the evenings and nights. Many children need to cross these riverbeds to access school, or use them as toilets, which becomes a threat in the rainy season and the evenings. In Kyangwali and Kyaka II – where they face long distances between places, mud, dangerous animals and abusive adults – children have created their own, 'safer' shortcut system to access the well or school, or to collect firewood.

## Conclusions

The humanitarian system is increasingly investing in ECD initiatives in East Africa's refugee camps. However – driven by donor agendas, scarce resources, poor coordination and a lack of institutional memory – the humanitarian system keeps trying to implement standardized and scalable, formal ECD centres, even in the long-term camps where 'emergency' is no longer the major issue.

Camp planning and refugee ECD policies and implementation strategies continue to overlook pre-existing community initiatives, family- and mother-led practices, and the effects of the built environment on children's development. Potential learning outcomes gathered from long-term camps' built environments and the perceptions of those who are affected by them – refugees and direct local hosts – are largely disregarded by the humanitarian system, and hence they are unknown and are not incorporated into the new assistance programmes. This greatly affects young children, whose voices are among the most marginalized.

Indeed, the current state of formal ECD centres is worrying. Both the broader literature on young children's development and the data that I have collected from these centres confirm that cramming children into an enclosed space with poor sanitation and scarce stimulation, with usually underpaid and undertrained caregivers, is not beneficial. Moreover, only 43 per cent of the camps' children attend them – and then, only for a few hours a day.[16]

Moreover, young refugee children in the cases that I have studied are most negatively affected by informal learning settings – in particular, the streets and their homes. The four main problems caused by these spaces are overcrowding in the home and settlement, poor sleeping arrangements, vulnerability in common spaces and the lack of play areas for young children. These effects are going almost completely unnoticed. On top of that, the non-formal initiatives that have the potential to improve the scarcity of formal ones, and to provide services closer and better adapted to each community, are not sufficiently funded, monitored, evaluated and promoted.

At present, the agency of the built environment that prevents or enables learning and the agency and knowledge of encamped refugee parents, caregivers, community members and children themselves are untapped resources. During the research presented in this chapter, I aimed to involve encamped populations throughout all stages of the discussion and in the creation of new knowledge. I believe that this collective means of knowledge creation, involving relevant actors currently marginalized from knowledge-production cycles, holds the key to developing a real understanding of the drawbacks and qualities of long-term refugee camps. Producing new, grounded knowledge can contribute to improving young refugee children's development in both existing long-term camps and new refugee-assistance interventions.

ECD initiatives can take a more empathic, nuanced and contextualized approach. Improving young refugee children's lifelong learning can be possible if the different processes and factors that affect early childhood development are taken into account, which include the encamped populations' perceptions and the role of the built environment as a learning source.

## Notes

1. Direct local hosts are the pre-existent residents of the areas where a camp is established. These individuals and their communities experience the physical, socio-economic and environmental impacts of refugee encampment in their daily activities and livelihoods.
2. Since the 1980s, renowned scholars and even the UNHCR have acknowledged in literature and policies that the temporary encampment of refugees has been failing (for example, Harrell-Bond, 1994, 1998, 2000; Kibreab 1991, 2014; Loescher and Milner, 2005; UNHCR, 1999, 2007, 2014, 2020).
3. For example, the New York Declaration and the Comprehensive Refugee Response Framework that was derived from it (UNHCR, 2016a).
4. Worldwide, 'Displacement is increasingly an urban and dispersed phenomenon, with settled camps becoming the exception. At least 59% of all refugees are now living in urban settings, a proportion that is increasing annually' (Crawford et al., 2015: 1). See diverse chapters in this volume for discussions of refugee experiences and encounters in both camp (for instance, Qasmiyeh, Chatterjee et al., Maqusi, Fiddian-Qasmiyeh) and non-camp settings (for example, Fisher et al., Tayob, Carpi, Loris-Rodionoff) in the Global South.
5. Some examples of this shift can be found in Kenya (UNHCR, 2016c) and Jordan (Dalal, 2015).
6. Even after the approval of the *Alternatives to Camps* policy in 2014 (UNHCR, 2014), several refugee camps have been established globally, including Azraq in Jordan (2014), Mahama in Rwanda (2015), Kalobeyei in Kenya (2016), Bidibidi in Uganda (2017) and Kutupalong

in Bangladesh (2017). For a discussion of the long-standing Palestinian refugee camps – in existence for over 70 years – see the chapters by Qasmiyeh, Maqusi, and Fiddian-Qasmiyeh in this volume.

7. In the early 2000s, Michel Agier initiated the discussion over the camp–city dichotomy (Agier, 2002: 322). Liisa Malkki questions the analytical use of comparing the camp with a city when the concepts of city and citizenship are, indeed, increasingly contested (Malkki, 2002: 354–6). Zygmunt Bauman praises Agier's urban-lenses approach (Bauman, 2002: 344). For more examples of works that discuss the camp–city dichotomy, see Diken, 2004: 83; Qasmiyeh and Fiddian-Qasmiyeh, 2013; Herz, 2008: 276; Herz, 2013; Pérouse de Montclos and Kagwanja, 2000: 205.

8. Clusters are groups of humanitarian organizations, both UN and non-UN, in each of the main sectors of humanitarian action – e.g. water, health and logistics. They are designated by the Inter-Agency Standing Committee (IASC) and have clear responsibilities for coordination (OCHA, 2015).

9. These are usually managed by NGOs and UN agencies, funded by international donors and built in somewhat permanent structures with a set curriculum, grades and accreditation once completed.

10. From the 1960s to the 1990s, Lynch developed studies on how young children and adolescents perceived and were affected by the built environment of the cities where they lived. He highlighted that a spatial analysis that shows people's perceptions and their use of the built environment leads easily into design proposals and policy recommendations.

11. With my team of research assistants, we delivered a total of 275 questionnaires to household caretakers – 25 of them in Kiziba; 11 in Kigeme; 8 in Mugombwa; 37 in Kakuma phase I, 15 in phase II, 14 in phase III and 14 in phase IV; 51 in Nakivale; 51 in Kyangwali; and 47 in Kyaka II. We undertook a total of 126 transect walks – 25 of them in Kiziba; 11 in Kigeme; 8 in Mugobwa; 7 in Kakuma phase I, 3 in phase III and 1 in phase IV. We held a total of 28 focus-group discussions with parent-teacher' associations (PTAs), women's and youth groups and community mobilizers – 2 each in Kiziba, Mugombwa, Kigeme, Kyaka II and Kakuma I and III; 3 each in Kyanwali and Kakuma II and IV; and 5 in Nakivale. These discussions included a total of 159 participants. We also held 33 focus-group discussions with young children in formal ECD centres: 4 in Nakivale, 5 in Kyangwali, 7 in Kyaka II, 2 in Kakuma I, 3 in Kakuma II, 3 in Kakuma III, 4 in Kakuma IV, 3 in Kiziba, 1 in Kigeme and 1 in Mugobwa.

12. From September to November 2017, in Kiziba and Kigeme camps, three participatory workshops were developed with a group of architecture fellows studying in Kigali and a group of refugees including mother leaders, PTAs, caregivers and NGO members in charge of education and child protection.

13. Among them was Resolution 64/290 of the Human Rights Council of the United Nations General Assembly, held in June 2010. It highlighted the right to education in emergencies (UN-HCR, 2012).

14. Ever since the 1970s, countries in Africa have slowly been developing ECD policies (Pence et al., 2008).

15. 'Child Friendly Spaces (CFSs) are a widely used tool to help support and protect children in the context of emergencies. Sometimes called Safe Spaces, Child Centered Spaces and Emergency Spaces for Children, CFSs are used by a growing number of agencies as a mechanism of protecting children from risk, as a means of promoting children's psychosocial well-being, and as a foundation for strengthening capacities for community child protection capacity' (Ager and Metzler, 2012: 2).

16. This is the average attendance enrolment in the centres. However, numbers fluctuate from year to year and actual attendance at the centres varies seasonally and across camps.

# References

Ager, Alastair and Janna Metzler. 2012. *Child Friendly Spaces: A Structured Review of the Current Evidence-Base*. London: World Vision.
Agier, Michel. 2002. 'Between War and City: Towards an Urban Anthropology of Refugee Camps', translated by Richard Nice and Loïc Wacquant, *Ethnography* 3 (3): 317–41.

Anderson, Allison and Marian Hodgkin. 2010. *The Creation and Development of the Global IASC Education Cluster*. Paris: United Nations Educational, Scientific and Cultural Organization.

Bauman, Zygmunt. 2002. 'In the Lowly Nowherevilles of Liquid Modernity: Comments on and around Agier', *Ethnography* 3 (3): 343–9.

Bronfenbrenner, Urie. 1979. *The Ecology of Human Development: Experiments by Nature and Design*. Cambridge, MA: Harvard University Press.

Consultative Group on Early Childhood Care and Development and INEE (Inter-Agency Network for Education in Emergencies). 2010. *The Path of Most Resilience: Early Childhood Care and Development in Emergencies: Principles and Practice*. New York: UNICEF.

Coombs, P.H. 1989. 'Formal and Nonformal Education: Future Strategies'. In *Lifelong Education for Adults: An International Handbook*, edited by Colin J. Titmus, 57–60. Oxford: Pergamon Press.

Coombs, Philip H. and Manzoor Ahmed. 1974. *Attacking Rural Poverty: How Nonformal Education Can Help*, edited by Barbara Baird Israel. Baltimore: Johns Hopkins University Press.

Crawford, Nicholas, John Cosgrave, Simone Haysom and Nadine Walicki. 2015. *Protracted Displacement: Uncertain Paths to Self-Reliance in Exile*. London: Overseas Development Institute.

Crisp, Jeff. 2001. 'Mind the Gap! UNHCR, Humanitarian Assistance and the Development Process', *International Migration Review* 35 (1): 168–91.

Crisp, Jeff. 2003. *No Solutions in Sight: The Problem of Protracted Refugee Situations in Africa* (New Issues in Refugee Research Working Paper 75). Geneva: United Nations High Commissioner for Refugees.

Dalal, Ayham. 2015. 'A Socio-Economic Perspective on the Urbanisation of Zaatari Camp in Jordan', *Migration Letters* 12 (3): 263–78.

Diken, Bülent. 2004. 'From Refugee Camps to Gated Communities: Biopolitics and the End of the City', *Citizenship Studies* 8 (1): 83–106.

Dovey, Kim and Ken Fisher. 2014. 'Designing for Adaptation: The School as Socio-Spatial Assemblage', *Journal of Architecture* 19 (1): 43–63.

Dryden-Peterson, Sarah. 2011. *Refugee Education: A Global Review*. Geneva: United Nations High Commissioner for Refugees.

Dryden-Peterson, Sarah. 2016. 'Refugee Education: The Crossroads of Globalization', *Educational Researcher* 45 (9): 473–82.

Edwards, Carolyn, Lella Gandini and George Forman, eds. 1998. *The Hundred Languages of Children: The Reggio Emilia Approach – Advanced Reflections*. 2nd ed. Greenwich, CT: Ablex Publishing Corporation.

Evans, Gary W. 1999. 'Measurement of the Physical Environment as Stressor'. In *Measuring Environment across the Life Span: Emerging Methods and Concepts*, edited by Sarah L. Friedman and Theodore D. Wachs, 249–77. Washington, DC: American Psychological Association.

Ferguson, Kim T., Rochelle C. Cassells, Jack W. MacAllister and Gary W. Evans. 2013. 'The Physical Environment and Child Development: An International Review', *International Journal of Psychology* 48 (4): 437–68.

Fiddian-Qasmiyeh, Elena. 2013. 'Transnational Childhood and Adolescence: Mobilizing Sahrawi Identity and Politics across Time and Space', *Ethnic and Racial Studies* 36 (5): 875–95.

Fiddian-Qasmiyeh, Elena. 2019. 'Memories and Meanings of Refugee Camps (and More-Than-Camps)'. In *Refugee Imaginaries: Research across the Humanities*, edited by Emma Cox, Sam Durrant, David Farrier, Lyndsey Stonebridge and Agnes Woolley. Edinburgh: Edinburgh University Press, 289–310.

Global Education Cluster. 2015. *Global Education Cluster 2015 Report*. Global Education Cluster.

Harrell-Bond, Barbara. 1994. 'Pitch the Tents', *New Republic*, 19/26 September, 15–19.

Harrell-Bond, Barbara. 1998. 'Camps: Literature Review', *Forced Migration Review* 2: 22–3.

Harrell-Bond, Barbara. 2000. *Are Refugee Camps Good for Children?* (New Issues in Refugee Research Working Paper 29). Geneva: United Nations High Commissioner for Refugees.

Herz, Manuel. 2008. 'Refugee Camps or Ideal Cities in Dust and Dirt'. In *Urban Transformation*, edited by Ilka Ruby and Andreas Ruby, 276–89. Berlin: Ruby Press.

Herz, Manuel, ed. 2013. *From Camp to City: Refugee Camps of the Western Sahara*. Zürich: Lars Müller.

Holzer, Elizabeth. 2015. *The Concerned Women of Buduburam: Refugee Activists and Humanitarian Dilemmas*. Ithaca, NY: Cornell University Press.

Kibreab, Gaim. 1991. *The State of the Art Review of Refugee Studies in Africa*. Uppsala: Uppsala University.

Kibreab, Gaim. 2014. 'Forced Migration in the Great Lakes and Horn of Africa'. In *The Oxford Handbook of Refugee and Forced Migration Studies*, edited by Elena Fiddian-Qasmiyeh, Gil Loescher, Katy Long and Nando Sigona, 571–84. Oxford: Oxford University Press.

Lefebvre, Henri. 1968. *Le droit à la ville*. Paris: Anthropos.

Lefebvre, Henri. 1973. *Le droit à la ville, I*. 2nd ed. Paris: Anthropos.

Lefebvre, Henri. 1991. *The Production of Space*, translated by Donald Nicholson-Smith. Oxford: Blackwell.

Loescher, Gil and James Milner. 2005. 'The Long Road Home: Protracted Refugee Situations in Africa', *Survival* 47 (2): 153–73.

Lynch, Kevin. 1960. *The Image of the City*. Cambridge, MA: MIT Press.

Lynch, Kevin, ed. 1977. *Growing Up in Cities: Studies of the Spatial Environment of Adolescence in Cracow, Melbourne, Mexico City, Salta, Toluca, and Warszawa*. Cambridge, MA: MIT Press.

Malkki, Liisa H. 1995a. *Purity and Exile: Violence, Memory, and National Cosmology among Hutu Refugees in Tanzania*. Chicago: University of Chicago Press.

Malkki, Liisa H. 1995b. 'Refugees and Exile: From "Refugee Studies" to the National Order of Things', *Annual Review of Anthropology* 24: 493–523.

Malkki, Liisa H. 2002. 'News from Nowhere: Mass Displacement and Globalized "Problems of Organization"', *Ethnography* 3 (3): 351–60.

McFarlane, Colin. 2011. 'Learning Assemblages'. In *Learning the City: Knowledge and Translocal Assemblage*, by Colin McFarlane, 15–31. Chichester: Wiley-Blackwell.

MINEMA. 2017. 'Refugees Camp and Transit Centers'. MINEMA. Accessed 31 January 2020. http://minema.gov.rw/index.php?id=69.

Montessori, Maria. 1984. *The Absorbent Mind*, translated by Claude A. Claremont. New York: Dell Publishing.

Newby, Landon. 2012. *The Education Cluster Thematic Case Study Series*. Inter-Agency Network for Education in Emergencies and Global Education Cluster.

Nicolai, Susan and Sébastien Hine. 2015. *Investment for Education in Emergencies: A Review of Evidence*. London: Overseas Development Institute.

OCHA (Office for the Coordination of Humanitarian Affairs). 2015. 'Cluster Coordination'. Accessed 10 March 2020. https://www.humanitarianresponse.info/en/coordination/clusters.

Office of the Prime Minister of Uganda. n.d. 'Ressettlement [sic] of Landless Persons and Disaster Victims'. Accessed 10 March 2020. http://opm.go.ug/ressettlement-of-landless-persons-and-disaster-victims.

Pence, Alan. 2011. 'Early Childhood Care and Development Research in Africa: Historical, Conceptual, and Structural Challenges', *Child Development Perspectives* 5 (2): 112–18.

Pence, Alan, Abeba Habtom and Francis R.W. Chalamada. 2008. 'A Tri-Part Approach to Promoting ECD Capacity in Africa: ECD Seminars, International Conferences, and ECDVU'. In *Africa's Future, Africa's Challenge: Early Childhood Care and Development in Sub-Saharan Africa*, edited by Marito Garcia, Alan Pence and Judith L. Evans, 487–501. Washington, DC: World Bank.

Pence, Alan R. and Hollie Hix-Small. 2007. 'Global Children in the Shadow of the Global Child', *International Journal of Educational Policy, Research and Practice* 8 (1): 83–100. Accessed 10 March 2020. http://web.uvic.ca/fnpp/documents/Pence_Hix-Small_Globalchildren.pdf.

Pérouse de Montclos, Marc-Antoine and Peter Mwangi Kagwanja. 2000. 'Refugee Camps or Cities? The Socio-Economic Dynamics of the Dadaab and Kakuma Camps in Northern Kenya', *Journal of Refugee Studies* 13 (2): 205–22.

Piaget, Jean. 1951. *The Child's Conception of the World*, translated by Joan Tomlinson and Andrew Tomlinson. London: Routledge and Kegan Paul.

Qasmiyeh, Yousif M. and Elena Fiddian-Qasmiyeh. 2013. 'Refugee Camps and Cities in Conversation'. In *Rescripting Religion in the City: Migration and Religious Identity in the Modern Metropolis*, edited by Jane Garnett and Alana Harris, 131–43. Farnham: Ashgate.

Slaughter, Amy and Jeff Crisp. 2009. *A Surrogate State? The Role of UNHCR in Protracted Refugee Situations* (New Issues in Refugee Research Research Paper 168). Geneva: United Nations High Commissioner for Refugees.

Stein, Barry N. and Lance Clark. 1990. 'Refugee Integration and Older Refugee Settlements in Africa'. Paper presented at the American Anthropological Association (AAA) Annual Meeting, New Orleans, 28 November–2 December 1990. Accessed 10 March 2020. https://msu.edu/course/pls/461/stein/FINAL.htm.

Stoddard, Abby, Adele Harmer, Katherine Haver, Dirk Salomons and Victoria Wheeler. 2007. 'Cluster Approach Evaluation – Final Draft', *Development* 10: 121–50. Accessed 10 March

2020. https://www.humanitarianresponse.info/sites/www.humanitarianresponse.info/files/2019/08/ClusterEvaluationFinal.pdf.

UNHCR (United Nations High Commissioner for Refugees). 1999. *Handbook for Emergencies*. 2nd ed. Geneva: United Nations High Commissioner for Refugees.

UNHCR (United Nations High Commissioner for Refugees). 2004. *Protracted Refugee Situations* (EC/54/SC/CRP.14). Geneva: United Nations High Commissioner for Refugees.

UNHCR (United Nations High Commissioner for Refugees). 2007. *Handbook for Emergencies*. 3rd ed. Geneva: United Nations High Commissioner for Refugees, 63–4.

UNHCR (United Nations High Commissioner for Refugees). 2008. *Protracted Refugee Situations: Revisiting the Problem*. Geneva: United Nations High Commissioner for Refugees.

UNHCR (United Nations High Commissioner for Refugees). 2012. *Education Strategy 2012–2016*. Geneva: United Nations High Commissioner for Refugees.

UNHCR (United Nations High Commissioner for Refugees). 2014. *UNHCR Policy on Alternatives to Camps*. Geneva: United Nations High Commissioner for Refugees.

UNHCR (United Nations High Commissioner for Refugees). 2016a. *Comprehensive Refugee Response Framework : From the New York Declaration to a Global Compact on Refugees*. Geneva: United Nations High Commissioner for Refugees.

UNHCR (United Nations High Commissioner for Refugees). 2016b. 'DRC Regional Refugee Response'. Information Sharing Portal. Accessed 24 February 2016. https://tinyurl.com/sglh5of.

UNHCR (United Nations High Commissioner for Refugees). 2016c. 'Kalobeyei Settlement'. UNHCR Global Website (June 2015): 2015–18. Accessed 10 March 2020. https://www.unhcr.org/ke/kalobeyei-settlement.

UNHCR (United Nations High Commissioner for Refugees). 2017. 'Population Statistics: Demographics'. Accessed 1 July 2017. http://popstats.unhcr.org/en/demographics.

UNHCR (United Nations High Commissioner for Refugees). 2020. 'Emergency Handbook: Camp Planning Standards (Planned Settlements)'. Accessed 10 March 2020. https://emergency.unhcr.org/entry/45582/camp-planning-standards-planned-settlements.

UNHCR Operational Portal – Refugee Situations. n.d. 'Horn of Africa Somalia Situation'. Accessed 5 March 2018. https://data2.unhcr.org/en/situations/horn.

UNHCR Uganda Comprehensive Refugee Response Portal. n.d. 'Refugees and Nationals by District'. Accessed 23 January 2018. https://ugandarefugees.org/analysis/refugees-and-hosts/.

United Nations. 2010. *The Right to Education in Emergency Situations*. New York: United Nations General Assembly.

Vygotsky, L.S. 1978. *Mind in Society: The Development of Higher Psychological Processes*, edited by Michael Cole, Vera John-Steiner, Sylvia Scribner and Ellen Souberman. Cambridge, MA: Harvard University Press.

Ward, Colin. 1978. 'The Child in the City', *Society* 15 (4): 84–91.

Ward, Colin. 1986. 'Children of the Streets', *New Society* 77 (1228): 23.

Zetter, Roger. 1995. *Shelter Provision and Settlement Policies for Refugees: A State of the Art Review*. Uppsala: Nordiska Afrikainstitutet.

# 25

# The Palestinian scale: Space at the intersection of refuge and host-country policies

Samar Maqusi

## Introduction

In 2017, the UNHCR published its 'Figures at a Glance' on the number of people forcibly displaced worldwide, recording this as 65.6 million. When I visited its website most recently, the 'Figures at a Glance' stood at 70.8 million. When confronted with such a significant number of displaced people, it feels both problematic and inadequate to just 'glance' at a number: displacement is a process that demands much deeper reflection. Yet, this is the language of the United Nations (UN). Inside the UN, of which I was a part for nearly a decade, numbers and figures count for more than advocacy and fundraising. Indeed, they form, and have long formed, the mode of operations that UN agencies adopt in designing relief and works programmes, as well as facilitating the way in which space in refugee camps is manifested in different host countries. In those camps that are managed by the UN (not all camps around the world are), the latter task is done through ensuring that the UN plans and builds the initial spatial layout of the camp while also taking responsibility for providing initial amenity services, in the form of collective water and sanitation areas. Yet, as the camp continues to exist, the UN gradually reduces its role in building space inside the camp until it encompasses only the rehabilitation of refugee shelters, while the infrastructure and amenities are often left to be built and maintained by international NGOs and host governments – the former with the permission (and, often, guidance) of the host government.[1] While UN figures and numbers are calculated by following specified protocols of humanitarian frameworks to plan aid and relief parameters in order to overcome an emergency phase of a displacement situation, they are in fact figures that entrench a 'crisis' through spatially upholding it. In turn, they make it necessary for members of displaced communities to construct other means of survival.

This chapter is concerned with the latter issue, through illustrating what happens on the ground when displaced people inhabit spaces of refuge that are 'designed and operated' by both host governments and UN relief agencies. In this case, Palestinian refugee camps in the Middle East, including 58 official camps, are presented as a space of refuge that is in a state of constant protraction, whereby refugees have been negotiating their refuge and displacement within a space that is deemed to be apolitical by the UN – here, specifically, the United Nations Relief and Works Agency for Palestine Refugees in the Near East (UNRWA), which has intentionally failed to admit and adopt a political mandate[2] for these spaces – camps. What results is a clear demonstration of refugees' refusal to accept the relief mandate and parameters within a highly political space. This is clearly illustrated through the ways in which refugees compensate for their denied political means by engaging in different forms of construction within their limited spatial means – that is, the humanitarian-refugee shelter. While this chapter showcases the creative spatial constructions and adaptations that Palestinian refugees have designed in a situation of protracted displacement, through utilizing a mode of what are bureaucratically categorized as 'spatial violations', it is important to keep in mind the fact that the reason the Palestinian camp continues to exist today, as such, is purely a Palestinian act.[3] This 'act' includes continuous forms of resilience and the reconstruction of space and lives, as well as the refusal to accept an unjust solution to their long-lived plight.

This chapter will first showcase the spatial, architectural evolution of the Palestinian camp, through illustrating the ways that Palestinian refugees have constructed space in order to overcome the limitations of a confined space – that is, the camp. It will then present various scenarios that both the Lebanese and the Jordanian governments have adopted in order to respond to the evolution and political utilization of the camp space by Palestinian refugees. I will map and explain these scenarios, which are concerned with refugee acts and responses to conflict inside the camp space, and both the host state's and refugees' own use of the architectural scale of the camp.

The research material for this chapter was collected during both my employment with UNRWA and, later, my PhD studies. The material emanated from my personal interest as both a researcher and a Palestinian, to document a spatial history of not only the growth of the camp but, more importantly, the negotiations, conflicts and compromises that have taken place during this growth. In addition, this work is done in order to explore what kind of impact this evolving constructed architectural Palestinian scale has on the ground, and for Palestinian refugees.

## Constructing the Palestinian scale inside the camp

The Palestinian camp (see Figure 25.1) was never meant to exist for 70 years 'as such'. Instead, it was planned as a transitional space, designed to control and manage refugees through the application of aid and relief (Malkki, 1992, 1994). This was done with the aim of making these spaces and their residents integrate socio-economically[4] in their host countries, as the political nature of those spaces – mainly embodied in Palestinians' Right of Return (UNGA Resolution 194) – was gradually stripped away.

### The transfer of space and people

The first spatial application of the Palestinian catastrophe (*Nakba*) was one of a physical *displacement-through-transfer*. What this entailed was that while displaced and dispossessed Palestinians were frantically trying to locate a space of protection, their spaces of origin were simultaneously

**Figure 25.1**   Burj el Barajneh camp, Lebanon 2016. © Samar Maqusi.

being re-formed to become Jewish-Israeli ones: *moshava* (colony), *kibbutz* (gathering) or a *moshav* (settlement).

If one tries to draw a timeline of the Palestinian–Israeli conflict, regardless of which time-specific events one chooses to link they are all imbued in some manner or another with either negotiations or illustrations of a 'transfer'.[5] Indeed, this 'transfer' is still ongoing today inside Palestine/Israel through land grabs and land transfer. The current 'transfer' is most commonly justified as necessary measures to ensure the security of Israel, from the occupied, overwhelmingly unequipped and unsupported indigenous Palestinian population. Hence, their location on top of hills (*lookout posts* in search of terrorists), in-between, and across Palestinian territories (Weizman, 2004: 227; 2007). Eyal Weizman further explains the political planning of the land initiated through former Israeli prime minister Ariel Sharon's and his political party Kadima's new grip on Israeli power, saying:

> Sharon saw in the depth of the West Bank, heavily populated by Palestinians, a sacred territory and a defensible frontier, a border without a line, across whose depth, around and between Palestinian towns and villages, a matrix of settlement could be constructed.
>
> Sharon's location strategy was based upon a close reading of the terrain and a decision made with the precision of acupuncture regarding where effort, usually in a form of a new settlement, could be applied. The fact that the word 'a point' (Nekuda) or 'a point on the ground' means 'settlement' in Hebrew is indicative of a planning culture that considers the positioning of a settlement less in terms of its essence, than in terms of its strategic location. (Weizman, 2004: 225)

## The spatial evolution of the Palestinian scale

The reality of displacement carries with it trauma inscribed within the social, psychological, economic and spatial experiences of the displaced. Yet, what remains true to scenarios of displacement around the world is the fact that displaced communities initially encounter a form of spatial containment once they arrive at their first space of protection, away from their home geography. Containment is, officially, meant to offer a first form of protection, whether formal – institutional protection by an international agency – or informal – through the local 'hosting' community, which offers 'in-transition' spaces of refuge in order to meet and contain the crisis at hand.

Arriving at the camp was a sombre moment of recollection for Palestinians as it was clear from the outset that these sites – camps – were perceived as *relief* sites by UNRWA and as *resistance* sites for Palestinian refugees, whose goal was returning to their homeland. Resistance is not a static notion but an active and operational one, and, in the case of the Palestinian camp, it is very much a spatial one. Architecture inside the camp is never built to attract or convince others of a possible new way of life – be it social, spatial or economic – as one only finds oneself building and inhabiting a camp out of urgency. Yet, as refugees find themselves inhabiting a camp for a protracted period of time, over 70 years in the case of Palestinian refugees, any external attempt to formally organize the camp will fail, and will be met with instantaneous restructuring by camp inhabitants.

Many scholars writing on the Palestinian camp directly associate the early architectural forms of the camps to the forms of Palestinian villages, as a way for Palestinian refugees to rebuild and replace familiar landscapes (Hilal and Petti 2019: 65; Hanafi, 2010; Misselwitz and Hanafi, 2010; Peteet 2005, 2016; Khalili, 2005). As Palestinian refugees moved into, or were moved into, camps, they produced similar characteristics of previous village inhabitation. This replication of habitual forms was not meant to recreate a village life, or even safeguard a spatial culture suddenly seized by force (nonetheless noting that these acts might have been in play on a subconscious level). The replication emerged, rather, out of a historical understanding of a relationship with land and space, though clearly interrupted and reformed as it comes into contact with a political spatiality – namely, the camp.

## Constructing the camp

The Palestinian refugee camp began spatially as a defined plot of land, 'temporarily' released by the host government to UNRWA for a period of 99 years (see Figure 25.2). Lebanon and Jordan host 12 and 10 Palestinian camps respectively, in addition to a number of unregistered spaces designated 'gatherings' by UNRWA. The first application of scale making inside the Palestinian camp was through relief tents, first provided by the International Committee of the Red Cross (ICRC) as an emergency measure before the establishment of the UNRWA. This haphazard distribution of tents on delineated plots was meant to serve as a spatial form of first aid. However, politics was a key element in this process as each tent correlated with a UN-allocated refugee number, making that tent one of the first forms of political agency that Palestinian refugees possessed: the refugee number meant that you were entitled to relief space and UN services – and, more importantly, to a political claim of your refugeehood.

After only five months of operation, UNRWA realized the urgent need to 'develop rules and procedures and instructions to standardize action in all areas' (UNRWA, 1951). Within a few years of creating the camp, UNRWA transformed the refugee shelter from that of an unregulated tent layout to one that was designed to both regulate and control (Malkki, 1992, 1994). This was done by subdividing the camp into a grid form consisting of 96–100m² refugee plots, something that I term the *relief*-scale (see Figure 25.3). This plot is the area granted as personal 'right-of-use' to each refugee family,[6] whereby each family was meant to adhere to the established rectangular parameters. The 'right-of-use' plots would house within them a 12m² room, termed the UNRWA shelter; these were made of straw/mud or prefabricated asbestos sheets and zinc roofing. The UNRWA shelter was based on a need to contain a large-scale crisis through material means, utilizing a familiar mode of production emanating from the desire to 'produce quickly and cheaply', very much resonating with the revolutionary production concept of Fordism (McKinlay and Wilson, 2012). To encourage refugees to become spatially self-supporting, UNRWA left basic amenities – the kitchen and bathroom – unbuilt, prompting the beginning of refugees' spatial self-support. Fully aware of Palestinian refugees' social values, along with their frustration with having to use public facilities for toilets and showers, it was only natural – seen as an existential need – to expect refugees' propensity to immediately construct amenities on their own plot, while incurring the cost.

This *relief*-scale that UNRWA placed over the political grounds of the camp was instantly met with refugees' acts of spatial appropriation. These acts, which I term 'spatial violations' – as they are considered

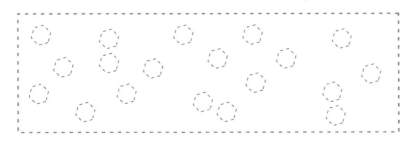

**Figure 25.2** The onset materialization of the Palestine camp, embodied in a haphazard layout of tents provided by the Red Cross. © Samar Maqusi.

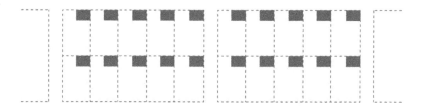

**Figure 25.3** Within the first two years of living in the camp, the UNRWA laid a new grid plan for each camp consisting of 96–100m² plots, housing within them a 12m² prefabricated room made of prefabricated asbestos sheets and zinc roofs. This plot is the area granted as personal 'right-of-use' to each refugee family. Water and sanitation services would be provided by UNRWA as collective points throughout the camp. © Samar Maqusi.

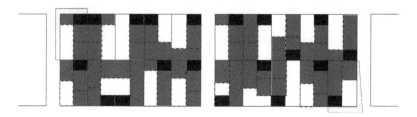

**Figure 25.4** Showing how some refugee families realigned the walls beyond the 96–100m² 'right-of-use' demarcation. © Samar Maqusi.

violations according to UNRWA and host-government policies, thus making the changes and additions open to removal whenever the host government deems it necessary[7] – demonstrated refugees' understanding of the humanitarian order, the *relief*-scale and displaced space before academics could even fathom what they entailed. Palestinian refugees challenged the *relief*-scale by first preserving more space – embodied in either retaining the relief tent next to the new UN plot to later become actual ground space, or by later realigning the UN plot border beyond the 96–100m² UN 'right-of-use' plot demarcation (see Figure 25.4).

As the 96–100m² 'right-of-use' plot boundaries gradually filled up with concrete rooms, concrete started to overflow beyond the wall in the form of thresholds (*attabat* in Arabic). These would become the first 'architectural element' to facilitate the changing scale of the camp (see Figure 25.5). Embodied in the act of *spatial violations*, the new scale – which I term the *political*-scale – being produced in the camp became a truly Palestinian one and would later redefine how conflict unfolds inside the camp.

As the camp's horizontal planes became saturated with cement (see Abourahme, 2015), some refugees devised another 'architectural

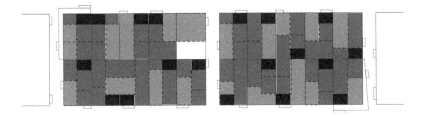

**Figure 25.5**  As the 96–100m² 'right-of-use' plot boundaries gradually filled up with concrete rooms, concrete would start to overflow beyond the wall in the form of thresholds. © Samar Maqusi.

**Figure 25.6**  As the horizontal planes became saturated with cement, refugees devised another 'architectural element' in the form of external stairs to serve as a facilitator to vertical expansion. © Samar Maqusi.

element' in the form of adding prefabricated external stairs to serve as a facilitator for expansion on a vertical plane. The temporality of the stairs' material would also preserve an encroached space until refugees and the camp grounds were ready to 'cement' this new, encroached-upon space (see Figure 25.6).

After over 70 years of displacement and the continued building up of needed space, the Palestinian camp as 'space' and the Palestinian as 'refugee' remain in a relationship that is co-constitutive (see Figure 25.7)[8] (Fiddian-Qasmiyeh, 2019). However, due to the act of *spatial violations*, this relationship stays in flux and continuously rescales itself proportionally to economies of inhabitation and disputes of political refuge.

What this constructed Palestinian, *political*-scale has done is ensure a mode of political negotiation between Palestinian refugees and their host governments in the Middle East. Through disrupting the UN *relief*-scale, Palestinian refugees have been able to challenge the spatial mode of control and surveillance inflicted on them. More importantly, through gradually constructing the *political*-scale, Palestinian refugees have generated a new political order that has thus far coerced the host governments into negotiating new terms of living with the protracted refugees. However, this 'new political order' has violence inscribed in it as the camp remains exposed to the threat of destruction by external sovereignties aiming to maintain spatial control.

**Figure 25.7**  The Palestinian *political*-scale inside the camp, constructed over 70 years of protracted displacement. (L) Burj el-Barajneh camp and (R) Ein el-Hilweh camp, Lebanon, 2017. © Samar Maqusi.

# Host-government responses to the Palestinian scale

Host governments have responded to the constructed Palestinian scale of the camp through different spatial modes, and yet what these host governments share is their stated need to regain spatial control over the camp since they all treat the Palestinian camp as a space of latent and ever-imminent conflict. In Lebanon, the government has traditionally resorted to either eliminating the camp by complete destruction, allowing the host government to reconstruct the camp scale to new dimensions to facilitate surveillance and control, or in other cases they have constructed prison-like architectural elements such as walls and gates to both regulate and confine the camp.

## Complete destruction of the camp

The conflict scenario of Nahr el-Bared camp in North Lebanon saw the complete destruction of the camp in 2007. The Lebanese military sought the destruction of a foreign militia group, the Fatah el-Islam militant group, which emerged inside the camp only months before the outbreak of the conflict. It is believed that the group's members inside Nahr el-Bared camp at the time of the conflict did not exceed 100 men, as opposed to over 27,000 registered refugees living in the camp – conveying a targeting, if you will, of said space and people (UNRWA, n.d.; Ramadan, 2009, 2010; Barakat, 2013; interview with Burj el-Barajneh camp resident, 2014). Initial negotiations to reconstruct Nahr el-Bared camp included attempts by the Lebanese Government to eradicate any possibility of reconstructing the camp on its original site, with the government mobilizing tropes of reported security concerns. The government even utilized the discovery of historic/archaeological, yet fragmented, ruins under a portion of the site to justify its demands, in spite of the fact that the country is full of such cases of unearthed ruins that have been left to decay without much governmental notice or intervention. Furthermore, Nahr el-Bared's location on the coast of northern Lebanon means that it is considered prime development land. These are among the arguments presented by the government in order to build a case for either reconstructing the camp elsewhere or reintegrating refugees from Nahr el-Bared into other existing camps, including in Baddawi camp, as discussed by Fiddian-Qasmiyeh in this volume (UNRWA, 2011; see also Qasmiyeh, this volume).

Eventually, and following arduous negotiations mobilized by the Nahr el-Bared Reconstruction Commission for Civil Action and Studies (NBRC) – a grassroots organization made up of refugees and

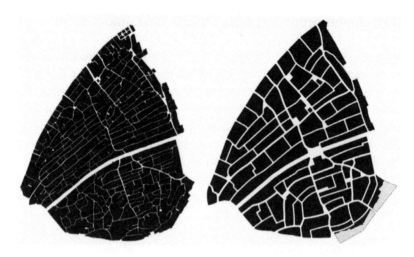

**Figure 25.8**  (L) Nahr el-Bared camp before destruction by the Lebanese military in 2007, showing the Palestinian scale built up over 58 years; (R) the new reconstructed scale, which requires the reconstruction of the camp's streets at 10–15m widths by the Lebanese Government. © UNRWA offices.

activists – the Lebanese Government agreed to reconstruct the camp on its original site, and to allow displaced and dispossessed refugee families to return to their home camp of almost 70 years. However, it did so on the condition of specific spatial demands. These demands amounted to the physical rescaling of the camp, by adopting spatial parameters very similar to the initial UN relief-scale (see Figure 25.8) (UNRWA interviews; Barakat, 2013; Sheikh Hassan and Hanafi, 2010).

## Confining the camp

In recent years, the Lebanese Government has embarked on a new 'mode of intervention' towards the Palestinian camp, consisting of confining the camp by building cement walls that surround the entirety of the camp: Ein el-Hilweh camp in southern Lebanon has provided the most recent example of this mode of intervention. In addition, the Lebanese Government installed metal gateways at the end of numerous pedestrian pathways that lead into and out of the camp, thus controlling and surveying the movement of each person trying to enter or exit Ein el-Hilweh camp (see Figure 25.9). While the wall and metal gates are not meant to cripple refugees' daily movement, they do intend to institute a new power relation, one that conveys the continuous assertion by the host government

**Figure 25.9**   (L) Concrete wall surrounding Ein el-Hilweh camp, and (R) camp gateways erected by the Lebanese Government in an attempt to contain conflicts inside the camp, Lebanon, 2017. © Samar Maqusi.

that it will always find ways to control the camp and its inhabitants. This kind of spatial behaviour – intervention – is reminiscent of what Gilles Deleuze refers to as measures of 'control', whereby he asserts:

> You do not confine people with a highway. But by making highways, you multiply the means of control. I am not saying this is the only aim of highways, but people can travel infinitely and 'freely' without being confined while being perfectly controlled. That is our future. (Deleuze, 2007: 322)

It is important to highlight here the fact that to enter Ein el-Hilweh camp, like most camps in Lebanon, people are required to pass through a Lebanese military checkpoint, whereby individual identification is requested and cars are subject to being searched. Therefore, it is not surprising that most refugees would not necessarily find the addition of a surrounding cement wall a mere hindrance but perceive it as a measure of 'control' and 'casting', which is what my interlocutors mostly relayed to me during my visit to the camp in the summer of 2017.

## Rescaling the camp

In the case of Jordan, whose government has historically had different power relations with Palestinian refugees living on its territory, the government opted instead to adopt a softer spatial mode of rescaling the camp. In Baqa'a camp, the Jordanian Government has been rescaling the

Palestinian camp by widening existing streets in order to disrupt the contiguity of the camp and allow for the quick entry of Jordanian gendarmes' tanks into it (see Figure 25.10). This enforced spatial measure was communicated to camp residents as a necessary means to provide them with better light and ventilation for their shelters.[9] The refugee families displaced as a result of these widened streets were then relocated outside the camp. Their compensation consisted of a new shelter, in the form of generic, cement apartment blocks that lack character, history or memory.

The cases of Nahr el-Bared, Ein el-Hilweh and Baqa'a camps are all examples that demonstrate how refugee spaces are continuously targeted for intervention. They further showcase the use of architecture and space as means to ensure the incarceration and control of the camp and its residents by the host governments, while the latter insist that they are improving the built environment for the refugees – including through enhanced lighting, ventilation and safety. Indeed, what architecture has

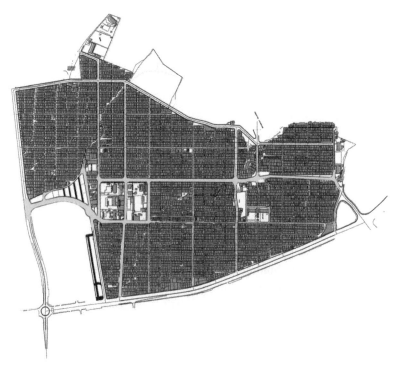

**Figure 25.10**   In Baqa'a camp, the Jordanian Government has been rescaling Palestinian camps by widening existing streets in order to disrupt the contiguity of the camp and allow for the quick entry of gendarmes' tanks. © Samar Maqusi.

been able to achieve in these sites is a 'concealment through space' of the intended control measures that the host governments build. In the case of Nahr el-Bared, this was an intention to widen the internal scale of the camp in order to make the camp fabric accessible to the Lebanese Army. In the case of Ein el-Hilweh, it was confinement in the name of safety, with the Lebanese Government surrounding the camp with the thick layer of a cement wall interrupted with metal gates. In the case of Baqa'a camp in Jordan, it was a declared need to divide a large camp into easily controlled and accessed quarters.

These examples bring to the fore the political instrumentalization of space and architecture, and their ability to conceal control measures behind architectural rhetoric of improving the physical environment.

## The Palestinian scale: In operation and response

### On Palestinian operation

The *'economy'* of spatial violations that construct the Palestinian *political*-scale inside the Palestinian camp interjects into all spheres of life of the camp: social; economic; and, most definitely, political. In this section, I will illustrate the latter through an example of how the Palestinian scale operates during conflict, and what kinds of spatial response host governments have adopted to the constructed *Palestinian* scale.

In the case of Burj el-Barajneh camp in Beirut (Lebanon), the constructed Palestinian scale operated as an existential element for Palestinian refugees as they came face to face with the Lebanese Amal militia during the War of the Camps, which lasted from 1985 until 1988. Confined within their camp for months at a time, with anyone who left the camp very likely to never return, Palestinians had to utilize the camp's spatiality to both confront the aggression and preserve their camp. The Palestinian scale to which the buildings had developed in Burj el-Barajneh camp created an advantageous proximity that enabled Palestinian refugees to create elevated walkways. Residents extended wooden boards between building openings that were opposite each other, thereby eliminating the need for movement on the ground, which would have otherwise made them more exposed and vulnerable in times of armed conflict (see Figure 25.11). In this way, they managed to gain an advantage – spatially – over Amal forces by utilizing the camp's *political*-scale to serve as a strategic 'economy': one which was both spatial and existential. This 'economy', in the form of resistance and survival

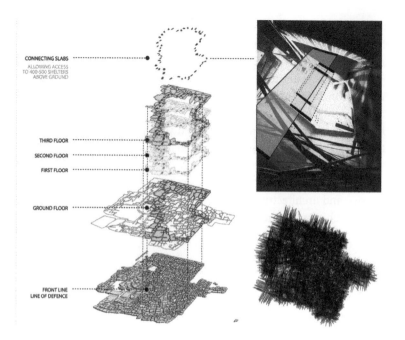

Labels on the diagram:

CONNECTING SLABS
ALLOWING ACCESS
TO 400-500 SHELTERS
ABOVE GROUND

THIRD FLOOR

SECOND FLOOR

FIRST FLOOR

GROUND FLOOR

FRONT LINE
LINE OF DEFENCE

**Figure 25.11**   Elevated walkways – the *political*-scale in operation.
Burj el-Barajneh camp, Lebanon. © Samar Maqusi.

employing spatial means, is where the Palestinian *political*-scale –
constructed inside a refugee camp living in a state of protracted displacement – acts as an example of real political agency for Palestinian
refugees. It has not only enabled refugees to safeguard their spaces and
their lives but moreover, and because of their survival, it compelled the
Lebanese Government to negotiate a truce.

## On host-government response

In Baqa'a camp in Jordan, as a result of the newly opened 'wide streets',
the camp fabric was bifurcated, providing the gendarmes' tanks with a
new spatial advantage that allows them to quickly and uninterruptedly
enter the camp tissue. It is worth mentioning here that conflicts occur
frequently in camps – sometimes resulting from the most mundane of
public acts, such as demonstrations and commemorations. Yet, never in
the history of Baqa'a camp had these conflicts resulted in the Jordanian
gendarmes' penetration into the camp's fabric.[10]

During my PhD research in Baqa'a camp, I witnessed and documented the first spatial scenario in the camp whereby the Jordanian

gendarmes were able to reach the central fabric of the camp, in an attempt to disperse a popular demonstration held in support of ongoing acts of Palestinian resistance to the occupation in both Gaza and the West Bank. The gendarmes were able to reach the centre of the camp by using the newly widened streets, which now enabled the tanks to roam around four different sections of the camp, as well as unleash their soldiers inside the camp fabric to chase and incarcerate the refugees themselves.

As the tanks unleashed their soldiers inside the camp, Palestinian refugees quickly dispersed, moving towards narrow and meandering pathways in order to mislead and escape the gendarmes (keeping in mind that Jordanian soldiers are not familiar with the camp's spatial tissue, and thus the camp scale worked to the refugees' advantage during the chase). However, it is crucial to highlight here that the advantages of rescaling the camp were not only concerned with this direct and quick access for the Jordanian gendarmes but also very much concerned with cost: literally, reduced monetary and personnel cost for the government security apparatus. This was achieved by replacing a mode of surrounding the camp for hours at a time, with tanks monitoring and confining the refugees within the camp during confrontations, to a mode of quick entry and dispersion requiring less time and fewer personnel. What results from this change is a clear attempt by the Jordanian Government to relegate role of Palestinian refugees to one lacking the agency to negotiate their own space while awaiting a political solution to their protracted refuge.

## Conclusion

As long as Palestinian refugees continue to inhabit this state of prolonged spatial displacement while their political state is relegated to an inferior – less *urgent* – *need* by external players and agencies, the camp will continue to exist for Palestinian refugees as a space where resistance continuously takes on various forms and scales. This is in an attempt to safeguard a space deemed existential not only for their *imagined* political state but also their individuated subjectivities and needs.

The Palestinian refugee camp remains a space in which the political problem – embodied in Palestinians' demand to their right-of-return to a Palestinian land and state, and the refusal to abandon this right to what is now being created as a 'pure' Jewish state – is constantly being negotiated inside the camp on multiple scales. This includes internally within oneself; with other refugees; and with the host government, which constantly reshapes the Palestinian camp through reshaping its architectural scale. Palestinian refugees have been able to construct a *political* value as space and people, through continuously building up the camp by encroaching on UN and host-government standards and parameters, in order to create what I have called in this chapter the Palestinian *political*-scale. This act of encroachment – spatial violations – over a protracted period of displacement, transgresses relief terms by building beyond UN spatial parameters. By doing so, the encroachment act practised over decades of living in refuge has challenged the very essence of relief standards and objectives, while replacing them with ones of power relations. These power relations are inscribed in the spatial practices of both refugees and host governments, in the form of constructing space. What the power relations reflect is Palestinian refugees' real agency to maintain a form of decision-making for their camps. Yet, as the spatial practices and aims are continuously negotiated and changed, so too are the power relations.

For Palestinian refugees, spatial practices are constantly negotiated and changed as a means to resist the imposed conditions of both protracted displacement and protracted immobility. Therefore, and directly related to the constructed Palestinian *political*-scale, the Palestinian refugee camp has been able to constantly challenge the imposed condition by demonstrating its spatial agency in various conflictual scenarios and through various spatial mechanisms, forcing the authorities to renegotiate the situation with camp residents in order to prevent a full-scale spatial conflict. Through diverse acts of spatial violation, which produce the *political* in the camp, refugees have been able to perform in diverse spatial economies.

By way of conclusion, I draw on Chantal Mouffe's treatment of conflictual spaces and the condition of 'antagonism' through an elaboration of 'agonism':

> What an agonistic approach certainly disavows is the possibility of an act of radical refoundation that would institute a new social order from scratch. But a number of very important socioeconomic and political transformations, with radical implications, are possible within the context of liberal democratic institutions. What we understand by 'liberal democracy' is constituted by sedimented forms of power relations resulting from an ensemble of contingent hegemonic interventions. The fact that their contingent character is not recognized today is due to the absence of counter-hegemonic projects. (Mouffe, 2005: 33)

What Mouffe is trying to showcase here is a rethinking of both the nature and the potential of existing, conflictual human relations. More specifically in this case, it is meant to be treated as a potential way of rethinking the conflictual relations between host government and host communities on the one hand, and refugees on the other. As we have been witnessing more generally around different parts of the world, these relations are often conflictual regardless of the communities involved. This is mainly as a result of a group of people being forced to live in a new space at the intersection of refuge and host-country policies. Thus, the challenge remains how we can reimagine and understand the new spaces of displacement that are being created and renegotiated around the globe, and the ways in which diverse forms of socio-spatial conflict can be meaningfully addressed.

## Notes

1. On the roles played by INGOs and local groups in providing learning environments for children living in camps in the East African Rift, see Amorós Elorduy in this volume; on the Calais camp, managed neither by UN agencies nor by the host government, see the contributions in this volume by Crafter and Rosen, Bailey, and Hooshyar Emami.
2. For more on UNRWA's mandate, please see Bartholomeusz (2009).
3. See Qasmiyeh in this volume, on 'Writing the camp: writing the camp archive'.
4. Please refer to 'UNRWA: A Brief History 1950-1982', accessed at UNRWA Archives.
5. See McMahon–Hussein Correspondence (14 July 1915–30 January 1916), Balfour Declaration (2 November 1917), and Faisal–Weizmann Agreement (3 January 1919). Available at UK National Archives: https://discovery.nationalarchives.gov.uk/details/r/C825496.
6. Please see https://www.unrwa.org/palestine-refugees, for UNRWA's explanation of the right-of-use granted to Palestinian refugees.
7. Please see Jordan's Department of Palestinian Affairs: http://dpa.gov.jo.
8. More recently, negotiations towards the Trump Administration's 'deal of the century' has revolved around eliminating the 'refugee' status of the Palestinians through: (1) eradicating UNRWA (the United Nations Agency for Palestine Refugees in the Near East), which services the camps, and, in retrospect, (2) working to eradicate the Palestinian camps. As of the time of writing the US has cut its funding to UNRWA, making it impossible for the agency to operate at the same scale and productivity as before. See Irfan (2018), Gardner (2018) and Fiddian-Qasmiyeh (2019).
9. While conducting fieldwork in Baqa'a camp in Jordan in the summer of 2014, I inquired about the process that took place on the ground to make way for the widening of the existing street. More specifically, I was trying to establish the nature of the power relations on the ground between the Jordanian Government and Palestinian refugees. Several refugees I spoke with conveyed to me the fact that while the Jordanian Government provided compensation for the affected, relocated families, it did so by providing the refugee family with one option: accept the compensation. This means that if a refugee family tried to argue that it wished to remain in the camp, the Jordanian Government would physically enforce its removal to make way for the new street.
10. This was related to me through interviews with refugees demonstrating in and others living around *Intifada* street (the main street where demonstrations take place in the camp) in Baqa'a camp, in August 2014 and July 2015.

# References

Abourahme, Nasser. 2015. 'Assembling and Spilling-Over: Towards an "Ethnography of Cement" in a Palestinian Refugee Camp', *International Journal of Urban and Regional Research* 39 (2): 200–17.

Barakat, Sultan. 2013. *Reconstruction of Nahr el-Bared Refugee Camp* (On Site Review Report). Beirut: United Nations Relief and Works Agency.

Bartholomeusz, Lance. 2009. 'The Mandate of UNRWA at Sixty', *Refugee Survey Quarterly* 28 (2/3): 452–74.

Deleuze, Gilles. 2007. *Two Regimes of Madness: Texts and Interviews, 1975–1995*, edited by David Lapoujade; translated by Ames Hodges and Mike Taormina. New York: Semiotext(e).

Fiddian-Qasmiyeh, Elena. 2019. 'The Changing Faces of UNRWA: From the Global to the Local', *Journal of Humanitarian Affairs* 1 (1): 28–41.

Gardner, David. 2018. 'Trump's "Deal of the Century" Offers Nothing Good to Palestinians', *Financial Times*, 5 September. Accessed 12 January 2020. www.ft.com/content/40d77344-b04a-11e8-8d14-6f049d06439c.

Hanafi, Sari. 2010. *Governing Palestinian Refugee Camps in the Arab East: Governmentalities in Search of Legitimacy* (Working Paper 1). Beirut: Issam Fares Institute for Public Policy and International Affairs.

Hilal, Sandi and Alessandro Petti. 2019. *Permanent Temporariness*. Stockholm: Art and Theory Publishing.

Irfan, Anne. 2018. 'What Jared Kushner's "Deal of the Century" Would Mean for Palestinian Refugees', *The Conversation*, 10 August. Accessed 12 January 2020. http://theconversation.com/what-jared-kushners-deal-of-the-century-would-mean-for-palestinian-refugees-101150.

Khalili, Laleh. 2005. 'Places of Memory and Mourning: Palestinian Commemoration in the Refugee Camps of Lebanon', *Comparative Studies of South Asia, Africa and the Middle East* 25 (1): 30–45.

Malkki, Liisa. 1992. 'National Geographic: The Rooting of Peoples and the Territorialization of National Identity among Scholars and Refugees', *Cultural Anthropology* 7 (1): 24–44.

Malkki, Liisa. 1994. 'Citizens of Humanity: Internationalism and the Imagined Community of Nations', *Diaspora* 3 (1): 41–68.

McKinlay, Alan and James Wilson. 2012. '"All They Lose is the Scream": Foucault, Ford and Mass Production', *Management and Organizational History* 7 (1): 45–60.

Misselwitz, Philipp and Sari Hanafi. 2009. 'Testing a New Paradigm: UNRWA's Camp Improvement Programme', *Refugee Survey Quarterly* 28 (2/3): 360–88.

Mouffe, Chantal. 2005. *On the Political*. London: Routledge.

Peteet, Julie. 2005. *Landscape of Hope and Despair: Palestinian Refugee Camps*. Philadelphia: University of Pennsylvania Press.

Peteet, Julie. 2016. 'Camps and Enclaves: Palestine in the Time of Closure', *Journal of Refugee Studies* 29 (2): 208–28.

Ramadan, Adam. 2009. 'Destroying Nahr el-Bared: Sovereignty and Urbicide in the Space of Exception', *Political Geography* 28 (3): 153–63.

Ramadan, Adam. 2010. 'In the Ruins of Nahr al-Barid: Understanding the Meaning of the Camp', *Journal of Palestine Studies* 40 (1): 49–62.

Sayigh, Rosemary. 1995a. 'Palestinians in Lebanon: (Dis)solution of the Refugee Problem', *Race and Class* 37 (2): 27–42.

Sayigh, Rosemary. 1995b. 'Palestinians in Lebanon: Harsh Present, Uncertain Future', *Journal of Palestine Studies* 25 (1): 37–53.

Sheikh Hassan, Ismael and Sari Hanafi. 2010. '(In)security and Reconstruction in Post-Conflict Nahr al-Barid Refugee Camp', *Journal of Palestine Studies* 40 (1): 27–48.

UNGA Resolution 194(III) Paragraph 11, available at https://undocs.org/A/RES/194%20(III), and at https://www.unrwa.org/content/resolution-194.

UNRWA (United Nations Relief and Works Agency). 1951. *Assistance to Palestine Refugees: Interim Report of the Director of the United Nations Relief and Works Agency for Palestine Refugees in the Near East*. New York: United Nations.

UNRWA (United Nations Relief and Works Agency). 2011. *Reconstruction of Nahr el-Bared Camp and UNRWA Compound: Progress Report, 1 September 2007–31 October 2010*. Beirut: United Nations Relief and Works Agency. Accessed 12 December 2020. www.unrwa.org/sites/default/files/2011042974549.pdf.

UNRWA (United Nations Relief and Works Agency). n.d. 'Nahr el-Bared Camp'. Accessed 10 March 2020. https://www.unrwa.org/where-we-work/lebanon/nahr-el-bared-camp.

Weizman, Eyal. 2004. 'Strategic Points, Flexible Lines, Tense Surfaces, Political Volumes: Ariel Sharon and the Geometry of Occupation', *Philosophical Forum* 35 (2): 221–44.

Weizman, Eyal. 2007. *Hollow Land: Israel's Architecture of Occupation*. London: Verso.

## 26

# Shifting the gaze: Palestinian and Syrian refugees sharing and contesting space in Lebanon

Elena Fiddian-Qasmiyeh

## Introduction

In this chapter, I propose the importance of analysing experiences of and responses to displacement with attention to what I call 'refugee-refugee relationality' (Fiddian-Qasmiyeh, 2016a). Drawing on the case of refugees from Syria who have sought safety in a Palestinian refugee camp in North Lebanon since 2011 – as part of a broader project funded by the AHRC-ESRC (AH/P005438/1) examining local community responses to displacement from Syria in Lebanon, Jordan and Turkey – I explore the complex dynamics, and limitations that underpin processes of 'refugees-hosting-refugees' and/or forms of 'refugee-refugee humanitarianism' (Fiddian-Qasmiyeh, 2016a, 2016b). Focusing on the nature and implications of refugee-refugee relations – in this case, people from Syria living alongside different groups of Palestinians in Lebanon – entails shifting our gaze away from relationships that have become archetypal in the field of refugee studies and refugee response: the relationship between refugees on the one hand and INGOs, UN agencies, states and citizens on the other.

Centralizing and critically analysing the role of displaced people as providers of assistance, solidarity and support for other people enables, and requires, us to transcend and challenge the frequent depiction of INGOs, UN agencies, states and citizens as either actively providing for or undermining the rights of passive and dependent refugees. It is notable that when refugees' agency *is* acknowledged in popular, political and policy frameworks, this is frequently either causally linked to the success of externally designed and implemented programmes (such as 'empowerment' and 'self-reliance' initiatives) or, conversely, done through securitization paradigms that reduce active refugees to threats against individual, national and international security (Fiddian-Qasmiyeh, 2016b; see Introduction in this volume). I would argue that acknowledging the assistance, support and solidarity provided *by* people who have been displaced provides an urgently needed counter-narrative to such depictions, which are themselves imbued with epistemic violence (Fiddian-Qasmiyeh, 2016a). However, in so doing, it is not my aim to either idealize responses led by displaced people or deny the significance of refugees' relationships with diverse actors on local, national or international levels. In effect, we must remain attentive to the structural inequalities that mean that refugee-led responses are both unsustainable and ultimately inadequate precisely due to the structural violence and barriers that both cause and perpetuate displacement and exclusion. Such attention must be situated within the context of the broader politics of states' responsibilities and duties to protect and uphold the rights of the displaced. As such, acknowledging the roles played by refugees must not be viewed as a way for states and international organizations to evade responsibility to provide refugee protection or to find political solutions to political crises (Fiddian-Qasmiyeh, 2019a).

With these caveats in mind, in the following pages I argue that focusing on refugee-refugee relationality is particularly essential when we explore the complex encounters that characterize contemporary displacement, including processes of 'overlapping displacement'. I use this term to refer to two intersecting dynamics. First, rather than refugees' journeys leading to safety, asylum and an 'end to the refugee cycle' (Black and Koser 1999), people often experience displacement on more than one occasion in their lives, both individually and collectively. This is the case for Iraqi and Palestinian refugees (amongst others) who had originally sought safety in Syria only to be displaced once more, alongside Syrian refugees, by the ongoing conflict there (Fiddian-Qasmiyeh, 2012, 2016a, 2019c). Second, since the majority of refugees around the world do not live in closed or isolated camps,[1] refugees are increasingly experiencing overlapping displacement in the sense that they often physically share spaces with other displaced people.

The implication of these intersecting processes is that people who have been displaced share, contest and (re)construct spaces over long periods of time with other people – citizens and refugees alike. *Inter alia*, this also means that, over time, displaced people often become members of communities that subsequently offer protection and support to others, including in conditions of ongoing precarity.[2] Such is the case of Baddawi refugee camp in North Lebanon, which I explore below, wherein residents of the camp – established in the 1950s to offer sanctuary to Palestinian refugees displaced from Palestine in 1948 – have 'hosted' refugees from elsewhere in the Middle East, including Syrians, Palestinians and Iraqis displaced by the conflict in Syria.

## Refugee-refugee relationality in situations of precarity[3]

In spite of the widespread reality of people being displaced for many decades, often being displaced multiple times during their lifetimes, and residing in diverse camp and non-camp spaces alongside both citizens and other groups of refugees, it is particularly notable that refugees' positions, identities, beliefs and behaviours in relation to other displaced people remain almost entirely unexplored to date (Fiddian-Qasmiyeh 2016a, 2016b, 2019a).

Indeed, a large proportion of studies of urban refugees focus on one particular group of people (typically defined by their nationality or ethnicity) in one city (see, for example, Lyytinen, 2015; Bartolomei, 2015), while multi-sited, comparative studies often focus on one group dispersed across a number of cities or divided across a city and a camp setting (for instance, Fiddian-Qasmiyeh, 2012, 2013; and Malkki, 1995 respectively) or compare the conditions and dynamics of one group of refugees in one city with another group in another city (as in Sanyal, 2014). In contrast, only a small number of studies explicitly examine the experiences of different refugees in the same city (for example, Brown et al., 2004; Fiddian-Qasmiyeh and Qasmiyeh, 2010). Of particular relevance to the argument that I make below vis-à-vis the 'relationality' of refugees in shared, if contested, spaces of refuge, Dale Buscher analyses the relative strength of social ties and networks within Somali, Congolese and Burundian refugee communities in the city of Kampala (Buscher, 2011: 21–2). While Buscher's article thus recognizes the overlapping presence of refugees from different countries of origin in Kampala, it seemingly highlights both the relative isolation of Somalis and Congolese refugees from other refugee communities and the extent to which fractures and mistrust characterize relations within the Burundi refugee community. This may helpfully demonstrate that segregation, rather than social integration via cohabitation, can maximize livelihood strategies for certain refugees (in this case, Burundian refugees), and yet this focus on nationality-based social networks continues to render invisible the *relationality* of refugees in spaces inhabited by multiple, and often overlapping, groups of refugees in urban contexts.

## From relative isolation to refugee-refugee relations

As academics, policymakers and practitioners have aimed to understand and appropriately respond to the needs and rights of displaced people in urban settings, refugees have often been viewed in isolation rather than in relation to other refugees. In effect, the *relationality* of refugees, and the extent to which they share and (re)create spaces (physically, socially, emotionally) with others, has typically been viewed through the lens of refugee–host relations (in itself a notably under-researched area), in which the host is conceptualized as the citizen-qua-host, hosting-the-non-citizen (on different forms of relationships with locally based citizens, see Declercq, Franceschelli and Galipò, Astolfo and Boano, Vandevoordt, all in this volume).

The focus on 'local host communities' and the 'national population' is understandable on policy (and political) levels in contexts of protracted displacement into urban areas. This is especially the case since integration is recognized to be a two-way process that depends on the 'readiness on the part of the receiving communities and public institutions to welcome refugees and meet the needs of a diverse community' (UNHCR, 2005; also see Declercq, and Vandevoordt, this volume). Nevertheless, the widespread reality of overlapping displacements prompts us to meaningfully recognize that newly displaced populations not only share spaces with or aim to integrate into communities of 'nationals' but also aim to do so into communities formed by refugees and/or IDPs of similar or different nationality or ethnicity (see Fiddian-Qasmiyeh 2016a, 2016b; Fiddian-Qasmiyeh and Qasmiyeh, 2018).

Ongoing cycles of displacement and the multi-directionality of movement deeply problematize the assumption that refugees are 'hosted' by settled national populations, highlighting the blurred nature of the categories of 'displaced person' and 'host' (Fiddian-Qasmiyeh and Ager, 2013; Fiddian-Qasmiyeh 2016b; Berg and Fiddian-Qasmiyeh, 2018). In some of these contexts, host communities are displaced by conflict or disaster and subsequently become 'the hosted', while in others the displaced themselves become hosts to newly displaced people (Fiddian-Qasmiyeh, 2016a, 2016b; Ramadan, 2008).

# Baddawi camp: the ambivalence of hosting

> Refugees ask other refugees, who are we to come to you and who are you to come to us? Nobody answers. Palestinians, Syrians, Iraqis, Kurds share the camp, the same-different camp, the camp of a camp. They have all come to re-originate the beginning with their own hands and feet. (Qasmiyeh, 2016 [also in this volume])

As I have noted above and elsewhere (Fiddian-Qasmiyeh, 2016a), initiatives developed by displaced people in response to protracted and new refugee situations directly challenge widely held (although equally widely contested) assumptions that refugees are passive victims in need of assistance from outsiders. My ongoing research in Baddawi camp, for instance, examines the encounters between its Palestinian residents and the increasing numbers of people from Syria with whom they now share the camp. These include not only Syrian refugees but also Palestinian, Iraqi and Kurdish refugees who had been living in Syria at the outbreak of the conflict and who have found themselves 'refugees-once-more' (Fiddian-Qasmiyeh, 2012). This encounter with refugees fleeing Syria situates Palestinians as active providers of support to others rather than as aid recipients – while, equally, reflecting the extent to which urban camps can become 'shared spaces', spaces to which 'new' refugees can head in search of safety (Qasmiyeh and Fiddian-Qasmiyeh, 2013; Fiddian-Qasmiyeh, 2016a).

Indeed, my interviewees in Baddawi repeatedly reiterated that as they fled Syria, 'we arrived in the camp' and just 'passed through Lebanon'.[4] Having crossed the Syrian–Lebanese border, they were physically on Lebanese territory and yet explained that they had travelled directly to, and arrived in, Baddawi camp, where established residents and local organizations offered them shelter, food and clothes. In many ways, the urban camp has superseded the (hyper-visible) Lebanese state, with many refugees from Syria explicitly stating that, from the very outset of their journeys, they had identified Baddawi camp as their intended destination. This is in spite of the extreme poverty and armed clashes that take place between the Palestinian factions that compete to assert their presence and/or to control different parts of the camp. While recognized as 'islands of insecurity' (Sayigh, 2000), Baddawi camp and others like it continue to be perceived by many 'new' refugees as being safer than any of the ('national'/Lebanese) spaces available outside of the existing Palestinian camps, as they are isolated from the national policies that increasingly restrict refugees from Syria in the country: *inter alia*, across Lebanon refugees from Syria face restrictions on registering for residence permits and are subjected to curfews, the demolition of their shelters and the risk of arbitrary detention and deportation to Syria (Al Jazeera, 2019).

Importantly, this is not the first time that Baddawi, as an urban camp, and its refugee inhabitants have welcomed 'new' refugees. Previous instances include the hosting of over 15,000 'new' Palestinian refugees who had been displaced from nearby Nahr el-Bared refugee camp when that camp was destroyed during the fighting between Fatah Al-Islam and the Lebanese Army in 2007 (see Qasmiyeh and Fiddian-Qasmiyeh, 2013; also see Maqusi in this volume). With an estimated 10,000 refugees from Nahr el-Bared still residing in Baddawi camp, these 'internally-displaced-refugees-hosted-by-refugees' have in turn become part of the 'established' refugee community in Baddawi hosting 'newly' displaced refugees from Syria (Fiddian-Qasmiyeh, 2016b). This demonstrates the centrality of spatial and temporal dimensions in such contexts of overlapping displacements and vulnerabilities.

As echoed in the following interview extract with a Palestinian from Nahr el-Bared camp, the current residents of Baddawi have themselves experienced complex histories of displacement *and* of hosting:

> While I was still in Nahr el-Bared Camp, my original place of residence, I hosted five Palestinian families displaced from Beirut in 2006 [during the Israeli bombardment of southern Lebanon] for a whole month.[5] We shared everything with them, the rooms of the house and the food, until they returned to their homes …

> When we left Nahr el-Bared [as a result of the destruction of the camp by the Lebanese authorities in 2007], the people poured into [Baddawi] camp in just one day and, the people here [in Baddawi] were waiting for us to lend a helping hand and to help secure shelter for us …

> [In 2012] I hosted a Syrian family in my house for fifteen days until I secured them a house of their own. I offered them food, clothes and necessary supplies during that entire period.[6]

Over the course of six years, this Palestinian man hosted six displaced families in his own home, directly experienced internal displacement and was hosted by other refugees in Baddawi camp – a clear reminder both of the precarity of many people's lives in displacement and of the diverse ways in which refugees respond to support the needs and rights of people affected by conflict and forced migration.

In addition to providing shelter and material resources – forms of assistance that are often designated as 'basic needs' by international humanitarian actors – local-level rituals are also regularly organized by, with and for different groups of camp residents. For instance, before and during Ramadan, local residents have collected *zakat* donations to prepare and distribute *iftar* food baskets with which families in need can break their fast. These donations – collected by, from and for refugees – are then distributed locally to families who are identified as having particularly precarious livelihoods in the camp, irrespective of their place of origin, legal status or how long they have lived in Baddawi: this includes long-term Palestinian Baddawi residents, internally-displaced-refugees from Nahr el-Bared camp and people from Syria alike.

## The creation of inequalities and tensions

While highlighting the relational nature of refugeedom and destabilizing the assumption that refugees are necessarily hosted or supported by citizens, the encounters characterizing refugee-refugee hosting are not to be idealized since they are also often framed by power imbalances and processes of exclusion and overt hostility by the refugee Self (the members of the 'original' refugee community) towards the refugee Other (the 'new' arrivals). In the case of Baddawi camp, these processes are further accentuated precisely by virtue of the overlapping, if temporally and spatially differentiated, experiences of displacement, dispossession and precariousness in this encounter and in the broader region.

Indeed, since 2011 Baddawi camp has become a space in which both of the United Nations' refugee agencies are present: the 'global refugee agency', the United Nations High Commissioner for Refugees (UNHCR), providing assistance and protection to all refugees from Syria *apart from* Palestinians, while the UN Relief and Works Agency (UNRWA) has a mandate to provide support *only* to Palestinian refugees – including both 'established' and 'new' Palestinian refugees in the camp. Following UNHCR's arrival in the camps, camp residents have transformed 'UNHCR' into a verb: the camps have been 'UNHCR-ized'. Through this process, Palestinians who had originally worked for UNRWA – the main employer in the camps – have shifted, when possible, to UNHCR positions, which are more highly paid (and more secure) than UNRWA roles (Fiddian-Qasmiyeh, 2019b). Palestinians who used to provide help to other Palestinians in the camp through UNRWA are now helping *Syrians* through UNHCR. Both institutions are struggling to support the needs and rights of the camp's expanding population.

In Baddawi, different groups of people who have fled the *same* conflict thus receive differing forms of assistance and different access to durable solutions depending on their nationality. On the one hand, Palestinians from Syria only receive limited assistance from UNRWA and can only access UNRWA-run educational and health services, which are increasingly underfunded and under strain (see Fiddian-Qasmiyeh, 2019b). On the other hand, non-Palestinian refugees from Syria (including Syrians, Iraqis and Kurds) are registered with UNHCR; are entitled to a wider range of services and programmes; and, most importantly for many residents in the camp, have the possibility of being referred by UNHCR to be resettled to a third country. Palestinian families who have resided in the camp since the 1950s remain stuck in the camp, observing the different forms of assistance and possible resettlement options that are officially available (even if they are not in fact provided) to new arrivals.

A number of internationally funded assistance programmes have also created tensions between different groups of people in the camp: for instance, while the arrival of people from Syria had initially led to the dynamic growth of Baddawi camp's local economy, the introduction of World Food Programme (WFP) food vouchers led to heightened concerns within the camp. This is because people from Syria holding WFP vouchers could only spend these in (Lebanese) stores *outside* of the camp, and not in Palestinian, Syrian and Kurdish-run shops *in* the camp. Such bifurcated structures and external interventions are thus *creating* tensions in this refugee camp rather than such tensions being inevitable.[7]

## Redefining response, and the poetics of undisclosed care

Indeed, in a protracted displacement situation such as that in Baddawi camp, which is characterized by extreme precarity, clearly not all residents are providing material assistance to people who have fled Syria. During his reflection on the roles that camp residents have played since his arrival in Baddawi, a 37-year-old Syrian man who has resided in the camp since 2011 shared his view that:

> I think that the biggest part of the local community *does not care about this* and their role does not transgress the limits of *observing*.[8]

While this may be because they don't 'care', another long-standing Palestinian resident of the camp explained that:

> I have not provided any assistance [to people from Syria]. I am personally in need of support, whereas the displaced people from Syria are provided with that support from many groups …

Irrespective of the presence or absence of material exchange or the 'provision' of aid, Baddawi camp residents clearly are responding in different ways – whether it is 'observing' the situation of people from Syria, 'accepting' their presence or offering 'moral support' and ensuring that their children 'are well among their foreign neighbours' – as a Kurdish refugee from Syria who has lived in Baddawi since 2012 reiterated in his interview:

> *It is enough* that they allowed us to live among them despite this great population pressure. In my view, the local community *is not interested in providing us with assistance. All they have to do is accept our presence* in these areas and *to offer us moral support*. For me, *it is enough* that my Palestinian neighbour greets me every morning and that I go to work being sure that my children *are well among their foreign neighbours* [emphasis added].

While the concept of the 'neighbour' in Arabic is an ambivalent one – demarcating proximity and charity on the one hand, and yet invoking antagonism on the other, as Yousif M. Qasmiyeh and I explore elsewhere (Fiddian-Qasmiyeh and Qasmiyeh, 2018) – what is pertinent in this context is this interviewee's usage of the phrase 'it is enough' not once but twice to refer to co-presence, everyday encounters and 'being well' in a shared space.

Here, the question of whether 'observing' without 'caring' can be conceptualized 'as' a response shifts to whether it can be viewed as an *acceptable* or *sufficient* form of response: What is the relative significance – from the perspective of different interlocutors – of the provision of material goods, spiritual support, conviviality, 'caring' and sharing space? Who determines what 'is enough' in such a situation of overlapping precarity? Is it sufficient, as Yousif M. Qasmiyeh and I have reflected elsewhere (Fiddian-Qasmiyeh and Qasmiyeh, 2018; Fiddian-Qasmiyeh, 2016a), for responses to be framed around 'being-with' and 'being-together' (following Nancy, 2000)?

In parallel with 'observing' without 'caring' is the possibility of 'caring' without being 'observed', including through what I conceptualize as the 'poetics of undisclosed care' (see Fiddian-Qasmiyeh, 2019c). In essence, a number of interviewees, when reflecting on the assistance that they *have* provided to other people – and when explaining their perspectives of how local communities *should* respond to the presence of refugees – drew attention to acts of kindness and solidarity that may be viewed as 'private' acts which should not be disclosed to others.

This private dimension of assistance, in the sense of acts undertaken discreetly, was described by one interviewee, a 31-year-old Palestinian man from Nahr el-Bared who has resided in Baddawi camp since 2007, as being 'only for God's sake':

> We collected clothes ... offered food and cash to refugees, but I hope you don't mention this except for reasons related to your research, because *we do this only for God's sake*.

In turn, a Syrian man who has lived in Baddawi camp since 2011 stated:

> Those people who offer assistance *without disclosing their names deserve respect*.

And a Kurdish man from Syria living in Baddawi camp since 2012 shared the saying:

> Be like the good tree that gives its fruits and *does not ask who took them*.

This desirability of discretion, silence and not asking questions was stressed by diverse interviewees in Lebanon, 'refugees' and 'refugee-hosts' alike, in line with the Qur'an – 'If you disclose your Sadaqaat (almsgiving), it is well; but if you conceal them and give them to the poor, that is better for you' (2.271) – and Hadith – those whom Allah will shade on the Day of Judgement include s/he ' ... who gives in charity and hides it, such that his left hand does not know what his right hand gives in charity'.

This commitment to *discreet* modes of supporting refugees is as strongly grounded in religious belief and practice as it is a powerful counterpoint to the international humanitarian system's long-standing preference for hyper-visible logos and public announcements of action.

## Conclusion

In Baddawi camp, not all people who have experienced displacement are positioned equally, nor have they been equally welcomed or had equal access to spaces, services and resources. Ultimately, while there are numerous examples of enacting solidarity and support for people displaced from Syria, it is clear that 'togetherness and being-together are not equivalent' (Nancy, 2000: 60). New hierarchies of refugeeness continue to emerge in this encounter, as do tensions – including those stimulated by the very interventions that are ostensibly developed on behalf of and to support refugees by international agencies and organizations such as the WFP, UNHCR and UNRWA.

While these hierarchies and tensions are often presented as not only common but also potentially inescapable, including through the application of the Derridean notion of *hostipitality*,[9] I would argue that these are neither inevitable nor organic. Indeed, as I have argued above, external interventions may challenge and even disrupt different forms of refugee-refugee relations – including dynamics of conviviality, solidarity and mutual support – with such interventions *creating* differences and hierarchies.

Throughout this short chapter, I have argued that it is essential to continue shifting our gaze in order to more carefully acknowledge and explore the nature and implications of refugee-refugee relationality. Doing so enables, and requires, us to acknowledge the diverse ways in which people who have been displaced not only *experience* displacement but also develop different ways of *responding* to their own situations and those of other people. Such responses include sharing space and shelter, providing material assistance and spiritual support, but also rejecting the presence of other refugees given their own conditions of precarity. Focusing on the relationship between different groups of refugees – in this case, Palestinians whose families have lived in Baddawi camp since the 1950s, internally displaced Palestinians from Nahr el-Bared camp and different groups of people who have fled the conflict in Syria – also draws attention to the ways in which external actors, including UN agencies, influence and interfere in the everyday lives of people living in displacement. As such, attention to refugee-refugee relationality must be as attentive to intersecting and overlapping processes of displacement as it is to the broader power structures and systems of inequality that refugees navigate individually and together. Far from a fatalistic approach, which presumes that hostility and tensions will arise, a focus on a range of scales and directionalities of thought and action are essential as we continue, collectively, to trace the realities of, and potential for, both 'being with' and 'being together'.

# Notes

1. This is the case in most parts of the world that are not characterized by restrictive encampment policies. See Amorós Elorduy on protracted encampment situations in the East African Rift (in this volume).
2. What I refer to as the process of overlapping displacement precisely recognizes the extent to which people continue to experience ongoing forms of vulnerability and precariousness over time – or, indeed, increased vulnerability as displacement becomes increasingly protracted, as noted by Barbelet and Wake (2017: 24).
3. An earlier version of this section of the chapter was published in Fiddian-Qasmiyeh (2016a).
4. Unless noted otherwise, all interviews were conducted by the author.
5. See Carpi (in this volume) for a discussion of NGO responses to the 2006 war.
6. This quotation – from an interview conducted by Refugee Hosts researcher and Baddawi camp resident, Mohammad Abu Iyad – and earlier iterations of the subsequent discussions on basic needs, rituals and the 'poetics of undisclosed care' originally appeared in Fiddian-Qasmiyeh (2019a).
7. Noting the extent to which external interventions, even when undertaken in a 'participatory' manner, create different forms of tensions, Perla Issa (2019: 7) draws on the case of Nahr el-Bared camp to explore the ways in which INGOs create systems of doubt and suspicion in the camp by working with 'locally recruited aid workers', who become implicated in the 'pervasive system of surveillance to monitor, evaluate, and compare residents' misery levels' introduced by INGOs 'in the name of distributing aid fairly'. Issa argues that this co-optation of local residents not only led to tensions within the camp but also 'ultimately hindered the community's ability to engage in collective political action' (ibid.).
8. This and the following extract are derived from interviews conducted by Refugee Hosts researcher and Baddawi camp resident, Mohammad Abu Iyad.
9. Jacques Derrida's notion of hostipitality *inter alia* starts from the premise that hospitality inherently bears its own opposition, the ever-present possibility of hostility towards the Other who has, at one time, been welcomed at the threshold. In this regard, the inherent conditionality of hospitality is underpinned by the paradox that to offer welcome is 'always already' to have the power to delimit the space or place that is being offered to the Other (Derrida 2000a, 2000b). For a longer, critical, discussion of hostipitality, see Fiddian-Qasmiyeh (2016a) and Fiddian-Qasmiyeh and Qasmiyeh (2018).

# References

Al Jazeera. 2019. 'Destruction of Syrian Refugees' Shelters in Lebanon Condemned', *Al Jazeera*, 5 July. Accessed 18 January 2020. www.aljazeera.com/news/2019/07/destruction-syrian-refugees-shelters-lebanon-condemned-190705102212768.html.

Barbelet, Veronique and Caitlin Wake. 2017. *Livelihoods in Displacement: From Refugee Perspectives to Aid Agency Response* (HPG Report). London: Overseas Development Institute.

Bartolomei, Linda. 2015. 'Surviving the City: Refugees from Burma in New Delhi'. In *Urban Refugees: Challenges in Protection, Services and Policy*, edited by Koichi Koizumi and Gerhard Hoffstaedter, 139–63. London: Routledge.

Berg, Mette Louise and Elena Fiddian-Qasmiyeh. 2018. 'Introduction to the Issue: Encountering Hospitality and Hostility', *Migration and Society* 1 (1): 1–6.

Black, R. and K. Koser, eds. 1999. *The End of the Refugee Cycle? Refugee Repatriation and Reconstruction*. Oxford: Berghahn Books.

Brown, Neil R., Sean Riordan and Marina Sharpe. 2004. 'The Insecurity of Eritreans and Ethiopians in Cairo', *International Journal of Refugee Law* 16 (4): 661–701.

Buscher, Dale. 2011. 'New Approaches to Urban Refugee Livelihoods', *Refuge* 28 (2): 17–29.

Derrida, Jacques. 2000a. *Of Hospitality: Anne Dufourmantelle Invites Jacques Derrida to Respond*, translated by Rachel Bowlby. Stanford: Stanford University Press.

Derrida, Jacques. 2000b. 'Hostipitality', translated by Barry Stocker and Forbes Morlock, *Angelaki: Journal of the Theoretical Humanities* 5 (3): 3–18.

Fiddian-Qasmiyeh, Elena. 2012. 'Invisible Refugees and/or Overlapping Refugeedom? Protecting Sahrawis and Palestinians Displaced by the 2011 Libyan Uprising', *International Journal of Refugee Law* 24 (2): 263–93.

Fiddian-Qasmiyeh, Elena. 2013. 'Inter-Generational Negotiations of Religious Identity, Belief and Practice: Child, Youth and Adult Perspectives from Three Cities'. In *Rescripting Religion in the City: Migration and Religious Identity in the Modern Metropolis*, edited by Jane Garnett and Alana Harris, 163–76. Farnham: Ashgate Publishing.

Fiddian-Qasmiyeh, Elena. 2016a. 'Refugee–Refugee Relations in Contexts of Overlapping Displacement', *International Journal of Urban and Regional Research*. Accessed 18 January 2020. www.ijurr.org/spotlight-on/the-urban-refugee-crisis-reflections-on-cities-citizenship-and-the-displaced/refugee-refugee-relations-in-contexts-of-overlapping-displacement/.

Fiddian-Qasmiyeh, Elena. 2016b. 'Representations of Displacement from the Middle East and North Africa', *Public Culture* 28 (3): 457–73.

Fiddian-Qasmiyeh, Elena. 2019a. 'Looking Forward: *Disasters* at 40', *Disasters* 43 (S1): S36–60.

Fiddian-Qasmiyeh, Elena. 2019b. 'The Changing Faces of UNRWA: From the Global to the Local', *Journal of Humanitarian Affairs* 1 (1): 28–41.

Fiddian-Qasmiyeh, Elena. 2019c. 'The Poetics of Undisclosed Care', *Refugee Hosts*, 21 May. Accessed 18 January 2020. https://refugeehosts.org/2019/05/21/the-poetics-of-undisclosed-care/.

Fiddian-Qasmiyeh, Elena. 2019d. 'Memories and Meanings of Refugee Camps (and More-Than-Camps)'. In *Refugee Imaginaries: Research across the Humanities*, edited by Emma Cox, Sam Durrant, David Farrier, Lyndsey Stonebridge and Agnes Woolley. Edinburgh: Edinburgh University Press, 289–310.

Fiddian-Qasmiyeh, Elena and Alastair Ager, eds. 2013. *Local Faith Communities and the Promotion of Resilience in Humanitarian Situations: A Scoping Study* (Working Paper 90). Oxford: Refugee Studies Centre.

Fiddian-Qasmiyeh, Elena and Yousif M. Qasmiyeh. 2010. 'Muslim Asylum-Seekers and Refugees: Negotiating Identity, Politics and Religion in the UK', *Journal of Refugee Studies* 23 (3): 294–314.

Fiddian-Qasmiyeh, Elena and Yousif M. Qasmiyeh. 2018. 'Refugee Neighbours and Hostipitality', *Refugee Hosts*, 20 March. Accessed 18 January 2020. https://refugeehosts.org/2018/03/20/refugee-neighbours-hostipitality/.

Issa, Perla. 2019. 'Fracturing Communities: Aid Distribution in a Palestinian Refugee Camp', *Journal of Palestine Studies* 48 (3): 7–20.

Lyytinen, Eveliina. 2015. 'The Politics of Mistrust: Congolese Refugees and the Institutions Providing Refugee Protection in Kampala, Uganda'. In *Urban Refugees: Challenges in Protection, Services and Policy*, edited by Koichi Koizumi and Gerhard Hoffstaedter, 76–97. London: Routledge.

Malkki, Liisa H. 1995. *Purity and Exile: Violence, Memory, and National Cosmology among Hutu Refugees in Tanzania*. Chicago: University of Chicago Press.

Nancy, Jean-Luc. 2000. *Being Singular Plural*. Stanford: Stanford University Press.

Qasmiyeh, Yousif M. 2016. 'Writing the Camp: Vis-à-vis or a Camp', *Refugee Hosts*, 30 September. Accessed 9 January 2020. https://refugeehosts.org/2016/09/30/writing-the-camp/.

Qasmiyeh, Yousif M. and Elena Fiddian-Qasmiyeh. 2013. 'Refugee Camps and Cities in Conversation'. In *Rescripting Religion in the City: Migration and Religious Identity in the Modern Metropolis*, edited by Jane Garnett and Alana Harris, 131–43. Farnham: Ashgate Publishing.

Ramadan, Adam. 2008. 'The Guests' Guests: Palestinian Refugees, Lebanese Civilians, and the War of 2006', *Antipode* 40 (4): 658–77.

Sanyal, Romola. 2014. 'Urbanizing Refuge: Interrogating Spaces of Displacement', *International Journal of Urban and Regional Research* 38 (2): 558–72.

Sayigh, Rosemary. 2000. 'Greater Insecurity for Refugees in Lebanon', *Middle East Report Online*, 1 March. Accessed 23 January 2020. https://merip.org/2000/03/greater-insecurity-for-refugees-in-lebanon/.

UNHCR (United Nations High Commissioner for Refugees). 2005. *Local Integration and Self-Reliance* (EC/55/SC/CRP.15). Geneva: United Nations High Commissioner for Refugees. Accessed 23 January 2020. www.unhcr.org/afr/excom/standcom/42a0054f2/local-integration-self-reliance.html.

## 27
# Different shades of 'neutrality': Arab Gulf NGO responses to Syrian refugees in northern Lebanon

Estella Carpi

## Introduction

This chapter explores different forms of humanitarian-assistance provision to refugees living in northern Lebanon and argues that aid provision cannot be explained by what is commonly known as a binary between 'apolitical humanitarianism' and 'political humanitarianism'. The Dunantist[1] approach to humanitarianism maintains that actors must conceal their political aims and intentions, and present themselves as holding no contextual interests (De Chaine, 2002: 363). However, it has often been assumed that it is impossible for state and non-state aid providers from 'the Global South' to uphold the humanitarian principles of impartiality and neutrality – that is, respectively, the principles of responding according to people's needs and of not taking sides in a conflict in order to make decisions independently (Mačák, 2015: 161).

In this chapter, I do not aim to trace whether it is empirically feasible or impossible to maintain neutrality and impartiality in the provision of aid in crisis situations.[2] Instead, I specifically seek to question what neutrality – even when employed as a rhetorical device – is able to engender at a societal level and in relations between aid actors and recipients in contexts of crisis management. To do so, I first show how different humanitarian models are based on nuanced understandings and practices of neutrality in northern Lebanon.[3] In this framework, I mark out the peculiarity of what I call a form of 'political realism' embraced by Arab Gulf-funded NGOs in Lebanon. I argue that political realism unravels different shades of the neutrality mantra, which, in turn, is far from merely being the vessel of 'Northern' humanitarianism.

To investigate the nuanced character of what Mark Cutts (1998: 7) refers to as 'operational neutrality' – that is, the attempt made by NGOs to enhance a *perception* of neutrality – in areas of humanitarian intervention, I draw on the aftermath of the July 2006 war between Lebanon and Israel, and the arrival of Syrian refugees in the villages of Akkar (a region in North Lebanon). Between 2011 and 2013, I conducted in-depth interviews and participant observation with Syrian refugees who had fled violence and political persecution in Syria. I also draw upon ethnographic research that I conducted with two groups of aid workers and NGO leaders. The first group included representatives of secular local and international NGOs: the Lebanese Amel Association, UNHCR, the Norwegian Refugee Council and the Danish Refugee Council. The second comprised representatives of Arab Gulf-funded NGOs overtly inspired by Islamic values, even though not all are officially registered as 'faith-based organizations': the Kuwaiti Association, the Qatari Initiative and the Saudi Taiba. At the time of fieldwork, all of these NGOs predominantly provided food, shelter, medical assistance and education in North Lebanon. Different Arab Gulf countries pursue diversified politics of aid in the region: in this chapter, I discuss their politics in relation to their own neutrality discourse and practices. All names used in this chapter are pseudonyms.

I start by demonstrating that the principle of neutrality not only plays a different role across different models of implementing humanitarian action but is also differently conceived of by various stakeholders. Departing from Jonathan Darling's definition of depoliticization (2014: 74) – that is, a set of tendencies and alliances that produces and maintains particular perceptual orientations – I aim to illustrate how Geneva-born humanitarianism, in the northern-Lebanese context, seeks to produce depoliticization as an actual condition for beneficiaries, which can better guarantee refugees' survival and their recovery from crisis. In contrast, Arab Gulf NGOs are viewed as adopting the framework of neutrality in order to produce a specific process of politicization, yet with means that are considered to be internationally accountable.

## Analysing neutrality on the ground: Beyond the logic of failures and successes

An expanding body of literature highlights the extent to which politics and religion have intertwined in various ways throughout the history of humanitarianism (Fiddian-Qasmiyeh, 2011; Zaman, 2012; Ager and

Ager, 2015; Carpi and Fiddian-Qasmiyeh, 2020). When war-affected people identify themselves as members of faith communities, they often tend to express their aims and motivations for responding to displacement through the use of religious language – which secular donors may associate with a religious agenda (Kraft and Smith, 2019). With religion being seen as a particularly powerful marker of identity in the crisis discourse (Wagenvoorde, 2017), secular Northern humanitarians often assume that faith-based acts of assistance are ill-placed to implement humanitarian neutrality and impartiality (Ferris, 2011). However, concern over promoting ideologies and world views to beneficiaries through the provision of aid is not limited to religious groups, since secular donors may also exercise their power over local communities (Lynch and Schwartz, 2016: 6–7, cited in Kraft and Smith, 2019: 39) or may believe in a civilizing mission vis-à-vis the people whom they assist.

In this context, international non-governmental organizations (INGOs) uphold different shades of neutrality, and yet the diverse ways in which neutrality plays out in INGO and NGO responses has received scant attention from scholars or even humanitarian peers.[4] Indeed, throughout my interviews with aid workers it transpired that, except for practitioners who neglect or oppose the official ideologies of the NGOs for which they work in war-affected areas, political neutrality and impartiality are often regarded as implementable and desirable on a practical level – or even as the only possible way to conduct humanitarian work in what are known as 'complex emergencies'. Several events in humanitarian history, however, have demonstrated that not all international humanitarian agencies intend to or do in fact *remain* apolitical on the ground.

Among the most telling examples, in 1994 the medical NGO, Doctors Without Borders (Médecins Sans Frontières, MSF), took a clear stance in the Rwandan genocide by denouncing the French Government's continued support of the Hutu regime (Groves, 2008). Similarly, and more recently, emergency food aid to Syria has unintentionally assisted the Assad regime by channelling most assistance through government-approved organizations. As a result, according to some experts (Martínez and Eng, 2015), foreign donors have helped Bashar Al-Assad's regime to fulfil the function of welfare provider and to pursue its military efforts by reducing expenditure on food distribution.

In such circumstances, neutrality turns into mere public rhetoric or the metaphysical ideal of philanthropists who purport to be neutral and impartial in their interventions. Nonetheless, the neutrality discourse *does* more than that. For instance, it can provide the foundations for negotiation between different warring parties, since the principles of impartiality and neutrality can, on the level of diplomacy, be compatible with conflict resolution.

Following the genealogy of international assistance, neutrality and humanitarianism have intertwined in the following two ways (Duffield, 2014). According to advocates of so-called 'apolitical' or 'prophetic' humanitarianism – which rests on the prophecy of rescuing lives and alleviating human suffering at any cost (Duffield, 2014: 76–82) – assistance must be seen as just and ethical in itself. Conversely, since the 1990s, according to proponents of a 'political' or 'new' humanitarianism, the just and ethical have, rather, become an *outcome* of assistance: this implies that the most just or ethical course of action may be withdrawing from providing aid. In essence, by refraining from supporting any side in a conflict, humanitarianism has gradually become an arm of politics and governance: yet another force to transform social order and public spaces. In this framework, some aid providers regard relief as the sole and ultimate end (when assistance is approached as 'prophetic'), while 'new humanitarians' (Duffield, 2014: 75) view aid as an instrument to promote social justice and rights.

Although such a relationship between humanitarianism and politics seems to be twofold, the tension does not merely lie between those actors who want to eradicate the underlying causes that make their beneficiaries vulnerable and those who limit their actions to alleviate human suffering. 'Operational neutrality' (Cutts, 1998: 7) is one of the factors that can reveal a much more complex picture of humanitarian neutrality than hitherto appreciated. It highlights how politics is discussed in humanitarian language and how it is also entangled in humanitarian practices. Specifically, operational neutrality aims to enhance our very *perception* of dealing with a neutral actor, rather than aiming to adopt neutrality in a deceiving manner as a standalone modality of aid management and policymaking.

It should be noted that the lines between NGO official ideologies and the ways in which aid workers imagine humanitarian neutrality remain blurred.[5] While international NGO workers act through the values of neutrality and impartiality – using them as a personal and professional drive and an aspiration tool – INGOs' neutrality politics vary considerably. While INGOs' neutrality rhetoric is mostly assumed to secure access to local beneficiaries by gaining the trust of local authorities and building up self-legitimacy, there is a common belief that Arab Gulf NGOs merely use neutrality to cloak political competition with a moral aura. Furthermore, NGOs that are (or are assumed to be) inspired by

Islamic – and, more generally, religious – values are often believed to have an inherently problematic relationship with neutrality (Ferris, 2011: 618).

My aim here is not to delegitimize all kinds of humanitarian action by ascribing to it mere political motivations. Instead, I intend to highlight the fact that these diverse – yet shared – humanitarian discourses of neutrality have not yet led local and international, secular and religious NGOs to achieve a common ground of communication and a deeper form of mutual knowledge.

## The multi-purposed survival of 'prophetic humanitarianism': Neutrality as an imperative ideal

While viewing Lebanon as a chessboard on which identity politics defines geographical and demographic spaces, specific factors bias the conditionality of aid provision and the implementation of neutrality and impartiality agendas. These factors include the provider's geographical location, the political origin of funding sources, the way in which funding is channelled and allocated, and the political orientation of humanitarian staff.

In this section, I provide different examples from local and international NGOs throughout Lebanon to show the diverse strategies that are employed to uphold standards of neutrality, while resorting to different understandings and configurations of neutrality. In spite of the ideological variety of NGOs' original manifestos, most of the INGOs that I interviewed in Akkar seek to uphold neutrality standards by refusing to address beneficiaries who are in some way involved with the political parties at war, and instead search for the 'ideal refugee' (following Fiddian-Qasmiyeh, 2010) who epitomizes the expectations of donors and aid providers.

Among the few large-sized local NGOs operating in the area, some have branches in different political spaces. For example, Amel Association,[6] while not operating in northern Lebanon, used to have a branch in 'Arsal (Beqaa Valley), where one of the informal bases of the Free Syrian Army (opposing the Syrian Government) was said to be located. At the same time, this NGO had a large branch in Haret Hreik, known as the urban heart of the Lebanese political party Hezbollah, which is the major local ruler and an ally of the Syrian regime. In our interview, Amel representatives often referred to the political diversity that exists in its territories of intervention in order to promote its accomplished strategies of 'political neutrality'. In contrast, Arab Gulf donors have largely funded the post-2006 reconstruction of Hezbollah-led South Lebanon (Barakat and Zyck, 2010), but they generally have not established branches in the south of the country.

Financial independence also constitutes one of the main avenues to obtaining operational neutrality. With regard to this aspect, an NGO worker from the Qatari Initiative operating in Wadi Khaled (Akkar)[7] argued that 'Unlike other NGOs, Qatar does not need to get money from anyone else. This allows the government as well as our NGO to make its own choices.' In a similar vein, the Norwegian Refugee Council does not accept funds from the US Government[8] for reasons of 'political sensitivity'; however, it welcomes financial support from other foreign governments – especially the European Community Humanitarian Office (ECHO), which aims to provide aid and civil protection. In turn, the latter seeks financial independence so as to not depend on the finances of UN agencies.

In sum, neutrality can be defined as an enhanced moral status gained by being funded by either NGOs or Islamic charities rather than by foreign governments, which would be too openly political. As a further example, the Lebanese leader of the Tripoli-based Kuwaiti Association[9] highlighted the association's financial independence from Kuwaiti politics, 'as [its] funding comes from NGOs that are located in Kuwait City rather than the Kuwaiti government'.

INGOs in Akkar also pursue operational neutrality by avoiding cash-in-hand policies and by providing payments to house owners to host refugees for a limited period of time.[10] Contrary to such politics of neutrality, which imply cash restrictions for beneficiaries – also including several Arab Gulf donors – the Saudi Taiba, previously located in Halba,[11] overtly embraced political and pragmatic realism by directly giving cash to refugees. Cash-in-hand programmes are considered to be a quick – although temporary – path to self-reliance, which has only recently been recognized as a dignity tool worldwide (Lehmann and Masterson, 2014; Harvey and Bailey, 2015: 2). Adopted in the first instance by the Saudi NGO in Akkar, cash-in-hand programmes are now increasingly promoted across the broader framework of international aid providers working on livelihoods in Lebanon.

A further avenue through which international aid providers pursue operational neutrality is by hiring humanitarian staff who supposedly hold different political opinions and orientations. Indeed, the majority of the secular INGO representatives whom I interviewed in Akkar in 2012 and 2013 stated that a small number of their workers tend to support the Syrian regime. However, they specified that all NGO workers are expected – and, indeed, requested – not to share their own political opinions in the workplace, in order to comply with apolitical humanitarianism.

In the framework of the presence of Syrian refugees in Akkar's villages since 2011, beneficiaries do not view neutrality as a key behavioural value but rather as hypocritical in nature.[12] In spite of different NGOs embodying differing approaches to neutrality, beneficiaries develop their own understanding of neutrality – within which their emotional and political reactions emerge. For instance, homogeneous forms of NGO neutrality discourses are perceived on the local level as a tacit strategy to uphold the legitimacy of the Assad regime – and thus, as part of a system that does not intend to eradicate the very source of the conflict and generalized violence. This also resonates in the words of a Syrian refugee interviewee:

> They [the staff of an INGO in Halba] said their role is not taking sides when I asked for medication. I have a maimed hand, as you can see … I was fighting in the Free Syrian Army. That's why they don't want to help me. It's because they still want Bashar [al-Assad] to be my president! This is the bitter truth.[13]

Aside from political neutrality being unrealistic in the encounter between humanitarian action and conflict processes, in this chapter I seek to question whether NGOs are able to use operational neutrality to provide a ground for future negotiations and rapprochements between warring parties or even to manage antagonism between humanitarian counterparts. Against this backdrop, what have NGOs' apolitical rhetoric and operational neutrality produced on a societal level within refugee and local communities in the villages of Akkar? Distress and increased fear and anxiety within the refugee community were often the response to such a 'discrepancy between environmental pressures and organisational culture' (Barnett, 2005: 728). The words of Ahmed,[14] a Syrian refugee relocated to the rural hamlet of Belanet al-Hisa, are meaningful in this regard: 'We don't want food and shelter to survive in Lebanon; we want you to help us to stop all this.' This invocation directly undermines the cornerstones of 'minimalist' humanitarian neutrality (Weiss, 1999), which never sides with the crisis-stricken victims but merely seeks to *heal* them and which, despite an evolution towards 'political humanitarianism', still predominate in the contemporary philosophy of humanitarian-aid provision.

## Political realism as a complex form of 'new humanitarianism'

Scholars have noticed the depoliticization of Muslim NGOs' work in recent years, in all likelihood as a result of NGOs being under pressure to adopt less overtly religious approaches to humanitarian endeavours (Wigger, 2005). In the ongoing Syrian humanitarian situation, while most INGOs still resort to operational neutrality as a way of cultivating international accountability, the representatives of NGOs funded by Arab Gulf countries whom I interviewed in Halba (Akkar) and the Lebanese city of Tripoli in 2012 and 2013 openly declared that they have started programmes that aim to support Syrian political opponents fleeing into Lebanon, thereby assuming a 'maximalist' stance (Weiss, 1999). More specifically, the Saudi Islamic organization Taiba and the Kuwaiti Association claimed to have been the first to establish systematic assistance programmes for refugees (from April 2011 onwards), and also the first to intervene to assist the war-stricken during the July 2006 war that Israel waged against Lebanon and, in particular, the country's Hezbollah-held areas.

This elucidation is meaningful due to the antithetical political stance of Arab Gulf countries on this matter: the Israel–Lebanon conflict was mainly experienced-Hezbollah leading the so-called March 8 Alliance, which has long supported the Syrian regime's presence in Lebanon (1976–2005) and inside Syria during the Syrian conflict (2011–). Likewise, Qatar and Saudi Arabia, currently at odds with each other in regional politics, both fund the 'Coalition of Charitable Organisations' (*I'tilaf al-Jam'aiyyat al-Khairiyye*) (Schmelter, 2019: 6), which coordinates the majority of Islamic local NGOs in Lebanon.

During our interviews, most of the beneficiaries of international and local NGOs expressed their desire for politically engaged and consequence-focused humanitarianism, such as clear-cut acts of support and advocacy that go beyond the mere provision of medical relief and social assistance. In other words, the only desire expressed by the beneficiaries whom I interviewed is that humanitarian actors help them renormalize their lives through international solidarity and action. Notwithstanding, this is commonly believed to come at the expense of a blatantly biased selection of beneficiaries.

The Gulf-funded NGOs that I researched in Akkar and Tripoli were explicit in their intention of providing relief to Syrians in order to support the anti-regime cause, therefore backing the Syrian opposition and bearing witness to the refugees' suffering. This form of humanitarianism was considered to be openly partisan, and, as such, it was harshly criticized by international and local NGO workers. Political humanitarianism is rooted in – and acts on – the grounds of practical and political consequences, and is still perceived as the antithesis of Geneva-born international neutrality, which is often deemed the worldwide upholder of good governance par excellence in times of conflict. This form of 'new' humanitarianism relies on realistic ways of operating – namely, by recognizing its own active role in crises – and it even elevates what I call 'political realism' – which here involves taking the victims' side – to a moral standard.

However, by diplomatically complying with either apolitical or political humanitarianism, secular and faith-based NGOs in northern Lebanon still mobilize their morality as a way in which to either counter or support the political agendas of other (in)formal actors. To provide an example, the July 2006 war became an opportunity for state and non-state actors alike to gain international as well as regional accountability by supporting the reconstruction efforts of the Hezbollah-led March 8 coalition across Lebanon. Similarly, the aid providers commonly known to be close to the opposing March 14 coalition,[15] which was led by Saad Hariri's al-Mustaqbal party, are now believed to be the political entity most heavily involved in the provision of aid to Syrians because of their political aim of toppling Assad's regime in Syria. According to members of the March 14-oriented NGOs whom I interviewed – mostly funded by Arab Gulf countries – the political realism of providing assistance in situations of conflict and displacement is not only unavoidable but also morally desirable.

Such an overt politicization of aid is, however, legitimized by declarations of good intentionality on the basis of philanthropic acts. Indeed, in this hybrid scenario, which is neither exclusively apolitical nor political, aid is adopted as a quick strategy to show or discard the impartial humaneness of certain political parties, confessional groups or NGOs close to the so-called March 14 Alliance. Providers who embrace political realism, like the representatives of the Arab Gulf NGOs whom I interviewed, generally do not disguise their political agenda but, as outlined above, hasten to point out that they do not merely intervene in line with political interests. Consequently, the ambivalence generated by their layered rhetoric and clear-cut stance regarding intervention complicates the notion of humanitarian neutrality, therefore wavering between apparent 'prophetic/apolitical humanitarianism' and 'new/political humanitarianism'.

In the contemporary proliferation of humanitarian programmes in Lebanon, the political seems to be accepted as long as it is exhibited with its moral face. Local politics, experienced as a constant source of instability and immorality, is a common historical denominator. As such, politics in Lebanon paradoxically constitutes a historical problem that needs to be fought and defeated, but that can scarcely be changed.

In essence, Arab Gulf-promoted humanitarianism drops neutrality as a moral standard while making the political moral. Furthermore, it indicates different shades of operational neutrality. Diverting attention from the successes and failures of humanitarian neutrality, the Geneva-born international humanitarian agencies aspire to be held accountable by their beneficiaries by embracing impartiality and asserting political neutrality. Conversely, Arab Gulf-funded NGOs overtly share their political aims while ensuring that their own practices *are not* perceived by their beneficiaries and other aid actors as neutral. However, at the same time, Arab Gulf-funded NGOs still present their intentions for providing aid as unconditionally humane. As an example, while the Qatari Initiative[16] remarks that its present work in the Syrian crisis is comparable with the assistance that they provided in the July 2006 war, it still acknowledges that the way in which they allocate aid provision normally reflects Qatar's foreign policy:

> Hezbollah's victory in the July war and an eventually successful regime change in Syria would represent two opposing regional scenarios. We intervened in both cases. Yet Qatar implements its humanitarian practices independently of political circumstances. However, it's *normal* that aid provision seeks to further the foreign policy of any state: at the time of the July war, Qatar needed to play a greater role in regional politics. At present, in the capacity of an established political actor, it would rather pursue goals that better suit its own domestic politics [my emphasis].

In summary, advocates of political realism in Akkar's villages consider humanitarianism to be a distinct and valuable form of politics, according to which the very ideology of political neutrality is unethical and impeachable. Although they can still be defined as 'solidarists' (Weiss, 1999), identifying totally with the victims and conveying their own political projects through assistance to the latter, they cannot be classified simplistically under the banner of 'new humanitarianism' (Prendergast, 1996: 42). In fact, these NGOs resort to more complex forms of neutrality discourses: while they aim to prevent external perceptions of dealing with a neutral actor in order for their practices to be deemed successful, they still resort to the rhetoric of impartial humaneness and neutrality to moralize their politics and to negotiate their own place within the arena of international aid. Arab Gulf-funded NGOs in Akkar instead reject operational neutrality in managing their political relations with beneficiaries, while mostly operating outside of the UN coordination system and rarely looking for partnerships. They likewise protect specific social groups in order to accommodate their own local politics of resource allocation.

It is by now evident that moral demands have increasingly populated the international and domestic political space. The ethical configuration of politics and the political character of humanitarian action are now widely recognized. Nevertheless, it is still worth researching how the interaction between ethics and politics impacts on Lebanese – and, in this case, Syrian – society. While the beneficiary, representing the ideal polity of the provider, becomes an a priori deserving member of humanity in 'prophetic humanitarianism', the beneficiary is recognized as 'human' only when adhering to a specific political partisanship in 'political realism'. On the one hand, prophetic humanitarianism deprives the victim subject of any political dimension and expects them to be apolitical. On the other, political realism expects the subject to be filled with social and political motivations that best correspond to its own primary purpose – which is, however, conveyed as humane to the wider public. Both tendencies, while showing an apparent polarization of humanitarian action, try to preserve the sociopolitical order that suits the desire to survive as a successful humanitarian actor.

## Imperative neutrality and political realism: Effects on the ground?

While contemporary humanitarian accounts show that apolitical humanitarianism is seen internationally as the norm for a large segment of INGOs in Lebanon and worldwide, Arab Gulf-funded NGOs seem to pursue political advocacy through aid provision. My interviewees have, however, emphasized how the latter explicitly aim to support the cause embodied by displaced Syrians while seeking to rhetorically 'humanize' their political agendas.

NGOs close to the two major political orientations in Lebanon – identified above as the March 8 and March 14 coalitions, in place since 2005 – increasingly promote their moral intentions of serving humanity through aid provision. Predominant attempts to 'humanize' politics enable humanitarian and political actors to enhance their accountability in international and regional politics. Nevertheless, such attempts remain ineffective before the widespread domestic disaffection of political and religious institutions in Lebanon. If neutrality is universally proven to endure as a strong rhetoric with which to campaign for humaneness and morality, it has so far failed as a device in crisis management, being unable to enhance coordination and effectiveness on the ground. Furthermore, it has brought no benefit in relation to regional protracted political failures, which underlie Lebanon's increasingly protracted emergencies.

Since the start of the Syrian crisis in 2011, both the prophetic and the overtly partisan NGO-ization of northern Lebanon have contributed to the political polarization of the country, through which the crisis has been misleadingly understood and approached. On the one hand, the neutral language developed by international actors – while supposedly bringing in 'good governance' without the aim of changing societies – ends up preserving the mistrusted political elites in Lebanon. On the other hand, partisan language inherently fosters and supports the cause of the social groups to whom it is addressed, who, in turn, must reflect the provider's political expectations and desires in order to be assisted.

Operational neutrality is often believed to positively contribute to peace negotiations or the avoidance of conflict but, as my fieldwork has shown, it has instead exacerbated people's mistrust of Lebanese institutions. Thus far, neutrality has seemed to be failing as a diplomatic instrument intended to expedite peace through aid provision in Lebanon's crises: it is, instead, employed in moral campaigns as a further political token of conflict and competition between international, regional and local actors. The widespread politicization of aid and the humanization of politics that I have traced above question Lebanon's political scenario as an arena of bipolar power circuits – simplified as the pro-Assad March 8 and the anti-Assad March 14 coalitions – that variously enact political competition along with competition over ethical values.

## Conclusion

Humanitarian and political actors in northern Lebanon adopt diverse strategies to bring humanity into politics and politics into humanitarianism. While prophetic/apolitical humanitarianism has traditionally been opposed to new/political humanitarianism, the Lebanese scenario of humanitarian provision appears far more hybrid and muddled than this binary model suggests. As illustrated in this chapter, international humanitarian actors deal in different ways with the recognition of their political consequences on the ground. Furthermore, Arab Gulf-funded NGOs adopt hybrid strategies of neutrality, seemingly complying with the Global North's standards of humanitarianism while simultaneously embracing political realism. As much as neutrality, the idea of 'being human' is used as a token of accountability by all humanitarian actors, while mostly secular – and mostly 'Northern' – actors have remained the ones that define what the very paradigms of humanitarian neutrality are.

Such a symbiosis of ethics and politics makes it challenging to identify the fluctuating dynamics of rapprochement between different political actors in Lebanon. The variegated prism of neutrality therefore gives birth to a hybrid arena of political competition that, by becoming *moral*, goes far beyond the simplistic binaries of Lebanese political tactics of power, accountability and survival.

## Notes

1. Henry Dunant was the founder of the Red Cross, a movement marked by neutrality and independence from governments. In modern humanitarianism, it is held that relief provision and politics should remain separate.
2. For a discussion – from the perspective of international and national law and migration policy – of how states justify and enact (non-)responses in humanitarian settings, see Wilde (this volume).
3. For analyses of refugees' encounters with diverse actors – including refugees of different nationalities and host governments – elsewhere in Lebanon, see the contributions in this volume by Qasmiyeh, Maqusi, and Fiddian-Qasmiyeh.
4. Skype conversation with Juliano Fiori, Head of the Humanitarian Affairs Team at Save the Children UK, 28 April 2017.
5. On the different strategies used by INGOs to promote support for LGBTI asylum seekers in the UK, see Raboin (this volume).
6. Interview with a staff member, 3 January 2013.
7. Interview conducted in Tripoli, Lebanon, 18 December 2012.
8. The Norwegian Refugee Council also receives funds from the United Nations High Commissioner for Refugees (UNHCR), which is, in turn, financed by Australia, Japan, the Arab Gulf, the US and the EU. Interview with the Program Support Manager in Lebanon, Beirut, 21 November 2012.
9. Interview conducted in Tripoli, Lebanon, 14 January 2013.
10. Interview with Danish Refugee Council (DRC) and UNHCR, al-Qobaiyat, February 2013.
11. Interview conducted on 14 December 2012.
12. Interview with Syrian refugees in Belanet al-Hisa and Halba (Akkar), March 2012.
13. Interview conducted with Hisham, a Syrian refugee and ex-Free Syrian Army combatant, Al-'Abdeh, 24 December 2012.
14. Interview conducted on 8 January 2013.
15. The March 8 and March 14 coalitions took their names from the dates of the demonstrations organized in 2005, which were respectively in support of and in opposition to the Syrian Army's presence in Lebanon. The so-called *Pax Syriana*, indeed, was supposedly meant to ensure the endurance of peace in Lebanon after the Ta'ef Agreements that concluded the Lebanese Civil War (1975–89/90).
16. Interview conducted in Tripoli, Lebanon, 18 December 2012.

# References

Ager, Alastair and Joey Ager. 2015. *Faith, Secularism, and Humanitarian Engagement: Finding the Place of Religion in the Support of Displaced Communities*. New York: Palgrave Macmillan.

Barakat, Sultan and Steven A. Zyck. 2010. *Gulf State Assistance to Conflict-Affected Environments*. London: Centre for the Study of Global Governance.

Barnett, Michael. 2005. 'Humanitarianism Transformed', *Perspectives on Politics* 3 (4): 723–40.

Carpi, Estella and Elena Fiddian-Qasmiyeh. 2020. 'Keeping the Faith? Examining the Roles of Faith and Secularism in Syrian Diaspora Organizations in Lebanon'. In *Diaspora Organizations in International Affairs*, edited by Dennis Dijkzeul and Margit Fauser. New York: Routledge, 129–49.

Ciro Martínez, José and Brent Eng. 2016. 'The Unintended Consequences of Emergency Food Aid: Neutrality, Sovereignty and Politics in the Syrian Civil War, 2012–15', *International Affairs* 92 (1): 153–73.

Cutts, Mark. 1998. 'Politics and Humanitarianism', *Refugee Survey Quarterly* 17 (1): 1–15.

Darling, Jonathan. 2014. 'Asylum and the Post-Political: Domopolitics, Depoliticisation and Acts of Citizenship', *Antipode* 46 (1): 72–91.

DeChaine, D. Robert. 2002. 'Humanitarian Space and the Social Imaginary: Médecins Sans Frontières/Doctors Without Borders and the Rhetoric of Global Community', *Journal of Communication Inquiry* 26 (4): 354–69.

Duffield, Mark. 2014. *Global Governance and the New Wars: The Merging of Development and Security*. London: Zed Books.

Ferris, Elizabeth. 2011. 'Faith and Humanitarianism: It's Complicated', *Journal of Refugee Studies* 24 (3): 606–25.

Fiddian-Qasmiyeh, Elena. 2010. '"Ideal" Refugee Women and Gender Equality Mainstreaming in the Sahrawi Refugee Camps: "Good Practice" for Whom?', *Refugee Survey Quarterly* 29 (2): 64–84.

Fiddian-Qasmiyeh, Elena. 2011. 'The Pragmatics of Performance: Putting "Faith" in Aid in the Sahrawi Refugee Camps', *Journal of Refugee Studies* 24 (3): 533–47.

Fiddian-Qasmiyeh, Elena. 2014. *The Ideal Refugees: Gender, Islam, and the Sahrawi Politics of Survival*. Syracuse, NY: Syracuse University Press.

Groves, Adam. 2008. 'NGOs in New Wars: Neutrality or New Humanitarianism?', *E-International Relations*, 15 March. Accessed 12 January 2020. www.e-ir.info/2008/03/15/ngos-in-new-wars-neutrality-or-new-humanitarianism/.

Harvey, Paul and Sarah Bailey. 2015. *Cash Transfer Programming and the Humanitarian System: Background Note for the High Level Panel on Humanitarian Cash Transfers*. London: Overseas Development Institute.

Kraft, Kathryn and Jonathan D. Smith. 2019. 'Between international donors and local faith communities: Intermediaries in humanitarian assistance to Syrian refugees in Jordan and Lebanon,' *Disasters* 43 (1): 24–45. Accessed 10 March 2020. https://doi.org/10.1111/disa.12301.

Lehmann, Christian and Daniel Masterson. 2014. *Emergency Economies: The Impact of Cash Assistance in Lebanon*. New York: International Rescue Committee.

Mačák, Kubo. 2015. 'A Matter of Principle(s): The Legal Effect of Impartiality and Neutrality on States as Humanitarian Actors', *International Review of the Red Cross* 97 (897/898): 157–81.

Prendergast, John. 1996. *Frontline Diplomacy: Humanitarian Aid and Conflict in Africa*. Boulder, CO: Lynne Rienner Publishers.

Schmelter, Susanne. 2019. 'Gulf States' Humanitarian Assistance for Syrian Refugees in Lebanon'. Accessed 12 January 2020. https://civilsociety-centre.org/paper/gulf-states%E2%80%99-humanitarian-assistance-syrian-refugees-lebanon.

Wagenvoorde, Renée. 2017. 'How Religion and Secularism (Don't) Matter in the Refugee Crisis'. In *The Refugee Crisis and Religion: Secularism, Security and Hospitality in Question*, edited by Luca Mavelli and Erin K. Wilson, 61–74. London: Rowman and Littlefield International.

Weiss, Thomas G. 1999. 'Principles, Politics, and Humanitarian Action', *Ethics and International Affairs* 13 (1): 1–22.

Wigger, Andreas. 2005. 'Encountering Perceptions in Parts of the Muslim World and Their Impact on the ICRC's Ability to Be Effective', *International Review of the Red Cross* 87 (858): 343–65.

Zaman, Tahir. 2012. 'Jockeying for Position in the Humanitarian Field: Iraqi Refugees and Faith-Based Organisations in Damascus', *Disasters* 36 (S1): S126–48.

# 28
# Navigating ambiguous state policies and legal statuses in Turkey: Syrian displacement and migratory horizons

Charlotte Loris-Rodionoff

## Introduction

State policies and legal status have diverse effects on displaced Syrians' everyday life in Turkey – and on their understanding of, and planning for, the future. In Turkey, where the largest population of displaced Syrians lives,[1] they hold the status of 'guest' (*misafer* in Turkish, *diuf* in Arabic) rather than refugee. Indeed, although Turkey is a state signatory to the 1951 Geneva Convention on the Status of Refugees it did not sign the 1967 Protocol, which lifted the Convention's original temporal and geographical limitations: this means that Turkey only recognizes people as refugees if they fled *from* Europe 'as a result of events occurring before 1 January 1951'.[2]

If being guests of the Turkish state did not appear to be an issue in the early years of displacement, the absence of official refugee status became increasingly problematic with the fading possibility of a near and safe return to Syria. Indeed, being considered guests in Turkey has created a feeling of instability and uncertainty concerning their future, since this status is only temporary and does not protect them from deportation to Syria – as refugee status officially would. Moreover, this guest status leads to a limitation of Syrians' rights as the great majority of Syrians live outside of guest camps and they receive very little state support, both factors having a strong impact on their everyday life. In addition, the absence of a stable and clear legal status that could ultimately lead to obtaining permanent residence or citizenship reinforces Syrians' uncertain present and future, as municipalities regularly stop issuing residence documents[3] without any apparent reason.

Based on 18 months of fieldwork[4] among Syrians in the city of Gaziantep, this chapter offers a thick description (Geertz, 1973) of the ways in which Syrians navigate state policies and legal statuses – which evolved throughout my research and in its aftermath – and the ways in which they inflect their perceptions of the future. Such an ethnographic approach allows us to show the multilayered effects of state policies and legal status on Syrians' everyday lives, their future-oriented decisions, their intimate and family lives, and the construction of a community in exile. Moreover, ethnographic description and anthropological analysis offer a valuable methodology to account for the multifaceted causes of migration.

This methodology offers a deep and nuanced understanding of both Syrians' dwelling in Turkey and their migration towards Europe. Indeed, one of the chapter's aims is to explain Syrians' migration to Europe in relation to the uncertainty and hostility that they have felt in Turkey and the fear of being sent back to war-torn Syria, feeling unprotected by their status. In addition, it explores the short- and long-term strategies that Syrians put in place in order to secure their living in Turkey. I first discuss Syrians' status in Turkey and show how it leads to a life in limbo: a precarious, uncertain and hostile everyday. I then examine the strategies that many of my Syrian interlocutors have built in order to inhabit and resist this hostile environment. I finally turn to the migratory horizons and paths that emerge from these circumstances.

## Being a 'guest': Legal limbo, precarity and the uncertain everyday

The feeling that Syrians are not guests in Turkey, despite being officially labelled as such, was widespread throughout my entire fieldwork. Pointing out the irony of the guest label, one of my interlocutors told me: 'We are treated nothing like guests and you know that very well!' In fact, my interlocutors understood that being given the status of 'guest' was just a tool for the Turkish Government to give them fewer rights than they would have if they were officially refugees. They argued that Syrians fall under the Geneva Convention international legal definition of a refugee – my interlocutors had fled Syria and could not return for fear of being arrested or killed since they had participated in anti-regime protests – and they held that Turkey therefore had the duty to grant them refugee status and its associated rights. Many of my interlocutors had first fled to Lebanon or Jordan before reaching Turkey, and acknowledged that the latter offered Syrians better living conditions than the former two – and yet they felt that it was not fulfilling its legal obligations towards them.[5]

Although in the international arena Syrians have been commonly described as refugees and became, in recent years, the emblematic figure of the refugee since the beginning of the so-called 'refugee crisis' (Fiddian-Qasmiyeh, 2016), they are not legally refugees in Turkey. Indeed, as noted above, refugee status has geographical and temporal restrictions in Turkey, since European citizens can be granted refugee status while other citizens are considered only temporary asylum seekers before they resettle in a third country through the UNHCR (Toğral Koca, 2016). However, Syrians have yet another status: as we have seen, they are called 'guests' and are granted a temporary protection status that gives them access to healthcare and education (Özden, 2013; Toğral Koca, 2016) if they hold a *kimlik* (the ID document issued to displaced Syrians in Turkey). This status officially means that they can stay in Turkey as long as the situation in Syria does not allow them to return. It is accompanied by three rules: an open-door policy, *non-refoulment*[6] and registration within Turkey (Özden, 2013). However, guest status is ambiguous and precarious as it is mostly defined by administrative circulars rather than laws, these three rules are not always followed and guest status is not always granted since obtaining a *kimlik* has not always been possible (Soykan, 2012; Toğral Koca, 2016).

Despite the fact that guests' living conditions are not totally dissimilar to those of refugees and asylum seekers (see Diken, 2004; Rotter, 2016; Sanyal, 2011; Sayigh, 1995), the major difference is that 'guest' is not a recognized legal category. Indeed, Syrians are only temporarily protected by the Turkish state; moreover, protection is not always granted nor is it always implemented. Many Syrians in Turkey are thus only rhetorically guests, as they do not receive any identification documents or the few rights that such documents ostensibly guarantee. Moreover, this protection is ambiguously defined and put into practice within a weak legal framework (Soykan, 2012; Ümit, 2014), for Syrians are treated following a logic of favour and charity rather than a legal one (Özden, 2013).

In 2015, *kimlik*s became compulsory for Syrians living in Turkey in order for them to reside there legally and access healthcare and education. Yet, *kimlik*s were not continuously issued by the Turkish authorities. Syrians were thus often put in a situation in which they were rendered illegal without the possibility of becoming legalized; in other words, they were placed in a legal limbo. This fragile position towards the law was reinforced by constantly changing (and inconsistently applied) regulations and laws, as well as the near absence of rights and aid (Ümit, 2014). In practice, this legal liminality affected all parts of Syrians' everyday lives. In what follows, I analyse the ways in which Syrians' legal status and the administrative situation in Turkey dramatically affected their everyday lives by limiting their work situation, living conditions, healthcare and education access. In turn, I describe the ways in which Syrians challenge this status quo.

## Consequences and subversions of Syrian guest status

Umm Khaled, a war widow from a provincial town in her early fifties, had lived in Turkey for a year and a half with her daughter and one of her sons when her sister, Umm Mohammad, fled Syria with her husband and three children. While Umm Mohammad's husband and Umm Khaled's son embarked on the perilous journey to Europe, the two sisters stayed behind with the children. Since Umm Mohammad's family was waiting to be reunited in Europe – this waiting was virtually unlimited since Abu Mohammad had to go through the asylum process and secure his own residency before being able to apply for family reunification, a process that could take between a few months and a few years – the two sisters and four children shared a tiny studio flat in Gaziantep. The studio was always overcrowded, as Umm Mohammad's children had no *kimlik* and so could not register for school.[7]

Yet, not having a *kimlik* not only affected Syrians' access to schooling, it also limited their access to healthcare, work and travel both within and outside Turkey. When her son was injured and needed to be taken to hospital, Umm Mohammad discovered that not all public hospitals accepted Syrians, despite being obliged to do so. The first hospital that she went to refused to treat her son. As she visited a second hospital, she was informed by a translator that the law would be changing in three days' time and that Syrians without a *kimlik* would no longer be eligible for free medical care after that point.[8] Moreover, as the family planned to visit the German Embassy in Ankara to start their family reunification process they were not allowed to board their plane for the internal flight. They had their Syrian IDs, which had been enough to travel inside Turkey until a couple of months earlier. However, during the 2015 general-election period, it had become obligatory to hold a travel authorization for any trip within Turkey, and this 'temporary' policy had apparently turned into a permanent rule.

The family's nightmare began when they realized that one needed a *kimlik* to obtain this authorization, and that the Gaziantep municipality no longer issued them. They were stuck in a Catch-22 situation: they could not travel to Ankara to obtain a *kimlik* without a travel authorization, but they needed a *kimlik* to secure this authorization. They thought of travelling to a nearby city to apply for the documentation there but, again, travelling without authorization could lead to their arrest and their deportation to Syria. Umm Mohammad eventually realized that rules, regulations and laws were not always implemented and followed by all, and managed to board a bus to Ankara. The fact that laws and regulations change quite often and are not published in Arabic, and the fact that they are not always followed, gave Syrians the feeling that they lived in a country without consistent laws, which contributed to the impression that they were living in a state of constant uncertainty.

This instability and unreliability made my interlocutors feel unsafe and uncertain, as it reminded them of the corruption and the quickly changing 'laws' in Syria. Around the time of the 2015 Turkish general election, conversations increasingly focused on who had managed to travel without authorization, and who had been stopped and why, as Syrians tried to extricate a general rule out of the diverse experiences that they had heard about. Yet, no one seemed to find a clear pattern: some were stopped in the airport when leaving Gaziantep while others travelled all the way to Istanbul without ever being asked for their travel authorization. It thus seemed to depend on the will of the officers concerned rather than on written law.

To deal with this situation, Syrians created different ways to overcome the everyday limits imposed by being guests. For instance, Arabic-speaking Syrians relied on Turkish-speaking fellow Syrians and/ or Turkish people who spoke Arabic to gain a better understanding of the system and to find ways in which to meet these restrictive conditions. However, the creative solutions to accommodate their uncertain and precarious status in Turkey were most visibly materialized in the 'Syrianisation' (Kodmani, 2016) of Gaziantep: the creation of a Syrian city within the Turkish one. This implied being able to speak Arabic, consume Syrian products, go to Syrian restaurants and shops, visit Syrian doctors and place one's children in a Syrian school. Having 'Syrian alternatives' was particularly crucial when it came to work, education and healthcare, given the limitations that Syrians' status entailed. For instance, Syrian medical practices, which are not legal but are tolerated by the authorities as long as they serve only Syrian patients, have increasingly emerged in Gaziantep alongside the growing number of displaced.

Thus, former shops and residential apartments became the homes of dental, gynaecological and other medical practices.

## Navigating Turkish and Syrian laws

In addition to the everyday limitations outlined above, on a legal and administrative level, Syrians displaced in Turkey have to respect Turkish law while still navigating Syrian law. On the one hand, Syrians' life in Turkey is subject to ever-changing – and not always respected – laws vis-à-vis healthcare, schooling, housing, work or travel regulations. On the other hand, when it comes to family law, the renewal of passports, and issuing marriage and birth certificates, Syrians have to deal either with newly established Free Syrian institutions,[9] and/or those of the Assad regime. This situation was particularly acute in the case of marriages, births and passport renewal.

My interlocutors often expressed the wish for their marriages to be registered in Syria so they would have an official contract – including being issued with a Family Record Book (*daftar al-ayleh*) – and would not face problems in the future. This was a very important issue for those whose children were born in Turkey since for most of my interlocutors, being officially married in Syria was the only way in which to later obtain official birth certificates and for the children to have a legally recognized father. Being officially married would allow them to live as a family in Syria in case they returned; having a Family Record Book would enable them to obtain a Syrian passport for their children, a crucial document for those applying for family reunification in Europe. Since Turkey only offers Syrians a temporary protection status, these are precious steps to prevent Syrian children from being stateless, in case of return to Syria or onward flight to Europe. Obtaining these documents thus led to great uncertainty as newly married couples and young parents struggled to find ways in which to acquire them.

Amal and Mohammad, a newly married couple in their thirties, were not able to obtain passports in Syria as they were wanted by the regime, and were seeking to acquire them so that they could travel and apply for a proper ID for their newborn baby. They faced two options: obtain a passport from the *Etilaf* (the National Coalition of Syrian Revolution and Opposition Forces) or from the Syrian Consulate. Most people did not trust the passports issued by the coalition, fearing that their worth was only temporary. However, securing a passport from the regime meant going through a humiliating process and paying at least US$800 for a document that would be valid only for three years. Moreover, on various occasions the regime had declared a passport as having been stolen, thus leading to the arrest of the holder and confiscation of the passport at a border-control point. Yet, the regime's passports were internationally recognized. Having proper documents was a major issue for the people whom I worked with. 'I will have no choice but to take a boat when my passport expires', I heard many times, as my interlocutors saw fleeing to Europe as a way to guarantee a clearer and more stable status,[10] with documents allowing one to travel more freely.

As shown in the context of Palestinians in the West Bank (Kelly, 2006) and Cypriots in Northern Cyprus (Navaro-Yashin 2012), the possession or otherwise of documents such as travel documents, residency permits, passports, marriage and birth certificates, and strategies to acquire them, have direct effects on people's everyday lives. The possession or absence of such documents is a factor in creating (un)certainty and (in)stability, and generates different future horizons as well as strategies to meet them. Legal status, processes and situations create a specific 'texture of life' (Kelly, 2006: 90). For my Syrian interlocutors, the suspension of their 'ontological status as legal subjects' (Butler, 2000: 81) contributed to rendering their life in Turkey precarious and uncertain. But this also led Syrians, as the war refused to finish, to increasingly consider fleeing to Europe.

## Syrian future horizons: settling in Turkey, fleeing to Europe

As I returned to Gaziantep in spring 2017, Syrians' legal status had changed quite dramatically. On the one hand, Syrians who held residency and university degrees were now being given the opportunity to apply for citizenship. On the other hand, Syrians working without the appropriate documents, or with documents issued in another city, lived with the constant risk of being returned to Syria or deported to Sudan.[11] This risk pushed Syrians who were employed in organizations and businesses to work from home in order to avoid arrest and deportation, or to quit their jobs. This also led to a loss of employment opportunities as employers feared being harassed by the police and Syrians feared being detained and/or deported. Moreover, the Turkish Government imposed a proportional quota system to increase the number of Turkish citizens working in Syrian organizations.

Although a minority of Syrians were able to obtain work-related residence and potentially access citizenship, through the temporariness and uncertainty of these new statuses their guest position still loomed.

This led a large number of Syrians to flee to Europe, where they hoped to find more stability and certainty for themselves and their children. Indeed, they hoped that being granted a more permanent refugee status – which they understood as being more clearly defined by a fixed law – would allow them to have a safer and more certain life and future in Europe. They also believed that they would finally access free schooling and healthcare services that increasingly became unaffordable in their precarious situation in Turkey.[12]

Some of my interlocutors had first tried to settle in Turkey as they hoped to eventually obtain citizenship, while others had found themselves stuck in Gaziantep. For example, Umm Khaled was ineligible to apply for family reunification in Sweden as her son was already in his twenties.[13] Moreover, she refused to attempt crossing the Mediterranean, despite her sister's and son's encouragements, for she was too scared to either lose her daughter or leave her orphaned. She thus tried to settle in Turkey. She sent her daughter to a Turkish school in the hope that they could more easily obtain residency documents and perhaps apply for citizenship through her position as a student of a Turkish university,[14] if her daughter managed to enrol at one in the future. However, the fear of falling ill and not being able to properly take care of her young daughter, as well as the worry of being unable to pay her rent and buy food if her son could no longer send her small remittances in the absence of aid, kept her in a state of permanent uncertainty and led her to continuously try to find a solution to be able to join her son in Sweden. She eventually tried to apply for resettlement in Sweden via the UNHCR, but was unable to obtain her husband's death certificate because of the high processing cost and therefore could not finalize her application. Every now and then, when I visited her, she told me about new hopes of obtaining citizenship in Turkey, and of new strategies to join her son in Europe, as she tried to secure a safer and more stable future for her daughter.

Similarly to Umm Khaled, many of my interlocutors who had first insisted on staying in Turkey – for they still hoped to be able to go back to Syria – and who wished to stay close to Syria or settle in a Muslim country, eventually fled to Europe when they realized that returning home had become a lost dream and staying in Turkey was increasingly difficult. Most of my interlocutors had been involved peacefully in the revolution in Syria in some way or another, from cooking for the protestors to joining the protests and treating injured demonstrators, which rendered their return to Syria unlikely as the Assad regime was still ruling. At the same time, the transformation of a revolutionary movement into an ongoing (proxy) war rendered any return to Syria perilous and prolonged Syrians' precarious and uncertain stay in Turkey. Moreover, with Syrians' status in Turkey being seen unfavourably by my interlocutors, Europe started to appear as a place where they could have a better life than the one that they had first sought at home (through the revolution) and in Turkey. Fleeing to Europe was thus an answer to Syrians' growing uncertainty regarding their status and their precarious everyday life in Turkey, as well as the impossibility of returning home.

'*Suria khalas* (Syria is over)', Umm Yazan told me with tears in her eyes as we took a break from packing her belongings and sat on her balcony enjoying the fresh breeze after a long, hot summer day. It was August 2015. Umm Yazan's daughter had been planning to cross the sea with her husband to join her sister in Germany, but Umm Yazan had never mentioned wanting to take that path. After her plan to return to Syria's liberated areas with her eldest son and his family failed, she seemed to have settled on staying in Turkey while waiting for her husband to join her from Lebanon. But the situation had suddenly changed. She had just lost her job a few days before our meeting, and was grim about her chance of being able to find a new one that would allow her to support her family. This would also make it impossible for her to pay for her youngest daughter's medical treatment, of which she was in dire need.

In the absence of institutionalized and substantial aid for the Syrian urban displaced in Turkey, a future in the country had thus become impossible. In contrast, Europe appeared as a place where being refugees would allow the family to access healthcare, education and work more easily. However, as for many of the families that I worked with, leaving Turkey was a wrenching move. They had hoped that they were only Turkey's temporary guests and that they would soon be able to return home. But the deteriorating situation in both Syria *and* Turkey pushed them further away into a more permanent exile.

## Conclusion: Syrian migratory paths

When I started researching Syrian revolutionary families in spring 2013 (Loris-Rodionoff, 2019), the hope that the revolution would eventually defeat the Assad regime and that Syrian displacement to Turkey was only momentary was high. Until summer 2015, Turkey's open-border policy allowed families to go back and forth between the two countries as the regime's repression of revolutionaries and their families moved from one town to another. Syrian spatio-temporal horizons then seemed to be mainly articulated around the revolution's destiny: they were waiting in Turkey for the revolution to succeed and to be able to return to Syria; they actively tried to settle in Turkey or Europe when they had lost hope that such success was still possible. Yet, Syrians' status in Turkey complicated this already delicate equilibrium as my interlocutors began to doubt that they really could settle in Gaziantep. Indeed, their 'guest' status, which had at first been a token of the Turkish Government's solidarity with the Syrian people and support for the opposition, eventually put Turkey's guests into a liminal position and pushed them to seek refuge elsewhere. This search turned Europe into an idealized horizon where Syrians thought that they would be able to obtain a more stable and certain status.

In this chapter, I have traced Syrians' condition in displacement in Turkey and explored what a life in legal limbo looks like. I have shown the consequences of being guests in Turkey on all dimensions of Syrians' everyday life, and how this has led to an uncertain and precarious present. Moreover, I have traced how Syrians navigate within their liminal position and create alternatives in order to resist the realities of their condition. Finally, I have suggested that these guests' limbo life is one of the major causes of Syrians fleeing from Turkey to Europe. On a methodological and theoretical level, using the ethnographic term *diuf* (guest) to describe Syrians' experience and status in Turkey made it possible to rethink displacement in new terms, and helped to unsettle reductive analytical categories to produce a more fruitful analysis that is also closer to Syrians' lived experience and legal status.

## Acknowledgements

This chapter was written with the support of the European Research Council-funded project Comparative Anthropologies of Revolutionary Politics (2013-CoG-617970).

## Notes

1.  At the beginning of my fieldwork (January 2015) there were 1,622,839 Syrians in Turkey and at the end (April 2016) 2,749,140, making up 20 per cent of Gaziantep's population in 2016.
2.  On changes in international law and migration policy beyond Turkey, see Wilde (this volume).
3.  Syrians are required to hold official documents in order to legally reside in Turkey. *Kimlik* is the Turkish word for 'identification'. The umbrella term includes the national ID cards held by Turkish citizens, but in this context refers specifically to the type of document delivered by the Turkish authorities to displaced Syrians in Turkey. *Kimlik* are usually automatically granted to any Syrian entering Turkey, but municipalities regularly stop issuing these. Tourist and work residences that open the opportunity to travel freely around Turkey (and to enter and exit it, for those who have visas) and to work, for the latter, are more complicated to obtain and have to be renewed yearly or bi-yearly.
4.  Mainly between January 2015 and April 2016, and including shorter visits in 2014 and 2016 as well as follow-up work, since the author has been living in Gaziantep since 2017.
5.  On the position of refugees (including Syrians and Palestinians) in Lebanon and Jordan, see Qasmiyeh, Chatterjee *et al.*, Maqusi, Fiddian-Qasmiyeh, and Carpi, all in this volume.

6. The principle of *non-refoulement* forbids the return or expulsion of any person to a territory where their lives or freedom would be at risk.
7. In 2015, about 400,000 Syrian children were out of school in Turkey according to a Human Rights Watch report.
8. This incident happened in autumn 2015.
9. Free Syrian institutions appeared inside and outside Syria, mainly in Turkey, as the result of the conflict between the Assad ruling regime and the opposition that rose up against it in the 2011 uprising.
10. This was based on the opacity and the national variation of refugee law in the EU and the fact that many were unaware (especially in the first years of displacement to Europe) of the difference between political and humanitarian refugee statuses, especially in Sweden and Germany, and the precedent of the deportation of Afghan refugees to Afghanistan and Iraqi refugees to Iraq after the country situation was deemed safe, regardless of the refugees' actual safety situation there.
11. At the time, Sudan was the only country that allowed Syrians to settle for an unlimited period of time without a visa.
12. On diverse challenges experienced by refugees throughout their journeys to and in Europe, see the chapters in this volume by Franceschelli and Galipò (Italy), Astolfo and Boano (Italy), Berg (UK), Vandevoordt (Belgium), Bailey (France), Crafter and Rosen (France), Mole (Germany), and Chatterjee *et al.*
13. Only parents of children under 18 or parents over 60 could apply for family reunification.
14. At this time, Syrian students at Turkish universities were given the opportunity to apply for citizenship.

# References

Abdulhadi, Rabab. 2003. 'Where is Home? Fragmented Lives, Border Crossings, and the Politics of Exile', *Radical History Review* 86: 89–101.
Butler, Judith. 2000. *Antigone's Claim: Kinship between Life and Death*. New York: Columbia University Press.
Diken, Bülent. 2004. 'From Refugee Camps to Gated Communities: Biopolitics and the End of the City', *Citizenship Studies* 8 (1): 83–106.
Fiddian-Qasmiyeh, Elena. 2016. 'Repressentations of Displacement from the Middle East and North Africa', *Public Culture* 28 (3): 457–73.
Geertz, Clifford. 1973. *The Interpretation of Cultures*. New York: Basic Books.
Kelly, Tobias. 2006. 'Documented Lives: Fear and the Uncertainties of Law during the Second Palestinian Intifada', *Journal of the Royal Anthropological Institute* 12 (1): 89–107.
Kodmani, Hala. 2016. 'Yassin al-Haj Saleh: "La Syrie ne s'est pas démocratisée, c'est le monde qui s'est syrianisé"', *Libération*, 9 May. Accessed 9 January 2020. www.liberation.fr/debats/2016/05/09/yassin-al-haj-saleh-la-syrie-ne-s-est-pas-democratisee-c-est-le-monde-qui-s-est-syrianise_1451478.
Loris-Rodionoff, Charlotte. 2019. 'Of Revolutionary Transformations: Life in Displacement at the Syrian-Turkish Border'. PhD thesis, University College London.
Navaro-Yashin, Yael. 2012. *The Make-Believe Space: Affective Geography in a Postwar Polity*. Durham, NC: Duke University Press.
Özden, Şenay. 2013. *Syrian Refugees in Turkey* (MPC Research Report 2013/05). Florence: Migration Policy Centre. Accessed 9 January 2020. koganweb.
Rotter, Rebecca. 2016. 'Waiting in the Asylum Determination Process: Just an Empty Interlude?', *Time and Society* 25 (1): 80–101.
Sanyal, Romola. 2011. 'Squatting in Camps: Building and Insurgency in Spaces of Refuge', *Urban Studies* 48 (5): 877–90.
Sayigh, Rosemary. 1995. 'Palestinians in Lebanon: Harsh Present, Uncertain Future', *Journal of Palestine Studies* 25 (1): 37–53.
Soykan, Cavidan. 2012. 'The New Draft Law on Foreigners and International Protection in Turkey', *Oxford Monitor of Forced Migration* 2 (2): 38–47.
Toğral Koca, Burcu. 2016. 'Syrian Refugees in Turkey: From "Guests" to "Enemies"?', *New Perspectives on Turkey* 54: 55–75.
Ümit, Devrim. 2014. 'Refugee Crisis Next Door: Turkey and the Syrian Refugees', *Nevşehir Hacı Bektaş Veli University Journal of Social Sciences* 3: 1–18.

## 29

# Exploring in-betweenness: Alice and spaces of contradiction in refuge

S. Tahmineh Hooshyar Emami

## Introduction

In the light of ongoing political turmoil around the world and diverse processes of displacement created as a consequence, investigation into the spaces and dynamics of refuge within an increasingly mobile world is imperative. The initial premise of this chapter is that through the mass movement of populations in recent years, a new form of cities and spaces has emerged. I refer to them as 'the cities/spaces of in-between', which blur and challenge the boundaries between our perception of temporariness and permanence.

The *in-between* city is a migratory and transportable entity that moves apace with its inhabitants, existing briefly in certain transient spatio-temporal conditions. The recently demolished 'Jungle' refugee camp (2014–16), an informal and organically developing settlement in northern France, epitomized the notion of transitoriness both in its age demographics and its geopolitical location at the crossing between the ports of Calais and Dover (on the Jungle, also see Bailey, Crafter and Rosen, and Qasmiyeh, all in this volume). Within this new subspecies of the city, which became a place of contradiction and refuge, traditional spatial conceptions no longer apply. Architectural necessities such as doors, walls and rooms – which have been long-established markers of domesticity and privacy, born out of the desire to set ourselves territorial boundaries – have become invadable thresholds in the context of refuge. The camp becomes a test bed to investigate these architectural objects, which stand in for larger-scale notions of checkpoints, borders and countries (also see Maqusi, this volume).

**Figure 29.1** 'Alice's Alternative Wonderland', extract no. 1. © S. Tahmineh Hooshyar Emami, 2015.

Concepts of sociological and political space come to play in juxtaposition against architectural forms in an attempt to decipher the formation and morphology of the in-between state of borders, roads and cities. Often, the new definition and perception of the architectural object is in full opposition to our normative understanding of it.

## Methodology and Alice in Wonderland

*Alice's Adventures in Wonderland* and *Through the Looking-Glass* (Carroll, 2015) have been chosen as a political allegory in fiction to underpin and structure a critical analysis of the spatial politics of refuge. Lewis Carroll's fictional works are a starting point for the author to analyse how our bodies are defined, shaped and influenced by space in this context. Steve Pile speaks of ALICE's[1] relation to, and reciprocal effect on, space as follows:

> ALICE was 'at odds with her space. Poor, dreaming, misfit Alice, while pursuing the time conscious white rabbit, was either too big or too small for her space; too sane for the Mad Hatter's Tea Party and dangerously outspoken in the Queen's Court. (Nast and Pile, 1998: xvii)

Investigating Carroll's dream spaces addresses fundamental questions surrounding concepts of spatial memory and perception, especially in children. ALICE becomes the vehicle that allows for a single-point perspectival view of the particularities of immigration. This fictional vehicle operates on several levels, the first of which is the geographical narrative of the dream world or, more specifically, the landscapes that guide and shape ALICE's pilgrimage through Wonderland. The scale-less pool, the nonsensical pathways that always lead back to the Looking-Glass house and the chessboard landscape of woodland and meadows all reflect the nineteenth-century rule-bound bourgeois society of Britain where, according to J.S. Mill, laws and social norms had combined to eliminate individuality (Siemann, 2012: 430). In the same fashion, the migrant trail through sea, crop fields and woodland can be interpreted as a compressed and miniaturized replica of the current political norms ruling the European Union.

The second level of operation is ALICE's character, which echoes her upbringing in a Victorian imperialist society. The child-imperialist (Bivona, 1986: 143) struggles to grapple with the non-conformist Wonderland dominated by rules and logic unknown to her. She tries to maintain her sanity by talking to herself, reciting poems to test her memory and to verify if she still is the ALICE that she was before her descent into the rabbit hole. Daniel Bivona states that the mind of child-ALICE lacks the ability to comprehend the operational modes of the dream world – perhaps due to it being a world dominated by older levels of mental organization, or else due to an absence in fixity of rules and regulations (ibid.: 168). Hence, despite the familiarity of Wonderland and the events that ALICE stumbles upon, she is soon to realize that this is a world which contradicts the logic-bound world of her reality by hovering between sense and nonsense, reality and fiction, variation and repetition, even linearity and circularity:

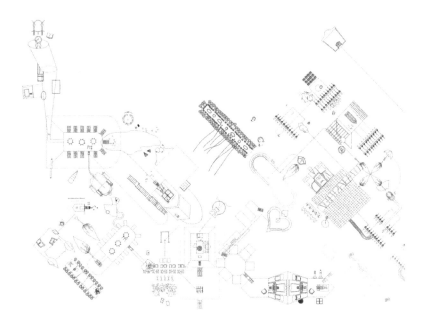

**Figure 29.2** Detail from a line drawing of spatio-temporal sequence of 'Alice's Alternative Wonderland'. © S. Tahmineh Hooshyar Emami, 2015.

> 'Come, there's no use in crying like that!' said Alice to herself, rather sharply; 'I advise you to leave off this minute!' She generally gave herself very good advice, (though she very seldom followed it), and sometimes she scolded herself … for this curious child was very fond of pretending to be two people. (Carroll, 2015: 13)

In Wonderland, unlike space, time exists in a psychological/perceptive sense. The static and reversed time of the dream world is overlaid with ALICE's normative understanding of it. Despite the fixity and stagnation of physical time at the six o'clock tea party, psychological time allows ALICE and the creatures to enter and leave the tea party and to expect the experiences of Wonderland to come to an end. Similarly, in the Jungle, time perception expands to the indefinite and continuous unfolding of events; whereas on the refugee trail, perception of time is highly compressed with a diluted content and is reduced to the sheer interval between two successive events/destinations.

The fifth level of operation of the ALICE vehicle is represented by the use of words and poems that follow the linguistic logic of Wonderland. The

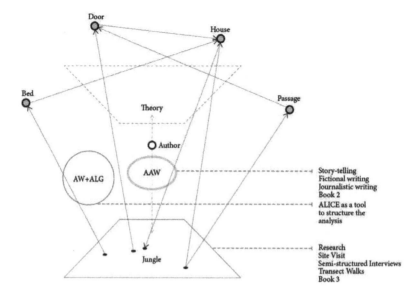

**Figure 29.3** Methodology diagram. © S. Tahmineh Hooshyar Emami, 2016.

inhabitants of the dream world have frequent altercations with outsider-ALICE and challenge common-sense references and dictionary-bound definitions. Carroll allows words to break from their dictionary definitions and adopt new/altered meanings:

> 'When I use a word,' Humpty Dumpty said, in rather a scornful tone, 'it means just what I choose it to mean – neither more nor less.'
> 'The question is,' said Alice, 'whether you can make words mean so many different things.' (Carroll, 2015: 205)

The transitoriness of refugee status emerges from a perpetual sense of movement and an absent sense of belonging, which create a strong connection to ALICE's status as an outsider in the fictional setting of Wonderland. The unlikely scenario of ALICE being a refugee in the nonsensical Wonderland is set as a hypothetical background in order to start a conversation on transitional spaces. Similar to her constant progression through dream spaces, coherently or otherwise connected, refugees pass through distinct, sequential spatial arrangements.

## 'Alice's Alternative Wonderland'

The exploration into various scales of spatial inhabitation in refuge starts with 'Alice's Alternative Wonderland', an inseparable part of the study, which adds fragments of the refugee trail narrated by child-*alice* and as imagined by the author, through the use of critical and creative storytelling. Comparable with ALICE's sudden and unintended descent down the rabbit hole and into the perplexing world of Wonderland, the condition of refugee-*alice* imposes a set of abrupt and unanticipated circumstances that she must conform to. Having ventured into the heart of unknown countries whose laws are alien to the story's subject, she must discern logic by transcending both immaterial linguistic/ legislative barriers and physical borders. *alice*'s memories – often real accounts composed from news extracts, data and travel journals – are complemented by fictional input from the author in order to create a less disjointed, highly detailed plot. The term 'critical imagination', coined by Jane Rendell, best defines the construct of the essay and the production of the narrative as an indispensable element of the chapter.

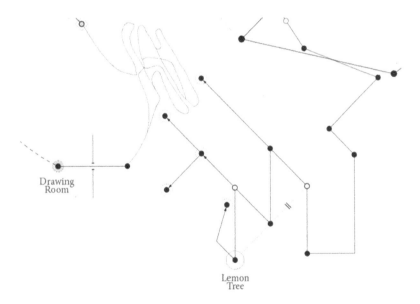

**Figure 29.4**   Detail from a line drawing of the Geometry of Journeys. © S. Tahmineh Hooshyar Emami, 2016.

Rendell describes this methodology as 'an analytic mode to outline the structure and form of her response, and memories – sometimes real, sometimes fictional – to create the content-filled detail' (Rendell, 2007: 185).

The character, *alice*, is the result of an amalgamation of factual and imagined realities reflected in story and journal writings; perhaps the author becomes the adult projecting her own self onto the child, or else it is the child that aspires to be the adult author. Much like Carroll's ALICE, who was fond of being two people, often scolding and contradicting, the voice of *alice* becomes the collective voice of refugee contributors, and it is thus used as a vehicle to facilitate the processes of anonymizing and ethicizing the research methodology and writing mode.

## The Jungle

As introduced earlier, this chapter evaluates the 'Jungle' refugee camp, in France. The 'Jungle' becomes a test bed for locating and identifying architectural motifs and, through the use of theoretical analysis, referring to their significance in different contexts and scales of refuge. It represents a moment of repose/stillness where, within a particular spatio-temporal condition situated outside the rules of the host country, one finds the freedom to express one's identity and nationality.

The study uses four motifs as metaphors to analyse architectural spaces and their significance in the context of the journey or that of the encampment. I move from the small scale of the bed to sequentially larger scales of human inhabitation such as the door; the house; and, eventually, the corridor/passage, alluding to the spatial sequence of

**Figure 29.5** 'Alice's Alternative Wonderland', extract no. 2.
© S. Tahmineh Hooshyar Emami, 2015.

ALICE *Through the Looking-Glass*. There, Carroll takes us from the space of the interior and interaction with small objects such as chess pieces to the larger mirror; Looking-Glass room; hall; and, eventually, paths, hills and woods.

First, the bed is of a scale highly comparable with that of the human body – virtually an extension of it in the times when we slide into the unconscious dream state. It dictates the position and form of our body through its size and proportions, which were in turn originally determined from standardized human measurements – it is perhaps the

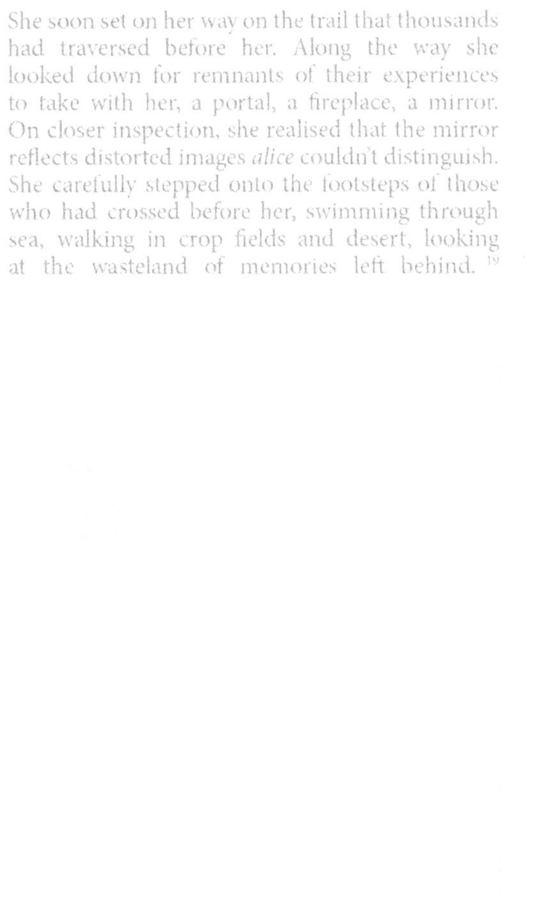

She soon set on her way on the trail that thousands had traversed before her. Along the way she looked down for remnants of their experiences to take with her, a portal, a fireplace, a mirror. On closer inspection, she realised that the mirror reflects distorted images *alice* couldn't distinguish. She carefully stepped onto the footsteps of those who had crossed before her, swimming through sea, walking in crop fields and desert, looking at the wasteland of memories left behind. [iv]

**Figure 29.6** Site-visit documentation. All photographs and sketches © S. Tahmineh Hooshyar Emami, Calais 'Jungle', 2016.

encapsulation of the idea of reciprocal effect between the body and object or the body and space.

Second, the door is the embodiment of the idea of passing from one state to the other, one space to the other and one room to the next. It becomes the establisher of interiority, the delineator of passage into personal space and the protector of territories in the context of the refugee trail.

Third, the house beyond the door, with its four walls, encloses the personal space, materializing its borders and symbolizing territories of the home or those of the country. Its walls can be as concrete and tangible as the walls of the room I am writing in now, or they can melt and vanish as suddenly as the spaces of Wonderland or Looking-Glass country.

Finally, the corridor symbolizes passage and transition. Through yet another door, one finds oneself in the Jungle, the ever-growing yet ever-shrinking city of contradictions, which condenses the experiences of the refugee trail within an area of 51.2 hectares. The Jungle, as a transient refugee camp, is merely a stopping point in the longest corridor between the Middle East and northern Europe. This last pinch point to cross over to Promise-land[2] is perhaps comparable to the small door standing between ALICE and the 'loveliest garden she had ever seen' (Carroll, 2015: 11). The last section therefore focuses on the larger, continental scale, analysing the European route and the transformation of countries into human corridors leading towards a destination that is a distorted mirage of the reality of asylum.

The investigation of architectural elements that epitomize the concepts of passage, connectedness, barrier and boundary is refined by referring to Georg Simmel's themes of social separation and connectedness reflected in architectural forms (Simmel, 1994: 5–10). In a highly metaphorical and fictional interpretation of sociological and geopolitical space, this chapter looks at the inherent and acquired significance of the four metaphors in relation to the refugee trail.

## Counting the beds

The bed is the first metaphor for the investigation of small-scale objects that embody cultural memory. It allows external circumstances and factors to morph its physical form, manifesting itself in various shapes throughout the journey. The *bed scale*, as we will call it henceforth, symbolizes and stands in for the multitude of objects transported from home that carry part of the sense of belonging. Concurrently, the bed evokes ALICE's sleeping and awakening – the original nature of her accidental descent into the dream-scape of Wonderland, which we are only aware of upon her awakening. It is not only representative of ALICE's unconscious state of mind but also stands for a level of interplay of scales within the novel. It can be interpreted as a standardized object of daily life, against which one might compare one's scale to make sure that one is the right size. Of course, for ALICE, the bed was the riverbank, under the shade of the trees – a first reference to the multivalence of the word itself: could a bed be anything?

Georges Perec argues that the bed is the individual space par excellence, the elementary space of the body, the space of dreams and nostalgia where, perhaps in a way similar to Wonderland, anything is possible (Perec, 2008: 16–17). The space occupied by the bed becomes a marker for the space of contemplation and fear, but also of desire and fantasy.

Contrary to the normative procedures of undertaking a population census, a more adequate criterion for carrying out a population census in the Jungle seemed to be counting the beds, sleeping bags or rugs. In this manner, one would easily determine the constant population of the camp, disregarding the minor fluctuations and exchange of individuals. Sleeping areas are often abandoned by refugees crossing the channel, but are immediately taken over by new arrivals.

**Figure 29.7** 'Alice's Alternative Wonderland', extract no. 3.
© Tahmineh Hooshyar Emami, 2015.

**Figure 29.8** 'Alice's Alternative Wonderland', extract no. 4.
© S. Tahmineh Hooshyar Emami, 2015.

Perec argues that the bed is an individual space, 'which even the man completely crippled by debts has the right to keep' (Perec, 2008: 16); in other words, it surpasses social class and statute. In the particular case of the beds that I have seen in the Jungle, the statute of the bed has changed from an indispensable commodity to a shared and, at times, political space.[3] Not unlike in most European capital cities, social stratification can be identified in various instances within the Jungle, although not as evidently, with subclasses with visible differences in financial ability. For instance, while some refugees may have the luxury of owning a bed as I described in my field notes, many others lack the ability to purchase a bed on the black market and will settle for a sleeping bag from the camp's donation-distribution points. These variations can be found in the underlying, less-visible layers of inhabitation but also in the larger setting of the camp. Similarly, there may be distinguishable differences in the physical construct of the different communities, with better-managed resources in one area and lack of provisions in another. This condition has resulted in unequal access to food or clothing and has been aggravated by the creation and silent operation of the black market, often controlled by one group of refugees (including on ethnic and/or national

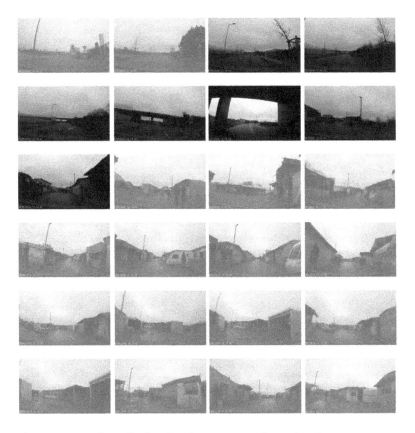

**Figure 29.9**  Film stills showing the sequence of entering the camp from the western border, driving south towards the exit. Film stills, film (Duration 03':02"), Calais 'Jungle'. © S. Tahmineh Hooshyar Emami, 2016.

lines) that webs across to other regions and sells donated goods at a high price. Perhaps with time, similar to many urban societies, the various strata will become increasingly accentuated, resulting in the growth and proliferation of certain enterprises and the collapse of others.

In this context, the bed becomes more of an identifier than a fingerprint. Objects and belongings often help to define the character and individuality of the domestic quarters in camps, and are a means of expression for the occupants of the shelter. The sleeping bag has been reclassified as the bed just as the shelter has become the house. It can speak of past financial and social status/provenance and has the power to express the present-day condition, such as duration of citizenship and occupation in the non-state of the Jungle.

She found *herself* confined in a long, low hall with locked doors all around. The only escape to safety was a small door which was half open. The door led into **the loveliest** garden you ever saw; oh, how she longed to get out of that dark hall and wander about among those beds of bright flowers and those cool fountains.[24] But the door was too small for her to get through and the garden of promises of hope and life, seemed beyond reach. [25]

**Figure 29.10** 'Alice's Alternative Wonderland', extract no. 5.
© S. Tahmineh Hooshyar Emami, 2015.

## The missing doors

The door, as an essential element in delineating thresholds, becomes imperative both as a metaphor for borders/frontiers but also as the signifier of interiority. Coincidentally, in Carroll's novels, doors often awaken senses of insecurity, hesitation and uncertainty in ALICE. They are difficult to open, difficult to walk through and their very reason for existence is questioned in various instances in the novel at which permission needs to be granted for safe passage. In the Alternative Wonderland, conflict is the inherent property of doors:

> 'Alice went timidly up to the door, and knocked.
> 'There's no sort of use in knocking,' said the Footman …
> 'Please, then,' said Alice, 'how am I to get in?'
> 'There might be some sense in your knocking,' …
> 'How am I to get in?' she repeated, aloud …
> 'ARE you to get in at all?' said the Footman …
> 'Oh, there's no use in talking to him,' said Alice desperately: 'he's perfectly idiotic!' And she opened the door and went in. (Carroll, 2015: 53–4)

Despite the similar scale of beds and doors, which have both been designed according to bodily dimensions, the latter architectural objects represent the vertical act of passing and are inherently active, whereas the bed represents the space of horizontality and stasis.

Thresholds of a larger scale are materialized by checkpoints and may shrink or expand according to changes in regulations, laws and individual circumstances such as nationality. In the context of the refugee trail, the concept of the door as threshold retains its architectural duality, both as an essential element in delineating personal space, cultural heritage and territory but also as an impassable barrier preventing access and integration. On a smaller scale, doors act as thresholds between personal space and the space of the outdoors, the space of solitude against the rest of the world. The multivalence of the checkpoint as an element of separation, connection, passage or interruption and a signifier of territoriality and identity can be substantiated in conjunction with the dual nature of doors. Frontiers or borders are dominant factors in delineating boundaries and contouring local identity; they become the manifestation of doors at large, urban scales. As well as a linear interpretation of doors as symbols of the permission of passage, a second – circular – interpretation is that of the door as marker of interiority and domesticity: a closed loop. The two perceptions enter into conflict in ALICE's spatial experience of Wonderland, in which the door often pertains to the idea of barrier between inside and outside:

> She came upon a low curtain she had not noticed before, and behind it was a little door about fifteen inches high … Alice opened the door and found that it led into a small passage, not much larger than a rat-hole: she knelt down and looked along the passage into the loveliest garden you ever saw. (Carroll, 2015: 11)

The missing doors in/of the Jungle camp are ones that can be invaded, and their power of separating spaces is undermined by their inherent conflict. On the rare occasions on which doors maintain their divisive potential, disproportionately large locks and chains are used to enforce ownership. For instance, community doors are usually more ornate and secure, ensuring the impartiality of public spaces and preventing their exclusive use by a particular group. Private areas for living may be broken off from the public realm by doors in the form of material thresholds or immaterial boundaries that have the power to filter and avert outsiders. The tents in the Jungle have permeable boundaries, lacking a physical or perceivable threshold to complete the internal space; thus, the space of domesticity is left exposed, incomplete. These semi-permanent shelters made of ply and chipboard, covered in tarpaulin sheets, are raised above the ground and require that one steps up, pushes the door open and takes off one's shoes in order to enter the space, imposing material or performative rituals before entering a well-defined space.

The entrances to the camp can be likened to checkpoints protecting border crossings between countries. Often, one or two entrances into the

**Figure 29.11** 'Alice's Alternative Wonderland', extract no. 6.
© S. Tahmineh Hooshyar Emami, 2015.

Jungle are guarded by riot police who prevent any interaction between outsiders and the residents of the Jungle. In the absence of the police, the entrances are made visible by markers such as handwritten signs, car-tyre markings or simply the flow and direction of people walking or cycling towards and away from the camp.

Similarly to the sleeping-bag reclassification, the door is reclassified as the checkpoint. Perec treats the two as similar concepts by stating that one cannot simply allow oneself to slide from the space on one side to the other without crossing a threshold, and that in order to cross that threshold one would have to communicate by showing credentials or, alternatively, knowing the password (Perec, 2008: 37). In the case of *alice*'s Alternative Wonderland, the door loses its role as provider of freedom and marker of personal boundaries and itself becomes the fine line between capture and release (Simmel, 1994: 7).

## The house beyond

The house beyond the door stands for ideas of territoriality and the delineation of borderlands through the use of an imaginary line. Similar to Wonderland and Looking-Glass country, where spatial compression and expansion were commonplace, geographical borders also change according to sociopolitical circumstances and respond to instances of conflict and resolution between counterparts. Carroll very rarely speaks of walls in the novel, and yet there is a curious tendency for spaces to vanish and

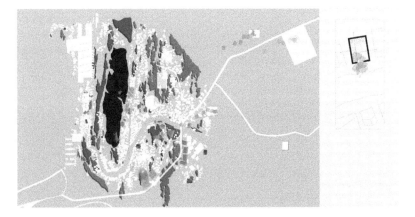

**Figure 29.12** Mapping, Calais 'Jungle'. Drawing © S. Tahmineh Hooshyar Emami, 2016.

for ALICE to find herself removed from one place and placed into another without a logical/clear spatial connector for the reader:

> the oars, and the boat, and the river, had vanished all in a moment, and she was back again in the little dark shop. (Carroll, 2015: 197)

Where the previous section dealt with permission and border crossings between two domestic or geopolitical spaces, here I speak of walls and fences – tangible or otherwise – at the scale of the body and that of the country. Within the Jungle, the issue of shifting edges and territories can be analysed through the lens of identity and nationalism, by observing regional conflicts and blurred boundaries between islands of communities. Susan Stanford Friedman writes of the historical appearance of a Thai epistemology of mapping, which allowed for great fluidity against the alien British concepts of a fixed imaginary line imposing the separation of territories. Similarly to the regional demarcations of Jungle communities, in Southeast Asia temporary borders were established during times of tension and conflict and disappeared with the re-establishment of friendly relations. Borderlands were spatial conditions that, according to the relations between different communities, would expand and contract, changing from spaces of open commerce and cultural exchange to spaces of confrontation (Stanford Friedman, 1998: 154).

The essence of the house can be reduced to the existence of a single room or can expand to the scale of a community or the camp. The room that I am writing in now is defined by four walls, but what if the walls vanished and I was left with my bed, writing desk, lamp, pen and books: what

The Jungle was the point where *alice's* journey was put on hold for the first time. This was the first barrier she faced, the first opportunity to sit down and rest her feet. She had been walking for days, thinking of the beautiful garden she yearned for and the Promise-land of her dreams. There was no way back and so she approached a few pitched tents along the road and entered one, only to see a family of four resting inside. She was welcome and rested for the night, dreaming of her home, the lemon tree and the garden she had left behind.[36]

**Figure 29.13** 'Alice's Alternative Wonderland', extract no. 7.
© S. Tahmineh Hooshyar Emami, 2015.

**Figure 29.14**  'Alice's Alternative Wonderland', extract no. 8.
© S. Tahmineh Hooshyar Emami, 2015.

would then define the room, or the house itself? As Simmel outlines in 'Bridge and Door', the need to draw boundaries and set territorial markings is primary in human nature. Together with the limitation that borders provide, people allow themselves the possibility to move them, readjust them or even step outside of them into freedom (Simmel, 1994: 7).

The Jungle was a space of contradiction, of conflict versus resolution, rapid annihilation versus rapid growth, a place of transition versus home, peace versus war and tragedy versus beauty. It hosted a 'transient community', in which individual inhabitants regularly changed but the integrity of the camp and its territorial markings remained consistent.

Within the Jungle, the physical construction and distribution of shelters is best described as typified and duplicated across the site. The division of the singular space of the shelter boasts of a stark contrast with the way in which we historically perceive domestic spatial arrangements. The seemingly simple and indivisible form of the singular internal space of the shelter is divided by immaterial spatial barriers into areas for sleeping, praying, eating or guest reception, which often overlap.

Robin Evans, in his essay entitled 'Figures, Doors and Passages' (1997) notes that in sixteenth-century Italy, buildings such as Villa Madama reflected social relationships and stratification through their organizational characteristics. The multitude of doors leading to one space was considered convenient and spatialized the journey between two opposite points of the domestic quarters as a labyrinthine experience.

Three centuries later, in Britain, concepts of privacy and division of social classes had penetrated domestic architecture and triggered changes

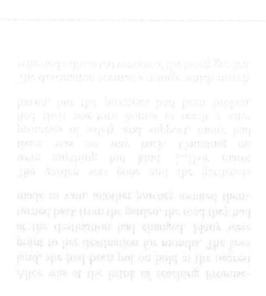

> Alice was on the brink of reaching Promise-land, she had been put on hold at the nearest point to her destination for months. The laws at the destination had changed. Many were turned back from the garden, the road they had made in vain, another journey awaited them.
>
> The garden was gone and the gardeners were anything but kind. [...]For many, there was no way back. Counting on promises of safety and support, many had fled their war-torn homes to reach a safer haven, but the promises had been broken.
>
> The destination seemed a mirage which merely reflected a distorted version of the lovely garden.[43]

**Figure 29.15** Untitled. © S. Tahmineh Hooshyar Emami.

to the typical arrangement of the house and patterns of inhabitation. The connecting matrix of rooms, which resulted in the intersection of activities, was reorganized by the introduction of a singular access door, marking the distinction between the inhabited space and circulation space. The statute of doors as establishers of privacy was progressively reinforced from that point onwards, and rather than being predominantly a connecting element they have been emphasized as elements that break spaces in two and allow one to retreat into solitude (Evans, 1997). This sequential arrangement of spaces has eventually evolved to dominate patterns of activities, physically shaping/changing the way in which we live. Walls and doors have become tangible divisions between spaces of sleeping, eating or receiving guests, changing our previous perception of interlinking spaces that bled into each other.

The moment of transition from one space to the other reinforces the in-betweenness of the Jungle. In some respects, the Jungle itself is a doorway: a doorway to reach Promise-land, which in this case is the United Kingdom, but also a doorway to adulthood. A large number of the inhabitants in the camp were unaccompanied youths on the brink of reaching their majority; hence, the moment of transition from one state to the other was twofold – both in the geopolitical position of the camp and also in its demographics and age groups.

## Conclusion

The 'Jungle' lived outside the laws and social principles of its host community, with a constantly changing and fluctuating population without which the camp would have stagnated. The settlement became the projection of a Promise-land that refugees aspired to reach, with its own legal system and emergency services, policing, educational curriculum and transportation. Of course, as previously mentioned, condensed periods of rapid growth and development were counterbalanced by rapid annihilation, which was coupled with violence and destruction. There was a proportional relationship between the rates of growth and annihilation: the faster and more developed the growth, the more frequent was the demolition – and larger areas were cleared.

The Jungle can be compared with early town settlements, which were established near sources of water. Here, the camp was built around the industrial lake located in the city outskirts, as well as by the Channel as a passage of exchange/commerce. There are various theories of city creation and growth to which we can refer in order to analyse and explain the situation of the Jungle; one would be the precedence of agricultural activities, which were essential to the growth of economies and, hence, cities. Another discusses the precedence of the city and the interdependence of rural and urban activities in development and progress (Jacobs, 1972: 15). The question here, I presume, is whether the Jungle was an anti-city or an in-between city? The contaminated industrial lake and unsuitable soil prevented growth and the spread of farming, whereas the channel was inaccessible for trade or movement. Hence, the city relied on sales and the vendor economy in order to sustain itself: it was an anti-city within the mother-city of Calais.

## Notes

1. ALICE in capital letters refers to Lewis Carroll's fictional character in *Alice's Adventures in Wonderland* and *Through the Looking-Glass*.
2. In the context of the refugee trail, Promise-land is the name I have given to the northern European countries, which have been a major destination point for those fleeing war.
3. The shipping containers provided by the French Government in the northern portion of the Jungle soon became symbols of forced removal/displacement at the heart of the EU. This was primarily due to the procedures of identification and fingerprinting to which refugees were subjected in order to enter the sleeping areas. Their provision became a mode of exerting control over an otherwise organic settlement.

## References

Bivona, Daniel. 1986. 'Alice the Child-Imperialist and the Games of Wonderland', *Nineteenth-Century Literature* 41 (2): 143–71.
Carroll, Lewis. 2015. *Alice's Adventures in Wonderland* and *Through the Looking-Glass*. Richmond: Alma Classics.
Evans, Robin. 1997. 'Figure, Doors and Passages'. In *Translations from Drawing to Building and Other Essays*, by Robin Evans. London: Architectural Association, 55–91.
Jacobs, Jane. 1972. *The Economy of Cities*. Harmondsworth: Penguin.
Nast, Heidi J. and Steve Pile, eds. 1998. Places through the Body. London: Routledge.
Perec, Georges. 2008. *Species of Spaces and Other Pieces*, edited and translated by John Sturrock. London: Penguin.
Rendell, Jane. 2007. 'Site-Writing: She is Walking about in a Town She Does Not Know', *Home Cultures* 4 (2): 177–99.
Siemann, Catherine. 2012. 'Curiouser and Curiouser: Law in the Alice Books', *Law and Literature* 24 (3): 430–55.
Simmel, Georg. 1994. 'Bridge and Door', *Theory, Culture and Society* 11 (1): 5–10.
Stanford Friedman, Susan. 1998. '"Routes/Roots": Boundaries, Borderlands, and Geopolitical Narratives of Identity'. In *Mappings: Feminism and the Cultural Geographies of Encounter*, by Susan Stanford Friedman, 151–78. Princeton: Princeton University Press.

## 30

# The imperfect ethics of hospitality: Engaging with the politics of care and refugees' dwelling practices in the Italian urban context

Giovanna Astolfo and Camillo Boano

## Introduction

With the increasing trend for the urban settlement of refugees, cities have a pressing responsibility to respond to the needs and rights of refugees and asylum seekers. While existing long before the mid-2010s, urbanism has become a salient subject of public discourse and a symbol of civil-society initiatives at various stages throughout the so-called 'refugee crisis' in Europe. Cities are places where both migrants and non-migrants interact, be it through working, studying, living or raising their families, or simply walking in the street. While cities offer great opportunities for migrants and refugees, at the same time they are also faced with challenges in creating opportunities for inclusion.

This chapter is situated within the context of the recent complex and multifaceted literature on urban humanitarianism (Fawaz, 2005; Campbell 2016: 23; Landau *et al.*, 2016; Woodrow, 2017), and is grounded within the Italian urban context. The aim is to shed light on the ways in which governments, host communities and aid agencies are challenged by myths of refugee camps as subjects and spaces of bare life and biopolitics, and to offer a perspective on the close and complex relationship that cities, refugee spaces and their residents have with each other, starting from the limits of the notion of hospitality in the current asylum system. Conceptually, the chapter is grounded in Jacques Derrida's reflection on hospitality and the Foucauldian framework of spatiology.

As Derrida has shown us, hospitality is not a panacea, and only a conditional, imperfect version of it is possible (2001). In turn, building on Michel Foucault, hospitality is essentially biopolitical in its management of refugees and migrants (Rozakou, 2012) and its production of subjects and bare lives. In this chapter, we first provide a brief overview of the concept of hospitality and then illustrate how it is enacted by and re-enacted into the practices of humanitarian organizations. We examine the city of Brescia, Italy, where the presence of refugees and migrants at different stages of their migration journeys has triggered a complex system of reception, assistance and hospitality. Since 2014, the authors have engaged in teaching-based research in Brescia in partnership with the Ambasciata per la Democrazia Locale a Zavidovici (Local Democracy Agency in Zavidovići – LDA). Amid a context characterized by contradictions as well as opportunities, further complicated by the politics of austerity, we have embarked on a long-term exploration of migrants' dwelling practices, the initial findings of which are included in the present chapter.

## The imperfect ethics of hospitality

### Reflections on the concept of hospitality

Hospitality has become a dominant notion in relation to asylum and immigration (see Berg and Fiddian-Qasmiyeh, 2018). Not only it is often used in public and state discourses but it is also prevalent in social analysis, as indicated by the established use of terms such as 'host country' and 'reception'. However, the notion of hospitality is ambivalent in nature, and requires closer examination.

As Derrida argues, 'Hospitality is culture itself and not simply one ethic among others' (Derrida, 2001: 16). Hospitality lies at the core of culture, because it concerns 'one's home, the familiar place of dwelling' (ibid.). Its importance, then, is related to the fact that it involves not only how we relate to others and to an imposed or a contingent alterity but also how we relate to the otherness within ourselves. Derrida discusses this condition of ethical openness towards the other in his writings on hospitality, and he critiques the current mode of operation in which hospitality is framed and practised through regulating and monitoring the mobility and rights of the other through laws and controls. He calls this 'conditional hospitality', as the other, the newcomer or the guest is obliged to follow specific routes in order to enter and remain in the host state; otherwise, his or her existence will be deemed illegal and he/she becomes a criminal.

The opposite, or what Derrida terms 'unconditional hospitality', is a much 'purer' practice – one that does not establish any conditions: 'pure hospitality consists in welcoming whoever arrives before imposing any conditions on him, before knowing and asking anything at all, be it a name or an identity "paper"' (Derrida, 2005: 7). Unconditional hospitality means the absolute action of accommodating anyone, without even knowing their names (as hospitality comes before language and communication) and without asking anything in return. Such an ethics of hospitality is not based on any 'calculations or projections' about the other. It should neither judge nor try to control the actions of the other. It should simply accept the other. Such an absolute version, in Derrida's own words:

> requires that I open up my home and that I give not only to the for-
> eigner, but to the absolute, unknown, anonymous other, and that I
> give place to them, that I let them come, that I let them arrive, and
> take place in the place I offer them, without asking of them either reci-
> procity (entering into a pact) or even their names. (Derrida, 2000: 25)

In order for such hospitality practice to materialize, 'the master must not allow for any debt or exchange to take place within the home. No invitation, or any other condition, can ever be a part of absolute hospitality. Hospitality, as absolute, is bound by no laws or limitations' (Westmoreland, 2008: 4).

In reality, Derrida's unconditional hospitality is an aporia: it exists only as an impossibility, as being 'possible as an experience of impossible' (Derrida and Prenowitz, 1995: 15). Nevertheless, he emphasizes the need to continuously deconstruct conditional hospitality by using the principle of unconditional hospitality in unexpected ways. In fact, for Derrida it is only through this process that the naturalness of the host–guest distinction and the accompanying political apparatuses (for example, nation states and borders) can be transformed (also see Fiddian-Qasmiyeh, this volume).

Unlike Immanuel Kant, who regards sovereign-state-regulated hospitality as the necessary and sufficient requirement for a peaceful cosmopolitan world order (Zavediuk, 2014), for Derrida law belongs to the sphere of violence and exclusion, whereas justice belongs to the sphere of the ethics of hospitality. Such an ethics of hospitality is guided by the call of justice, but it needs the law to materialize itself; it is a continuous process of transforming the law beyond calculability and conformity so as to make it more accommodating to the needs of the other (Derrida and Prenowitz, 1995). With this suggestion, laws and regulatory frameworks become the territories in which different forces and ethics negotiate the development of possible small, incremental and transformative forms of justice.[1] The latter could manifest simply as temporary alliances that open space for the ethics of hospitality to occur and perform, acknowledging their very same impossibility to exist.

What is emerging here is the ambivalent nature of the concept of hospitality. For Kant (Zavediuk, 2014), hospitality is the visitor's right not to be treated with hostility.[2] For Derrida, on the contrary, hostility presupposes hospitality. As Derrida (2000) put it, hospitality includes since the beginning the possibility of rejection, or hostility – 'it bears its own opposition' (see also Fiddian-Qasmiyeh and Qasmiyeh, 2018). Hence Derrida's coinage of the concept of 'hostipitality', which is a blend of hospitality and hostility. *Hospitalité* and *hostilité* (Derrida, 2000b: 57), or *phyloxenia* and xenophobia, are in fact two sides of the same coin, of the control and management of others and the danger that they embody. Likewise, Leonie Sandercock reminds us that 'our ambivalence towards strangers expresses fear and desire fused into one, and is thus doubly unsettling' (Sandercock, 2000: 23).

## 'Conditional hospitality' and how it is reflected and enacted in host countries' policies

Borrowing from Derrida, hospitality becomes operative only in conditional form when certain spatial and temporal conditions and restrictions apply. Hospitality is assumed to be temporary, and so is the offer and establishment of the space for the guest. Seen in the form of a gift, conditional hospitality includes the guest in the host's social and spatial realm – albeit on the condition that this inclusion is temporary, and spatially limited. Reviewing national policies on migration and asylum is revealing in this sense. In the Italian context, refugees are hosted on the condition that the number of refugees is limited, there is sufficient evidence of persecution in the country of origin and refugees commit to behaving according to certain cultural rules (including learning the local language). As Katerina Rozakou puts it, refugees are hosted only on the condition that they prove to be 'worthy' guests (Rozakou, 2012: 568; also see Mole, this volume). Further restrictions apply during the process of requesting asylum, as asylum seekers are not allowed to participate in economic activities (although they engage in the informal economy) or to engage in political activities (such as being part of a political party, and voting); they have limited mobility (as they cannot travel outside the city, unless they notify the local police); and further restrictive rules apply to their accommodation (see below). All of the above conditions of hospitality are forms of escalating violence, from the apparently innocent request that refugees learn the language to the expectation that they will 'integrate' within the host community.

One of the mechanisms through which conditional hospitality works is that of spatial and social separation. Reception centres are located outside the reach of the host community, ensuring that refugees are separate from local residents to avoid an 'unprepared encounter' (Darling, 2009: 192), minimizing the conflict over scarce resources and ensuring that control and aid are delivered efficiently. As Romla Sanyal puts it:

> singling out refugees for assistance contributes widely to the process of marginalization because such practice can adversely affect the ability of refugees to integrate into host societies. It also raises questions of how help can be provided in urban areas where local populations live in similar socio-economic conditions [without creating] double standards between international humanitarian protection and local 'civil rights'. (Sanyal, 2012: 639)

Opposing such spatial and social segregation,[3] Derrida points out how face-to-face encounters between the host and guest groups could be vital for the materialization of an ethics of hospitality. In a Levinas-inspired passage, he writes that 'face-to-face is the original ethics' (Derrida, 1999: 68). Face-to-face interaction not only involves two parties (host and guest; migrant and citizen), it also involves a third element – that is, 'a call for justice' (ibid.).

Conditional hospitality happens also through mechanisms such as externalization, differential inclusion or inclusion through exclusion. From a Heideggerian perspective, the discourse around hospitality deepens the idea of otherness by implying the treatment of the other as an outsider. Refugees and migrants embody the exteriority of the urban system since it is the host who always defines the rules of engagement. Hospitable practices symbolically place the host in a hierarchically superior position and the guest in moral debt and an inferior position (Herzfeld 1993; Fassin and Pandolfi, 2010; Rozakou, 2012). An extensive body of literature addresses refugees as 'bare lives', as being included in the system though exclusion; in this sense, refugees represent the outlaws who sit outside the law but at the same time are necessary for the law to exist.

Thus, a refugee-hosting policy symbolizes exception because it operates both within the host state (and with its permission) and outside it and its laws (by having separate rules, administrative structure and budgets), simultaneously challenging and upholding state sovereignty. Unlike Derrida's ethics of hospitality, which leaves room for limited ethical acts as long as they are driven towards unconditional hospitality, Giorgio Agamben's ethics has a tendency to straightforwardly:

> reject all sovereign apparatuses that produce or threaten to produce 'bare life'; this makes it difficult to think about 'imperfect, yet necessary, political formations of conditional hospitality.' (Darling, 2009; 650)

To return to Derrida (2000, 2005), the concept of hospitality extends to all human relations. It governs relations between the self and the other, not only between the host and the refugee. It is a relationship that is binary but not static, as it evolves over time. We could argue that it is a transformative process through which the guest becomes the host, and the host becomes the hostage. As Derrida reminds us, the word hospitality – he cites '*Hospitalität*' in this case – has a 'troubled and troubling' Latin origin, 'which allows itself to be parasitized by its opposite, "hostility"' (Derrida, 2000b: 3). This leads us to think that refugees are carriers of transformative processes, and it is in this logical vein that the LDA partners in Brescia (Italy) manage the Sistema di Protezione Richiedenti Asilo e Rifugiati (System for the Protection of Asylum Seekers and Refugees – SPRAR) in an effort to subvert the forms of violence produced by unconditional hospitality at the basis of current hosting policy. The LDA enacts what Derrida terms an 'ethics of hospitality', which materializes in small ethical acts such as the construction of spatial opportunities for encounter and the recognition of the political existence of migrants. Despite its limited and temporary success, the LDA practices ethical openness and respect for human life that can create a disruption within the exclusionary regime and provide a template for a new urbanism to come.

## The politics of care in the Italian urban context

Amid austerity, financial stagnation and xenophobia

Italy has long been one of Europe's thresholds for people from sub-Saharan Africa, although it receives a smaller number of asylum requests than other countries and has low immigration rates (Eurostat, 2015;

UNCHR, n.d.). Both features are due to a number of disparate factors, including the current politics of austerity and cuts to welfare and social services, increasing unemployment and homelessness, and a proportional surge of nationalism and xenophobic sentiments – which makes Italy a less attractive port of entry than other countries such as Germany. The financial crisis and the politics of austerity affect local communities, economic migrants and refugees alike. As homelessness is on the rise, houses and benefits offered to refugees within protection programmes have become unpopular and have been targeted by right-wing propaganda. Humanitarian organizations (and, increasingly, the private sector) with budgets to run reception centres provide a parallel (and often very profitable) system of governance that allows refugees to survive in ways that low-income groups cannot; this creates double standards between humanitarian protection and local civil rights – leading to conflict between host communities, whose members feel they are not receiving assistance from the state, and refugees who receive economic support from the EU, the state and aid organizations. Such double standards exacerbate already tense situations in which host communities are not willing to welcome refugees. It is within this polarization that the struggle of local humanitarian organizations needs to be understood, particularly in terms of developing political and civic consensus.

## The hosting system: Heterogeneity, fragmentation and informality

The Italian hosting system is a complex, multifarious and fragmented apparatus of humanitarianism, control and containment, resulting from chronic policy failure. Over time, administrative devices – as well as technical and humanitarian measures aimed at accommodating, containing or detaining refugees and asylum seekers – have produced a constellation of more or less segregated urban and peri-urban centres, dormitories and shared accommodations, with disparate temporal and legal requirements and governance, where refugees often face precarious living conditions. Established to respond to short-term emergencies rather than to address refugee situations that persist for years and decades, the asylum-and-hosting system fails to respond to real needs. Insularity, combined with the temporariness of the system and the high number of asylum rejections (50 per cent), ultimately results in a process of expulsion, illegality and informality. According to Médecins Sans Frontières (Medici Senza Frontiere, 2016, 2018), for every 100,000 refugees and asylum seekers who are hosted in government-run structures, there are almost 10,000 who live in informal settlements close to urban areas without any access to water, sanitation or basic healthcare.[4]

Without delving into the complex aberrant details of the system,[5] asylum seekers and refugees (at the time of writing) have access to a reception system that is split into first and second reception lines. First-line reception consists of around 3,000 Emergency Accommodation Centres – 'CAS' (Centro Accoglienza Straordinaria) distributed across the national territory. A lack of adequate structures and services – coupled with the protraction of the refugees' stay as well as mismanagement, corruption and a violation of human rights – characterize these centres. Furthermore, there is little clarity on their exact location, governance and management system, as there exists no obligation by law to disclose information about the CAS (Cittadinanzattiva, LasciateCIEntrare and Libera, 2016). Second-line reception consists of a number of shared-housing accommodation units within the SPRAR, and it is based on the 'diffused hospitality' model whereby small groups of refugees are hosted in separate accommodations in urban and peri-urban areas.

## 'Diffused' hospitality: Another form of conditional hospitality or the first step towards an 'ethics of hospitality'?

The 'model' of diffused hospitality is neither new nor novel, as it stems from the bottom-up initiative of Italian families hosting Bosnian refugees fleeing war in the 1990s.[6] Based on the assumption, in the early 2000s, that small groups of refugees could have a better chance of integrating into the local community and life than larger groups in segregated and overcrowded centres, such a practice was 'institutionalized' and incorporated into the SPRAR programme,[7] which is currently active in 95 cities and towns across Italy, hosting 25–30,000 people (potentially marking a policy shift towards urban-dispersal reception).[8] It is based on the spontaneous initiative of local municipalities, which retain considerable control over the process and are tasked with generating political and civic consensus around its implementation. It is, in principle, an attempt to overcome the mechanism of separation (at least at the spatial level) entailed by conditional hospitality as we have highlighted above.

This strategy appears to fit the specificity of the Italian territory and its social fabric, formed by a constellation of small and medium-sized cities and small (usually very internally homogeneous) communities. However, the temporariness of the programme largely compromises the effort in establishing relations with the local community. In turn, the very idea of employing a redistributive system – relocating refugees in small towns – raises issues, including the perpetuation of forms of control and policing that ultimately fail to achieve the integration of individuals in a given community, as well preventing them from developing modes of political action by atomizing their presence in the urban space (Manara and Piazza, 2018).

## The dilemmas of conditional hospitality from the perspective of humanitarian organizations

Scholars have already highlighted the dilemmas of humanitarian practices faced by both recipients and providers of aid (for instance, Fassin and Pandolfi, 2010; Feldman, 2007; Rozakou, 2012), and the Italian politics of care is no exception here. According to Agostino Zanotti, the director of the LDA, an NGO that collaborates with local municipalities in the management of the SPRAR programme in Brescia, Italy, 'the most relevant dilemmas can be represented through some key words: *suspension, standardisation, autonomy and awareness*' (Zanotti, 2016: 13). Suspension is related to the very long and convoluted asylum-request process that hinders the beneficiary's ability to find sufficient stimuli to define or redefine his/her own path of development and existence. Standardization is required for the sake of providing everybody with the same opportunities, but it generates a homogenization of individual needs, aspirations and expectations. In turn, autonomy is about enabling the manifestation of one's own individuality and culture, which becomes impossible within a system of protection that performs control. Finally, awareness implies acknowledging and working within the above-mentioned dilemmas, and the inherent conflict resulting from individual ethical positions.

Well aware of the unavoidable risk of reproducing the violence of conditional hospitality, the LDA's current effort opposes the conventional humanitarian approach whereby the refugee is seen as a voiceless victim, the receiver of aid and a passive object of policymaking. Instead, the LDA supports avenues for refugees' agency to challenge and fragment power with different goals in mind. This is done by moving forward from the idea of hospitality as shelter provision, towards enabling or consolidating a network of relations around each single refugee.

## Engaging with refugee dwelling practices

### Home as a place or as being in the world?

As part of a long-term teaching-based research project conducted with UCL's MSc BUDD[9] students and staff over four years and coordinated by the LDA in Brescia, we have been investigating refugees' dwelling practices in the city. In the form of a three-day intensive field exploration – including interviews, transect walks and focus groups – we have, each year, engaged with around four different groups of young male refugees and asylum seekers (around 15 in total) hosted within the SPRAR.[10]

It is within the SPRAR houses in which refugees are hosted that the violence of conditional hospitality (restrictions and rules, separation, externalization, and so on), as well as the dilemmas of the humanitarian organization (such as suspension, standardization and autonomy), have become manifest to us. Within the houses, hospitality turns into a device of control as it ensures protection at the expense of individual freedom, while the humanitarian organization transforms itself into a policing body.

After going through identification, asylum registration and several relocation processes since their arrival on Italian shores, refugees and asylum seekers allocated to the SPRAR in Brescia are accommodated in small groups in shared flats. The host and owner of the flat is either the municipality or the country's Ministry of the Interior. The host institutionalizes rules in order to retain its authority – mostly banning the consumption of alcohol; barring the presence of women and guests; and imposing a curfew, and maintenance and cleaning duties. Although it is not 'their' house, the guests are asked to maintain it with the same care as if it was. Broken rules lead to fines, and in certain cases might lead to expulsion from the programme. Such rules largely limit people's freedom in the house, and deeply affect its emotional and social meaning.

These same rules also deeply affect care workers by turning their work into that of policing. Particularly affected are those who engage with passionate political sensitivity with the refugees and who struggle to deal with such limitations in order to reconcile the legal meaning of protection with the universal right to freedom and the political imperative to host and help. As rules betray the law of absolute hospitality and result in forms of violence that turn the home inside out, where do refugees find home (and the attributes of home)? With this question in mind, we embarked on an attempt to understand different forms, perceptions and spaces where dwelling is temporarily manifesting itself.

According to the interviews and conversations that we have held with different groups of refugees in Brescia since 2014, it has emerged that their lives are trapped within a number of paradoxes produced by hospitality, including the mobility of a long migration journey and forms of immobility imposed by legal and bureaucratic processes, the possibility of permanence in the host country and the risk of constant transience, exclusion from the local host community and inclusion in supranational aid communities, economic dependence and pressure to obtain an autonomous livelihood. Each of these paradoxes tends to influence the physical, social and emotional meaning and perception of the house. Shifting meanings are related to individual trajectories, and to cultural and economic factors. For many refugees, the journey to Italy is a protracted one with multiple departure points.

Italy is not necessarily the intended 'arrival country' for refugees; most often it is a transit country (on their way to Germany for Syrian refugees, and to the UK for refugees from Senegal and Nigeria). Choices about final destination countries are often related to welfare and benefits, job opportunities and language, which are or may seem greater in countries such as Germany and the UK. The amount of time and effort that refugees and asylum seekers invest in maintaining the house, purchasing personal objects and building relationships with the host community highly depends on such a trajectory.

Meanings of home are diverse and often contradictory. As Michael Jackson (1995: 122) puts it, home is 'always lived as a relationship, a tension … like any word we use to cover a particular field of experience, home always begets its own negation … It might evoke security in one context and seem confining in another'. Similarly, we have found that for some refugees, home is a familiar and comfortable space where particular relationships are lived. In this sense, the idea of home relates to privacy, intimacy, domesticity and comfort according to cultural origin and context. Sometimes home is perceived as a safe, enclosed domain opposed to perceptions of external space as dangerous and unknown, as a protected inside in an increasingly alienating outside. However, the house is not a space that offers freedom. Given the presence of house rules, a sense of intimacy and privacy turns into oppression, as was explained to us by a significant percentage of interviewees, who are subject to forms of control in the home environment. Instead of being a 'private space' distinguished from the public realm – a refuge, removed from public scrutiny and surveillance – the home of refugees might turn into the opposite of home. Hence the contradictory feelings around the idea of home as a space of belonging and alienation, intimacy and violence, desire and fear.

Feelings around 'home' may greatly change and vary during refugees' stay within the programme, according to the positive or negative outcome of their asylum-application processes. The latter becomes an obsessive thought that obscures and prevails above any other, and sometimes hinders action. Alternative feelings towards the idea of home vary between:

1) a sense of safety, trust and euphoria at the beginning of the programme
2) a sense of immobility and frustration soon afterwards, when refugees find themselves stuck in the legal process, when they struggle with learning the language or with performing an identity that is compatible with the legal requirement for protection
3) a sense of disengagement and withdrawal, when protraction decreases motivation and willingness to engage with the process, the local community and housemates
4) a sense of rejection, despair and/or renewed uncertainty at the end of the programme, when they find themselves homeless again, no matter whether they have obtained the papers or not.

In the case of a positive outcome, the meaning of home changes completely and starts relying on ideas of tenure, and personal and familial security. As soon as they have their papers, refugees are compelled to leave the programme – often without having secured a job or sufficient means to cover their rent.

During our transect walks and urban explorations with refugees and asylum seekers, research participants shared/showed the existence of networks (often of a religious nature) and social interactions occurring at different and distant locations around the city. This is revelatory of a multi-sited appropriation of the urban territory and a certain level of mobility, despite refugees' difficulty in accessing public-transport systems due to difficulties of information and the fragmentation of the services. Turning to the question – Where do refugees find home? – it seems to us that many attributes of home such as privacy, safety and security are found outside the house; and discomfort is sometimes felt inside the house, when refugees feel homeless at home. We could argue that for people on the move, rather than home being a fixed place it is a condition: the experience of being at home in the world.

## Conclusion

The spatial element of reception, its materiality and locality, is sidelined in discussions around practices of hospitality in Italy. Engaging with the pressing contemporary problematics of refuge and its spatial semantics forces us to think about the city as the unfinished foreground of the malleable nature of human–nonhuman interactions. It also demonstrates the ways in which people and social forms partake of, and are shaped by, multiple systems and forces with variable degrees of agency. The practice of the LDA, as well as that of other organizations operating within the parameters of similar humanitarian and ethical dilemmas, requires political, social and cultural change in the way in which we see, manage, conceive of and practise urban spaces (Zanotti, 2016: 11).

We hope to have briefly provided an understanding of the political nature of urban reception infrastructures and the practices of hospitality, unravelling how they make the city. Hospitality practices in general, and those of the LDA in particular, inevitably emerge not just as the material embodiment of the ambiguities of humanitarianism but also as their complicit and instrumental medium. To admit as much is to recognize the extent to which a material organization and the spatiality that it forms not only reflect but also reinforce social orders, thus becoming a contributing factor in recurring forms of containment, suspension and control. The LDA's work suggests that hospitality not only involves the creation of ethical subjects in the form of the host, the guest and their relations of identity and difference, and welcome and rejection, but that it inevitably also produces space. Hospitality, then, is a form of 'spatial relational practice with affective dimensions' (Bulley, 2016: 7), and so requires us to unpack and problematize not the simple, given space of hospitality in the form of assistance (camp, centre or house) but the micro, banal, humble and everyday practices of the spatial politics of refuge.

What appears important in the LDA experience, and the UCL MSc teaching-based experience attached to it, is the possibility of steering the process towards practical, material recommendations that could potentially improve the lives of those who are pressured by the city (Rodgers and O'Neill, 2012: 6). This not only calls for renewed social responsibility in thinking differently about the spaces of refuge but, importantly, also directs action towards their realization, invoking the need to redesign the spatial taxonomies of humanitarianism manifesting, in the case of the LDA, as seemingly disentangled, neutral and temporary entities in local city-making processes.

## Notes

1. See Wilde (this volume) for a discussion of the implications of recent and ongoing legal and policy changes in the field of migration.
2. On the 'hostile environment', see Berg (this volume).

3. On different forms of social and spatial differentiation in displacement, see Tayob (South Africa), Maqusi (Lebanon and Jordan), Fiddian-Qasmiyeh (Lebanon), Loris-Rodionoff (Turkey), Hooshyar Emami (France) and Vandevoordt (Belgium), all in this volume.
4. These individuals (1) are waiting to submit their asylum application; (2) have had their asylum application rejected; or (3) have never applied because they are not intending to remain in Italy but have not yet secured the resources to leave. Furthermore, even individuals who are currently hosted in the reception centres or are part of protection schemes could potentially end up living in informal settlements, if their asylum application is unsuccessful or if they cannot afford a house on the market once they have obtained their papers.
5. The so-called reception system is more articulated and convoluted than briefly outlined here, also including a 'first aid and assistance' component formed by the Hotspots. Hotspots facilities have been created following the European Agenda on Migration in 2015; they are located close to the arrival routes with the initial purpose of identification and fingerprinting procedures, before transferring refugees and asylum seekers to first-line or second-line reception centres (on one of these 'hotspots', Lampedusa, see Franceschelli and Galipò, this volume). They have now partly changed their function, having become 'places for migrants' redistribution on land' (Garelli and Tazzioli, 2016; Tazzioli and Garelli, 2018) and often places for protracted (illegal) detention where human-rights abuses and poor living conditions are well documented (Amnesty International, 2016). Similar precarious and inhumane conditions are well documented within the infamous detention centres called Centres for Identification and Expulsion – CIE (recently renamed Deportation Centres – CPR) (LasciateCIEntrare, 2016).
6. See for instance www.balcanicaucaso.org/aree/Bosnia-Erzegovina/Dentro-il-conflitto-94400.
7. Article 32, Law 189/2002, 'Modifica alla normativa in materia di immigrazione e di asilo'.
8. Each municipality has a quota of 2.5 refugees per 1,000 inhabitants. See for instance: www.interno.gov.it/it/notizie/sprar-verso-modello-unico-accoglienza-i-numeri-2015; http://viedifuga.org/asilo-e-accoglienza-lunhcr-superare-i-cara-lo-sprar-come-modello/; http://viedifuga.org/wp-content/uploads/2015/03/Nota-Direttive_Final-04-02-2015.pdf; www.vita.it/it/article/2016/09/01/di-capua-sprar-diffondere-a-livello-nazionale-i-modelli-di-accoglienza/140578/.
9. The MSc Building and Urban Design in Development is one of the postgraduate programmes offered at the UCL Development Planning Unit. The programme examines the ways in which humans' activities shape and influence their spatial environment, and how the physical environment in turn affects and influences human activity with specific attention on participatory design in the context of the Global South.
10. More information on the programme can be found at https://www.sprar.it/english and at https://openmigration.org/en/glossary-term/sprar/. The LDA is predominantly hosting young men and, in rare cases, some families. In our specific engagement, we have engaged with two Syrian families – but mostly with young men.

# References

Amnesty International. 2016. *Hotspot Italia: Come le politiche dell'Unione Europea portano a violazioni dei diritti di rifugiati e migranti*. London: Amnesty International. Accessed 4 June 2017. www.amnesty.org/en/documents/eur30/5004/2016/it/.

Berg, Mette Louise and Elena Fiddian-Qasmiyeh. 2018. 'Introduction to the Issue: Encountering Hospitality and Hostility', *Migration and Society* 1 (1): 1–6.

Bulley, Dan. 2016. *Migration, Ethics & Power: Spaces of Hospitality in International Politics*. London: Sage Publications.

Campbell, Leah 2016. 'Stepping back: understanding cites and their systems'. ALNAP Working Paper. London: ALNAP/ODI.

Cittadinanzattiva, LasciateCIEntrare and Libera. 2016. 'InCAStrati. Iniziative civiche sulla gestione dei centri di accoglienza straordinaria per richiedenti asilo'. Accessed 11 March 2020. https://www.cittadinanzattiva.it/files/primo_piano/giustizia/inCAStrati-report.pdf.

Darling, Jonathan. 2009. 'Becoming Bare Life: Asylum, Hospitality, and the Politics of Encampment', *Environment and Planning D: Society and Space* 27 (4): 649–65.

Derrida, Jacques. 1999. 'Hospitality, Justice and Responsibility: A Dialogue with Jacques Derrida'. In *Questioning Ethics: Contemporary Debates in Philosophy*, edited by R. Kearney and M. Dooley. London: Routledge, 65–83.

Derrida, Jacques. 2000a. 'Hostipitality', translated by Barry Stocker and Forbes Morlock, *Angelaki: Journal of the Theoretical Humanities* 5 (3): 3–18.

Derrida, Jacques. 2000b. *Of Hospitality: Anne Dufourmantelle Invites Jacques Derrida to Respond*, translated by Rachel Bowlby. Stanford: Stanford University Press.

Derrida, Jacques. 2001. *On Cosmopolitanism and Forgiveness*, translated by Mark Dooley and Michael Hughes. London: Routledge.

Derrida, Jacques. 2005. 'The Principle of Hospitality', *Parallax* 11 (1): 6–9.

Derrida, Jacques and Eric Prenowitz. 1995. 'Archive Fever: A Freudian Impression', *Diacritics* 25 (2): 9–63.

Diken, Bülent and Carsten Bagge Laustsen. 2005. *The Culture of Exception: Sociology Facing the Camp*. London: Routledge.

Eurostat. 2015. 'Asylum Applicants in the EU'. Accessed 27 January 2020. http://ec.europa.eu/eurostat/web/main/news/themes-in-the-spotlight/asylum2015.

Fassin, Didier and Mariella Pandolfi. 2010. *Contemporary States of Emergency: The Politics of Military and Humanitarian Interventions*. New York: Zone Books.

Fawaz, Mona. 2005. 'Agency and Ideology in Community Services: Islamic NGOs in a Southern Suburb of Beirut'. In *NGOs and Governance in the Arab World*, edited by Sarah Ben Néfissa, Nabil Abd al-Fattah, Sari Hanafi and Carlos Milani, 229–55. Cairo: American University in Cairo Press.

Feldman, Ilana. 2007. 'Difficult Distinctions: Refugee Law, Humanitarian Practice, and Political Identification in Gaza', *Cultural Anthropology* 22 (1): 129–69.

Fiddian-Qasmiyeh, Elena and Yousif M. Qasmiyeh. 2018. 'Refugee Neighbours and Hostipitality', *Refugee Hosts*, 20 March. Accessed 18 January 2020. https://refugeehosts.org/2018/03/20/refugee-neighbours-hostipitality/.

Garelli, Glenda and Martina Tazzioli. 2016. 'The EU Hotspot Approach at Lampedusa', *OpenDemocracy*, 26 February. Accessed 27 January 2020. www.opendemocracy.net/can-europe-make-it/glenda-garelli-martina-tazzioli/eu-hotspot-approach-at-lampedusa.

Herzfeld, Michael. 1993. *The Social Production of Indifference: Exploring the Symbolic Roots of Western Bureaucracy*. Chicago: University of Chicago Press.

Jackson, Michael, ed. 1995. *At Home in the World*. Sydney: Harper Perennial.

Kelly, Sean K. 2004. 'Derrida's Cities of Refuge: Toward a Non-Utopian Utopia', *Contemporary Justice Review* 7 (4): 421–39.

Landau, Loren, Caroline Wanjiku-Kihato, Jean Pierre Misago, David Obot and Ben Edwards. 2016. *Becoming Urban Humanitarians: Engaging Local Government to Protect Displaced People*. Washington, DC: Urban Institute. Accessed 27 January 2020. www.urban.org/sites/default/files/publication/84356/Urban%20Institute%20Research%20Report%20-%20Becoming%20Urban%20Humanitarians_FINAL.pdf.

LasciateCIEntrare. 2016. *#20GiugnoLasciateCIEntrare: Mobilitazione nazionale della societa' civile per la richiesta d'accesso nei centri per migrant in occasione della giornata mondiale del rifugiato 2016*. Rome: LasciateCIEntrare. Accessed 4 June 2017. www.asylumineurope.org/sites/default/files/resources/20giugnolasciarecientrare.pdf.

Manara, Martina and George Piazza. 2018. 'The Depoliticisation of Asylum Seekers: Carl Schmitt and the Italian System of Dispersal Reception into Cities', *Political Geography* 64: 43–52.

Medici Senza Frontiere. 2016. *Fuori Campo: Richiedenti asilo e rifugiati in Italia: Insediamenti informali e marginalità sociale*. Rome: Medici Senza Frontiere. Accessed 27 January 2020. www.medicisenzafrontiere.it/wp-content/uploads/2019/04/Fuoricampo2016.pdf.

Medici Senza Frontiere. 2018. *Fuori Campo: Insediamenti informali: Marginalità sociale, ostacoli all'accesso alle cure e ai beni essenziali per migranti e rifugiati: Secondo rapporto*. Rome: Medici Senza Frontiere. Accessed 27 January 2020. www.medicisenzafrontiere.it/wp-content/uploads/2019/04/Fuoricampo2018.pdf.

Rodgers, Dennis and Bruce O'Neill. 2012. 'Infrastructural violence: Introduction to the special issue', *Ethnography* 13: 401–12.

Rozakou, Katerina. 2012. 'The Biopolitics of Hospitality in Greece: Humanitarianism and the Management of Refugees', *American Ethnologist* 39 (3): 562–77.

Sandercock, Leonie. 2000. 'When Strangers Become Neighbours: Managing Cities of Difference', *Planning Theory and Practice* 1 (1): 13–30.

Sanyal, Romola. 2012. 'Refugees and the City: An Urban Discussion', *Geography Compass* 6 (11): 633–44.

Sanyal, Romola. 2014. 'Urbanizing Refuge: Interrogating Spaces of Displacement', *International Journal of Urban and Regional Research* 38 (2): 558–72.

Tazzioli, Martina and Glenda Garelli. 2018. 'Containment beyond Detention: The Hotspot System and Disrupted Migration Movements across Europe', *Environment and Planning D: Society and Space*, 1–19. Accessed 19 January 2020. https://doi.org/10.1177/0263775818759335.

UNHCR (United Nations High Commissioner for Refugees). 2010. *2009 Global Trends: Refugees, Asylum-Seekers, Returnees, Internally Displaced and Stateless Persons*. Geneva: United Nations High Commissioner for Refugees. Accessed 11 April 2017. www.unhcr.org/statistics/country/4c11f0be9/2009-global-trends-refugees-asylum-seekers-returnees-internally-displaced.html.

UNHCR Operational Portal – Refugee Situations. n.d. 'Mediterranean Situation'. Accessed 27 January 2020. http://data2.unhcr.org/en/situations/mediterranean.

Westmoreland, Mark W. 2008. 'Interruptions: Derrida and Hospitality', *Kritike* 2 (1): 1–10.

Woodrow, Nina. 2017. 'City of Welcome: Refugee Storytelling and the Politics of Place', *Continuum: Journal of Media and Cultural Studies* 31 (6): 780–90.

Zanotti, Agostino. 2016. 'In Transit'. In *Seeing the City Anew: Designing for Refugee Integration* (BUD-Dlab 8), 11–12. London: Bartlett Development Planning Unit.

Zavediuk, Nicholas. 2014. 'Kantian Hospitality', *Peace Review: A Journal of Social Justice* 26 (2): 170–7.

Zetter, Roger and George Deikun. 2010. 'Meeting Humanitarian Challenges in Urban Areas', *Forced Migration Review* 34: 5–7.

# 31

# Producing precarity: The 'hostile environment' and austerity for Latin Americans in super-diverse London

Mette Louise Berg

## Introduction

Recent years have seen a hardening and securitization of borders and rhetoric in different parts of the Global North vis-à-vis migrants and refugees from the Global South (De Genova and Peutz, 2010; Jones, Reece, 2017; Perl, 2019). In the US, policing, criminalization and deportations have been steadily on the increase (Brennan, 2018), while in the UK, the government has explicitly sought to create a 'hostile environment' for what it calls 'illegal immigrants' (Burnett, 2016; Travis, 2013), a contentious and misleading term.[1] The 'hostile environment' manifests itself *inter alia* in an 'astoundingly complex web of regulations, rules, exclusions and addenda around the eligibility of migrants to a range of public services and benefits' (Oliver, 2014), and has been shown to affect a wide range of migrant groups and ethnicized minorities (Jones, Hannah *et al.*, 2017).[2] The 'hostile environment' approach requires service providers to perform 'everyday bordering' (Yuval-Davis *et al.*, 2018) as part of their jobs, and puts them under direct and indirect pressure to exclude rather than include.

The 'hostile environment' measures were introduced during a period of harsh austerity policies in the UK and against a background of new forms of diversities, dubbed 'super-diversity' (Vertovec, 2007), in London and other major UK cities.[3] Super-diversity refers to the increasing diversity of ethnicities and countries of origin among urban residents, who are further differentiated by socio-economic status, distinct patterns of labour-market integration, language, religion, migration trajectory and immigration status, as well as different gender, age and generational profiles (ibid.). The 'hostile environment' and super-diversity together create multilayered and complex dynamics of differentiation, hospitality and hostility – including those among and between migrants with different migration trajectories and legal statuses, and refugees and asylum seekers sharing, negotiating and contesting urban spaces. The impact is felt particularly at the very local level: in streets, neighbourhoods and on housing estates (see, for example, contributions to Berg *et al.*, 2015; Hall, 2012; Wessendorf, 2014).

Focusing on Latin Americans in a super-diverse inner London borough – namely, Southwark – this chapter traces the implications of this complex environment on service access for newly arrived migrants, as seen from the perspectives of differently positioned front-line service providers or 'street-level' bureaucrats (Lipsky, 1980). Latin Americans constitute a relatively recent but growing and internally diverse migrant group in London. The 'community' includes people who have arrived as migrants, asylum seekers or refugees, either directly from Latin America or as secondary migrants from Spain and other European countries (McIlwaine, 2011). Many do not speak English on arrival, or speak it only poorly, and although many arrive with secondary or even tertiary education they tend to be incorporated into London's labour market in low-pay, part-time jobs in commercial cleaning and hospitality. Irrespective of their legal position they are often in situations of vulnerability and precarity for reasons explored in this chapter. I argue that examining the barriers to service access for new migrants in London provides a window onto the production of precarity and new inequalities. I invoke Judith Butler's notion of precarity here in order to emphasize a '*politically induced* condition in which certain populations suffer from failing social and economic networks of support and become differentially exposed to injury, violence, and death' (Butler, 2009: 2, my emphasis). In other words, precarity is produced by structural inequalities and exclusionary legal frameworks; it is not a quality inherent to particular groups. It offers a different framing from the notion of 'vulnerability', which has been criticized for essentializing certain groups rather than accounting for the wider structural processes that produce marginality (Fiddian-Qasmiyeh, 2019).

I begin by describing the research on which the chapter is based. Following this, I describe the local context in Southwark and then home in on the Latin American community in the borough and the multiple barriers that its members face in accessing services. In the conclusion,

I reflect on the production of precarity for migrants, refugees and asylum seekers placed at the intersections of austerity and 'hostile environment' policies.

## Research methods

The chapter is based on research conducted as part of an Economic and Social Research Council (ESRC) Knowledge Exchange Fellowship 2014–15, during which I was a 'researcher in residence' with Southwark Council on a part-time basis.[4] During the Fellowship, I worked closely with council officers from the Community Engagement Division and also with the Latin American Women's Rights Service (LAWRS), a well-established charity run for and by women from Latin America.[5] As a super-diverse borough with many new and small migrant groups, and high turnover rates among its residents, Southwark faces particular challenges in planning and delivering services – especially in a context of central-government funding cuts. Following on from its pioneering collaboration with LAWRS, Southwark Council wanted to know more about the barriers that its Latin American residents experience in accessing services.

Cathy Trejos, an experienced LAWRS outreach worker who also had previous research experience, worked with me on the project as research assistant and was an important interlocutor. She contributed to all stages of the research, from designing the interview guide and identifying interviewees to conducting interviews and interpreting results. Between us, we conducted 27 semi-structured interviews with 35 Southwark-based statutory and non-statutory service providers in the public sector and third sector between May and July 2015. We included a wide range of services including employment support, language tuition, schooling, housing, health, legal advice, domestic violence and support for disabled people. We also organized a workshop for and with Southwark Council staff in relevant departments and services.[6] Finally, we participated in relevant community events during the period of research (for more details, see Berg, 2019).

In the light of the paucity of data on the Latin American population in London in general and Southwark in particular (see McIlwaine and Bunge, 2016), I commissioned a series of detailed tables based on microdata on country of birth and passports held for Latin Americans in Southwark, including educational attainment and household characteristics. The census analysis was conducted by Anna Krausova (Krausova, 2015). This chapter draws on both interview and census-analysis material.

# Latin Americans in London: Invisibility and community organizing

Latin Americans have settled in London since the 1970s, but the majority living in the city today have arrived since 2000 (McIlwaine and Bunge, 2016: 22). They have, however, gone largely unnoticed by policymakers and the general public (McIlwaine *et al.*, 2011). As a new migrant group, they are 'invisible' in the census, constituting one of the 'hidden communities' in the capital (Pharoah and Hopwood, 2013). This means that any particular challenges and barriers that they face are unlikely to be addressed.

Notwithstanding their census invisibility, people born in Latin America and the children of Latin American-born mothers make up a significant group. They were estimated to number about 145,000 in 2013, making them 'the eighth largest non-UK born population in London and larger in size than Somalian, Chinese and Romanian migrants' (McIlwaine and Bunge, 2016: 8), all of whom have a much higher degree of policy, media and public visibility. As a group, Latin Americans are characterized by considerable internal diversity not only in country of origin but also in language, education and class background. Added to this are differences between cohort-defined migrant generations (Berg and Eckstein, 2015 [2009]) – for instance, differences between those who arrived in London as political exiles in the 1970s versus more recent labour immigrants and refugees; and differences in migration status and trajectories, such as between those who have migrated directly from Latin America versus those who have migrated to London via other European countries, principally Spain (McIlwaine and Bunge, 2016: 5, 18; McIlwaine *et al.*, 2011: 43–4). Many in the last-named category hold EU citizenship and have therefore not, until Britain's departure from the EU at least, needed visas and/or work permits. Degrees of formal entitlement to services vary considerably between those with EU and those with Latin American passports, yet community groups find that most Latin Americans (regardless of citizenship and entitlements) face difficulties in terms of employment, language barriers and the recognition of qualifications.

Latin Americans live across all of London (McIlwaine *et al.*, 2011), but two areas are especially identified with them: Seven Sisters in Haringey, north London, and Elephant and Castle in Southwark, south London, on which this chapter focuses. Both areas feature clusters of Latin American shops and businesses catering to a co-ethnic as well as a broader clientele, and both also regularly feature cultural events, such as the *Carnaval del Pueblo* in Southwark. There are other shared features too: both areas are undergoing large-scale public- and private-led regeneration projects that are likely to dramatically increase rents in the areas and lead to a loss of 'ethnic' businesses (Román-Velázquez, 2014). In Southwark, the Elephant and Castle area, which has become the centre of a small 'Latin Quarter' (ibid.), is at the centre of these changes.

## The Southwark context

Historically, what is today the London Borough of Southwark has been a working-class settlement characterized by intense poverty. The borough is today characterized by considerable and growing linguistic and ethnic diversity, and represents a typical site of urban super-diversity (Poppleton *et al.*, 2013). More than 120 languages are spoken in Southwark and about one in ten households have no members with English as their first language. Fully 39 per cent of its residents (an estimated 113,667 people) were born outside of the UK. Diversity is most evident among younger residents, and three-quarters of reception-age children in the borough are from black and minority ethnic (BME) groups. New and growing demographic groups in the UK including 'white other' and 'mixed' ethnicities, and African and Latin American ethnicities represent a relatively larger share of Southwark's population than the national average (Krausova, 2015; Pharoah and Hopwood, 2013). In short, the population in the borough is fluid and stratified, and consists of many small and internally differentiated groups, some in positions of considerable precarity, and with differential entitlements and degrees of visibility to service providers but also different needs and expectations of services and how they are delivered.

As well as this migration-driven diversification, dramatic processes of gentrification mean that the borough is increasingly marked by stark and visible juxtapositions of wealth and deprivation among its residents (Berg *et al.*, 2019).

## Latin Americans in Southwark: Housing, labour-market incorporation and community organizing

According to the census, about eight thousand Latin Americans lived in Southwark in 2011, representing just under 3 per cent of the population, and 8 per cent of the residents who were born outside of the UK, equally split between men and women (Krausova, 2015: 4). Both London-wide and in Southwark, the main countries of origin for Latin Americans are

Brazil and Colombia (Krausova, 2015; for London as a whole, see McIl-waine and Bunge, 2016: 10).

There is a significant shortage of affordable housing in Southwark, reflecting a London-wide problem. Notwithstanding, the borough has a niche market of relatively cheap private housing – some of it of sub-standard quality, and sometimes operated by rogue landlords – and it is in this section of the housing market that many newly arrived Latin Americans and other recent migrant groups find themselves (Pharoah and Hopwood, 2013: 48).[7] Latin Americans are also attracted to Southwark because many have friends and family members living in the borough, and because of the Latin American shops and services in the Elephant and Castle area. However, the language barrier; low incomes; and, in some cases, insufficient understanding of rights puts many Latin Americans in vulnerable positions vis-à-vis private landlords.

Service providers commented on the poor and overcrowded hous-ing conditions of many Latin American service users, including families. The detailed census analysis supports their observations, although it is likely to under-report the true scale of the problem. According to the cen-sus, the majority of residents in Southwark lived in 1–2-person house-holds (63 per cent), with only 8 per cent in households with more than five members. Latin American households by contrast tended to be larger, with only 47 per cent living in smaller (1–2-person) households and 14 per cent living in households with five or more members.

Across London, nearly 90 per cent of Latin Americans are of working age and their rate of employment is high at almost 70 per cent. Despite half of the community having university-level education (43 per cent for Latin Americans in Southwark), they tend to work in low-pay, elemen-tary jobs, particularly commercial cleaning, and are more deprived than the average for London (McIlwaine and Bunge, 2016: 31). All service providers commented that Latin Americans are 'hard-working', that the vast majority are in employment and that they often find jobs through word of mouth. However, many lack English-language skills – making it difficult to get jobs that match their qualifications:

> Latin Americans are very good at getting jobs quickly. Approximately 80 per cent of Latin Americans of working age are in employment, and on Spanish or Portuguese passports. But there is a big issue of why they work below their qualifications, including in cleaning and hospitality. They work, earn their salaries, pay their taxes; they are entitled to be here, but we are losing something – they have qualifi-cations that are not being used. (Job Centre manager)

The cleaning sector, which provides jobs for many Latin Americans,[8] is largely unregulated and characterized by low pay and fragmented, unsocial hours (McIlwaine, 2007; Però, 2008). Reflecting their labour-market incorporation, Latin Americans seeking support from legal-advice clinics present with issues of retention of payment, non-payment of wages, pay below minimum wage, unfair dismissal, non-payment of sick pay, holiday-entitlement issues and discrimination, reflecting wider issues in the low-pay end of the labour market (Equality and Human Rights Commission, 2014: 30). Not speaking sufficient English to understand a payslip, make a simple telephone call or to be able to attend a job interview constitutes a considerable barrier to inclusion, participation and social mobility for Latin American migrants (Carlisle, 2006; Granada, 2013; McIlwaine et al., 2011). Given that many Latin Americans work almost exclusively with other Latin Americans, they are not picking up more than rudimentary English in their workplaces.

Adding to this marginality, many have to combine several jobs with different employers in order to get by, which in itself can have an impact on entitlements and which negatively affects their opportunities for learning English. For instance, most Latin Americans are in employment, and do not claim income-related benefits (although some may be entitled to them). Therefore, they are not considered a 'priority group' and so do not qualify for subsidised ESOL[9] language classes (Granada, 2013). However, their pay is often so low that they cannot afford to pay for courses at market rates – and fragmented, unsociable and unpredictable hours make it difficult for them to attend classes regularly (see also, Carlisle, 2006; Granada, 2013; McIlwaine et al., 2011). Many consequently find themselves trapped in low-paying jobs despite qualifications from their country of origin. Trade unions and community groups are providing some accessible and free language training, combined with training in employment rights and entitlements. This includes trade-union-organized language classes part-subsidised by one of the Latin American embassies and scheduled at times that make it possible for Latin Americans to attend.

Overall, Latin American migrants' pattern of labour-market incorporation – in combination with welfare cuts, service restructuring and an acute shortage of affordable housing – interacts with census invisibility and the growing complexity of entitlements in producing precarity. Responding to this, community groups have mounted campaigns for more visibility for Latin Americans – so far leading to ethnic recognition by Southwark Council in 2012, followed by Lambeth, Hackney and Islington councils.

## Access to and provision of services for Latin Americans

Service providers interviewed for the research underpinning this chapter generally had a nuanced understanding of the multiple and interlinked barriers that their clients faced in accessing services. They discussed these barriers within a wider socio-economic context, including public-spending austerity – which also affected other service users, migrants or otherwise – and a complex and changing structure of service provision. All service providers, whether in the public or third sector, were under pressure not only because of austerity measures but also, and especially, because of the increasing complexity of entitlements, which makes it difficult to establish which services residents can access and which they cannot. Others have written about instances in which service providers are so overworked and dealing with such complex cases that it simply becomes easier to refuse migrants access 'rather than risk making the wrong decision' (Oliver, 2014: 25; see also Phillimore, 2015: 579).

Generally, service providers found that Latin Americans have the same needs as other Southwark residents regarding advice and services. However, unsocial working hours and poor English-language skills mean that Latin Americans face greater barriers in accessing appropriate support. Community groups and service providers all expressed concerns regarding the vulnerabilities of some Latin Americans, while also recognizing their agency. They described Latin American residents through terms such as 'resilient' and 'strong work ethic', and commented on 'high levels of community support'. Yet while advice via word of mouth and internal and informal support structures within the Latin American community somewhat mitigate the impact of language and other barriers, word of mouth does not always convey the complexity of rules and entitlements for individuals. Other significant barriers that emerged in the research were employment-related ones; barriers to accessing affordable and good-quality housing; barriers to schooling and education; and health-service barriers (see also Carlisle, 2006; McIlwaine *et al.*, 2011). Importantly, these different barriers interact with each other while gender and immigration status intersect with all of them, creating different degrees and conditions of precarity for men and women, children and adults, EU and non-EU citizens, and between individuals subject to different legal statuses and with different migration trajectories. In what follows, I discuss these different barriers in turn, while showing how each is related to the others. I focus especially on the difficulties that Latin Americans face in learning English, and the wider ramifications of the increasingly restrictive access to English language tuition for non-English-speaking migrant groups.[10]

## The language barrier and 'literacy in how the system works'

There is broad consensus in the policy literature on the importance of ensuring that new migrants are able to speak English sufficiently well to participate in wider society (Kere and Bell, 2017; Casey, 2016). Increasingly, however, English-language tests and skills have been instrumentalized as part of the 'hostile environment' in order to facilitate exclusion. Rather than seeking to enable and widen access, funding has been cut, making it difficult for new migrant groups to access affordable classes at suitable times of the day and week – especially for those, like Latin Americans, who work unsociable or changing hours. Thus, there is a tension between a recognition that enhanced language skills are important for integration and inclusion and, at the same time, an institutionalization of language skills as requirements that facilitate exclusion and expulsion.

All service providers interviewed for this research mentioned the crippling effects of poor English-language skills for Latin Americans in London. Cathy McIlwaine's detailed analysis of the 2011 census found that around one in five of all Latin Americans in London cannot speak English or cannot speak it very well, rising to more than a quarter of those resident in Southwark, but with significant variations between Latin Americans of different national origins (McIlwaine and Bunge, 2016: 20–1).[11] Importantly, recent and precarious migrants with uncertain status, who are more likely to speak English poorly or not at all, are also less likely to be included in the census, suggesting that the issue may be under-reported.

Recognizing the language barrier, some service providers have been able to draw on staff and volunteer language skills to reach out to Latin Americans, and have seen a considerable surge in demand – sometimes leading to saturation. Service providers commented that Latin Americans demonstrate agency and resilience in overcoming language barriers, often using a 'trial and error' approach as illustrated here:

> Latin Americans come to this library because a friend has told them that there is someone who speaks Spanish and helps with information, so they feel confident coming to a person that will speak in Spanish with them, someone who understands their needs ... Sometimes the library becomes like a GP [General Practice] surgery ... They come for

any kind of thing, how to enrol their children into school, looking for English classes, benefits, how to register to vote, anything, you name it. It's like a focal point for the community ... It would seem that the Latin Americans do not have many places that cover their needs for information and support ... They are new in the UK and they have no knowledge of how things work in the UK ... They are missing information or places to go. (Spanish-speaking librarian)

Service providers emphasized the fact that the language barrier was linked to an overall patchy understanding of UK public-service provision:

You can send out letters, like the council does, but they are very difficult to understand if you don't understand and read English. Translating alone isn't going to help, it's also about context: these are complex issues. You need to sit with people and explain in their own language. (Advice worker)

Latin Americans need basic literacy in how the system works, more signposting to services, and training in how to make basic telephone calls to the council. (Community outreach worker)

As well as identifying what this third-sector service provider calls 'basic literacy' in understanding services, culturally embedded expectations of services also effectively constituted a barrier. For instance, many service providers found that Latin Americans were reluctant to claim benefits to which they were entitled, including Working Tax Credit and Child Benefit.

Compounding these issues, many Latin Americans who seek legal advice are not able to document the length of their residence in the UK, which is needed to prove entitlement to benefits; they may have moved and changed jobs many times, they may have multiple employers, and their income may go up and down from week to week. Many have not kept payslips and tenancy agreements going back five to eight years, or may have been paid cash in hand and/or rented without contracts without realizing that this would have an impact on their entitlements in the future – and, in any case, many have little power to change their situation.

## Gender-related barriers

Service providers agreed that women tend to be more affected by the language barrier than men, as was also seen for other migrant groups (Casey, 2016: 95). Spanish- and Portuguese-language services supporting women affected by intimate partner abuse additionally reported socially and culturally embedded barriers. These included a lack of trust in the police and authorities more generally, making women reluctant to report incidents of domestic violence, and a normalization of gender-based violence in intimate relationships. As this domestic-violence advice worker commented, there is a link between political violence in wider society and intimate partner abuse – which, in the case of women from conflict areas, had normalized abuse (see also, McWilliams and Doyle, 2017):

> It has been my experience that there are many Latin American women who can't recognise when they are in a violent or coercive relationship … it has become a normalised way of interaction between the couple and family. This is also relevant because I had some cases where the social circle was very harsh and made the women feel guilty as if they had done something very wrong by denouncing their aggressive partner … Many women still only depend on their friends' advice to make decisions due to their lack of interaction with other parts of the community, including services … They endure these situations because many of them come from hard or socially insecure situations in their home countries.

Such barriers make it particularly difficult for women in abusive relationships to seek support in a socially legitimate manner, suggesting a need for culturally sensitive service outreach that can reach women in their own language. Just like for other groups, the shortage of affordable and accessible housing makes it more difficult for women to leave abusive relationships (Miles and Smith, 2018).

## Housing

There is an acute shortage of decent affordable housing across London, affecting recent migrants particularly. Some service providers found that recent migrants have also been adversely affected by the requirement that landlords check the immigration status of tenants. Because of the complexity of the requirement, landlords prefer to turn away migrants rather than risk being fined. This requirement, part of the 'hostile environment' policy, particularly affects recent migrants, while language and wider service literacy issues mean that they may not be aware of benefits rights and entitlements, or are reluctant to claim them; service providers reported a low take-up of housing benefits even among Latin Americans who are entitled to them.

## Access to schooling and education

Latin American community groups were concerned about the difficulties faced by many of their users in accessing schooling for their children. Community groups agreed that there has been an increase in families arriving and waiting for school places, and that some schools are reluctant to take children who do not speak English because of a lack of resources and concerns about the potential impact on the school's ranking. As with other services, a stumbling block for parents is insufficient English and a lack of awareness of how the system works:

> There is a lack of information around education, many parents are not aware of the education system and they send their children to classes without really knowing what the levels, exams, or steps are. (Language teacher, NGO)

Once children are enrolled in schools, there are issues around learning English to a sufficient level in time for key exams, which can then impact on access to further and higher education. There are also challenges related to maintaining a good level of written and spoken Spanish or Portuguese. This is how a secondary-school teacher explained the situation in his boys-only school, which has a relatively high proportion of Latin American children:

> Some families arrive here and the boys come to school in 1–2 weeks, but some have been out of school for up to a year. The Latino boys we see are mainly here as a result of secondary migration from Spain, but some come direct from [Latin America] … Parents often don't realise the importance of GCSEs [General Certificate of Secondary Education, taken at ages 14–16], e.g. 15-year-olds might not be able to speak English well enough to be able to get good grades.

As well as the language barrier and the challenge of providing up-to-date and accurate information in an area in which policies change frequently, access to schools is also linked to immigration status – as discussed below.

## Immigration status

Immigration status was seen as a major issue by many service providers, who cited an unmet need for affordable, reliable and accurate immigration advice. A recurrent problem is substandard immigration 'advisers' who are not adequately trained:

> People pay for sub-standard immigration advice ... There is a real crisis in access to good quality, affordable immigration advice ... I have fears about people paying for poor quality immigration advice, it's often people from within the communities who are exploiting people. (Advice worker)

The issue needs to be understood in the context of legal-aid cuts, increasingly complex immigration legislation and a proliferation of immigration statuses with different levels of entitlements resulting from the 'hostile environment' policy. In the words of a legal adviser with more than ten years' experience in the field, the differentiation in entitlements for different kinds of benefits has become 'extremely and unbelievably complicated' with distinctions between EU and non-EU nationals complicated by non-EU residents who are married to EU nationals or whose children have EU or UK citizenship.

A particular issue of concern for immigration advisers, is family-reunification cases. Many Latin Americans who arrive in London have left family behind in either their country of origin or in another European country, often Spain, and hope to reunite with their family once they have established themselves. Several countries of origin for this group are undergoing complex processes, which mean that family reunification is not only desirable but also necessary. However, given their concentration in low-pay and part-time jobs, Latin Americans have been especially affected by the threshold of a minimum annual salary of £18,000 from a sole employer in order to be entitled to family reunion (amounting to more than someone working full-time on the minimum wage would earn). Thus, the particular intersection of immigration status and the nature of Latin Americans' incorporation into the labour market produces barriers to securing the right to family life as outlined in the European Convention on Human Rights (European Court of Human Rights, 2019).

## Barriers to accessing health services

It is well documented that migrants face multiple barriers to accessing healthcare (Fernández-Reino, 2019). In a focus group for Latin American women specifically, conducted by LAWRS and Healthwatch Southwark, participants identified challenges in registering with medical practices, difficulties in making appointments and in accessing interpretation services, and negative attitudes from staff. Participants reported that they use private healthcare in addition to or instead of National Health Service (NHS) services to which they may be entitled.[12] Depending on immigration status, some migrants have been required to pay for certain health services since October 2014, creating barriers especially for pregnant women and mothers with young children. Confusion and lack of knowledge among both health providers and migrants about entitlement – particularly for undocumented migrants and migrants with uncertain immigration status, including visa over-stayers, refused asylum seekers, those who have been trafficked into the UK and spousal migrants escaping domestic violence – mean that migrants are not always able to access the care that they need (Fernández-Reino, 2019).

Several service providers pointed out that Latin Americans, like other recent migrant groups, do not always know about the full range of services offered by General Practice doctors, or the difference between primary- and secondary-care providers. The complexity of entitlements makes word of mouth particularly unreliable, and many Latin Americans therefore do not understand or know what their entitlements are, or how to access care.

As for other migrant groups and the population at large, health and well-being are related to socio-economic conditions: overcrowded accommodation, social isolation, poverty, unsocial work schedules and work stress, are all known to contribute to ill health, including mental ill health (Fernández-Reino, 2019).

## Conclusion: Super-diversity, austerity and the production of precarity

When Steve Vertovec coined the term 'super-diversity' in 2007, he argued that the proliferation of legal statuses was a 'fundamental dimension' with which local service providers had yet to catch up (Vertovec, 2007: 1036). Not long afterwards, the then UK coalition government began its programme of public-sector austerity, including the retrenchment and restructuring of services, and a redrawing of boundaries between the public, private and third sectors. Local governments were especially affected by budget cuts (Lowndes and Gardner, 2016). Vivien Lowndes and Alison Gardner have dubbed this 'super-austerity' in what seems an implicit nod to super-diversity, although they do not make this point. With super-austerity, they clearly seek to capture something similarly complex and qualitatively new, defining it as a situation in which 'new cuts come on top of previous ones, compounding original impacts and creating dangerous (and unevenly spread) multiplier effects' (ibid.: 358–9).

Importantly, super-austerity has affected already-deprived local authorities more than others, and these are often also the very same local areas that are the most diverse, including central London boroughs (Poppleton *et al.*, 2013). At an immediate level, super-austerity means that small community-support groups are facing diminished or no funding. Meanwhile, larger, mainstream service providers do not have the resources or cultural and language skills needed to reach out to new, small and hard-to-reach groups, whose understandings of service access and entitlements may be incomplete due to the complexities described in this chapter. Such groups are thereby less likely to be able to access services to which they are entitled (see also Phillimore, 2011 and 2015). Several service providers interviewed identified issues regarding such 'service literacy' among their users. Critical literacy scholarship has long advocated an approach to literacy that places it within a wider socio-economic context imbued with unequal power relations (Rockhill, 1993; Street, 2003). Melissa Steyn has helpfully linked this critical work to diversity scholarship in the form of 'critical diversity literacy', defined as an 'ethical socio-political stance' (Steyn, 2015: 379) that acknowledges the constitutive role of power in issues of diversity. As Steyn argues, it can be understood as:

> an informed analytical orientation that enables a person to 'read' prevailing social relations as one would a text, recognizing the ways in which possibilities are being opened up or closed down for those differently positioned within the unfolding dynamics of specific social contexts. (Steyn, 2015: 381)

Key here is the need for service providers to have the time and resources required to examine and understand the multiple, structural and interacting barriers that their users face, and how best to facilitate access and inclusion – especially when this goes against the grain of a 'hostile policy' environment. Yet this capacity is being undermined by pressure on services, funding cuts and increasing complexities of entitlement. Meanwhile, service users – including Latin Americans and other new migrant groups – are struggling to gain access to the building blocks, including English-language skills that would enable them to obtain a more comprehensive degree of service literacy.

As has been shown in this chapter, 'hostile environment' policies not only exacerbate pre-existing and growing inequalities in service access but also introduce further barriers and exclusions. Direct and indirect barriers interact with each other and create exactly the kinds of dangerous multiplier effects described by Lowndes and Gardner (2016) as an integral part of super-austerity. For new migrant groups such as Latin Americans, these intertwined developments entail high risks of entrenchment of precarity, with women and children especially at risk of 'falling through' the increasingly threadbare nets of service provision.

## Notes

1. As migrant scholars and activists have long argued, 'no-one is illegal'; migrant 'illegality' is a status produced by migration legislation (De Genova, 2002). It is more accurate to talk of unauthorized, irregular or undocumented migrants (Bloch and McKay, 2016).
2. The devastating consequences of the policy, especially on the so-called Windrush generation, were exposed in a series of articles in the *Guardian* newspaper in the spring of 2018, which led to the resignation of the then Home Secretary Amber Rudd. Her successor, Sajid Javid, renamed the policy the 'compliant environment', but no substantive changes were introduced (Gentleman, 2018a, 2018b, 2019). See also Wardle and Obermuller (2019); for a discussion of a similar policy in Denmark, see Suárez-Krabbe and Lindberg (2019).
3. On the urban dynamics of migration, displacement and hosting, see the chapters in this volume by Tayob (South Africa); Vandevoordt (Belgium); Astolfo and Boano (Italy) and Loris-Rodionoff (Turkey).
4. https://www.compas.ox.ac.uk/project/servicing-super-diversity-esrc-iaa-knowledge-exchange-fellowship.
5. http://www.lawrs.org.uk.
6. These included Children's and Adults' Services, Community Engagement, Corporate Strategy, Customer Service, Education, Housing, Improvement and Development, Mental Health, Public Health, Regeneration, Social Services, Translation Services and Young People's Services.
7. Across the UK as a whole, recent migrants are overwhelmingly living in private rented accommodation. Private lettings are often informal, sometimes without legal agreements, and some involve illegally converted outbuildings or obliging people to share with strangers. See http://www.compas.ox.ac.uk/2012/what-is-the-evidence-about-migrant-living-conditions-in-the-private-rented-sector-and-how-could-they-be-improved.
8. For instance, 80 per cent of users of the advice service of the Indoamerican Refugee and Migrant Organization (IRMO: http://irmo.org.uk), a community-led NGO, work in cleaning jobs.
9. ESOL stands for 'English for speakers of other languages'.
10. Public funding for English-language classes for adults has been severely cut in recent years; see https://www.theguardian.com/uk-news/2017/jan/05/theresa-may-faces-calls-to-implement-regional-immigration-policy
11. This was also reflected in demand for Southwark's translation service in 2014–15, when Spanish accounted for a far higher number of requests than any other language (data supplied to the author by Southwark Council).
12. See 'Community Focus Group with Latin American Women's Rights Service (LAWRS) Findings & Recommendations', July 2014, https://www.healthwatchsouthwark.org/sites/healthwatchsouthwark.org/files/hws-and-lawrs-final-report.pdf; and 'Latin Americans: a case for better access to sexual health services', March 2014, http://www.clauk.org.uk/wp-content/uploads/2014/06/CLAUK-and-NAZ-Latin-Americans-a-case-for-better-access.pdf.

# References

Berg, Mette Louise. 2019. 'Super-Diversity, Austerity, and the Production of Precarity: Latin Americans in London', *Critical Social Policy* 39 (2): 184–204.

Berg, Mette Louise and Susan Eckstein. 2009. 'Introduction: Reimagining Migrant Generations', *Diaspora: A Journal of Transnational Studies* 18 (1/2): 1–23.

Berg, Mette Louise, Ben Gidley and Anna Krausova. 2019. 'Welfare Micropublics and Inequality: Urban Super-Diversity in a Time of Austerity', *Ethnic and Racial Studies* 42 (15): 2723–42.

Berg, Mette Louise, Ben Gidley and Nando Sigona, eds. 2015. *Ethnography, Diversity and Urban Space*. London: Routledge.

Bloch, Alice and Sonia McKay. 2016. *Living on the Margins: Undocumented Migrants in a Global City*. Bristol: Policy Press.

Brennan, Denise. 2018. 'Undocumented People (En)counter Border Policing: Near and Far from the US Border', *Migration and Society* 1: 156–63.

Burnett, Jon. 2016. *Entitlement and Belonging: Social Restructuring and Multicultural Britain: An IRR Discussion Paper on the Housing and Planning Bill 2015 and the Immigration Bill 2015*. London: Institute of Race Relations.

Butler, Judith. 2009. 'Performativity, Precarity and Sexual Politics', *AIBR: Revista de Antropología Iberoamericana* 4 (3): 1–13.

Carlisle, Frances. 2006. 'Marginalisation and Ideas of Community among Latin American Migrants to the UK', *Gender and Development* 14 (2): 235–45.

Casey, Louise. 2016. *The Casey Review: A Review into Opportunity and Integration*. London: Department for Communities and Local Government.

De Genova, Nicholas P. 2002. 'Migrant "Illegality" and Deportability in Everyday Life', *Annual Review of Anthropology* 31: 419–47.

De Genova, Nicholas and Nathalie Peutz, eds. 2010. *The Deportation Regime: Sovereignty, Space, and the Freedom of Movement*. Durham, NC: Duke University Press.

Equality and Human Rights Commission. 2014. *The Invisible Workforce: Employment Practices in the Cleaning Sector*. London: Equality and Human Rights Commission.

European Court of Human Rights. 2019. *Guide on Article 8 of the European Convention on Human Rights: Right to Respect for Private and Family Life, Home and Correspondence*. Strasbourg: Council of Europe. Accessed 28 January 2020. www.echr.coe.int/Documents/Guide_Art_8_ENG.pdf.

Fernández-Reino, Mariña. 2019. *Health of Migrants in the UK*. Oxford: Migration Observatory, 13 August. Accessed 11 March 2020. https://migrationobservatory.ox.ac.uk/resources/briefings/the-health-of-migrants-in-the-uk.

Fiddian-Qasmiyeh, Elena. 2019. 'Looking Forward: *Disasters* at 40', *Disasters* 43 (S1): S36–60.

Gentleman, Amelia. 2018a. 'The Children of Windrush: "I'm Here Legally, But They're Asking Me to Prove I'm British"', *The Guardian*, 15 April. Accessed 20 January 2020. www.theguardian.com/uk-news/2018/apr/15/why-the-children-of-windrush-demand-an-immigration-amnesty.

Gentleman, Amelia. 2018b. 'Windrush Row: Javid's Apology Overshadowed by New Removal Figures', *The Guardian*, 21 August. Accessed 20 January 2020. www.theguardian.com/uk-news/2018/aug/21/sajid-javid-says-sorry-for-18-windrush-removals-or-detentions.

Gentleman, Amelia. 2019. 'MPs Refer Home Office to Equalities Watchdog over Windrush Scandal', *The Guardian*, 1 May. Accessed 20 January 2020. www.theguardian.com/politics/2019/may/01/mps-refer-home-office-to-equalities-watchdog-windrush-scandal-hostile-environment-institutional-racism.

Granada, Ana Lucila. 2013. 'Latin Americans in London: Language, Integration and Ethnic Identity'. PhD thesis, Aston University.

Hall, Suzanne. 2012. *City, Street and Citizen: The Measure of the Ordinary*. London: Routledge.

Jones, Hannah, Yasmin Gunaratnam, Gargi Battacharyya, William Davies, Sukhwant Dhaliwal, Kirsten Forkert, Emma Jackson and Roiyah Saltus. 2017. *Go Home? The Politics of Immigration Controversies*. Manchester: Manchester University Press.

Jones, Reece. 2017. *Violent Borders: Refugees and the Right to Move*. London: Verso.

Kere, Anna and Richard Bell. 2017. *Interim Report into Integration of Immigrants*. London: All Party Parliamentary Group on Social Integration.

Krausova, Anna. 2015. *Latin Americans in Southwark: A Census Analysis Report*. Oxford: COMPAS.

Lipsky, Michael. 1980. *Street-Level Bureaucracy: Dilemmas of the Individual in Public Services*. New York: Russell Sage Foundation.

Lowndes, Vivien and Alison Gardner. 2016. 'Local Governance under the Conservatives: Super-Austerity, Devolution and the "Smarter State"', *Local Government Studies* 42 (3): 357–75.

McIlwaine, Cathy. 2007. *Living in Latin London: How Latin American Migrants Survive in the City*. London: Queen Mary University of London.

McIlwaine, Cathy. 2011. 'Super-Diversity, Multiculturalism, and Integration: An Overview of the Latin American Population in London, UK'. In *Cross-Border Migration among Latin Americans: European Perspectives and Beyond*, edited by Cathy McIlwaine, 93–117. New York: Palgrave Macmillan.

McIlwaine, Cathy and Diego Bunge. 2016. *Towards Visibility: The Latin American Community in London*. London: Trust for London. Accessed 11 March 2020. https://trustforlondon.fra1. digitaloceanspaces.com/media/documents/Towards-Visibility-full-report_QqkSbgl.pdf.

McIlwaine, Cathy, Juan Camillo Cock and Brian Linneker. 2011. *No Longer Invisible: The Latin American Community in London*. London: Queen Mary University of London. Accessed 28 January 2020. www.qmul.ac.uk/geog/media/geography/docs/research/latinamerican/No-Longer-Invisible-report.pdf.

McWilliams, Monica and Jessica Doyle. 2017. *Violent Conflict, Political Settlement and Intimate Partner Violence: Lessons from Northern Ireland* (Political Settlements Research Programme Research Report). Edinburgh: Global Justice Academy.

Miles, Charlotte and Katie Smith. 2018. *Nowhere to Turn 2018: Findings from the Second Year of the No Woman Turned Away Project*. Bristol: Women's Aid.

Oliver, Caroline. 2014. 'Muddied Waters: Migrants' Entitlements to Public Services and Benefits'. In *Migration: The COMPAS Anthology*, edited by Bridget Anderson and Michael Keith, 24–5. Oxford: COMPAS.

Perl, Gerhild. 2019. 'Migration as Survival: Withheld Stories and the Limits of Ethnographic Know-ability', *Migration and Society* 2 (1): 12–25.

Però, Davide. 2008. 'Migrants' Mobilization and Anthropology: Reflections from the Experience of Latin Americans in the United Kingdom'. In *Citizenship, Political Engagement, and Belonging: Immigrants in Europe and the United States*, edited by Deborah Reed-Danahay and Caroline B. Brettell, 103–23. New Brunswick, NJ: Rutgers University Press.

Pharoah, Robin and Oliver Hopwood. 2013. *Families and Hardship in New and Established Communities in Southwark*. London: Southwark Council.

Phillimore, Jenny. 2011. 'Approaches to Health Provision in the Age of Super-Diversity: Accessing the NHS in Britain's Most Diverse City', *Critical Social Policy* 31 (1): 5–29.

Phillimore, Jenny. 2015. 'Delivering Maternity Services in an Era of Superdiversity: The Challenges of Novelty and Newness', *Ethnic and Racial Studies* 38 (4): 568–82.

Poppleton, Sarah, Kate Hitchcock, Kitty Lymperopoulou, Jon Simmons and Rebecca Gillespie. 2013. *Social and Public Service Impacts of International Migration at the Local Level* (Research Report 72). London: Home Office. Accessed 28 January 2020. https://assets.publishing.service.gov.uk/government/uploads/system/uploads/attachment_data/file/210324/horr72.pdf.

Rockhill, Kathleen. 1993. 'Gender, Language and the Politics of Literacy'. In *Cross-Cultural Approaches to Literacy*, edited by Brian Street, 156–75. Cambridge: Cambridge University Press.

Román-Velázquez, Patria. 2014. 'Claiming a Place in the Global City: Urban Regeneration and Latin American Spaces in London', *Revista Eptic Online* 16 (1): 84–104.

Steyn, Melissa. 2015. 'Critical Diversity Literacy: Essentials for the Twenty-First Century'. In *Routledge International Handbook of Diversity Studies*, edited by Steven Vertovec, 379–89. London: Routledge.

Street, Brian. 2003. 'What's "New" in New Literacy Studies? Critical Approaches to Literacy in Theory and Practice', *Current Issues in Comparative Education* 5 (2): 77–91.

Suárez-Krabbe, Julia and Annika Lindberg. 2019. 'Enforcing Apartheid? The Politics of "Intolerability" in the Danish Migration and Integration Regimes', *Migration and Society* 2 (1): 90–7.

Travis, Alan. 2013. 'Immigration Bill: Theresa May Defends Plans to Create "Hostile Environment"', *The Guardian*, 10 October. Accessed 20 January 2020. www.theguardian.com/politics/2013/oct/10/immigration-bill-theresa-may-hostile-environment.

Vertovec, Steven. 2007. 'Super-Diversity and Its Implications', *Ethnic and Racial Studies* 30 (6): 1024–54.

Wardle, Huon and Laura Obermuller. 2019. '"Windrush Generation" and "Hostile Environment": Symbols and Lived Experiences in Caribbean Migration to the UK', *Migration and Society* 2 (1): 81–9.

Wessendorf, Susanne. 2014. *Commonplace Diversity: Social Relations in a Super-Diverse Context*. Basingstoke: Palgrave Macmillan.

Yuval-Davis, Nira, Georgie Wemyss and Kathryn Cassidy. 2018. 'Everyday Bordering, Belonging and the Reorientation of British Immigration Legislation', *Sociology* 52 (2): 228–44.

## 32

# Encountering Belgians: How Syrian refugees build bridges over troubled water

Robin Vandevoordt

## Introduction

The man who opened the door was bald and taller than me. His dark, friendly eyes, buried deep in their sockets, welcomed me into his home as he forcefully shook my hand up and down.

'Olan!' he shouted.

'Robin' I shouted back.

'Pleased to meet you!'

Olan was one of the first Syrian men whom I encountered in my research. His social worker had put us in touch, and he had insisted we meet at his place, a small studio in a village in Flanders, the Dutch-speaking part of Belgium. He welcomed me with a big smile and impassioned gestures, pleased, I presumed, to receive a guest.

'Sit! sit!' he said, pointing to a beige sofa. He had put cookies, crisps and a pot of tea on a small glass table. Behind the table an old television was playing cartoons, dubbed in Dutch. I smiled, nodding to the cartoons. He grinned: 'like this, I practice Dutch!'

Olan had been in Belgium for 18 months, and had been granted protected status a year ago. He had immediately subscribed to Dutch-language classes, but it was going slowly, he found, much too slow:

The grammar, I understand, 90 per cent. But talking, listening, writing is difficult. To whom should I talk? I can't practice! It's difficult. I'm learning, every day. But if people speak dialect, it's difficult, I can't understand. And a lot of people only speak dialect all of the time!

I asked him whether he had contact with Belgians. Without hesitating he responded:

> Oh! They're very, very nice. If I ask them where is the shop or where is this or that, just on the street, they help me immediately. They're very nice, very friendly.

'And did you make any Belgian friends?' I asked. He sighed, long and deep. 'No. It's difficult. I have one Belgian friend. I met him at the bus stop. We were waiting. And we started talking, because the bus was late. And we talked. And then I asked if he wanted to become my friend. My first Belgian friend.' His grin reappeared. 'After that, we met a few times, in the city. But it's not easy. You know, he's a bit, handicapped. He's got a problem with his voice. He can't speak very well. And he's got problems to sleep as well.'

It took me a while to understand: the man he had met at the bus stop was taking the bus back to the rehabilitation centre where he was recovering from a severe traffic incident that put him in a coma for 11 days. After 18 months of trying, that man was the only Belgian whom Olan described as a friend: a man recovering from a serious injury, waiting for the bus.

Olan's story was far from unique. After conducting several dozen interviews and countless casual conversations with Syrian refugees in Belgium, I learnt that many were in similar situations. They were eager to bond with Belgians, yet only a few managed to do so. Several months after meeting Olan, I spoke with Mustafa and Mohammed, two cousins aged just over 30 who had travelled to Belgium alone before being reunited with their wives and children. When I asked them whether they had regular contact with Belgians, Mustafa replied:

> Actually, we don't have any relations with Belgian people at all. But when I go to the supermarket, or any market or any place, I think they are friendly. It's easy to make contact. We would like to have more relations with Belgians, to enter the real culture. Talking with the person in the supermarket is not really making contact. It's the same with my Belgian teacher.

Most of the Syrians I spoke with struggled to move beyond such superficial encounters with Belgians.[1] Khaled, one of my key informants who translated the conversation with Mustafa and Mohammed, summarized their situation afterwards: 'They are trying to find the key to open the door to Belgian society. They want to break [down] that wall. But [for] now, they're still outside. They can't get in.'

One way in which social scientists have described such social relations is through the concept of 'social capital' (Ager and Strang, 2008; Bourdieu and Wacquant, 1992; Putnam, 2000, 2007): social networks provide individuals with emotional and material support, as well as practical information on the ways in which social institutions work (for example, how and where to apply for which types of work, where to look for education or find affordable housing) (Ryan *et al.*, 2008; Ryan, 2011). Those who possess social capital have easier access to other forms of 'capital', such as cultural (for instance, language skills, knowledge of local customs and culture, education) and economic capital (work, housing, benefits). And vice versa: those who possess a great deal of economic capital (money) and cultural capital (for example, education) will generally find it easier to acquire resourceful forms of social capital such as influential, knowledgeable or affluent friends (Bourdieu and Wacquant, 1992).

Newly arrived refugees and migrants generally find themselves in a situation in which the social, cultural and economic capital that they possessed in their country of origin has lost much of its value. Having influential friends in Damascus, the ability to communicate fluently in Arabic or having a postgraduate degree in Law, for instance, may be considered useful assets in Syria, but they are usually of little value in Europe (Csedő, 2008; Erel, 2010). Yet acquiring such forms of capital is crucial to refugees' and migrants' livelihoods, as well as their overall sense of well-being and belonging.

To analyse the social capital that immigrants possess, scholars often use Robert Putnam's (2000, 2007) distinction between 'bridging' and 'bonding' social relations (Ager and Strang, 2008; Nannestad *et al.*, 2008; Patulny and Svendsen, 2007; Ryan *et al.*, 2008; Ryan, 2011). Whereas the former concept denotes weak ties with people who are 'unlike me in some important way', the latter refers to stronger ties 'to people who are like me in some important way' (Putnam, 2007). While bridging relations are thought to help people 'get ahead' and learn the local language or find a better job, bonding relations are thought to provide the emotional support and the odd temporary job that allows one to 'get by'.

Other scholars have argued, however, that the distinction between bridging and bonding social capital is not always that clear-cut. Evidently bridging relations, between Belgians and Syrians for instance, can be strong and affectionate too. Conversely, relations within one's own ethnic community may be rather weak and practical (for instance, drawing on the help of a friend of a friend in order to secure a better job). In addition, scholars have made the fairly obvious point that migrants' social relations vary not only in terms of ethnic affiliation but also along the lines of class, religion, gender, urban/rural divides, political beliefs and lifestyle (Erel, 2010). Indeed, young cosmopolitan men from Damascus may find it easier to establish ties with Brussels' international students than with many of their fellow Syrians.

To further nuance the concept of social capital, Louise Ryan *et al.* (2008) have argued that newly arriving immigrants in particular tend to have dynamic social networks that change rapidly depending on who they meet and what they need. Scholars have therefore called for an examination of the ways in which migrants develop their bridging social capital through a qualitative, microsocial perspective that includes the particularities of the barriers with which they are faced and the strategies that they adopt to overcome these barriers (Erel, 2010; Favell, 2008; Ryan *et al.*, 2008; Ryan, 2011; Svendsen, 2006; Williams, 2006).

This chapter responds to that call by exploring why most of the Syrian participants in this research had only weak, if any, ties with established Belgian citizens. What are the barriers that they encounter in developing such ties? Which strategies do they use to overcome these barriers?

## Methods

This chapter draws on 26 in-depth interviews with 39 Syrians who had applied for asylum in Belgium after the summer of 2011, and numerous informal encounters (see Vandevoordt, 2017; Vandevoordt and Verschraegen, 2019b). In the interviews, participants were asked to discuss part of their 'life histories', starting from the moment that they arrived in Belgium (Ghorashi, 2008; Vandevoordt, 2017; Vandevoordt and Verschraegen, 2019b). While the interviews generally concentrated on their overall *experiences* in Belgium, specific questions explored the social networks that they had developed since their arrival: how they established their first contact in Belgium, which individuals were crucial to them at particular points in time, how their first encounters with Belgian citizens came about and how they experienced them. After the interviews I conducted an ego-centred network analysis (cf. Williams, 2006), in which I mapped the intra- and inter-ethnic relations that participants had developed over time, and how these fed into economic (for example, work, benefits, affordable housing) and cultural (for example, language proficiency, knowledge of local customs) forms of capital.

Participants were selected so as to represent a variety of legal statuses, socio-economic backgrounds and ethnic-religious affiliations. Although I tried to include respondents of both genders, 30 out of 39 participants were male, and 7 of the 9 participating women were members of Syria's religious and/or ethnic minorities. While most Syrian refugees who have recently arrived in Belgium are men, the main reason for this imbalance was that I – as a white, male researcher – struggled to gain access to female Syrian respondents. In most cases in which I tried to establish contact with Sunni Syrian women, I was told in a variety of ways that it would be inappropriate for me to converse with them rather than their husbands, sons or brothers. As a young, rather inexperienced researcher grappling with their lack of consent, I decided not to insist further and to focus instead on including respondents from a range of class, ethnic and religious backgrounds. Obviously, this gender bias has implications for the generalizability of my research findings: it seems likely that Sunni Syrian women face specific challenges in establishing contact with Belgian women and men, and develop strategies of their own to bridge these barriers (cf. Saeys *et al.*, 2018).

While I conducted the interviews between March 2015 and February 2016, three key informants with different ethnic, religious and gender profiles played a crucial rule in the research. This included one Sunni Arab man, one man from a religious and ethnic minority, and one woman from a religious minority. These informants translated from Arabic to Dutch conversations with 23 out of 39 persons – in this chapter, interview excerpts in English have been translated from Dutch by me – and they continually challenged my observations and reflections. This means that we informally discussed my tentative analyses, after which I, drawing on their ideas and remarks, gradually adapted the topics that were discussed in the subsequent interviews. The analyses presented here are thus strongly dependent on my informants' insights and their constructive criticisms of the preliminary ideas that I presented to them. More concretely, the codes that I used to analyse the data emerged from three sources: the scholarly literature, mostly on the lived experiences of legal citizenship statuses and migrants' social networks (see Vandevoordt and Verschraegen 2019a); the issues that my key informants emphasized in our discussions, which included respondents' accounts of dependency and dignity (Vandevoordt and Verschraegen, 2019a and 2019b); and codes that emerged from the data itself, such as the symbolic significance of food and hospitality (Vandevoordt, 2017).

In this chapter, I focus on one particular part of these analyses: Syrians' social relations with Belgians. First, I discuss the barriers that

Syrians experienced in developing social ties with Belgians before, second, detailing some of the strategies that they used to address these barriers.

## Troubled waters: Barriers to Belgian bonds

The first barrier focuses on individual Syrians' cultural capital: their ability to apprehend a new language and its dialects. The second and third barriers focus more on the structural characteristics of Belgian society: racial and religious discrimination, and the formal organization of Belgian social life.

### Language and dialect

Most Syrians who have recently arrived in Belgium do not speak English, French or Dutch. This was a particular problem for middle-aged Syrians like Olan, Mohammed and Mustafa, who had never mastered a foreign language and who struggled to learn Dutch in spite of their efforts. Their lack of a particular form of cultural capital (that is, linguistic skills) thus prevented them from acquiring bridging social capital. As a result, their encounters with Belgians remained largely limited to superficial encounters in public places. Mustafa for instance, said that he and his cousin Mohammed:

> would really like to have relations with Belgian people, enter the Belgian culture. I will learn the language, but now, even if we need someone and we want to start talking with him, we cannot say anything. Right now we cannot say anything. We don't have a problem with anyone but we cannot speak with them, this is the problem I believe. But in the street, and the market and anywhere [we meet Belgians], it's good, it's good. We can speak with them, [in] English. We ask people where we can go, they help us. It's not bad. But we don't have relations. Maybe we will have in the future. We are, consider us, apart from the social, out of the social. Because the language, it's a problem.

To Mustafa, language was the primary cause of their social exclusion.[2] Without mastering Dutch, they lacked the ties that they needed to weave themselves into Belgium's social fabric. To some extent, this resonates with an increasingly dominant (neo-communitarian) discourse that sees migrants' efforts to learn the local language as a first step towards their social integration (Pulinx and Van Avermaet, 2015; Van Puymbroeck and Saeys, 2014). Since 2014, refugees receiving full legal status are obligated to attend Dutch-language courses, which are organized by Flemish government agencies. Several of my respondents, however, complained that these courses were insufficient as they consisted of just one weekly three-hour class. More intensive courses have been available at Flemish universities, yet at a much higher cost of €400 per month and more.

After completing their classes, Syrians were confronted with a new challenge: the standard Dutch that they had learnt in class is generally spoken only in white-collar professional contexts and in the mass media. The difference between standard Dutch and the wide variety of local dialects drove Syrians like Olan and Mustafa to despair. In slow but relatively fluent Dutch, Roha, a single woman in her early thirties, shared some of her experiences with me. When I first met her, she had been working for more than six months in a Belgian firm as part of a social-employment scheme. Although she was surrounded by Dutch-speaking colleagues, she had not been able to develop any meaningful social relations at work. She was convinced that this was at least partly due to the local dialect:

> The language is my problem actually, still now, because people speak dialects. And I find it really difficult to understand, sometimes, because what I learn in school is something else you know. Really, this is how you get in touch with people and you hear people, every day speaking and this and that. You start to learn and it takes time, to communicate. It's really not easy. It's not easy at all.

While the Dutch that Syrians learn in class may lead them to develop weak ties with colleagues or neighbours, developing stronger social bonds based on emotional support, mutual trust and friendship requires a higher degree of either Dutch or English. In that respect, a handful of Syrians who possessed 'cosmopolitan habitus' or 'cosmopolitan sociability' (Glick Schiller *et al.*, 2011) – a transnationally valid set of dispositions, embodied skills and knowledge – seemed better able to create such bridging bonds. Syrians who already spoke English before they arrived in Belgium; belonged to a Christian or secular minority in Syria; and/or were familiar with intercultural, super-diverse settings felt much more at ease in connecting with (similarly cosmopolitan) Belgians. They possessed a form of cultural capital that migrated with them: in contrast to most of their compatriots, their existing social and language skills were valid in the country of arrival (Erel, 2010).

Consider Cemal, a single man in his late twenties. Prior to his residence in Belgium, he had lived for several years in a cosmopolitan area in a Turkish city (on Syrians' situation in Turkey, see Loris-Rodionoff, this volume). As a result, he explained, he felt more like a 'secular Turk' than a 'traditional Arab':

> A friend of mine, one day he was talking about nationalities and stuff, and he asked me, what do you feel like? You are Syrian or what? I said I feel that I'm Turkish. And they said no, we think that you are more Western. Maybe that's why I have many Belgian friends, because, you know, when you want to be a friend of someone, you have to have, like, mutual things or ideas with them. Otherwise you will not be friends, anyway. That's why I have many, many foreign friends in general, like not just Syrians.

In other words, Cemal claimed that he had been able to establish deeper bonds with Belgians due to his cosmopolitan disposition and the sociocultural intercultural skills that he had accrued in Turkey. Contrary to Cemal, however, most Syrians who had been in Belgium for a longer period of time and who were relatively fluent in Dutch still faced what they saw as a problem in itself: a lack of meaningful social relations with Belgians. In the following sections, I therefore focus on barriers that emanate not so much from migrants' skills and dispositions but from Belgian social structures.

## Racial and religious discrimination

A second barrier that emerged from my participants' stories was discrimination, usually based on markers of racial and/or religious difference (on racialization and xenophobia in urban spaces, see Tayob, this volume). Especially in Belgian villages with no prior history of immigration, they had to deal with a sudden 'visibility' (Fiddian-Qasmiyeh and Qasmiyeh, 2010: 304–5): they were quickly recognized as, or assumed to be, Arabs and/or Muslims, which led to popular associations with fear and mistrust (see Fiddian-Qasmiyeh, 2016 and 2017). Mohammed, a man in his early twenties, told me of the village where he had lived for seven months. When I asked him whether he had had any contact with Belgians there, his answer echoed those of several young Syrians living in the Flemish countryside:

No. If I would see them on the street, they would really just prefer to cross the street to avoid me. People looked at my beard, frowned their eyes and looked away. They were afraid. It was difficult to meet people. When I went to the library, people were friendly. I had no pass or anything, but they let me just sit inside and read. Comics and books for kids, you know.

He laughed. 'The kids even came to me and said, "Oh, you need to read this, this is a good one!" But on the street, no. It was difficult. So I moved to [a larger city].'

Roha, the young woman who struggled to connect with her colleagues, told me of an encounter with a Belgian woman on the bus. They started talking, and as soon as the Belgian woman found out that Roha only spoke English she asked her where she was from:

> She was shocked to hear that I'm from Syria. They're underestimating us, a lot of Belgians. We don't all ride camels and wear headscarves you know. And it's the same thing with doctors. I had something, but not because I'm Syrian or something but I'm, because I'm a foreigner. I felt like I was underestimated by the doctor.

A few months earlier, she had faced a serious medical problem. She visited a doctor, who made a diagnosis and sent her to hospital for immediate surgery. At the time she felt too uncertain to speak up against the doctor and the nurses. Afterwards, the diagnosis proved to be wrong and caused irreparable damage to her health. I cannot claim for certain that race played a crucial part in these events, although numerous studies have traced a strong link between race and the nature of encounters with medical practitioners in diverse contexts (Akhavan and Karlsen, 2013; Castañeda, 2012; Mulinari, 2016). What is certain is that Roha felt that she was not taken seriously, and, based on her earlier experiences, she ascribed this directly to her being a foreigner unable to speak Dutch fluently.

Most Syrians were quick to emphasize, however, that most Belgians were 'not really racist' in the sense that they would physically or verbally assault them. It was more a question of distrust and avoidance, rather than direct violence. When I asked Mustafa if he had experienced any kind of hostility or racism, he answered, 'Mh, not racism. Most Belgian, Flemish people are not racists. But sometimes people look at you, [and] it's not direct racism, but on the bus, they look angry. I don't think they look the same way at other people. But it's not *really* racist.'

Yet the felt consequences of such covert, implicit racism are quite intense. Ali, a man in his early twenties, elaborated on the small, subtle prejudices that he experienced and how these fed, at times, into more offensive forms of racial prejudice:

> You know, when you are getting on the tram or the bus, you feel like, people are looking at you, like you are not them. You know what I mean, like you are the stranger here.

'I can imagine', I replied. 'Was that specifically in the city of X?'

> Like in X it was, when I was working in the refugee centre, I don't know if you've ever been there, there is a lake, close to the centre. And we used to walk there. Sometimes there are people, fishing, sitting there, Belgian people, and they have bicycles. When I was walking in the street, I saw them running to their bicycle to bring it closer to them. Okay, I could understand why, they are scared and worried and blah blah blah. But at the same time there is a Belgian person that just passes by, and they do not act. I understand why they are doing that, because, a lot of people they are stealing bicycles and so on. But they seem to, I mean … you have to be careful about your stuff. But when you do something like that, don't show it to the person who is, in front of you. He could be a person who is going to steal your bicycle, but at the same time he could be not. And that gave, really, a fucking bad feeling.

I have known Ali for quite a while now, and he has always put great pride in his efforts to convince Belgians that he, his cousins and the Syrian people as a whole are hard-working, friendly, trustworthy people. Yet in January 2015, he snapped as these race- and religion-inflected encounters mounted up to an unfathomable height. After the *Charlie Hebdo* terrorist attacks in Paris – which were claimed by Al-Qaeda – a Belgian woman added a comment on Ali's Facebook account, writing something along the lines of 'you see now, what you Muslims are doing. Go back to fucking Syria!' This time, Ali responded to the comment and received more and more angry replies from the woman, both on Facebook and on Twitter. His efforts to bond with Belgians received a blow:

> I'm sick of it, really, I'm done with it. I thought my future was in Belgium, but I don't know. People don't want us here. I feel like I don't want to stay. It's useless.

## Formalized structures of Belgian social life

While the potentially exclusionary effects of language, race and religion have been frequently researched, other barriers have received less attention. One of them, I argue, is the relatively closed or formalized structure of Belgian – and, by extrapolation, West European – social life (cf. Rutter *et al.*, 2007; Spencer *et al.*, 2007). The ways in which social encounters take place, how we assume they ought to be experienced and what it means to be friends differs across different social groups. To many of my Syrian participants, Belgians appeared as closed, slightly introverted people that were hard to connect with, even if both sides had the best of intentions.

In some cases, Syrians associated this closed nature with specific cities like Antwerp or Brussels where, in contrast to smaller cities like Ghent or Hasselt, people were difficult to approach. Abdul, a 22-year-old man told me, 'you know in Antwerp, people, they just walk, like, quickly. And they look angry, on the bus, on the street.' Such accounts were strikingly recurrent among the Syrians with whom I spoke. Mahmoud, a 28-year-old man, for instance, said something very similar: 'yeah in Antwerp at the tram, people are just like, like zombies. If you try to talk to someone, they just get angry.'

At the same time, however, such experiences also emerged in the small villages where some Syrians had stayed. Ebrahim for instance, a 44-year-old father of three, noted with a wry smile that 'in X [our village] my neighbours are always looking angry. They don't smile. I try to speak, but they don't speak back. I say good morning, good morning, and if they say it back than it's a big success.'

In a similar vein, Moussa, a 32-year-old single man who had been living in a village for seven months, told me how he unsuccessfully tried to make eye contact with the locals. He had tried to talk to people on the street, but they turned away:

> In seven months I did not have any contact with any of the locals. No contact at all. They [local Belgians] were like, they were busy with their work and their lives, and we [he and other asylum seekers] were living in this [social] house.

'Okay', I replied, 'and did you think that people were friendly or not so friendly?'

I didn't have a real problem. I cannot answer because really there was no contact at all. Even when I tried to make eye contact in the street, people looked away. One day, we had a problem with the electricity. And someone needed to call an electrician. But we could not speak Dutch, just a little bit of English. And we didn't know anyone. So we asked our neighbour, an old woman. And she helped us: she made a call and the electrician came. But then she just shut the door, without saying goodbye. She helped us, it's nice. But there's no contact.

As in their accounts of discrimination, most participants were quick to emphasize that not all Belgians were closed. Jamal, a 26-year-old man, told me how the municipal social service of the village where he was given accommodation had organized a meeting to introduce him and a few other asylum seekers to the locals. 'It was good. That's where I met Anna', a middle-aged woman who later helped him find an affordable studio, to arrange all the bureaucratic requirements to move and to explore the possibilities for continuing his study at university. At the same time, however, this woman was identified as being an exception:

I was really nervous. I felt like we were in the zoo. The people [from the village], they were just, like, looking at us. They said hello and that was it, we didn't talk or anything. We were on this side of the room, they were on that side.

A few months later, Jamal – who had grown up in one of Syria's larger cities – moved to the nearest city. In the village, he said, 'there were only old people. I didn't, like, have anything in common with them. So I came here.' Even though the introductory meeting event provided him with a crucial friend who effectively helped him – a form of social capital that was converted to cultural and economic capital – a distance remained between him and most locals, including those who were willing to join the meet-and-greet event.

Most of my interlocutors ascribed the difficulty to establish bonds to Belgians' collective character. This resonates with what could be described as an Occidentalist reversal of Orientalism (Said, 1978): compared with the spontaneity, warmth and passion of Middle Eastern cultures, the West appears cold, reserved and rational. Adopting a more sociological perspective, these experiences of distance seem partly due to the *formal* structure of Belgian social life (see Vandevoordt and Verschraegen, 2019a). One dynamic that many Syrians struggled to grasp was that if they wanted to meet someone, even a friend, they usually had to arrange a date and place a few days or even a week in advance. Cemal, the young man with the cosmopolitan habitus and a large number of Belgian friends, drew a striking comparison:

> With us Arabs, when friends meet it's more like, you call two hours in advance what are you doing? You're closer to your friends. But like here, it's just in the weekend.

When I asked Samir, a 20-year-old man waiting to be reunited with his wife and son, if it was easy to make friends with Belgians, he gave a similar answer:

> What friendship means for Belgians, friendship for Belgians is like 'hey hey' [*he waves his hand*]. That's it. But, in Syria, for Syrians, friendship is just [he imitates holding a phone with his right hand] 'What are you doing today? I am doing nothing, come drink some tea.' Not beer but tea. For Belgians, I don't think it's like that.

Many participants contrasted the formalized, reserved manner of meeting friends in Belgium with a more spontaneous lifestyle. 'I miss the *Arab* way of life', Mohammed said. 'You know, hanging around, taking the car for a ride. Meeting people. Just being together, you know.' Roha mused on her former lifestyle too: 'I miss the Syrian way of being together. Just relaxing, together. Eating something, talking, music, maybe some dancing.' What they described closely resembled what Georg Simmel (2011) once called 'pure sociality': meeting one another for the simple sake of being together.

In Western Europe and North America, however, we often assume that our social networks are rooted in formalized associations such as music schools, sports clubs, neighbourhood committees and social movements. Putnam (2000, 2007), for instance, conceives of social capital largely as individuals' participation in such formal associations. Migration scholars have criticized this assumption, as it does not necessarily fit with how immigrants construct their social networks or live their social lives (Ryan *et al.*, 2008; Williams, 2006). Depending on their class, religion, legal status and gender their networks may be organized – or better, they may flow – in different, more informal ways. Hence, individuals' exclusion from bridging social capital may be caused partly by the formalized structure of Belgian social life. As I show below, however, the Syrians who did establish a network of Belgian friends and acquaintances often did so by participating in such formal associations. In that sense, the formal structures of Belgian sociality appeared to function as a gateway into Belgian social life.

## Building bridges: Syrians' strategies

In spite of the challenges posed by language, race, religion and the formality of Belgian social life, Syrians developed a range of strategies in order to establish bridging social bonds. In this section, I discuss two such strategies: chance encounters and personal persuasion on the one hand, and engaging in volunteering work on the other.

### Chance encounters and personal persuasion

Ahmed, a 34-year-old single man, told me of the first Belgian that he encountered: a middle-aged woman to whom he had given up his bus seat. She wanted to thank him, and quickly learnt that he did not speak Dutch, only English. They started a conversation and exchanged contact details when he got off the bus at the asylum centre. After they had met again a couple of times, she asked if he wanted to help paint her living room in return for some pocket money. Ahmed repeatedly described to me how he had gained her trust, and how that led her to support him when he left the centre and needed furniture and other basic household materials: 'It all comes back to you, you know. You have to show people that they can trust you, that you're a genuine person.'

A year later, Ahmed worked in a factory through a social-employment scheme. There he faced a space where colleagues were strangers to one another. On top of that, two of them were racists, accusing him of taking Belgian people's jobs. His response was compelling:

> Yeah, I invited them, to my apartment. With food, drinks, anything, for free. I asked do you want to come here? And they said you're a weird person. We've been working here for 12 years, and we've never been at each other's homes. Yeah, and after it, they started visiting each other a little bit. But before, they never did.

The day his employment ended, he deployed a new variant of the same strategy. He boasted how he had surprised all of his colleagues by handing them a white rose. Even the two racists, he claimed, 'said they were sad that I was leaving', after which he showed me the supportive text messages that they had sent him. Whether or not he actually managed to change his colleagues' attitudes towards one another is, of course, an open question. But the strategy that he used to bring that change about recurred more frequently with the few Syrians – 6 out of 39 – who were able to establish bridging social bonds with Belgians. They made a point of showing, through acts of personal reciprocity, that they were trustworthy; honest; and, in Ahmed's enigmatic words, 'genuine person[s]' (see Vandevoordt and Verschraegen, 2019a and 2019b).

Yasser, a 33-year-old single man, similarly developed his first contacts in Belgium by helping an older lady carry her bag onto the bus. As they engaged in conversation in rudimentary English, it transpired that she was a volunteer at a civil-society organization helping newcomers. Even though Yasser only spoke a few words of English and close to no Dutch at the time, he regularly met the woman and her volunteering friends in the subsequent months. As with Ahmed and several others, Yasser thus used a chance encounter to persuade individual Belgians that Syrians were good people. Again, for such a strategy to succeed, a great amount of cosmopolitan cultural capital was required: a minimal knowledge of English prior to their arrival in Belgium, a charismatic appearance and perhaps a smooth way of establishing contact. The walls were high, but they were gifted climbers.

## Syrian volunteers

As mentioned above, the entry to Belgian social life often seemed to pass through the gates of formal associations. Several Syrians volunteered in such associations, usually after being advised to do so by their social workers or by the one Belgian with whom they had become acquainted (on refugees supporting refugees in Lebanon, see Fiddian-Qasmiyeh in this volume). Syrians often viewed their volunteering work as an explicit strategy to heighten their social capital (establishing bonds with Belgians), as well as their cultural capital (by becoming familiar with local customs and dialects) (cf. Rutter *et al.*, 2007).

Ahmed, for instance, was strongly advised by the Belgian woman he had met on the bus to register with a local volunteering organization to help the poor. It was there that he made most of his friends. He emphasized the fact that they worked together, as equals (Vandevoordt, 2017). 'I don't really go there to get help or anything. It's more to help, and to build relations. That's where I met Kevin' – currently his closest Belgian friend, who has helped him to find affordable housing, fill in his paperwork and to work out a plan to start his own business. In his case, it was a combination of a chance encounter, personal persuasion and doing volunteering work that made it possible for him to acquire bridging social capital.

At the same time, I should add, Ahmed represented a somewhat exceptional case. He spoke fluent English before he arrived, which enabled him to converse directly with Belgians. In addition, he regularly received remarks that he looked more like a 'South-European' – in his case, Italian or Greek – than an Arab. While this may seem trivial at first, it does raise questions on how the racial typographies that white Europeans impose on Middle East migrants (see Fiddian-Qasmiyeh and Qasmiyeh, 2010; Saunders *et al.*, 2016) may form barriers to genuine social encounters.

Zayed, a 25-year-old man, told a similar story. He served as a volunteer with one of the civil-society organizations helping the thousands of refugees who were stranded in Brussels in the late summer of 2015. There he befriended several people from Belgian and of other nationalities – again, in a setting in which they worked as equals:

> I [had] already met Belgian and French people here. There are a lot of people working here, so somehow, we became colleagues. We're all working together. So I started in the [civil-society refugee-support organization] and I made three Belgian friends here. We're still in touch.

In turn, Rashid, a 28-year-old single man, volunteered at the reception centre where he had once resided himself. After learning some English in the centre, he befriended a Belgian couple with whom he later went to Greece to help other refugees. What initially started out as volunteering work later turned into temporary employment with a larger NGO active in the Mediterranean Sea, where he served as a translator and cultural mediator. In his case, it was a specific combination of a cosmopolitan type of cultural capital (learning English, rather than Dutch) and a locally rooted yet transnationally validated form of social capital (establishing a stronger, emotional bond with the Belgian volunteers) that fed into the economic capital represented by a job – albeit a temporary one.

## Building bridges: Belgian support

Whether these Syrians overcame barriers in order to take part in Belgian social life was, of course, not merely a matter of their own strategies.

Many of my interlocutors were supported by Belgian citizens, either through the latter's volunteering work or, in a more personal manner, by introducing them to their own social networks.

## Belgian volunteers

As most Syrians felt that the language courses that they were given were too slow, they sought other ways in which to practise their Dutch. Several of them joined conversational groups in which Belgians volunteered to help migrants practise Dutch. Mohammed, for instance, commented that 'I'm going to integration courses and language course. And they're offering, every day Friday or Saturday, there's like volunteers, and they organize a meeting between us and them, and then we can talk, so we will learn the language.'

For some Syrians these were their only informal contacts with Belgians. When I asked Ebrahim if he had been able to talk to Belgians, he replied, 'Yes, when I go to the volunteer centre, there a man speaks with me, for one hour, every week. His name is Kenneth. Kenneth, he's a good man. He speaks with me, every week, one hour. He's a very nice man.' Abdullah, a 29-year-old father of two, offered a similar answer: 'Yes, I go to [the village of] X, to the centre of volunteers. They speak with me, one hour, per week. [I always speak with] Marc. He's a good man, he speaks with me, one hour every week.'

While these conversation groups were part of a strategy to improve migrants' language skills, they were, in some cases, also effective in establishing social relations that transcended the organized conversations. When I met Olan again, a few months after our first interview, he told me that he had befriended a Belgian couple whom he had met at such a language-volunteering organization. He did not describe them as friends yet, but he told me that they were meeting outside the language events. Based on the stories of Syrians who possessed a great deal of bridging social capital, I would expect that if Olan needed or desired it, this befriended couple, as a weak bridging tie, might be able to provide him with some kind of social, cultural or even economic support.

## Belgian gatekeepers

Participants who were able to establish deeper rapports with Belgians, often did so after befriending one person who introduced them to their own circle of friends, neighbours and relatives. These Belgians often guided Syrians into entering formal associations like music schools, sports clubs and cooking societies. They functioned as gatekeepers, using a phrase by Khaled, one of my informants, 'holding the keys' to entering Belgian social life.

Ahmed's story has already evidenced this practice, as it was the Belgian woman whom he met on the bus that put him in contact with the volunteering organization at which he later made most of his Belgian friends. Similarly, one family had befriended Martha, a Belgian woman who was volunteering at the reception centre where the parents had been staying. Martha provided substantial support to them by looking for a place for them to rent; introducing them to her own friends and relatives; and by helping them with arranging their gym subscriptions, health insurance, practising Dutch and enrolling the children into music schools. When I asked Soraya, one of the daughters, whether she had met many Belgian people, she replied, 'Yeah for me, I feel, it was easy. They are so nice people, in the music academy and at the community centre. Martha helped us so much. And when we need her, we just call, and she's there.' Subsequently, she was invited repeatedly to play as a Syrian musician at reception parties and cultural events, thus paving her way into Belgian social life.

Similarly, two sisters, Amala and Nasra, came to know Elisabeth, a Belgian woman, through the Belgian branch of a faith-based organization for which they had volunteered in Syria. Elisabeth immediately gave them shelter in her house, which meant that the sisters were not forced to sleep on the street as thousands of asylum seekers had done in autumn 2015. Sharing their views on life, spirituality and work, they soon became close friends. Eventually, Amala and Nasra were lucky enough to be housed in a collective reception centre that was only 45 minutes away from Elisabeth's home. During their stay at the centre they frequently met, and Elisabeth's friends quickly became those of the Syrian sisters. In Nasra's words:

> So I feel like we were very lucky. In two or three months, we met great Belgian people like A and B. They are our friends, really. And also X and Y, they're really great people, very warm. So two weeks after we arrived, it was like home to us.

This emotional sense of belonging also fed into practical forms of support, making it easier to navigate the new environment of Belgian state and society. As soon as the sisters were granted refugee status, they searched for a property to rent together with Elisabeth, figured out the best neighbourhood in which to live and planned a sound trajectory towards education and work. Unlike most other refugees, they did not need to rely on professional social workers as they could simply turn to their newly made friends. Thus, by befriending this Belgian woman, partly through a pre-existing form of transnational social and cultural capital (membership of the same volunteering organization, English language proficiency), they quickly accumulated new forms of localized social and cultural capital that seemed necessary in order to acquire economic forms of capital such as affordable housing and a realistic trajectory to work.

## Conclusion

Most Syrians whom I encountered were eager to engage in meaningful social relations with Belgians, yet only few actually managed to do so. This chapter has explored why this was the case, and how they have tried to build bridges over these troubled waters. Syrians were faced with three barriers in particular: insufficient proficiency of Dutch and its Flemish dialects, indirect forms of racial and religious discrimination, and the formal structure of Belgian social life. My interlocutors tried to overcome these barriers in two ways: by making personal efforts to gain Belgians' trust and by taking up volunteering work. In doing so, some Syrians were supported by Belgian volunteers, both through formal initiatives such as conversation groups and through informal actions by individuals introducing Syrians to Belgian social life.

What does this tell us about the conditions in which meaningful social relations can flourish between newly arrived refugees and established citizens? On the one hand, establishing bridging social capital requires transferable skills (for instance, the ability to learn a new language or to gain people's trust in spite of prejudice) that are unequally distributed among Syrians. On the other hand, accumulating such capital requires a hospitable social environment that is void of racial and religious discrimination, and which contains, instead, benevolent individuals who proceed beyond their formal duties as volunteers or social workers. The forging of social bonds, therefore, can only be done by a party of two.

# Notes

1. On the historical case of Belgian refugees in the UK, and how they were received by local communities and developed their own communities and systems of support during the First World War, see Declercq (this volume).
2. Also, see Berg (this volume) on the case of Latin American migrants and refugees in London.

# References

Ager, Alastair and Alison Strang. 2008. 'Understanding Integration: A Conceptual Framework', *Journal of Refugee Studies* 21 (2): 166–91.

Akhavan, Sharareh and Saffron Karlsen. 2013. 'Practitioner and Client Explanations for Disparities in Health Care Use between Migrant and Non-Migrant Groups in Sweden: A Qualitative Study', *Journal of Immigrant and Minority Health* 15 (1): 188–97.

Bourdieu, Pierre and Loïc J.D. Wacquant. 1992. *An Invitation to Reflexive Sociology*. Chicago: Chicago University Press.

Castañeda, Heide. 2012. '"Over-Foreignization" or "Unused Potential"? A Critical Review of Migrant Health in Germany and Responses toward Unauthorized Migration', *Social Science and Medicine* 74 (6): 830–8.

Csedő, Krisztina. 2008. 'Negotiating Skills in the Global City: Hungarian and Romanian Professionals and Graduates in London', *Journal of Ethnic and Migration Studies* 34 (5): 803–23.

Erel, Umut. 2010. 'Migrating Cultural Capital: Bourdieu in Migration Studies', *Sociology* 44 (4): 642–60.

Favell, Adrian. 2008. 'The New Face of East–West Migration in Europe', *Journal of Ethnic and Migration Studies* 34 (5): 701–16.

Fiddian-Qasmiyeh, Elena. 2016. 'Representations of Displacement from the Middle East and North Africa', *Public Culture* 28 (3): 457–73.

Fiddian-Qasmiyeh, Elena. 2017. 'The Faith–Gender–Asylum Nexus: An Intersectionalist Analysis of Representations of the "Refugee Crisis"'. In *The Refugee Crisis and Religion: Secularism, Security and Hospitality in Question*, edited by Luca Mavelli and Erin K. Wilson, 207–22. London: Rowman and Littlefield International.

Fiddian-Qasmiyeh, Elena and Yousif M. Qasmiyeh. 2010. 'Muslim Asylum-Seekers and Refugees: Negotiating Identity, Politics and Religion in the UK', *Journal of Refugee Studies* 23 (3): 294–314.

Ghorashi, Halleh. 2008 'Giving Silence a Chance: The Importance of Life Stories for Research on Refugees', *Journal of Refugee Studies* 21 (1): 117–32.

Glick Schiller, Nina, Tsypylma Darieva and Sandra Gruner-Domic. 2011. 'Defining Cosmopolitan Sociability in a Transnational Age: An Introduction', *Ethnic and Racial Studies* 34 (3): 399–418.

Mulinari, Diana. 2016. 'Postcolonial Encounters: Migrant Women and Swedish Midwives'. In *Changing Relations of Welfare: Family, Gender and Migration in Britain and Scandinavia*, edited by Janet Fink and Åsa Lundqvist, 155–77. London: Routledge.

Nannestad, Peter, Gunnar Lind Haase Svendsen and Gert Tinggaard Svendsen. 2008. 'Bridge over Troubled Water? Migration and Social Capital', *Journal of Ethnic and Migration Studies* 34 (4): 607–31.

Patulny, Roger V. and Gunnar Lind Haase Svendsen. 2007. 'Exploring the Social Capital Grid: Bonding, Bridging, Qualitative, Quantitative', *International Journal of Sociology and Social Policy* 27 (1/2): 32–51.

Pulinx, Reinhilde and Piet Van Avermaet. 2015. 'Integration in Flanders (Belgium): Citizenship as Achievement: How Intertwined Are "Citizenship" and "Integration" in Flemish Language Policies?', *Journal of Language and Politics* 14 (3): 335–58.

Putnam, Robert D. 2000. *Bowling Alone: The Collapse and Revival of American Community*. New York: Simon and Schuster.

Putnam, Robert D. 2007. '*E Pluribus Unum*: Diversity and Community in the Twenty-First Century: The 2006 Johan Skytte Prize Lecture', *Scandinavian Political Studies* 30 (2): 137–74.

Rutter, Jill, Laurence Cooley, Sile Reynolds and Ruth Sheldon. 2007. *From Refugee to Citizen: "Standing on My Own Two Feet": A Research Report on Integration, "Britishness" and Citizenship.* London: Metropolitan Support Trust and Institute of Public Policy Research.

Ryan, Louise. 2011. 'Migrants' Social Networks and Weak Ties: Accessing Resources and Constructing Relationships Post-Migration', *Sociological Review* 59 (4): 707–24.

Ryan, Louise, Rosemary Sales, Mary Tilki and Bernadette Siara. 2008. 'Social Networks, Social Support and Social Capital: The Experiences of Recent Polish Migrants in London', *Sociology* 42 (4): 672–90.

Saeys, Arne, Robin Vandevoordt and Gert Verschraegen. 2018. *Samenleven in diversiteit: Kwalitatief onderzoek naar de perspectieven van vluchtelingen.* Brussels: Agentschap Binnenlands Bestuur.

Said, Edward W. 1978. *Orientalism.* London: Penguin.

Saunders, Jennifer B., Susanna Snyder and Elena Fiddian-Qasmiyeh. 2016. 'Introduction: Articulating Intersections at the Global Crossroads of Religion and Migration'. In *Intersections of Religion and Migration: Issues at the Global Crossroads,* edited by Jennifer B. Saunders, Elena Fiddian-Qasmiyeh and Susanna Snyder, 1–46. New York: Palgrave Macmillan.

Simmel, Georg. 2011. *Georg Simmel on individuality and social forms,* edited by Donald N. Levine. Chicago: University of Chicago Press.

Spencer, Sarah, Martin Ruhs, Bridget Anderson and Ben Rogaly. 2007. *Migrants' Lives beyond the Workplace: The Experiences of Central and East Europeans in the UK.* York: Joseph Rowntree Foundation.

Svendsen, Gunnar L.H. 2006 'Studying Social Capital in Situ: A Qualitative Approach', *Theory and Society* 35 (1): 39–70.

Vandevoordt, Robin. 2017. 'The Politics of Food and Hospitality: How Syrian Refugees in Belgium Create a Home in Hostile Environments', *Journal of Refugee Studies* 30 (4): 605–21.

Vandevoordt, Robin and Gert Verschraegen. 2019a. 'Citizenship as a Gift: How Syrian Refugees in Belgium Make Sense of Their Social Rights', *Citizenship Studies* 23 (1): 43–60.

Vandevoordt, Robin and Gert Verschraegen. 2019b. 'Demonstrating Deservingness and Dignity: Symbolic Boundary Work among Syrian Refugees', *Poetics* 76: 1–11. Accessed 20 January 2020. https://doi.org/10.1016/j.poetic.2018.12.004.

Van Puymbroeck, Nicolas and Arne Saeys. 2014. 'Nationalisme in de integratiesector: Een proces van verstatelijking en centralisering'. In *Over gevestigden en buitenstaanders: Armoede, diversiteit en stedelijkheid,* edited by Gert Verschraegen, Clemens de Olde, Stijn Oosterlynck, Frédéric Vandermoere and Danielle Dierckx, 187–206. Leuven: Acco.

Williams, Lucy. 2006. 'Social Networks of Refugees in the United Kingdom: Tradition, Tactics and New Community Spaces', *Journal of Ethnic and Migration Studies* 32 (5): 865–79.

# Index

and distant suffering, 146; ethics, 418, 424–7; history of, 416–17; new humanitarianism, 418, 422, 424; political and apolitical, 415, 418, 421, 423, 424, 426; 'prophetic humanitarianism,' 418, 419, 423, 425, 426; 'refugee–refugee humanitarianism,' 402, 408, 411; urban, 461. *See also* faith; humanitarian; NGO; refugee-led responses to displacement

humanization, 40, 168, 189, 425, 426

Hungary, 169, 286

Hurricane Katrina, 183

Icelanders, 127

ideal: refugee, 2; victim, 6; idealization, 15

identity: essentialized, 27; in exile, 86; and faith, 291; formation, 34, 35; humanitarian, 239; individual and communal, 195, 329–30, 339; loss of, 326; markers, 5; and particular social group, 275; performance of, 105, 106, 107, 205, 472; politics and, 171, 204, 419; refugee, 34–6, 38, 39; religion and, 48, 83, 417, 83, 499, 500; and sexuality, 276, 278; suspended, 213; territory and, 453, 455. *See also* ethnic; gender; label

immigration, restrictions, 82, 117, 157, 164, 169, 464

immigration status, 28, 75, 143, 144, 349, 408, 429–38, 478, 480, 484, 485, 487–90, 492n1, 508; climate-change-refugee status, 129; protected status, 496; refugee status, 39, 201, 204, 205, 207, 238, 273, 277, 310, 323, 340n4, 399n8, 444, 502, 514; settled status, 75. *See also* guest; refugee status determination; 1951 Geneva Convention

immobility, 1, 5, 6, 170, 171, 172, 398, 470, 472

inclusion, 78, 97, 111, 461, 471, 483, 485, 491; differential, 465; temporary, 464. *See also* integration

inequalities: and care, 232, 235, 240; creation of, 408–412, 478; power and, 13, 37, 228, 232, 408, 491; in research, 30, 330; structural, 5, 16, 17, 313, 478

informal: care and caring, 228, 229, 232, 234, 235, 239–41; labour, 172, 464; learning centres, 374, 376; settlements, 440; support, 484; trade, 350, 351, 356, 358, 360n11

infrastructure: camp, 336, 382; destroyed, 87–8; public, 309; reception, 473

inhabitation, 357, 446, 449; scales of, 446, 449; space and, 444, 457

inhabitants: of Baddawi camp, 52–3, 55–7, 58–61, 65–70, 404–12; of Baqa'a camp, 393–4; Burj el-Barajneh camp, 395; of Calais camp, 233, 440, 454, 456; of camps in the East African Rift, 362; of Ein el-Hilweh camp, 393; of the Palestinian camps, 383, 386; of Talbiyeh camp, 336, 338

integration, 142–3, 205, 404, 453, 468–9; courses, 512; cultural activities and, 323, 328, 329; labour-market, 478; and language, 485, 502

interdisciplinarity, 5–6, 95, 215, 317, 329, 330

internal displacement, 113, 289; in the First World War, 80, 82; in Georgia, 290, 295, 297–300. *See also* IDP

IDP (internally displaced persons), 12, 80, 82, 113, 289–90, 293, 295, 296–302, 306, 405, 412; IDP settlement, 260, 262, 293, 296–8, 302

International Association for the Study of Forced Migration (IASFM), 113

International Gay and Lesbian Alliance (ILGA), 148, 155, 273, 281

International Organization for Migration (IOM), 80

international organizations, 33, 35–7, 403, 412. *See also* NGOs, UN, UNHCR, UNRWA; *and separate names*

international protection, 276; for LGBTI asylum-seekers, 145, 276–7. *See also* immigration status

International Committee of the Red Cross (ICRC), 386, 427n1

intersectionality, 5, 8, 17. *See also* identity; inequalities; violence

Intifada, First Palestinian, 311, 313

intimacy, 153, 154, 233, 471; physical, 234; sexual and affective, 147. *See also* violence

invisibility, 1, 3, 28, 32, 114, 233, 480; social, 154; spaces, 351, 354; strategic, 33–4, 36–8, 40, 197, 279, 281. *See also* visibility

Iran, 86, 256, 276, 277; Iranians, 205, 211, 276

Iraq, 10, 12, 58, 86, 160, 161, 195, 208, 249, 250, 252, 266, 271, 286, 439; Iraqis, 4, 166, 211, 340, 404, 406, 409, 439; Iraqi Kurdistan, 194–5, 208n8, 249, 252, 266; Iraqi Kurds, 194–5, 208, 249; Iraqi military, 249

irregular migration, 118, 323–5, 492n1

ISIS: *See* Islamic State

Islamic State (including ISIS), 83, 167, 249, 250, 264

Islamophobia, 5. *See also* discrimination; Orientalism; racism; xenophobia

island: communities, 125–31; of hospitality, 94–8, 100–9. *See also* Lampedusa; Kos

Istanbul, Turkey, 172, 200, 433

Italy, 10, 15, 16, 79, 80, 90, 95–6, 108, 112, 115, 117, 119, 158, 165, 177, 194, 196–8, 201, 205, 206–8, 214, 439, 457, 461–2, 464, 466–74, 492; Italian coastguard, 177; Italian government, 102; Italian media, 105–6, 109, 119–20, 198, 201–7; Italian police, 108, 465; Italians, 82, 205, 468, 511

Jewish migrants and refugees, 42, 76, 82, 204

Johannesburg, South Africa, 44, 349

376, 377n1, 385, 405, 465, 506, 507; local-history groups, 77; organization, 337, 406, 416, 419, 422, 423, 467; perspectives, 98, 317. *See also* barriers; knowledge; language; municipality; NGOs

Local Government Board, 79, 82, 90n18

Local Democracy Agency (LDA), 462, 466, 469, 470, 473, 474n10

London, UK, 153, 207, 210, 214, 279, 477–91

loneliness, 32, 113, 326, 331, 339

*Lontano dal Kurdistan*, 194, 198

*Lost in Translation*, 41–3, 45–7

Malek, Alia, 183, 184

Malian refugee, 353

Malina, Judith, 201, 203, 204, 208n11

map, 148, 149, 151, 155n8, 219, 328, 363, 367, 368, 383

material: assistance, 408, 409, 410, 412, 498; conditions of reception, 163, 164, 290; frames, 184; materiality, 144, 368, 373, 472; reality, 173

May, Theresa, 161

Médecins du Monde, 232

Médecins Sans Frontières (MSF), 232, 417, 467

media: and climate change, 123, 129, 130, 133; coverage, 75, 77, 82, 84, 85, 87, 98, 101–2, 105, 106, 115, 141, 169, 170, 178, 180, 182, 183, 185, 187, 193, 197, 198, 355, 492n2; digital, 155n12, 188; social-media, 166, 168, 171. *See also* journalism; *and specific titles*

Mediterranean, 79, 95, 112, 112, 115, 117, 177, 178, 185–6, 205, 436, 511. See also *Crossing the Sea*, deaths; Kurdi, Alan; Lampedusa

memoir: *See* autobiography

memory: and the camp archive, 53, 54,57, 69, 70; cultural, 207, 448; documenting, 337; of elders, 337; erased from, 87; institutional, 369, 376; public, 75, 76, 77, 174; spatial, 442, *See also* commemoration

men: 290; Belgian, 79, 83, 86; in Georgia, 291, 298, 299, 301; Syrian, 178, 500; Yezidi, 249; young, 113, 119, 313. *See also* boys; gender; LGBT

mental health: *See* health

metaphors: architectural, 446, 448; borders, 324, 325, 451; 'invasion,' 77; 'waves' and 'masses', 2

Mexico, 44

Miami, USA, 329

Middle East, 53, 83, 167, 173–4, 195; 199, 218, 403, 511. *See also* Orientalism; the other; UNRWA; *and country entries*

minority: ethnicized, 477; ethno-religious, 249; religious, 500, 502; sexual and gender minority, 154n2, 273,275, 279, 281, 284. *See also* black and minority ethnic (BME) groups; LGBT; Yazidi

mobility, 125, 128; limited, 462, 465; regimes, 231; rights to, 97; social, 88, 483. *See also* immobility; transnational

Morocco, 112, 113, 114, 117; Moroccans, 114, 115, 119

mosque, 58, 59, 65, 66, 356, 359

Mozambicans, 296

Mugombwa camp, Rwanda, 371, 372, 378n11

multiculturalism, 48, 146, 188, 190

municipality, 430, 433, 438, 468, 469, 470, 474n8, 507

Murphy, Joe, 210. *See also* Good Chance Theatre

museum: exhibition, 9, 139; Flanders Fields Museum, 77; and health and well-being, 327; Imperial War Museum, 87; Migration Museum, 144n1; UCL Grant Museum of Zoology, 215

music, 211, 508, 513; Kurdish music, 198, 200; and well-being, 329, 330, 334; and Yezidi shamans, 256

mutuality, 17, 48, 412, 419, 502. *See also* solidarity

Nahr el-Bared camp, Lebanon, 68, 391–2, 394–5, 407, 408, 411–13

Nakivale camp, Uganda, 368, 376

Nancy, Jean-Luc, 410, 412

narration, self-, 44, 62, 65

narrative, 3, 33, 179, 182, 184, 198; of commemorations, 75; counter-, 2, 157, 193, 197, 403; defensive, 83; discourse, 147; distancing, 87, 147–8; of exceptionalism, 4; historical, 80; homonationalist, 150; humanitarian, 178, 185, 232; humanizing, 189; in literature, 44, 45; national, 78; personal, 29, 52, 105, 274, 285; public, 77; Refugee Week, 75; of refugeehood, 33, 38, 84, 179, 279; rescue, 149, 150, 151; saviour narrative; of travelling, 45; visual, 100

Nassau, 126

nationalism, 118, 168, 189, 467

neighbour; in Arabic, 410; camp, 35, 57, 65, 66, 67, 69, 410; helping a, 153; the inhuman, 189; pre-displacement, 298; relationship with, 502, 506, 507, 512; neighbouring country, 4, 80, 205; neighbourhood, 35, 38, 478, 508, 514

neo-colonial, 17, 150

the Netherlands, 90n8, 131, 169, 286n7; Belgian refugees in, 79, 80, 81, 84, 85

Neufeld, Josh, 183, 184, 185, 186

neutral, country, 85, 90

neutrality, humanitarian principle of, 415–27

New Zealand, 129

NGO, 231, 232, 424, 461, 469; criminalization of, 79, 91n19; discourse, 146, 148; and education, 368; responses 417; worker, 238, 370, 416, 418, 420, 421, 423, 469, 488. *See also* humanitarian; local; neutrality; *and NGO names*

Nicaragua, 132

Nigeria, 96, 471

Nineveh Plains, Iraq, 249

nomad, 42, 127, 128, 223

*non-entrée* policy, 157, 159, 162, 164

present, tense, 45, 47, 54, 67, 178,
prayer, 56, 57, 59, 300, 456; room, 354
precarity, 57, 140, 404, 407–10, 412, 413n2,
    431, 469, 478, 479, 490
private: and discrete assistance, 411; housing,
    310, 453, 482, 492n7; initiatives, 373;
    sector, 354, 467, 481; sphere, 38, 285,
    359, 453
protracted: displacement, 315, 363, 364, 365,
    383, 398, 405, 406, 409; immobility,
    298; refugee camps, 362, 363–4, 376,
    377, 383, 386. *See also specific camps*
psychosocial, 290, 301, 313, 315, 331. *See also*
    well-being
public, 147, 151, 153, 154, 480; services, 105,
    477, 479, 484, 486, 490; space, 38,
    187–8, 213, 235, 283, 359, 453, 501;
    memory, 75, 76; opinion, 83, 94. *See*
    *also* audience
Punamäki, Raija-Leena, 310–11, 312, 313,
    326
push-backs, 157, 158, 159. See also
    *non-refoulement*

Qasmiyeh, Yousif M., 3–4. *See also* poetry;
    refugee writing
Qatar, 422, 424; Qatari Initiative, 416, 420,
    424
queer, 151, 152, 154, 274, 276, 278, 279,
    283, 285, 286n3, 286n7; democracy,
    150; happiness, 153; Muslim, 285;
    liberalism, 149, 154; migration,
    146, 148, 274; optimism; politics,
    149; racialized, 148, 155. *See also*
    homonationalism, LGBT

race, 5, 111, 114, 149, 275, 351, 504, 505,
    506, 511; citizenship and 152;
    democracy, 349; racial profiling, 350,
    351; racial segregation, 351, 354, 359;
    racialization, 5, 14, 16, 118, 146, 148,
    155n10, 170, 351, 359, 370; racialized
    queer, 148, 155. *See also* Black; black
    and minority ethnic (BME) group;
    intersectionality; White
racism, 188, 504, 505. *See also* apartheid;
    discrimination; Islamophobia;
    xenophobia
Ramadan, 35, 408
Rawls, John, 97
reception: centre, 465, 467, 474n5, 511, 513;
    culture, 74, 75; historical, 81, 86,
    91n20; system, 102, 462, 468. *See also*
    hospitality
recognition, 28, 34, 36, 45, 46, 48, 49, 50,
    144, 213. *See also* refugee status
    determination
reconstruction: of destroyed camp, 228, 391,
    392; post-war, 87
Red Cross: see ICRC
refuge: crisis of, 170; place of, 226; political,
    390; spaces of, 351, 354, 358, 359,
    383, 385, 404, 440; spatial politics of,
    441, 444, 471, 472–3; theatre and,
    226, 227. See also *Refugia-ti*

Refugee Convention, see 1951 Geneva
    Convention Relating to the Status of
    Refugees
refugee history: *See* history
Refugee Hosts, 18n1; 53, 413n6, 413n8
refugee literature: *See* refugee writing
refugee studies, 402; invisibility in, 36
Refugee Week, 74, 75
refugee writing, 52–71. *See also* poetry
refugee-led responses to displacement, 3, 52,
    54, 335, 350, 383, 395, 396, 402–12,
    433. *See also* invisibility; voice;
    volunteers; *We Are Movers*
refugee–refugee humanitarianism, 402, 408,
    411
refugee–refugee relationality, 402–12
refugee-status determination, 145, 238, 284.
    *See also* immigration status
Regina Pacis detention centre, Italy, 198, 202
relationality, 4, 5, 14, 17, 144, 402–12, 473
religion, 70; and coping, 250, 299, 300, 313;
    and donations, 408; duty of hospitality,
    96, 411; duty to migrate, 114; religious
    belief, 411; religious discrimination,
    502–4, 514; religious festivities,
    35, 356, 408; religious identity, 83,
    499, 500; religious spaces, 365;
    persecution, 204, 250, 75; and
    sexuality in asylum claims, 282, 284–5;
    and support and assistance, 411, 417,
    422, 472, 508. *See also* discrimination;
    faith; Islamophobia; minorities; racism
remittances, 127, 436
repatriation: See durable solutions
representation, 2, 3, 6, 141; of camps, 36; of
    death, 173, 203; of identities, 34, 37;
    of lifeless body, 110, 166, 168, 171,
    172, 174n1; self-, 106; of women,
    197, 200, 203. *See also* advocacy;
    comics; discourse; Kurdi, Alan; media;
    performance; photography; video; visual
rescue, 98; boat, 205; narrative, 150, 151
resettlement: *See* durable solutions
resilience, 307–318, 327. *See also*
    psychosocial; well-being
resistance, 36, 37, 38–9, 316, 317; sites, 386,
    395–6. *See also* agency
Ressler, Oliver, 172
Revolution: Libyan, 325; Tunisian, 119–20;
    Syrian, 436, 437
Reznikov, Hanon, 201, 203
*Rifugia-ti* (2005), 194, 200–7, 208n2
rights, 97; civil, 465, 467; cosmopolitan,
    97; migration, 113; of migrants and
    refugees, 106, 161, 185, 190, 461; to
    mobility, 97; and political rights, 115.
    *See also* human rights; law; social justice
risk, 102, 112, 114; factors, 306–11; at risk of
    future harm, 276, 283, 284, 285
Robertson, Joe, 210. *See also* Good Chance
    Theatre
Roma, 329
Russia: Russian Federation, 212, 273–7,
    280–5, 291, 292; LGBT asylum-seekers
    and refugees, 273–85

testimony, 54, 202, 279, 283; testimonial comics, 50, 178, 185
'The Road to Germany: $2400', 183
theatre, 193–208, 210–15, 225, 226, 227; exercise, 32, 39; Goffman, Erving 104; interactive forum theatre, 142; life as theatrical performance, 104; national traditions of, 212; political theatre, 196; space, 211–14; Theatre Reportage, 10, 196, 207; and well-being, 213, 327, 329. See also audience; Good Chance Theatre; performance; Teatro di Nascosto; and separate play titles
There are no Syrian Refugees in Turkey, 172
threshold, in the camp 58, 65, 67, 388, 389, 413n9, 440
time: and the camp, 55–67, 69, 71; slower, 183. See also history; temporality
togetherness, 410, 412
torture, 113, 185, 198, 202, 203, 206, 326, 330. See also Helen Bamber Foundation
tourism, effects of displacement on, 101, 102, 106
translation, 279, 432, 486; cultural translator and mediator, 24, 27, 511; interpreting, 24, 490; in research, 497, 500; self-, 43, 45
transnational: capital, 514; community, 85; mobility and movement, 84, 111, 117
trauma, 40, 185, 188, 295, 308, 309, 310, 311, 335. See also Post-Traumatic Stress Disorder
Tunisia, 101, 102, 119–20,
Turkey, 172, 184, 194, 195, 203, 206, 249, 429–38, 503

UCL Grand Challenges, xxx, xxxi, 18n2, 108n1, 314
Uganda, 150, 296, 313, 366, 373; Ugandan Asian refugees, 76; camps in, 366; child soldiers, 313; IDPs, 296; refugees, 150. See also Kyaka II camp; Kyangwali camp; Nakivale camp
UK Border Agency, 276
UK Lesbian and Gay Immigration Group (UKLGIG), 151, 154n4,
Ukrainians, 48, 89
UN Relief and Works Agency for Palestine Refugees in the Near East (UNRWA): and camps, 383, 386–90; in Lebanon, 57, 65, 66, 408, 409, 412; in Jordan, 355, 336, 340n4
unaccompanied minors: care for and by, 229, 231, 236, 237, 238–9, 241; label, 28; as peer-researchers 24–25; travel of, 114; and well-being, 310. See also child
unemployment, 113, 125, 335
United Nations High Commission for Refugees (UNHCR), 33, 164, 340n2, 363; in camps, 372, 373, 377, 382, 408–9; in Lebanon, 416, 427n8; and refugee identification, 96; and resettlement, 431, 436

UNHCR Guidelines on International Protection with reference to Claims to Refugee Status based on Sexual Orientation and/or Gender Identity, 277
UNHCR Policy on Alternatives to Camps, 363
unions, trade, 86, 483
United Nations Human Rights Council (UNHRC), 273
USA, 168, 174n3
universalism, critiques of, 145–6, 149
Unofficial Women and Children's Centre, Calais, 229
urban: refugees, 377n4, 404, 405, 406, 437, 461, 465–72, 478; camps, 404–7. See also city names
us and them, 3, 4, 17, 58, 207, 235

Vanuatu, 130, 131
victim, 2, 5, 6, 50, 150, 173, 197, 290, 406, 421, 423, 424, 425, 469; and gender and sexuality, 281, 285; silent, 98; victimhood, 33, 35; -island, 102
violence, 2, 3, 49, 289, 290, 309, 311, 325, 336, 421, 478, 487, 504; against LGBT people, 281, 282, 283, 284; borders and, 179, 324, 325; of conditional hospitality, 465, 466, 469, 470, 471; domestic violence, 486–7, 490; epistemic, 6, 197, 403; intimate violence, 486–7, 490; of labelling, 30; and the law, 463; political, 166, 169; in research, 27, 28, 30; representation of, 182; sexual, 172, 231, 234, 282, 311, 375; in South Africa, 349, 350, 351, 355, 357; of storytelling, 40; structural, 117, 190n2, 403; xenophobic violence, 349, 350, 357. See also persecution; police
visas, 42, 112, 118, 119, 129, 157, 164, 438n4, 439n12, 480, 490
visibility, 1, 30, 37, 38, 197, 503; and camera, 105; hyper-visibility, 2, 28, 33, 34, 36, 38; imposed, 37; public, 480, 481, 483. See also invisibility
visual, culture, 94; research, 94, 95, 98–100, 104, 108; narratives, 100; politics, 174; production, 104, 167. See also comics; film; photography; representation
voice: and belonging, 143; disembodied, 172–3; dominant, 23; one's own, 358; 'refugee voice', 7, 33, 36, 197; in refugee writing, 59, 61, 62, 68; in research, 24, 26, 30, 107; and strategic invisibility, 32–4, 36–7; in theatre, 199, 201, 207; as response, 281; voiceless, 469. See also invisibility; silence; speech
voluntary or forced migration: See category; choice, conceptual boundaries
volunteers, in Belgium, 510, 511, 512, 513, 514; the Calais camp, 212, 229, 230, 240; in Jordan, 337; in London, 330, 331, 485; Syrian, 510–11, 513. See also Clegg, Liz